TIME AND CHANCE

James Callaghan entered Parliament as the
Labour Member for Cardiff South and Penarth
in 1945. He retired in 1987 after 42 years'
service, during the latter part of which he had
been 'Father of the House' as the longest serving
Member. He is now a Knight of the Garter and a
Peer. In addition to the many political offices he
has held, he is President of University College,
Swansea, Honorary Freeman of the cities of
Cardiff and Sheffield, and holds honorary
degrees from the Universities of Birmingham,
Wales, and Gujerat in India.

By the same author

A House Divided

James Callaghan

TIME AND CHANCE

Collins/Fontana

First published in Great Britain by
William Collins Sons & Co. Ltd 1987
First issued in Fontana Paperbacks 1988

Copyright © Collins 1987

Printed and bound in Great Britain by
William Collins Sons & Co. Ltd, Glasgow

To my wife,
our children and grandchildren,
and to the electors of Cardiff who made this
book possible

'I returned, and saw under the sun, that the race
is not to the swift, nor the battle to the strong,
neither yet bread to the wise, nor yet riches to men
of understanding, nor yet favour to men of skill; but
time and chance happeneth to them all.'

ECCLESIASTES 9 vs. 11

CONTENTS

CONTENTS

LIST OF ILLUSTRATIONS

———◆———

A WORD OF THANKS

This book has been on the stocks for a number of years and now, as it leaves the slipway, is the time to express my grateful thanks to all those who took part in its construction.

Lord Donoughue was there when we laid the keel, to discuss the structure of the book, to suggest lines of development, and to point me in the right direction. He kindly read the manuscript and I am very grateful for his constructive help. Dr Nigel Bowles was also in at the beginning. He did much of the early research and in the process of sorting and indexing my papers spent many winter hours in a cold loft at the top of the house. Not surprisingly, after this ordeal he left me for Edinburgh University. It was my loss. He was assisted by Carey Oppenheim and I am very grateful to them both.

For the last two years I enjoyed the assistance of Dr Caroline Anstey, whose knowledge of international affairs saved me from a number of errors, and who at the end took charge of the manuscript and oversaw all that needed to be done before it was delivered to the publishers. On several occasions she gave up smoking, but the manuscript was too much even for her determination and on as many occasions she succumbed once more.

I have been a nuisance to many people during the writing. First I thank the staff of the House of Commons Library who have gone beyond the call of duty to answer my queries, to furnish useful information and to respond speedily to every request. They were, no doubt, relieved to hear that the book is complete and that I shall not be standing for Parliament again. Next, I thank the staffs of the Treasury, the Home Office, the Foreign and Commonwealth Office and the Cabinet Office. It may seem like lese-majesty to throw all these august Departments together in one compendious sentence, but I must say to each and every one of them that it would not have been possible for the book to provide a degree of detailed background without their ungrudging help. The Treasury had no difficulty in identifying half-remembered conversations and producing the papers; the Home Office stacked a tall cupboard completely full of the files I asked for (and some I didn't); the Foreign and Commonwealth Office's index of my discussions and papers was awesome in its comprehensiveness; and the Cabinet Office lived up to its reputation by never flinching from any of my requests. I am greatly in their collective debt.

I had the benefit of talking with Sir Brian Cubbon, Permanent Under-Secretary to the Home Office, and to Sir Antony Acland, Permanent Under-Secretary to the Foreign and Commonwealth Office, both of whom I am proud to say had been my Private Secretary at an earlier stage in their careers. Like everyone else I have mentioned, they bear no responsibility for the contents of the book. Sir Tom McCaffrey was with me at the Home Office, and later at my request joined me at the Foreign Office and at 10 Downing Street as Chief Press Secretary. He was good enough to read the manuscript and recalled matters that I had forgotten as well as making a number of suggestions for which I am grateful. I must also thank Merlyn Rees for reading the manuscript. He helped to clarify a number of points and corrected errors I had made.

My publishers have been forbearing in not nagging me to complete the book several years ago and I am particularly grateful to them for allowing Richard Ollard to act as my editor. No one could have been more understanding or knowledgeable. He and I served together in the Navy more than forty years ago and his expert advice more than repaid the longstanding debt he owed me from the days when I lashed up his hammock for him in Portsmouth Barracks.

Ruth Sharpe, my secretary for nearly thirty years and a friend to all our family, typed the early pages. Since her death I have had a succession of helpers – Sue Nye, Jill Sindall, Janet Godden, Judy Ray, Maria Evans, Jane Hannaford and Ann Thomson have all grappled with my handwriting and I thank them all, as well as Joe Hazard for his many kindnesses.

The role of the Parliamentary Private Secretary is to be always with his Minister in the House and at official and Party engagements, to be observant but usually to be silent – except when they are alone together. For this reason Merlyn Rees, Gregor Mackenzie, Roland Moyle, John Cunningham and Roger Stott hardly feature in this account in their capacity as Parliamentary Private Secretaries; but this does not lessen my immense debt to them for all their personal and political advice and friendship in good times and bad. It seemed as though when one of them gave up to become a Minister he knew automatically the right person to hand over to. We all became close friends and remain so.

To this list I should also like to add Lord Brooks of Tremorfa and the constituency officers of Cardiff South and Penarth, who have given me unstinting support throughout my Parliamentary life. Finally, I owe Audrey more than I can write and once more I have to thank her for putting up with hours of silence whilst I scribbled, without a word of complaint, and for always putting my consideration ahead of her own.

PART ONE

INTO POLITICS

I

Earliest memories – Portsmouth and the First World War – we move to Brixham – schooldays

Memory is a capricious companion. Like the wind of St John's Gospel, 'It bloweth where it listeth, and thou hearest the sound thereof, but canst not tell whence it cometh.' So with memories. We do not know why we remember some things clearly whilst about others our memories are fitful and even fail altogether. Nor in later life do we understand what triggers off our early recollections.

Sometimes my wife and I compare notes about events in the near sixty years that we have known each other. We have many common memories but the emphasis of her recollections is different from mine. She focuses more on people; on friends whom we have known well, and on passing acquaintances, their fortunes and misfortunes. She recalls their families and personal lives. I tend to remember dates and events. Perhaps this has something to do with the difference in our characters. Although her opinions once formed are hard to shift, she is unfailingly thoughtful about others, generous and considerate in her actions. And our friends are in no doubt about who is the nicer character.

As I have confessed to a selective memory, can anyone trust that what I write is accurate? I hope so; it will certainly not be my intention to deceive, and I shall hope to do at least as well as Huckleberry Finn, of whom Mark Twain said: 'There was things which he stretched but mainly he told the truth.' A reading of these pages will soon show that there are differences between what I saw as the truth and the recollections and diaries of others. The reader will have to judge.

We have seen some diaries published and I cannot deny their usefulness, especially as I have read only the extracts serialised in newspapers, and not the complete volumes. Historians of the future will certainly know more, thanks to the indefatigable energy of Dick Crossman, Barbara Castle, and perhaps Tony Benn, when his voluminous records appear. But the weakness of diaries is that they are written in haste, and therefore lack perspective about the totality of the writer's relationship with his colleagues. I have myself reproduced verbatim extracts from a few conversations, but am generally cautious about diaries. In general, diary extracts, even when correctly reported, rarely catch either the inflexion of voice or the gesture that modifies the spoken word. Nor does such conversation when written down convey the notion that sometimes a man talking with his colleagues may be arguing as much with himself as with them, modifying his own views in the very process of exposing them.

Dick Crossman had a particularly emphatic way of expressing himself and would never have admitted such a possibility. His reputation for changing his mind came not only from his own intellectual flightiness but also because in the course of argument, at the very moment that he was engaged in destroying the other's case, he consciously or unconsciously absorbed what his opponent was saying. A week later, the listener might well be astonished to hear Crossman repeat as his own opinion the very argument that he had demolished with such ferocity at their previous encounter. It was this trait that instilled in me a mistrust of Crossman's judgement – and this within a month of our first meeting in the Smoking Room of the House of Commons after the great General Election of 1945, where the excitement of hearing that powerful mind at work had at first carried me away.

I am reinforced in this by an undated letter from Crossman which I found recently among my papers. It ran as follows:

Dear James
I made a thorough exhibition of myself talking to you and Hugh last night. Please accept my regrets and also my assurance that I am NOT as bad as that!! If you can't forget what I said, at least don't hold my remarks against me as settled convictions.

                                                        Dick Crossman

To be candid, I cannot remember the occasion, the subject, or whether Hugh Dalton or Hugh Gaitskell was the third person present. But it was because of this spontaneous and characteristic response and contrition of Dick's that we always remained on friendly terms, and I found stimulation in his company, even if I was not always convinced that he was expressing his 'settled convictions'. And his weekly diaries should be read accordingly.

I do not say that it is impossible to reproduce conversations, but that it is difficult. As a Minister in various capacities, I marvelled at the ability of some civil servants to reproduce conversations on paper. Their memories seemed almost faultless. Sir Kenneth Stowe, who later became Permanent Secretary at the Department of Health and Social Security, was my Private Secretary for the whole of the period I served as Prime Minister. Stowe had an awesome capacity to distil the essence of conversations with visiting heads of government, without seeming to lose any nuance. His skill was that he not only remembered accurately but he also understood the inner and sometimes unspoken meaning of what had been said. Stowe, however, rarely used direct reported conversation in his written summaries, and I have great scepticism about total recall of the exact words used in a long dialogue. I have known only one man, Dick Plummer, one-time editor of the *Daily Express*, and MP for Deptford, who could do it.

People vary a great deal in how far back their memory reaches, but for a particular reason I can pinpoint exactly one of my earliest memories. It is from the early days of November 1914 when I was two years and seven months old. The First World War had begun the previous August. I had been born in Portsmouth in March 1912 where my father served in the Royal Navy. For the previous ten years he had been a member of the ship's company of the former Royal Yacht, *Victoria and Albert*, in which he served as an able seaman. On the outbreak of war the ship's company had been dispersed, several of them, including my father, joining the 27,000-ton battlecruiser HMS *Agincourt* at Scapa Flow where the Grand Fleet lay.

One of the other members of the crew of the Royal Yacht and a near neighbour of ours had been sent to join the armoured cruiser HMS *Good Hope*, which was despatched to form part of the British Squadron in the South Pacific for the protection of British trade and shipping. On 1 November 1914 the records show that HMS *Good Hope*, with another British cruiser, *Monmouth*, encountered Admiral von Spee's Asiatic Squadron; both British ships were sunk with great loss of life. Among those killed in action was our neighbour.

It took a few days for the news to filter back to Portsmouth, and when it did I have a clear memory of clutching my mother's hand as she walked down the street to visit and comfort the widow. I was conscious of the grief in that room. What engraved the visit indelibly on my memory was the sight of the young widow suckling her new baby at her breast. This was something I had not seen before, or so I thought, and no doubt the two mothers considered that a little boy of two and a half would hardly notice.

My mother must have had a deep feeling of sympathy for the widow, for she had herself been married before. Like my father, her first husband also served in the Navy, and lost his life when the liberty boat on which he was returning to his ship one night was cut down by a destroyer in Plymouth Sound. She was married and widowed before she was twenty-one. A year or two later she met my father in Devonport and married him in 1903.

The family story goes that my father, who was born a Roman Catholic, was refused permission to marry my mother by the Catholic Naval Chaplain, as she was a Protestant. My father robustly said that if he had to choose between the Church and my mother, then he would have nothing further to do with the Church. My elder sister, Dorothy, was born in 1904 and she and I were brought up as Baptists.

My father was high-spirited and adventurous. As a lad he ran away from home because he wanted to join the Navy, giving the recruiting officer a false name and age so that his parents would not be able to trace him. The recruiting officer accepted what he was told and so my father, born James Garoghan on 21 January 1877 in Birmingham, enlisted under the name of James Callaghan, giving his date of birth as 21 June 1878. My father was neither the first nor the last to enlist in the Forces under an assumed name, and I am happy to say that Admiralty records from then on show that his character was consistently 'very good' and his efficiency 'superior'. He rapidly passed for promotion to Petty Officer, served in the battleship HMS *Benbow*, the cruiser HMS *St George* and other ships during the 1890s. He took part in expeditions to Benin City and to Zanzibar, qualified as a deep-sea diver and among his other accomplishments, such as expertly dancing the hornpipe, he was very handy with his needle and ran up uniforms for his messmates in order to make a little extra money.

My mother had no contact with my father's family during his life, nor after his death early in 1921, but fifty-five years later there was an interesting sequel. When I became Prime Minister in 1976, the *Sun* enterprisingly delved into parish records and constructed and published a family tree. It revealed that my father had been one of ten children, five boys and five girls. His father (my grandfather), whom I never knew, had been a silversmith in Sheffield and Birmingham. This, and the fact that my father had changed his name on enlisting, was a revelation not only to me but to one of my father's very elderly relatives, still alive.

My mother's relationships with her family were very different. She was one of five children born in Devonport, and unlike my father she kept in close touch with them throughout her life. Her father, William Cundy, born in Tavistock in 1831, had been a naval shipwright in HMS *Impregnable*; her grandfather, Robert Cundy, a quarryman, was also born in Tavistock, in 1775 or 6. On the other side of my mother's family, her grandfather was a shoemaker in Devonport, who died when young leaving five children under the age of thirteen. His widow, my great-grandmother, was described in the census of 1851 as a 'widow pauper, fish seller'. I was grateful to the *Sun* for unearthing this information.

At about the same time that my father volunteered to join the Royal Yacht, he also made application to join Scott's expedition to the South Pole in HMS *Discovery*. Scott's sledge teams probed deep into the Antarctic Circle and I have no doubt that the risks and hardships would have suited my father's ardent temperament, but my mother, perhaps remembering the loss of her first husband, and being of a more cautious disposition, dissuaded him from the Antarctic and he settled down to a more humdrum, although in our eyes more prestigious existence on the Royal Yacht.

The Yacht was based at Portsmouth and my mother removed there from Plymouth after her marriage. I suspect that my father did not relish spending so much time in harbour. The Yacht had had an unfortunate start: when she was floated into the water at her launch, she heeled over at an acute angle and almost capsized. Queen Victoria seems to have been mainly responsible for the mishap, for during the building of the Yacht she continued to make suggestions for new additions which, when piled one upon another, made the ship top-heavy. But no one liked to disagree with the old Queen and it was not until the ship was launched that the mistakes showed up and the design faults were put right.

My father made a number of foreign voyages in the Royal Yacht, especially when King Edward VII was on the throne, although my mother used to say that Queen Alexandra's dislike of sailing on her was the reason she spent most of her time in Portsmouth harbour. The routine was for my father to go aboard in the morning and come home in the late after-noon to the terraced house he had rented, where both my sister and I were born. His naval pay was good enough for us always to have plenty of good plain food and we never went without a fire in the winter.

Men in Portsmouth mostly worked in the Navy, the dockyard or in the supporting services. Women did not go out to work, and the standard of life was quite sufficient for most as long as the man survived. But it was different for widows and fatherless children; when the breadwinner was gone, they lived in hardship. My sister Dorothy, who was eight years older than me, recalled one widowed neighbour of ours who survived by washing and finishing blankets for sixpence each, plus a bar of soap. It was hard work. Her children, with whom we played, were given meal tickets in class to take to a food centre.

There were many voluntary organisations with the aim of relieving poverty. The chapels too did their best. I remember that on the Sunday before each Christmas, one of the deacons at the Baptist Chapel would load up a handcart with groceries which we pushed round the streets, calling at homes we knew were in need to leave a pound of sugar, a pound of sultanas and margarine to help towards the Christmas pudding. We knew families in deep poverty and there was a sense of sharing. The biggest worry was being ill and having to pay the doctor's bill, though as a naval family we were lucky. Hospital operations were expensive, and a kind of primitive insurance was invented. Subscriptions of a few pence were made to the local hospital when they could be afforded and in return subscribers were given 'tickets' for the amount of the subscription. When an operation became necessary, they counted the value of 'tickets' they had accumulated, and if there were not enough they would try to borrow the balance from friends and neighbours. These were taken to the hospital and the operation could then be performed.

When my sister Dorothy needed an operation as a small girl, she walked to the hospital with my father in the morning, before he went aboard his ship. He left her there and called for her in the evening, wrapped her in a large blanket, and carried her two miles back home for my mother to nurse.

The fever van was a familiar sight in the street, calling to take children to the fever hospital. I do not recall any vaccinations other than those against smallpox. My sister used to argue that we were brought up in Sunday School to accept that child mortality was a natural event, and that we should look forward to going to Heaven as a reward. In support she quoted a hymn we were taught to sing:

> 'Around the Throne of God in Heaven
> Thousands of children stand,
> Children whose sins are all forgiven
> A holy happy band.
> Bright things they see,
> Sweet harps they hold,
> And on their heads are crowns of gold.'

I cannot say I was thrilled by the notion. My mother was deeply religious and fundamentalist and she looked forward to the Second Coming of the Lord when all who had been saved would be taken up to Heaven. This would be for her a joyful day, one to which she looked forward, and the expectation enabled her to bear her present troubles. As a child I imbibed this same belief, but to me it was a dread prospect. Only God and I knew what terrible sins I had committed: *I* knew that I was unworthy to be taken up to Heaven with all those who were saved; and what shame my mother would feel when she ascended to Heaven but I was left on earth as unworthy. To a seven-year-old the fear was real and tangible. I came home one day from school to find the house empty and silent and I knew at once that it had happened. The Second Coming had taken place, my mother had been taken up to Heaven and I had, as I had always feared, been rejected. For a moment near-panic set in and then, with a relief almost too great to describe, I heard the sound of my mother's voice. My sense of shame was so great that I was never able to tell her how I felt, but it left its mark and even in adult life I have never been able wholly to shake off a sense of guilt.

Our Sunday School was typical in having over six hundred 'scholars' and one hundred teachers. We lived up to our name of scholars. When we were young we learned by heart long passages from the Bible. As we grew older, our Sunday School teachers set us written examinations and, if we passed well, we were allowed to choose a book as a prize. I still have on my bookshelves *The Coverley Papers* from the *Spectator* which I chose as my prize in 1927, for I was then a devotee of Joseph Addison.

The chapels were much more centres of the community than they are today. Almost every night of the week there were different activities: Monday, Band of Hope; Tuesday, Christian Endeavour; Thursday, prayer meeting; Friday, juvenile choir practice. Our Sundays were spent at chapel. Sunday School started at 9.30 in the morning. From there we went into chapel at 11 o'clock. Home to Sunday dinner, which was usually cold ham and mashed potatoes, and at 2.30 we returned to afternoon Sunday School. Finally to Chapel at 6.30 in the evening with sometimes a Sunday School tea in between. We were not permitted to have playing cards in the house and we did not read newspapers on Sundays. I was allowed the *Children's Encyclopaedia* but nothing else secular. At home we began each day with a short Bible reading before leaving for school, and of course we never omitted to say Grace before meals, a practice that has fallen into disuse in most homes. I noted many years later that the

practice was maintained by President Jimmy Carter and his wife Rosalynn
when we breakfasted together at the White House, and it is my impression
that the practice is more usual in the United States than in Britain.

My schooldays began in 1916 at a large infants' school at Copnor,
Portsmouth. The classrooms were big and high-ceilinged with a floor that
was staged in order that the teachers, who had sixty children in each class,
could see what those at the back of the room were getting up to. We had
five rows of desks arranged in six blocks, two children to each desk and
we began almost straightaway to learn the alphabet and multiplication
tables. We also learned not to speak to a teacher unless she spoke first to
us; and we spent many hours sitting 'at attention' with our hands behind
our backs, a procedure that I guess modern children who live in today's
freer climate would find very strange. Not that we were unhappy. Anyone who had a reasonably good memory and who could learn the multiplication table by heart and could recite the capes and headlands of
England from St Abb's Head to St Bee's Head could escape trouble. The
teachers were conscientious and hard-working and it never occurred to
us, or perhaps to them, that education means more than committing
facts to memory and that at its best it involves sparking the imagination,
thinking for oneself and striking ideas off one another.

My schooldays were spent at elementary or secondary schools in
Portsmouth except for an interlude of four years, from 1919 to 1923, spent
at the fishing village of Brixham in South Devon. I recall the time I spent
there with great affection, despite the deep shadow cast when my father
died in 1921. He had been discharged from the Navy in 1919 after twenty-
six years' service but was fortunate to be accepted for the Coastguard
Service and was sent to Brixham. We left Portsmouth and moved into
the coastguard station overlooking Torbay. It was a simple, small cottage
standing next to the sea.

Thinking back over the changes in everyday life since those days, I am
struck by the great improvements in even the most ordinary home. Not
only are they much more comfortable to live in but the commonplace
gadgets of today, which were not known sixty years ago, have all but
abolished the slavery of the housewife. The scrubbing board for the
Monday morning wash is unknown; the copper in which she boiled the
clothes has gone, as has the safe to keep the food fresh. The linoleum on
the floors has been replaced by carpets. The washing machine, the fridge
and the vacuum cleaner are commonplace. No longer does the average
house possess only one cold tap situated in the kitchen over a yellow sink;

or a zinc tub hanging outside to be brought in for the Saturday night bath in front of the living-room fire, the hot water for which was carried in pails from the copper which had been especially lit for the purpose. The marble wash-stand and jug have gone from the best bedroom, together with the candle and candlestick which used to light our way upstairs. No longer do we shiver in winter as we move from the one and only warm room in the house with its coal fire or oven range to an unheated bedroom. Nor does mother do the filthy job of black-leading the fireplace and the range. The single hissing gas jet in the middle of the front room (which was the best room in the house), with its fragile gas mantle, has been replaced by numerous electric points, and the television set and video have taken the place of the piano.

I do not wish to appear complacent about our progress. There are too many homes in our country where this standard of amenities still does not exist. But in general there has been a transformation, and a great deal of the credit is due to the higher standards imposed by local authorities in their council house building programmes, as well as to the desire of the new generation of owner-occupiers for self-improvement.

Because women's physical labour has been immensely lightened by domestic inventions during my lifetime, their independence and their opportunities to undertake activities outside the home have increased. Women now play an important role in most of the public aspects of our community, in the political parties, and especially in local government. They are often the most lively spirits in organisations like the Parent Teacher Associations, which themselves were unknown in my early days; or in organizing cultural and sporting activities for the young. As their household chores have eased and become more widely shared by the present generation of husbands and young fathers, so women's lives have become fuller. They take up social problems with zeal and enthusiasm, showing tremendous energy and determination to achieve their ends. They set an example to the men. If I may dare say so, as I get older I find them much more interesting and attractive companions than in my youth.

My father's duties at the coastguard station were not as onerous as my mother's in the house. His principal task was to keep watch for ships at sea from a small watch cabin perched within a few yards of the top of Berry Head, a 300-foot high cliff that marks the entrance to Torbay. His station was connected by morse to other watch stations on the Devon and Cornwall coasts, and the coastguards reported passing ships to one another, gave notice of bad weather, and kept a look-out for vessels in distress.

Sometimes, when I was not at school, he would take me to keep watch with him. How I looked forward to this. We would rise early and set off from the coastguard cottages, walk past the vicarage where the Reverend Henry Francis Lyte had written the hymn 'Abide With Me', then pass through the old forts built to prevent Napoleon's invasion, until the vista opened out and we looked down at the open sea all around us, and the neat steep Devon fields. There we would sit together, just the two of us in the tiny cabin, whilst he taught me the morse code and the signal flags. In summer we would venture out over the close-cropped turf and would walk past bushes of golden gorse to search for gulls' eggs at the cliff edge. This was a slightly hazardous occupation, and despite my father's enthusiasm I never thought the fishy taste of the gulls' eggs made the prize worthwhile. It could be very frightening to come unexpectedly upon a gull on its nest three hundred feet above the sea, when it would whirl into the air, wheeling and turning, and uttering raucous cries just above your head.

The seasons of autumn and spring gales were thrilling. Huge seas dashed against the foot of the cliffs, and the winds set the wire guy ropes that anchored the frail watch cabin to the cliff top singing and straining. Our shelter seemed to rock in the wind and my father kept extra watch. We were careful how we set foot outside, for sometimes the gusts were strong enough to sweep a man off the cliff.

Late one winter afternoon there came a distress call from a ship that had gone aground a short distance further down the coast. My father was not on watch at the time, but he and everyone on the coastguard station were called out to man and transport the life-saving equipment overland to the wreck. A farm cart pulled by two horses appeared; the gear was loaded, lanterns were lit and everyone set off including we boys from the station, our oilskins and sou'westers glistening in the light of the swinging lanterns as we followed the straining horses pulling the equipment across muddy fields, through rain and wind, to the edge of the cliff face where the wreck had struck. We could make out the faint line of white foam at the foot of the cliff and see a dim light shining aboard the vessel. The coastguards unloaded their equipment while my father used a signal lantern to send messages to the men of the wreck that they intended to fire a rocket across the ship. These rockets trailed a thin life-saving line to straddle the wreck. The wind was so fierce that the first shot was blown hopelessly wide. A second rocket was fired but again the gusts blew so fiercely up the cliff face that it fell short. Eventually the coastguards made sufficient allowance for the wind and a line was got on board. To this they attached a heavier rope and a breeches buoy which the ship's crew pulled on board. A breeches buoy was nothing more than a pair of strong canvas shorts into which a man could thrust his legs and, by holding fast to the rope, be hauled to safety up the cliff face. It was a perilous journey for the exhausted men. The winch slipped continuously and everyone took a hand on the tope. Even we boys were pressed into service to hold on with all our might as the men were hauled up. The handful of men were all saved, no one even injured, and we marched back together, wet and cold, taking the crew to our homes across the fields. We boys were too excited to feel tired and we talked of the adventure for many months after-wards. I am sure the shipwrecked men did not see it in the same light.

The sea was the whole of our daily lives. Only a few feet of grass separated our cottages from the rocky beach where we searched for crabs and prawns and fished for bass. Occasionally we had great good fortune. One evening in the hot summer of 1921 the porpoises hunting shoals of fish came so close to the beach that mackerel trying to escape were driven to the water's edge, and we scooped them out with our hands without either rod or net. I took the catch home proudly for my mother to cook. Nothing tastes better than mackerel fried and eaten within the hour.

In those days there were no school dinners or school buses, and we walked back and forth four times a day. Our journey took us around the harbour, and some of the bolder spirits whose fathers worked aboard the trawlers would sometimes loosen a rowing boat from the stern of one of the fishing smacks tied up alongside so that we could scull across the water and so shorten our walk to school. It followed that we left the boat on the wrong side of the harbour, and we fled up the hill to safety, pursued by irate shouts from the trawlermen on the quay. When we emerged from school in the late afternoon the boats would slowly be coming to life as they prepared for sea. This was the time to clamber unobserved down the. vertical ladders, and if we got aboard safely, to make our way to the ship's galley in search of the great blocks of coarse chocolate which the fishermen used to make hot steaming cocoa. I do not know whether they still make these blocks or whether I would now enjoy the taste, but at the age of ten it was sheer ambrosia. Even today, whenever I catch the smell of tarred nets and ropes my mind goes back immediately to Brixham harbour sixty years ago.

From the windows of the coastguard cottage I would watch the fishing fleet sail as dusk fell, as many as seventy or eighty boats at a time. Their red and brown canvas sails clustered together, and if the wind was off-shore they would seem so close to the cottages that I felt as if I could almost reach out and touch them.

At certain times during the year the larger fishing smacks would sail 'round Lands' to Newquay, Padstow and Milford Haven, and would be away for several days or weeks, but mostly they came back to harbour in the early morning following a night's fishing. As we went to school, we would stand and listen to the auctioneers selling the catch on the fish quay: plaice, whiting, herring, mullet, mackerel, John Dory, Mary Ann, according to the season; and from time to time tiny boats would come in to the quay, awash to the gunwales with a cargo of sprats. In the mornings the quay was a cheerful, bustling scene that regularly tempted us to be late for school.

In summer, the high spot was the Torquay and Brixham Regatta which is still held every year. There was keen competition to be allowed to sail aboard a fishing smack in the trawler race, although I think we boys used to enjoy the huge slabs of cake and hot cocoa as much as the race itself.

We were familiar with the large racing yachts, the predecessors of the modern 12-metres which compete for the America's Cup, such as King George V's *Brittania*, *White Heather* and *Shamrock*. These sailed down from Cowes to compete in their classes, but we did not envy them; we thought we had a jollier time taking part in the sculling and swimming races round the harbour, while the most daring attempted to walk the greasy pole and always fell in. I never even tried.

Summer ended and autumn began with a Harvest Festival of the Sea. Those trawler skippers and crews who worshipped at the Baptist Chapel would decorate it with fishing nets, oars, sails and lobster pots. On either side of the pulpit was hung a lighted red and green lantern for port and starboard, and all our hymns were of the sea. The Area Superintendent of the Baptist Church came to preach the sermon, dignified in a long frock coat. He was the Reverend Durbin, father of Evan Durbin, a brilliant boy who became a contemporary and friend at Oxford of Hugh Gaitskell. They joined the Labour Party together and in 1945 Evan won Edmonton for the Labour Party. I got to know him well after we both entered Parliament. Unfortunately he was drowned whilst on holiday in Cornwall when he had been a member of the House for only two years. Had he lived, his talent and his strength of character were such that he might

even have surpassed Hugh Gaitskell himself, and would undoubtedly
have had a great influence on Labour Party policy in the 1950s and 1960s.
Both Attlee and Dalton thought very highly of him.

Harvest Festival over, fishing settled down for the winter. The trawlers
did not go out to sea quite as often, for winter held its dangers. One tragic
evening in March 1922 the fleet put to sea in a rising storm which increased in force and grew worse during the night. But by morning it had
largely subsided and we made our way to school, down to the harbour
on one of those bright, shining early mornings when an angry yellow sun
follows the storm of the night before. The fish quay was empty; the
auctioneers had no fish to sell. The boats had not come home, and several
wives and mothers had gathered on the quay wall to watch and wait. We
arrived late at school that day and were not reproved, for the fathers of
our class-mates were still at sea. The life of the harbour seemed suspended.
As the day wore on, the trawler fleet, which had been scattered by the
gale, came struggling home, one by one, with stories of nets lost, sails
rent and masts broken. As afternoon school finished we ran down to the
harbour wall. The groups of women were smaller, but some were still
there hoping against hope. Two smacks never did come home – the *Love
and Unity* and the *Majestic*. Both were lost at sea with all their crews,
including one of our friends who had left school only the previous
Christmas at the age of fourteen.

Further disasters of a different nature were to follow. The sailing
smacks of the early 1920s were gradually ousted by steam, and I recall
our curiosity when the first steam trawler arrived, too big to enter the
inner harbour, and we learned that she had come from as far away as
Fleetwood and could freeze her catch on board. From then on, the sailing
smacks were doomed and their passing was hastened by the heavy loss of
nets caused, we were told, by the number of wrecks lying on the sea bed.
A local insurance scheme which protected the trawlers against such mis-
haps could only be financed by premiums too heavy for the men to bear.
So, over the years the fishing fleet dwindled and the boats were either
sold or broken up. I believe that today only three of these splendid, sturdy
Brixham sailing smacks remain.

My father became ill in the autumn of 1921 and was taken to the Naval
Hospital at Plymouth where he died after a painful illness at the early age
of forty-four. This ended the shortest and happiest period of my childhood.

I do not have a day-by-day, continuous memory of my father. I was only two years old in 1914 when he joined the Grand Fleet at Scapa Flow, and I do not recall him coming home during the war, although I suppose he did. He was demobilised when I was seven and died when I was nine. The only real time we spent together was during the two years before he died. It is those days that are among my happiest memories. I remember him as a jolly man, ready with a practical joke and a fund of exciting adventure stories. I would sit in the cabin at Berry Head while he told of his exploits as a naval diver, of how his ship had bombarded Zanzibar from the sea, and of fighting in the tropical jungles of Africa.

My mother used to say of him, 'Jim could always spin a good yarn' (and my wife thinks I have inherited the same trait), but it never occurred to me to disbelieve him. Indeed, I have some confirmation that his stories contained a good measure of truth, for when I became Parliamentary Secretary to the Admiralty in 1950 I looked up his naval record. This showed that he had served in the cruiser HMS *St George* when she was Flag Ship to the Africa Squadron, based at Simonstown in South Africa. While there, she had led the naval expedition to avenge the murder of the British Deputy Consul at Benin City in Nigeria. When the expedition arrived, companies of sailors from HMS *St George* were landed on the marshy banks of the Benin River and cut their way step by step through dense tropical jungle under spasmodic attack and constant threat of ambush. The column had several wounded and some died. As they neared Benin they found evidence of fresh human sacrifice lying across their path. These were believed to have been slaves who had been beheaded by the defenders of Benin as a sacrifice to the gods in order to turn back the expedition.

In due course Benin was captured, after fierce fighting in which several lives were lost on both sides. Some of the Deputy Consul's personal effects were found, lending colour to the belief that he had been murdered. My father related how shocked he and the others were by evidence that mass slaughter had taken place in the city before they captured it. Whilst they were there fire broke out, spread rapidly and completely destroyed the city. There was suspicion about how the fire had been started, though the official record maintained that it had been an accident. There is no doubt, however, that they were glad to leave behind 'this most bloody city' and march back to their ships.

My father recounted various versions of this story to me. Nearly seventy years after the Benin expedition, when I was appointed Chancellor of the Exchequer in 1964, I received out of the blue a letter from a very elderly retired naval officer, Captain Llewelyn RN. He had been a seventeen-year-old midshipman in HMS *St George* at the time of the expedition to Benin and had been in the thick of the fighting. He wrote because he wanted me to know that he remembered my father well as the boatswain's mate of his watch. I was naturally pleased to have this confirmation of my father's stories.

I remember my father as being more indulgent than my mother. It was she who had to undertake the less enjoyable role of disciplinarian of the family while he was away. After his death his body was brought back to Brixham for burial. I can still feel my intense sense of loss and of grief as we drove in a carriage behind the horse-drawn hearse, bearing his coffin draped in the White Ensign. The fishermen on Brixham quay took off their caps, as was the custom in those days, and fell silent as the procession passed them on its way to the churchyard. My father's fellow coastguards bore the coffin to the grave. I wish that he had lived longer and that I had known him better.

After his death the Board of Trade allowed my mother to remain in our coastguard cottage for some months but, eventually, we had to make way for someone else. She had nowhere to go, but we were taken in by the family of one of the deacons of the Brixham Baptist Chapel. At that time my mother received no pension, and even in later life she never told me how she had managed for food, fuel and clothes. On Saturday mornings I was sent with a large sack to the shipyard where I was allowed to pick up the discarded pieces of wood from under the keels of the trawlers that were even then being built. This helped us out with fuel.

Two days a week, on my way home from school for midday dinner, I was told to call at the sheds on the quay of one of the fish auctioneers who attended the Chapel. He would wrap a packet of fish in newspaper for me to take home. When there was no fish, the midday meal sometimes comprised no more than bread and dripping with a cup of cocoa made with hot water. I cannot say that I felt deprived at the time, but one consequence was that when I entered Parliament I became, and shall always remain, an advocate of universal school dinners.

The four-year interlude at Brixham came to an end in 1923. For some reason my mother decided that we should return to Portsmouth and my chief impression of the next few years is of living in rented rooms in other people's homes.

One of these temporary homes was that of Mrs Long, a Scotswoman whose husband, a dockyard worker, had been transferred from Rosyth dockyard. She started me off on my lifelong attachment to the Labour Party, for she was a member of the old Independent Labour Party and a strong member of the Cooperative Society. During the 1923 and 1924 General Elections she pressed me into service to run between the polling station and the Labour Party committee rooms, carrying the numbers of those who had voted. She also assisted my mother to prepare a claim to the Ministry of Pensions on the grounds that my father's death had been due to his war service. This was conceded by the short-lived Labour government of 1923/4, together with an additional allowance for my upkeep until I reached the age of fourteen. Our total income became twenty-six shillings per week, £1.30 in modern parlance, and with this my mother was able to rent unfurnished upstairs apartments in a private house, where I enjoyed a small bedroom to myself. When I passed the examination for entrance to the local secondary school, the Ministry of Pensions agreed to pay the school fee of two guineas a term, conditional upon my making good progress, and so at the end of every term a copy of my examination results was sent to the Ministry in London. I am sorry to say that for the first two or three years these reports were nearly always indifferent, if not downright bad, and the holiday would be clouded by a stern letter from the Ministry of Pensions bearing the threat that unless my work improved they would stop paying my school fees.

Those were unhappy days. I had to endure my mother's reproaches, my headmaster's anger, emphasised by frequent canings, and the distant but disquieting threats of the Ministry. I must have been wanting in common sense, for on looking back I do not understand why I did not do a little work. I could have kept out of trouble quite easily, but I idled my time away, except for reading anything I could lay my hands on. With each succeeding rebuke I became more uncooperative, withdrawn and obstinate, although it was constantly held in front of me that if I had to leave the school I would become an errand boy. My mother did her best to get me to work but neither her strict discipline nor her cajolery made me change my ways in my early teens.

The secondary school itself had been newly established with the primary purpose of preparing boys for work as apprentices in the naval dockyard, or for entry to the Navy as engine room and electrical artificers. These boys left school at the age of fourteen and fifteen. A small group stayed on and sat for what was then called the Senior Oxford School Leaving Certificate, and of this handful some entered the dockyard as shipwright apprentices and one or two achieved distinction. Perhaps the most notable was Charles Sherwin, three years older than me, who in later life became a senior naval constructor and designed the old *Ark Royal*.

I was in an awkward position because I failed to do any work except for following my undiscriminating interest in English and history, so it was of little avail to enter me for the artificer or dockyard apprentice exams. My mathematics and science were poor; indeed it was some time before I discovered that I could understand them at all.

In the school holidays I spent many hours in the Carnegie Public Library, reading omnivorously. The works of Dickens and Walter Scott I followed up with those of Thackeray, Henry Fielding, Samuel Richardson and Macaulay. The Public Library was a quiet place in which to read, and in winter it was also warm, which was a great consideration. Unfortunately its contents were limited to writers of the nineteenth century and earlier, and it was not until after I left Portsmouth that I discovered there were twentieth-century writers of repute.

Having realised that with a modicum of effort I could keep out of trouble and even pass examinations, my mathematics suddenly showed a startling improvement and the headmaster decided I should enter for the Senior Oxford Certificate, which I passed easily enough, with exemption from matriculation. I was told that this would qualify me for entry to a university, although such a far-fetched idea had never entered my calculations. At home it was tacitly assumed that the Senior Oxford Certificate marked the apogee of my education, so I sat for, and passed, an exam to become a Civil Service clerk.

This was an occasion for rejoicing at home, for I had fulfilled my mother's ambition that I should secure a permanent job offering a pension at sixty. It was not much of an ambition to hold out to a boy, but I suppose she was influenced by her own past insecurity. She rarely displayed her emotions, but on this occasion my sister and I persuaded her to climb on to the kitchen table and dance a little jig. We did not always have such fun – although I am sure she loved us, she did not easily convey it.

In her youth my mother had been a very good-looking young woman with a fine carriage, and I recall her in later life sitting bolt upright in her chair until near the end. I came to realise how fiercely she guarded her independence and respectability and how unwilling she was to rely upon others.

After my father's death she must have suffered greatly, if silently, from the indignities forced upon her by the need constantly to move from one set of rooms to another. As I write this I can count eight different houses in which we rented rooms in the short period of five years, and there may be more that I have forgotten. It was an unsettling time in which the Chapel acted as an anchor. And in the 1920s there was high unemployment. Whenever we walked past the Labour Exchange, we could see the long, quiet dole queues waiting every day. Unemployed men called regularly at the door offering notepaper for sale in order to make a few pence. When the first flakes of winter snow fell, they would come with brooms and ask to sweep the pavement in front of the rows of terraced houses. It was natural that with such a background my mother's first thought should be for our security. Her constant iteration, however, inhibited any feeling of adventure, although I do recall discussing with one of my schoolmates whether we should apply to go to New Zealand under a farm training scheme. He went and I stayed.

Except for election times, when I continued to run with the numbers from the polling station, we had little to do with politics, although I naturally thought of myself as Labour. There were other Labour supporters among our friends at the Baptist Chapel, and if we had been asked we would have agreed with a comment made many years later by Morgan Phillips, the General Secretary of the Labour Party, that the Labour Party owed more to Methodism than to Marxism.

My mother's joy at my success in the Civil Service examination was dampened when I received a letter from the Civil Service Commission instructing me to report to the Inland Revenue Tax Office at Maidstone, Kent. I would be paid £52 per year, plus a cost of living bonus, bringing my total pay up to £1 15s. 9d. per week. We knew no one in Maidstone, but the Baptist Chapel rallied round and I was found lodgings. As a leaving present I was presented with a large Bible signed by the Pastor and Sunday School Superintendent and inscribed with the text 'The steps of a good man are ordered by the Lord.' I still have it. As my mother and I stood waiting for the coach that would bear us to London on the first leg of my journey to Maidstone the Sunday School Superintendent, a jobbing builder, cycled up bearing a huge bag of ripe pears which he presented to me and, clutching this kind gift, I set off to an entirely new life, different from anything that had gone before. I was about to earn my own living.

2

Work at the Inland Revenue – political awakenings – marriage – the Second World War and naval service – victory at Cardiff South

Brixham had meant the freedom to roam in safety in total harmony with the sea, the rocks and cliffs, clambering in and out of boats and fishing trawlers in the harbour and absorbing the sense of close living in a small community. In Portsmouth, by contrast, the long rows of streets were anonymous and inhuman; living meant a series of rooms in terraced houses. The secondary school was housed in a church hall without a playground, much less a playing field, and only football on Saturday mornings at the public recreation ground to give any sense of space. The noises were urban noises. Of course we created our own enjoyment. One excitement was to run out from the pavement into the road to try to cling, unseen, to the tailboard of the horse-drawn carts as they clattered by, whilst other more envious boys would shout to the driver 'Whip behind, Guv'nor' as we rattled along. But although we made our own fun, Portsmouth streets gave a sense of restriction, a feeling of being hemmed in.

Maidstone was different from both Brixham and Portsmouth. It was a country town based on agriculture and some small industry, with the River Medway winding slowly past the parish church. The atmosphere was of the countryside, for no matter in which direction you walked you would be among fields within a very short time. Even in the lodgings that I shared with another young man in the centre of the town, we would wake up on certain mornings in spring and autumn to find the roads outside blocked by seemingly never-ending flocks of sheep being driven to the fair down by the river. At Portsmouth we had lived in the mighty shadow of the Navy and the dockyard. By contrast, in Maidstone the principal employers made custard, jellies and creamy toffees – hardly awe-inspiring.

The pace then was more leisurely than it is today. In the tax office on Saturday mornings there was always time to steal out to a nearby restaurant for coffee, and when the senior clerk discovered that I had begun to play tennis he used to make up a foursome from within the office, and we would leave for a couple of quick sets in the late afternoon during the summer.

The office would become busy on market days, with farmers coming from the surrounding villages with their problems. These chiefly concerned their unwillingness to pay the tithe duty, a small tax that must have cost more to collect than the revenue it yielded, and which has long since been abolished. The villages bore names like Boughton Monchelsea, Hollingbourne and Mereworth, names which still carry in my ears a faintly romantic sound.

When I joined the Inland Revenue in 1929, income tax was levied at four shillings in the pound – 20 pence in today's terms. But hardly any farmers paid tax, nor could they afford to, for agriculture was in the doldrums. Nor did the average industrial worker pay much, if any, tax. The main revenue was collected from companies and firms and from those working in the professions, such as solicitors, doctors, accountants and teachers, as well as from local council clerical staff. It was only with the onset of the Second World War that the majority of industrial workers became ensnared in the income tax net from which they have never escaped. Before the war the main interest of the annual Budget for the industrial worker and his wife was whether it proposed an increase in the tax on beer, cigarettes or tea.

There was no formal instruction in my duties as a tax clerk, but every new entrant was issued with three large loose-leaf books which set out what Somerset House thought we should know. They might as well have been written in Greek for all I understood of them at the beginning. We learned by watching and asking. We were told that after three years' practical experience we could sit for a written examination in London which, if passed, would qualify us for promotion. Equally, it was made clear that we would not be promoted automatically even if we did pass. We would have to wait our turn and it might be several years.

Although we were given no formal instruction in our duties, the Board of Inland Revenue made certain that every new entrant understood that he was required to follow a strict code of conduct. I had been in my new office for only two or three days when I was taken before a dignified and bearded Commissioner of Oaths. It was a momentous and solemn experience, for I, who had never taken an oath in my life, was required to swear that I would not disclose any taxpayer's affairs to others, with the inference of unmentionably awful penalties if I did. He gave me a lecture to the effect that I had a duty to point out to a taxpayer any relief that he might have omitted to claim. I was to be scrupulously fair; I must not involve myself actively in local or national party political activities. He made clear that I could count myself fortunate that the Inland Revenue had been willing to employ me. I was very impressed, but later, when I had reached the age of eighteen and was worldly wise, or so I thought, I realised that my mentor was a local Commissioner of Income Tax and, if there was the slightest doubt in any appeal, he would find for the tax-payer and against the Revenue. Nevertheless, there was much in what he said, and as I gained experience I found that members of the Tax Service regarded themselves as belonging to an elite which had no equal among the other clerical grades of the Civil Service. It did not matter whether this was true or not for it certainly resulted in a high degree of personal self-esteem, esprit de corps, and of loyalty to the Inland Revenue Department, all of which I gradually absorbed.

Leaving Portsmouth I had been transferred, as it were, from the bosom of one Church to the care of another, and found myself in a familiar and stable background.

I became a Sunday School teacher and it was in Sunday School that I met Audrey Moulton. She was a tall, slim sixteen-year-old, in the first year of the sixth form at the local grammar school. I recall clearly what she said to me at our first meeting, for at that moment in October 1929 I felt she was quite unlike anyone I had ever met before. I still think so. So began a liking that developed into affection and lasting love, over nearly sixty years. In due course I learned that she played tennis and so I bought a tennis racket. She was a very good player whilst I, although keen and enthusiastic about all ball games, never possessed a good eye or coordination. Fortunately she overlooked this blemish. Her father, Frank Moulton, was both Superintendent of the Sunday School and also a Deacon of the Church and, perhaps because of this, felt some Christian responsibility for a young man away from home. Audrey's family were very kind and invited me to table on Sundays, to picnics and to visits to the seaside, all of which I eagerly accepted. I benefited very much from being allowed to become so much a part of the home and family, and from joining in their activities. They were a stable and happy family with a strong sense of responsibility for others, yet enjoying themselves in ways that were quite outside my experience. I was young and impressionable and may have seen in Audrey's father a substitute for my own. At any rate I developed a lifelong admiration for his quiet sense of purpose, his integrity and his kindly patience with me, even when I argued vehemently for my half-thought-out views against his mature understanding. His daughter has inherited his qualities.

It was at Maidstone that I began a voyage of political discovery as a consequence of one of my seniors in the tax office introducing me to new books. Until then I described my politics as Labour because of our Portsmouth neighbours and our environment. I was to discover that there was a socialist philosophy with thinking and writing of a high order. I read all I could find of Bernard Shaw, H. G. Wells, H. N. Brailsford, G. D. H. Cole, Harold Laski and many others, and had a sense of exhilaration when I discovered that my boyhood sympathies were backed by a convincing criticism of the shortcomings of society, as well as by a well-argued philosophy of the alternative. Despite the injunction I had been given by the Commissioner of Oaths, I quietly joined the Maidstone Labour Party and endeavoured to overcome the great gaps in my education by joining WEA evening classes in social history and economics, in which our tutor, an Oxford graduate by the name of de Vere, even dipped a toe into *Das Kapital*.

I wanted to tell everyone about my discovery of socialism and must have been a very trying young man. This new experience that I was living through seemed much more real and true than the fundamentalist religion in which I had been brought up, and I impetuously dashed off a letter of resignation to the Secretary of the Maidstone Baptist Chapel. This created something of a stir. It was apparently acceptable for someone unostentatiously to stop going to church services and gradually drift away, but it was practically unheard of formally to resign membership. So it was arranged that one of the Senior Deacons should have a conversation with me. He was a wise man who argued that although he disagreed with my new-found socialist beliefs, there need be no conflict between them and Church membership. Many tenets of the Christian faith were reconcilable with socialism. He rather surprised me by adding that I should not believe that every Christian subscribed to the kind of fundamental beliefs in which I had been brought up, and I need not fear that I would be behaving hypocritically if I remained a Church member. So I stayed, but from then on, my activities in the Labour Party and Trade Union Movement increasingly had the first charge on my energies, although I never forget the immense debt I owe to a Christian upbringing, nor have I ever escaped its influence.

I joined the Association of Officers of Taxes, the AOT, a small but remarkable trade union, which managed to attract a 95 per cent voluntary membership without the benefit of a closed shop and despite the fact that its ten thousand members were scattered in six hundred separate towns and offices throughout the length and breadth of Britain. This was mainly due to the vigour and organisational ability of the General Secretary, Douglas Houghton, who was then a young man in his early thirties. His example and success were such that I have never been a devotee of the closed shop, although I know that industrial conditions on the shop floor are now very different from those at that time. Although I did not meet Douglas Houghton until some years later, he was to have a great influence on my early life and my involvement in the Trade Union Movement.

One of his inspirations was to fill the gap left by the failure of the Board of Inland Revenue to provide new recruits with any systematic instruction. He decided that a course should be prepared to enable us to pass the qualifying examination for promotion and, with the voluntary aid of other members of the union, a course of tuition was prepared which covered the syllabus for the examination. He then submitted the proposed course to the Inland Revenue Department and received their informal blessing, although they did not officially recommend it to new recruits. The tuition course was a very useful bait to draw new members into the AOT, for even those who could find no other reason for belonging to a trade union understood this to be a positive attraction. For the sum of fifteen shillings (75p), the AOT was ready to provide new recruits with a six-month correspondence course: a written paper to answer, which arrived regularly once a fortnight, and a voluntary tutor allocated to each student, drawn either from within the student's own office or from a nearby town. All this was voluntary work of a high order, and with such detailed care the new recruits could hardly fail to pass the examination, which we did in large numbers. Houghton gathered around him a remarkable group of young men and I put this on record as but one of many examples of his capacity for constructive and imaginative thinking and positive organisation.

At that time, the Civil Service was rigidly stratified. The clerical class, of which I was a member, was drawn from the secondary schools, the executive class from the sixth forms of the grammar schools, and the administrative class from the universities. Once in the clerical class you could rarely, if ever, escape from it by any internal means. It followed that in a period when higher education was less accessible than it is today, there were many young people confined to the clerical class who were quite as able as some university entrants.

Douglas Houghton saw this clearly and pressed the Board of Inland Revenue to hold an internal examination that would enable members of the clerical class to be promoted to the tax inspectorate. After much negotiation, he persuaded the Department to hold an examination from which ten clerks a year would be selected. It was hardly a revolution but it was the opening of a door, though much ability was squandered and frustrated until the class system was modified under the pressure of war.

More immediately pressing were our living conditions. The Inland Revenue recruited by examination in a short period at the end of the 1920s more than a thousand boys and girls of sixteen years of age, despatched them from their homes to live in lodgings in strange towns where they were expected to survive on thirty-five shillings a week with an increase to £2 10s per week at the age of eighteen. After two or three years they were often up-ended again and sent off to a different town or to London. But there were few resignations. We knew we were lucky to have permanent jobs and we put up with it, although not without protest. Conditions did not improve and the new young entrants banded themselves together, using the publicity facilities of the AOT to begin an agitation for better pay and conditions. I had reached the ripe age of twenty and found myself at the centre of this activity. I became the organiser and Secretary of this new movement, and Stanley Raymond, who was a year younger than me, was elected Chairman. Raymond, who had been brought up in an orphanage, was extremely dogged and tenacious, a man of great courage and loyalty. Later on he was one of the ten clerks a year to escape from the clerical class as a result of the internal examination. After war service he carved out a career with British Railways and rose to become Chairman of the Board, but then fell out with Barbara Castle, a fate he shared with me, and resigned. In the fullness of time I was able, when I was Home Secretary, to appoint him as Chairman of the Gaming Board for Great Britain in 1968.

Raymond and I formed a good combination – I was the more impetuous and he the steadier of the two. In my capacity as Secretary I despatched angry articles to the union journal, wrote countless letters, called well-attended and boisterous meetings in London and Manchester, and bombarded the union's Executive Committee with demands for improvement in our conditions. When all this failed, I personally visited the awesome precincts of Somerset House and delivered a pompous message to the Chairman of the Board of Inland Revenue, informing him that the AOT no longer represented us new entrants and that we wished the Chairman to deal with us direct. To my consternation he ignored this bombshell. Our older colleagues were shocked and angered by this behaviour and, looking back, I would have felt as they did. They were especially incensed by my apparent intention to split the union, although I was acting more out of ignorance than malice. I was described as 'an impatient and unreasonable young man in a hurry', a verdict that was probably true. One of my older critics who had emerged unscathed from the Great War wrote: 'Oh to be in Mr Callaghan's shoes with his life before him and opportunity looming ahead. I can understand his youthful ardour to smash through to better conditions but I do deplore the querulous tone of his article.' How truly he wrote, though I doubt whether he foresaw the tremendous opportunities and satisfaction that trade union and political life were to give me.

All our agitation met with no immediate success but the efforts of Raymond and myself, backed by several hundreds of angry young men and women, had created a genuinely popular movement, and alerted Douglas Houghton to our problems and to the need for proper representation. As a result, in 1933, when I was twenty-one, I was elected by the union's Annual Conference to the National Executive Committee.

A short time later I was transferred from Maidstone to a tax office in London and as a result came closely in touch with Houghton. He was thirty-six at that time and seemed several generations older than me.

I have already written of his creative and organising ability. He thought on a bigger scale than his contemporaries and used his eloquence and negotiating skill to bolster the union's membership, and to establish a unique place for himself in Civil Service trade unionism. He was pugnacious and capable of wild outbursts when crossed. We all suffered but none of us ever knew how far he simulated these in order to get his way with more cautious colleagues who did not grasp a new idea as quickly as he. But the measure of his leadership was that he gained the lifelong loyalty and admiration of the membership. They knew he was different, and his contemporaries have cherished him all his life as an outstanding leader, who forged their union for them and achieved conditions they could not have won without him. It speaks volumes that as late as 1986, when those of his contemporaries still alive were in their eighties, over sixty of them gathered in the House of Lords to pay tribute to him.

In the late 1940s, Douglas Houghton became a well-known radio broadcaster, and he was in due course Member of Parliament, Chairman of the TUC, a Minister of the Crown, and Chairman of the Parliamentary Labour Party, before going to the House of Lords. But his first love has always been the small union which he took over as a young man in his early twenties, and built into the present-day Inland Revenue Staff Federation.

When he first knew of me he was not well disposed, because our new entrant movement seemed to threaten the unity of the AOT. But once I had been elected to the National Executive Committee, he went out of his way to encourage me and, three years later in 1936, partly due to his influence, I was elected by the Executive Committee to the post of full-time Assistant Secretary. I was then twenty-four. This meant my resignation from the Inland Revenue Department, a letter announcing which I sent off without a pang of regret.

A natural doubt about taking such a step was expressed by my mother. Was it not, she asked, a serious risk to give up a pensionable post in the Civil Service? How could I be sure the Association would survive? Was there any guarantee that the job would be permanent? I did my best to reassure her but I failed to overcome her doubts. For myself, I had none. I knew this was what I wanted to do more than anything else. A new life beckoned which would give me the chance to put into practice what I believed. The material rewards were not to be sneezed at either, although they were secondary. The Federation paid me £350 per annum, much more than I had ever received in my life. I enjoyed the luxury of a room to myself and, even more surprising, a telephone and a part-time secretary.

I plunged with enthusiasm into the work, fighting cases on behalf of individual members, learning the art of negotiation, watching Houghton's handling of committees. There were failures as well as successes. On one occasion I led a small team to conduct negotiations with the Board of Inland Revenue. Houghton was, no doubt, trying me out. We had a good case and it fell to me, as principal spokesman, to put it. I was eloquent and forceful, pressed it to the extreme, rebuffed the rather weak opposing arguments with ease and with scorn, and altogether gave what I thought was a brilliant display of fireworks. But pride goes before a fall and, at the end of the afternoon, despite the easy wicket I had been batting on, our team came away without having gained a single halfpenny. I was furious and could not understand what had gone wrong. But D. N. Kneath, one of the older and more silent members of the negotiating team from south Wales, knew. And the next day he told me. 'Remember, my boy, more flies are caught with honey than with vinegar.' And that has remained one of my negotiating maxims ever since.

I had better luck on another occasion with a claim heard by the Civil Service Arbitration Tribunal, a group of three members representing the Treasury and the Staff, with an independent chairman. Professor Harold Laski of the London School of Economics, a member of the Labour Party National Executive Committee, was the Staff nominee. Not only did I win the case but Laski wrote to me when it was over congratulating me on my presentation and inviting me to see him at the LSE. When I did so he urged me to study for a degree as an external student, promising he would oversee my studies and progress. This was a great opportunity but I did not accept, for trade union and local Labour Party work was taking up all my thought and energy. Despite this, he arranged for me to use the LSE Library and kept in touch with me in the years that followed, using his good offices to put my name forward as a potential Parliamentary candidate.

I devoured his books on the grammar of politics, sovereignty and other subjects, as did so many young people at that time. He had a great influence on his students, especially those who came from the overseas Empire and Dominions: India, Australia, Canada, Malaya. During the next three decades, whenever I travelled abroad I would meet men occupying high positions in politics or in the Civil Service of their country who would speak with affection and gratitude of his kindness and influence upon them. Although he did not know it, it was many of his former students who helped to keep the Commonwealth together during the transformation from imperial rule. In India, even today, there is a Harold Laski Institute devoted to his memory.

In personal conversation he fascinated the young and unsophisticated man that I was. He would speak familiarly and casually of his conversation on the day previously with Attlee, of how Churchill had sent for him to ask for his opinion, of his correspondence with Roosevelt. In later years, I am sorry to say, I had to conclude that on occasion he was romancing, but at the time he made me feel I was indirectly in touch with the great world of politics where the real decisions were taken. Harold Laski had his critics but, like many others, I remain grateful to his memory, for the trouble he took to help an unknown and rather prickly young man.

Like many other trade unionists before and since, I felt a natural affiliation between my work as a trade union officer and my political convictions. But I could not push these too far, for most of the members of the AOT were not Labour Party supporters. The fact is that before the Second World War the Labour Party did not achieve a high degree of 'respectability' with white-collar workers as a Party with which they could associate, and for which they could vote. Civil servants, unlike most other white-collar workers, were generally well organised in trade unions, but that did not lead naturally to a feeling of affiliation with the Labour Party. 'White-collar', I note, is a post-war description of such workers. In the 1930s the more usual term was 'black-coated' worker, and today, to judge by dress, even 'white-collar' is old hat as a correct description of what the fashionable non-manual worker wears. Indeed in dress, as in other matters, non-manual and manual workers, both men and women, are becoming more indistinguishable, and whilst I rejoice at this I confess I become tired of seeing jeans and trainers on all occasions.

Pre-war, the white-collar trade unions operated in an even more hostile climate than the manual unions. The employers had a secure grip on the white-collar workers. Sacking was easy, white-collar solidarity was low, many were badly paid, and jobs were hard to find. One of many efforts to improve their lot was made by the Fabian Society, which called a conference in 1936 of professional and non-manual workers to press the need for trade union combination. About fifty organisations attended, including the TUC and a number of Labour MPs. But one of the more notable speeches was made by a Conservative, Harold Macmillan, who was the MP for Stockton. I can still recall him, elegantly dressed, precise in speech, almost artificial in manner, but the delegates were ready to forgive his mannerisms for it was a coup to have him with us. He moved a resolution calling on government to formulate immediately a national plan of public works to relieve unemployment, and his earnestness made us forget his manner and carried us along with him. How ironic it is that fifty years later it was necessary for him to repeat the same arguments. I have listened to Harold Macmillan in the House of Commons many times and, however much I may have disagreed, I could never deny that throughout his life he has been consistent in his detestation of unemployment and in his belief that government has a major role to play in solving this human problem.

I remember his 1936 speech, but I have never reminded him that he was preceded by a young man who called for the repeal of the Trades Union Disputes Act, 1927. This had prevented the Civil Service unions from affiliating to the TUC and it was an injustice we were determined to remove. My resolution was carried and, ten years later, as one of the new generation of Labour Members in the House of Commons, I took part in removing this hated Act from the statute book.

The modern example of how little governments learn from their past mistakes is the decision to compel the staff of the Government's Head-quarters Communications Centre to resign from membership of their unions. I have no doubt that in due course this particular folly will also be tipped into the garbage bin.

When the general election was declared in 1935, I was certain that the Labour Party must be the favourite to win. There were no public opinion polls in those days and we felt that the whole nation must be as scornful as we of the so-called National Government, which was Conservative in all but name. It had failed to overcome mass unemployment and the miserable poverty of the north of England, Scotland and Wales persisted. I visited them all in my capacity as Assistant Secretary to the union. We read the evidence of the Rowntree Report, which revealed substantial malnutrition among some children and the elderly.

We were deeply critical at the failure of the British Government to take effective action in the League of Nations to assist Abyssinia when Musso-lini declared that independent country to be a Protectorate. We denounced Italy's action as an imperialistic hangover from the nineteenth-century European carve-up of Africa, and at Labour Party meetings I argued that Mussolini would be compelled to disgorge his prey if only the British Government would give a lead to other members of the League of Nations in favour of sanctions against Italy's trade and her supplies of materials. Against this background we were sure, in our youthful idealism, that the rest of the country would respond to our call that the rule of law be upheld as the best way to preserve world peace. In the event sanctions against fascist Italy were never enforced, so no one can say what success the League might have had. In the light of later experience we may have been unduly optimistic, but it is certainly true that the collective failure to act gave Mussolini and later Hitler a psychological boost in planning further aggression against Austria and Czechoslovakia.

The Peace Ballot of 1935 had given a clear signal to the Government of public support for sanctions. More than eleven million people voted in a massive door-to-door canvass, conducted by many thousands of sup-porters of the League of Nations. More than ten millions voted in favour of taking economic and non-military measures against an aggressor, and nearly seven millions were in favour of military measures. Surely, I thought, the fact that the Government had so flagrantly flouted this great upsurge of opinion, added to their miserable record on unemployment and poverty, would lead to their being swept from office. Not so. Labour won only 154 seats whilst the Conservatives, with 432 seats, were given an undeserved vote of confidence. There were political repercussions on the left, some of our contemporaries arguing that Labour should refuse to cooperate in government measures to relieve unemployment and poverty, because capitalism was rotten and near collapse and our assistance with such measures would only prolong its death throes. They concluded objectively, therefore, that any help by the Labour Movement would only prolong the misery of the masses. This was a view that I could never stomach and which most of us rejected.

Abroad, fascism was on the march and the democracies dithered. The publications of the Left Book Club, which was in the hands of Victor Gollancz, John Strachey and Harold Laski, poured out a stream of evidence that Europe was on the brink of a war between fascism and communism. The outbreak of the Spanish Civil War in 1936 lent colour to this, with the Soviet Union backing the legitimate Republican Government with arms, while Germany and Italy armed Franco's rebels. Audrey and I joined wholeheartedly in the protests and demonstrations against the British Government's refusal to send arms to the Spanish Government and I managed to convince the Federation's Conference that they too should organise a fund to send medical supplies to Republican Spain, basing my argument largely on the grounds that Franco had denied trade union rights to the workers. I led a deputation of protest from the Lewisham Labour Party to Hugh Dalton, who was then the National Executive Committee Spokesman on Foreign Affairs. We had a lengthy meeting in the House of Commons and Dalton disappointed us when he said that the NEC could not support an all-out demand for the supply of arms.

Dalton was known to be one of the strongest and most steadfast opponents of the appeasement doctrine, and at the time I could not understand his attitude. Later I concluded that the NEC had taken this decision because the Labour Movement was not united upon the issue. Many of our Catholic supporters were divided in their minds because the struggle seemed to be between a Christian Franco and an atheist Russia.

Hitler's menacing influence grew larger year by year, bringing terror to both Jews and socialists inside Germany as he destroyed that country's democratic institutions and rule of law. When he had done this, he turned his malign attention to Germany's neighbours. We seemed to witness a new crisis every year, each one more intense than the last, as Hitler in a succession of calculated steps denounced the Locarno Pact, re-militarised the Rhineland, broke the Versailles Treaty by building an army half a million strong, created a German Air Force, built powerful so-called pocket battleships, and sent fighter planes and tanks to support Franco. When he turned his attention to Germany's neighbours, the world was bombarded with loud cries for *lebensraum* as he constantly increased his pressure on Austria, Czechoslovakia and Poland. I seem to recall, though this may be exaggerated, that never a weekend went by without the wireless reporting some 'grievance' of Hitler's that he argued must be remedied without delay. These demands were made at huge rallies, and we listened to him ranting and screaming abuse at his opponents against the mindless cries of '*Sieg Heil, Sieg Heil*' from his hypnotised followers. As fast as one grievance was removed, he manufactured another. Slowly the British people began to believe that nothing could finally satisfy him.

This attitude was not shared by most of the press nor by the Conservative Party, both of which were desperately anxious to believe that peace could be ensured if only Hitler's grievances were removed. Moreover, the Government shared his hatred of Bolshevism. Most of us on the left were unduly ready to give the benefit of the doubt to Stalin but we were more clear-sighted about Hitler's wickedness. A consequence of the terrible losses of the Great War of 1914–18 was that my generation had grown up with a horror of war. We hated it as much as we detested Hitler and the Nazis, and this led many of us to oppose the rebuilding of Britain's defences. Some of our leaders like Churchill, Hugh Dalton, and Ernest Bevin understood better, but even as late as 1939 I recall arguing that the Government's proposals for conscription constituted an interference with our individual liberties, and urging that we should rely on the voluntary principle. I was wrong, but I carried my principle into practice by volunteering for service in the Navy in May 1940.

In political terms, the 1930s were a disaster. Unemployment at home, the feebleness of the democracies abroad, the palpable shadow of the war all combined to give many young people like myself a feeling of political hopelessness. In personal terms, though, the 1930s were a very happy period. Audrey and I were both living in lodgings in London, as she had qualified as a domestic science teacher, and we explored its many delights together. We squeezed into the hard seats high in the gods of the Old Vic, and watched Sybil Thorndike play St Joan. We listened to *Peer Gynt*. We went to the Queen's Hall, then adjoining Broadcasting House but later blitzed, to listen to the Promenade Concerts at a price of two shillings (or 10p), heard the newly established BBC Orchestra night after night, conducted by Henry Wood and Thomas Beecham, and shared the experience of listening to the Italian conductor Toscanini taking us through all the Beethoven symphonies with his metronome-like precision.

We bought a 1921 Wolseley drop-head coupé with a dickey seat for £8 10s. It carried us to and from Audrey's home at Maidstone at week-ends and even took us as far as Cornwall and back, although we needed two days for the journey. We sold it shortly before we were married for £1 10s. It was still running but we could not afford the garage rent and had to confess that it was not very reliable. We went for long walks in the Kent countryside, heard Bernard Shaw, H. G. Wells and others lecture at the Friends' Meeting House, and played a great deal of tennis.

While I busied myself with Federation work, Audrey enrolled on a four-year external London University course in economics organised by the Royal Arsenal Cooperative Society. The tutor was a young lecturer with a growing reputation, who was also a Labour candidate for Parliament, and so began a lasting friendship. His name was Hugh Gaitskell. Audrey completed the course successfully, specialising in the causes of children's malnutrition and its remedies. This awakened her life-long interest in children's welfare, in which field her life has followed a consistent and rewarding theme. We married on her birthday, 28 July 1938, and rented a semi-detached house in Norwood for one pound a week. It was a new experience for me, since I had lived in other people's homes for most of my life.

Alas, we had no sooner settled ourselves than Hitler staged the latest of his crises. A few months earlier, in March 1938, he had sent the German Army to occupy Austria, where they met with no resistance, and during the summer he turned his attention to Czechoslovakia. He used the demands of the Sudeten Germans to bring pressure to bear on the Czech Government to cede the Sudetenland to Germany. The Czechs resisted and seemed ready to fight. Week by week the pressure and the tension increased. All of Europe had its attention focused on the problem, and everywhere there was talk of the inevitability of war. Hitler was con-vinced that France and Britain would not fight, and in this was correct, for after Neville Chamberlain had visited the German Chancellor at Berchtesgaden, the British Government brought pressure on the Czechs to give way. Deserted by France and Britain, the Czechs did so, and

Sudetenland was handed over to Germany. Six months later the whole of Czechoslovakia was occupied by Hitler. I still recall the mingled relief and shame with which I heard the news of the Munich settlement. It was only human to feel relief that our new life together, so lately begun, was not to be disrupted by war, but I was ashamed of feeling such relief, and ashamed too for the action of my country in unjustly sacrificing the Czechs to an evil dictator.

Audrey and I decided that we would do some small thing by way of recompense, and we got in touch with an organisation in London which was extending hospitality to refugees from the Nazis. They referred us to Bernhard Menne in Prague, a German journalist and Social Democrat, who suspected his arrest would come at any time. The Home Office had issued special dispensations for such categories and we invited him to London to live with us. He stayed for some months, gallantly putting up with our English ways. His wife later escaped from Prague to Katowice in Poland in August 1939 and reached London just before the war began. When she arrived they removed to north London where they remained throughout the war. He was deeply hurt at being classified an 'enemy alien', and when the war was over returned to Germany, his spiritual home, and became the editor of the newspaper *Die Welt*. We remained in touch until his death.

Frau Menne was vehement about Hitler and the Nazis, and after one conversation I made notes which give a flavour of our mood at the time. I had defended the early RAF flights in which they had dropped leaflets and not bombs on Berlin. Surely, I said, they would make the German people realise the depths of Hitler's depravity. Frau Menne would have none of it. I recorded her as saying, 'Bomb them. Until they feel the bombs in Berlin they will not think they are at war. Leaflets are interpreted as a sign of weakness. The only thing the mass of Germans recognise is superior strength.' Bernhard demurred and predicted with remarkable accuracy the length of the war. He forecast that it would be very long, at least six years, and that Germany would have immense successes during the first two years. But Britain and France must not give up. We would win in the end.

I expressed my bitterness about the Soviet Union's betrayal of socialist principles in their invasion of Poland. Menne said that it was no more than he would have expected. He had been a member of the German Communist Party until he had paid a visit to the Soviet Union in 1927 and disliked what he saw. The German communists, he argued, bore a heavy responsibility for the growth of the fascist state in Germany. They had held democracy in the same contempt as the Nazis and it was from them that the Nazis had learned their revolutionary techniques.

I replied that Allied policies since 1918 also bore a responsibility for Hitler's rise and I quoted Stresemann's words, that if he had just received one word of encouragement from the Allies, 'I could have won this generation for peace.' Menne was not convinced.

In October 1939, one month after the war began, I set down my personal aims:

1 Our colonies to be put under an International Commission and Britain to cease its monopoly of colonial trade and preference in the Dominions' markets.
2 India to be given genuine Home Rule and not just a makeshift substitute.
3 Britain to cease enduring two millions unemployed; the Bank of England to be controlled and a National Investment Bank to be established; coal-mining, cotton, woollen and agriculture industries to be planned in the national interest.
4 Hitler and the Nazi idea to be destroyed.
5 Do not create new small European states whose artificial boundaries would cause political tension. Rather we should remove economic barriers so as to encourage free exchange of trade and ideas.

I concluded that it was impossible for a Conservative Government under Chamberlain to adopt all of these aims. Therefore, until there was a change in government, I could be only a conditional supporter of the war. I have reproduced these notes as I set them down in the autumn of 1939, not because they have any intrinsic merit but to illustrate how one young man felt at the time. The reader will see that my mood was far from heroic – we were too close to the 1914–18 War for that.

As soon as war was declared we obediently stuck long strips of narrow brown paper criss-crossed over the windows as we had been instructed, in order to lessen the danger of flying glass. We bought blackout material for curtains but Audrey's heart was in preparing our tiny spare bedroom for the arrival of the baby she was expecting. Our neighbour, a prudent man, had spent the summer digging a small semi-underground shelter at the bottom of his garden, and on the first Sunday in September, as Chamberlain told us that war had been declared, the air raid siren wailed and he and his family went to their shelter. After the siren there fell the silence of a peaceful Sunday morning and a few minutes later, since nothing had happened, he emerged and called us over to join them. Together we sat in the gloom looking at one another and waiting for we knew not what. We had listened to many accounts of bombing by German and Italian aircraft in the Spanish Civil War, and we expected our ordeal to be swift and severe. I had been told on impeccable authority by someone who had been in Spain that if a bomb fell near by, and one's back was touching the shelter wall, death would certainly result through shock, as a result of the vibrations through the earth. I passed on this information and we all leaned forward on the wooden benches. We speculated whether huge armadas of German aircraft were at that moment flying towards us to appear overhead and drop their bombs on the London suburbs. But everything remained quiet and we continued to sit and wait. The sun was shining warmly outside the shelter, which began to feel a little damp. The grass needed cutting; the Sunday dinner was in the oven; and after a consultation, we all agreed that it might be safe to venture out, provided we did not go too far, so that if we heard the bombers approaching we could run back quickly. Nothing happened during the afternoon, nor that night, nor in the weeks that followed. It seemed an anti-climax.

No fighting took place during the winter of 1939–40. So far as I personally was concerned, the major casualty of the winter was the loss of two front teeth through walking into a postbox in pitch-black darkness because of the blackout whilst on my way home from visiting our newly born baby daughter, Margaret, and her mother in hospital.

The winter passed and in the spring of 1940 Chamberlain told the nation that Hitler had 'missed the bus'. Almost as he said it, the German Army occupied Norway and Denmark without great difficulty. In May 1940 Hitler invaded the Netherlands, Belgium and France. This was the war we knew, a replay so to speak of 1914, but we were totally unprepared for the swift collapse of the French Army, which was held in exaggerated awe by laymen in Britain. The Germans turned the impregnable Maginot Line, overran it on their way to the coast, and France was psychologically betrayed and defeated almost before the fighting got underway. Her defeat created a hurricane of activity in Britain. Chamberlain was replaced by Churchill who immediately appointed Ernest Bevin as Minister of Labour. One of his first engagements was to address a thousand trade union delegates in the Westminster Central Hall at a conference called to rally support behind the new Government.

Bevin appeared at the foot of the platform; mountainous as ever, and

rolling heavily from side to side, he climbed the steps and began to speak.
He read a message from the new Prime Minister emphasising the gravity
of Britain's situation following the defeat of France, and asking the trade
unions to throw their full support into the struggle. We sat silent as
Bevin gave us an outline of his plans to mobilise the workers. It was
obvious that in so many words he was asking delegates to set aside many
of the sacred trade union rights and practices that they had preserved
for decades. From any other man and in any other circumstance it would
have been an impossible pill for them to swallow. But I, as a young delegate, was struck by the skilful way in which he balanced his demands by
undertaking with great force and emphasis to seek all possible advantages
and amenities for the workers in their changed circumstances, and to set
up machinery to ensure that they did not lose out. For this purpose,
trade union officials were to be seconded to the Minister of Labour as
inspectors; the Department would take personal charge of the welfare
of the workers as far as billeting and feeding were concerned. Bevin was
gentle with the miners in calling for longer working hours; growled at
the employers, 'I feel happy now – as you will realise – that I can assist
in sacking the boss. Big Business has failed'; and spoke even at that early
moment of the task of reconstruction that would face the nation after we
had won. Everything should meanwhile be subordinated to using our
resources of labour as efficiently as possible to support our comrades in
the battle line, and the 'beautiful lads' in the Air Force. He concluded:
'Nothing stands between you and enslavement but the bodies of your
own sons with the courage of their own souls to resist.' He swept us along
by the sheer power of his personality and the force of his conviction, and
when the vote was taken only four delegates dissented.

One moment remains forever imprinted on my memory: the shock
that ran through the Central Hall as Bevin delivered the news that the
retreat of the British Expeditionary Force towards the coast could not
be stopped; the Belgians and French were laying down their arms. Indeed, it seemed as though the Germans might totally destroy the British
Army, and we would have to start again from scratch. There is no reference to this dramatic moment in the official record of Bevin's speech
published by the TUC. Several years later I wrote to Walter Citrine,
that most meticulous of TUC Secretaries, to enquire if my recollection
was accurate. He confirmed that it was and added that it was omitted
from the printed report because it was 'secret'. Three days after Bevin
spoke, the evacuation of our Army began by sea from Dunkirk, and only

a miracle of improvisation and good weather enabled most of our troops to be brought back to Britain, though without their equipment.

In the same month I visited the local recruiting office and volunteered for service in the Royal Navy. It was my intention to enlist as a seaman but I was told I could be accepted only as a ship's cook. I returned home and wrote an indignant letter to the Admiralty, addressing the envelope to the Lords Commissioners in person. Two weeks later, with the confusion and disorganisation of the Dunkirk operation only just behind us, I received a polite and formal letter from a Lieutenant Commander at the Admiralty to inform me 'that Their Lordships have been pleased to accept you for service as an Ordinary Seaman'. But I was not permitted to join at that stage, for directions issued under the Emergency Powers Act described full-time trade union officials as being in a 'reserved occupation', and as Douglas Houghton said he could not spare me, I had to stay where I was. This was a source of friction between us until he eventually agreed that I could go. In fairness, I now admit that he was probably right to hold on to me in view of the vast amount of work thrown upon the Federation office by the transfer of the Inland Revenue Headquarters at Somerset House to its new home at Llandudno in North Wales.

Foiled in my effort to secure my release, I joined the newly established Local Defence Volunteers, whose name was later changed to the Home Guard. We drilled with .303 Lee Enfield rifles at a nearby cricket ground, paid one visit to Bisley to practise shooting, and at nights left our homes to guard the cricket pavilion and a railway bridge. We were determined enough but if the expected German parachutists had arrived we would have been sitting ducks. We also mastered the air raid precautions drill which came in useful in the autumn of 1940 when the Germans began to drop a type of small fire bomb nicknamed 'Molotov cocktail' on the London suburbs. We extinguished several of these by climbing into neighbours' lofts armed with nothing more than stirrup pump, pails of water and sandbags. I whiled away the hours on nightly watch with a neighbour, Gordon Denniss, who had also recently married. We came to know each other well and have remained friends ever since.

The main topic of our nightly talks was the imminent threat of German invasion. The Molotov cocktails had extinguished all traces of my rather pompous 'conditional' support for the war. During the summer of 1940 the mood of the country was for swift decision and drastic action, however unpalatable, and Churchill was the man for the job.

I reproduce some notes that I made in October 1940 to illustrate the change in my attitude:

> In the last 12 months Poland, Norway, Denmark, Holland, Belgium, France and Roumania [have all] fallen under Hitler's control. A year ago such a prospect would have seemed fantastic. Had I been told, I should have said that in such circumstances we ought to pack up because there was nothing more we could do. But here we are only just beginning to fight. We didn't really start until France went under, and irrationally enough we are more sure now that we cannot be beaten than we were in 1939. Russia remains out, interested only in herself. Stafford Cripps is our Ambassador. How ludicrous that would have seemed a year ago. The USA is practically in the War and will be right in very soon. Japan is hesitating but I don't think she will come in. It is not worth her while. Spain is holding the balance but she will stay out until our chances are worse than they appear today.

Party political activity had been all but abandoned but trade union work went on at a fast pace. Douglas Houghton despatched me to Llandudno to acquire a suitable office for the union. I found an empty boarding house on the north shore at Llandudno, and we removed to it a substantial part of the union's records and furniture.

At the top of the house was a useful flat and Audrey, with our infant daughter Margaret, moved there as a kind of housekeeper. From then on, I divided my time between London and Llandudno, sleeping when in London in the basement of the Federation office at St George's Square near the Embankment. This was a safe place for it had been shored up with strong wooden beams to protect us in the event of the office collapsing during a bomb attack.

The Blitz had begun and as offices were required to provide their own fire-watchers I served a useful dual purpose as a semi-permanent basement dweller. The Pimlico and Victoria areas suffered heavily during the bombing. The nights were a mixture of the whistle of bombs as they fell, the counterpoint of anti-aircraft fire, the acrid smell of brick and plaster dust that filled the air as the Victorian houses were hit and collapsed, the ash swirling around the streets after fire-bomb attacks. Huge craters and piles of rubble that once had been dwellings blocked the roads as each morning broke. For the first time in my life I came face to face with violent death. During one attack, as we sheltered in our basement, we heard and felt the vibrations of a particularly heavy explosion that rocked our building so violently that we knew the bomb must have fallen very close by. Despite the blackout we did not need torches to find the area it had hit. Flames were leaping from burning upper floors and roofs, and from broken gas mains in the street. Fifty yards away in Lupus Street a whole block of houses had been devastated by a land mine. All that remained was a huge crater together with a tangled pile of masonry, beams and bricks. And then someone caught sight of an arm. It was protruding from the rubble, palm wide open, fingers outstretched, a ring on the third finger. We knew that no one could have survived but it was impossible to stand by and do nothing. We tore fruitlessly at the rubble, piece by piece, until the Fire Brigade arrived.

The men and women of the Fire Brigade, the police, the ARP wardens, the ordinary citizens of London – how matter-of-fact, how calm, how stoical, how heroic they were as they carried out their duties, night after night, with hardly a respite. I was more fortunate than they, for at regular intervals I escaped to Llandudno. But we could rarely persuade Douglas Houghton to leave London. He remained at St George's Square throughout the war.

I continued to ask him for my release to the Navy and shortly after our second daughter, Julia, was born in October 1942, Houghton agreed. One reason for his change of mind was that he could replace me with my friend Cyril Plant, who was somewhat older than me. Plant took my place as Assistant Secretary and in due course became General Secretary of the Federation, Chairman of the TUC and later Lord Plant of Bessenden. His characteristics were honesty, straightforwardness and infectious enthusiasm in everything he did, including his many years of voluntary service to the Civil Service Sanatorium Society.

As soon as Houghton had agreed that I might be replaced, I began to regret it. I discovered that after all I did not want to leave my wife and two small daughters. But the die was cast and having been such a pest, I could hardly admit it. I had a notion that it would be rather daring to serve in motor torpedo boats. These were light, fast craft with small crews whose great speed enabled them to cross the sea quickly at night to the enemy's coastline, observe what he was doing, and shoot up targets of opportunity before returning as quickly as they had left. My experience provided a lesson never to trust the name on the package to describe the contents accurately.

It seemed logical that the motor torpedo boats should be part of the Royal Navy Patrol Service. I therefore asked to join this service and was accepted and ordered to report to Lowestoft. It was when I arrived that

I discovered my bloomer. Instead of joining the fastest ships in the Navy, I had volunteered for the slowest. Lowestoft was the home of mine-sweepers and anti-submarine trawlers, not of the MTBs, which were based further along the east coast. By then it was too late to change.

My life as a recruit was as unremarkable as that of any other ordinary seaman. We were given nine weeks' tuition in the elements of seamanship before being drafted to a ship. We learned to distinguish enemy aircraft from our own but were not always correct, with unhappy results. We were taught how to tie knots and we discovered how to launder our new, dark blue collars so that they appeared as faded and washed-out as those of any veteran seaman. We risked the wrath of the chief gunner's mate by cutting the tapes of our collars so that they showed a U-front instead of the regulation V-front, and we made sure we had seven horizontal creases (no more, no less) in our bell-bottomed trousers. All these matters were important to us.

Being rather taller than my mess-mates I was christened 'Lofty', a name which stuck with me throughout my service. I enjoyed the open air, marching and drilling, especially as the squad grew to know one another and to manoeuvre as one. My closest friends were Scottish fishermen from the Outer Hebrides and the Isle of Skye. The round plastic identity disc that hung from my neck showed that I belonged, like them, to the Church of Scotland, and I marched with them to Church of Scotland services on Sunday mornings. This had its advantages for, in addition to spiritual refreshment, the Church of Scotland canteens were superior to any other. The pride of them all was the canteen at the top of the steps at Waverley Station, Edinburgh, where it was possible to get for breakfast a vast helping of hot porridge and a plate of eggs, bacon and sausages at a time when these were unknown luxuries to the civilian population.

My home port at the end of training was Lamlash in the Isle of Arran, where I was drafted to a small ship. At seamanship I was enthusiastic but clumsy, and I wilted under the look of disgust on the face of a leading seaman as I stood on a plank suspended over the ship's side, trying to paint the hull. However, I regained a certain respect when they found that I picked up the rudiments of navigation easily, although the Captain regarded me with some suspicion when the ship's officer, who censored our mail, found that one of my correspondents was Professor Harold Laski. The Captain must have been a fair-minded man, for he recom-mended me for promotion to Sub-Lieutenant, perhaps arguing to himself that as Russia was by then fighting on our side, my promotion might be tolerated.

In due course I left the ship to be trained for promotion, but to my chagrin the doctor's examination revealed tuberculosis and I was despatched to Haslar Hospital near Portsmouth. I languished there for several weeks, disliking the food, the inactivity, the treatment and the sense of having landed in a backwater, for I did not feel at all unwell.

I pestered everyone to be discharged, and eventually was told that I could be released for shore duties. A job was found for me as the Training Commander's Messenger in Portsmouth Barracks. My main duties were to make and light his coal fire before he arrived in the morning, to keep it stoked during the day, supply him with continuous cups of tea and run his errands. My mother's warning had come full circle. This hardly occupied my full attention and I rapidly perfected a comprehensive collection of methods for absenting myself from the Barracks and re-entering without being challenged by the petty officers at the main gate. I became so adept at this and so daring that I booked a room by the week at the nearby Salvation Army hostel and slept there undisturbed every night, so avoiding slinging my hammock on the overcrowded mess deck in the Barracks. No one ever split on me and I was never found out.

This existence could not last, however, and I was told to report to the Admiralty in Whitehall. There I found scores of naval officers but no one dressed as a seaman, I saluted everyone who passed by and eventually was ushered before a Commander who told me that the doctor had ordered that I stay on shore for six months before returning to sea. I could fill my time, he said, by writing a manual on Japan. I was staggered and protested that I knew nothing about Japan, and in any case, Sir, it was hardly the duty of an ordinary seaman. As to the first, he said I could find out. As to the second, he thought I had a case. If I had not gone to hospital, I might even have been promoted. So, he said, the Admiralty would assume I had completed the promotion course and I could be promoted to Sub-Lieutenant forthwith.

With such a bait dangled in front of me, he had made an offer that I could not refuse. My Commander made arrangements for me to be given facilities at the Royal Institute of International Affairs at Chatham House in St James's Square and, with their invaluable aid, I wrote and completed the manual within the required time of six months. It was given a code number BR 1212 and the title *The Enemy Japan*, and was widely distributed to the fleet as background information to prepare for the time when the Battle of the Atlantic would be won and the Navy would move to the Far East. It was in the form of twelve talks to be given aboard ship about the history and people of Japan and the progress of the war in the Far East since 1941. I never saw anybody read BR 1212 but I was gratified to discover when I recently made enquiries that the Admiralty Library still holds a copy. Forty years later I became one of the three Presidents of Chatham House.

I re-applied to return to sea but, with impeccable logic, was told that as I was now an 'expert' on Japan, I would be sent in due course to Australia to join the British Pacific Fleet. I protested that I wished to go to sea at once, and as soon as the request was granted took passage in HMS *Activity* to join the East Indies Fleet in Ceylon. HMS *Activity* was a 'Woolworth Carrier', so called because she was a former merchant ship converted to flying duties by building a flight deck.

By this time there was a growing air of war-weariness on the mess deck. Many men who had served for four years in the Atlantic on convoy duty believed that they had done enough and did not relish the prospect of having to start over again in new and hostile waters. The Japanese had a reputation as desperate fighters who would never surrender, and the general belief was that we would have to fight to the last man on every Pacific island before we reached Japan itself. Ships' companies continued to do their duties readily enough but the Dunkirk spirit had evaporated. The men wanted to return to their families and one way in which this showed itself was their attitude to Churchill's broadcasts, which were relayed whenever possible to the mess decks through the ship's broadcasting system. In the early and middle years of the war, ships' companies had gathered round to listen, quiet and intent, but as victory in Europe grew more certain, so, paradoxically enough, Churchill's popularity began to decline. He had rallied us against Hitler in 1940 with words that stirred us as nothing else could have done, but by 1944 he was felt to be too enthusiastic about fighting a second war which would draw men thousands of miles away from their homes. When Churchill came on the air, I noticed that men no longer listened. It was no surprise to many of us in the Forces that, when the general election eventually came, the servicemen voted Labour in overwhelming numbers. The 1945 election was held at a time when the European war had been won but the Japanese war seemed likely to be prolonged. None of us knew that such a terrible weapon as the atomic bomb existed. None of us could realise the devastating effect it would have on the people of Hiroshima, or that it would bring the Japanese war to such an unexpectedly swift conclusion.

We indulged in a great deal of speculation about what we hoped for from the post-war years and one event in December 1942 crystallised all our feelings. This was the publication of the Beveridge Report on Social Insurance. Alan Bullock did not exaggerate when he called the report 'one of the key dates in the wartime history of Britain', and added that no official report had ever aroused greater interest or enthusiasm.

Beveridge set out in detail a comprehensive plan of insurance to safeguard every citizen against the effects of poverty, sickness, unemployment and old age, together with proposals for a free National Health Service, full employment and family allowances.

Those who are too young to recall pre-war days and who grew up to think of the welfare state as part of the natural order can hardly understand the excitement and enthusiasm which greeted these proposals. They were no less than a charter of human rights. They meant that the quality of life in post-war Britain could, if we chose, be entirely different from that before the war. They meant greater equality, they meant that the worst evils of poverty and old age would be swept away. They were achievable and practicable. I bought my own personal copy and carried it with me in my kit bag as a missionary would carry the gospel. The test of where a man stood on the Beveridge Report was the benchmark of whether he was friend or foe.

In the Services those of us who were politically minded had the field to ourselves as we preached the need for the report to be implemented, and in doing so we gave men something to hope for when the war would eventually come to an end.

Harold Laski had encouraged me to stand for Parliament, and when D. N. Kneath, a member of the Executive Committee of the Inland Revenue Staff Federation, suggested that I should put myself forward for Cardiff, I eagerly agreed. When I arrived home on leave, Kneath took me to meet Bill Headon, the Secretary of the Labour Party in South Cardiff.

In his home I was received with hospitality and warmth. But the initial question that Mrs Headon shot at me was totally unexpected: 'Are you a Catholic?' she asked. I replied that I was a Baptist. I suppose my name confused her, as it has many others, and I did not realise until I got to know her better that if I had given the wrong answer (from her point of view) she would have supported my chief rival for the seat who was a Methodist, the son of a Welsh miner and a Cardiff schoolteacher, by the name of George Thomas.

The Headons warned me of another possible candidate who also happened to be the son of a Welsh miner. They said he had been to Oxford University and was a brilliant young man. His name was Roy Jenkins. But it was thought that as he was only twenty-three years old he would be too young. At the time I was thirty-one and George Thomas thirty-four, so none of us was old. I do not know whether Roy was ever approached but in the end he did not appear in Cardiff and fought Solihull instead.

When the selection conference was held in 1943 I received one more vote than George Thomas, which I attributed to the glamour of my naval uniform and not to my merits. I left for Birkenhead as soon as the selection conference ended to rejoin my ship, which was escorting a convoy to Iceland, and did not set foot in Cardiff again until the general election campaign began.

In addition to looking after the children Audrey kept up the connection with Cardiff, even speaking at a May Day meeting after which Bill Headon, an admirer of hers who always tried to save me from a swollen head, wrote to tell me that she had made a much better speech than I would have done.

When VE Day finally arrived in May 1945 I was aboard the battleship HMS *Queen Elizabeth*, and in company with the French battleship *Richelieu* we spent the day in a fruitless chase of two much faster Japanese cruisers across the Indian Ocean. The *Queen Elizabeth* had been Beatty's flagship in the First World War but by now was old and slow, and the Japanese gave us the slip.

With the war in Europe won, the Coalition Government broke up and a general election loomed. The Admiralty had kept a record of all Parliamentary candidates and my Captain received a signal authorising my return home. I had to make my own arrangements for transport and managed to get passage in the baggage compartment of an RAF York aicraft which lumbered home via Bombay, the Gulf and Cairo. The journey took a week and was the most uncomfortable I have ever made in a lifetime of flying. But my spirits were high, for I was going home. In some ways that last journey epitomised my time in the Navy: usually uncomfortable, frequently bored and only sometimes in danger. Civilians living in London during the Blitz or the days of the flying bombs endured hazards quite as great, although I would not derogate in the slightest from the magnificent endurance and courage over a period of years shown by the brave men in the Royal and Merchant Navies who sailed the convoys across the submarine-infested Atlantic or to Murmansk.

Modern war is total war, in which civilians are exposed to danger and risks alongside the men and women in the Forces. The Second World War encircled the globe. Seventeen million armed men and eighteen million civilian non-combatants were killed. It was the most destructive war in human history. But even that tale of horror would not compare with the destruction and death that would ensue were nuclear weapons ever to be used. Pray Heaven the nations keep their sanity and disarm.

I arrived home to find my wife nursing Margaret and Julia who were both suffering from measles. After a brief stay I set off for Cardiff without them although Audrey, uncomplaining as ever, arrived later in the campaign with both girls.

Cardiff had been a Conservative seat for more than twenty years with a two-year intermission, but from the beginning it seemed as though the mood had changed. Bill Headon, my agent, who was born and bred in the constituency, reported that more and more 'blue noses', as we vulgarly referred to our opponents, were unlikely to vote at all or might even vote Labour.

Nationalisation of the coal mines was an important issue. In South Wales there was little argument against our proposals, for it was generally accepted that the mine owners had had their day. The miners were justifiably bitter about their treatment at the hands of private enterprise and the owners were in deep financial trouble, having few funds available for post-war development. It made no sense for the South Wales coal seams to be mined haphazardly by different owners operating within artificial underground boundaries, drawn with small regard to geological faults or other natural handicaps. We had the best of the argument that to win the most coal in the most economical way and give the miners a fair return, it was necessary for the South Wales coalfields to be operated as one. The case was not seriously challenged by the Conservatives. There was more opposition to Labour's proposal to nationalise steel, for the local works was modern and well run by a paternalistic firm which had cared for its workers.

I made many speeches in favour of our proposals for a universal Health Service and comprehensive social security, and campaigned for a vigorous prosecution of the war against Japan. But most of the questions were about demobilisation from the Forces or about housing shortages. In my innocence and in good faith I promised rapid action on both, and during the campaign my main slogan became, 'We built the Spitfires. Now we can build the houses.' The result was a stunning victory. Our majority in Cardiff was bigger than even we had dreamed possible, and I had the experience of being carried shoulder-high from the City Hall in triumph through a host of our supporters.

Labour won all three Cardiff seats from the Conservatives. George Thomas, who had been adopted for Cardiff Central, received the same exuberant treatment and together we were borne precariously away.

Men and women twice our age who had hoped all their lives to see this day were overcome with emotion, and amid the cheering I saw tears of joy. They were thinking that never again would our people return to the unemployment of the 1930s. Never again would sons and daughters leave their homes so that their parents could avoid the means test. No longer would men and women be crushed by blind economic forces. Instead, we would use economics to serve the people's needs. Hospital treatment, decent houses to live in, and pensions in old age would banish want. Nothing was impossible. We were unconquerable.

On that day a bond was forged between the people of Cardiff and myself that remained unbroken for over forty years. I felt part of a large extended family and joined in their successes, their failures, their problems. I have watched successive generations grow up, and nowadays when I go to school prize-givings I find myself handing certificates to children whose names are familiar and whose parents tell me that many years before they, in their turn, had received their prizes from me.

The bond between an MP and his constituency is something that the Boundary Commissioners who carve up and redistribute our constituencies are not expected to take into account. They have the task of determining a strict, arithmetical electoral quotient and applying it across the country. I recall that when I was a member of the Shadow Cabinet we were once faced with proposals for a wholesale redistribution of constituency boundaries which would tear long-standing areas in two and sink well-known names without trace. Clem Attlee was in the chair and at one point he asked who had been the chairman of the Electoral Commissioners. He was told the name. 'Thought so,' he said crisply. 'Cambridge man. All statistics. No sense of history.' Like him, I am on the side of history and opposed to the slide-rule in determining constituency boundaries I recognise that regard must be paid to some measure of arithmetical equality between constituencies, but we should not allow ourselves to be dominated by a system in which the Boundary Commissioners seem to have as much influence on the composition of the House of Commons as does the electorate.

3

When the taxi-driver who drove me to the Beaver Hall in London on Saturday 28 July 1945 realized my destination was the first meeting of the newly elected Parliamentary Labour Party, he delivered me free, refusing to accept the fare. Like millions of others he was full of excitement at the massive political upset that had taken place and at the prospect of the first ever Labour Government with a substantial majority.

393 Labour MPs had been elected and more than 250 of us were entirely new to Parliament. Attlee, Morrison, and the Party managers must have gazed down from the platform and wondered whether they would ever be able to lick us into an effective government majority. For me, the happenings at our first meeting passed in a dream.

We carried unanimously and enthusiastically Ernest Bevin's vote of confidence in Clem Attlee as Party Leader and Prime Minister. Many of us were in uniform and I am sure that my other colleagues home from the Forces were as innocent as I of the manoeuvrings that had taken place during the previous forty-eight hours to replace Clem Attlee with Herbert Morrison. If it had come to a vote Attlee would have won for we newcomers, who were the majority, would have seen no reason for change. We felt a part of great events as Attlee announced that he and Bevin must leave the meeting to go to Potsdam immediately to continue with the peace negotiations begun by Churchill with Stalin, Truman and de Gaulle. It was exciting, but I had more domestic events on my mind and left the meeting as soon as I could. It was Audrey's birthday and it was the first we had spent together in some years.

The Chamber of the House of Commons had been blitzed and the Peers lent the Commons their Chamber for our meetings. There were fresh excitements when we met some days later to elect a Speaker. The Labour majority was so large and the Lords Chamber so small that we overflowed from the Government side of the House onto the Opposition bench below the gangway. The Tories, huddled together behind their front bench, seemed a small, beleaguered garrison. Numbers of new Members could find room only by standing at the Bar of the Chamber and were therefore technically outside the House. As latecomers arrived, the front rows were pushed across the Bar into the Chamber itself. This was a major sin. Stalwart badge messengers physically tried to push us back behind the Bar of the House without success. One of them, panting with exertion, shouted to a Labour Member, 'Come on, Captain Bellenger. You know better than this.' Bellenger was about to be appointed a junior Minister at the War Office, but that afternoon neither he nor anyone else could control the surging crowd.

It was exciting for us new young Members returned from the war to see Winston Churchill. As he entered the Chamber a Conservative Member in uniform and sporting a monocle rose to his feet and led the Conservative benches in singing 'For he's a jolly good fellow'. I discovered later that the leader of the choir was Colonel Thornton-Kemsley, MP for Angus and Mearns (Kincardine and Western), who in later sessions was one of the few Members to maintain the tradition of wearing his top hat in the Chamber on the day of the King's Speech. But Clem Attlee was our hero and when he arrived we immediately retaliated by singing 'The Red Flag', begun by George Griffiths, a miners' MP who was standing next to the Speaker's Chair. The Speaker Elect, Colonel Clifton Brown, looked on bemusedly during these happenings and when both sides had finished said mildly that he had not realised he was being called upon to preside over a glee club. This calmed us down.

George Thomas and I sat side by side on the third bench above the gangway during the election of the Speaker. I am sure that neither of us thought on that afternoon that more than thirty years later we should sit together again while his own election as Speaker took place. His quick wit and his sensitive feel for the mood of the House made his term of office as Speaker quite exceptional. The broadcasting of our proceedings and his Welsh baritone crying 'Order, Order' became known throughout the country. As long ago as 1947, in the days before microphones were in use in the House, I wrote of him: 'George is a delight to listen to. His ringing voice can be heard throughout the Chamber and his Welsh lilt gives him the ear of all Members immediately.' He maintained that capacity throughout, as he showed in July 1981 when he read the lesson at the wedding of the Prince of Wales in St Paul's Cathedral and his ringing tones were heard throughout the world.

George has a warm heart and generous disposition but people often overlook the fact that before he became Speaker he was a most effective politician, capable of dealing some very hard blows. It was a privilege to stay with him in the miner's house in Tonypandy in which he lived with his mother and stepfather – a disabled miner who suffered from the disease pneumoconiosis, the scourge of the pits. After his stepfather's death George took care of his mother, and no one ever had a more devoted son. Her comfort and well-being were his first charge. He also stood a little in awe of her: quite late in life I have seen him put out his cigarette if she was coming, and I do not think he ever admitted to her that now and again he might accept a little alcohol. In 1945 George introduced me to his friends in the Rhondda Valley and they showed me for the first time the hard lot of the Welsh miner. I became convinced that the two toughest callings in Britain were those of the miner and the fisherman, and throughout my political life I have felt an instinctive sympathy with both. The miners for their part supported me loyally in the various offices I held and I cherished my connection with a grand body of men. Although in the early years there was a certain rivalry between George Thomas and myself, with the passage of years we became more intimate and I developed an affectionate appreciation of his foibles. Fortunately when we were younger our interests lay in different fields and we did not openly clash but confined ourselves to minor disagreements such as who should have the right to speak in the best position at our public meetings.

In the years after 1945 we held joint meetings once a month on a Sunday evening in a large cinema in the centre of Cardiff. The meetings were timed to begin at 8 o'clock so as not to interfere with evening chapel. In those days we did not have to compete with television and we two young unknowns could regularly draw an attendance of up to a thousand people. It was a period of high political interest and expectation, and at our meetings speakers and audience felt a sense of joint participation that cannot nowadays be achieved through television.

In both our constituencies and in Parliament we were ardent and impatient to sweep away the vestiges of the 1930s and to begin the new post-war era. We were sent to Parliament to change the condition of Britain and we intended to do so.

Jim Griffiths, the South Wales miners' leader, had become Minister of National Insurance and more than doubled the retirement pension from ten to twenty-six shillings a week. We passed a Bill to provide, for the first time in the history of our country, for every man and woman under pensionable age to be insured against hardship caused by sickness, unemployment and retirement. Aneurin Bevan triumphantly carried through a bold and imaginative scheme to establish a universal Health Service to give everyone, no matter how rich or poor, the same access to diagnosis and treatment of illness, free of charge. The Beveridge Report that I had carried with me during my days in the Navy was becoming reality and I was there to see it happen. The Report had called for a crusade to slay poverty, ignorance, disease, squalor and idleness, and the Labour Government of which I was a part was using Parliament day by day to make the biggest and swiftest changes in our social and economic framework that this century had witnessed. Morale ran high on the Labour benches.

We nationalised the coal mines, and rejoiced as the official notice boards were planted at the top of every pit bearing the sign 'This colliery is now managed by the National Coal Board on behalf of the people.' We said it and we meant it. And Manny Shinwell, the Minister of Fuel and Power, at once gave meaning to what we had done by bringing in a five-day week for the miners.

We proceeded to the Second Reading of the Bank of England Bill and the huge figure of Hugh Dalton, then Chancellor of the Exchequer, loomed over the front bench, elbows firmly planted on the dispatch box as he held up for all the Tory benches to see a copy of the twelve-page Labour manifesto on which we had fought and won the election. It was evidence for our mandate to take the citadel of capitalism into public ownership. The Tories despised Hugh's gesture as a piece of theatre, especially as it came from an old Etonian who, they sneered, had deserted his class. But they could deny neither our manifesto nor our majority and whatever they thought, we newcomers loved it.

In fact, the Conservatives had little stomach for serious opposition to the nationalisation either of coal or of the Bank. Winston Churchill had said during the war that the principle of publicly owned coal mines was accepted by all, provided proper compensation was paid. This took the sting out of the criticisms of Anthony Eden who led the opposition to both Bills for, despite our inexperience, we young backbenchers were quick to detect his lack of enthusiasm for the fight.

We were great singers too. When we voted to nationalise the coal mines, Jim Griffiths led us through the Division Lobby to a mighty chorus of 'Cwm Rhondda'. If some Tory sharp-shooters held up the progress of legislation late at night, we would gather undaunted in the Members' Tea

Room and sing the hours away with hymns, ballads and revolutionary songs.

Friday was usually a day for relatively unimportant business, and some of us made a habit of going into the Chamber to take part in a process that Dick Crossman labelled 'batting practice in the nets'. We studied beforehand the matter under discussion, whether it interested us or not, and then deliberately intervened in the debates in order to gain experience and confidence. A few Conservative Members were always ready to take us on, notably Earl Winterton, an Irish Peer, who had been elected to the House as long ago as 1904. He had been Parliamentary Private Secretary to Joe Chamberlain but advancing years had not cooled his spirit. He told me that in his younger days he would hunt in the Midlands throughout the day, then catch the train to London in the evening to harass Campbell-Bannerman's Liberal Government late into the night. He was an irascible but kindly man who would belabour us without mercy and then walk out of the Chamber without waiting to listen to a reply. After one of his peppery Friday interventions I remarked that he 'blew in, blew up, and blew out'. Winterton liked this.

We younger Labour Members invaded the Smoking Room which previously had been the main sanctuary of the Tories. Sitting there in a corner I found myself listening to conversations conducted with verve, self-confidence and humour by new acquaintances such as Dick Crossman, Raymond Blackburn, Maurice Webb, Seymour Cocks, Evan Durbin and Tom Driberg. Many of them with university backgrounds knew one another before they arrived. To me it was a new world and I was enthralled. In those early days I could truthfully say:

> 'Bliss was it in that dawn to be alive
> But to be young was very heaven.'

And our happiness was added to when Michael, our youngest, was born on Michaelmas Day, 1945.

The Map Room was a part of the Library which had been reserved by custom and prescription for the trade union Members, among whom the miners' MPs were predominant. It was presided over unofficially by George Dagger, the Member for Abertillery, who had been a miners' agent and who could usually be found in the winter of 1945 standing in front of the Map Room's huge coal fire, faultlessly dressed in wing collar and spotted bow tie, conducting a never-ending discussion and criticism of the new Labour Government's industrial and social programme.

The atmosphere of the Map Room was more sober than that engendered by the exciting theories of the young revolutionaries in the Smoking Room. The trade union Members were older. They were the contemporaries of recently appointed Ministers, and were well represented in the Cabinet by men like Jack Lawson, George Tomlinson and George Isaacs. If the talk was not as highfaluting as in the Smoking Room, it was informed by a much wider background of industrial and social experience. They were a group of men with little formal schooling who had worked first in industry and later in their trade unions until entering the House of Commons. They possessed a native homespun understanding and some were widely read. At the time, thirteen Welsh constituencies were represented by miners; today there is not one.

Some of these men had attended school only until the age of thirteen, when they left to follow their fathers into the pits. Underground, they had learned the hardness of life and the essential need for mutual support. Dependability ranked high in the list of virtues, as did loyalty. As they grew up the most promising would be offered scholarships to the Central Labour College in London by the South Wales Miners' Union, paid for from the miners' own funds. As students they existed on a pittance and were steeped for two years in left-wing teachings. It was here that Aneurin Bevan, Jim Griffiths, Ness Edwards, George Dagger, Will Mainwaring and others were first brought into contact with Marx and Engels, Kautsky, Bukharin and Trotsky. The effect of this teaching never completely left them, but equally the Labour College never produced a stereotype because its students were not callow youngsters straight from school. They were mature men, hardened by practical experience, who accepted Marxist analysis as a new and enlightening tool for understanding economic problems but were not willing to swallow whole the doctrine or its absolutism. Unlike so many present-day academic Trotskyites and Marxists, they had been able to test the theories against their own industrial experience, and had found them wanting.

Shortly after the general election John Parker, the Parliamentary Under-Secretary at the Dominions Office, asked me to become his Parliamentary Private Secretary. The duties were not onerous but the experience gave me an early interest in Commonwealth affairs which I have since maintained.

I spent much time in both Map Room and Smoking Room and felt equally at home in either. We also sat and listened to debates in the Chamber even when we were not taking part, something which is rather unfashionable today. There were even fewer facilities for Members then than now. A new Member was allocated a locker about two feet by one in which to store his papers. This was the only space he could call his own, but if he could find a seat in the Library he was free to sit there and write letters to his constituents. I have held the key to locker Number 47 for over forty years. The adjacent lockers were held by Nye Bevan and Simon Ramsay, a Conservative Member of about my age. Nye's locker overflowed with papers of all descriptions, and he had a highly struggle to shut it.

One evening I emerged flushed and heated from the Chamber at the end of a debate and turned to Simon Ramsay with the words, 'Isn't this place exciting?' His reply was like a douche of cold water. 'Do you think so? I dislike it more every day.' It was not surprising that he did not remain a Member. There was a sequel. Several years later I visited Rhodesia and received an invitation to stay with the Governor General, the sixteenth Earl of Dalhousie, at Government House. I accepted and when I arrived was greeted by the great man who turned out to be none other than my former neighbour Simon Ramsay. I was not very knowledgeable in 1945.

Only slowly did the economic consequences of Britain's exhausting war effort come home to those of us who had been in the Services and therefore out of touch with domestic affairs. We were well aware that Lend Lease from the United States had underwritten Britain's requirements for war ammunition, weapons, raw materials and even food, and whenever we came into contact with the American Services overseas we had the impression that they had access to an overflowing cornucopia. In 1944 I went ashore in Iceland, following convoy duty. I was given access, for what reason I forget, to the American Quartermaster's Stores in Reykjavik. I bought a huge tin trunk which I stuffed with purchases of luxuries unseen in Britain since the war began. I always remember the delight with which Audrey greeted the sight of silk stockings, tins of canned meat, tinned fruit and chocolate.

But although we were sharply aware of the luxuries long foregone, I had not realised how much the British people depended upon American Lend Lease for even the basic essentials of our daily lives. Ministers in the Coalition Government knew the position only too well, but when Lend Lease was ended suddenly – even brutally – just three weeks after we had taken our seats in the new Parliament, few of the new Members appreciated the seriousness of the economic problems inherited by the Labour Government.

Consider the timescale. The Labour Government met Parliament for the first time on 2 August, 1945. The Japanese war ended days later on 14 August. Seven days after that, on 21 August 1945, President Truman signed the order that cut off Lend Lease with immediate effect. I cannot recall feeling alarmed or even upset when I heard about this catastrophic blow, nor did I realise that it was to cast a blight over the Labour Government's economic policy throughout the six years of its life. T. S. Eliot has a line, 'We had the experience but missed the meaning', which seems to sum it up.

It is said in defence of Harry Truman's action that he had become President unexpectedly following Roosevelt's death only four months earlier, and did not fully appreciate the serious implications of his decision for Britain. I doubt this. The record shows that American opposition to a continuation of Lend Lease had been building up steadily in Congress. Just two days before Roosevelt's death a measure to kill its use for post-war reconstruction had resulted in a tied vote in the Senate and was defeated only by the casting vote of Vice-President Truman. So the subject was known to him and it seems more likely that Truman allowed his many domestic difficulties with Congress to outweigh the serious effects on Britain of his decision.

The Labour Cabinet was not ignorant of the facts even if we newcomers were. Hugh Dalton has told us since that he circulated a paper to the Cabinet in order 'that my colleagues should be informed without delay of this most grim problem'. Our gold and dollar reserves totalled only £500 millions: a sum wholly inadequate for the purchase of necessary food and raw materials.

Keynes gave his opinion that 'Britain would face a financial Dunkirk if she failed to secure post-war American aid', and the upshot was that he was sent to the United States with others to negotiate a loan sufficiently large to take the place of Lend Lease and to see us through until 1948. During the ensuing three years it was expected that millions of men and women in the armed forces would be demobilised, our wartime industries would be reconverted, the factories would hum again, we could rebuild our export trade and so earn our living once more. This at least was the Cabinet's hope. Three months of intense negotiation followed, at the end of which Britain secured an inadequate loan of $3.75 billions instead of the estimated required minimum of $5 billions. Nevertheless, Keynes recommended acceptance. Britain also undertook to join the Bretton Woods Agreement.

The Government's immediate problem was caused by a pledge to make sterling freely convertible against the dollar at the end of twelve months. In effect, this meant ending the Sterling Area which had embraced the Commonwealth countries and some others. It was not difficult to see the potential for disaster, but the Cabinet were in a fearful dilemma. Hugh Dalton wrote:

> I was under no illusions as to what would follow if we got no dollar credit. We would go deeper into the dark valley of austerity than at any time during the war. Less food, except for bread and potatoes – less than an Irish peasant's standard of living – in particular less meat and sugar. Little cotton, and therefore less clothes and less exports. Heavy and growing unemployment in many industries. Worst of all, from the point of view of public morale, practically no smokes, since eighty per cent of our tobacco cost dollars.

The British people were expecting some relaxation from the gruelling wartime demands made upon them. The imposition of fresh sacrifices would have met with little understanding for, as Hugh Dalton said, 'Every shortage would be attributed to the Government's incompetence.' It is not easy at this distance in time to convey the frustration felt by the British people who had been subjected to years of bombing, food shortages and rationing, coupons to buy standard clothing, and shortages of fuel and of housing. They deserved an easement.

Although I was practically unknown to Hugh Dalton when I entered Parliament, he befriended me from my earliest days. He co-opted me as a member of the Parliamentary Party's Finance Group after I caught his eye in a Finance Bill debate. As Chancellor, he kept in weekly touch with our group, and by the late autumn even I was alerted to the gravity of our position. He left our group in no doubt that it was vital to accept the loan, yet I found it difficult to stomach the crippling conditions that were attached. I conveyed my doubts to A. V. Alexander, who had been First Lord of the Admiralty during the war, and who retained this post when the Labour Government was formed. I found him very sympathetic and he told me privately that a small number of the Cabinet, including Nye Bevan and Manny Shinwell, were opposed to the scheme. Armed with this information I tackled Hugh Dalton again in the Smoking Room late one night, where a small group of us sat talking. I told him I thought the British people should be made to understand, as I was coming to do, what financial perils we faced, and that we should all need to tighten our belts

even further. In reply, Hugh Dalton gave one of his portentous winks.
He did not mind, he said, if some of us voted against the loan and the
Agreement. It would show the Americans that the Labour Government
was not a pushover, and had its own domestic problems.

The debate on 13 December 1945 was made memorable for me by an
outstanding speech from Bob Boothby, a brilliant and entertaining Conservative Member who would have made an outstanding Minister but
for some political misfortune. What he said was music to my ears. He was
opposed to the loan because Britain would not be able to carry out the
obligations she had undertaken. America was behaving like someone
giving a man a lift in an aircraft, taking him nine-tenths of the way across
the Atlantic and then, when a hundred miles offshore, throwing him out
and telling him to swim for it. We could not possibly know what the
exchange value of the pound sterling would be in the post-war period.
The agreement would prise open the markets of the world for the benefit
of the United States. Lifting exchange controls would open the sluice
gates for sterling while we were still weak. He paused and said he was
taking too much time. We shouted, 'Go on, go on', and he did. He did not
want to see the world divided into two opposing systems. An alternative
existed – the Sterling Bloc, based upon the British Empire and fortified
by the countries of Western Europe. I quote his conclusion:

> We have heard a lot about mandates recently. It may be that the Govern-
> ment have a mandate to nationalise the gas works. I do not deny it. And
> on this question of whether this will be good for the gas works or the
> public I would not venture to dogmatise. But there is one mandate which
> His Majesty's Government never got from the people of this country and
> that was to sell the British Empire for a packet of cigarettes.

He stopped and, with a histrionic gesture, dived into his pocket, produced
a pack of cigarettes, waved it above his head and sat down to loud cheers.

His speech was what many of us wanted to hear and it was he and not
Hugh Dalton who made up my mind finally to vote against the loan. It
was not acceptable on such onerous terms; Churchill was said to be in
favour of the Tory Party voting for the loan but the Smoking Room
intelligence was of disagreements in the Shadow Cabinet and their front
bench abstained. About seventy Conservatives voted against the loan
together with a number of Labour Members, of whom I was one. On the
following day I resigned as PPS to John Parker, and gave up my office in
a converted passageway between the Foreign Office and the Dominions

Office. No one had taken any notice when John Parker appointed me, and likewise nobody noticed when I resigned.

The debate on the American loan and its consequences had an unsettling effect, for it shook many settled convictions and prejudices. Until then, if questioned, I would have been in no doubt that Britain was a great power – one of the big three who had won the war in partnership with the United States and the Soviet Union. Winning the war placed us in a different category from France, which had surrendered, or Germany, Japan and Italy which we had defeated. I had no doubt that to hold a British passport entitled the user to special consideration when he travelled abroad as a citizen of the world's largest empire, of which London was the centre. And I was suddenly mortified to discover that our economy was in such bad shape that we must borrow from the United States on terms which demonstrated our weakness.

I was by no means anti-American at the end of the war. On the contrary, I admired American know-how, their 'can do' attitude in facing problems and the boldness and openness of the national character. But because I underestimated both their strength and our losses, I saw no need for our policies to be slavishly yoked with theirs.

Nor was I at that time convinced by Churchill's famous speech at Fulton, Missouri in March 1946, when he first used the metaphor of an Iron Curtain descending across and dividing the continent of Europe from the Baltic to the Adriatic. This dramatic figure of speech created a great sensation, especially as it stood in such stark contrast to the wartime perception of a smiling Uncle Joe Stalin leading a heroic and desperate resistance by the Russian people against the Nazi invaders.

We did not know at that time of the many frustrations experienced by the Coalition Cabinet in their dealings with the Soviet Union during the war years. These did not become public until later, and most of us in the Armed Forces had been too much engaged in the war against fascism to realise the significance of the Yalta Declaration or to have studied the Soviet Union's intentions towards Eastern Europe.

A. V. Alexander frequently used sulphurous words about Russia's behaviour when we talked, but I thought he was rather right-wing and discounted some of what he said. The truth was that wartime secrecy and censorship had created a wide gap between the way Ministers saw the reality of Russian policy and intentions and the image that was filtered through to the average citizen.

In the run-up to the election in 1945 Bevin had expressed the hope that 'left could speak to left', but the reality proved different. Immediately after the war was over the Soviet propaganda machine focused its attacks on Britain, leaving the United States relatively untouched. Britain was so obviously the prime target that many Americans felt it was not in their interests to become involved in what was essentially an Anglo-Soviet dispute. There was talk and some signs of an American return to isolationism. But the dismal catalogue of events that followed hardened opinion within both the Labour Government and the American Administration: in 1946 the crisis over Iran; in the summer of 1947 Stalin's refusal to participate in the Marshall Plan, and his embargo on Czech participation despite Czechoslovakia's willingness; in February 1948 the communist overthrow of the Czech Government, and four months later the Soviet blockade of Berlin.

The piecemeal but relentless extension of Soviet control in Eastern Europe steadily wore away any remaining Western hopes. In 1947 the American Government responded with the Truman Doctrine. By 1948 Bevin was convinced of the need for a North Atlantic Alliance that would bind the Western states together. In March he was instrumental in establishing the Brussels Treaty between Britain, France and the Benelux countries; one year later, the North Atlantic Treaty was forged. I found myself following rather reluctantly in Bevin's wake, as he moved to a position of greater hostility. Perhaps those of us who thought there were prospects for cooperation were naive, but ours were not foolish hopes for a generation that had just emerged from world war.

It is difficult to recreate the early post-war atmosphere of Western Europe, but it was a mixture of expectation, fear, and defeatism. There was even talk of another war in those European countries which feared that Russia would make demands on them. On his side, Stalin too was said to fear that the Americans would begin hostilities against the Soviet Union. Fear was everywhere.

Jean Monnet, a great Frenchman and practical visionary, wrote in the summer of 1950: 'Britain has no confidence that France and the other countries of Europe have the ability or even the will effectively to resist a possible Russian invasion. Britain believes that in this conflict continental Europe will be occupied but that she herself with America will be able to resist and finally conquer.' As I recall, this statement was no more than a small exaggeration of our sentiments.

Whilst Monnet was writing this the world was shaken by events in Korea: the North Korean army, trained and equipped by the Soviet

Union, crossed the border separating it from South Korea and invaded that country in June 1950. Stalin had boycotted the United Nations but the other members met immediately and demanded that North Korea withdraw, calling on all members to assist South Korea.

Shortly before this, the Prime Minister had transferred me from the Ministry of Transport, where I was a junior Minister from 1947 onwards, to become Parliamentary and Financial Secretary to the Admiralty. As these events unfolded and, for a day or two, the world trembled between action and inaction, my heart sank. I saw the affair as one of the early tests of the new world body that had succeeded the League of Nations. Were we to witness once again the futilities and failures of the 1930s, when members of the League of Nations failed to act effectively against aggression by Japan in the Far East and by Italy in Africa? If so, we were doomed eventually to fight another war. There would be no lasting peace. Such was my mood. There was little I could do, but I did intensify my single-handed campaign in the Admiralty to save the wartime 'H' class destroyers which were on the point of being scrapped. I feared they would be needed.

Then one morning a day or two later the clouds lifted. The door to my room in the Admiralty was thrown open. It would be wrong to say that Earl Mountbatten entered. That was not his style. He swept in, and you could almost see the wake he left behind. He was about to take up his new post as Fourth Sea Lord following his return to the Navy after he ceased to be the Viceroy of India. The room in which he would be working was next to mine, and we had got to know each other. 'Have you heard?' he said, 'Truman has promised to send the American Navy and Air Force to Korea. Now we shall do the same.' He was a good prophet, for Clem Attlee announced shortly afterwards that the United Kingdom would also send a contingent to resist North Korea's aggression. I came to learn that Dickie Mountbatten was usually first with the news.

The thoughts of Munich disappeared from my mind. On this occasion, instead of shrinking from the challenge the United States had taken it up, and I felt that even if Truman's decision might lead to a limited war, such action would at least prevent the world war that was widely feared in Europe and elsewhere.

These moves had important consequences. In retrospect Harry Truman's response, together with the Allies' decision to undertake the Berlin Airlift, were the two important turning-points in reversing the Western withdrawal that had followed the deterioration of post-war relations with Stalin's Russia.

During the summer of 1950 I was appointed a delegate to the Council of
Europe, and mixed with delegates from the other member countries. In
December, we launched a rearmament programme and shortly after I
gave my impressions: 'My first visit to the Strasbourg European Assembly
was a depressing experience. Many European Parliamentarians seemed
to feel themselves in the grip of forces stronger than they and helplessness
seemed to have settled on the Continent . . . There is no doubt that during
the last three years the mainland of Europe has suffered from a very real
fear of invasion by Russia.'

I went on to say that the success of the Berlin Airlift had been a turning-
point and Europe's will to resist had increased, thanks to the United
States being willing to make her forces available as a nucleus of resistance
to the expected invasion. 'I do not agree that war is inevitable. Our rearmament programme has convinced Russia that we are determined to
resist and we can establish communication with her again, confidently
because of our strength.' I concluded that it was beyond belief that the
Western powers themselves should start a war against the Soviet Union.
Therefore, 'we have to find a way of living with her.'

This has remained my constant view. While the West must never lower
its guard when dealing with Russia, equally it must always be ready to
reach a mutually advantageous accommodation. We should compete
where we must and cooperate where we can. Such experience as I have
had in dealing with the Soviet Union convinces me that they scorn weakness and are ready to take advantage of it. If they are offered a concession
for nothing, their response is to pocket it but never to allow such a gesture
to affect their future attitude. On the other hand, provided the Soviet
Union believes that the West is determined and has the will to act, there
will be no prospect of her overstepping the mark in Europe.

Soviet policies, together with Europe's economic prostration and political defeatism, brought together a group of idealists with the intention of
establishing a European Federal Union. They believed that national
decision-making by European countries on the most basic issues should
be transferred to a supra-national government and parliament. The
group translated these ideas into draft treaties, institutions and agreements. The Schuman Plan for a steel and coal community, the Council
of Europe itself, plans for a European Army, and draft legislation to
establish a federal Europe all came tumbling out in quick succession and
were placed before the people of Europe. As idealists usually do, they
carried all before them for a short while by a combination of dedication

and hard work. They attracted great support, especially from the young.

There was a serious division between the so-called 'federalists' and those who, like the British and the Scandinavians, took up an alternative idea which they called, rather clumsily, the 'functional approach through the creation of specialised authorities'. These specialised authorities would be established by means of industrial and other across-border activities, of which transport was a good example. It seemed to me, as a 'functionalist', that the Schuman Plan for Coal and Steel was such a project and I was therefore in favour of Britain taking part in the negotiations to establish it. I wrote to Ernie Bevin to say so.

But there were two objections. First, it was clear that the Parliamentary Labour Party, having just emerged from lengthy struggles to nationalise the basic industries of coal, gas, electricity and steel, strongly opposed handing over decisions about their future policy and conduct to an international body. This was understandable.

Ernie Bevin asked me to see him. 'They don't want us, Callaghan,' he said, emphasising as he always did the hard 'g' in my name. I was not able to convince him, but in the light of what has been published since, there was much truth in his assessment. Jean Monnet, who was the true author of the Plan, wanted to tie the French and German coal and steel industries indissolubly together because of his fear that German industry would in due course grow faster and be more efficient than that of France. His purpose was to prevent the domination of France. But beyond this, he saw the coal and steel industry as an expression of political will, a symbol of federal Europe, and Britain's membership of the Coal and Steel Community was of interest to him only if we accepted the federal concept, which neither Labour nor the Conservatives did.

This did not prevent the Conservative Opposition from trying to make mischief for the Labour Government, and they succeeded for a time in convincing other European Governments and Parliamentarians that the Labour Government was dragging its feet, and that things would be much easier if they were in power. The controversy itself made little impression on people in Britain, nor I think in Europe, and the Conservatives did not enjoy the advantage for long. When they came to power in 1951 and adopted much the same position as Ernest Bevin had done, the Continental federalists quickly rumbled them.

As time went by it became clearer that the federalists themselves did not wholly represent their own public opinion, and as early as the Council of Europe session of November 1950, I heard a Belgian delegate admit that only three votes would be cast in favour of federalism in his Parliament, while both Italian and French delegations estimated that there would be no majority in their own Assemblies.

An obscure argument also broke out between 'maximalists' and 'regionalists'. Maximalists were those who would agree to federation only if Britain and Scandinavia, as well as all the other major western European democracies, became part of the new entity. 'Regionalists' were ready to proceed immediately even though only a limited number of countries would join the new federation. Hugh Dalton was the leader of the Labour Government's delegation and I was the junior spokesman. With Dalton's consent and with a brief cleared by the Cabinet, I made a speech at Strasbourg to the effect that, although the Labour Government would not agree to federate with others, we would 'vote in favour of allowing those countries which wished to federate partially to do so'. In other words, we gave the regionalists the green light if they wished to proceed without us. I argued that, as federation could not be imposed upon Britain or Scandinavia, these continuing theoretical discussions took up time that could be better devoted to considering what functional specialised authorities Europe might establish, with which Britain and the Scandinavians could be associated. I concluded, 'We have linked ourselves with Europe through many economic and military ties in the last five years to a much closer degree than ever before. There is hardly an Englishman who does not realise that we are part of Europe and must work with Europe.'

These debates in the Council of Europe, although repetitive, were passionate and sincere. The delegates believed firmly that we were engaged in shaping post-war Europe, as indeed we were. Georges Bidault, who had been Prime Minister of France only a few months earlier, passed me a note when I sat down:

Strasbourg   23 November 1950

Dear Mr Minister,
Mes compliments pour votre discours. Vous avez tort, au moins à moitié, si vous me permettez de vous le dire, mais vous avez tort d'une manière qui donne envie de vous suivre. Pardonnez moi de résister à la tentation.

                                                    Amicalement
                                                    Georges Bidault

I fell under Georges Bidault's spell from then on.

One other great issue defeated us, namely, the possibility of establishing a European Army. The idea had been conceived by France for the same reasons that led her to propose the Coal and Steel Community – to prevent a new German army from becoming a menace to France and to peace. French Ministers were well aware of the large number of American troops that had been withdrawn from Europe. They also knew that United States strength was being heavily taxed by her involvement in Korea. It was the strain of this which led America to propose the rearmament of Germany, an event which in the eyes of many Frenchmen was unthinkable. Their alternative proposal was to set up a European Defence Community as a means of integrating a German contingent into a Combined Armed Force at the level of the smallest possible unit, so as to achieve a complete merger under a single military and political authority. It was known simply and shortly as the European Army. I found myself very much in sympathy with the idea, although at the time I was strongly opposed to rearming Germany. The Second World War was still too close.

Winston Churchill joined us at Strasbourg as Leader of the Conservative Party and, with all his great prestige, made a speech that was construed as being in favour of the European Defence Community. Certainly the continental delegates wanted to believe this, but his words were truly ambiguous and, in reality, he did not make clear whether he favoured a European Army that would be a complete merger of all national forces at the level of the smallest possible unit, or whether in fact he was supporting a combined force that would remain under independent national control.

I was still Parliamentary Secretary to the Admiralty and had been involved in a recent joint naval exercise in the Channel. One afternoon a group of us were given an indication of Winston Churchill's own ambivalent thinking. We were sitting with him in the Delegates' Lounge in Strasbourg, when the subject of the European Army came up. I said that I wondered whether he was fully aware how far we had taken the developments in joint exercises between the ships of the Western Union powers. For instance, in a recent exercise, a squadron of Netherlands naval aircraft had been embarked in a British aircraft carrier, had joined in joint anti-submarine patrols with British and American aircraft, using standardised radar and signalling equipment and instruments. All the participating nations had been under the direction of a French ship with a French Admiral in overall control. Sir Winston looked at me. 'That all sounds very satisfactory, Mr Callaghan. Very good – except for the French Admiral.'

He enjoyed great attention at Strasbourg. He relished every minute and his movements in and around the Chamber became small processions. He was followed with undisguised interest and admiration by the public and the press, and played unashamedly to the camera, quite outshining the British Government delegates at the first Assembly. We were led by Herbert Morrison and Hugh Dalton, and Morrison's chagrin showed. He went home half-way through the session, leaving me as his substitute.

Every night one of the national delegations gave a sparkling reception at which the champagne flowed freely, to be followed by dinner in one of Strasbourg's many restaurants, which served some of the most delicious food to be found in France. It was a quite different way of living for me but I did not find it hard to become acclimatised. Hugh Dalton took the culinary education of our delegation upon himself and, under his guidance, we formed an acquaintance with many different Alsatian wines and liqueurs.

The weekends were especially memorable. As soon as the Assembly adjourned we would motor out through the lovely small villages of Alsace, each giving its name to a local wine to be sampled, until we had reached the Vosges mountains where we would find a small inn, dine with the greatest good humour, and the next day walk in the autumn sunshine through the Alsace woods. Hugh Dalton loved trees, and would usually arrange for us to be accompanied by a local forester. It was during such weekends that I first became friends with Tony Crosland and Denis Healey.

One Saturday we persuaded a reluctant Ernie Bevin to join us for dinner in a small inn high up in the Vosges. His health was deteriorating, and after dinner he decided he must return to Strasbourg. He clearly was not at all well. During the meal I asked him, 'Isn't the countryside magnificent?' I always remember his sad reply. 'I don't know,' he said, 'I didn't look.' Six months later he died.

The pressure for Germany to rearm persisted in one form or another. I was lobbied hard and continuously by the United States Embassy in London, whose members did not believe the European Army was a practical possibility under either a Labour or a Conservative Government. I was still in favour, if it could be achieved, and tried to persuade Hugh Dalton in this direction. The best instruction we could obtain from the

Cabinet was that we need not oppose the principle of the idea, but we were to vote against on the procedural grounds that the Statute of the Council of Europe specifically excluded the subject of defence from the Assembly's powers. I was young and inexperienced at the time, and if I were given such instructions today I would not accept them, for as I quickly discovered, they left me open to ridicule. I made the best of them, however, and was immediately followed by Robert Schuman, then the Foreign Minister of France. He began by referring to 'my friend, Mr Callaghan', which put me on my guard, and then made much of a speech of mine at an earlier meeting of the Assembly in which I had used the idea of the European Defence Community as evidence that the nations of Europe were prepared to pool their sovereignty. Schuman drew the obvious conclusion that if the British Government's objection, as expressed by Hugh Dalton and me, was to the letter of the Statute and not its concept, 'Would our colleague, Mr Callaghan, be prepared to vote for a motion for the amendment of the Statute in such a way as to eliminate every suspicion of such incompatibility?' He pressed me for a reply which as spokesman for the Government I could not give.

At the end of the session I received a note from Bevin's Private Secretary, Eddie Tomkins, who much later became our highly successful Ambassador in Paris. He wrote that the Foreign Secretary 'thinks you had a very difficult and thankless task to do and that you handled it extremely well'. Although I always purred to have a word of appreciation from Ernie, this was one occasion on which I did not find it a consolation.

The Labour Government was defeated in October 1951, and when we went into Opposition the National Executive Committee of the Labour Party moved closer to the idea of a European Defence Community, believing that it provided the best solution for the reintegration of an armed but peaceful Germany into Europe. But by that time the sands were running out. The German Bundestag and Bundesrat both ratified the treaty that had been prepared but, as some had always suspected, the idea was finally buried by the French Assembly itself which refused to support the treaty, both Gaullists and Communists voting together. As one commentator said at the time, 'it was a combination of nationalists and neutralists'.

So the European Defence Community was finally killed and I was subsequently greatly influenced by Hugh Dalton's attitude of complete opposition to rearming an independent Germany. I could not be as entirely negative as he was and went so far as to put forward proposals of my own, setting out conditions for the reunification of Germany, with a disarmed zone between East Germany and Poland, and with guarantees of frontiers by all the European states plus the United States and the Soviet Union.

There was no prospect, however, of such ideas catching hold. The post-war mould had set. The Americans had made up their minds that German rearmament must go ahead in some form or other and the Soviet Union had no intention of relinquishing control over East Germany. I had been told in Moscow in early 1946 that under no circumstances would Russia ever again permit Poland to be used as a pathway for invasion, and by the late 1940s the Soviet Union had extended that doctrine to East Germany itself, and had permitted the formation of an East German paramilitary force to form a glacis against any invader from the West.

Two criticisms of the Labour Government's post-war European policy were frequently made during those years. First, it was said that if the West, and in particular the United States and Britain, had adopted a more accommodating and understanding attitude towards the Soviet Union, we would not have faced the unbridgeable gulf that opened up between the former wartime Allies. The second criticism was that Britain threw away a glorious opportunity, freely offered to her by Europe, to take the lead in restructuring the devastated countries of the Continent. In 1945 I had some sympathy with the first criticism but this quickly evaporated as events unfolded.

The first criticism came from the Keep Left Group, who criticised Britain's foreign policy as too pro-American. In the preceding November more than a hundred Labour MPs abstained in a vote on foreign policy for similar reasons. This criticism subsided after the Marshall Plan, which provided essential resources for the recovery of Europe, but it is worth for a moment looking at the situation which the Government had to grapple with. At the end of the war Britain's financial problems were so severe as not only to jeopardise Labour's economic programme but to extend the harsh demands of rationing well into the next decade. In addition, it appeared to Ernest Bevin that there was a real danger that the United States might revert to pre-war isolationism. Britain would be in no position to hold the line against the Soviet Union alone at a moment when fear of war was rife in Europe, with France and Italy economically crippled and politically divided. To Bevin the United States was Western

Europe's only possible source of defence and economic support. But this did not mean subservience on our part. Over the European Recovery Programme, the recognition of China, and the proposed use of the atomic bomb in Korea, the Labour Government was able to demonstrate both independence and influence.

Bevin came to office desirous of good relations with Russia. Many of us felt sympathy for Soviet concerns about security – but not security at the expense of denying freedom and security to others. If the price of good relations with the Soviet Union was that the West should acquiesce to every Soviet demand, it was a requirement we could not meet.

Another obstacle was the basic Soviet concept that there must always be antagonism between capitalist and communist states. This had been drummed into me by those I met in Moscow when I first visited it as member of a British delegation of younger people sent in December 1945. As a newly elected supporter of the Labour Government, I took some offence and argued vigorously that Britain was no longer following the policies of the 1920s and 1930s, with its vast army of unemployed and its fatal appeasement in the face of the rise of Italian fascism and German Nazism. This argument was dismissed. There could be no shade of grey. If we were not marching towards communism then we were a capitalist country. I was told by Russian spokesmen of their belief that Eastern Europe would be invaded by the West, led by the Americans, once Germany had revived. I was never certain whether they genuinely believed this, but they acted as if they did.

Russian fear of Germany was immovable. The Soviet Union had experienced at the hands of the Germans much wanton destruction and purposeless killing. It led her to demand that German industry should be dismantled and plant and factories bodily removed from the country. I recall only too vividly the scenes of desolation presented by the cities and towns I visited immediately after the end of the war. The centre of Kiev was no more than a pile of rubble, the buildings deliberately burnt to the ground as a reprisal for partisan attacks. The Nazis sent the older schoolchildren away from their homes to Germany to work as slave labour, and then re-opened the empty schools for German children who had been evacuated to escape British and American bombing attacks. I wrote in my diary at the time: 'The people have no pity in their hearts for the destruction of Berlin.'

Whilst I was in Kiev in January 1946 I attended a war crimes trial. It was held in a large newly built hall, filled to capacity with about 1,500 members of the public who listened intently to the evidence. Three military judges, high-ranking members of the Soviet Army, sat on a raised stage, flanked by the State Prosecutor and the defending lawyers.

In a large and specially constructed dock sat the twenty German officers on trial. One of them was the Major General who had been in command of the 213th Division in the Ukraine, another was the Lieutenant General in command of police in the Kiev region, and a third the Rear Commander of the Sixth Army in the Don Basin. On the day I was present, the examination was taking place of Georg Heinisch, a Nazi who had been in command of the Melitopol Region, an area to the south of Kharkov. He was described as an Obersturmbahnfuhrer of the Nazi SS. In the courtroom I made a note of his evidence as my interpreter translated. This is it.

Heinisch answered the questions freely and volubly. His role had been to round up the villagers and children and send them to work in Germany.

QUESTION: Why?
ANSWER: Because Germany was so short of labour.
QUESTION: Did the villagers protest?
ANSWER: Oh, yes. Quite frequently. Then they were imprisoned or in some cases were shot.
QUESTION: How many were shot?
ANSWER: Perhaps four thousand. In one case a whole village rose in revolt and the only way to suppress them was to shoot the whole population and burn down the village. After that, protests ceased for some time.

He sent many children to work in the marshy bed of the River Dnieper.

QUESTION: Did any die?
ANSWER: A number of them caught malaria but he did not think many died and, in any case, they worked only in the summer and not in the winter.

His other job was to see that the crop quota fixed by the German authorities was extracted from the peasants. It normally ranged from 75 to 100 per cent of the total crop, but he always aimed at securing more than the quota because of the food shortage in Europe.

QUESTION: Had he taken part in the killing of Jewish children of Russian nationality?
ANSWER: No. That had all been done before his arrival. But the killing

of mixed Jewish-Russian blood had taken place while he was there.
QUESTION: Had he taken part in it?
ANSWER: No. It was not in his province but he had heard about it.

At this, the officer sitting next to him, a Major General, nodded his head
in agreement.

QUESTION: Was it not his duty to protest against the inhuman slaughter
of such children?

And then came the most dramatic moment in his evidence. Heinisch
shrugged his shoulders and raised his voice a tone. 'As a Nationalist
Socialist, I could not but approve of their deaths.' A murmur of horror
and anger washed over the spectators even before the translation from
German into Russian, for whether we knew German or not, his attitude
had told us the answer.

My interpreter was so shaken that she was unable to concentrate
properly on the answer to the next question about the method of putting
the children to death, and she asked me not to require her to translate
the reply. I did not press her to do so.

The dock was guarded by Red Army soldiers, but when the court rose
many of the audience crowded round to get a closer sight of the accused.
Some shook their fists, but the Germans feigned indifference as they filed
out of the dock. This scene, and others, had a profound effect on me.

From Kiev we flew in an old Dakota over a snowy landscape to Stalino,
a coal-mining city that was the centre of the Don Valley (rechristened
Donetsk after Stalin's death) and thence to Stalingrad (now Volgograd).
One of my companions was Lawrence Daly, a young miner from Fife in
Scotland, who was later to become the General Secretary of the NUM.
We spent six weeks in each other's company and, as a result of that journey, developed an affinity that defied the passage of time and our political
differences. When I became Prime Minister the relationship we developed
during our Russian journey stood us both in good stead on more than one
occasion, when Daly accompanied Joe Gormley to see me at 10 Downing
Street on behalf of the miners.

As part of the British delegation to Russia, I was asked by A. V.
Alexander to put on my naval uniform and represent the Navy (I had not
then been demobilised). Also represented were the Army, the Air Force,
the Women's Services, the Bevin Boys, the Women's Land Army, the
Merchant Navy, and other groups. Most of us wore uniform and these

attracted much attention, especially from the Nazi officers in the dock at Kiev.

We spent much of our time in the company of other young people, and what I saw and heard during our six-week visit gave me a lasting sympathy for a people who had suffered and endured but whose spirit, even in those dreadful days, seemed unconquerable. We were subjected to large daily doses of indoctrination but whenever we talked, as we usually did, with the ordinary non-political young Soviet citizens in factories, universities, on farms and in the coal mines, we were greeted with great kindness, cheerful good humour and spontaneous and simple hospitality.

We were not to know that while we were in the Ukraine nationalist partisans were continuing to fight, but we glimpsed beneath the surface enough of an authoritarian, bureaucratic regime with a morbid preoccupation with security to ensure that we did not return to Britain wearing rose-coloured spectacles. Nevertheless for some time afterwards I would tend to explain the inexcusable by the Russians' need to rebuild their plundered and shattered country.

My feelings were torn between my liking for the Russian people and my growing dislike of Soviet actions. Bevin's cry that 'Left can speak to Left' remained unanswered, and I came reluctantly to the conclusion that the very nature of Stalin's regime made an affirmative reply impossible.

It is not so easy to give an assured answer to the question as to whether victorious Britain missed a chance to take the lead in reconstructing postwar Europe, politically and economically. Undoubtedly a strong wind was blowing in Britain's direction as Europe emerged from Nazi occupation, bombed and defeated, to struggle to her feet. Men and women in every occupied country admired the defiance of the British people when we stood alone and responded to Churchill's resolute leadership. This had lifted their spirits and captured their imagination during the Occupation.

In the first post-war winter of 1945, few on the Continent could see the way forward. They looked for help and hope whever it could be found and would have willingly accepted Britain's lead. But, as the early debate on the American loan had shown, Britain already had enough difficulties to cope with: food and clothes rationing, the repairing of houses and cleaning up of bomb damage, controlling the distribution of an inadequate supply of raw materials, with shortages of every kind. In addition there was the problem of how to bring back to this country several millions of war-weary men and women serving throughout the world, to demobilise

them in an orderly way and to find jobs for them all. It was hard enough
to feed liberated Europe without taking bold political initiatives.

A hard-pressed Labour Government acted humanely. Grain from
America that had been intended to feed the British people was re-
directed to the Continent. Australian grain ships coming to this country
were diverted to India to avert a threatened famine. Britain was ready to
ration bread, something that had never been necessary even in wartime.
With care, enough remained for everyone, but this gesture was used by
the Opposition and the press not to praise a selfless action but to allege
that the Labour Government was incompetent.

We concentrated on rebuilding our shattered economy but it was not
this alone which prevented us from taking the initiative in Europe. The
major obstacle was the view we took of ourselves and our future. We
were the Mother Country, centre of the British Commonwealth, to
whose aid the Dominions had come immediately war was declared.
During hostilities we had lost part of our South-East Asian colonies to
the Japanese but these had been won back. We had difficulties in Egypt
but it would remain a British base. Despite all the perils and problems of
the Arab-Jewish conflict, Palestine was our responsibility and we would
handle that too. Our extensive African colonies and Protectorates remained intact and so did the West Indian colonies.

The King's Speech, delivered by George VI on the opening of Parliament on 15 August 1945, had promised India early self-government in
fulfilment of undertakings given 'to my Indian peoples'. The speech
undertook to press on with the development 'of my Colonial Empire'.
The word 'independence', was not mentioned for the new Labour
Government did not know how long this would take. Devoted socialists
like Arthur Creech Jones, Fenner Brockway, Reginald Sorensen and
others had worked out a line of political and economic advance that
would need substantial resources of money, manpower, technical aid and
educational training. In some countries we thought it might take as many
as forty or fifty years to achieve complete independence.

One other factor was the way Britain saw her 'special relationship'
with the United States. The armies and navies of the two nations had
fought together, frequently under one Allied Commander. We had
shared each other's intimate secrets, including, most recently, the awesome knowledge of atomic weapons. We spoke the same language. The
common law was known to us both. In 1945 America and Britain together formed the most powerful and influential combination in the

world. Anglo-American joint decisions would shape the future of the immediate post-war world.

I do not remember that I consciously reasoned to myself in this way. There was no need to do so. The facts were self-evident and they led to the apparent conclusion that, although it was vital to rebuild Europe, we would assist from the outside in joint partnership with the United States. Europe had become yet one more of our manifold world-wide responsibilities. No one can say whether our attitude to Europe would have been different if we had been told that the post-war pace of colonial development would lead to rapid decolonisation within a period of twenty years, or that the Dominions would seek other relationships as the decline in Britain's political influence and economic strength became apparent.

Neverthless, the signs were there. America's productive capacity had grown by 50 per cent or even more. Her leaders recognised clearly enough that Britain was a junior partner in the joint enterprise. The American loan had been negotiated on unfavourable terms and, although the United States did not ask for Britain's formal support for the Bretton Woods Agreement, there was no doubt that our negotiators were influenced by the fact that British support for Bretton Woods would make the passage of the loan through Congress much easier.

The House of Commons vote in favour of the Bretton Woods Agreement led effectively to the dismantling of the Sterling Area, together with the further condition that sterling would become freely convertible into other currencies within the following twelve months. In a world crying out for dollars the inevitable happened. As soon as sterling became convertible on 15 July 1947, many countries holding large sterling balances immediately scrambled to convert them into dollars to pay for purchases from the United States. The intended purpose of the dollar loan had been to support Britain during three years of reconstruction. But on 20 August, only five weeks later, the drain on sterling had been so overwhelming as our creditors rushed into dollars that the Bank of England was compelled once more to make sterling inconvertible against the dollar.

With dollars drained away, even Britain's essential raw material imports became subject to drastic restrictions. The end of American Lend Lease had caused food to be rationed more strictly than during the war. Drastic reductions took place in every walk of life. Stafford Cripps, who had become Chancellor of the Exchequer when Hugh Dalton resigned after a Budget indiscretion, headed a great export drive to earn dollars to pay for Britain's food and raw materials. The British domestic market was stripped, the pottery industry, for example, being ordered under wartime controls to export practically all of its finest china, except for 'seconds'. The poor British housewife who had been hoping to restock after the privations of the war years made do with a utility brand of china. The motor car industry was threatened with the loss of its allocation of steel if it failed to export more cars. Cripps was booed loudly when he spoke at the annual dinner of the motor industry, whose dealers naturally preferred to meet the huge pent-up home demand for cars rather than export them to earn dollars. The Opposition made the most of it, and Labour paid heavily in the constituencies.

The consequence of making sterling convertible had been foreseen by some. Thomas Balogh, the economist and adviser to the Labour Party, had forecast that it would prove a rash and premature step. Robert Boothby saw it clearly. I have already written of his preference for a commercial loan from America to enable Britain to plan her future, as he said, as part of 'the Sterling Bloc based upon the British Empire and fortified by the countries of Western Europe'. It was an imaginative, forward-looking concept. We shall never know whether the rush towards decolonisation would have rendered it void, or whether Europe would have been more united, and her relations with the Third World closer. There is small virtue in looking back, but it might have been worth a go.

Britain's decision to continue working in partnership with the United States gave impetus to those European politicians who sought closer collaboration between their own countries. Britain did not seek to impede this, nor did we turn our backs on Europe. Clement Attlee had made Britain's position clear in the debate in the House of Commons on the plan to create a combined coal and steel industry in Europe: 'In the world as it is placed today it is ridiculous to try to stand for the absolute sovereignty of the individual state. We have always been willing and are now to enter into international arrangements. There are great possibilities of moving forward on functional lines towards European unity.'

In 1950 I repeated these words when I addressed the European Consultative Assembly in Strasbourg, and continued: 'We regard ourselves as part of Europe. We desire to work with Europe and our intention and aim is that there should be the fullest cooperation between us all. Today all of us are interdependent. I must remind those who advocate a federal arrangement for Europe that theirs is not the only method by which sovereignty can be pooled and merged into something larger.'

I went on to quote an earlier remark by Sir Winston Churchill that he could not conceive that Britain would be an ordinary member of a federal Europe in the foreseeable future. And I took pains to deny a suspicion which, while never publicly uttered, went the rounds in Strasbourg and elsewhere, that in the event of war Britain would withdraw behind the English Channel. 'That is not true,' I said. Europe's defence was Britain's need. Those who believed they could create a federal Europe almost overnight were not impressed by Attlee's functional approach. They went ahead without us, although some hoped that eventually Britain might join them.

I have written about matters in which I played no more than a walk-on part some forty years ago, because some of the problems we discussed then still remain unresolved. True, Britain has thrown in her lot with the European Community and nothing will disturb this relationship. On the other hand, Europe is politically becalmed and lacks economic vitality. The idealism of the federalists has evaporated and nothing has taken its place, for Europe has no clear vision of what it wishes to become, nor of how it can achieve a closer unity.

The profound industrial and economic changes since the end of the Second World War have turned a searchlight on the inadequacies of national frontiers and artificial trade restrictions. The time is overdue for a new European leap forward that would match the dynamism of Japan and the combined strength of the United States of America.

Nor is the West clear about what it expects in its relationship with the Soviet Union. Second World War cooperation became a state of Cold War, followed by a thaw which resulted in the Helsinki Agreement. Soviet rearmament and the invasion of Afghanistan led to American calls for trade sanctions and a war of overblown rhetoric. As I write, the meetings between the new Soviet leadership under Central Secretary Gorbachev with President Reagan have cooled the temperature for the time being, but the Alliance still has no steady compass by which to steer. The phrase 'constructive engagement' may be a cliché, but it embraces, I believe, the shortest definition of the best way for the West to conduct itself. Nuclear energy, pollution, population, the use of scarce resources, the conservation of the environment and the cleanliness of the seas in order that our successors may enjoy them, are all areas of common concern in which East and West, as well as North and South, should seek to work together. Cooperate where we can. Compete if we must, but never forgetting that man's scientific achievements have rendered our planet too dangerous to allow our technological ingenuity to outrun our moral sense.

I have already referred in passing to my appointment as Parliamentary Secretary to the Ministry of Transport in 1947 and to the Admiralty in 1950. But I might have become a junior Minister even earlier, in 1946, and my experience then showed how large a part chance can play in such appointments.

I had visited Czechoslovakia in September 1946, before the communist takeover, and on the day I returned to London I found there ad been a Ministerial reshuffle. The Chief Whip sent for me a day or two later and said that it had been intended to promote me to Parliamentary Under-Secretary at the War Office under Manny Shinwell. However, as I had been out of the country and the matter could not wait, the Prime Minister had appointed Frank Pakenham (later Lord Longford) in my place. All this in a matter-of-fact voice. I was mortified, but at least it showed that neither Clem nor the Whips held against me the rebellious attitude I had adopted when dealing with the problems of the men and women in the Armed Forces.

I had been elected as Chairman of the Party's Defence Committee in 1945, and knowing how the men who were still overseas felt, I spent much time harassing Ministers on Service questions, especially those concerning demobilisation, post-war service conditions and the length of conscription. Demobilisation was the most pressing topic: men were weary and anxious to resume their civilian lives. In some overseas posts there was a state of near mutiny. I prodded Ministers to demobilise more quickly so that those who had served overseas for as long as four or five years without seeing their families could come home as early as possible. We younger Members, fresh home from abroad, pressed that the period of overseas service be reduced to three years and the maximum peacetime conscription period to twelve or eighteen months, with the Government retaining no more than 1.6 million men in the forces one year after the end of hostilities.

These demands were given immense publicity throughout the Services with the result that I received a very large correspondence from men all over the world. Looking through my replies I note that I entertained no doubts that everyone would find work and that the returning service-men would not repeat the wretched experiences of their fathers after the 1914–18 War. There existed a united determination in the country about this, and all Parties in the wartime Coalition Government gave a solemn undertaking to maintain a high level of post-war employment. I never doubted that a Labour Government could ensure that this binding promise was fulfilled. I notice that one of my stated reasons for pressing for faster demobilisation was my forecast that Britain would not be able to achieve the government target of boosting exports by 175 per cent over pre-war levels, because industry would be starved of manpower.

The problems of demobilising millions of men could have caused great social and industrial unrest had they not been handled by Labour Ministers and their Departments with skill and understanding. Much has rightly been written about the giants of that Government – Attlee, Bevin, Cripps, Morrison and Dalton – and of the great innovators in health and social insurance, Nye Bevan and Jim Griffiths. But there were others too: Jack Lawson, the Minister for War; George Isaacs, the Minister of Labour; George Tomlinson, Minister of Education – all men without much formal education themselves but possessed of moral purpose and firm character, and blessed with common sense, shrewdness and understanding, and a care for their fellows. These three (and there were others) were cast in a similar mould of hard industrial experience. All three left their elementary schools at eleven or twelve years of age, Lawson to become a pit boy at Boldon Colliery, Durham; Isaacs, a reader's boy in a London printing works; and Tomlinson, a half-timer in a Lancashire cotton mill. All were self-educated. Jack Lawson wrote *A Man's Life*, a book that was his own record and became a Labour classic. They did not practise sophisticated arts but all of them knew how to speak straight to the hearts of working men and women. In their homely tones and everyday phrases, they brought hope and understanding to millions of workers who asked only of society that it should give them and their children a fair deal in life, the chance to live decently, to bridge the gap between great riches and harsh poverty, and to ensure dignity in their old age. In those early post-war days I was sometimes impatient and critical of these men's unhurried pace. But looking back, I now know better.

One morning in October 1947 I received a message from the Whip's office that the Prime Minister wanted to see me. I knocked on the door of 10 Downing Street and was shown to the small ante-chamber outside the Cabinet Room. The Prime Minister's Private Secretary put his head round the door and called me in. Clem was sitting in the Prime Minister's place at the centre of the long Cabinet table. He motioned me with his pipe to sit beside him and, as far as I can recall, said only three sentences. First, he appointed me to be Parliamentary Secretary to the Ministry of Transport. Then, 'Remember you are playing for the first eleven now, not the second eleven. And if you are going to negotiate with someone tomorrow, don't insult him today.' With that he nodded and said goodbye and I was out of the Cabinet Room in less than two minutes.

I walked down Whitehall towards the House of Commons feeling very elated and a few yards before reaching the House met Alf Robens. Intuitively, both of us knew that we had been separately to No. 10 but we had both been instructed to tell no one, and neither of us said a word. George Brown and Michael Stewart were promoted at the same time, and all of us went on to serve in Labour Cabinets.

Alfred Barnes, the Minister of Transport, was the son of a London docker. His main interests were the Cooperative Society, and making metal statuettes and ornaments. He had been trained as a gold and silver designer and never lost his skill. Nor did he ever lose his temper. In the House he was always calm, polite and dull. This last attribute was an asset in carrying through the nationalisation of the railways and of road transport. His patience and quiet approach disarmed the most prickly Conservative and he got his Bills through the House more easily than other more entertaining but controversial Ministers. It was a lesson I learned from him and sought to apply on occasion when at the Dispatch Box, especially when I became Chancellor of the Exchequer. When in trouble, keep your head down, read your speech notes closely, speak in a monotone, never raise your voice or look up if you can help it, and be as uninteresting as possible. Alf Barnes practised these techniques whether he was in difficulty or not.

The Ministry of Transport was responsible for shipping and docks and I was given the enjoyable task of touring all the major ports in the United Kingdom. This fitted in with my interest in the future of Cardiff Docks and the other South Wales ports.

I soon realised that their fortunes were interlinked, but, alas, there was great rivalry between them, and even more between South Wales and Bristol which was a lively, enterprising municipally owned port. The great London and Liverpool docks enjoyed the first choice of traffics and cargo liners and although ships were stacked up waiting for berths at which to unload in these two ports, many shipping lines were reluctant to use others. Shipowners had great influence with the Ministry of Transport shortly after the war and it seemed to me that their idea of

Utopia was to persuade the Minister to direct all government traffic through Liverpool and London whilst other ports scrambled for the crumbs. I was strongly opposed to this on grounds of regional employment policy as well as for defence and strategic reasons. Forty per cent of South Wales docks capacity was unused and I fought a continuous battle to ensure that they and the Scottish ports got a share of the traffic.

In the early post-war period the Government frequently bought in bulk and there were many government-owned cargoes whose port destination could be adjusted in order to secure a rational use of port facilities and manpower at a time of great shortage of tonnage. But I was swimming against the tide and as post-war government buying decreased, shippers and shipowners used London and Liverpool to an ever-increasing extent, despite the long delays incurred. Shipowners and dockers in these two ports brought much of their future trouble on their own heads by their inflexibility. Among the best run ports at that time were Bristol, Manchester and Southampton. Some parts of the London docks were well run but the Port of Liverpool was certainly below standard.

Alf Barnes hardly involved me at all in major policy decisions but I plunged into administration with enthusiasm, and like all new brooms, tried to sweep clean. Alf was very kind, and whatever he thought of my attempted reforms, he never complained. I campaigned for the Department to provide short answers to parliamentary questions and, when I achieved some success, signed a minute of thanks to the office following congratulations from the Prime Minister who had listened to my replies during Question Time. I tried to speed up the time it took to reply to letters from the public, amalgamated various provincial offices, shortened the six-month interval that elapsed between a bus company making an application to increase fares and receiving the answer, improved coastguard uniforms, stirred up trouble about ship-building and repair costs which were too high, fought a battle (which I lost) to prevent ships loaded with explosives from using commercial ports and, ever-mindful of South Wales, persuaded Alf Barnes to agree that a slip road should be built from Merthyr Tydfil to the top of the Valleys. The cost was £220,000 to build three and one third miles, including three bridges. I also cajoled the Permanent Secretary into allocating £20,000 to abolish the last toll road between Cardiff and Penarth.

Alf Barnes gave me one totally independent post, that of Chairman of the Road Safety Committee, in which capacity I had my first meeting with Princess Elizabeth. One of my first tasks was to visit the Road Research Laboratory, where I uncovered two projects languishing because the Laboratory had not been able to procure sufficient resources from the Department.

The first idea was to paint the road at pedestrian crossings with broad white stripes that would show up in the dark or on a gloomy day. I was enthusiastic when I saw the full-scale models and persuaded the Minister to adopt the notion. Inevitably the crossings became known as zebra crossings.

The second idea was for catseye studs. These had been invented before the war by Percy Shaw, a Yorkshireman. He eventually made a fortune out of his idea but he probably never knew that he owed part of it to me. Catseyes had already been used in a limited way but officials in the Ministry of Transport were strongly opposed to their use on trunk roads, and I had to use all my powers of persuasion before I eventually overrode the Department. The principal objection of one official was that to place the studs on the crown of the road would encourage car-owners to drive in the middle during a fog and a dreadful series of collisions would follow.

I treated experts with respect, but while at the Ministry of Transport I had a taste of their fallibility. Officials were planning at that time the post-war motorway system, and one of the greatest transport experts of the day was in charge of the exercise. I recall one meeting at which he told us that the number of licensed motor cars on the roads at that time was 1.9 millions and that we could safely plan on the assumption that the total number was never likely to exceed 4.5 millions. In fact it reached that figure ten years later in 1958. (At the latest count in 1985, incidentally, the number of cars on the roads was 16,453,000.) This gave me a healthy scepticism about the value of statistical forecasts which has persisted throughout my Ministerial life, although when I was Chancellor of the Exchequer I sometimes had to act on them in default of anything better.

I was also given a piece of practical advice by Sir Cyril Hurcomb, the Permanent Secretary at Transport, who became the first Chairman of the British Transport Commission. When I became a Cabinet Minister, he said, I should set in hand anything I wished to be done within the first three months of taking office. 'After that, it gets much more difficult, if not impossible.'

While these Departmental matters were occupying my time, energy and enthusiasm, great events had happened in the world. India secured her Independence, Israel proclaimed hers and the Arab League invaded. Britain exploded an atomic bomb and the Soviet Union blockaded

Berlin. In Britain we nationalised electricity and gas, clothes rationing was done away with, but other rationing continued. The National Health Service had been launched, the pound was devalued and exports were roaring ahead. But the Labour Government's standing steadily declined. The British people were not enjoying the easement they felt they had a right to expect after six years of war, and the press encouraged them to believe that prosperity was withheld only by the malevolence of the Labour Government.

I was an observer rather than a participant in these great happenings, for I had fallen a victim to a disease to which junior Ministers, absorbed in the excitements of their first office, are prone. I was beguiled by 'departmentalitis'. Those who are afflicted by this disease suffer from distorted vision. They can see their own Department's needs and concerns very clearly, almost obsessively, but they show strong signs of detachment from the general fortunes of the Government. They work hard in their Departments but exhibit a certain listlessness about the day-to-day Parliamentary battle, and may attend only when urgently summoned by a three-line Whip. Sometimes they enjoy the illusion that because their own Department's affairs are in good order, there can be little wrong with the Government as a whole. Junior Ministers who hold marginal seats are often immune from such attacks, and in all cases the symptoms invariably disappear with the onset of a general election.

I was clearly recovering from my attack by the end of 1949, for I made a note of a conversation with Douglas Jay, then Economic Secretary at the Treasury. As I have said, I did not keep a diary, but from time to time I made notes of interesting conversations such as this. He had said that Stafford Cripps was taking the attacks on his integrity following the devaluation of sterling very badly: 'He is one of the chief protagonists of a March [1950] election because he refuses to introduce another Budget until he has been fortified by the electorate. Most recent indications are that he had been persuaded by the Prime Minister to change his mind.' I myself was not in favour of an early election. I preferred the summer, as did Douglas Jay and most of my colleagues. I wrote, 'I think the mood of the people is for another period of Labour government. Of course, we could lose it through our crass stupidity but given that we shall behave reasonably I think we shall form the government again. But for the moment we have exhausted the vein of thinking that served us from 1918 to 1945 and are being carried along by our initial momentum. Unless we have thought out and got over to people our attitudes on the problems of 1950 to 1960 we shall lose the election *following* this one – and will deserve to.' And that was what happened. I have not always been as accurate in forecasting the results of more recent elections.

We junior Ministers were given an indication of Stafford Cripps's frame of mind at a meeting of the Cabinet Production Committee. The food situation was still difficult and Cabinet Committees received regular, detailed statistical reports on the stocks of food and materials held in the country to enable scarce dollars to be allocated to various priorities, and so indirectly to determine the level of food rationing in every household.

John Dugdale, the Parliamentary and Financial Secretary to the Admiralty, was a member of the Committee. Like the other junior Ministers present at the meeting he knew an election might be coming, but having been Attlee's Parliamentary Private Secretary, he was bolder than them. As we concluded the last item on the agenda he broke in to say that stocks of cheese seemed much higher than they had been in the past and he hoped that the Chancellor would not keep them unnecessarily high in view of certain developments expected later in the year.

Stafford looked at him witheringly over the tops of the half-moon glasses he wore. 'It would not be proper to be imprudent because of the approach of an historical accident,' he said. John was silenced and the meeting broke up.

Stafford had his way and Attlee called an early general election which took place on 23 February 1950. The weather was terrible. It rained throughout the day and we were all wet through more than once. There were few cars and it seemed heartless to urge elderly pensioners to venture out on foot to vote, but most of them were keen to do so. They could compare conditions of life after the last war with those after 1918. I was returned with a satisfactory majority and it was then that the Prime Minister appointed me to the Admiralty as Parliamentary and Financial Secretary. This was welcome in many ways, and as the First Lord of the Admiralty, Viscount Hall, was in the Lords, particular responsibility fell upon me to answer in the Commons. George Hall had originally been a miner in the Aberdare Valley and had begun work in the pits at the age of twelve. He became a check-weighman and miners' agent before entering the House in 1922. He was softly spoken, well dressed and invariably polite, but was approaching seventy when I arrived at the Admiralty and was not looking for radical change. The fact that we both represented South Wales seats led him to be indulgent to my schemes and criticisms.

Although I was very happy to be at the Admiralty, the future was uncertain. The Government had been returned with a majority over all
other parties of only ten, and Clement Attlee had said in the King's
Speech that Parliament was 'more evenly divided than any House had
been for the last hundred years'. None of us foresaw at that time that in
1964 a Labour Government would be elected with an overall majority
of only four, or that in 1974 we could govern with a majority as low as
three. On this last occasion we succeeded by a combination of good Party
discipline, efficient Whips, some unorthodox decisions and a variety of
stratagems which enabled us to defeat every vote of no confidence for a
period of nearly five years. And during this time we put through most
of our programme.

The difference was that in 1976 we made a compact with the Liberals,
and Ministers were fresh and eager, but in 1951 senior Ministers were
tired, a number of them having been in office for eleven years, nearly
six of these at war. The Tories felt that in 1950 they had only just missed
victory and one more heave would put them in. So they made life in the
Commons as uncomfortable and as unpleasant for Ministers as they could.
Their attitude did not distress us junior Ministers for, with all the self-
confidence of comparative youth, we felt able both physically and mentally
to handle anything the Opposition could throw at us, and indeed to hurl
it back.

I had made it my business to keep up with post-war developments in
the Services, and when I presented the naval estimates to the House only
three weeks after my arrival at the Admiralty I was presumptuous enough
to make a speech lasting for fifty minutes without a written text. I would
never dare to do it today.

In 1950 the Navy was going through a difficult transition. After the
end of the war there had been a rapid demobilisation, the active fleet was
living on accumulated wartime stockpiles and a process of scrapping
ships was in hand. The Admiralty had already decided that the major
threat for the future was the growing submarine fleet of the Soviet Union,
and was altering the balance of the post-war fleet to meet it. A new anti-
submarine frigate had been designed, and research and development was
taking place on anti-submarine weapons such as helicopters and listening
buoys.

The Board's policy was that Britain should possess a fleet which could
fulfill the task of protecting Britain's trade routes around the world.
Their policy was to scrap older ships and to rebuild so as to maintain a

constant supply of up-to-date vessels. In the period of financial stringency
we were living through I felt, on the other hand, that this policy led to
ships being scrapped whilst still having a useful role, and in my capacity
as Financial Secretary I fought a running battle to keep certain types of
wartime ships in the reserve fleet so that they could be refitted quickly
in an emergency.

Ships in reserve deteriorated swiftly and the Admiralty had developed
a process of drying a ship out by first sealing the exits, then sucking out
the moist, damp air and finally pumping dry air into the empty spaces.
I had been urging this policy for some months when I found I was doing
no more than following in the footsteps of my predecessor, Samuel Pepys.
In 1684, in writing about the reserve fleet, he spoke of 'general rot'. The
ships' decay, he said, was due to 'want of graving and bringing into dock,
neglect to clean and air the holds till I have gathered with my own hands
toadstools as big as my fists'. The problem had hardly changed.

I was engaged in trying to prevent the scrapping of the Hunt class
destroyers which had done invaluable convoy duty during the Second
World War when Britain found herself called upon as part of a United
Nations force to repel the invasion of South Korea. This came at the
moment when the Navy was about half-way towards converting from its
end-of-war state to its projected long-term shape and size. Looming over
our heads was the great anxiety caused by the assessment on which the
Cabinet was acting, namely that there was a possibility of a major war
with the Soviet Union at any time within the following three years. The
Korean crisis led to much improvisation and the Admiralty was able to
bring sixty ships out of reserve immediately and add them to the active
fleet. The naval staff did an about-turn on the Hunt class destroyers and
decided to refit them. Dickie Mountbatten, who had been on my side,
said after one Board meeting ended that if a major war did come, I could
regard myself as a saviour. I replied that this would be cold comfort to
both of us. Another piece of good fortune was that fifty thousand trained
naval reservists were working in civilian jobs, of whom a number were
called back for a period of eighteen months to man the reserve ships.

One harsh decision was the retention of long-service men who had
completed their period of engagement and were about to retire. All of
these men had joined before 1939, served throughout the war, and had
then remained in the Navy during the post-war rundown. Now we were
asking them to stay on once again. I managed to sweeten the pill by
securing a substantial increase in pay from the Treasury. During the

whole period of conscription, the Navy never had trouble in securing the volunteers it needed. In fact, it accepted only a token number of two thousand national servicemen every year as a gesture towards its part in the national conscription scheme.

In 1982 I was reminded of the Korean War during the campaign to retake the Falklands. Public and press rightly praised the speed and efficiency with which the Navy set out on the Falklands expedition within a matter of days of the Argentine's invasion of the Islands. They expressed surprise at the promptness of the action, but in 1950 much the same thing had happened. When South Korea was invaded, Britain's Far Eastern Fleet was a thousand miles from base, but within three days it had reached the west coast of Korea, was engaged in operations and had sunk a number of North Korean E-boats. Within eight days of the invasion, the aircraft carrier HMS *Triumph* was flying successful sorties to the mainland. There was one important difference: in 1950 the Navy had far more ships, men and reserves than it has today.

The Royal Marines of 41 Independent Commando fought most gallantly in Korea. They began with landings on the coast and later advanced to join up with the United States Marines. They did their share of 'yomping', although they would not have recognised the word. At one stage they were nearly overrun and were forced to carry out a fighting withdrawal, marching for three days without food or sleep. Conditions were atrocious. The temperature was forty degrees below zero as the men struggled up high mountains and plunged through deep snow drifts. After one terrible night their commanding officer, Colonel Drysdale, wrote, 'I thought the morning would never come', but they battled their way successfully to Hungnam, losing a number of brave men on the way. There was a thirty-year gap between Korea and the Falklands. The battles were fought by different generations but the fighting spirit had endured.

Because our parliamentary majority was small and the 'harrying' of the Government persistent, it was not possible for me to leave the Admiralty to see as much as I would have liked, but at Whitsun 1950 I managed to pay an enjoyable visit to the fleet. Audrey, the children and I stayed with the Commander-in-Chief at Plymouth, from whose house there is a breathtaking view across Plymouth Sound. My mother was thrilled when I told her of our plans, because as a young girl she had stood and watched the grand carriages drawing up at the door, never expecting that her son would one day stay there.

It was Navy Week and for the last time before they were finally paid off I was able to visit a number of ships, including the battleships *Vanguard* and *Anson*. I then sailed in the cruiser *Euryalus* to Gibraltar. Her Captain, 'Egg' Burnett, was one of a group of commanders whose determination had helped us win the Battle of the Atlantic, and he and the ship's company made me feel at home.

I took my midday meal in a different mess every day with the petty officers or seamen and visited all parts of the ship. The crew's spirit was impressive, especially among the young men, although the older ones who had served throughout a long war did a certain amount of what they called 'tooth sucking'. When we reached Gibraltar I was less than impressed by one or two of the shore-bound senior naval officers I met, some of whom were politically right-wing and even pro-Franco. Their partiality chimed oddly with my recollection that during the war the aircraft carrier in which I was sailing was ordered not to enter Gibraltar before nightfall, and to leave before morning in order to avoid coming to the notice of German agents whom Franco allowed to operate in La Linea.

The atmosphere between my hosts and myself was cool, and in order not to make it worse I weakly consented to their proposal to entertain me by taking me to a bullfight at which Vincent Charles, the English matador, was performing. I disliked both the event and the atmosphere, and have never been since. My hostess was ecstatic.

Although I was happy to meet some former naval mess-mates with whom I had served and enjoyed a pleasant day with the Governor of Gibraltar, I was relieved when we sailed for Malta. When we arrived, the reception by my naval hosts was much more agreeable, and I was impressed by the general keenness and enthusiasm when I toured the dockyard and paid visits to establishments, ships and submarines. It was on this occasion that I met Dom Mintoff for the first time. He was even then the fiery young leader of the Opposition Labour Party. He told me that when he gained power he would press for Malta to become the equivalent of an English county, with representation at Westminster. If that was not acceptable, then he would demand independence for Malta and be ready to offer the dockyard and base facilities to the United States. I asked him about the Soviet Union. He replied No, because he would be the first to be shot. He was probably correct.

Dom Mintoff is an able, mercurial and warm-hearted man who led Britain a merry dance in the years that followed. But it must be said for him that, although irascible and erratic, his purpose was to secure the best deal he could for the island and people of Malta which lacked so many natural resources. In private life he was generous and good fun, married to an English architect who was as calm as he was volatile.

At the time of our first meeting he was in the midst of one of his interminable disputes with the dominant Catholic Church, and when the austere and elderly Archbishop came to visit at the front entrance of the Verdala Palace, where I was staying, we had to smuggle Dom out of the back door.

Not every British Governor lived in grandeur and I felt sorry for the Governor in Verdala. His house was large and gloomy, the lighting was inadequate, the plumbing was bad, the furniture was grand but sparse, and my bedroom was as large as a railway station, with a vaulted roof in which the slightest noise echoed and reverberated. But my hosts were kindly and welcoming and did all they could to make my visit enjoyable.

Six months elapsed before I was able to escape from the Admiralty again. On New Year's Day 1951 I left a dark and freezing Northolt airport to arrive at Malta in warm bright sunshine. The sight of the fleet in the Grand Harbour always stirred the blood and as they put to sea the ships made a splendid picture. Cruisers, destroyers and frigates – more than twenty ships in all sailed in company towards Greece, carrying out exercises on the way.

One frigate, HMS *Magpie*, was commanded by Prince Philip who was then twenty-nine years of age. His ship enjoyed a good reputation, borne out on the following day when, during an anti-aircraft shoot at sea, *Magpie* was the first ship in the flotilla to open fire. We reached Argostoli Bay, an anchorage in the Ionian Islands, and some of the destroyer and frigate captains came aboard the flagship for dinner. This was the first occasion on which I met Prince Philip and it was clear that he was an officer of outstanding keenness, with a passion for efficiency and for his profession, and an outspokenness which few of his contemporaries copied. When they came aboard the flagship he talked the sort of sense it was good for his seniors to hear. The first impression I formed that night remained with me: he did not suffer fools gladly, nor would he allow slipshod thinking to go unchallenged. Everyone Prince Philip worked with must adopt his own high standards of performance. This has not made for a placid existence.

Thirty years later he had not changed. I was part of the British delegation led by the Duke of Edinburgh to the state funeral of Marshal Tito of Yugoslavia in 1980. There is one unchanging rule at state funerals:

when the ceremony is concluded it is a matter of honour that every one of the dignitaries should try to leave before the others. Confusion reigns. On this occasion the only way the British delegation could leave the scene was for the Duke of Edinburgh, Prime Minister Mrs Thatcher and me to squeeze ourselves into the rear seat of a small car a little larger than a Mini, with accompanying detective and driver. In the ensuing conversation, if that is the appropriate word to describe the comments of my two companions on the arrangements, I recognised at once the force of their characters and decided that my best contribution to the general happiness would be to remain quite quiet. I escaped unscathed.

As Captain of his ship, Prince Philip had shown in the Mediterranean that he knew how to get things done well, quickly and with the enthusiasm of his ship's company. When I returned I reported this to the Prime Minister in an account of my visit. He replied on 15 January 1951, in a handwritten letter, that he shared the same impression of the Duke's qualities as a sailor, and that he was right to carry on his naval career. The Prime Minister added that Prince Philip would have a difficult job when he became Prince Consort, and he would see what could be done to give him more experience of home affairs when he took up his next shore job. Unfortunately, King George VI died before this could be done but the Duke had no difficulty in carrying out his own particular role in public affairs, prodding where necessary, not hesitating to state his opinions, and placing his energy behind many worthwhile causes. As Britain changes the Crown must adapt, and the wide knowledge acquired by the Duke in many fields has been of great benefit to the Sovereign in making her long reign appear both stable and relevant in an age of transition. Just as important, he has always provided a protecting arm and sure support.

I parted from the fleet at Patras and flew in an RAF Anson at 120 knots to Athens. Flying so slowly at less than ten thousand feet was often more uncomfortable than the stratospheric journeys of today, but it had the advantage that you could see where you were. We flew in sunshine over a sea of deepest blue, level with snow-covered Mount Parnassus. There followed a clear view of the Corinth Canal before we landed to be received by a Naval Guard of Honour in Athens.

Very early on the next morning I paid my first visit to the Parthenon. I challenge anyone with a sense of history not to feel deeply moved at the sight of this monument of an ancient civilisation, and found myself picturing the many scenes it had witnessed. It conveys a greater sense of life and history than the remarkable ancient temples of the Upper Nile, perhaps because we know more of those who lived at that time. The buildings of the Moghul Empire in India vie with the Parthenon in beauty but in age they are no more than monuments of yesterday.

From the Parthenon we journeyed to Poseidon's Temple, where I could clearly make out Byron's name carved on one of the pillars. We drank a Greek wine, Domestica, and ate small tender *brisolakoi* lamb chops in the home of Demosthenes. My host, the head of the British Naval Mission in Greece, told me that he had been one of the handful of Englishmen who had been present at the burial of Rupert Brooke. He had been a young midshipman at the time, and on his return to Greece as Head of Mission he had revisited the grave to find it kept in perfect condition, despite its isolation.

I had talks with Field Marshal Papagos, the Greek Prime Minister, but as he did not speak English and I spoke no Greek, translation made the exchanges rather heavy-going. But he, the Minister of Defence, senior naval officers and a number of politicians made clear their objection to Britain's decision to reduce her presence in the Eastern Mediterranean and to allow the Americans to take our place. They lost no chance to emphasise their preference for the British to stay. The United States was already paying much of the costs of training the Greek Armed Forces, however, and in our straitened circumstances there was an overwhelming case for not duplicating the training effort. The second major topic of our talks was their fear of war with the Soviet Union. They feared an attempt by Stalin to take over Greece through the instrument of the Greek communists who were training in Albania and constituted a potential threat. They urged me to convince Mr Attlee that the British should stay. It was a measure of Britain's high standing at this time that they should urge that Britain's role was to be both the arbiter between the European powers and the voice of Europe in its exchanges with the United States.

I returned to the United Kingdom with mixed feelings but eventually made the only practicable recommendation, namely to reduce the British Mission's numbers and our training commitment, and to carry out what training we undertook from Malta instead of in Greece itself. These recommendations were implemented. I could not fail to be impressed by the deep fears I heard of a Soviet invasion but I was by no means convinced that war with the Soviet Union was inevitable.

In a minute to Lord Mountbatten, then Fourth Sea Lord, I wrote: 'I believe, as I think you do, that we must try and live with [the Soviet Union] and it is in the interests of our society that we should do so.' It was obvious that 'in the next twenty years the major transformation of power will take place in the Middle East, Asia and in the backward territories'. Nevertheless, it was not possible or prudent to dismiss the widespread fears of war throughout Europe and I fully supported the programme of rearmament that the Labour Government had embarked upon.

In December 1950 the Cabinet, under American pressure and in agreement with other NATO European countries, took a decision to rearm, and a few months later, in April 1951, Nye Bevan resigned. The proximate cause of his resignation was the determination of the Chancellor Hugh Gaitskell to impose charges on medicines and dental treatment in order to raise revenue for the Health Service, but in his resignation speech to the Commons Nye Bevan widened his disagreement publicly for the first time by also declaring his opposition to the rearmament programme.

This was a surprise to those who had not been party to the Cabinet discussions, and caused great bitterness. It led to the creation of the Bevanite Group, and the rearmament issue became the major factor in the debilitating controversy which divided and weakened the Labour Party in the 1950s. Let me therefore say how I regarded the matter from the standpoint of a junior Minister who was not part of the Cabinet decision but served in a Defence Department.

When we had prepared the Navy's part of the rearmament programme during Christmas week, 1950, it was absolutely clear to all of us, whether Ministers or officials, that the programme could only be achieved provided we received supplies of raw materials and machine tools from the United States with the same high degree of priority as Britain had enjoyed during the war. So far from disguising this necessity from public view, the Board of Admiralty took every opportunity to emphasise it because of their private doubts as to whether America, despite pressing us to carry out this vast programme, would be willing or able to fulfil her own part.

We knew of the debate that was raging in the United States between President Truman and a considerable part of the Republican Party. Their attack went to the very heart of Truman's European policy, for the Republicans disputed his constitutional right to deploy four additional American divisions to reinforce Europe without Congressional approval. The Republican Party also complained that the President had been weak in his dealings with communist China, and they used these issues to attack Truman and to overthrow their own leaders, who had followed a broad bi-partisan policy since the Japanese attack on Pearl Harbor in 1941. In Britain we lived in some apprehension that the Republican Party would use the American setbacks in Korea to weaken Europe, by withdrawing American troops for service in the Far East.

Europe was fortunate that General Eisenhower was in command of the NATO forces. He knew the weakness of the West and resisted very strongly any attempts to take American troops away from Europe. His reputation was so considerable in the United States that the very fact that he backed Truman rather than the Republicans may well have saved the day, but we could not know how the battle would turn out when the Government embarked upon a rearmament programme.

What was uppermost was that the American President was under great pressure, that the American press and public were calling on Continental Europe to do more to help itself, and that if there was no adequate response not only might we lose the prospect of four additional American divisions at a time of tension, but Europe might face further troop withdrawals.

The number of divisions that the Russians could have used may have been fewer than was believed at the time, but I do not think the Cabinet overestimated Europe's military weakness or the dangers that flowed from it. Germany was totally unarmed, the armed forces of the Low Countries were tiny, those of the French had been substantially rebuilt but were already engaged in a vain effort to hold on to French Indo-China, and only the much reduced British and American forces stood between a Soviet advance and the English Channel, if Stalin had been so minded.

These were some of the reasons which led the Labour Cabinet without serious dissent to agree that Britain should undertake its formidable rearmament programme. I repeat that the records show the emphasis that was placed upon the necessity of receiving adequate American supplies if the programme was to be carried out. These were not political conditions added by the Cabinet, but constituted the essential conditions laid down by the Service Departments. In public they professed confidence that the conditions would be satisfied, but that was not the private expectation.

In the defence debate in February 1951 Clement Attlee deliberately introduced all the necessary words of caution. After Nye Bevan's resignation together with that of Harold Wilson and John Freeman, I made a much less important speech to the Enfield Labour Party on 29 April 1951. 'There are shortages of manpower, scarcities of raw materials and an insufficient number of machine tools,' I said, adding that we looked to the United States to make up the gap. I went on to say that the American people should understand that, if they chose to improve their own standard of living by diverting the materials that were necessary for the rearmament programme, it would be impossible for Britain to carry out her part of the bargain. I summarised my view about the way Nye Bevan had dealt with this issue in his resignation speech: 'It has not surprised anyone who follows the programme of rearmament to hear these facts [about shortages] restated this week by those who have resigned. We have always been uncomfortably aware of them. But that is no reason to resign at this time. They have left us either too late or too soon. Too late if they opposed the programme – too soon if they believe it will fail.'

The resigning Ministers made much of the impossibility of fulfilling the programme because of shortages. No one could complain about that, but the left took over the issue as though only they had the patent rights to express such doubts, and a week later in the Miners' Hall in Merthyr Tydfil I returned to the subject, saying that I did not agree with those who said that the rearmament programme showed up a difference between left and right in the Labour Party. I went on: 'I meet Tories who share the views of resigning Ministers but that does not make them left-wing socialists nor Nye Bevan a rabid Tory.'

The story of Aneurin Bevan's resignation and its consequences for the Labour Party has been fully told from the points of view of the principal protagonists. There is no need for me to go over all the ground again except to recount my slight personal involvement in trying with some others to prevent his fateful resignation.

I happened to be among a group of junior Ministers who had foregathered by chance early on Budget Day to make sure of securing our seats in the crowded Chamber. One of our number was Arthur Blenkinsop, who had been Parliamentary Private Secretary to Nye Bevan during the time when he was Minister of Health. He told us that he personally believed the truth of the strong rumours that Nye was considering resignation if the Chancellor, Hugh Gaitskell, went ahead with charges for Health Service treatment. The rest of us had been inclined to discount such rumours but as Arthur Blenkinsop was a junior Minister at Health, we thought he was in a good position to judge and we were aghast at the prospect. The Prime Minister was lying ill in hospital, Ernie Bevin was out of action, in fact dying, the Government's standing was rickety and we expected a general election at any time. Surely another hammer blow could not fall on us on Budget Day? There and then I impetuously seized a sheet of notepaper and drafted a short letter to send to Nye, which the other junior Ministers all signed in turn. Here it is:

April 10

Dear Nye,

All sorts of rumours exist about your position. None of us knows the merits until we hear the Budget. But we know the Party's interests will only be served if we *all* go into a general election *together*. Any fragmentary resignations will split the Party in the constituencies, and we shall be not only defeated in the election – but routed. In the Party's interest we urge you to wait until the Party Meeting has expressed itself tomorrow.

Ever yours,
Jim Callaghan
Alfred Robens
Michael Stewart
Arthur Blenkinsop
Fred Lee

The signatories were by chance a fair representation of the Parliamentary Party, with Robens on the right, Michael Stewart, Blenkinsop and me in the middle, and Fred Lee on the left. We delivered the letter by hand and Nye Bevan sent for me immediately. Thirty minutes before the Budget we paced up and down the corridor behind the Speaker's Chair. Nye was clearly agonising and used me as a talking post. He began by complaining, but not in an unfriendly way, that because our letter had come from a representative cross-section we were making his position very difficult, and he gave me to understand that he had already decided to resign. Then he burst out: 'Hugh is a Tory. Why do they put me up against it? They have known my position for weeks.' I replied that because of the Budget secrecy, none of us knew the details of the disagreement or its seriousness and I urged him very strongly to take no action until the Party held its budget inquest at a meeting on the following day.

I certainly did not go away from that conversation believing, as others have said, that Nye was looking for an excuse to resign. On the contrary, I felt he was tormented as to whether he was taking the right course. I suggested that we might meet again when the inquest had been held and at this stage Nye, bowing to the sentiment of us all, said that he would not resign for the time being in view of the appeals that had been made to him.

In the afternoon we met as arranged and he was much more composed. I asked him how the dispute could be resolved so that he could remain in the Cabinet at least until we had got through the coming election. He replied that the Bill on Health Service charges must be postponed, for if it went ahead, amendments might be pressed in the House by Labour Members who felt as he did. Because of the Government's tiny majority, these could be carried with the aid of mischievous Tory votes looking for any opportunity to defeat the Government. Such votes would make his position impossible if he was still a member of the Cabinet and he pointed out to me vehemently and eloquently the difficulties that would arise if Clem called an election in just two months' time, in June. Therefore the Bill must not be presented. The dispute was about an insignificant item of £13 millions and he said this could be found 'by altering the Service', although he did not spell out how this would be done. He then reverted to the impossibility of carrying out the rearmament programme, and the necessity of re-examining it.

I sympathised with much of what he said, although I argued with him that this was not the right moment to go back on an arms programme that had been launched by the Government less than three months previously and had been sustained by his own brilliant speech defending it in the House. Surely he could let events determine the fate of the programme in due course? He refused to listen but then diverted his rising wrath from me by making another attack on Hugh Gaitskell.

I told the junior Ministers who had been signatories to the original letter about this conversation, and it was agreed that I should see the Chief Whip. He listened and then passed me on to the Home Secretary, Chuter Ede. Both of them were belligerent and angry with both Hugh and Nye. Chuter Ede kept me for a full hour while he berated them. Hugh Gaitskell, he said, was an intellectual and was not easy to handle. There was no chance of him giving way. As for Aneurin, he said it was impossible for the Cabinet to go on with him, if his present behaviour continued. Chuter Ede told me that the Prime Minister had earlier that day given him the election date in confidence. No one should rock the boat at this moment. Neither Nye Bevan nor Herbert Morrison would win the Party leadership if Clem Attlee retired following his illness, because both of them calculated too much the effect of every move on their chances.

Chuter Ede claimed that he had himself won an important concession on the Bill – namely, that the Bill itself should contain no date as to when it could come into force. He could go no further. He had done all he could.

It was one of those fudges that are made from time to time in politics, where both sides must give ground if they are to continue to live together, and it would have enabled the Government to go united into an election. The next step should have been for me to see Hugh Gaitskell, as we were on friendly terms and it was the obvious thing to do. Yet for some inexplicable reason this does not seem to have crossed my mind, nor did the others, in my recollection, suggest it when I reported to them what had passed. Instead, armed with Chuter Ede's hint about an early election and the prospect that the Bill would carry no operational date, they agreed that I should tell Nye that although we understood how strongly he felt, we all thought the Cabinet's decision should be accepted. I did so. Nye was impervious and that ended our attempted intervention. We sat and waited while this unnecessary tragedy played itself out over our heads and beyond our influence.

Life is full of 'if's. If Attlee, instead of being in hospital, had been in full control at the crucial Cabinet meeting; if Ernie Bevin had been at the height of his powers instead of seven days from death; if Nye Bevan had not underrated Gaitskell's determination; if Hugh Gaitskell had enjoyed a longer period to establish his general authority, as a Chancellor must do if he is to survive – even if only one or two of these 'if's had been fulfilled, they might have been sufficient to prevent the resignation of the most charismatic figure in the Government over a trivial sum of £13 millions – a sum that must seem trumpery to the detached outsider.

In fairness to Hugh Gaitskell, he was not the first nor the last Chancellor to dig in his heels at a particular moment and cry 'Enough! I will go no further.' One of his successors, Peter Thorneycroft, resigned as Chancellor in the Conservative Government in 1957 and took all of the Treasury Ministers with him because he could not persuade his colleagues to reduce their demands by £50 millions. I recall fighting bruising rearguard actions to save the last £5 millions in a Departmental budget when I occupied the same office. Every Cabinet Minister dreads the long, exhausting meeting in which they are called upon to squeeze sums ranging from a few millions upwards out of their budgets.

Every Departmental battle is fought separately. All Ministers believe they have an unanswerable case for their particular level of expenditure. And yet, at the end of the day, none of the figures we fight so hard about ever is or can be exact. I confess that when I became Prime Minister and faced long drawn out battles over the last few million pounds of a vast Budget in which we had achieved 99 per cent of our objective, I would sometimes find it convenient to adjourn the Cabinet on the pretext of lunch and then omit to call it together again, only to find that the sum we needed seemed to have got 'lost in the wash'. But a Prime Minister must be careful not to bruise the Chancellor or the Chief Secretary too much in matters they regard as vital, for a Chancellor must expect to be able to rely upon the Prime Minister's backing in a dispute with other Ministers. He has no one else to turn to and his job is, in my experience, the most thankless in the Cabinet.

I understand Hugh Gaitskell's feelings. He must have felt himself very much alone in expenditure disputes, with his Prime Minister ill and he himself possessed of no more than five months' experience as Chancellor. He was a man of passion and emotion which he did not often show. He had a deep sense of personal responsibility, a strong sense of duty from which he could not be deflected when he had made up his mind, and a steely will which was a source of his courage. Once he had amassed and mastered the facts and figures, argued through the alternative courses of action, and reached logical conclusions, the only problem left, as he saw it, was how to convince those of his colleagues who had not followed him through the same rigorous process.

His view was that because we were rational human beings, once his colleagues understood the matter they would be bound to see it in the same light as himself. Compromise did not come easily to him although later, when he became Leader of the Party, he recognised the need for accommodation. And in the Shadow Cabinet he would sometimes allow a contrary view to his own to prevail, letting it pass with a deep, deep sigh at the irrationality of his colleagues. But, on certain issues, notably immigration and the rights of West Indians to come to this country, he was unshakeable, whether his views were popular or not. On all important matters of policy he radiated the assurance that if you and he shared the same beliefs they would be safe in his care and he would not betray them, even if under pressure you yourself weakened. He was therefore a source of strength to his friends and admirers, with a personal kindliness and a sense of fun whenever he relaxed. His loss was a great tragedy. He would have been a strong Prime Minister if he had lived.

Nye Bevan underrated Gaitskell's qualities. Shortly after his resignation, a group of us sat in the Smoking Room with him while he told us that the Labour Movement would sweep Gaitskell away. He was certain of this and nothing would shake him. He held this view, I believe, because Hugh, for all his brilliance, did not at that time have Nye's deep hold on the party. Hugh had enjoyed a phenomenal rise to attain the office of Chancellor of the Exchequer when he had only five years' experience as a Member of Parliament. No one else has done it in this century. During his short period in the House he had gained support among many Labour Members of Parliament who had observed his qualities at close quarters, but the Party in the country did not know him nearly as well or for as long as it had known his opponent.

Nye was a senior Parliamentarian who had been a Member for over twenty years, and a prominent controversialist in every major Party dispute during that period. He was an important symbol to many of the Party's rank and file of what a true socialist should be. He had been a miner; the miners were the true aristocracy of the Labour Movement, and although he was sometimes not politically in tune with the miners' leaders, nevertheless no one could deny his authority to speak on mining and industrial matters. In those days the NUM had more members than the Engineering Union or the General and Municipal Workers and was only a little way short even of Ernest Bevin's Transport Workers, so he possessed the weight that numbers carry. He was a proud man, proud of his origins and of his class, and he wore the air of one who consciously represented his community, the working people of Britain.

By contrast, Hugh Gaitskell did not have a power base that was comparable in any way. True, he had been a faithful, hard-working Party member throughout the 1930s. But, as I have said, he was little known to the Party at large until he became Chancellor and, unlike Nye, held no nationally elected office in the Party. He had not had time to gain the confidence of the rank and file, and Nye must have believed that in a conflict the Movement would have backed him.

The Prime Minister himself must have realised that in the exposed post of a Labour Chancellor it was preferable to have someone who was a tried and trusted figure in the Party, and therefore more likely to survive the inevitable left-wing attacks. But Attlee's choice was limited. Dalton was ruled out by the earlier indiscretion which had led to his resignation. Of the others it is not at all clear that Nye Bevan himself wished to do the job, and with the possible exception of Herbert Morrison, no one else had the right combination of experience and Party roots. Herbert was in any case past his best by this time, having suffered a serious illness. Nye did not suggest anyone else. Harold Wilson was technically equipped for the task but he too had been in the House no more than five years and had no better Party standing than Gaitskell. So, in the absence of any suitable senior figure, Gaitskell's outstanding qualities made his appointment inevitable.

He and Bevan differed in their approach to problems. The tool of Marxist analysis that Bevan employed to underpin his criticism of the social and economic system attracted many followers but he was too much of a romantic and poet to believe that the aridities of Marxism, especially as distorted by Stalin, could be a cure for our ills. In personal relations Nye emanated great charm and conversation with him was a delight. The talk bubbled and his flashing intelligence touched what he said with vividness so that new insights seemed to pour from him. At his best on the public platform or in the House of Commons he was magic. He could lift an audience so that they shared with him new heights of understanding and awareness; he could fell his enemies – and sometimes disconcert his friends – with a single devastating phrase, and disarm opponents with a droll wit if the mood was on him.

And yet at the end of the dispute with Gaitskell in 1951, he found himself on the outside, and throughout that decade when his great gifts might have united the Party, and even he himself seemed to have become tired of the dispute, it was the use of his reputation by others that kept it divided. Without this handicap, we might have escaped thirteen continuous years of Tory rule. No one should doubt Bevan's absolute sincerity in his ambition to maintain an entirely free Health Service. But, like other Ministers I have known, he eventually lost the sympathy of his Cabinet colleagues, not on the merits of his case but because by their lights he seemed the less amenable of two uncompromising characters, when Ministers thought they had found a possible solution.

When Nye, for the first time in public, widened the dispute to make known his opposition to the size of the rearmament programme, I disagreed with him for the reasons I have given, but I did not know then that at a much earlier stage he had argued against the size of the programme, but had nevertheless accepted the Cabinet's decisions and spoken in its favour. We might have understood his attitude a little more had we known this at the time.

Many of us knew in broad terms that he was dissatisfied with aspects of Government policy, for in those days the South Wales Members would usually travel together by train to and from Paddington, appropriating two or three neighbouring compartments, and pass the hours enjoyably in argument and gossip. It made for good comradeship. The building of the motorways has put an end to this agreeable practice.

On one such Friday morning at the end of October 1949, Nye joined us at Paddington. Stafford Cripps had devalued sterling amid a great sense of shock and Nye had defended the Government in a brilliant speech in the House. We settled in our compartments but the talk was noisy and some time later he called me out into the corridor. He was in pessimistic mood and dispirited about our prospects at the next general election. It would be fought on an unworthy platform because Herbert Morrison was insisting on the need for consolidating what had been done. On the contrary we must go forward. We should not stand still. The Government had become timid, Herbert Morrison was frequently wrong, and Ernie Bevin's health would not allow him to hang on for much longer. Nye went on: 'After the election in 1950 both Ernie and Clem should set a date for their retirement.' If they did not he might consider not joining the new Government. I protested at this and said something to the effect than when Clem did go Nye would be as well placed as Herbert Morrison for the succession. At that stage Hugh Gaitskell, who had been in the House for only four years, had not come into the running.

Nye looked at me. 'Look boy, don't think the lot of the Prime Minister is enviable. No one should want to become Prime Minister. But,' he went on, 'at some stage in a man's life, he may become the custodian of the hopes and aspirations of others. At that moment he is no longer a free man and his situation is personally not enviable.' Soon after that the train plunged into the darkness of the Severn Tunnel, the corridor filled with acrid fumes, and we returned to the compartment, but the impression left on me was that despite Nye's ambivalence he would contest an election for the leadership sometime in the future, not out of naked ambition but because he felt he would be able to contribute more than anyone else to save the Party and the country.

It was eighteen months later that his resignation took place, but when he finally left the Government with Harold Wilson and John Freeman our fate was sealed. In the closing months, there was one final flicker of personal interest for me when Viscount Hall, the First Lord of the Admiralty, resigned in May 1951. As I had carried full responsibility for the Admiralty in the Commons, I hoped Clem would appoint me to succeed him. However, Frank Pakenham, who had taken my intended place at the War Office four years earlier, was appointed. I was naturally disappointed but he and I were and have always remained good friends. The Prime Minister wrote a letter which did not altogether mollify me: 'You have done excellently in both the Ministries in which you served and I shall expect to see you in due course proceeding to more responsible work.'

The post-war Labour Government came to an end in October 1951. Its senior Ministers were tired after eleven years in office, the Party was wracked by differences and disputes and no vein of fresh thinking had been discovered. And yet, although the Conservatives won more seats, the Labour Party actually polled the highest number of votes that either Party has recorded at any election since the war. During their period of office the 1945 Labour Government gained many supporters and kept their confidence, despite our problems. Creeping inflation was one. Another was a chronic weakness in the balance of payments. The country had endured bread rationing for a period, petrol continued to be rationed and many goods were not available in the shops. But the growth in productivity was higher than before 1939, despite a siege economy and the consequential physical controls. The basic industries on which the economy depended were nationalised. The Local Authorities had begun to launch a great campaign of house building. And above all, people remembered that unlike the period after the First World War this time there was work for all. No ex-soldiers rattling collecting boxes in the streets, as they displayed their medals and their mutilated limbs; no South Wales miners marching to London, playing mouth organs on the way, looking for work and hoping for assistance as they passed through towns and villages. The war wounded were cared for. Labour's system of universal insurance provided protection for all against injuries at work, the accident of sickness and the dwindling capacity of old age. The new Health Service brought higher standards of medical care, especially in industrial areas. It was universal in its application, and neither drugs nor surgery nor treatment was denied on grounds of cost. The Labour Government's challenging idealism had won a new dignity for the working people of Britain.

4

---

*Post-war colonial policy – visit to West Africa in 1946 – demands
for independence – the Central African Federation*

The affairs of the Commonwealth and colonies have played a large part
in my political life, and perhaps never more so than when Nye Bevan,
who had been the Party's spokesman on these matters for some time after
Labour left office, moved from them to take over responsibility for Foreign
Affairs in 1956. I jumped at the chance when Hugh Gaitskell asked me to
succeed Bevan for I was part of the generation that cared deeply about
the decolonisation and independence of East and West Africa, the future
of the Central African Confederation and the problem of raising the
standard of life of what we then called the undeveloped countries.

At a time when Labour was deeply divided by the bitter Bevanite
controversy, these were matters on which we could agree. I was not
regarded as being on the left of the Party and I saw a chance to work with
left and right in a field in which there was broad unity. My eyes had first
been opened about colonial problems at a much earlier date during naval
service in Ceylon. This was followed by an extended visit to the four
West African colonies of Nigeria, the Gold Coast, Sierra Leone and the
Gambia in 1946 and 1947. We ruled the British Empire on the cheap.
The colonies were a source of wealth, raw materials and minerals, and
the Empire was sustained by a cluster of naval bases strung across the
oceans from Gibraltar to Hong Kong. We had been miserly in the use
of British manpower, and India was the reservoir of military strength,
with an army whose soldiers safeguarded not only their own country but
also Britain's interests from the Middle East to Malaya.

These interests had in their turn influenced the direction of our trade,
our military strategy, our communications and even our domestic labour
and economic structure. Many young working men, bereft of prospects
at home because of unemployment, tried their luck in the white dominions. Others from better-placed families sought and sometimes found
their fortune as planters and settlers. Yet others became traders and
agents for large and wealthy English and Scottish companies based

mainly in London, Liverpool and Glasgow. The disputes with native peoples to which these activities gave rise required the appointment of overseas administrators and the involvement of the British Government. And so the Empire grew. But its direction slowly changed and after the First World War concern began to grow that the balance had tipped too far against the interests of the native peoples and too much in favour of Britain's commercial interest in exploiting the natural resources of the colonial peoples.

The Duke of Devonshire laid down Britain's colonial policy in 1923 when a conflict had arisen between the indigenous Africans and immigrant Asians: 'His Majesty's Government think it necessary definitely to record this considered opinion that the interests of the African natives must be paramount, and that if and when those interests and the interests of the immigrant races conflict the former should prevail.' This was often quoted by African leaders but was frequently honoured more in the breach than in the observance, and with the adverse effects of the world depression of the 1930s felt so severely in Britain and the obsession of governments with balanced budgets, very little money was spent on strengthening the infrastructure of the colonies, on educating their children or preparing them for self-government.

The Second World War shook the foundations of the Empire and Malaya, Singapore and Burma all fell in quick succession. Nationalism rose to new heights in India but even so the Empire emerged once more after the defeat of Japan. When we new young Members of Parliament returned from the Second World War, we felt no embarrassment in using the term 'British Empire' in our speeches. It was an accurate description, recognised as such by elderly Colonel Blimps and socialists alike. The difference between us lay in the way we expected the future to unfold.

The Labour Movement had been nurtured in the tradition of anti-imperialism, opposed to exploitation of class by class, or race by race. We declared that our purpose was to transform the subject people of the colonies into equal partners with Britain.

At the end of the Second World War there were more than fifty British dependent territories in many of which the production of raw materials and the extraction of minerals had been Britain's main interest – not food. I was told during my visit to Gambia in 1946 that up to the outbreak of the 1939–45 war, the Colonial Administration had imported every grain of rice needed to feed the people; this basic foodstuff was shipped round the Cape of Good Hope from distant Burma. The Labour Government's first aim was to encourage peasant countries to increase food production so that they would be self-sufficient. Our next stated aim was to promote education and industrial development and to encourage political advance, so that in due time Britain would be able to transfer power to some form of democratic government in each territory. We had come to power ready with a colonial policy, and if (as in the case of Indian independence) some of the grand changes did no more than confirm trends that were inevitable, nevertheless the thrust from Westminster and Whitehall was intended to meet and match the changed spirit in the colonies after the War.

Three separate Government Departments were concerned with different aspects of these matters: the Dominions Office, the India and Burma Office and the Colonial Office, all headed by Cabinet Ministers. It was at the inspiration of the new Parliamentary Under-Secretary at the Colonial Office, Arthur Creech Jones, that the Westminster Branch of the Empire Parliamentary Association despatched an all-Party delegation to West Africa late in 1946.

I was included. We were the first official MPs to visit the territories after the war, and our objective was to restore the contacts that had been neglected during the war period and to strengthen the ties of Empire. We were hospitably received in every territory but, whilst the Africans made clear their pleasure at the initiative of the Empire Parliamentary Association, they were not reluctant to voice their needs and their requests. They did so with great firmness.

One of our early encounters was with the leaders of Nigeria's largest political parties at a meeting in Lagos Town Hall on 1 January 1947. Britain's efforts during the war were admired and respected even as far afield as West Africa, and the Nigerian African leaders reflected this when they told us with no reluctance or affectation that they were 'proud' (that was their word) to be a part of the British Empire and were happy to remain so. They looked forward to self-government in due course, yet despite much talk, there was no sign of action. When would a start be made? If the Governor of Nigeria would consult them, they would willingly cooperate with him. But instead, they said, the Colonial Administration seemed to block their efforts to help themselves. For example, why were they not allowed to build their own teacher-training college? There was a desperate shortage of teachers and they said it was not uncommon for as many as six hundred children to present themselves at school for admission at the beginning of the year, to find to their disappointment that only fifty could be accommodated. Moreover, the present type of education was too literary. More education should be technically based and greater opportunities should be given to women, so that Nigeria would be able at some time in the future to stand on her own feet as a self-governing country. Until that day arrived, they requested that we should inform the British Parliament that they wished to be treated as equals and with the respect due to all members of the British Empire. All this was put forcibly and knowledgeably by the leaders of the Zikist Movement, the railway workers, the Nigerian Women's Party, the Teachers' Union and others. They knew what they were talking about and in some spheres had a better grasp of the problems than did the Colonial Administration.

Later on that same day I talked with the Acting Governor, an able official of long experience, without illusions, and with a genuine sense of responsibility for his African charges. His view was typical of many that we were to hear frequently during our seven weeks' journey. It was not possible, he said, to set a date for the achievement of self-government. In Nigeria the period of preparation might need to be as long as forty or fifty years, and to fix a date so far ahead would have no meaning for the present generation, for it might take until the twenty-first century. If we were to leave Nigeria, the country would revert to a disease-ridden malarial swamp and jungle, and the inhabitants to cannibalism. It would help him and his colleagues very much in their work if Britain ceased her constant and hypocritical emphasis on being in Africa for the benefit of the Africans and made it clear that we stayed there for our own good, though this might also benefit the Africans.

In the course of one day I listened to two diametrically opposite opinions from black and white, views which were reiterated many times in the following weeks. One name seemed to crop up in every conversation: Zikwe, or more accurately Nnamdi Azikiwe, at that time the General Secretary of the National Council of Nigeria and the Cameroons. Naturally I was keen to meet a man who attracted so much support. It was soon obvious that he was not popular with the colonial administrators and as our delegation headquarters were at Government House, we felt compelled to accept official advice that we could not meet him since he was not welcome there. This setback made me even more keen and despite a marked lack of official enthusiasm, I arranged a private and almost clandestine visit to the cramped, upper-floor rooms in an old part of the city which served as his headquarters.

I went alone and was greeted by a tall, imposing, rather reserved man, quite unlike the violent and venal figure described by Government House officials, most of whom had never met him. When Zikwe had finished school in Lagos he studied at an American university and developed into a first-class athlete. It was said that his hostile attitude arose partly from slights about his colour received during his sporting career. In our conversation he strongly attacked the colour bar practised by Government House, and said that until this was changed he would refuse to visit there, even if invited. He did not put a date to self-government but was uncompromising in his demand that it should be recognised as a practicable goal within a reasonable period. His force of character was obvious, as was the influence he exercised through a series of regular and angry articles written in his capacity as editor of the *West African Pilot*. Unfortunately, the Administration felt strong enough to ignore him and their ignorance induced a false and exaggerated picture in Government House of an impossible agitator. Time after time in that first talk he returned to the indignity caused by the inferior status of the African. Self-government was a means to an end – the achievement of equality. I have tried to remember this in more recent years, whenever I have met a seemingly unnecessarily prickly African official.

The superior attitude of the whites was at its strongest in the Central African Federation in the late 1950s, where European political leaders who had been long resident in both Rhodesias would remark complacently that they never discussed political problems with African politicians, and saw no need to meet them. Such attitudes brought the inevitable comeuppance. In the case of Nigeria, good sense prevailed before irreparable damage was done. Fourteen years after my first meeting with Azikiwe he made his official entry into Government House, appointed by the Queen, as the constitutional Governor General and Commander-in-Chief of all Nigeria, and later when Nigeria became a Federal Republic the Right Honourable Nnamdi Azikiwe became the first President.

Among a number of senior colonial administrators there was a failure of imagination, but they did their jobs faithfully. Many colonial civil servants who could neither sympathise with nor understand men like Azikiwe nevertheless felt a devotion and a responsibility that was little short of patriarchal for their charges. During our visit I enjoyed the hospitality of youthful field district officers who carried sole responsibility for territories far from Lagos, several hundreds of square miles in area and comprising populations of 150,000 or more.

In their company I listened to appeals for money for a proper water programme. We were told that a programme could be started in Nigeria if Britain would supply as few as twenty water drills and fifty men trained in their use. Not far from Ubiaja in mid-Western Province we saw for ourselves what the lack of a water supply meant. Women and small children walked in a long line every day as much as fifteen miles for a pail of water. At every village the needs and the demands were similar.

One unforgettable figure was the Onogie of Uromi who was reputed to be a hundred years old. He had prepared to receive us by decorating his bare torso and forearms with a pattern of dried mud, to which he added several strings of beads, a pair of dark sunglasses, and on his head a much too large topee. We regarded him with some awe, for despite his age he told us he had about eighty wives – although he added that he had not counted recently. He led us to the wives' compound where we were introduced to his newest bride, a shy girl of fifteen. Through an interpreter he told us that he paid the equivalent of £10 in dowry for each wife which, if he was fortunate, he recovered in due course, and he could make a profit if the wife bore him several daughters. A jug of dark brown fluid with some cups was placed on the table in front of us. I took this to be tea until the interpreter explained that it was not tea but water, the sediment colouring it brown, which was the best they could draw from a very deep well, the only one in the community. Like others, he repeated the demand for a supply of water.

We moved on to Benin which I was anxious to see in view of my father's stories. There was a link with his time as the ruler, Oba Akenzua II, was the grandson of Oba Ovevami who had ruled Benin at the time of the murder of Deputy Consul Phillips in 1897. The city had more than recovered from the disastrous fire that had destroyed it, and in 1947 we were told the population was a quarter of a million. At the time of our visit it was efficiently governed by a Native Council which raised substantial revenues and even accumulated financial reserves. This was a much more advanced community than many others and the Oba's chief preoccupation was to enlist our aid to secure a place for his son at Oxford University.

The next morning before the sun was up we left Benin to travel by car to Ife, about 150 miles away, an eight-hour journey because of the state of the roads. We arrived late in the afternoon, our clothes stained with red sweat and our lips and faces caked with dust from the laterite roads. We were given no time to rest and after a quick, cold shower and a change of clothes we were escorted to greet the Oni of Ife who had been waiting for some time with his assembled elders in the new Council Chamber. After an exchange of compliments, he invited us to walk to his compound which we did in a straggling procession. At the head went the Oni's bugler, sounding an untidy blast to clear the path. He was followed by the official court jester, a man of melancholy mien. Then the Oni himself, our party, the elders and a crowd of curious onlookers. It was in the Oni's compound that I first saw the famous life-size bronze and terracotta human heads. At that time these masterpieces of art were almost unknown to the outside world and had not achieved the recognition they have since. I had not even heard of them and, after a long and tiring day, I was not in the most receptive mood. The collection was not displayed to any advantage, dusk had fallen and the exhibits were badly lit, but tired as I was, I knew I was in the presence of unique and beautiful works of art. We were told that they had been unearthed during the early war years and that they were a thousand years old. I was ready at that time to believe it. The Oni was justly proud of them and these examples of an ancient, lost civilisation will always serve as a reminder to those who forget that the African has a long history and culture.

On our seven-week journey, which had taken us from Gambia, through Sierra Leone and the Gold Coast to Nigeria, we heard many conflicting political views, but there was no difference of opinion about the principal needs of the people. These were put most graphically by Dr Mackay, the Senior Medical Officer in the Gambia: 'Every African you see has suffered at some time from yaws, sleeping sickness, malaria or hook worm.' His condition was made worse by the so-called 'hungry season', a term which described the months of the year when food was in short supply. We saw for ourselves the extreme poverty of the people, the inadequacy of the Government's Development and Welfare Fund to meet their manifold needs and the dilemma of colonial civil servants who had to choose between spending money on long-term projects to increase the territories' wealth or alternatively establishing much-needed social improvements.

On my return to London, I summed up as follows:

> I can see no reason why Britain should not continue to seek commercial and strategic advantage in partnership with her colonies, but top priority must be given to the task of increasing the standard of life of their people and encouraging them to become self-governing. It is only on those grounds that we shall retain any moral right to stay in the colonies, or indeed that we shall find it physically possible to stay, as nationalism grows among the backward peoples. Let us relate this to West Africa.

The first principle that must underlie all our actions is that the country belongs to the Africans and not to us. We can take to Africa many benefits, our skill, machinery, organizing ability, honest administration, and the advantage of being economically linked with a powerful industrial nation. But our reward for that should be a reasonable management fee, and not the cteam of the profits. Next, we must be certain that 'welfare' does not degenerate into paternalism. It is not sufficient to say to the African: 'Here are our plans for your advancement. Now, we know they are the best for you, and you will find when they are in operation that they will bring you considerable benefit.' The African must be associated closely at the formative stage with what it is proposed to do, and he must understand what is being done, and be allowed to make his own mistakes and profit from them. (*West African Review*, June 1947, p. 668)

In the matter of political advance, my instincts were most strongly reinforced by the Governor of the Gold Coast, Sir Alan Burns, with whom we stayed in his beautiful residence at Christianborg Castle, a white fortress built on the seashore by the Swedes in 1652. When we met, he was nearing retirement age but combined a mature wisdom with youthful enthusiasm. His service in the colonies had begun more than forty years before, in 1905, and I listened intently as he gave us the benefit of his experience on the timing of self-government. The greatest danger, he said, lay in excessive caution arising from our fear that people were not fit for responsibility. If we waited for too long, political concessions would be forced out of us, attitudes would harden, and Britain would lose African goodwill. The African could become fit for responsibility only by exercising it and by learning responsibility by making his own mistakes. This opinion, held by an experienced colonial governor who had joined the Colonial Service when the Empire was at its height, fitted my own perceptions. Nevertheless, a nagging doubt grew stronger the further we travelled. Was the Africans' concentration on securing independence so single-minded that they ignored or underestimated the economic problems they would face when they became independent?

On my return home in February 1946 I wrote a cautionary letter to the *Daily Guardian* in Freetown, Sierra Leone:

I certainly hope to see West Africa attain independence in my lifetime, but may I urge my friends in Africa to realise that India contains lessons for them as well as for the British. As India is now seeing, self-government is only the commencement of her difficulties, not the end of them, and from the angle of 'economic self determination' . . . West Africa will be in a more difficult position than India when she becomes self-governing. We have to recognise that in the twentieth century the nations of the world (with the possible exception of the USSR) are becoming economically more dependent on each other, and not less, and the only nations that really achieve economic self-determination are those that combine in their own borders enough food to feed themselves, a vast industrial machine, and a handful of atomic bombs.

My hope, therefore, is that West Africa and Britain will jointly recognise the advantages to each of them of integrating their economies, and instead of pulling apart, will bind themselves closer together in a partnership from which Africa will reap the advantage of being allied to a powerful industrial machine to secure the consumer and capital goods and the skill she is short of, while Britain will find her export trade and her foodstuffs position considerably helped. In other words, [the plea for] 'economic self-determination' must not be allowed to degenerate into a narrow economic nationalism.

These attitudes, which were formed early in my Parliamentary life, had a considerable influence in later years, notably when I became the Party's Spokesman on Colonial Affairs in the middle 1950s, and I found myself then very much in tune with Iain MacLeod, who was Colonial Secretary in the Conservative Government at that time.

The Labour Government had faced the problem of India's future the moment it came to office. Gandhi received tumultuous support for his campaign calling on Britain to 'quit India'. Jawaharlal Nehru, Harrow-educated, a complex character and a convinced socialist who was to become India's first Prime Minister, had been released from his eighth spell in jail and was actively preparing his next blow against Britain. Many other Congress leaders were also recently released from jail, men who would later become Ministers in their own country. India was a tinderbox ready to burst into flame. There was talk of unrest and possible mutiny in some Indian regiments, and despite Gandhi's huge moral authority and his commitment to attain India's freedom by peaceful means, if violence had broken out it would have swept through the sub-continent.

Supposing Churchill had won the 1945 general election instead of the Labour Party? What would Nehru have made of Churchill's defiant statement: 'I did not become the King's First Minister to preside over the liquidation of the British Empire.' Would Churchill have refused self-government, and would colleagues like Oliver Stanley and Rab Butler have allowed him to do so? We do not know. But Lord Moran records in his diary that some years later in conversation Churchill complained that Britain had given India away, and said that it would have given him pleasure to fight for it. If he had been Prime Minister and followed his instincts, post-war Britain might have been involved in a long and debilitating conflict in a vain attempt to hold down the whole subcontinent by force. Such a conflict would have weakened Britain's exhausted economy still further and no doubt would have met the same fate as the attempts by France and Holland to hold their Asian empires.

We would not have prevented India from gaining her independence but it would have been won by her people after a bloody conflict, leaving behind bitter feelings between them and us. Fortunately, the election of the Labour Government spared both India and Britain from the possibility of any such folly. It fell to Clement Attlee to take the momentous decision to offer India her freedom. With his knowledge of India he had no hesitation, and his leap into the unknown proved to be the wisest as well as the most courageous decision in the whole lifetime of the Labour Government.

I write this despite the terrible slaughter that followed the partition of the country and the creation of Pakistan. Since those days, Pakistan has left the Commonwealth, although from time to time there have been hints that she would not be averse to rejoining. At present this would not be possible, though I hope it would not be ruled out in different circumstances.

India on the other hand, under Pandit Nehru, took the decision to remain a member of the Commonwealth with the result that the friendship of the Indian and British peoples has grown as the years pass and I, like thousands of others, have been the recipient of many tokens of genuine and sincere Indian affection. Indeed, I am proud to say that in Andhra Pradesh a housing estate is named after me.

When the Bill to grant independence to India came before Parliament, Churchill framed his opposition in a speech which contained a memorable phrase. He spoke of the grief with which he watched 'the clattering down of the British Empire'. But his followers were divided. Some agreed with him, most did not. How were they to vote on the Bill? The Conservative Party did what every Opposition does in such a situation. It put down a so-called 'reasoned amendment' which blurred the differences between its members and under which they could all huddle in safety. The amendment did not oppose the grant of independence in principle, but it attempted to assuage those Conservatives who were opposed by leaving out any date for its implementation. A toothless beast indeed, and it was rejected by an overwhelming vote.

If it had been carried it would have aroused intense anger in India. A story went the rounds at the time that may be apocryphal but illustrates perfectly Churchill's wit and his prejudices. It was said that when the Tory Shadow Cabinet met to consider whether it should oppose the Indian Independence Bill, the former Colonial Secretary, Oliver Stanley, who was the principal Tory spokesman, was not present at the beginning of the meeting. Churchill took advantage of his absence to deliver a diatribe and by the time he had finished, Oliver Stanley, a member of the Derby family, had arrived and was sitting listening, rather boot-faced. Churchill turned to him as he finished: 'Come on, Oliver. You agree we must oppose this Bill.' Stanley shook his head. Winston urged him again and once more Stanley refused. The old man turned on him: 'You are like all the Derbys,' he snorted. 'You arrive late on the battle-field and when you get there you won't fight.' It was a splendid quip but it did a grave injustice to Oliver Stanley who, on this matter, was more far-sighted than Churchill. Stanley was one of the wittiest and most effective of Conservative spokesmen in the immediate post-war days, and his Party suffered a severe loss by his early death.

Our post-war expectations were for a sober, steady march by each territory towards self-government. This would be self-sustaining as a result of a period of preparation in which the level of literacy was raised, agricultural production increased and industrial skills learned, concurrently with a steady broadening of the franchise leading to the final transfer of executive and legislative powers. This was a convenient blueprint but in reality all was telescoped by the headlong rush towards independence that began in West Africa in the 1950s. Nkrumah emerged as the outstanding leader in the Gold Coast and, after serving a term of imprisonment (an almost necessary pre-condition for leadership), he was released to become the first Prime Minister of the country in March 1952, and ushered in the new state of Ghana five years later in 1957.

Along the coast Nigeria, fired by the example of Ghana, moved rapidly in the same direction. The three major regions of the country, although displaying great tribal differences, came together for the purpose of electing a legislature for the whole country, armed with federal powers, in 1957.

By contrast, the East African territories moved more slowly. This was not surprising for, unlike West Africa, where Britain's principal interest was trade, the East African territories had been the subject of a substantial white permanent settlement, and so presented bigger problems in handing power to their African inhabitants. We were to find this especially true in Kenya and the Central African Federation.

In post-war days the House of Commons took its colonial responsibilities seriously, devoting several debates to them each year. The Colonial Secretary's Question Time in the Commons was a lively and informed occasion, and during the 1950s the Conservative Government possessed in Alan Lennox-Boyd a Colonial Secretary who was combative, self-confident, strong-minded, right-wing and able. He had sympathy with Africa's advancement.

Members of Parliament singly and in groups exercised a continuous watch over the affairs of the colonies through regular visits, and built up considerable expertise by forming friendships with African and European leaders. There was concern in schools, too, and there were frequent invitations for Members to speak to sixth forms. The newspapers carried special articles and editorials. This was particularly true of the Scottish press, whose historical relationship with parts of Africa, formed through the Church of Scotland Missionary Society, gave it an authoritative and influential standing on African problems. Party Conferences held informed annual debates on colonial issues, and although I do not claim that they ever became a dominating political issue (except perhaps in Scotland over the future of Nyasaland) there was in the 1950s a more knowledgeable and sustained interest in colonial questions than at any other period. I was fortunate to be concerned with these matters at such a vital time.

Nye Bevan did not give up his interest in colonial affairs when I replaced him as Party Spokesman, and he continued to act as Chairman of the Commonwealth Committee of the Labour Party's National Executive Committee. I was happy about this for it was helpful to have such a powerful ally on these sensitive matters. He asked me to be his Vice-Chairman and so we were able to dovetail both the Party and Parliamentary aspects of colonial affairs. He also carried great influence at the time with some of the rising colonial leaders.

The Party appointed John Hatch (now Lord Hatch) as full-time Commonwealth Officer at Transport House. He had lived in South Africa, possessed a wide knowledge of African affairs and was a good organiser. He took up his post in 1954. Under his direction the Labour Party took full advantage of the tide of public interest and increased its influence in the dependent territories. We made it our business to get to know the young overseas students who came to study in Britain, and held regular meetings with them in London. We offered them simple hospitality in our homes, and made special arrangements for them at our party conferences. It was a seminal period and its influence lasted for the following thirty years. Labour Party Headquarters became an essential port of call for overseas visitors, and looking at some old records I see that in one relatively short period we held discussions at Transport House with the Prime Minister or chief Ministers of Singapore, Ghana, Malta and Jamaica. During this same short period, the record shows that other callers included Julius Nyerere, Seretse Khama, Harry Nkumbula, Dr Hastings Banda, Tom Mboya and Oginga Odinga, all later to hold high office in their own countries.

In 1957 the Party called a highly successful conference of Commonwealth socialist and allied organisations at Beatrice Webb House, Dorking. This was a very suitable venue as it was her husband, Sidney Webb who, as Secretary for the Dominions and Colonies in the 1929 Labour Government, had reinforced the Devonshire pledge that if any conflict of interest arose between immigrant races and Africans, the interests of the native inhabitants must be paramount. Representatives of organisations from seventeen separate Commonwealth territories attended the conference, which lasted ten days. They were addressed by Hugh Gaitskell, Nye Bevan, Jim Griffiths, Barbara Castle, Vincent Tewson, the General Secretary of the TUC, and by me.

I took as the theme of my discussion 'The Problems of the Transfer of Power', and concentrated on what were then known as plural societies, namely countries in which people of different races and at different levels of development lived side by side. They were to be found in many parts of the Commonwealth but I was especially concerned with European-African relations in countries like Kenya and the Central African Federation. The Labour Party had recently completed a study of these territories and I was deputed to outline our conclusions. The basic dilemma was that Europeans wanted a self-governing society based on European attitudes and values to which, in their view, the African majority should and could aspire, whilst retaining their traditional culture. The African concept was diametrically opposed: namely, that the minority Europeans even though more advanced that the Africans, should take their places in a state whose values would be basically African, although the Europeans might be accorded (temporarily) a privileged position.

How was this dilemma to be resolved? The answer we gave was that legislation should be introduced to outlaw racialism and establish truly democratic societies while protecting the rights of minorities. Prior to drawing up a basic constitution for each territory, elections must be held on the basis of full adult suffrage. But, as this was not yet possible in some territories, Britain should not transfer power to minority (by which we meant European) groups until universal adult suffrage was in existence.

The right to vote would mean weakening the influence of the tribal chiefs. We did not wish to remove that completely, even though some of them were little more than paid government servants, and one possibility I put forward was to establish a second Chamber of tribal chiefs and give it an advisory role. In order to safeguard the future of Europeans (and Indians) who had brought technical skills and investment to their new homes, it would be necessary for Governors of territories to retain reserve powers to protect minorities against excessive nationalism.

Looking back on this outline, it is apparent that our cast of mind was limited to the traditional Westminster mould. We envisaged adult suffrage, elected representatives, parliamentary government, even a second Chamber, as the essential furniture of the state. Perhaps we were not sufficiently imaginative but there is no need to apologise for our desire to outlaw racialism and to place our trust in democracy. Nor were we isolated from African opinion at that time. Kenneth Kaunda, who later became President of Zambia, invariably invoked the principle that all men are born equal in the sight of God, and that Africans would not be justified if, when they came to power, they turned on their oppressors and subjected them to the indignities they had suffered. He wanted Northern Rhodesia to develop as a non-racial society: 'To my mind democratic government on the lines of the British pattern provides the only kind of government in which human beings are regarded as human beings.'

Nor was he alone. Dr Azikiwe used similar words when he delivered his inaugural address as Governor General of Nigeria in 1960: 'Representative government as it has been adapted to Nigeria is based on the rule of law and respect for individual freedom which have been bequeathed to us during our political associations with Britain . . . The Westminster model of parliamentary government and democracy has been proved by us not only to be capable of being exported to Africa but practicable in this part of Africa.' So, if we were too optimistic about the prospects of transferring successfully the Westminster pattern of democracy to a different culture, we at least erred in knowledgeable company.

The delegates to the 1957 Dorking Conference, who came from many parts of the world, and most of whom were meeting one another for the first time, found great enjoyment in talking with like-minded comrades, told one another of their struggles and experiences, argued, discussed and swopped confidences long into the night and gave Beatrice Webb House a general air of excitement and cheerfulness. It was almost a fore-runner of later Commonwealth Heads of Government meetings, with many of the same personalities attending. In some instances their knowledge of how to organise a political party was rudimentary, but they were anxious to learn and Len Williams, the Labour Party's national agent, made arrangements for some of them to be attached to Transport House for short periods of training. This too had its repercussions for, following his retirement, Sir Len Williams became the Governor General of Mauritius at the invitation of the Prime Minister, Seewoosagar Ramgoolam.

Such meetings and the regular correspondence that passed between us led to lifetime personal friendships among many who later held im-portant offices, and some of whom became Heads of Government in their own countries. It encouraged the leaders in several territories to join the Commonwealth when their countries became independent and the friendships made at a time when we were young sometimes eased the political differences that arose in later life between our countries.

The most brilliant of them all was Tom Mboya, a member of the Luo tribe in Kenya. He was a good-looking man in his middle twenties, straight-backed, tall and with immense charm, even though he used to deny it saying that his motto was 'Growl now, smile later'. His father had been a sisal plantation worker and Tom joined a trade union at an early age. His ability carried him to the office of General Secretary of the Kenya Federation of Labour while in his early twenties. He won a scholarship to Ruskin College, Oxford, where he spent a year. Margery Perham, one of Oxford's distinguished scholars with an intimate knowledge of the African continent, said that she had never met an African with an abler brain or a stronger will. He had something of Nye Bevan's intuitive imagination and mercurial temperament and they got on well together. He understood the strategy and tactics that would be most effective in Kenya's march to independence, and was second in influence only to Jomo Kenyatta, who was old enough to be his father and who came from the much bigger Kikuyu tribe.

Despite Mboya's youth, it was inevitable that he should become

Minister of Economic Planning as soon as Kenya became independent
and he exercised great influence on all aspects of government policy,
although his self-confidence and sheer ability was the envy of some of his
less able colleagues. The last occasion on which he came to Britain was
to take President Kenyatta's place at the Commonwealth Prime Ministers'
Conference in London in January 1969. Six months later Tom Mboya
was assassinated by a political opponent while shopping in Nairobi. He
was only thirty-eight at the time. No one can tell to what heights he
would have risen: although because of his tribe and origin he might not
have succeeded Kenyatta as President, I have little doubt that in one
field or another he would have become a world figure.

Mboya was one who faced the problem as to whether democracy
could thrive in an underdeveloped and tribal society. He was more
sceptical than his fellow Africans as to whether forms of Western democracy could be grafted on to an African background. He argued that a
society should be regarded as democratic if the people were freely and
structurally associated with the control and functioning of the government, and provided that it could be shown that democratic voluntary
bodies, like free trade unions and cultural and professional associations,
were able to exist. Given these conditions, he did not believe that two or
more political parties were a necessary condition for democracy in the
then state of African development. He also argued that different political
institutions would be required to replace the existing colonial structures.
The Civil Service, for example, should cease to serve European interests.
He contrasted his view of African socialism with the Marxist brand. Man
was not a means to an end but both an end in himself and an entity in
society – a basic concept which he claimed fitted African thought processes
and traditions and would assist that continent in its struggle to find a new
identity.

He was one of the first to suggest that African background and experience would be better served by an economic programme in which
agricultural development had priority over industrialisation. This showed
both his insight and his willingness to swim against the current fashion,
for at that time other African leaders were scrambling for new industrial
projects even though their people were not growing enough food to
feed themselves properly.

Julius Nyerere was another socialist in his early thirties, who studied
at Edinburgh University and much later became leader of his country.
When that happened, I found myself travelling to the independence

celebrations in the same aircraft as his former Scottish landlady, whom he always remembered with gratitude and invited to be his guest at State House. Like Tom Mboya, in those early days of transition from British colonial administration Nyerere demonstrated his capacity for looking beyond the immediate problems. He saw the difficulties that independence would bring in delimiting the boundaries of the new states. The straight lines on the map which European countries had drawn when marking out their various spheres of influence in the nineteenth century had been frequently delineated in complete disregard or total ignorance of the fact that they might divide a tribe between two different countries. He foresaw that the divided tribes might seize the moment of independence as the best chance they would have to reunite, for the situation would be at its most fluid. Nyerere took a clear line. The internal economic problems of the new states would be severe, he said. If African countries added to them by launching claims on one another's territories to redress historic grievances, Africa might fall into anarchy, and spend money on arms that would be better devoted to health and education.

I have no doubt that his great influence in the African councils at that time saved the new, young independent countries from making serious territorial mistakes. He advocated the formation of regional associations that would achieve a larger African unity by means of inter-state coordination of economic and educational plans, but an attempt to do this by forming an East African Federation of Kenya, Uganda and Tanzania broke down.

The future of the Central African Federation took much of my time as Colonial and Commonwealth Opposition Spokesman. The Federation had been formed in 1953 by bringing together the territories of Southern Rhodesia, Northern Rhodesia and Nyasaland. The last two were British Protectorates under the control of the Colonial Secretary in London. Southern Rhodesia was the odd man out. It had a relatively large established white population whose pioneers had marched north from South Africa with Rhodes in the 1890s and had conquered the local Matabele and Mashona tribes. The Europeans had followed up their victory by establishing a unique form of self-governing colony with neither the legal status of an independent Dominion like Australia nor yet that of a Protectorate like Northern Rhodesia.

The British Government had reserved the right to control certain aspects of native policy, in contradiction of the settlers' assertion that they were self-governing, but in the years between the wars Britain failed to exercise this right and the Europeans had consolidated political power firmly in their own hands, establishing a form of cabinet government headed by a Prime Minister. The majority African population was totally excluded. With such a background, the white Southern Rhodesian Government was always sensitive lest British colonial policy in other territories threaten their supremacy. The Europeans had been alarmed by the 1923 Devonshire Declaration, and concluded that white supremacy would be safer if Northern Rhodesia ceased to be the responsibility of the Colonial Office and its rich mining areas were added to Southern Rhodesia instead.

The Second World War put an end to such ideas, and they were not revived until other African states began to win their independence during the 1950s. The white Rhodesians disliked African majority rule, whose contagion they feared would spread, but they had little more sympathy with the South African solution of apartheid which had triumphed when Afrikaner Nationalism came to power in 1948. Southern Rhodesians were afraid to seek closer ties with South Africa because they might become subject to a larger and more dominant Afrikaner influence and Afrikaner language. They believed they were caught between the devil and the deep blue sea. They looked for another way out and found it in the idea of federation. It has been said that it was put into their heads by Oliver Stanley, the former Conservative Colonial Secretary, but wherever it came from they took it up eagerly and persuaded Jim Griffiths, who had become Labour's Colonial Secretary after the February 1950 election, to agree that officials should make attempts to draft a constitution that would set out the powers of a possible federation between the three territories whilst meeting the Colonial Office's intention to maintain the British Protectorates of Northern Rhodesia and Nyasaland.

When the results of the officials' work was published, and a conference was convened, Jim Griffiths and Patrick Gordon Walker, the Commonwealth Secretary, faced substantial African opposition. The Nyasaland African delegation refused to discuss the details of the plan and presented themselves only to express their opposition to the very principle of federation. Their fears were justified, for as the conference sessions progressed it became clear that the intention of Southern Rhodesia was to dominate such a federation and that, whatever safeguards might be written into a new constitution, it would be the policies and practices of Southern Rhodesia which would determine the future of the Africans in all three states. They would have none of it. The Africans pointed out that unlike the two Protectorates, in Southern Rhodesia more than half the land was reserved for a handful of European farmers, and it added to their sense of grievance and suspicion that this land had the best communications, was closest to the markets, and contained the most fertile soils. They were resolutely opposed to the racial nature of Southern Rhodesia's housing policy and the onerous requirement placed upon a Southern Rhodesian African that he must carry a pass and identification with him on pain of imprisonment. The Africans accepted the potential economic advantage of federation but nothing the Southern Rhodesian Government could say would convince them that federation was a scheme with any other major purpose than to preserve European supremacy and to deny them the right to win their own independence in due course.

Jim Griffiths refused to push the draft scheme through in face of such strong opposition, but the Labour Government was defeated shortly afterwards at the general election of 1951 and the incoming Conservative Government announced that they regarded the case for federation as an urgent necessity and would press ahead with it. Early in 1952 they began consultations with the Southern Rhodesian Government. This was a meeting of Europeans only: African representatives were not invited. Later, when the British Government called a second conference, this mistake was corrected but Africans refused to attend. A draft constitution was drawn up which clearly weakened the safeguards that the Africans in the two Protectorates had enjoyed up to then and, in Jim Griffiths' words, 'this destroyed any chance of securing African agreement'. It was a tragedy of shortsightedness, added to by insensitivity, especially when the British Government stated that the overwhelming majority of Africans neither knew nor cared about federation and the Government ought not therefore to take African opinion into account. The Federation could not have got off to a worse start.

The Government carried the draft constitution through Parliament against the votes of the Labour and Liberal Parties. At the same time, a referendum on the issue was held in Southern Rhodesia and secured a substantial majority of European votes. It seems extraordinary now to recall that of more than three million Africans living in the country no more than 380 were entitled to vote. So the Federation came into being on 1 August 1953.

The British Government expressed their belief that once Federation was in being, African opposition would gradually die away and the Colonial Office would be able, if all went well, slowly to relinquish its responsibilities for the Africans in the two Protectorates to the Federal Government. When that stage was reached, Britain would be justified in granting full independence and 1960 was the year fixed for a review to decide on independence for the Federation as a whole. But contrary to the Government's hopes, vocal African opposition in Northern Rhodesia and Nyasaland did not die away. On the contrary, it grew louder, especially as the passage of time made it clear to them that the British Government had already relinquished to the Federal Government the responsibility for making proposals to extend the African's franchise. Hitherto, Africans in the Protectorates had looked to negotiations with the British Governor or the Colonial Secretary for this purpose. From now on it seemed they would have to look to Salisbury.

In a debate in the House of Commons in June 1957 I set out the problem faced by the Federation. In short, unequal oxen had been yoked together with the result that Northern Rhodesia and Nyasaland could not attain their overriding objective of self-government at the same pace as Ghana, Nigeria and other African territories. In my view, the racial policies practised by the Europeans in Southern Rhodesia were spreading into the northern territories, whereas the reverse should be true and the Colonial Office policies for advance should be spreading from north to south. Demonstrations and boycotts were inevitable and would grow unless the Federal Government recognised the increasing representative nature of the African National Congress and extended the franchise. My conclusion was that, although African leaders in the northern territories did not demand self-government immediately, they would judge the Federation's value in 1960 by whether the Europeans, who were in total control, had helped them to reach their goal. The British Government understood this perfectly well yet they had decided to back the Federal leaders to the hilt.

Later in 1957, in an attempt to present a better image, the Commonwealth Parliamentary Association invited an all-Party group of Members of Parliament, of which I was one, to visit the three territories and report back. Our delegation was led by Richard Wood, who has since become Lord Holderness, and I was appointed deputy leader. Wood was Parliamentary Secretary to the Minister of Pensions at the time and had special responsibility for the welfare of disabled ex-servicemen. This appointment was particularly appropriate for he himself had lost both his legs during the war when he was crushed by a tank. Although our journeyings were arduous he managed with the minimum of fuss, stumping over rough ground and rocks and up and down hills in a manner that won our admiration.

I recall one occasion when we landed on a grass airstrip in the bush and had to scramble out of a tiny aircraft without steps, making our exit by means of a half-jump to the ground. Richard went first, and by leaning out of the cabin door and pointing his two sticks stiffly towards the ground, he leapt into space and swung himself perilously to safety. I was hesitating in the doorway as he turned round and looked at me solicitously. 'Can I help you down?' he asked.

He was never ostentatious or assertive and had that genuine sense of *noblesse oblige* that sometimes comes with a privileged background. As a Minister he was never a bare-knuckle fighter in a rough-house, but would win consent by his gentleness and popularity – he had no difficulty with our delegation. His father, Lord Halifax, had given valuable support to the Labour Government at the time of India's independence.

We spent five weeks in the three territories. My first impression of Salisbury was of the mass and beauty of the jacaranda, a superb ornamental flowering tree growing fifty feet high, with fern-like leaves and smothered in masses of purple blooms not unlike lilac. In the bright tropical sun, set against the blue sky, these trees were a picture of delight in Salisbury's main streets. Parts of the town with the old-style colonial buildings and houses had changed little since Rhodes's day. I have never been back but I am told that modern Harare is a city of skyscrapers.

Everywhere we travelled throughout Southern Rhodesia there were visible signs that industry was expanding and new enterprises opening up. The European business community repeatedly told us of their confidence in the future. We noticed that the standard of living enjoyed by the immigrant European skilled workers, who had left Britain after the war, was much higher than they had been used to at home. But there was a total lack of contact between them and the African workers and our all-Party delegation said with emphasis that this rigid racial separation represented a large danger to the future of the Federation. However, industry was booming, European wages were high and no notice was taken.

By way of contrast when we moved through Nyasaland we found little industry. Its beautiful lakes, green hills and deep valley gorges were committed to agriculture and this, as well as the future of land tenure, was the constant concern of those we met. We found a deep-seated fear in Nyasaland and later in Northern Rhodesia that federation would mean that the Africans' land would be taken over and farmed by Europeans. The example of Southern Rhodesia was quoted to us time after time. It had happened there and federation would lead to the same result in the other territories. Nothing would reassure those we met. The Federal Government, in reply, pointed to the increased aid that Nyasaland had received as a result of federal revenues, and our delegation agreed at that level that federation had helped.

Southern Rhodesia possessed vast real and potential wealth: two-thirds of the world's known resources of metallurgical grade chromite were to be found there, along with gold, nickel, platinum and coal. The country was a leading producer of asbestos as well. Some part of the revenues from these were used by the Federation to strengthen Nyasaland's services. We met some Europeans who supported federation because they genuinely believed that it would be the best instrument for a more equal development of all the territories and this would be in the interests of both Africans and themselves. But they were in a minority.

Too many Europeans openly advocated the unity of the three territories on the grounds that federation was an instrument that would prevent rapid political advance by the Africans. These Europeans said so loudly and often, and seemed to think the Africans were deaf. It was hardly surprising that the African leaders told us they were ready to sacrifice any economic or financial advantage that federation might bring if only they could be rid of it.

Of all the three territories, opposition to federation was most intense in Nyasaland. In our written report we said, 'Virtually all those with whom we spoke, whether chiefs, African Members of the Legislatures or leaders of Congress and leaders of Asian organisations, were unanimous in their opposition.' The conclusions of our report were clear and it was signed by all of us – Conservative and Labour Members. We said that if federation was to have any chance of surviving, the African community must be given a large political stake in its future. This would require a bold increase in African participation in the Federal Government and a substantial widening of the African franchise in the election of Members to the federal Assembly. Our report said that these steps were essential, and responsibility for initiating them lay with the Europeans who controlled the Federal Government.

We were not surprised that this was badly received. The Federal Prime Minister, Roy Welensky, was scornful both of our credentials and our opinions, overlooking the fact that it was the branches of the Commonwealth Parliamentary Association in the three territories that had jointly invited us and had specifically asked us to write a report on our findings. No doubt, if our conclusions had been more palatable we should have been told how percipient and wise we were.

I fear our delegation did not get on well with Roy Welensky, whose bluff manner had little regard for the niceties. Richard Wood was hardly his type and Welensky naturally disliked my African politics. He told us that he met and listened to the views of the African chiefs, a number of whom were little more than salaried civil servants, but we were all surprised when he said that he had never met the leaders of the African National Congress. He could therefore have no detailed knowledge of the characters and objectives of African leaders such as Nkumbula, Kenneth Kaunda, Chipembere, Joshua Nkomo and Hastings Banda, whose words carried great weight with their followers. At a dinner in our honour, I claimed provocatively that as I had regularly met, talked and corresponded with these African leaders whom he ignored, I at least had first-hand knowledge of what they were saying, whereas he did not. Welensky was contemptuous. He had swum and played with Africans when he was a boy and he knew what the real African wanted.

Welensky was, of course, a big character. In his youth he had been a heavyweight boxing champion of the Rhodesias, a railway engine-driver and a trade unionist who founded the Northern Rhodesia Labour Party. From trade unionism he turned naturally to politics and it was a measure of his very considerable ability that he held the office of Prime Minister of the Federation for seven years from 1956. Because he had grown up among African children, he believed he knew the limits of their abilities as well as their capacity. But in my view, it was a disabling feature of his leadership that he could never come to terms with the irresistible tide of independence that swept through the African continent after the end of the Second World War. In some ways he was aware of this for he once said to me that he felt the need to leave the Rhodesias at least once a year and visit Europe in order to get a wider perspective. It must also be said that many of those he led were far less understanding than he and would have totally disowned his leadership had he shown sympathy with rapid African political advance. I admired his rumbustious character even though we disagreed, and later, when the Federation had been dissolved, our relationship improved. He developed substantial criticisms of the Smith regime following the Declaration of Unilateral Independence, and we became friends, corresponded, and remain in touch even now.

I returned from our extended tour sceptical about the future of the
Federation but willing to suspend final judgement until 1960, when the
conference to review its progress was to be held. In the same spirit, the
Labour Party National Executive Committee issued a statement in March
1958 which I had helped to draft, calling for the elimination of racial
discrimination in social relations and industry, urging an inter-racial
policy in education, a broadening of the franchise and an increase in the
numbers of African Members of the Legislative Council. The Executive
Committee stated that if a Labour Government was elected, it would
decide its attitude to the future of the Federation in 1960 by reference to
its progress in these matters.

The Southern Rhodesian Europeans were headstrong, however. Instead of attempting to win the Africans they pressed for early Dominion
status which would have taken the control of all African affairs in the two
northern territories out of the hands of the British Government. This
aroused ever stronger resistance among the Africans, who campaigned
vigorously against any major change in the existing arrangements, and
aroused hostility at Westminster among those who believed that Britain
held the Protectorates in trust for the Africans. Colin Leys, a student of
Africa, summed up the situation as it had developed: 'The imposition
of federation made the Africans of the Protectorates politically conscious:
experience of it has been making them into nationalists, if not racialists.'

Matters continued to deteriorate. The Africans held out no hope for
the 1960 conference and began a sequence of strikes and riots in the three
territories. The security situation got worse and in turn each state was
forced to proclaim a state of emergency which was followed by the arrest
and imprisonment of the African leaders and many of their followers.

My contacts showed that privately and secretly some members of the
Colonial Administration in the northern territories were deeply disillusioned with the Federation's policies and had reached the conclusion that
it could not continue. They were convinced that the imposition of federation upon the Protectorates was the primary cause of their difficulties.
It was clear that matters could not go on as they were, and Alec Douglas-
Home, who had become the Commonwealth Secretary, proposed that
another all-Party commission should be sent out from London to advise
the federal Government, as well as the British Government, on the constitutional programme and framework best suited to the advance of the
objectives contained in the constitution of 1953.

The Prime Minister Harold Macmillan appointed Walter Monckton, who was a skilled conciliator, as Chairman. Monckton saw Gaitskell and told him that he would be happy if I were to represent the Labour Party on the commission and asked Hugh Gaitskell to propose my name to Harold Macmillan. Unfortunately for Monckton, Roy Welensky was insisting that members of the commission must be Privy Councillors and it was suggested that his purpose was to prevent Barbara Castle or myself from serving. Then came a surprise. Harold Macmillan formally invited me to become a Privy Councillor, saying that he was ready to submit my name to the Queen, and thus overcome Welensky's objections. Hugh Gaitskell and I talked. I told him that for me to accept a Privy Councillorship from a Conservative Prime Minister would be as if a Welsh rugby forward had accepted an England cap (in those days such a thing was unknown, but times have since changed). In any case, I said, there was a more fundamental objection. From the way matters had developed, I concluded that the only slight chance of keeping the Federation together would be if the Monckton Commission was empowered to hear evidence and recommend on the issue as to whether any one of the territories could choose to secede in 1960 if it so wished. I had Nyasaland particularly in mind, believing that it was certain to go, but thought Northern Rhodesia might remain if there were considerable improvements in African voting rights. Hugh Gaitskell agreed and took up this and other matters with the Government. But Macmillan was not willing formally to consider this and the Shadow Cabinet then decided that they would not nominate anyone to represent the Labour Party.

This was the second occasion on which I had missed my chance of becoming a Privy Councillor. The other had been at the time of the Coronation in 1953, when I was told by the Chief Whip that Clement Attlee had put my name forward but had been asked by Winston Churchill to withdraw it, as he wished to propose the name of Harold Holt, the Australian Minister of Labour who later became Prime Minister and subsequently disappeared while swimming near his home.

Lord Monckton and his commission reached conclusions not dissimilar from those of the Labour Party. It was ironic that one of their most important recommendations was about the precise issue of secession which had been the cause of the initial breakdown between Macmillan and Gaitskell. Paragraph 298 of their report said: 'A declaration of the intention of Her Majesty's Government to permit secession by any of the Territories ... would have a favourable effect and might be decisive in securing a fair trial for the new association.'

Monckton had correctly seen the reality of the situation behind the smokescreen of propaganda. His report called for an extension of the franchise, more seats for Africans in the Assembly, drastic changes in racial policies, and removal from federal laws and practices of all instances of unfair racial discrimination. In the light of this, we could fairly claim that the Monckton Commission vindicated the Labour Party's stand on what changes were necessary to make the Federation acceptable to the Africans. But no favourable response came from the Europeans in Southern Rhodesia.

The Conservative victory at the 1959 general election brought important changes at the Commonwealth and Colonial Offices. Alec Douglas-Home became Foreign Secretary and was succeeded at the Commonwealth Office by Duncan Sandys. The Colonial Secretary, Alan Lennox-Boyd, retired from politics and was succeeded by Iain MacLeod. As a result of these changes, we began to detect a rather different note in the speeches of the new Ministers. Sandys spoke of the desirability of preserving the Federation and said that the condition for this to happen was the creation of a real partnership between the races. Nevertheless, he and MacLeod increasingly conveyed the impression that they felt they might have arrived on the scene too late to save the day.

As happened throughout the history of the Federation, the Southern Rhodesian Government continued to make a bad situation worse. They brought in a notorious Law and Order Act which was not only oppressive in itself but also discriminated against the African population. Misused so as to prevent African political parties from functioning, the Act created a political vacuum.

Peaceful demonstrations, boycotts and strikes were all made illegal. Then, having firmly blocked the avenues of political and peaceful protest, the same Act introduced serious penalties for acts of violence and sabotage. It was a truly downward spiral. And, as usually happens, repression made violence worse. The new law was so offensive in character that it brought about the resignation of the Federal Chief Justice, Sir Robert Tredgold, who was without doubt the most respected judge in Southern Rhodesia. This was a shock to public opinion in Southern Rhodesia and in Britain. He gave as his reason that the Law and Order Act 'outrages almost every basic human right'. I quoted this in a debate on the Monckton Report as an example of the difficulties of British Government policy but I added:

It is still possible for Europeans in Southern Rhodesia to step back from the course upon which they seem to be embarked. We know that there are divisions of opinion there. We know of the great disquiet that exists among many people about the path that they seem to be treading. They will have to choose between association with the northern territories or their own racial policies, with all the consequences that flow from them – the increasing isolation, the undoubted break-up of the Federation which cannot be sustained if Southern Rhodesia pursues her present racial policy. They must make their choice. The choice for them is which they value more – their racial policies or their association with the two northern territories. The situation in Southern Rhodesia is so critical that the British Government should call a conference, widely based, of the Southern Rhodesian Government. They should ask that there should be included in that conference representatives of all the political parties there, leaders of every opinion, like Sir Robert Tredgold, the churches, and the trade unions. Above all the Africans should be brought in.

The Southern Rhodesia Government and their supporters did not listen. They had decided that their overriding priority was to preserve European supremacy at all costs and to prevent African political advance. In doing so, they not only condemned the Federation to a lingering death but sealed their own fate at a later date.

Iain MacLeod's new realism resulted in Nyasaland's leader, Dr Hastings Banda, being released from jail and he pledged immediately that he would take his country out of the Federation as soon as he had secured its independence. In the Northern Rhodesian Legislature, Kenneth Kaunda and other members voted to secede from the Federation at the earliest date. Such events sounded the death knell of the Federation, and Ministers recognised the futility of continuing this shotgun marriage. It was finally killed off in 1963, just ten years after it had been brought into existence.

A little later the African leaders in Northern Rhodesia and Nyasaland legally negotiated their independence and these countries became full members of the Commonwealth, as Zambia and Malawi. But for a long period afterwards Southern Rhodesian Europeans refused to recognise reality or to accept Britain's terms for a negotiated independence of their country. Britain's main interest was to ensure the political advance and equal racial status of the Africans. Ian Smith, who had become Prime Minister, rejected this and unilaterally declared Southern Rhodesia's independence from Britain in November 1965. This illegal act remained a thorn in Britain's side for the next fifteen years.

Looking back to my days in the Labour Government in 1965, at which time I was Chancellor of the Exchequer and wrestling with the problems of sterling and the balance of payments, I now regret that my preoccupation with these matters prevented me from urging forceful action by Britain to compel Rhodesia's return to legality. We should have used whatever means were necessary to apprehend and arrest Mr Smith and his followers, for Smith's Declaration of Independence was a plain act of rebellion against the Crown. A number of the most senior officers of Southern Rhodesia's armed forces were in great mental turmoil at being required to forswear their Oath of Allegiance to the Queen, and we might have successfully capitalised on these feelings to bring about Smith's quick capitulation. I must accept my full share of collective responsibility for our decision to limit our action to taking trade and financial sanctions – and there were arguably good reasons for going no further – but I do not disguise my regrets nor my belief that more forceful action by us at the time might have saved Britain from many uncomfortable moments in later years.

Following the death of Aneurin Bevan in 1960, Hugh Gaitskell asked Harold Wilson to take over his responsibilities for Foreign Affairs, and then invited me to succeed Harold Wilson as Treasury spokesman. My period as Shadow Spokesman for Commonwealth and Colonial matters came to an end, but it had been a valuable experience in the course of which I travelled widely and learned a great deal. I attended a Commonwealth conference in New Zealand, visited Australia and Singapore, India, Indonesia and Burma, and paid many visits to the African continent. The 1950s was a decade of great change. Harold Macmillan went to South Africa and made his famous speech about the winds of change blowing through the world, encouraging all those who opposed apartheid in that country to redouble their efforts. His speech aroused great expectations in all parts of Africa and shortly afterwards, when I was in Kenya to see Jomo Kenyatta, I met a senior underground fighter who told me he looked to China as his mentor rather than to the Soviet Union or to the West. I asked him what was his ultimate objective. He replied, 'To march straight through to Cape Town.'

The Chinese made considerable advances in parts of Africa at that time at the expense of the Soviet Union and the West. In the eyes of many Africans the Russians were too much like us, whereas the Chinese seemed like them and worked side by side with them. They gained much credit for this. In Asia, too, the Chinese communist influence was spreading. Their message was simple and direct. They asked what the word 'freedom' meant to the tens of thousands of families without homes, who were condemned to live and sleep on the sidewalks of Asia's cities and towns. Their propaganda asked whether freedom had a meaning for educated high-school students whose only prospect for the future was between the shafts of a rubber tyre pedicar pulling their human freight like beasts of burden.

I must admit that we were too optimistic about Africa's future, but I would claim that we showed more realism than those who buried their heads in the sand and opposed the African's march to independence. Africans may have attained their political goals but they have discovered that economic advance is much harder to come by, and hunger, disease, poverty, corruption and illiteracy continue to disfigure the African continent, not by any means always the result of their own mistakes. Politically the Westminster model of party government that we sought to transplant never took root and was too alien to survive in the state of development of differing ethnic groups and tribes. Some leaders can proudly claim that they have endeavoured to sustain basic human rights, but in other countries we have witnessed frequent and inhuman breaches. But it is not enough for the West just to condemn. Africa needs our help too.

PART TWO

CHANCELLOR
OF THE
EXCHEQUER

5

Hugh Gaitskell's death – Labour wins in 1964 – problems with sterling and relations with the United States – tax reform and the National Plan.

Some events remain forever printed on the memory. We recall afterwards the inconsequential things we were doing at the very moment that we felt their stunning effect. Such an occasion for me was Hugh Gaitskell's death in January 1963. I was walking to my home in Cardiff from a Labour Party meeting when someone came running from the house I had just passed to call to me: 'Hugh Gaitskell has died. They have just announced it.' I was stunned.

Hugh was fifty-six years old. Like many others, I admired his exceptional qualities of honesty and courage. They were to cause him trouble during his leadership, especially his determination to change the Party's constitution on public ownership and his bitter fight against unilateral disarmament. But by the time of his death he was leading a united Party that seemed poised for victory at the approaching general election.

I am sometimes asked what kind of Prime Minister he would have been and I suppose not one of us can be sure how we will react until we are put to the test. On the whole I believe great responsibility does not alter a leader's abilities, but enlarges them and may awaken them if dormant.

In Hugh's case, his penetrating and informed mind would have shown itself in a clear vision of the direction in which he wanted to take a socialist Britain. He had formed strong views about equal opportunity and abhorred racialism, and he possessed a passionate belief in Britain's future. His strong determination to master obstacles and his wide experience of government, gained during his years as a civil servant and Minister, would have enabled him to brush aside official excuses for inaction. His deep sense of Britain's history and her greatness would have led him as Prime Minister to offer a strong lead on world issues. He was pro-Europe but anti-Common Market because, like others among us, he was a strong believer in the Atlantic Alliance. And he cared deeply about the Commonwealth. Perhaps, had he lived to see our former colonial territories in the

Commonwealth forming other alliances and in the process growing away from Britain, together with our lessening importance in the eyes of the United States, he might have changed his mind about membership of the European Community.

He was strong-willed (stubborn in the eyes of his opponents) and he would have needed Ministers who were prepared to argue hard with him in Cabinet. I thought he was wrong in the matter of changing the Party constitution but could not dissuade him. On the other hand, I supported him through thick and thin in his fight against unilateral disarmament and worked hard to help him successfully to reverse the decision.

Once he had taken up a position he was very certain about what he was doing and gave us a feeling of assurance that he had made a thorough examination of the facts and weighed the alternative courses before deciding to take action. Our confidence grew by the very fact that it was he who had done it. His death was undoubtedly hastened by overwork for he never spared himself on the Party's behalf. Within a short space of time we had lost the two biggest leaders in the Party – Hugh Gaitskell and Aneurin Bevan. A new generation was maturing and in the contest to elect a new Party Leader I stood against Harold Wilson and George Brown. My principal nominators were Tony Crosland and George Thomson. But such quality was not enough. Harold automatically got the vote of the left and George scored heavily with the right, while I secured only the votes of those who preferred neither candidate. This was not a very solid base and I came bottom of the poll. In the run-off Harold Wilson was an easy winner. This was the right result, for although George Brown exceeded us all in his darting imagination, his demonic energy and his persuasive power, Harold Wilson had the stability and unifying influence that the Party needed.

As soon as he became Leader, he took advantage of a deep decline that had become apparent in the fortunes of the Tory Party. After their huge success in the 1959 general election, the country began to turn against the Conservatives and nothing could reverse the trend. The poor results of bye-elections revealed their unpopularity and reduced the authority of Harold Macmillan as Prime Minister. By comparison, Harold Wilson, more than twenty years younger, seemed representative of a new spirit in Britain, determined to reverse the industrial decline which was becoming apparent to the British people. Harold Wilson's theme that Britain's revival could be ensured by harnessing socialism to science stood in sharp contrast to the 'thirteen wasted years' of Tory rule.

In a speech to the Labour Party Conference, he correctly forecast that the 1960s and 1970s would 'embrace a period of technological change, particularly in industrial methods, greater than in the whole industrial revolution of the last 250 years'. He spoke of the need to accept automation; there would be no room for Luddites. He talked of the coming impact of the computer age and of the significance of technological change for employment prospects, especially in the service industries and among white-collar workers. He coupled this analysis with scathing attacks on those he called the 'Tory amateurs in the boardrooms of Britain who were unable to think or speak the language of our scientific age'.

He caught the mood of the British people and even elicited a hearing from industry and commerce, the readier to listen because they had become impatient with successive balance of payments crises in the Tory years of 1955, 1957 and 1961. On every occasion these had resulted in industrial production being brought temporarily to a halt, and industry listened with attention to Labour's argument that this could be avoided by a form of national planning.

They were ready to give it a chance if the result would be less frequent alterations in the rates of purchase tax, the conditions attached to hire purchase agreements and changes in investment tax allowances. These measures were used regularly first to stimulate and then to slow down industrial production, and industry complained that these 'stop-go' policies made it difficult for them to plan ahead and resulted in increased production costs and difficulties with the work force.

In 1961 Selwyn Lloyd, who was the fourth successive Conservative Chancellor of the Exchequer in five years, knocked production on the head when he increased indirect taxes by 10 per cent, made bank credit more difficult and cut public expenditure. These measures put a severe brake on production, which stagnated in the following twelve months. Spokesmen of industry, as well as academic and business economists and the press, began openly to echo the Labour Party's criticisms of 'stop-go', and the Government's popularity continued to sink.

In the summer of 1962 R. A. Butler and Iain MacLeod, who had made little secret of their disagreement with the Chancellor's policies, urged the Prime Minister to replace him. They probably got more than they had bargained for when Selwyn Lloyd and no fewer than six other Cabinet Ministers, one third of the Cabinet, were dismissed overnight in a 'July massacre'.

One of Selwyn Lloyd's most effective critics at the time was Nigel Lawson, who himself became Chancellor some twenty years later but was then a financial journalist. He wrote at the time of the 'dreadful follies' of the Government's strategy; that our low level of production was 'the final unanswerable condemnation of the criminal lunacy' of Treasury policies. He urged Reginald Maudling, who took over from Selwyn Lloyd, to throw these discredited policies overboard. His remedy at that time was for the Chancellor to expand Britain's production urgently. This was strong stuff but Lawson was one of many commentators who helped to create a national mood from which Labour's election prospects benefited. Yet when Maudling became Chancellor, he himself soon fell into disfavour with the critics, who alleged that he was too slow in taking remedial action. One popular newspaper headline was 'STOP DAWDLING MAUDLING'. This was unfair to him, for he had taken action quickly, but it takes time for the results to show.

The accent was on the need for faster growth and the Labour Party adopted as its target a steady 4 per cent growth in the economy each year. This figure was given added authenticity by the work of the National Economic Development Council, which reported that 4 per cent steady growth was a feasible proposition. Somewhat later the Conservative Party, under Maudling's influence, also adopted the same figure for growth and their 1964 election manifesto included as 'first priority' that 'Britain's national wealth can expand by a steady 4 per cent per year'.

On the public platform our riposte to this death-bed conversion was obvious: 'Then why haven't you done it already?' We argued that thirteen years of Tory rule had demonstrated that this rate of growth, which was now admitted to be necessary, could not be achieved as long as the economy was left to look after itself. Britain needed structural changes to take advantage of new technology and science-based industries.

These objectives could be reached by socialist planning. Labour would set up a Ministry of Economic Affairs and in cooperation with both employers and trade unions would prepare a National Economic Plan stretching throughout the lifetime of one Parliament and beyond. It would be a framework for industrial investment and production, whose object would be to increase exports and replace imports. The whole plan would be constructed on the potential capacity of each separate industry for production and export. Every industry would be able to see where it fitted into the national economy and would be able to make long-term plans more safely than hitherto in the expectation of steady industrial growth throughout the rest of the economy. This strategy would solve recurring balance of payments crises followed by the inevitable 'stop-go'.

The story that the idea for the Ministry of Economic Affairs was born in a taxi-cab conversation between Harold Wilson and George Brown is a myth. The proposal had been thought out and widely discussed in Labour Party circles for some years and gained momentum rapidly as the Treasury's reputation declined because of its alleged mishandling of the economy under successive Chancellors. I supported fully the proposals for the establishment of a new Ministry of Economic Affairs and the ideas of indicative planning which we had inherited from the experience of France, but as Party Spokesman on Treasury matters, I tended to be more cautious about our prospects than some of my colleagues.

At Tony Crosland's suggestion and with his help, a small group of economists were assembled who agreed to advise me. Among them were Nicholas Kaldor, Robert Neild, Donald MacDougall and Kit McMahon – all of whom subsequently had distinguished careers. We held our meetings at Nuffield College, Oxford, of which I had been made a visiting fellow some years earlier, thanks to the Warden, Norman Chester.

Not having attended a university in my youth, I enjoyed these visits and the university atmosphere and learned a great deal. But one field of experience was not included among my advisers, namely a first-hand knowledge of how the City of London works; its strengths and its weaknesses. Like most if not all Chancellors, I did not learn the ways of the City until I had held the post for some time, and consequently made mistakes. Perhaps I should add that one of my advisers, Kit McMahon, subsequently became Deputy Governor of the Bank of England, but it was a quarter of a century too late for me.

There was a mutual liking and confidence between Maudling and myself. During his tenure of office he did not hesitate to talk privately and frankly to me about his concerns. I reciprocated during my period at the Treasury and also later in the Home Office, when he was my opposite number as Shadow Spokesman.

By the spring of 1964 Maudling's reflationary measures and his deliberate increase in public spending on health, housing and education had geared up the economy to the extent that it was expanding at more than 6 per cent per annum. Earnings were increasing by nearly 9 per cent a year and profits were growing fast. Maudling's strategy was based on the expectation that production would increase sufficiently rapidly to satisfy both increased home consumption and the need for more exports, thus enabling him to accelerate out of the balance of payment deficit.

There were, however, already signs of trouble. The cost of imports, which had been relatively stable for some years, had begun to increase, both in cost and in volume. Over a period of two years the cost of Britain's imports grew by nearly £1,000 millions, but exports increased by only £450 millions with a consequent deterioration in our balance of trade.

Maudling could see difficulties coming. In January 1964 he told me that he would prefer the approaching election to be held in the spring in order to be more free to take any necessary corrective action during the summer. But Sir Alec Douglas-Home had become Prime Minister as recently as October 1963 and understandably wished to defer the election until the last possible date to give him as much time as possible to play himself in.

The last of our regular conversations prior to the general election of 1964 took place in the Chancellor's room in the House of Commons on 18 June. Maudling was his usual unruffled, amiable self, reflectively sipping a large whisky and soda. He confessed he could see no sign of the high level of imports diminishing, so he expected troubles ahead for sterling. Nevertheless, he did not regard the economy as overheated and intended neither to restrain the rate of growth nor to increase the bank rate. If it became necessary to restrict imports, the best way to do so would be through the use of some kind of financial control. He said privately that he expected Labour would win the election, although he warned me that he would do his best to stop us.

In the post-election period he thought it would make sense to approach the French and Germans for a large loan to fend off the attack on sterling that he expected, and he would ask the International Monetary Fund for a large borrowing for the same purpose. But suppose all these measures failed to halt the attacks on sterling? 'Then,' he said, 'devaluation would be the solution – but in the very long term.'

Knowing the dislike of financial markets for uncertainty, I was fearful that there would be a run on sterling during the month before the election if it seemed possible that Labour would win. We had been out of office for thirteen years, and there would be speculation that our first step might be to devalue sterling. I asked Maudling if he would be willing, in the event of such a run on sterling, to issue a statement jointly with me to the effect that neither Party would devalue following a general election. He said that this would be very difficult to do during an election campaign. He told me he would like to introduce a 'proper' Capital Gains Tax in order to reduce the rate of Income Tax. His final word was to recommend William Armstrong as Permanent Secretary to the Treasury, as he was the best civil servant he knew.

Throughout the whole of the post-war era of fixed exchange rates, the stability of sterling had been a never-ending source of concern to successive Chancellors. Gone was Britain's nineteenth-century dominance of world trade, which had brought with it the worldwide use of sterling by other countries, both for trade and as a safe refuge for their currency reserves. By 1945, much of sterling's role had been replaced by the dollar. Nevertheless, habit, convenience and trust led many countries to continue to handle and hold large quantities of sterling. All these transactions were very profitable for the City of London, which built up a formidable reputation and expertise in the handling of other countries' deposits, but such transactions become an added source of strain on a currency if it is suspect and is insufficiently liquid. This happened after 1945, when Britain suffered because her wartime effort had left her with an insufficient level of currency reserves to provide a safe margin if overseas depositors should make a combined demand for the return of their assets.

In overseas eyes it was not a sufficient safeguard that Britain's total overseas assets were always greater than the Bank's total overseas liabilities. The doubters hinted that it might not be possible to realise such assets quickly. As a result, troubles often arose during the early stages of an expansion of the British economy when the country imported more than it exported and the overseas accounts showed a deficit.

Anxious noises would then be heard in the foreign currency markets. Speculators would add to this – the Gnomes of Zurich as we called them – increasing the pressure by selling sterling in exchange for other currencies in the hope of making a quick profit. Doubts would spread from the City to Fleet Street; uncertainty fed upon itself as newspaper headlines hardened question marks into the certainty of crisis. Furthermore, during the Labour Government's term of office genuine overseas anxieties were sometimes exaggerated in the hope of political advantage and even the possibility of bringing about a change of government.

Confidence is the surest guarantee of stability for a currency. The biggest enemy is doubt; rumours can all too often turn a flurry into a hurricane. In those days of fixed exchange rates every Chancellor was sensitive about domestic events that might affect sterling. In the early 1960s the world was at the beginning of a communications revolution.

This made banking conversations between the international financial centres a routine occurrence, minute by minute or even second by second. A whisper in London could become a shout in Wall Street. At such moments the foreign exchange markets, which in calmer times serve a valuable and legitimate purpose, can be exploited so that they become no better than a casino.

There were other anxieties. Post-war Labour and Conservative Governments felt a special sense of obligation to Commonwealth countries. Many of them, including some of the poorest like India, as well as the most wealthy, such as Australia, held a large part of their currency reserves in sterling and stood to suffer seriously if the sterling exchange rate was pushed lower than the then existing level of £1 to $2.80.

Maudling took a rare pessimistic view of world financial developments. At times we talked of his concern that the growth of world trade and production might be held back if there was an insufficient total supply of dollars, sterling and gold to finance it. He had no more wish than I to see sterling expand its world trading role and thus become even more exposed, but in public speeches the Chancellor began to suggest that other additional methods of financing world trade should be found which would not impose extra strains either on sterling or on the dollar. In a notable speech he suggested that such methods might take the form of a new internationally backed paper currency that could become transferable between countries as a means of settling their debts, and would be officially accepted as a currency reserve asset. I applauded his initiative and President Kennedy gave it a welcoming nod. But the United States Treasury was very sniffy, believing that Maudling's idea cast reflections on the strength of the dollar, which in their eyes at that time was impregnable. Some Continental bankers eyed Maudling's ideas suspiciously, believing that his real intention was to find a means to enable Britain to slide out of the obligations she had incurred during the war.

By the time I succeeded Maudling, there was considerable international interest in these matters. In due course, it was my turn to become Chairman of the Finance Ministers of the group of ten industrial countries and, in conjunction with Otmar Emminger of the German Federal Reserve Bank, we had the satisfaction at a conference at Lancaster House in London of securing the consent of the Ten to the introduction of a new currency reserve asset to be called the 'Special Drawing Right' (SDR). This became accepted as an internationally recognised asset for settling inter-governmental debts.

The use of SDRs has grown substantially since they were launched in 1969, and the International Monetary Fund has ceased to draw up its accounts in dollars and values all its assets, such as gold and national currencies, in terms of SDRs. In addition, it has specifically allocated over twenty-one million SDRs (worth about £15 billions) to its members. It would have been better for the world had the conversion been quicker. Although Maudling's ideas for an additional international asset were beneficial and were eventually accepted, in the short run his initiative served to increase doubts about the future level of sterling.

I could not understand the Continental, and especially the French, post-war attitude towards sterling. They privately thought and sometimes said that Britain enjoyed an undeserved advantage from sterling's world-wide use, yet they gave us no help during my period as Chancellor to reduce its role, and as time went on I became convinced that sterling's role as an international currency was more of a burden than a blessing.

The Continental bankers' suspicions inhibited us more than once from pressing as strongly as we might have done for reforms that would have stregthened the Bretton Woods monetary system. The Americans wished the world to believe that the dollar was as good as gold. There were whispers in the mid-1960s that the dollar might come under suspicion, for there were growing doubts as to whether the United States could sustain the obligation it had assumed at the end of the Second World War to buy or to sell gold from their stock to any central bank freely, without limit, and at a fixed price of $35 for an ounce of gold.

This policy had seemed feasible in 1945. At that time the United States owned nearly two-thirds of the total world gold stock, and their willingness to accept the liability was based on the confident belief that the war-time economic dominance of the United States would survive, and accordingly that the central banks of other countries would be willing to hold dollars in their reserves equally with gold, knowing that they could freely exchange one for the other. But the post-war recovery of Europe gathered pace and this, together with the rise of Japan, undermined the foundations of America's policy. Doubts began to emerge as to whether the dollar would remain as good as gold. From time to time during the 1960s this led some countries, and especially France, to sell part of their dollar holdings to America and to take gold instead. Slowly at first but with gathering momentum, America's gold reserves began to run down, and with each reduction in America's gold stock, doubts about the value of the dollar grew stronger.

By an interesting convention the Americans did not physically part with the gold bars they sold to the French or elsewhere. In the early 1960s I visited the vaults of the New York Federal Reserve Bank, deep below the level of the Hudson River. Men wearing heavy boots with reinforced toecaps were wheeling trolleys of gold bars from one part of the vaults to another. I asked the purpose and it was pointed out to me that vaults were divided from floor to roof into a series of heavily padlocked, strong wire cages – all of them visible from any angle. Some cages contained a large stack of gold bars, others had fewer, and on the door of every cage was a printed label carrying the name of a different country. In these cages were stored their reserves of gold.

I enquired what was the procedure when one country wished to settle its debts with another in gold, or to exchange its dollar holdings for America's gold. 'Oh,' they said, 'we go to the wire cage of the selling country, load the required number of gold bars on to a trolley and then wheel them into the wire cage of the purchasing country.' I thought that this convenient and sensible way of settling the world's debts showed a justifiable trust by overseas countries in the good faith of the New York Federal Reserve. It also occurred to me that were it not for the magic hold that gold has on man's imagination, any other metal or commodity of which there was a controlled or limited supply could have logically served the same purpose.

As doubts about the dollar grew, the run on America's gold gathered momentum and in the early 1960s President Kennedy felt impelled to give two personal public commitments to try to stem the outflow. First, he repeated the pledge that there would be no departure by the United States from their obligation to supply gold whenever they were offered dollars by another country. He went further. He pledged that the price of gold would not increase beyond $35 to the ounce. In other words he was saying that the dollar would not be devalued. There was some disappointment at the Bank of England about President Kennedy's pledge, for the British reserve included a large gold holding and there were hopes that if the official price of gold was increased, this would automatically increase the value of the British reserves and thereby make it more difficult for speculative attacks on sterling to succeed. But as this had not happened, it seemed in the summer of 1964 that if the Labour Party won the general election we would take over a rapidly growing economy, sucking in imports, but with a serious balance of payments deficit and the possibility of a run on sterling before an election or immediately afterwards.

After Harold Wilson asked me to become Shadow Chancellor, I had paid regular visits to America to get to know the American Treasury and the Federal Reserve, and had struck up a relationship with Al Hayes, the President of the Federal Reserve Bank of New York. He was a knowledgeable practitioner and a man of integrity. In May 1964, as the British general election grew closer, I had a long talk with Hayes in London, and expressed my concern at the prospect of speculative attacks on sterling in the event of our expected victory. He was more optimistic than I. He thought that Continental bankers had realised that a change of government was likely and had got used to the idea of a Labour Government. He said that the attitude to sterling would be influenced by how Labour looked as a Government, and he had found fears in the City of London both about our proposals for a Capital Gains Tax and about our handling of Britain's balance of payments.

I explained to him our intentions for tax reform, and that we would probably need import controls to reduce the trade deficit. I further explained the Party's steel nationalisation plans. Hayes' view was that we might have to make a large increase in the bank rate in order to protect sterling, but perhaps only for a short time. He spoke very frankly about the strains on the dollar and repeated more than once his belief that the best prospect for effective action in monetary matters depended upon Britain and America working together. Above all, he promised that he would do everything in his power to help us repel speculative attacks during the first few months of a Labour Government, and gave me his firm assurance that the New York Federal Reserve would throw everything into preventing a run on the pound from becoming serious. Some months later, when the testing time arrived, he could not have been more helpful and was every bit as good as his word.

Sterling's value has seesawed so dramatically in recent years that it is difficult to recreate at this distance of time how violently public and international sentiment opposed any idea of devaluing the second most important reserve currency in the world. It was almost a moral issue. One or two of my Oxford and Cambridge advisers, notably Professor Kaldor and Robert Neild, were in favour of an incoming Labour Government devaluing as soon as we took office, and they never swerved from that view. But theirs was a minority view which I resisted both for political and economic reasons. The Conservatives would have crucified us. It had taken several years for Labour to live down the taunts directed at us following Cripps's devaluation in 1949, and if we had devalued on coming to power in October 1964 the Tory Opposition as well as the press would have hammered home day after day that devaluation was always Labour's soft option, and took place whenever a Labour Government was elected. The extreme fluctuations that have recently taken place under Conservative government will I hope have destroyed that myth.

I was reinforced in my view when the result of the election became known and we emerged with a tiny working majority. If a devaluation is to be successful it must result in a reduction in the standard of living of the people. Given our minute majority, I did not see how we could hope to win the second general election that was bound to follow within a short time, with a sterling devaluation hanging around the Government's neck. But, more important, I held the view that the amount of sterling's overvaluation could be corrected and its value maintained provided Britain fulfilled two conditions. First, industry must increase productivity and efficiency. This we were determined to achieve through the instrument of the National Plan. Second, trade unions and employers must show prudence and moderation in wage increases and labour costs.

There were other important arguments. We should be embarking on a course the consequences of which I could not see. As all other nations at that time were opposed to a sterling devaluation, there was a danger that unilateral action by Britain might lead them to follow suit and protect themselves by devaluing their own currencies. In the process, they would deprive Britain of the competitive advantage we might otherwise gain.

Again, sterling's devaluation would add to the difficulties of the dollar and might dislodge the Bretton Woods system, as in fact happened when sterling was eventually devalued in 1967. Then again, devaluation in 1964 would certainly hit those Commonwealth countries hardest who had voluntarily maintained their reserves in London, for it would have reduced their value in other currencies. And, finally, I feared that a devaluation that took the pressure temporarily off the pound would be regarded by my Cabinet colleagues as an opportunity to increase spending on all the schemes for social improvement with which we had come to office. Whereas, in truth, if it is to be successful, devaluation demanded the opposite.

Accordingly, I made speeches in the summer of 1964 prior to the election to the effect that the Conservative Government's enlarged programme of public expenditure was as big as an incoming Labour Government could sustain, given the existing rate of growth of the economy.

Maudling, naturally, quoted this against me and visited Cardiff for the purpose of emphasising the point.

This was not popular with some of my colleagues, and I might as well have saved my breath for all the notice that was taken. I usually found that my endeavours to explain the interrelated problems of the sterling exchange rate, the effects of devaluation on standards of consumption, and the importance of overseas confidence in a reserve currency as difficult as convincing a dipsomaniac of the virtues of barley water. Intelligent people's eyes glaze and their ears shut when they are asked to focus on such problems.

My apprehension grew and in the summer of 1964 I summarised in note form a list of actions that might be necessary once a Labour victory had been gained. It went in part like this:

- See Governor to (declare) Bank Holiday
- Curb drain on foreign exchange (through) borrowing from the IMF
- Raise bank rate
- Capital issue control on foreign borrowers
- Control imports by levies
- Review cost of overseas bases and close some of them
- Special deposits – use regulator to restrict consumption
- See trade union leaders for a wages holiday
- Tax reforms ready for April 1965
    - (i) corporation tax
    - (ii) capital gains tax
    - (iii) export rebates
- Operate on prices.

In due course, we found it necessary to put into force most of the items contained in this list.

During the election campaign, Harold Wilson repeated his promise that a new Labour Government would usher in one hundred days of dynamic action. Like other Labour spokesmen, I undertook an extensive speaking tour and the enthusiasm among Labour members and workers led me to expect a bigger majority. But the Conservative Party held on, led by Sir Alec Douglas-Home, and although a number of Ministers lost their seats there was a neck-and-neck finish, with Labour gaining sixty-one seats but ending up with a working majority of only three. There was no substantial increase in the Labour vote, but a large number of Tory voters stayed at home. It was not until the afternoon of the day after the election that our victory seemed certain and I was still in Cardiff when I received a telephone call from Peter Jay at the Treasury telling me that Harold Wilson was already at No. 10, and urging me to come to London immediately. From Paddington I drove straight to No. 10, where I was at once shown into the Cabinet Room.

Thirteen years had gone by since I was last there. Harold was standing by the Prime Minister's chair, and in the emotion of the moment I embraced him. His prosaic reply was 'Where have you been? I'm waiting for you before I can announce the first list of Ministers.' I stayed with him for only a few minutes and then walked in a state of some excitement along the corridor to the front door of No. 10. I was about to leave when a dark figure glided (I can use no other word) to my side from the internal door that joins No. 10 to the Chancellor's residence at No. 11. 'Good evening, Chancellor,' he said. 'I am Ian Bancroft, your Private Secretary. The Permanent Secretary, Sir William Armstrong, is in the study, and we wondered whether you would care to have a word with him.'

I stepped through the communicating door for the first time to No. 11, where the Permanent Secretary was waiting. He handed me a foolscap typed volume at least two inches thick of background economic information, with a polite intimation that I might wish to read it before the morrow. It began with the words: 'We greet the Chancellor', but the rest of the contents were not so happy. I was still glowing with anticipation, and it was only later that I came across the remarks of the Marquis of Halifax in 1698 about a colleague who wanted the Treasury – 'charmed with the name of the place where the money groweth, forgetting the drudgery and trouble of it'. I soon discovered how wise Lord Halifax had been.

Next morning I was sitting at what had been Reggie Maudling's desk in the ground-floor study at 11 Downing Street. While I was reading the briefs which Treasury officials had prepared against the possibility of a Labour victory, he was in the upstairs flat with his wife, packing their belongings. On his way out, he put his head round the door carrying a pile of suits over his arm. His comment was typical: 'Sorry, old cock, to leave it in this shape. I suggested to Alec this morning that perhaps we should put up the bank rate but he thought he ought to leave it all to you. Good luck.' And with that he ambled off down the garden path to the rear exit of Nos. 10 and 11, avoiding the waiting press photographers outside the main entrance.

Maudling was very likeable and extremely intelligent, with a first-rate mind and understanding of the workings of the economy. He was impatient with much conventional City wisdom and this led him into serious policy differences with the Earl of Cromer, who had shortly before become Governor of the Bank of England at the comparatively young age of forty-two. Neither approved of the other and I always believed this had adverse consequences for Reggie Maudling a year later, when he contested the leadership of the Conservative Party following Alec Douglas-Home's resignation. I met Maudling at a function on the day after he announced his challenge and asked him about his prospects of victory. I remarked that I was glad he had placed his hat in the ring, and his reply was again typical: 'Yes, but now I don't know what to do with it before it's kicked out again.' Reggie Maudling had many qualities that were needed in a leader of the Conservative Party, but he was too easy-going and uncritical of his business friends. When he spoke in the House of Commons he appeared to lack passion, but that did not mean he was without conviction. He was a generous man who could recognise that his opponents had a point of view even when he did not accept it, and this made him more acceptable to the Labour Party than some of his other colleagues. A man of great ability and understanding, but without the overwhelming drive and single-mindedness that was necessary to carry him to the Tory leadership in 1965. He was none the worse for that and I have little doubt that if he and Iain MacLeod had lived, they would have had small patience with Conservative policies after 1979.

Harold Wilson, George Brown and I held the first of our many meetings in the Cabinet Room on Saturday morning, 17 October 1964. From where I sat I could see the autumn colours in St James's Park, heightened by the bright sunshine, and I felt we were beginning a great adventure. We had discussed our early action often enough, and the first item on our informal agenda did not take long to dispose of. It was to decide formally whether to devalue the pound. We did not need to call in the officials for each of us knew before the Prime Minister began what our answer would be, and we quickly reached a unanimous conclusion to maintain sterling's exchange rate.

In view of the significant part sterling played in the fortunes of the 1964 Labour Government, it is noteworthy that our election manifesto made no mention of the issue. The only indirect reference was to the need to 'give priority to closing the trade gap' – a necessary but unstated condition for a strong currency. Our basic objective was to avoid a recurrence of the 'Stop-Go' economy which three times during the Tories' period of office had brought them into disrepute. Our remedy was to induce a high rate of industrial activity that would generate fresh investment, and encourage the modernisation of our industrial system. We would work with both sides of industry and stated without equivocation that we would introduce a national incomes policy as the best means of avoiding inflation.

Two new Ministries were set up to achieve these aims: a Department of Economic Affairs, headed by George Brown, and a Ministry of Technology under Frank Cousins, who was seconded from his job as General Secretary of the Transport and General Workers Union. Both men were dynamic, forceful and self-confident.

It did not seem unrealistic to aim for a high rate of growth, for this was in tune with what industry and the economists had been calling for. The International Organisation for Economic Cooperation and Development, comprising the world's major industrial nations, had set as a target for its members a growth rate of 50 per cent for the decade 1960–70. An incoming Labour Government after thirteen years in Opposition could not aim lower than that.

We knew that one major weakness in our plans was the tendency for imports to rise faster than exports because of a lack of competitiveness in British industry. There was little doubt that some parts of industry were under-financed, badly managed and technologically backward, and as an encouragement for them to do better my task was to overhaul the tax system so as to stimulate higher investment in new plant and machinery. Our objective was clear – to put right the failure of the United Kingdom to keep pace with the technological advance of Germany, Japan and America.

Twenty years later, the government is still saying much the same. Our analysis was correct in the early 1960s, but neither country nor government was then willing to face the degree of change that was necessary to put the situation right. I am not certain that we in government fully understood how big were the changes that would be required if Britain's industrial decline was to be reversed. It was not until British industry faced a worldwide recession in the early 1980s, whose adverse effects were accentuated by the Conservative Government's policy, that rigid ideas and practices were shaken loose. So far this has led to no improvement in the dreadful unemployment figures.

In 1964 we soon discovered that the decision to set up two new economic Ministries headed by two powerful Ministers created difficulties with the older Departments, and especially with the Treasury and the Board of Trade. Douglas Jay, who had become President of the Board of Trade, had foreseen this before we took office and had argued strongly against the creation of a Department of Economic Affairs. His view was that it was a fallacy, if a government Department (for example the Treasury) was not doing its job properly, to believe that you could solve the problem by creating another Department to do the job in its place. His experience during the Attlee Government was that this led to overlapping responsibilities, to ambiguity of function and eventually to frustration. He argued in a well-written memorandum that the right solution was to see that the responsible Department was led, organised and staffed to do its job properly.

He was right, but the Prime Minister had a problem of Cabinet balance and needed to satisfy the tremendous talents and energy of George Brown. I came to the conclusion that it was useless to oppose the creation of the DEA, and instead tried to ensure that there was a workable division of responsibility between the Treasury and the new Ministry. This was to take the form of a so-called 'Concordat', and immediately we took office, a small committee of officials was given responsibility to draft the outline. Sir William Armstrong, the Permanent Secretary to the Treasury, together with Sir Eric Roll and Donald MacDougall of the DEA were the main members; Secretary of the group was Peter Jay, who had married my eldest daughter, Margaret, and was at that time an outstanding young civil servant in the Treasury with a brilliant future ahead, had he not later resigned. He was at the time Private Secretary to the Permanent Secretary, Sir William Armstrong, and shortly after I became Chancellor of the Exchequer it was suggested to me that in view of the family connection, it might be in Peter's interest if he ceased to occupy such a sensitive post. Accordingly, he was moved to a much less interesting post in the Treasury. I should not have agreed to this.

Despite the assembled brainpower, several meetings failed to produce a formula for the Concordat that was acceptable to both George Brown and myself. This was not simply a case of *amour propre*. The problem was more fundamental and George Brown put his finger on it when he noted at the time that 'the problem of conflicting [economic] priorities lies at the bottom of our difficulties over drafting'. He rightly argued that because the responsibilities of the two Departments were different, they were bound to have a different set of priorities.

His solution was that both Departments should accept that responsibility for final decisions did not rest exclusively with the other. For some reasons that I could not follow, he believed that this made two Departments desirable. I believed otherwise. I argued that if the Government was to have any chance of succeeding it would be necessary, when there was disagreement, for an umpire to step in without delay to settle the differences. Only the Prime Minister had the authority to act in this manner, but experience was to show that as George and I continued to argue alternative courses of action, final decisions were sometimes too long delayed.

After many weeks we reached an agreed version of the 'Concordat'. The DEA was to be responsible for the long-term aspects of economic policy, for physical resources, incomes policy, economic growth, regional and industrial policy. George Brown would take over from me the chairmanship of the National Economic Development Council. The Treasury's responsibilities were for short-term economic policy and finance: the Budget, public expenditure, the balance of payments, exchange control and overseas financial relations. George had the better of the argument but the Concordat represented a verbal truce rather than a true meeting of minds with a genuine and rational division of responsibilities. The principal officials in the Treasury and the DEA tried to make the agreement work, but there were what the Americans call frequent 'turf fights'. It was sometimes said that No. 10 believed in something called 'creative tension' and that the friction between the Departments would produce the desired pearls. This was not my experience.

George Brown was dissatisfied almost from the start and he wrote later: 'It had to be laid down that the Department of Economic Affairs was the senior economic Ministry, and the Treasury would have to take on something of the style of a continental Ministry of Finance. The Prime Minister never did this.' Nor, I may add, would I have been willing to fill this role. In addition to his disagreements with me, George also found himself involved in similar disputes with Douglas Jay at the Board of Trade and Frank Cousins at the Ministry of Technology, some of whose functions he tried to absorb.

As time went by, the two principal Departments grew further apart. The Treasury began to regard the DEA as unrealistic, and the DEA considered the Treasury obstructive. Both had some right on their side, but both erred because Ministers failed to come to a clear and uncluttered conclusion on what our first priority should be. Should we begin by getting the balance of payments right and, subsequently, expand on the foundation of a secure sterling currency? This was my view. Alternatively, should we go full steam ahead with a fast rate of expansion in the hope that sterling would not be toppled? This was the policy of the DEA.

It could be argued that the decision which Harold Wilson, George Brown and I took at our first meeting committed the Government to getting the balance of payments right as our first objective. Certainly that was my conclusion. On the other hand, after we had won the second election in 1966 George Brown would be legitimately entitled to argue that there was a stronger case for devaluing, as the debilitating attacks on sterling did not cease.

We had been in office for only three weeks when the first large attack against sterling was launched from the Continent. It was in essence an attack by speculators which I had been half expecting and had believed I was mentally braced to overcome. But in all the offices I have held I have never experienced anything more frustrating than sitting at the Chancellor's desk watching our currency reserves gurgle down the plug-hole day by day and knowing that the drain could not be stopped. I could not even share the misery with others, because the market operators at the Bank of England insisted that the daily losses should be kept secret so that speculators would not know how much damage they were inflicting.

Each day turned into a game of bluff. It would begin with reports being placed on my desk in the early morning recording the amount of Continental sterling sales since, with the time difference, their foreign exchanges opened an hour before London. There might follow a lull until lunchtime when up-to-date figures of the morning selling in London and further sales on the continent would arrive. It was early afternoon in London before Wall Street got to work and early reports of their dealings would arrive at teatime. Finally, very late at night, there would come news from the Far East where they were already starting another day. The process never stopped.

It was like swimming in a heavy sea. As soon as we emerged from the buffeting of one wave, another would hit us before we could catch our breath. Whatever my inner feelings as the losses mounted, I must have outwardly looked more confident than I felt. Ian Bancroft (later Lord Bancroft and Head of the Civil Service), who was then my Private Secretary and an expert in psychological warfare, said to me in the House of Commons on one particularly bad day of heavy losses, 'Chancellor, why don't you go for a walk through the lobby and show them how composed you are?' He never told me subsequently whether he was being sardonic.

Other Chancellors during those post-war days of fixed exchange rates had experienced similar sensations, and Hugh Dalton in particular had told me how shaken he had been by the run on sterling in 1947. The loss of one tenth of one per cent in the value of sterling in those days was taken by the money markets to foreshadow calamity. In recent years, now that sterling is free to float upwards and downwards, no one seems to notice if sterling loses ten times that amount in a single day.

Not even the Cabinet were told the figures of the daily losses and I confided only in Harold Wilson and George Brown. George was somewhat detached for he had thrown himself into his Departmental affairs with tremendous zest, but Harold gave me unfailing support and encouragement, helping me through a most trying experience. I was very grateful to him.

After the Prime Minister, the First Secretary and I had taken the decision not to devalue on Saturday morning, a larger group of Ministers and officials from the Treasury, the Department of Economic Affairs and the Board of Trade met under George Brown's chairmanship in the afternoon. Our first conclusion was that with unemployment as low as 1.6 per cent, that is, 376,800, we should reduce the pressure on the economy, although George Brown asserted immediately that the slightest increase in unemployment would be politically intolerable. Our next decision was to prepare a national incomes policy. George urged me not to wait until the spring Budget before bringing in a new Capital Gains Tax but to do so immediately, as delay would hinder the acceptability of an incomes policy. It was further agreed that I should use fiscal means to encourage the private sector to use our scarce manpower resources more efficiently. Our next decision was to review the previous Government's priorities on public expenditure with the aims of switching resources from enterprises such as building Concorde and the TRS2 aircraft, whose costs were rapidly mounting, to other industries such as the motor car industry, whose leaders were crying out for labour. They informed us that they were being forced to decline export orders from overseas because of insufficient manpower. All these matters were at once taken up with the enthusiasm expected from Ministers who had been in the wilderness for thirteen years.

One of my first tasks was to establish contact with the United States Treasury. In the first of many telephone calls that passed between Douglas Dillon, its Secretary, and myself, I informed him that we had decided not to devalue. He was relieved at the news. With more than a touch of bravado I also told him that the United States could assume that despite our tiny majority the Government was planning to stay in office for a full five years.

Sir Alexander Johnston, the Chairman of the Board of Inland Revenue, came to see me and I informed him that I would need his help to bring in an immediate Budget and that, in the medium term, the Budget of April 1965 would contain substantial tax reforms, particularly a new Capital Gains Tax and a new Corporation Tax. It was my hope that an announcement of our intentions would buttress the discussion about an incomes policy on which George Brown was already embarking. The Chairman explained with great force the difficulties of such an inadequate period of preparation, but in response to my urgings, revenue officials did everything in their power during the ensuing months to meet the deadline I had given them.

I have already noted that the outgoing Conservative Government's reflationary programme had saddled us with large expenditures, and that in the months preceding the election I said in public speeches that no responsible Government could take on more commitments at the existing levels of taxation and saving. During the first week, therefore, I embarked on longer discussions with Treasury officials about what was to be done and found one of their main concerns was the prospect that defence expenditure would rise substantially in the years after 1964.

Our pre-election discussions had agreed in general terms that the Government should endeavour to reduce defence expenditure by disarmament agreements and economies in procurement of weapons. Treasury officials went further and argued for a reappraisal of the whole of Britain's overseas strategic commitments. This went rather against the grain; as a staunch supporter of the Commonwealth, I did not like to be brought up sharply against the costly realities of our worldwide role, but when I examined the figures I had to agree that officials should begin such a general review.

While I was busy with these matters George Brown worked flat out to prepare a considered statement on Britain's economic position. I had been unpleasantly surprised on arriving at the Treasury to find that estimates of the balance of payments deficit for 1964 were as high as £750 to £800 millions. By contrast, the deficit for the year before had been only £35 millions and there had actually been a surplus of £14 millions in 1962. Never previously had there been a deficit of such size, and it was clear that a large part of it was the result of the huge growth in imports caused by our predecessors' election boom. The Treasury forecast for 1965 was not much better as the best they could say was that the deficit would be somewhat less than £800 millions. The Prime Minister, George and I were agreed that, faced with the need to finance these two huge deficits, we should act at once to slow down imports and boost exports.

Days of intensive discussion followed in which Douglas Jay, as President of the Board of Trade, argued that the best control would be a restriction on the volume of imports entering the country. This had the advantage of being allowed by existing international agreements. On the other hand, George Brown and I argued for deterring imports by fiscal means. This method of restriction was not encouraged by international agreements, but he and I believed it was preferable because it would be less likely to restrict consumer choice or to freeze trade in particular channels.

The First Secretary and I carried the day and within a week he was ready with a scheme to impose a 15 per cent surcharge on all imports with the major exceptions of foodstuffs and raw materials. On the other side of the balance sheet, we planned to encourage exports by relieving exporters of part of the burden of indirect taxes. These schemes were included in a broader statement that covered other matters: our intention to begin immediate discussions with the TUC for an incomes policy; the establishment of a commission to keep price increases under review; and our intention to seek a joint review of the Concorde aircraft project with the French Government.

George Brown called a press conference in Church House, Westminster, on 26 October 1964, to announce these plans. He was the star and I attended in a supporting role. For the first time the country learned of the serious deficit of £800 millions. We emphasised this heavily as our justification for the import surcharge scheme – too heavily, as events were to show, for the health of the foreign exchange markets. The assembled press corps seized on the import surcharge and asked very searching questions which George handled with great bravura, though some of the detailed points had not been worked out.

Typical of the detailed questioning was that of a Dutch correspondent who asked me if imported tulip bulbs would be subject to the surcharge. I had no idea and skated around his question, but it was an early indication of the difficulties we would face. But the question that gave most indication of the storm that was about to break over our heads was whether we had consulted with other countries before making our announcement.

We replied that we had informed our trading partners but had not consulted them. This failure to consult was to be our undoing. In our enthusiasm we had tried to jump too many hurdles at once, despite warnings not to do so from Douglas Jay. In retrospect, it would have been much better to take longer over our initial moves and to have sought the understanding of other countries before we acted.

The Americans took no offence at the absence of consultation and gave us full support. Not so the European countries. Uproar ensued and they accused the Labour Government of every crime in the international calendar. They were aided and abetted by the Conservative Opposition, whose indignation was grossly overdone.

We had announced that the surcharge would be temporary and before long we were under pressure to say how long 'temporary' was. In the hope of regaining a little international goodwill we named a date for ending the scheme, but to no avail, for once the date was known, overseas comment began to speculate on the future of sterling if a large payments deficit still persisted at that point. The whole episode had an adverse effect on sterling's strength to which we had ourselves contributed.

At this time I received two significant visits. The first was from Jonkheer van Lennep, the Secretary of the European Monetary Committee, who suggested that it might be appropriate to devalue sterling by about 12 per cent if such a step could coincide with an agreed realignment of other currencies. But he did not explain whether other countries would agree and it seemed very unlikely that they would.

My second caller was Bob Roosa, the United States Under-Secretary of State for Monetary Affairs, who was strongly opposed to a sterling devaluation and gave me the reverse advice. He said there were whispers in Germany that the surcharge was a cover to prepare the way for devaluation and this was very unsettling. He was emphatic that an international currency realignment was impracticable and if the idea was floated the subsequent failure would be disastrous for the stability of the international monetary system.

Roosa was a very able banker who had been the originator of the so-called 'Roosa bonds', a device he invented to persuade European central banks to hold guaranteed American securities as a substitute for exchanging their dollars into United States gold. He was helpful and sympathetic about our import surcharge and urged me not to weaken sterling's role as a reserve currency.

Despite American help and support, from this time on we were never able finally to quash continual doubts and rumours about the British Government's commitment to maintain sterling's value. The Gnomes of Zurich took advantage of every piece of bad economic news in order to take a gamble against sterling maintaining its parity. We could have ridden out these squalls if our gold and dollar reserves had been adequate, but they were too exiguous to permit the Bank of England to ignore the raids.

General de Gaulle was one of the most unhelpful actors in this drama. His announced dual ambition was to end the role of sterling as a reserve currency and, more importantly, to bring down the mighty dollar. His method was to require the French central bank to offer the dollars in France's possession to America at regular intervals in exchange for gold. Under the terms of their undertaking, the United States Federal Reserve could not refuse these offers and America's gold stock, which had stood at such a high level at the end of the war, was continually depleted. Our own Government's policy was not assisted by some of our economic advisers who discussed the merits and demerits of devaluation with their academic friends as freely as if the Government were engaged in an interesting intellectual experiment, and not conducting the affairs of a great nation.

Among the Labour Party's election pledges was an undertaking to make a substantial increase in old-age pensions and to abolish charges for medicines. I was as much party to these promises as my other Cabinet colleagues and I had other improvements also in mind. One sprang from a personal piece of family background which had wider application. My mother was one of many widows whose husbands had died as a result of the First World War and the pension she had been awarded was tiny. There was also a particularly mean 'earnings' rule for widows who found work, as I knew from my experience in Cardiff. The rule was that for every shilling a widow earned over £8 a week, she suffered an equal deduction of one shilling from her pension. I was determined to remove these two injustices and did so in my first Budget on 11 November by abolishing the widow's earning rule and increasing the war widow's pension from ten to thirty shillings a week.

I had not overlooked the danger that speculators would seize on these measures as evidence of a lax attitude towards public expenditure, and my Budget also proposed that these and other concessions should be paid for by increasing income tax by 6d (2½p) in the pound, the duty on petrol by 6*d* a gallon and by an increase in National Insurance contributions.

The net effect of the Budget was probably slightly deflationary and the Conservative Spokesman, Reggie Maudling, admitted as much. I did not object to this because I wished to avoid the pressure of demand building up any further than I had found it on taking office. In view of the speculation about sterling I believed the Budget was a model of rectitude, but that was not how the speculators and foreign holders of sterling saw it. In their eyes the Labour Government was at fault for not cutting social benefits. They had excused Tory inaction because an election was approaching and they were inherently supportive of them, but they had no such indulgence for a Labour Government.

Foreign holders and speculators began selling sterling almost immediately after the Budget, and day by day the losses mounted. Friday was the worst day of the week because Continental bankers argued that if devaluation was planned it would take place at a weekend while the major markets were shut. Ten days after the Budget, speculative fever had mounted to such an extent that the Bank of England was forced to sell $180 millions on one day in the face of strong but baseless rumours about devaluation. Even Al Hayes and the New York Federal Reserve, which had been staunch in its support, was infected and half convinced that we were about to throw in the sponge.

The Prime Minister had called an informal meeting at Chequers for the weekend of 20 November 1964 to discuss future defence policy with the Chiefs of Staff. It was late on Friday evening when I arrived, bearing the figures of the day's losses. Lord Cromer, the Governor of the Bank of England, had advised earlier in the week that the bank rate should be increased by one per cent, and I had urged this on the First Secretary and the Prime Minister, but George Brown had been strongly opposed and no action was taken. Now it was clear that we must act and as soon as I had arrived at Chequers I returned to the charge. As so often, the delay meant that the necessary action was greater than it would have been had we acted earlier, and instead of an increase of one per cent we decided to increase the bank rate by 2 per cent. This was announced on the following Monday morning, 23 November, and those speculators who on the previous Friday had sold sterling they did not possess were caught short. When the market closed on Monday evening the Bank had recovered as much as $70 millions of the earlier losses.

On the next day, however, the speculators had second thoughts. It was said that the bank rate increase had been the Government's last desperate throw, and that devaluation was inevitable because our reserves were at a very low level and would soon disappear. These rumours spread quickly, and by noon on Tuesday 24 November Continental selling orders for sterling were once again flooding in from France and Germany. At the end of the day the Bank of England had not only lost all of Monday's gains but also a further $211 millions. If this continued our reserves would indeed soon be exhausted, and the Governor came hot-foot to see me on Tuesday evening, bringing the Deputy Governor, Leslie O'Brien, with him.

He was unusually emotional as he told me that we were facing a complete lack of overseas confidence in the Government's policies and were in a position of extreme crisis. He agreed that the policies themselves were perfectly sensible, but their piecemeal presentation – first the surcharge, next the Budget and later an increase in the bank rate – had lost the advantage they might have possessed had they been put forward at the same time. The markets had no confidence in a policy which increased social benefits ahead of measures to improve the balance of payments. The country was living too high on the hog at a time when overseas countries were looking to us for restraint. No government, he continued, could devalue sterling as a calculated act. It would be extremely irresponsible and Britain would have no friends left in the world. It was his opinion that the best way forward would be for the Government to introduce a real credit squeeze, together with legislation to remove trade union restrictive practices, a specific figure for restrictions in government expenditure and the abandonment of steel nationalisation. These measures would re-establish confidence.

The Deputy Governor was more restrained and the main thrust of his comments was that there was something fundamentally wrong with the economy, and that our actions so far had done little to put it right. As we had been in office for only five weeks at the time, I failed to see what fundamental improvement could have been expected and a fairly rough exchange followed between us which concluded with my saying that I would take them to see the Prime Minister immediately.

Harold Wilson has described what took place at that meeting, including his dramatic threat to ask for a dissolution of Parliament and seek a further general election. Lord Cromer pointed out that by the time a general election was held we should have no reserves left, to which the Prime Minister replied that in such an event sterling would be allowed to float. In the circumstances of those days this was akin to assailing the Holy

Grail, and the Governor fiercely said that a floating pound could precipitate a world financial crisis. Harold Wilson replied that as there was a general interest in preventing such a calamity, the world's central bankers should cooperate against the speculators.

Harold's threat of a further general election had a big impact on the Governor's attitude. I did not know on that evening that the alarm bells had already sounded on the other side of the Atlantic. Charles Coombes, the Director of the Foreign Exchange Operations for the New York Federal Reserve, has written about that day: 'On that morning of 24th November 1964, market traders were gripped by the immediate and exciting chance that sterling – and perhaps the Labour Government as well – might from one day to the next be toppled.' His own view was more objective. He went on to say that the few short weeks since Labour had taken office was not a long enough period to constitute a test of the efficacy of the Government's policies. 'It seemed to me,' he said, 'that the market was challenging not only the British Government's defence of sterling parity, but also the whole structure of international financial cooperation built up since Bretton Woods.'

Charlie Coombes explained the situation to his banking colleagues throughout the afternoon of the 24th in a telephone discussion that involved linking several reserve banks in the United States. He warned them that if Britain's reserves ran out and we were forced to devalue, the next step might be an extremely dangerous attack on the dollar. He recommended, and the American authorities agreed, that they should try to assemble during the next few hours a huge credit package of $2 billions to buy up any sterling that was offered in the markets and so prevent speculators from getting the upper hand. Immediately the decision was taken, Coombes informed Maurice Parsons, his opposite number in the Bank of England, adding that the Americans would take action when Britain requested them to do so.

I assume that this message had not arrived at the Bank when the Governor came to see me, for I was given no inkling of it. However, on his return from meeting the Prime Minister and myself, Lord Cromer got in touch with the New York Federal Reserve and told them, as Charles Coombes has recorded, that 'after consultations with the British Government, they (the Bank of England) were now prepared to go for a new credit package and would welcome our assistance'.

The Prime Minister had obviously made a deep impression on Lord Cromer. During the remainder of that night the Bank of England and the

Federal Reserve Bank of New York began a series of telephone calls to
their other central banking colleagues around the world. When they are
of a mind, central bankers move much faster than their governments do,
and within a matter of hours the coordinated activities of London and
New York had assembled credits from the central banks of eleven separate
countries for the huge sum of $3 billions, which they put at the disposal
of the Bank of England. The public announcement of this formidable
backing ended the feverish speculation of the previous day, as the speculators recognised that the odds against them had heavily increased.
Attacks on sterling fell away immediately, although they did not cease
entirely and were resumed from time to time.

One such occasion was early in 1965 when Kuwait, which up until
then had held its large reserves entirely in sterling, announced that it had
decided to replace 50 per cent of its holding with dollars. There was a
further flurry following a telephone call I received early one Saturday in
January 1965 from the French Finance Minister, Giscard D'Estaing, informing me that France was about to offer a large quantity of dollars to
the United States in order to acquire gold. Giscard was speaking under
instructions from President de Gaulle and emphasised that the French
action was not primarily directed against Britain, but expressed France's
dissatisfaction with the existing currency system and with America's role
in it.

Thankfully, as the winter of 1964/5 drew on, the feverish daily fluctuations of sterling, which had been my overwhelming concern almost from
the first day on which we assumed office, took up less of my attention. In
his biography of Frank Cousins, Geoffrey Goodman alleged that it was
'emphatically the case that American support for sterling was secured at
the price of tacit British acceptance of American action in Vietnam'. I do
not know what evidence exists to justify this statement, but equally
emphatically I must record that I encountered nothing said or implied
to this effect. The evidence is that American support for sterling arose
from the American perception of the threat to the dollar and to the international monetary system. It is surely significant that it was the Federal
Reserve Bank and the United States Treasury that made the running
and not the White House. Much later in 1967 I was to learn of an attempt
to make a specific link between American support for sterling and British
support for American policies, but when I learned of this I refused to
proceed.

George Brown and I had already met the General Council of the TUC, on 9 November 1964. We had told them of the seriousness of our balance of payments position and had said that this made an effective prices and incomes policy imperative, as the viable alternative to the now discredited policy of deflation. George did not ask for a wage freeze, but he sought a public statement from them of their willingness to agree that normal increases in earnings should be consistent with increases in productivity and the rate of economic growth.

The TUC's response was couched in equally general terms but was favourable in tone and reflected the general consensus in industry and elsewhere that the Government should take every possible step to solve the problems caused by the payments deficit other than putting the brake on production. Their veiled response was that the active cooperation of all sections of the industrial community was required and they 'were confident that trade unionists would respond readily to proposals by the Government'.

This was enough for George Brown. He plunged ahead with his usual energy and enthusiasm and by dint of private arm-twisting and public exhortation persuaded both the TUC and the leading organisations of employers to agree at a conference in December 1964 to launch a much-heralded joint approach by Government, employers and unions. Both sides of industry announced their intention to keep money incomes in line with increases in national output and to get rid of restrictive practices, at the same time guaranteeing workers a greater sense of security. For its part, the Government stated an intention to set up machinery to keep a continuous watch on the movement of prices and incomes of all kinds, and employers and unions jointly and formally undertook to cooperate in keeping wages, salaries and other forms of income in line. This statement of intent received widespread publicity and during the following twelve months became the touch-stone by which the success or otherwise of Government policy was judged.

Unfortunately, various groups were looking for different results. The foreign exchange markets and the employers watched to see whether incomes remained in line with national output. The TUC watched to see that nothing was allowed to interfere with a fast rate of economic growth. George Brown was vigilant lest decisions by the Government should give employers or trade unions the excuse that we were making it impossible for them to carry out their side of the bargain.

As Chancellor, I was put in the position of making up my mind about the Budget in April 1965 with no more than a statement of intent to guide me about the future levels of money incomes. Certainly, the Government had been given a promissory note which enjoyed the backing and active goodwill of the TUC, but there was a large element of doubt as to whether it would be honoured because it was vigorously opposed by the largest union, the TGWU, whose General Secretary, Frank Cousins, was a member of the Cabinet.

I decided that the April 1965 Budget could not ignore the undertakings that had been given by both sides of industry, for to have done so would have given the other parties an excuse to back away. I therefore threw all my weight behind George Brown's endeavours to turn the statement of intent into a reality. He gave it some credibility by setting up a Prices and Incomes Board under the chairmanship of Aubrey Jones, a former Conservative Cabinet Minister. Its remit was to examine undue increases in particular industries or companies but it was no more than a voluntary body and its influence was limited. He further announced at the time of the April 1965 Budget that the norm for income increases should be 3 to $3\frac{1}{2}$ per cent per annum.

A quarter of a century ago when Chancellors prepared their Budgets they consciously aimed at four separate targets – full employment, a high growth rate, steady prices and a balance in Britain's overseas payments – but they rarely if ever succeeded in hitting all four at once, for the Budget was partially an exercise in interpreting inaccurate Treasury forecasts and in diagnosing the subconscious. If, for example, the Chancellor's conclusion was that the economy should grow faster, was the best method to achieve this to reduce personal taxation? If so, would the extra in people's pockets be spent or saved? If spent, would the money go to home manufacturers or to imported goods? If it went to imports, would that drag our overseas payments balance into unacceptable deficit? He would also need to form an opinion on the right levels of increase in earnings to ensure stable prices, taking into account any increases in productivity. And so the questions flowed.

Treasury officials produced calculations and statistics of the recent past from which they would attempt to forecast the future. The most recent set of such figures would be placed before the Chancellor in February of each year and he would peer into the entrails. Harold Macmillan, who very sensibly occupied the post of Chancellor for less than a year, compared the preparation of a Budget to using last year's timetable to catch a train. And Derick Heathcoat Amory, who was Chancellor in the late 1950s, once told me that after he had pored over all the figures he would come to the conclusion that the only thing to do was to 'fly by the seat of of my pants'. We were all so much more innocent in those days. Nowadays there are computers and economic models, yet they still manage to get it dreadfully wrong.

There was a primitive form of control of the money supply through a system of special deposits by the commercial banks with the Bank of England, but this method was frowned upon and not thought to be as useful as moving interest rates up or down. Some even argued that it was a purely cosmetic device.

Having decided on his overall budgetary requirement, the Chancellor would embark on a series of discussions in early February and March with the junior Treasury Ministers and officials. Jack Diamond, the Chief Secretary to the Treasury, and Niall MacDermott shared the task with me. Jack's accountancy background and Niall MacDermott's legal training combined to produce a competent, loyal, hard-working team which successfully piloted through the House of Commons some controversial and complicated Finance Bills. Between them, they took a very heavy weight off my shoulders.

During the Budget's preparatory period, we would receive and consider scores of written representations and, in some cases, Ministers would meet with the more important interests to listen to their case for budgetary changes. The CBI and the TUC among other bodies always offered their own advice on the Budget's total shape and size. While this was happening, the Board of Inland Revenue and the Customs and Excise would be asked to submit various alternative proposals showing how much money could be raised by juggling with the tax rates, purchase tax, petrol duty and suchlike, and officials would calculate the impact of such alterations on the Retail Price Index. Once I had this information, it was my practice to have a session with the Prime Minister and the First Secretary and discuss the possible contenders for tax changes.

And then came the time of decision; a period when the Chancellor was visited by his officials at intervals as Budget Day drew nearer to warn him of the different cut-off dates by which he must decide on the various tax changes. Politely they would warn him if he overshot the cut-off dates Departments would not be able to make the necessary administrative arrangements, with the result that some decisions were taken a month or more ahead of Budget Day. By the time the newspaper commentators got around to offering their public thoughts, most of the major decisions had already been taken.

In deciding what had to be done, my colleagues and I went through days of intense self-questioning but my recollection is that once I had taken the final decisions and the die was cast, a quiet peace descended. For better or worse, there was nothing more I could do. The same could not be said for my officials. They were the recipients of written passages from other Ministers which they claimed were vital for my speech. My Private Secretary would winnow these and prepare a first draft. At the same time, other officials were already sending out instructions in heavily sealed envelopes marked 'TOP SECRET' to all those who would put the changes into motion on Budget Day. They prepared briefing notes and explanations for Jack Diamond, Niall MacDermott and myself so that we would be well armed to meet the British and overseas press and my television broadcast on Budget night.

My favourite interviewer was Robin Day, and I would send messages to the BBC asking that he should be given the task. I liked his tough manner of questioning and although he could be a bit of a bully if his victim seemed to flinch, I hardly ever found that he took unfair advantage.

On the day before a Budget, the Cabinet met and I disclosed my proposals to them. In those days, this was the first inkling most of the Cabinet had and they met at a time when it was too late to make changes. Although I took full advantage of this convention at the time I am in no doubt, in retrospect, that it was an unsatisfactory method and that things are better ordered nowadays. Much of the secrecy behind which the Chancellor sheltered to preserve his prerogatives was unnecessary and has rightly vanished.

During my period as Chancellor, Tony Crosland, Dick Crossman and other Cabinet Ministers sought greater opportunity to express their views prior to the preparation of the Budget and this pressure grew in the years following 1966. By the time I became Prime Minister ten years later, it was the custom for the Cabinet to have a full-dress discussion on Budget prospects in early spring, well before the time for taking final decisions. This was not only a means of preserving greater unity in the Cabinet but has been of benefit to the Chancellor's decisions. There are many matters of administration and policy that profit from open discussion before a Budget is launched.

An example from my own experience was the introduction of Corporation Tax in the 1965 Budget. This was a landmark in our fiscal history which, the accountancy profession declared, 'represents a prodigious feat of parliamentary administration'. I had announced the proposed outline of the changes in November 1964, and subsequently spent many hours discussing various important aspects with Inland Revenue officials. The purpose was to differentiate between the taxation of individuals and the taxation of companies, and to encourage the latter to undertake more capital investment. The changes also made tax-dodging rather more difficult. It was a complicated Bill and, in retrospect, our task would have been easier and we would have produced a better Bill if I had taken another year for a detailed discussion of our proposals by a Committee of the House of Commons. Members of Parliament could have examined officials of the Inland Revenue, heard evidence from bodies of accountants and other interested groups, and produced amendments based on their conclusions. In the days of which I write no such procedure existed and I must confess that after thirteen years in the wilderness I was impatient to succeed, and crammed on all sail, causing some mental sea-sickness among tax practitioners and others, who did not have sufficient time to familiarise themselves with the legislation before it became law. Inland Revenue officials performed miracles in order to meet my deadline and I cannot praise their efforts too highly. The Opposition fought fiercely against the new tax, and with our small majority, Jack Diamond and Niall MacDermott had a most difficult time. Eventually, the Finance Bill was passed only with the aid of the Parliamentary guillotine, yet despite all the sound and the fury, the essential structure of our Corporation Tax remains on the Statute Book, although there have of course been many amendments.

The Budget of April 1965 also included what Maudling had called a 'proper' Capital Gains Tax. Taken together, these two measures were probably the biggest tax changes of the century and the immediate effect was that my Budget speech was of record post-war length, namely two hours and twenty minutes, although this did not begin to match the four and three-quarter hours of Mr Gladstone's Budget in 1853.

The major income tax change was an increase of sixpence in the pound. This caused near apoplexy in some quarters of the City of London. A television programme showed one outraged City gent standing in Throgmorton Street and declaring that the Budget was 'a most disgusting attack on anyone who wants to make his way in the world. It's Marxism: they want a communist state. Personally, I shall fight like hell on the beaches, and on the streets and in the farms we will fight them.' Major-General Sir Edward Spears, the Chairman of the Institute of Directors, pronounced an equally daft verdict on the new Corporation Tax: 'Its purpose was to upset the whole of the capitalist system with the object of introducing a socialist state. It was a revolution to achieve exactly the same results that they did with the guillotine in 1790 in the French Revolution.' Such remarks revealed the implacable hostility of some elements in the City to the very existence of a Labour Government, but this absurd extremism brought a yawn from the rest of the nation which, as far as I could tell, took little notice. Public opinion polls said that on the whole the Budget was thought to be fair.

The General Council of the TUC issued a strong statement of support and I was very pleased to have letters of congratulation from Tony Crosland ('old Hugh [Dalton] would have been terrifically proud'), from Roy Jenkins ('a tremendous triumph') and a characteristic note from George Brown which I quote in full:

> *Storey's Gate, SW1*   13th April 1965
>
> Dear Jim,
> You must be feeling very pleased with the way the Budget has been received and, of course, with the way your own speeches have gone down. As I did not wholly agree with the make-up of the Budget I thought it only right I should tell you how glad I am at the outcome! The more so because I remember so vividly a meeting in my room at the House one Friday morning which now seems ages ago, when you were rather miserable and I told you that these things have a way of levelling themselves up and that I thought that certainly within six months relative publicity values would be totally changed. I obviously made my date with something to spare!
>
>   Yours
>   George

George could be generous as well as trying, and such spontaneity meant that he was never a lasting enemy. To balance these welcome notes, I should quote a critical letter which appeared in *The Times* during the same period: 'Sir, There have only been two sorts of Chancellors since the war – those who have left in disgrace and those who got out in time. Successive holders of the office have acted merely as book-keepers and traffic-light operators.'

Whilst I had been busy with the Budget, the First Secretary pressed ahead with the preparation of the National Plan, the first time in our history that such a huge task had been attempted. He persuaded, cajoled, and hectored both sides of industry to assist in its preparation, and chose the period 1964–70 for its fulfillment. His blue-print traced an analysis of available manpower, future hours of work, skill requirements and shortages, and possible productivity increases. It set down the Government's future public expenditure plans as well as projecting Government overseas spending. It based itself firmly on the need for an effective prices and incomes policy. Estimates of the level of investment and of exports and imports up to 1970 were set down, producing a balance of payments forecast which for 1970 showed a surplus of £270 millions.

The Plan then examined each major industry in turn. In the case of the chemical industry, for example, the First Secretary persuaded as many as 250 firms to supply estimates of their expected output, their manufactured requirements, their investment and their overseas trade for the following five years. The result was that the chemical industry forecast shortages of scientific manpower and technicians as well as probable delays caused by a shortage of capacity in the chemical plant industry. Under the heading 'Conditions for Growth' the Plan recommended the chemical industry to consider its future on a worldwide scale in planning the installation of future plant. The industry's own summary was that it could expand its output up to 1970 at a rate of 8 per cent per annum, increase its productivity by 59 per cent with a slightly smaller labour force, and double the level of its net exports. It reported that as a result of the discussions, management and workers' representatives both recognised their responsibilities for the changes that would be required, and were ready to implement them.

I recount this as one of many similar exercises that were undertaken for Britain's major industries. The critical element of the Plan was that each industry, in preparing its own report, was invited as its starting point to take a figure of 25 per cent as the projected growth of national output from 1964 to 1970. This figure implied an overall growth rate over the period of 3.8 per cent per annum. During the previous five years growth had been smaller at 2.75 per cent per annum.

The National Plan acknowledged the historic dilemma that fast growth was accompanied by huge overseas deficits, and George Brown admitted that this was the central challenge to the Plan's success. He founded the Plan on the expectation that if the Government set a fast but steady growth rate, then a low level of inflation and unemployment, with an agreed prices and incomes policy, would result in high increases in productivity, modernisation through more investment, and a fast increase in exports. This combination was expected to prevent the huge overseas deficits that had crippled previous attempts. The Labour Government was certainly not wrong to try – indeed, we had committed ourselves to do so during our thirteen years in Opposition.

The climate was right in which to make the attempt, as both sides of industry supported it. Treasury officials such as Sir William Armstrong were personally committed to the attempt to break out of our economic problems by achieving a fast growth rate, but when they examined the Department of Economic Affairs figures the Treasury's calculations showed that they did not add up to a consistent whole. In the Treasury we discussed our doubts and I decided to present them to the First Secretary. But my officials, like those of the DEA, were dealing with forecasts, not facts, and we could not prove that their figures would turn out wrong. We were dubbed half-hearted defeatists and George Brown's huge enthusiasm overbore any doubts when the Plan was launched. This over-optimism was a basic mistake which damned the Plan from the outset.

The other new Department, the Ministry of Technology under Frank Cousins, was also hard at work. Cousins understood the need for British industry to match its foreign counterparts in the use of modern technology and took up the issue with great zeal. One of his ideas was to set up an 'Industrial Reorganisation Corporation' but this fell foul of George Brown who claimed that such an important instrument should come under his own Department of Economic Affairs in addition to its control of prices and incomes policy. Frank Cousins offered fierce resistance but George Brown won. This was only one of a series of running battles on which a great amount of energy was expended.

These 'turf fights' took place because the newly-born DEA was anxious to establish once and for all a pre-eminent position against the other economic departments. So it fell foul not only of the new Ministry of Technology but also of older and longer established departments such as the Board of Trade.

There were strong personalities involved which the Prime Minister sought to reconcile or pacify. In his personal relationships, Harold is a kindly man who does not enjoy knocking heads together, nor does he easily ride roughshod over his colleagues' feelings. He has probably forgotten saying to me on one occasion when he had to ask a Minister to move to another Department: 'It has torn at my heart strings to move him.'

I believed him then and I still do. He was never a butcher. Although none of us would have been pleased, probably the only way in which the boundaries of the new Departments could have been settled would have been for the Prime Minister to have been ruthless in laying down the law.

He and I were in agreement that the National Plan would never get off the ground unless we could surmount the gyrations of sterling, and we frequently discussed what we could do in the short term to put an end to these. In June 1965 a visit from France's Finance Minister Giscard D'Estaing confirmed our view that President de Gaulle was after much bigger game than sterling. He confirmed that France would continue to exchange dollars for American gold and he argued that other countries would increasingly do the same. The gold exchange standard was doomed and would die a natural death. The French did not feel it necessary to put forward proposals designed to kill it off for once the existing system collapsed, the present gold price of $35 to the ounce would increase. Therefore, France was not willing to embark on a reform of the monetary system, although she would be ready to participate in a debate about the future. We must wait for the existing system to break down before the role of the reserve currencies would become clear. It was obvious that General de Gaulle would be unlikely to turn a receptive ear to any thoughts Britain might have of securing large credits on a ten- to twenty-year basis to put sterling out of danger and convince the speculators that they should abandon the game.

I suggested to the Prime Minister that I might visit the United States to talk to Henry 'Joe' Fowler, my opposite number at the United States Treasury. Harold agreed and sent a message to President Lyndon Johnson, asking him to see me in order that I might test whether there was any validity in a number of ideas that were being floated at the time, some more realistic than others.

On our side of the Atlantic, the most far-fetched unofficial proposal was for an amalgamation of the pound and the dollar so that the two currencies would become as one, and American and British financial policies would be effectively linked together. In the United States a proposal, again unofficial, had emerged under which the exchange rates of the dollar and the pound would be linked and both would float together against the Continental currencies. I record these ideas, not because I believed that they would have proved feasible in the form proposed, but because I was ready to examine any long-term viable solution that would have secured a breathing space and given the National Plan a chance.

I had seen enough to know that, despite the advantages Britain gained from the world's use of sterling as a reserve currency, there were counter-vailing serious disadvantages, and I was beyond the stage of believing that sterling's reserve role must be preserved at any cost. As time went on my problem was to persuade others to share sterling's reserve role with us, but this was something that neither the French nor the Germans were willing to do.

It was high summer in 1965 when I reached Washington. Joe Fowler was sympathetic to the idea of a large, multilateral long-term loan of several billions of dollars, but the United States Treasury was sensitive about launching something that looked like an Anglo-American plan, and proposed instead that Britain should take the initiative with the European countries. Joe said he would indicate that the United States would be willing to join in any plan that Europe could agree. This was not as helpful as I had wished. American influence with all the European states except France was still considerable enough for a joint scheme to have carried the day, if the Americans had been agreeable. In New York Al Hayes and his officials were sceptical of the success of an approach to Europe by Britain, and in the light of my talks with Giscard I could not disagree. Such talks would have been conducted in private but the number of governments involved would have resulted in rumours about the dis-cussions reaching the press and would have set off more speculation against sterling. If Britain were to be rebuffed, the effect on sterling would be horrendous and could easily force the devaluation we were seeking to prevent. I concluded that Joe Fowler and the United States Treasury were not sufficiently concerned about the effects of a sterling devaluation on the strength of the dollar to take any action. Joe Fowler was a modest, courteous, painstaking lawyer whose great asset to President Johnson was that he was respected by Congress, was popular and carried conviction with them and so managed to smooth the path of the President's Great Society budgets. There was no side about him, and when he flew the Atlantic he invariably travelled tourist class which caused some mild consternation among dignitaries who met him at airports. They would stand at the first-class cabin exit, waiting for Joe to appear, while he would hop out at the tourist end and take his place in the queue to go through immigration controls. He was a good servant of the United States.

The most memorable talk during my visit was with Bob MacNaramara, the Secretary for Defence. He had been a hard-driving President of the

Ford Motor Company, and carried these same attributes into the Pentagon. This was the first time we had met, and he took me aback by making a fierce onslaught on the Labour Government's overseas policy. He had obviously been well briefed on a recent Cabinet decision, taken only ten days before my visit, to limit defence expenditure to £2,000 millions a year by 1970. This was one of the results of the Defence Review that I had set in hand during my first weeks in the Treasury. He swept into the attack. Many aspects of British naval policies were luxuries, he said, and were no more than duplications of the naval fleet of the United States. Our government should realise that if we were to change our political commitments in order to keep within the £2,000 millions limit, for example by cutting back east of Suez, then the United States would have to reconsider its whole defence posture. The American Congress would not tolerate a situation in which the United States was the sole world policeman. The country was already overcommitted politically in Asia, and in no circumstances would it assume Britain's present responsibilities in countries like Malaya nor would it extend itself further in the Middle East. Other countries should do more to help themselves.

MacNamara had the element of surprise, as I had not been expecting this, but I responded rather tartly that Britain's overseas military expenditure as a percentage of our national product was much larger than that of the United States. Warming up, I added that Britain could not carry her present level of foreign exchange expenditure on defence and, as Chancellor, I would throw my weight against her doing so. If Britain was to be a sound ally of the United States then she must survive and prosper as a viable economic unit and it would be shortsighted if American officials did not understand this. With tongue in cheek, I said I had noted his views about the Royal Navy, and enquired if he had similar views to offer about the value of the Royal Air Force or the British Army. After these early broadsides we settled down to a more profitable discussion on how to minimise Britain's balance of payments problems. We discussed various possibilities such as building ships for the American Navy in British shipyards, moving military bases from France to Britain, and arranging better credit facilities for American equipment. Since that first meeting I have got to know Bob MacNamara well, and take no offence at his hard-hitting style. In later years his determination and drive served the developing countries well when he left the Pentagon and became President of the World Bank for Reconstruction and Development.

Joe Fowler took me to see President Johnson in the Oval Office at the

White House. Two or three television screens flickered but the sound was turned down, and L.B.J. literally bounded out of his chair to greet me. It was a most enjoyable interlude, but the President was in no mood to talk serious business. His chair in the Oval Office had been placed in such a way that he sat at a higher level than his visitors and he loomed over and leaned down at me. From this unequal position we gossiped for an hour, talking politics and telling anecdotes as he explained his method of handling awkward correspondents and sent for some of their letters for me to read. I listened to his exposition of the worries of the Texas cattle ranchers and the best method of handling small-town bankers, business-men and trade unionists: 'Bring 'em in and wrap your arms around them.' I felt that was what he was doing with me.

At one stage, he spoke with passion and determination about Vietnam. He expected a rough ride but he wished Britain to know that he would be careful and prudent in extending operations any further. He paid a generous tribute to the help he was getting from Australia and asked me to thank our Prime Minister for his efforts, which he hoped would be continued. The hour passed quickly but I had no opportunity to raise any serious financial matters as he relaxed and enjoyed himself. Our talk ended when his secretary prised him loose, but even then L.B.J. took me with him to greet a group of fifty high-school seniors who had been patiently waiting to meet him. Finally, he led me to the press conference that I was to hold and acted as Master of Ceremonies before he left. On subsequent occasions I have been received by other Presidents and had serious talks but I must confess that I have never since enjoyed such a rollicking afternoon in the Oval Office with so huge a personality – and one who, despite his faults, was a very warm-hearted and human man.

After the press conference we left for New York and as there were no engagements in the evening Chaim Raphael, the Treasury Press Officer, and I went to see a new musical, 'Fiddler on the Roof' with Zero Mostel in the lead. Raphael had been an Oxford don and his hobby was writing successful thrillers under a pseudonym. He is also a distinguished Jewish scholar, whose book *The Springs of Jewish Life* is one of the most compel-ling accounts of the dynamism of the Jewish people that I have read. Chaim is a good-humoured and lively companion and we enjoyed the performance. I saw it again later when it was produced in London, but it never reached the same level of perfection as in New York. We finished the evening at the 21 Club. Sitting at a nearby table was the former Vice-President, Richard Nixon, in company with Ginger Rogers. She made

my day, and the four of us sat talking politics and theatre for some time.
Three years later, Nixon won the 1968 Presidential election, so by coinci-
dence on the same day I had met both the sitting incumbent of the White
House and his successor.

My conversations in America showed that their officials were following
our economic progress very closely, and the firmness of Aubrey Jones's
reports on prices and incomes had created a good impression. His most
recent strictures had been directed at the road haulage industry, whose
plans for price increases were, he said, excessive. His report urged the
industry's customers to resist but neither his admonitions nor the exer-
tions of George Brown could keep prices and incomes within our targets
and as the summer wore on, Joe Fowler began to ask questions about the
prospects for our voluntary policies which I found increasingly hard to
answer.

A generally bad atmosphere developed in the foreign exchange markets
during June 1965. I could prevail upon the First Secretary to agree only
to some small steps to lessen the pressure in the economy, but with the
aid of a loan from the IMF and with the help of the United States
Federal Reserve, the attack on sterling was once more repelled. Joe
Fowler now began to display increased anxiety for the stability of the
dollar and told me of his concern about the American balance of payments. The Vietnam war was an increasingly heavy burden and the gold
drain from the United States was continuing. He told me frankly that if
sterling came down, the dollar would take its place in the front line and
be under attack. In this the interests of our two countries coincided. He
believed, as I did, that Britain could correct her situation without reducing
the exchange value of her currency if she took the necessary steps to keep
incomes in line with increased productivity.

I kept the Prime Minister and First Secretary fully informed and the
idea began to crystallise that the voluntary nature of Aubrey Jones's
Prices and Incomes Board should be strengthened by giving it statutory
powers to defer the operation of proposed price and wage increases, to
give the Board power to decide on these and enforce their decisions. Joe
Fowler encouraged me in this line of thought and we, in our turn, were
heartened when this possibility was reported in the press and resulted
in a favourable upward movement in sterling.

The TUC Annual Congress was due and George Brown, who had
now become convinced that the situation was serious, made a superhuman
effort to convince the General Council of the need to give the Prices and

Incomes Board statutory powers. The TUC swallowed their doubts and on the first day of the Congress, Monday 6 September 1965, adopted the Government's proposals. The state of Britain's economy was a perennial source of foreign press headlines and the remarkable turnabout of the TUC attracted favourable coverage in many countries and improved sentiment markedly.

The Federal Reserve Bank of New York and the Bank of England had previously made plans to take advantage of any favourable decision by the TUC Congress. Secretly they prepared a big offensive operation against the anti-sterling speculators, and quietly approached the central banks of other countries which, with the usual exception of France, agreed to join in the attack. They waited for four days after the TUC decision, and then on Friday 10 September at a pre-arranged time the New York Federal Reserve simultaneously placed massive orders with dealers offering to buy sterling from every major bank operating in New York at the prevailing exchange rate. The impact was stunning. Charles Coombes, the senior Vice-President of the Federal Reserve, masterminded the American end of the operation, and described the effect as 'electrifying'. Dealers were caught short, the sterling rate of exchange shot upwards within minutes, and many speculators who had sold sterling they did not possess were caught in an expensive trap when they were called upon to deliver.

The Federal Reserve and the Bank of England thrashed the speculators thoroughly and later cleaned up. Skilful operations on both sides of the Atlantic enabled the Bank of England to recover all the dollar losses it had incurred during a period of several months, and to repay the credits Britain had been given. After so many doleful Fridays, this was particularly satisfying. I stayed at the Treasury while the dollars flowed in. The immediate result was to put sterling beyond the reach of the speculators for many months to come, and I was not troubled again with daily figures of sterling losses until the spring of 1966.

Without the decision of the TUC Congress to accept the prices and incomes legislation, the two Banks would not have felt enough confidence to make their bold bid in the market, and although this was not their intended purpose the period of stability that was ushered in and which took sterling out of the headlines played a major part in helping the Labour Government to win its large majority in the subsequent general election in March 1966. We had the TUC, the Federal Reserve of New York and the Bank of England to thank for their parts. Even so, the prices and incomes legislation made slow progress in Parliament during the winter of 1965, and had not been completed by the time of the general election on 31 March 1966.

6

---

*The general election of 1966 – sterling's effect on the dollar –
strikes and the Six Day War – devaluation, 1967*

The timing of the general election, eighteen months after the indecisive result of 1964, was faultless, as was Harold Wilson's conduct of the campaign, and Labour cruised to victory. He turned a majority of one at the time of the election into a majority of ninety-seven, and we owed our victory to his tactical skill, his determination, his orchestration, and the confidence he conveyed to the electorate.

He asked me to take the lead at the daily press conferences because, he said, I had a safe pair of hands, and also in a television confrontation with Iain MacLeod, who had become Shadow Chancellor and was one of our most formidable opponents. With sterling out of the headlines, MacLeod knew he was on difficult territory with the Tory Party promising in the same breath both higher public expenditure and lower taxation. It was difficult to reconcile the two. He was on good ground when he criticised the different emphasis given to our economic problems by the DEA and the Treasury; and I was grateful to him for making no mischief about the currency. He strongly upheld the policy of not devaluing sterling.

During the election, the Government continued to enjoy a considerable psychological advantage. The Tory Party had not had long enough to live down the feeling of drift that accompanied their last years in office, whereas Labour was felt to be tackling the country's problems with fresh vigour, even if success had eluded us. I was able to report that exports were increasing far more quickly than imports (7 per cent against one per cent), partly due to the import surcharge. Unemployment was low and investment by industry was high and steady. Above all, in 1965 the dreaded visible trade deficit we had inherited in 1964 had been halved.

During my election speeches I repeated on several occasions that I could not promise an easy Budget when we won, and that the prospects were wide open. But I had given a hostage to fortune in my last speech in the Commons prior to the elections when I had said, 'I see no reason for severe increases in taxation this year. I use the word carefully.' I made

My father watchkeeping at Berry Head, Brixham, in July 1921. He died three months later from war service.

2 My mother in the 1930s. She was twice widowed by the age of forty-two: both her husbands served in the Royal Navy.

My sister, Dorothy, and I (aged twelve and four), taken in 1916 to send to my father in the Grand Fleet.

4 Myself aged twenty-one, or thereabouts.

5 Audrey when a student at college.

6 Ordinary Seaman Callaghan's Pay and Identity Book
– three shillings (15p) per day.

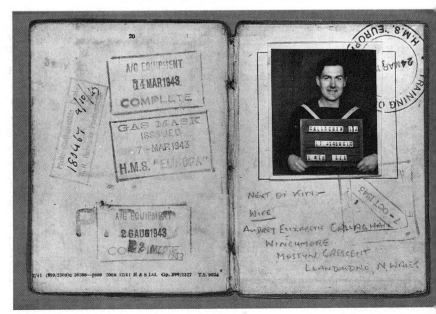

7 ABOVE: Carried shoulder high from City Hall, Cardiff, after the 1945 election victory. George Thomas and Hilary Marquand, who won the other Cardiff seats, are also in the picture.

8 BELOW: In Nigeria, the first Parliamentary delegation to the Empire after the war. Standing on the right of the Chief is Colonel J. J. Llewellin, leader of the delegation. On the Chief's left, Sir Edward Keeling (Twickenham), myself, and Cyril Dumpleton (St Albans) wearing a topee.

9 ABOVE: The railways still used horses in 1949. Presenting prizes at the Easter Parade at Broad Street Station.

10 RIGHT: Launching a road safety campaign in 1949 with the actress Linda Joyce to add glamour.

11 BELOW: Canvassing in Cardiff Docks in 1950, where I received strong support from the seafaring community.

12 ABOVE: The Board of Admiralty, 1950. Viscount Hall was
First Lord; Admiral Lord Fraser of North Cape,
First Sea Lord; Admiral Earl Mountbatten, Fourth Sea
Lord. On my left is Stoker Wally Edwards, Civil Lord.

13 BELOW: Visit to Supreme Allied Headquarters. Godfrey
Nicholson (Farnham) is on General Eisenhower's

right and I am on his left next to Air Chief Marshal
Hugh Saunders and General Al Gruenther, who
succeeded Ike. Standing next to Field Marshal
Montgomery is Tony Greenwood. Others include
Stanley "Featherbed" Evans, Roy Jenkins, Sir Cyril
Black, Dick Crossman, Frederic Bennett,
Tony Barber, Eddie Shackleton and Tony Crosland.

14 ABOVE: Hugh Dalton, the life and soul of the party, at a Fabian Easter School in 1953 with Tony and Hilary Crosland, Bill Rodgers (General Secretary), Audrey and me.

15 BELOW: On holiday in Pembrokeshire 1955. Margaret (sixteen), Julia (thirteen) and Michael (ten).

RIGHT: With Aneurin Bevan at the Scarborough Labour Party Conference, 1958.

BELOW: Clem Attlee in full fig at an LCC Reception in 1954. Audrey can just be seen on the left.

18 Hugh Gaitskell at the Brighton Conference in 1962,
the last before his untimely death. Harold Wilson was
Chairman of the Conference and George Brown, Deputy
Leader of the Party. At the back, Leonard Williams,
Party General Secretary.

no attempt to mislead, for I had called a meeting of top Treasury officials during February 1965 to begin our preparations for the Budget and my speech had reflected the consensus of view that was expressed by officials at that meeting.

Nevertheless, as Chancellors frequently discover, the rosy hues of dawn often give way to overcast skies by mid-morning, and I returned from the hustings to find longer faces at the Treasury; the forecasts had changed for the worse. I was naturally put out for I knew I would be accused of having misled Parliament, but I settled down to examine what taxation increases would cause least damage and be politically most acceptable. I was also anxious to continue with the programme of tax reform that had begun with Corporation Tax and Capital Gains Tax, and I had previously decided that the 1966 Budget should contain proposals to fortify the revenue with a new betting tax.

Forty years earlier, Winston Churchill had tried to raise revenue from this elusive source. 'I am not looking for trouble,' he said, 'I am looking for revenue.' But the bookmakers were too quick for him. Very little money was collected and the tax was repealed three years later. By the time I came to re-examine the idea, social attitudes had changed and legal betting shops were in existence. These provided a framework which made the taxation of betting a realistic proposition and I found the Customs and Excise officials, despite their earlier failure, full of confidence that legislation would be effective. Iain MacLeod as Shadow Chancellor thought otherwise, and in addition to his public arguments against the new impost, he privately sent me a copy of a very famous racing novel, *The Calendar*, written by Edgar Wallace in the 1920s, whose plot described how bookmakers had evaded Winston Churchill's levy. I enjoyed the book but was not convinced. There were shouts of 'wishful thinking' from the Opposition when I told the Commons that I expected the tax to bring in a reasonable amount of revenue, but the record confirms that view. Nearly a quarter of a century has passed and no Chancellor has repealed the tax which in 1985 brought in £745 million.

It was obvious that a new betting tax by itself would not bring in the revenue needed in the spring of 1966 but I was not anxious to increase the rate of income tax once again, and George Brown had strong objections to raising the duties on spirits and tobacco because these would increase the retail price index. I turned back to an idea that Professor Kaldor, my taxation adviser, had discussed with me during our days in Opposition. It built on a proposal that had been made by Selwyn Lloyd during his period as Chancellor of the Exchequer. His idea had been to increase the cost of the employee's National Insurance stamp and use the revenue from this as an economic regulator. Kaldor's idea was more sophisticated. He suggested that we impose on employers a flat-rate tax for every person they employed, but differentiate the tax so that it favoured manufacturing industry against the service industries.

The argument, as set out by him, was that Britain was suffering from manpower shortages in industry and that these held back the high rate of growth that we aimed for and which was necessary if we were to achieve our objective of fast growing exports. Therefore, by taxing services more heavily and relieving manufacturers, we would not only raise the revenue which was needed but would encourage the service industries to be more economical in their use of manpower. In the long run this might slow down their recruitment and so make more manpower available to industry. I daresay this seems hard to understand in the 1980s, given the collapse of some of Britain's basic industries and with more than three millions out of work.

The Treasury, the Inland Revenue, and the Customs and Excise went to work with a will and by a prodigious effort a scheme was ready for me to introduce in the Budget five weeks after election day. But I made a mistake in presentation that had an adverse effect on sterling. Instead of announcing the scheme early in my speech, I left it until near the end, to achieve a better effect. It was an indulgence a Chancellor should not permit himself. The foreign exchange markets had been expecting tax increases and became increasingly disappointed as the tickertapes flashing the progress of my speech were read. The first flash read that there would be no extra taxation on beer, tobacco and spirits. The next flash read that I ruled out increases in the purchase tax. Moments later, they heard I intended no increase in income tax. The exchanges did not wait to hear more. They made up their minds that this was a bad Budget, and when a little later I announced my proposals for the Selective Employment Tax, they entirely ignored them and did not wait to judge their intended effect.

Purchases of sterling began to dry up and after a day or two of hesitation, selling began. We might have recovered from this, but nine days later came another blow that set the sterling rate sliding fast. British seamen went on strike and dramatic television pictures appeared abroad and at home of ships tied up by the quayside, silent docks, and stationary cranes. The strike lasted for seven weeks, during which there were intensive and prolonged waves of sterling sales overseas. The central banks took a more rational view of our longer-term prospects and once more halted the drain by assembling a billion-pound dollar credit package, specifically designed to protect sterling's position as a reserve currency. Nevertheless, the seamen's strike was to weaken us in the long run.

The first day of July 1966 was a significant day. The seamen's strike came to an end; the Government published its Bill to nationalise iron and steel; Lord Cromer retired as Governor of the Bank of England and Leslie O'Brien, the Deputy Governor, succeeded him. Lord Cromer had tendered his resignation to me five months earlier, in advance of the general election, but had suggested that in order to avoid any upset in the currency markets during a nervy period, the announcement should be delayed until the election was over. He had not been happy working with the Labour Government, and we had had many disagreements. He expressed his opinions very frankly but was never less than courteous, and the high opinion in which he was held by overseas central bankers helped us enormously in the difficult negotiations he conducted to secure substantial international credits to support sterling. Our politics differed greatly but we have remained on good personal terms ever since those stormy days nearly a quarter of a century ago.

I was attracted to the idea of Leslie O'Brien taking Lord Cromer's place as Governor, for he had entered the Bank of England on the bottom rung without the advantage of family or school. He had become an expert professional and I could see nobody in the City who would do the Governor's job better so I recommended him strongly to the Prime Minister who was of the same mind. I invited him to come and see me and offered him the post. He sat back in astonishment. 'I thought you had asked me here to tell me who you had decided on and ask me to continue serving as Deputy Governor!' And after a moment, 'May I ring Isabel?', his wife. I never regretted our decision. Modest, quiet, considerate of the views of others but firm in his own beliefs, he was technically proficient and donned Lord Cromer's mantle with ease. The Americans called him a 'tough little scrapper'.

On the morning of 1 July the Prime Minister, the First Secretary and I had met in the Cabinet Room for a discussion on longer-range strategic planning and the use we should make of the forthcoming visit of M. Pompidou, the Prime Minister of France. We agreed to carry our discussions about joining the European Community a stage further to test his reactions, and the First Secretary undertook to have a paper prepared. Our conversation then turned to the outlook for the domestic economy, and the Prime Minister asked if I expected to come to Cabinet with any fresh economic measures before the recess four weeks later. With the seamen's strike ending that day, I replied that I hoped and expected we would get through the rest of the summer without any need for further measures, and that by September the collection of the Selective Employment Tax would have begun and would be biting rather hard. The economy was not overheated.

Such is the frailty of a Chancellor's hopes and forecasts. I had scarcely left the Cabinet Room and returned to the Treasury when I learned that serious selling of sterling had begun that very morning, despite the ending of the seamen's dispute. Two days later Frank Cousins, the Minister of Technology, resigned from the Cabinet, and the monthly figure showing the size of Britain's reserves was published, which, because of the seamen's strike, showed a considerable fall. Cousins' departure was serious because he was known to be opposed to the Government's prices and incomes policy and it was assumed that he would be a powerful reinforcement to those who sought to reverse the TUC's support. In America, where these events were watched very closely, news of Cousin's resignation proved particularly disturbing to market confidence.

'When sorrows come, they come not single spies but in battalions.' The French Prime Minister and the Foreign Secretary, Couve de Murville, delivered the next blow when they came to London for bilateral talks. Pompidou's manner was cordial but the content of his remarks was uncompromising. We began with the Common Market and under the guise of a lengthy historical disquisition on the development of French economic history during the preceding decade, it was clear that he expected us to draw the moral that if Britain was to be in an economically healthy state to join the European Community we would need, as France had done, to devalue our currency and combine such action with a further large dose of deflation. Pompidou was expansive; Couve his usual austere self, adding little to the exchanges; and George Brown by turns persuasive, abrasive and effusive. When they returned to Paris, the French acquainted the press with the kernel of their remarks, which fitted into de Gaulle's bigger strategy for breaking up the dollar/sterling reserve currency axis, and sales of sterling grew larger in anticipation of devaluation.

Prime Minister Pompidou's lecture changed George Brown's mind.

Despite his early staunch defence of the sterling parity, I knew that he had growing doubts about the policy and the talks with the French convinced him that we should not continue to hold the parity at $2.80 to the pound. He broached the subject in his most sober and impressive mood over dinner at his flat. Our destiny lay with Europe and he wished me to devalue in order to secure a quick entry into the Community. This was George the statesman, but George the politician was never far behind, and he would not entertain my argument that if devaluation was to be successful, it must be accompanied by a measure of deflation. So there was stalemate.

At about this time, estimates for the rest of the year's balance of payments became available. Our original estimates for 1966 had forecast a deficit of about £100 millions, which could easily have been financed, but as we neared the finishing-post the deficit grew larger and in July 1966 the figure had been revised to £350 millions. This was as high as the 1965 deficit and would be liable to have an adverse effect when it became known.

I intended to report this estimate to the Cabinet but the Prime Minister asked me not to give a figure, but to say only that the underlying deficit was not improving fast enough. There was a case for this in the sense that the forecasts were not at all reliable, although they were the best the Treasury could produce. I accepted this request unhappily. As Chancellor, my complaint was that we usually interpreted figures in the most optimistic way, even when sufficient justification did not exist. Later, in answer to a question in the House, I made it clear without giving a figure that the Government expected a trade deficit, and this accentuated the run on sterling, which in turn provoked dissension between Harold, George and me as to whether action should be taken to stem the flow. I made proposals for a substantial cut in overseas defence expenditure and a reduction in the Civil Service, coupled with a tightening of hire purchase restrictions. George would have none of these and the only matter on which we could agree was to increase the bank rate by one per cent, which turned out to be too little, too late.

My concern grew for we were losing tens of millions of dollars and our dollar reserves were approaching danger point. For the first time since I had become Chancellor in 1964, I began to feel that our inability to reach crucial decisions was making devaluation inevitable. Yet I also knew that if there was a forced devaluation there was a strong likelihood that the Cabinet would not accept the restrictions that should accompany it. On the contrary, some Ministers in discussion seemed to believe that devaluation would spell a blessed release from bondage and from the budgetary constraints that had hampered them in carrying out their plans. Robert Neild and Nicky Kaldor, my two advisers, had always been in favour of devaluation although, unlike some Ministers, neither of them had any illusion that the British people could escape from the consequential lower standard of living. The subject had become an unspoken obstacle to a totally frank exchange of views, but I was depressed and felt the need to talk. On 13 July I had a long talk with them, accompanied by the Permanent Secretary, Sir William Armstrong, and my Private Secretary, Ian Bancroft. The floodgates opened and we talked without reserve. George Brown had at last given a measure of agreement to a package of measures to stop the outflow of dollars but as we talked, I found we all shared the same view that they would be quite inadequate for the purpose. We would be embarking on deflation without a clear objective.

The Prime Minister called a further meeting with the First Secretary and myself but we could not agree, and in the end we decided to make only a general statement, indicating our intention to bring forward new measures at a later date but giving no immediate details. This was done on 14 July. The announcement went down like a lead balloon.

Our respective positions at this time could be summed up as follows: the Prime Minister was opposed to devaluation but understandably disliked being pushed by irrational foreign exchange markets and speculators into taking action that he believed was unnecessarily harmful to the domestic economy. The First Secretary had turned in favour of immediate devaluation, and therefore tactically opposed any fiscal or other measures that might prevent it. I was strongly against devaluation, and believed it could be avoided, but I reluctantly concluded that our lack of action was rendering it inevitable.

Twenty-four hours later the situation had worsened, with further losses, and the Prime Minister came to the overnight conclusion that far-reaching measures must be taken immediately. This at once resolved my doubts about our capacity to sustain the exchange rate, but George continued to argue strongly and considerable tension built up. Not unnaturally, the Cabinet became aware of these differences. The Prime Minister left for Moscow for a brief 48-hour visit to attend the British Trade Fair, and during his weekend absence there seem to have been exchanges between Ministers that led to a demand by the Cabinet for a full review of the way the three of us were handling the economy.

Audrey and I were in the country during the weekend, staying with our friends Gordon and Violet Dennis, and as no one knew where I was I escaped any approaches from other Ministers. Thanks to some highly impressionistic information conveyed by George Wigg, the Paymaster General, to the Prime Minister on his return, he however believed that a plot was being hatched to replace him as Prime Minister. I did not and do not believe this was true. There was certainly unrest in the Cabinet and a number of rather feverish consultations about the health of sterling and the economy, and these resulted in a temporary coalition of convenience between some of the left-inclined and the right-leaning members of the Cabinet.

Harold called an evening Cabinet as soon as he returned from Moscow, on 19 July, and the meeting took place in a tense atmosphere and lasted for nearly five hours. For the first time since 1964 he launched into a full discussion on the merits of devaluation as an alternative to an economic package prepared by me but not agreed upon by the Prime Minister and George Brown. This new package included items such as tightening hire purchase controls, a 10 per cent increase in the duties on drink, tobacco, petrol and purchase tax, a 10 per cent surcharge on surtax and a cut of at least £100 millions in military and civil overseas expenditure. The package was striking in itself, but not as startling as the additional proposal facing the Cabinet for a total standstill on prices, wages and salaries for a six-month period.

I had no doubt that if the Cabinet agreed all these measures there would be no need to devalue sterling, and at the meeting I set out the case strongly. George Brown rebutted it with equal vigour and argued the case for devaluation. He said he wished to make a 'breakthrough', a phrase that conjured up an attractive image but did not represent the reality that our post-devaluation situation would be as harsh as the present one. Having made his case, George then announced that he would reserve his position and sat silently for most of the evening. The Prime Minister invited every Minister to express his view. We went round the table, one by one. Six were in favour of devaluation – George Brown, Roy Jenkins, Dick Crossman, Tony Crosland, Barbara Castle and Tony Benn. The remaining seventeen, including Harold Wilson, Denis Healey and myself, were opposed. The economic package was the preferred option and on the following day the Prime Minister announced it to the House of Commons.

The newspapers were well aware of our differences, and their headlines helped to fan the feverish atmosphere. The Tory Front Bench also joined in and Mr Heath announced that the Government was in the worst crisis since 1951. Typical of the speculation was a report that if overseas defence expenditure was cut Denis Healey and the Chiefs of Staff might resign in protest. There was no truth in this. Harold Wilson was even attacked for using the weekend to visit the Moscow trade fair, the main purpose of which was to sell British exports. Many British businesses exhibited there, and Mr Kosygin, the Soviet Prime Minister, had himself visited the exhibition with Harold Wilson. Eager hands reached for every stick to beat us, although we were spared the Tory Front Bench and the editorial writers advocating devaluation as a solution.

During the 1960s the pound sterling sign had been turned into a symbol of national pride, only somewhat lower than pride in the national flag, and no matter how compelling the arguments of the economists, press and public regarded devaluation as a major blow to Britain's prestige and a serious defeat for the Government. The possibility of this had been freely touted and the House was expectant when the Prime Minister rose to make his statement, the Chamber crowded with Members standing in a solid mass at the bar. The Opposition were jubilant, and ready for the kill. Our supporters were dejected, for in addition to our other woes, a bye-election in Carmarthen had taken place and we had lost Megan Lloyd-George's seat to Gwynfor Evans, the President of Plaid Cymru.

Harold Wilson was a fighter who never lacked courage when his back was to the wall, and he needed every ounce of willpower, for the anger and noise of the Opposition exceeded anything I had heard since the terrible Suez debates ten years before. I sat beside him for such moral support as I could offer, and as he answered question after question I could feel the atmosphere begin to change. After a time the storm in the Chamber blew itself out. I regarded the statement as my responsibility and had pressed him to allow me to make it, but he insisted on doing it himself, partly to protect me and partly perhaps wishing to prevent any intensification of my differences with George Brown. As soon as Harold Wilson had resumed his seat, I left the Chamber in the knowledge that he had won the day, to prepare for a flight to Bonn.

This visit had been planned as part of my campaign to reduce our defence expenditure by securing a larger payment from the West German Government to cover some of the heavy and increasing costs of maintaining the British Army of the Rhine. Our Ambassador, Sir Frank Roberts, had invited Herr Blessing, the President of the Bundesbank, to be among the guests at dinner, and when I arrived Herr Blessing received me with a beaming smile. He had been given an account of the Prime Minister's statement in the House of Commons, and he told me with great enthusiasm that if we could carry through the measures that had been announced, sterling would be secure. He was anxious I should know that as a measure of Germany's confidence, he had that evening given instructions that the Bundesbank should be ready to sell German DM and purchase sterling to any necessary quantity to stabilise the sterling exchange rate as soon as the foreign exchange markets opened the next morning. With this encouragement and with similar messages of support being sent by other countries, I believed sterling was set fair for a strong recovery. Once more I was disappointed.

Two events marred the next day. News reached the Continent that the First Secretary had carried out his implied threat at the Cabinet meeting and had submitted his resignation. Later we heard that he had withdrawn it, following a talk with the Prime Minister, but this did not undo the damage. I missed the drama of the night, but awoke early in the morning and lay listening to the mournful sound of the Rhine barges, fitting my mood, as they chugged past my bedroom window in the Ambassador's Residence. I had hardly recovered when further news came that our former colleague Frank Cousins had announced in his resumed capacity as General Secretary of the TGWU, the largest union in the country, that he would not cooperate with the wage freeze. This resulted in a further setback for sterling in Continental markets, for they regarded an effective prices and incomes policy as a touchstone by which British prospects should be measured. Although overseas holders of sterling had undoubtedly been impressed by the voluntary declaration of intent signed by the employers and the trade unions, they were disillusioned by the results, as I was myself, for in the twelve months up to July 1966 earnings had increased by 8 per cent per annum but productivity had only gone up by 1.5 per cent. It was obvious that Britain's competitive position had been further eroded.

The news of Frank Cousins' declaration and the prospect of a revolt by the TUC led the Americans in particular to prepare a contingency plan to protect the dollar in case the trade unions' attitude resulted in sterling devaluation, but as the weeks went by and the prices and incomes freeze held firm, sterling began to recover. The policy was generally accepted by the country, because it was seen to apply to all, but both unions and employers regarded it with distaste.

George Brown, having decided to stay in the Government, threw all his famous energy into persuading Parliament to pass the prices and incomes legislation. Day after day and night after night, he never spared himself and I admired his stamina and commitment. I did not know then that the Prime Minister had promised that once the legislation was complete, he and Michael Stewart would exchange posts and that George would achieve his long-standing ambition to become Foreign Secretary. The thought that his labours at the Department of Economic Affairs would soon be ended must have spurred him on.

With Michael Stewart's arrival at the DEA it seemed to me to be the right moment to make an attempt to redefine the unsatisfactory division of responsibility between his Department and the Treasury, and I asked to see the Prime Minister. Normally, there was no difficulty when I wished to see Harold. It is well known that between the Chancellor's residence at No. 11 Downing Street and No. 10 there is an internal communicating door which was always unlocked, and either of us could walk through to the other. In the House of Commons, the Prime Minister's room and the Chancellor of the Exchequer's room also adjoin. Unfortunately for me, I had given an interview a day or two before to William Davis, the Financial Editor of the *Guardian*, which had displeased the Prime Minister. I had replied to one question by saying that I thought a period of two years at the Treasury was long enough, and that I would be ready for a change in the autumn. Davis had responded by suggesting that the Foreign Office would be a suitable alternative, and I had incautiously agreed, although I had given no serious thought to this or any other Cabinet post. The interview when written made it seem as though the proposition had come from me and had been interpreted at No. 10 as meaning that I was manoeuvring to become Foreign Secretary.

No Prime Minister cares to have his freedom of choice circumscribed, and I of course did not know of Harold's offer to the First Secretary. I became aware of a certain coolness and when I asked to see the Prime Minister there was an unusual silence. The evening newspapers appeared on my desk with accounts that Michael Stewart and the Department of Economic Affairs were to occupy the role they had during George Brown's regime, and it appeared that my intention to talk the matter over with the Prime Minister had been pre-empted. After waiting for a few more hours, I wrote a note to Harold telling him of my frustration, and this produced an immediate call to see him in the House of Commons. He was seated alone at the table, eating a meagre cold supper from a tray, and was obviously very tired. I at once launched into the same, well-trodden argument that I had pursued on other occasions.

It ran like this: the division of economic responsibility and the effort needed to get agreement with George Brown and sometimes to overcome his opposition often lost the Government vital days when quick decisions were needed on operational matters concerning the Bank of England or the Board of Trade. Sometimes the delays cost us heavily in the foreign exchange markets. At other times we spoke with different voices. The Prime Minister would remember, I continued, that I had told him when we were in Opposition that the arrangement would not work. But subsequently when we were elected with a bare majority of three, I had promised to do my best. The experience had convinced me however, that my initial reactions were correct, and the position was now more stable because we had a large majority. Although Michael Stewart would be an easier colleague to work with, I was not prepared to go through the frustrations which would exist as long as the unsatisfactory division of responsibility between the two Departments continued.

I remained standing whilst I delivered myself of this demarche, for I was determined not to be side-tracked. But Harold, as so often, disarmed me. He looked up from the table. 'Sit down, Jim,' he said. 'I am in great trouble, and I must tell you about the events of the last fortnight,' and before I could interrupt he swept on with a detailed account of how his own position as Prime Minister had been placed in great jeopardy during the weekend of his visit to the Moscow Trade Fair. He elaborated in great detail on the colleagues who were involved, but exonerated me of any knowledge of the so-called 'plot': 'You were on the side of the angels.'

Eventually, when I could interrupt, I said that such plotting was 'pure parlour politics', and there was no one who could replace him, no matter what criticisms existed of his leadership. I told him that was not the way the Party worked, and I was rather curt about the little group of tale-bearers who seemed to have his ear. With some difficulty, I got the conversation back to the issue, and eventually he suggested that a solution might be to bracket Michael Stewart and me together as third in order of precedence in the Cabinet, following himself and George Brown, the Foreign Secretary. But I was concerned about status only inasmuch as it would enable me to secure a unified and coherent approach to our economic affairs, and his suggestion would not do this. We needed a new definition of responsibility. I continued to argue but got no further so I climbed on my high horse and said I must resign.

Poor Harold must have been exasperated. He must have had enough of major colleagues threatening to resign or doing so, but he had an almost inexhaustible supply of patience, and pointed out that I would never forgive myself if I resigned whilst sterling was in a parlous state. This called my bluff, but I recovered sufficiently to say that because of the economic measures, sterling would be much steadier by the autumn and I would therefore wait until the IMF meeting had taken place at the end of September, and the Party Conference was over. But, I said, unless the responsibilities of the DEA and the Treasury were clearly delineated by then, I would not be willing to go on. The Prime Minister said he had already told Michael Stewart that in the future the DEA should concentrate on increasing productivity, and there should be fewer clashes than in the past. He promised that we would have a further talk after the holidays, and with this he departed for the Scillies and I for the Isle of Wight.

On our return, I sought out Michael Stewart. He and I were old friends, and I explained why my experience had led me to conclude that the existing arrangements would not work. I set out my view that the issue which most mattered for the survival of the Government was how we handled the economy in the short run, for unless this succeeded there would be no long run and the National Plan for which he was now responsible would be aborted. I also told him of my disbelief that the National Plan's forecasts for the balance of payments in 1970 were practicable. Michael was a good listener with calm judgement, and at the end of a serious and rational conversation he said that he had not been long enough at the Department of Economic Affairs to form his own views, and would reserve his opinion. Meantime, he hoped we would be able to work together.

I then saw the Prime Minister, who had returned from his holiday fresh and invigorated. But I found him unyielding. He said he remained of the same mind as earlier. I said: 'So do I.' There followed some flattering remarks that if he fell under a bus, the Party would elect me as Leader, although he added with a typical flash: 'Mind you, I take good care not to go near a bus nowadays.' He urged me to remain as Chancellor and prepare the 1967 Budget, and if I would do so he volunteered to work out a new concordat between the Treasury and the DEA, adding that he would give instructions to officials to do this. I returned to the Treasury to tell my officials to be ready to join in talks to work out the new arrangement, but nothing more was heard. As time went by, Michael Stewart and I sorted matters out informally between ourselves. Perhaps that was what the Prime Minister intended all along.

It was unfortunate for Harold that some of those around him felt so insecure that they fed on a regular diet of conspiracies against the Prime Minister. There was sometimes some smoke, but very little fire. Amongst others Cecil King, the Chairman of the Daily Mirror Group, tried his hand at replacing the Prime Minister, but it was no more than a piece of amateur theatre. Dick Crossman, who had an inventive mind, even affected to believe at one moment that I was in league with some unnamed group in the City of London to bring about a national government under my leadership. If the suggestion had come from anyone else I would have been insulted but Crossman's diaries reveal his obsessional search for hidden motives behind the most transparent actions of his colleagues. This trait was a singular weakness in a powerful intellect, and the passion for conspiratorial politics which he shared with George Wigg and some others had a divisive and weakening effect on Cabinet unity.

I would not claim that the prices and incomes freeze was ever popular, but there was no general upsurge of revolt and the average trade unionist was prepared to acquiesce for a period. Some trade union activists set out to fan the embers of discontent, but we might still have hoped to maintain the policy on a voluntary basis had Clive Jenkins, the General Secretary of the Supervisory Staffs Union, not taken a case on behalf of one of his members to the county court, asking for a judgement on whether a wage increase which had been promised during the period of the freeze should be paid. On 29 September 1966, at the very moment that the Labour Party Conference was foregathering at Brighton, the court gave a decision in his favour. This decision opened the way for countless similar cases which would effectively have ended the freeze, and Michael Stewart had to consider the disagreeable option of abandoning the voluntary basis and activating powers in the statute which would make the freeze legally binding.

The Prime Minister called a meeting of the full Cabinet in the Grand Hotel, Brighton, on Monday evening at the end of the first day's conference proceedings. In the light of Michael's report, we decided quickly but regretfully to exercise the Government's powers of compulsion. The arrangements for the conference had provided for a full day's debate on prices and incomes, and we were conscious that our decision could provoke an explosion among the delegates. Michael Stewart was not a member of the National Executive Committee, and it was ruled that he could not handle the debate for the platform. This weakened the Government's position unnecessarily, and was not even justified by precedent, for Ernie Bevin had replied in similar circumstances to a debate on foreign affairs during the days of the Attlee Government. George Brown was, of course, best qualified to speak, and was a member of the Executive Committee, but he had opted to handle the foreign affairs discussion at conference, so the lot fell upon me.

Both Clive Jenkins and Frank Cousins were due to move hostile motions on behalf of their unions condemning the Government's policy. I decided to attack. I argued that if a pay standstill was to operate, it must apply to all, including the better paid. There had been widespread acceptance of the standstill, and if that had been universal the voluntary system could have been preserved. But some said publicly: 'We will challenge the Government at every opportunity and exert our legal rights to the full.' I went on that this attitude faced the Government with a hard choice, for if a trade union which refused to cooperate was left to go its own way, no other union would be able to justify to its members why they should stand back. That would mean the prices and pay standstill was effectively at an end. 'That is what some people want; that is why they issued the challenge. They are unwilling to stand back and some of the most vociferous, who are also some of the most highly paid, are determined that nothing will stop them.' This reference to Clive Jenkins and his members met with loud applause from the delegates, showing that the Government's position was not without support.

Clive Jenkins followed me immediately. His colourful personality and gift for a phrase always attracted the attention of the press and, anticipating a noisy row, the photographers crowded around him, holding up the proceedings. He made ironic play with the contradictions in the Government's position but although the Conference delegates laughed at his wit, they maintained a stubborn commonsense and he did not win their sympathy. There was much private criticism because his union had appealed to the courts, and at the end of the debate the Government's policy was upheld by a substantial majority of 4.283 million votes to 2.085 million. The TGWU motion met a similar fate.

Following this endorsement by the Labour Party Conference, the wage freeze was loyally observed, and it was only necessary for the Government to use its compulsory powers in a tiny handful of cases, affecting 56,000 workers in all. For the six-month period of the freeze from July to December 1966 there was no increase in weekly wage rates. For the following six months there was a rise of 2 per cent in average earnings. During the same period the retail price index increased by 2 per cent. So there was no doubt about the benefits over the twelve-month period to those living on pensions and fixed incomes.

Nevertheless, I was no more enamoured of the statutory powers than were our critics. My own trade union experience had taught me that anomalies would be thrown up, and none of us could judge how far wage increases were only postponed, not foregone. I held strongly to the view that the country would get the best results when the unions themselves recognised the wisdom of voluntarily and freely linking their pay claims to increased productivity, and I had vainly hoped that George Brown was right and that their signatures on the statement of intent in December 1964 meant they would do so. I used every public opportunity to argue for this, including my frequent visits to my constituency in Cardiff.

Wales's capital city was not only growing in importance as a commercial centre, but was a natural meeting-place for South Wales industrialists and the regional headquarters of most of the national trade unions. During this period we organised several lunchtime gatherings specifically for these industrialists and trade unionists. These lunches attracted over four hundred people, and enjoyed considerable popularity and prestige because they provided an opportunity to question and discuss difficulties with the Chancellor of the Exchequer at close quarters. They also gave me a valuable insight into the true state of opinion at the sharp end of industry. My refrain hardly varied. A prices and incomes policy was needed so that Britain could once again become competitive and maintain a high level of employment. If Britain could not stand up to foreign competition, unemployment would surely follow. I urged that they agree these matters between themselves 'so that the Government could bow out of the arena.' I emphasised that increased exports were a top priority and the Government would not be able to finance a consumer-led reflation as an alternative. I preached the need to eliminate restrictive practices, and to improve the quality of management; called for more investment in modern plant and machinery, and emphasised that the country needed, and a Labour Government would foster, an efficient, flourishing private sector. I spoke on these lines to all and sundry, not only in Cardiff but at many other functions from Regional Councils of Labour to the Lord Mayor of London's banquet for top bankers and merchants. It was a speech to be made many times by Chancellors of both parties.

As the weeks went by without a major revolt on pay, sterling steadied and once more slipped out of the daily headlines. There was no immediate crisis. Out of sight, out of mind, and I could feel the sense of urgency beginning to fade, and opinion in the country becoming forgetful. By November 1966 the TUC was pressing Michael Stewart and myself to stop the Government's 'deflationary dive'. This was not a unanimous view, and we received valuable support from Bill Carron, the President of the powerful Amalgamated Electrical Unions, who urged that the Government should not listen to pleas to increase demand.

I came under increasing pressure every month at meetings of the National Executive Committee of the Labour Party to increase economic activity. Frank Chapple, the General Secretary of the Electrical Trades Union, was particularly vociferous and scathing about the fact that as many as 450,000 men and women were out of work. Jack Jones, also a member of the Executive Committee at the time, was more effective in his criticism because of his natural courtesy and understanding. In retrospect, when these criticisms are set against recent levels of unemployment, they seem out of proportion. But all such matters are relative and at the time they received much support.

I had achieved part of my objective to secure a substantial reduction in the Government's overseas expenditure, and this had improved the balance of payments. I was aiming for total public expenditure to grow in future years at a lower level of 3 per cent per annum, and for an annual economic growth rate of 3 per cent per annum from 1968 onwards. I had to acknowledge that these targets were lower than those contained in the original National Plan, but I justified them to Michael Stewart on the grounds that they made the other objectives in the Plan more viable.

Our critics were impatient for quick results. Sterling remained strong during the winter months of 1966; our reserves increased, and we felt confident enough to reduce the bank rate to 6 per cent; exports rose in value by 6.5 per cent; there was a dramatic improvement in the balance of payments and we ended 1966 with a small deficit of no more than £61 millions on our current account – a welcome improvement over the figure of £393 millions in 1964. But as these figures became known, so far from convincing the critics that our policies were working, the complaints grew louder, and the calls to increase public expenditure and reflate the economy became ever more insistent. By this time unemployment in London and in the Midlands stood at 1.4 per cent, and even in Scotland, Wales and the North it was only 3 per cent. At no time during the winter of 1966–7 did the national figure rise above 500,000, or about 2 per cent, but this was made the basis of a constant drip of criticism of the Government by the Tribune Group of the Parliamentary Labour Party, which subjected me on more than one occasion to blistering attacks at Party meetings.

At the beginning of 1967 I recommended to my Cabinet colleagues the major provisions in our economic policy for the year ahead. I proposed as follows. First, the compulsory powers to control prices and incomes should not be renewed after they expired in the summer. Second, the Government should announce that negotiations for pay increases in 1967 should be linked with productivity, with only a few exceptions. Third, the Government should activate that part of the Prices and Incomes Act which gave it the power to order a thirty-day standstill on any proposal to increase a particular price or charge or wage, and be ready to refer such increase to the national Board for Prices and Incomes for them to adjudicate. Fourth, we should seek the agreement of the TUC and the CBI to this policy, taking into account the fact that prices were hardly rising.

I met privately with George Woodcock and Lionel Murray of the TUC on the day I made these recommendations to seek their reactions, and told them further that we were aiming at an annual surplus in the balance of payments of £100m per annum from 1967 to 1970. More generally, I proposed that the 1967 Budget should not tilt towards a higher percentage increase in public expenditure than in earlier years. The Prime Minister held similar views, and this general approach was agreed by the Cabinet.

At the same time I was discussing with officials in the Treasury the future of sterling and the dollar now that the atmosphere was less feverish. The Prime Minister lent me Chequers for a weekend to enable me to act as host for a meeting of Finance Ministers to discuss monetary cooperation. We all agreed we should aim to reduce interest rates as quickly as possible. As usual the French Finance Minister, Michel Debré, made a strong plea for an increase in the price of gold, which was another way of asking the Americans to devalue the dollar, and as usual Henry Fowler, the United States Treasury Secretary, dismissed the French proposal with general backing from all the other countries present. Our own Treasury discussions about the future took place on the firm assumption that there would be no devaluation of either the pound or the dollar, but we also privately reviewed two other options, namely letting the pound float to find a new level and, as an alternative, devaluation to a new fixed parity. Apart from officials in the Treasury no one other than the Prime Minister was aware of this review, for had it become known to some of the more gossipy members of the Government the information would have reawakened the traumas of an earlier period, and a quiet and reflective discussion would have been presented as a panic scramble to avert a desperate situation.

The Prime Minister and I were close in our thinking on this issue. There seemed reasonable grounds for expecting a surplus in the balance of payments for the two years 1967 and 1968, and beyond that date I hoped that the savings of overseas expenditure caused by the reduction of our defence arrangements in the Far East would result in a further easement and enable us to get through to 1970 without undue strain on sterling's parity. What lay beyond that date would depend on our economic progress at home, and on whether and when Britain would join the European Community. Neither the Prime Minister nor myself had any doubt that joining would have a serious adverse effect on our balance of payments, but Harold's emphasis was a little different from mine. While he was very determined to avoid devaluation, he thought it was probably unavoidable at some stage during or after our entry into the European Community. On the other hand, while I thought this was a strong possibility, my preferred objective (and probably his) was that our sustained work in improving Britain's industrial structure combined with a substantial increase in exports should suffice to see us through with an unchanged parity. Neither he nor I were or could be dogmatic, unlike some of our colleagues who accepted the popular Party belief that once devaluation took place our difficulties would evaporate.

The option of allowing sterling to float during the early months of 1967 had some attractions, for we were living through a quiet period where it might have been possible to adjust without a dramatic fall in the value of the pound. However, at the end of our series of discussions I reached the conclusion that we should not take such a step. Some of our reasons were good, others do not stand the test of time. For example, it was believed that a floating currency would make trade credit and overseas banking almost impossible. Experience has shown that this was not true. But our major reason for not floating the pound in January 1967 was that we believed that the market would assume that the sterling situation must be bad if we were prepared, by taking such a step, to breach the general principles of the IMF and face the hostility of the holders of sterling credits. If that became the view of the market sterling might sink rapidly, instead of floating. A run could develop which might tempt those Commonwealth countries which held their reserves in sterling to sell and buy dollars. The rate would then be carried down even further. It was a matter of sheer conjecture as to where it would hit the floor. A further difficulty was that a lower pound would result in higher domestic prices and therefore make it difficult to adhere to the prices and incomes policy, which itself was necessary to improve our competitive position. Our final argument was that it was impossible to know whether a voluntary float would set off a round of competitive devaluations by other countries, with the end result that Britain might finish off very little better than before. In short, my conclusions were that the immeasurable risks of floating sterling were greater than the intangible gains. Some of the Party's economic advisors held a different view and were profuse in their criticism, so I take this opportunity to show that there were respectable and serious arguments to the contrary. Many of these same reasons were also applicable to a voluntary devaluation to a new fixed rate.

In February 1967 an American idea surfaced at a fairly low level for a multi-billion-dollar long-term international loan with a duration of not less than twenty-five years, and possibly irredeemable. Such a loan would have enabled us to fund our sterling debts and shake off the speculation about sterling that had proved so inhibiting. The attraction to the Americans was that the loan would have been coupled with the creation of a dollar/sterling area of members who would not demand gold from the United States, and this would have given the United States more room to manoeuvre. I followed up this idea as a hopeful development, but it never got further than first base. Unlike the Central Banking operation in 1965, American political officers became involved and sought to inject into the proposals a demand that Britain should continue to play a substantial role in the defence of the Far East. This was unacceptable. It was clear that if Britain was to reduce government overseas expenditure significantly it would be necessary for us to withdraw from Malaya and Singapore, and although I hankered after close defence links with Commonwealth countries, including of course Australia and New Zealand, it was not sensible to maintain a world-wide influence on borrowed money. Nor would this stance sit easily with the visits that the Prime Minister and the Foreign Secretary were making to various European countries to advance Britain's application to join the Community. General de Gaulle certainly would have believed his suspicions proven: that Britain would be a Trojan horse in the European Community. He held the opinion that British membership of the Community was incompatible with the preservation of the special relationship between Britain and the United States, and that until this was ended, Britain could not be permitted to join the Community.

If discussions of the multi-billion-dollar loan had been left to negotiations between the monetary and financial experts in Washington and London, without any attempt to attach political conditions, there is just a chance that such a loan could have been negotiated, and Congress convinced of its usefulness. Such a conclusion would have had longer-term beneficial results not only to sterling and the dollar but also to the maintenance of the international monetary system for a further period, although Bretton Woods could not have been sustained indefinitely.

We kept the discussions alive for a time against the possibility that a situation might develop in which I could suggest to the Prime Minister that a high-level approach to President Johnson might be worthwhile. I made two attempts to carry the idea further. One was on a lovely June evening in 1967 when the Port of London Authority kindly loaned me their yacht, *St Katherine*, in order to entertain to dinner Joe Fowler, the Canadian Minister of Finance Mitchell Sharp, the Governors of the Bank of England and of Canada, and Federal Reserve Board Governor Dewey Daane. As we sailed under London Bridge past cranes and wharves and reached Greenwich Palace, with its hilly backcloth, we held a private talk about sterling and the dollar at which I returned to the idea of a multi-billion-dollar loan at a low rate of interest, large enough to put sterling out of reach of the speculators. In addition to strengthening our reserves, I proposed that the proceeds be used to pay off any government which held its reserves in London and wished to recover them. The attraction for the United States Treasury was that it would remove their constant fear that a forced devaluation of sterling would lead inevitably to an attack on the dollar and heavy depletion of their gold stocks. This was exactly what took place a year later in 1968. Joe Fowler undertook to consider the matter and to resume contact at a later date, but no progress had been made by the autumn of 1967, when the storm finally broke and took sterling down.

I also held a discussion with the Finance Ministers of the Community at which I floated similar ideas. Emilio Colombo, the Italian Minister of the Treasury, who was always extremely helpful and most keen that any obstacle to Britain's membership of the Community should be removed, at once took the lead and proposed that experts should look into the matter and a further meeting of Finance Ministers be held at a later date. But objections were raised by Michael Debré, the French Finance Minister, and although we had German support, Colombo was not able to carry the other Finance Ministers with him.

Despite the devaluation gale that was to sweep us away in November, the year 1967 had begun quietly enough. The sterling exchange rate was steady and the currency was under no speculative attacks that would have distorted my judgement in preparing the spring Budget. The purpose of the 1967 Budget was to create the conditions that would produce the best balance between a high level of economic growth and low levels of unemployment and inflation, so as to end the year with a satisfactory balance of overseas payments. The Treasury's economic assessment in early spring was that no major changes were necessary to achieve these ends, and when I told Audrey of my general conclusion, her sensible advice was that there was no need for a long speech, but I should stand up and announce what the tax rates would be for the coming year and sit down again almost at once.

I was ready to make further progress in tax reform but the Chairman of the Board of Inland Revenue made a heartfelt plea for the Department to be spared. He said that Revenue could not absorb further changes in 1967, but undertook to make a renewed effort in 1968 and we agreed we should concentrate then on the abolition of Estate Duty, which had become little more than a voluntary tax paid only by the public-spirited or those who disliked their heirs more than the Inland Revenue. In place of Estate Duty we proposed to tax capital when it was transferred from one person to another. My resignation in November 1967 put an end to this, and it was not until Denis Healey became Chancellor that this overdue reform was made, in his 1975 Budget. However, the great body of the major tax reforms introduced in the three years from 1964 stood the test of time and remained on the statute book after we left office. The only unsuccessful new venture was the Selective Employment Tax.

As tax reform was ruled out, and there was no need for major changes in economic policy, I had no great new issues to discuss and I delivered an unexciting homily: our existing measures were doing what we expected; we should avoid sudden switches of policy, and should follow through the policies that we had successfully begun. Not very much red meat for an expectant House of Commons, in the days when Budgets held a greater significance than they do nowadays.

I could have made a better fist of it if I had announced a new scheme prepared jointly by the Treasury and the Department of Economic

Affairs to assist the Development Areas by paying a premium of thirty shillings (£1.50) per week for a period of seven years for every worker employed in areas of high unemployment. This would certainly have attracted publicity but Michael Stewart wished to announce these developments himself, and I did not press him. Instead, I gave a long lecture on the international monetary system, its principles, its difficulties and its need for reform. The House did not seem to care very much but the newspapers did. 'Rotten, lousy, threadbare, poor . . .' were some of the less abusive epithets. I had concluded the Budget speech with a phrase that has often been quoted: 'I sum up the prospects for 1967 in three short sentences. We are back on course. The ship is picking up speed. The economy is moving ahead. Every seaman knows the command at such a moment – "Steady as she goes"'. This was a hostage to fortune which rapidly returned to haunt me. But I feel no remorse for I know of no one who foretold that within two months of the Budget the Six Day Arab/ Israeli War and the closure of the Suez Canal would cause sterling to run aground, and that by November both sterling and I would be shipwrecked.

The immediate effect of the Six Day War was to cause a flight from a number of currencies, including sterling, into the dollar, this being regarded as the safest currency at a time of crisis. There were well authenticated threats from Arab sources too that they would follow suit. We incurred immediate heavy additional costs by routing ships and tankers on the long haul around the Cape and this, together with a large increase in the price of oil, had a serious adverse effect on the balance of payments. This was particularly disappointing as calculations made by the Treasury during the summer of 1967 showed that our overseas payments had actually been in surplus for the first half year and forecast a small surplus for the year as a whole. This was subsequently amended to a forecast that Britain would be in surplus for the year as a whole if the temporary additional cost of the Suez Canal closure was omitted. That seemed a reasonable proposition. So in mid-summer the prospects were not frightening, provided we were able to change the psychology of the market. This proved impossible.

World trade was slowing down, commodity prices were falling and oil price increases were causing the less developed countries to run deficits. Suspicion developed in the markets and some newspapers began to speculate that there must be a sterling devaluation. The press was always in a dilemma at such time. Clearly it had a legitimate right to comment, but the state of the currency was a national interest and was undermined when unfounded speculation caused sterling sales, so making the prophecy self-fulfilling. The *Observer* was regularly gloomy and because it was (wrongly) thought to be close to Treasury Ministers, Monday mornings often brought a spate of sterling sales. One of the most costly articles ever written must surely have appeared in the *Wall Street Journal* during August 1967. The author stated flatly, without qualification and without evidence, that there was growing weariness in London in the fight to preserve sterling's parity and a growing acceptance that devaluation was inevitable. This was true neither of the First Lord of the Treasury nor of the Chancellor of the Exchequer, and we together carried the major responsibility. The article had a serious effect in the New York markets, and on the day it appeared the Bank of England had to support the pound to the tune of £56 millions. I noted that while there was no rational need for devaluation, the effects of such defeatist articles could force our hands if they continued to influence overseas holders of sterling. Nevertheless, for most of August the foreign exchange markets were placid enough and the first half of September also passed without incident. But then began the series of events which were to force devaluation two months later in November.

The fuse was lit by a walk-out of dockers in Hull, London, Liverpool and Manchester, which began in a ragged way on 18 September and continued in London for a period of more than eight weeks, officially being brought to an end ten days after sterling had been devalued. Ironically, the strike started because of the introduction of Lord Devlin's recommendations to decasualise dock workers as a means of making their jobs more secure. As the Member for Cardiff Docks, I knew that South Wales dockers among others had been pressing for such an historic reform for many years, and it was the declared objective of the TGWU. I was astonished when the dockers walked out, although it must be said that the new scheme did not seem to have been well explained to the dockers in certain ports. This in itself, however, did not justify the strike.

It was one of those occasions, familiar in industrial relations, where misunderstanding arises because of a breakdown in communications, and advantage is then taken by militant leaders to foment the difficulties. At no time did the TGWU support the strike, which remained unofficial, and Frank Cousins the General Secretary did his best to halt it. But the dockers were traditionally resistant to any lead from Transport House and they ignored Frank's appeals to return to work. The official leader-

ship was frequently undermined by a group of Trotskyists and communists who were close to the dockers and kept the grievances alight long
after they could have been satisfactorily settled.

Once again, the newspapers published dramatic pictures of idle ships
and motionless cranes together with a graphic account of how Britain's
overseas trade was grinding to a halt. Sub-editors captioned the pictures
with every well-known cliché in the book, with the inevitable result that
sterling became more and more unsettled.

Strangely, by a statistical convention that I was not aware of at the
time, imports were treated differently from exports in making up our
balance of payments. Cargoes waiting to be unloaded from the ships at
the quayside were regarded as having been already delivered, and were
debited to our overseas account. But, conversely, the British goods waiting at the dockside to be sent abroad were regarded as not having been
exported and so were not credited. It was estimated that there were £100
millions of such exports with the result that the recorded figures for our
balance of trade during October and November were hopelessly wrong
and showed apparently yawning deficits, while in July we had been in
overall surplus. The dealers in the foreign exchange markets were no
more aware of this statistical quirk than I, and an overly pessimistic
picture was painted. Even an acute operator like Charles Coombes of the
Federal Reserve Bank of New York believed the figures revealed a permanent weakening in British exports.

Heavy selling of sterling took place as soon as the trade figures became
known. Two months later after the docks strike was over our exports
immediately jumped by an extra £100 millions, but of course by this time
devaluation had taken place.

I have already referred to the adverse effect of the closure of the Suez
Canal and there was one other piece of ill fortune. The Common Market
Commission had engaged in a long-term study of the role of sterling as
a reserve currency and published their report in the autumn of 1967. By
implication, this expressed the doubts we had already discussed about
our long-term prospects for holding the sterling rate steady if we were to
become full members of the Community.

Couve de Murville, the French Foreign Minister, seized on this as an
additional reason for obstructing Britain's entry and in a well-reported
speech repeated the outlines of M. Pompidou's argument when he had
visited London the previous year. He drew a parallel between Britain's
position and that of France in 1958, when the French Government de-

valued the franc prior to the establishment of the Community. The moral was as clear as he intended, the foreign exchange markets took their cue and sterling weakened still further.

The atmospherics did not improve at home. The two railway unions embarked upon one of their long-drawn-out manning disputes which resulted in daily newspaper reports of threats of strike action and counter action. In addition, some members of the Parliamentary Labour Party were up in arms about the Government's defence policy and announced that they intended to challenge the Prime Minister at a well-publicised Party meeting. Everything conspired to come together at the same moment to create the most unfavourable circumstances, and sterling sales contrived to gather momentum from October until we were finally pushed over the edge.

I am in danger of getting these events out of perspective so I should add at once that while these factors were important in precipitating devaluation on Saturday 18 November 1967, they were not the basic cause of devaluation. The fundamental reason was that the world was not convinced that Britain could establish a long-term equilibrium in its balance of payments. Writing as I do twenty years later, at a time when Britain's balance of payments would be substantially in deficit if the vast and temporary benefit of Britain's oil were put to one side, no one can say that the international observers were wrong. Nevertheless, devaluation by itself was not even a short-term remedy unless accompanied by other measures. The Labour Government of 1964 had set out with the right priorities – structural industrial change, redeployment of labour, training for the new technology, reduction of the burdens of overseas defence, and maintenance of wage increases in line with productivity.

I was not ready until nearly the end to give up the struggle to find our salvation through these measures. Nor was I alone. The American Treasury and Federal Reserve held the view right up to the week of devaluation that the pound was not intrinsically overvalued, but in the end they did not back their opinion with their money. If they had taken up the question of a long-term loan more energetically, when it was discussed in the early summer of 1967, there would have been time to negotiate the arrangements before the storm hit us in October and November.

In the end they came round to the idea too late, at a moment when we had already reached our decision to devalue and the lengthy procedure to make it effective had already begun. Moreover, a loan would have been hedged with political conditions that made it unacceptable. Germany and

Italy were opposed to sterling's devaluation, but France and Belgium were in favour. We wondered whether the French franc would follow sterling down at once, but it was some months before the French Government was forced to do so.

One event followed another helter-skelter during November. Harold Wilson has recounted that on 1 November the Governor of the Bank of England told him that he did not intend to recommend devaluation, despite the effect of the apparently awful trade figures on sterling. But the very next day a personal and 'top secret' packet was placed on my desk from Sir Alec Cairncross, at that time the Head of the Government Economic Service and subsequently to become the Master of St Peter's College, Oxford. Alec had been one of the staunchest of the praetorian guard determined to maintain sterling's parity, so it had a profound effect on me when I opened the packet and found it contained a personal and pessimistic typed memorandum on the outlook, together with a covering, handwritten letter from him for my eyes alone. In this, he said that, having started with the conviction that I was right to try as hard as possible to solve our problems without devaluing, he had after long consideration changed his mind and was now a 'convert to devaluation'. He continued by saying that world opinion would have condemned devaluation at an earlier date but would now be understanding because it was known how hard the Government had tried to avoid it. He added that he had consulted no one before writing and did not intend to canvass any other opinion.

I read this with emotion and then read it again in case I had missed an important meaning in trying to decipher Alec's spidery and difficult handwriting. But I found no qualification. His view was clear. We should devalue and 'if it cannot be avoided, the sooner it is over and done with, the better'. I folded the paper and placed it in my breast pocket, where it stayed, burning a hole, throughout the rest of the day and long into the night. I spent Friday 3 November wrestling with the problem in isolation : we had gone over the ground often enough; there were no new arguments to rehearse, no new facts to be discovered. No one else could take the decision except me. If those like Alec Cairncross who throughout the previous three years had not wavered were now privately reaching such conclusions, was I justified in continuing the struggle? Or would I be serving only a wrong-headed stubbornness?

By Saturday morning my mind was clear. It would not be sensible to continue any longer to defend the existing parity of sterling against continual attacks if our only support was by means of short-term credits from other countries needing to be renewed every few months. This was living from hand to mouth. It left the currency without long-term adequate reserves. We ought therefore to give our friends and allies due warning that one of the two major reserve currencies in the world was now preparing to devalue. They, like us, had more than once discussed the possibility that sterling's devaluation could break up the whole structure of the world's post-war monetary system. I continued to argue with myself. If they regarded that as undesirable, they must come forward at once with a long-term solution to the perennial problem of sterling balances. They had missed other opportunities and I was doubtful that they could do so in the short time available, but we owed it to the international community to give them the opportunity before taking our action, the results of which were unforeseeable for the world's financial systems.

All this was in my mind as I walked from my study in 11 Downing Street through the communicating door to No. 10 on Saturday morning, and over a cup of coffee discussed with the Prime Minister our narrowing alternatives. The two of us sat alone in the quiet Cabinet Room looking out on to Horseguards Parade. Everything was peaceful. People were strolling through St James's Park on their Saturday pursuits. No one out there had any idea of the welter of emotions I felt. My mind went back to a similar Saturday morning three years before, when the three of us had held our first discussion and decided against devaluation. I felt that the three years of struggle had been of no avail.

Harold sensed my feelings of failure and was kindness itself. As soon as I had told him of my change of heart, I felt relief to have shared my anxieties. He was encouraging and I came away reinforced in my decision and ready to set in motion the necessary action. It is a common experience that whatever doubts and terrors assail us in making up our minds, once a decision is reached a calm descends and I personally enjoy the tumult of the follow-up.

My first step was to invite Jonkheer Emile van Lennep, the Chairman of the Monetary Committee of the European Community, to meet me on the following Monday. I gave Joe Fowler a hint in guarded terms over the transatlantic telephone. I followed up with a letter which told him that we would not carry on in a hand-to-mouth existence. I concluded, 'There are ways and means by which the market can be quietened down and the incalculable consequences of fresh action by us, avoided. I use the word "incalculable" because I think that is the exact description. Denis

Rickett will talk these matters over with you and I can only reiterate that the time for long-term decisions one way or another is very close at hand.' I did not need to use the word 'devaluation'. Joe Fowler knew well enough what I meant.

Sir Denis Rickett, the Second Secretary of the Treasury in charge of international monetary matters, flew that day to Washington and during the following six days he travelled to Germany and then back to Washington before finally coming to rest in London, in his attempts to assess the prospects of a solution.

At first, encouraging reports filtered back. The Americans were clearly alarmed – one source said 'horrified' – and came forward with certain proposals which they said would require the cooperation of some of the European central banks. They repeated their general assessment that sterling was not over valued and they expected that if the Suez Canal reopened, our balance of payments would improve and we would be able to resume our progress in 1968 without devaluation. A large supporting figure of $3 billions was spoken of – the very figure that I had proposed five months earlier. Further conversations revealed additional details and although I thought the amount sufficient, there were two stumbling blocks: the period of the loan; and the conditions, which were not such as I could recommend to the Cabinet.

The Governor of the Bank of England, Sir Leslie O'Brien, also went into action, consulting with his central bank colleagues in Basle, and keeping in touch with me by telephone at each new development. At one point on Monday morning, 13 November, he telephoned from Basle to enquire whether the Government would be ready to accept a smaller loan of say $2 billions from the IMF, with milder conditions than those initially proposed by the United States. I asked him whether in his judgement $2 billions would be enough to provide a long-term solution, to which he responded that it would 'stop the rot' and earn a breathing space. I told Sir Leslie that at this stage it would be wrong for us to embrace a solution that would secure no more than relief for a year or two, especially as I did not think the sum was large enough. Therefore, despite his efforts, I told him I would prefer to retain the Government's freedom to devalue and the international financial community would have to face the consequences, as we ourselves would.

For all practical purposes, that was the end of active attempts to put together a long-term solution. The Governor arrived back from Basle and reported to me on the evening of 13 November, and thereafter both of us went to see the Prime Minister. My mind was made up and Harold did not dissent. Incongruously after a short exchange, we all three hurried away to change into full evening dress in order to attend the annual Lord Mayor's Banquet for Her Majesty's Ministers. This is a glittering occasion, but I fear I was in no mood to be caught up in it. Fortunately, my only role was to listen to the speeches, but I felt sorry for the Prime Minister whose responsibility was to reply to the principal toast in front of a huge audience of bankers, ambassadors, archbishops, aldermen and councillors, not to mention the statues of Wellington and Pitt, neither of whom seemed much interested. No one could have told from the Prime Minister's demeanour that anything was amiss.

We returned at 11.15 p.m. after the dinner and speeches and, still in evening dress, went immediately to the Cabinet Room at No. 10 where Sir William Armstrong and Sir Burke Trend, the Cabinet Secretary, were awaiting us. Harold and I had no doubts about the decision and from that moment our discussions were about such practical matters as the level at which the new rate should be fixed and the many administrative details that followed. We decided on a devaluation of 14 per cent so that the pound would acquire a new exchange value of $2.40 instead of $2.80. Our choice of a new rate was successful. In the end, only a handful of other countries devalued of whom the most important were New Zealand and Denmark.

It was difficult to carry on with other normal work and behave as if nothing unusual was afoot. The first step was to enlarge the circle of Ministers who needed to know. I asked Tony Crosland to see me and privately told him of our intention. He was relieved and did not share my gloom. I had already intimated to the Prime Minister that it was my firm decision to resign once the devaluation operation was complete and I had accounted for myself to the House of Commons. I recommended to him that Tony should succeed me as Chancellor and I had thought that the Prime Minister shared my opinion. Tony had been a devaluer for some time, but unlike some of our Cabinet colleagues he understood that devaluation was not a soft option, and that if it was to be successful it must be accompanied by some measures that the Cabinet and the country would not like. Tony's view, which in my view was correct, was that these unpleasant measures should be taken within a week or two of the decision. The Prime Minister also recognised the need for such measures but preferred to defer their full effect until the following year's Budget in April 1968. This was too late.

The Prime Minister urged me very strongly to remain at the Treasury for the time being, but I felt unable to do so in view of the undertakings I had given in good faith as lately as the previous September that sterling would not be devalued. I had made one such pledge when the Kuwaiti Ambassador put a direct question to me at the request of the Emir. I had known the ruler personally for many years and on the strength of my reply, Kuwait had maintained very substantial sterling balances in London which would in future be worth much less.

The Prime Minister, knowing I could not be dissuaded, asked what other office I would like. This was generous and I told him that if I stayed in the Government my first choice was to be Secretary of State for Education, an office to which I had always been attracted. He told me that he did not wish to have too big a reshuffle and if he promoted Crosland this would create a chain reaction. To avoid this I agreed to make a straight exchange with Roy Jenkins who had built up a formidable reputation at the Home Office. Roy soon showed himself at home in the Treasury. He mastered the complexities of the situation with apparent ease, and quickly gained the authority that every Chancellor needs in dealing with his Cabinet colleagues. I cannot write too highly of Harold Wilson's personal consideration and kindness during this period. He was as tired as I was and was beset by many concerns other than devaluation but he never showed impatience or irritation, and I was greatly indebted to him.

The public reaction to devaluation was hostile. As I had always anticipated, the newspapers told the public that the country had suffered a severe national defeat and the Government's reputation plunged. Not for the first time, Dick Crossman offered the Prime Minister ungenerous and ill-timed advice on the stance he should take. He wrote, 'Jim must be the Chamberlain of our times and you the Churchill.' I blame him for the fact that Harold's first post-devaluation press conference struck a false note.

For the next fortnight as I walked back each night from the House of Commons I would find a small knot of youthful Conservatives gathered on the pavement opposite 11 Downing Street, and at my approach they would burst into loud cries of 'Traitor . . . resign'. They waited patiently for hours for the chance to do this and at first seemed genuinely angry. But when this had happened for several nights with the same group, any real anger seemed exhausted, and after they had got their ritual chants off their chests, they would shout, 'goodnight, sir' very politely and make their way back to Whitehall.

Recollecting Stafford Cripps's 1949 devaluation, I was not at all surprised that it took some time for the emotional effects to wear off in the press and elsewhere. The man in the street felt let down because he had been led to believe that if devaluation took place, it would be a consequence of the Labour Government's incompetence. There was too little understanding at that time that devaluation reflected the world's opinion that Britain was not sufficiently competitive with other trading nations, and our sterling reserves were never large enough to permit us to withstand that opinion.

One further comment. Our economic advisers and those others who had advocated devaluation for so long always underrated the political damage that such a step would cause. Not only did the Government's fortunes plunge immediately, but in my view the adverse effects were still being felt at the time of the 1970 election. Nowadays the press has a different perspective. It has transferred the national angst from sterling to our football and cricket failures.

As some of us had always feared, sterling's devaluation was far from being a signal that the international crisis was over. Indeed it had just begun. The results of our action were like those of the climber on the mountainside who dislodges a stone, which in turn sets off the avalanche that engulfs the valley below. Sterling had for many years been the weaker of the world's two reserve currencies, and once devaluation of the pound was accomplished international attention focused on the dollar. The question that had once been whispered was now loudly shouted. Could the United States' post-war pledge to exchange every dollar they were offered for gold at $35 to the ounce be maintained? Increasing doubts arose despite United States' reassurances, and before long the American Treasury was put to the test.

Four months after sterling's devaluation in early March 1968 the Americans had to disgorge $400 millions worth of gold from their vaults in a period of three days in exchange for dollars held by other countries. On the fourth day they expected to need a further $400 millions. There was consternation in Washington and President Johnson made contact with the Prime Minister in the evening of 14 March with an urgent request that the London gold and foreign exchange markets should not open on the following morning. This would have effectively blocked dollars from being offered in exchange for gold. Harold Wilson at once agreed, but this course needed an Order of the Privy Council to make the closure effective. An Order in Council does not require the full attendance of the

Cabinet, and Harold called together the requisite number of Ministers (I was not one of them) to wait upon the Queen. George Brown, the First Secretary, was also not among those who would have been present, and it was this that caused his resignation from the Government.

Closure of the markets was an acknowledgement by the United States that it could no longer live up to its post-war undertakings to regard gold and dollars as freely interchangeable. Coming so shortly after the devaluation of sterling, this action was a further stunning blow at the post-war international monetary system, and from then on its disintegration was only a matter of time.

The next step was the devaluation of the French franc, despite President de Gaulle's fierce opposition. This was followed by the revaluation of the German Deutsche Mark. The United States had led the post-war world through many crises, but at this moment when leadership was needed the Nixon administration seemed afflicted by paralysis. Some of us were incredulous when we heard American officials saying that the dollar 'is our currency but your problem'. This was translated into another widely used phrase, namely that the Administration's policy towards the dollar was one of 'benign neglect'. The result of this naivety was to make the dollar a one-way bet for the currency speculators, who could hardly believe their luck. The working of the international monetary system was dependent for its success on the coordination of the United States Treasury and Federal Reserve, and when this was smothered by lack of political understanding no other country was strong enough to pick up the ball and run with it.

There were officials in the United States Treasury and the Federal Reserve who recognised the seriousness of the Administration's dollar policy for the world's monetary system, but their arguments did not prevail and eventually President Nixon was forced to make a formal announcement that the United States would no longer sell gold for dollars on demand. With that announcement the dollar ceased to be as good as gold and the Bretton Woods era effectively came to an end.

With the advantage of hindsight it is very doubtful that the post-war system could have survived in the long run, however skilfully it was managed. The development of free capital markets in Britain and elsewhere, the extraordinary increases in the price of oil, the remarkable growth of Japan's external trade, and the world's falling rate of improvement in productivity would have placed intolerable strains upon a system of fixed exchange rates.

But we should not forget that for nearly twenty-five years the world had possessed a workable system of international monetary cooperation that brought great benefit. When that system broke down and its generally accepted rules, conventions and undertakings vanished, no other set of principles was devised to take its place. The result is that the world's monetary arrangements are a mess, and practices exist that should not be acceptable.

It is for example deplorable that central banks should add a veneer of respectability to speculation by shifting their own reserves from time to time into other currencies, merely to make a profit. The exchange rate of a country's currency can no longer be relied upon as a measure of its competitive trading position, as long as more than 90 per cent of the transactions on the New York money market are for the purpose of shifting footloose capital from one country to another. The time is overdue for an extension of the use of Special Drawing Rights to settle commercial transactions between banks themselves and their countries, so that the SDRs can develop into a true international currency.

The communications revolution which began in the 1960s has altered the scale of the problems, but although the world cannot go back to another Bretton Woods era, it badly needs a new set of international monetary principles and a supervisory body to monitor and enforce them. The irresponsibility of bank borrowing and lending to the Third World left the poorest people on the face of the earth worse off than they were before, and in some cases has destroyed their ability to finance their most elementary needs. The sophisticated West has a responsibility it should fulfil and Third World governments need both assistance and a better sense of priorities.

History will show the 1980s as a decade in which the world stood at a crossroads. Either the nations retreat into more narrow, restrictive and nationalistic monetary, fiscal and economic policies or they move forward to a willing merger of some aspects of their sovereignty. In international economics as in world politics, the manifold interdependence of all nations makes the second course imperative.

PART THREE

HOME SECRETARY

7

The Home Office – care and control of children – crime and punishment – prisons and prisoners

Moving from the Treasury to the Home Office involved not only a change of offices but also a domestic upheaval, involving giving up the Chancellor's official residence at 11 Downing Street, whose living accommodation, incidentally, is far superior to that of the Prime Minister's next door. Our own house was let and occupied, and Audrey wanted time to think about what we should do next, for our children had grown up, our first granddaughter had already arrived and our family needs in the years ahead would be different. Fortunately George Thomson, a long-standing friend, had recently been appointed Commonwealth Secretary, an office which enjoyed an official residence, and we gratefully accepted his kind offer of the use of his own private home.

We made the most of our last Christmas at No. 11, and Audrey turned it into a huge and enjoyable family party. The State Drawing Room was the ideal length for carpet bowls, while the large number of rooms and the staircases were just right for the younger members of the family to play a game they had newly invented – 'Hunt the Dispatch Box'.

Audrey and I talked about what we should do. Thirty years earlier I had shared with a friend, Gordon Denniss, an ambition that one day we would go farming. He had done so, shortly after the war, and despite his early difficulties his hard work and energy had won through and he became highly successful. We had remained friends and in the intervening years he frequently urged me to follow his example. Now he took matters into his own hands and persuaded Audrey that a farm usually had the additional attraction of a big old house. Audrey, looking ahead, could see the need for space to accommodate not only married children but also in due course more grandchildren. She was right – we now have ten. In a further gesture of friendship Gordon Denniss offered to become a partner in the enterprise. That settled it. We looked for and found a farm in the Sussex Weald which could be bought cheaply, together with an old house in need of improvement, and I became the apprehensive half-share owner. We sold our home in London, arranged a substantial mortgage and overdraft and embarked on learning a new way of life which neither of us has ever regretted.

As the years went by I leaned less on Gordon's experience and attained sufficient competence to take policy decisions on what crops to grow and how best to fertilise them, buying and selling and making my own mistakes. So much depends upon the weather and I grumble along with my neighbours when on one and the same day I need rain to make the grass grow for the stock and dry weather to combine the arable crops. But to grow and harvest fields of wheat, barley or oats, to rear a good crop of lambs or some sturdy bullocks satisfies a deep instinct, and the occasional successes bring so much pleasure that they offset the winter mud, the flooded fields and the inevitable failures.

Whilst I was engaged in politics our children had grown up, all too quickly. Margaret, the eldest, won an Exhibition to Girton College, Cambridge, but decided to go to Somerville, Oxford, where she met and later married Peter Jay. She has since pursued a successful career in television. Julia, our second daughter, always practical and independent, decided to attend Kidbrooke Comprehensive School in South London, one of the earliest and for many years the most famous of the then new comprehensives, whose Headmistress, Miss Green, set a high standard for similar schools to follow. After striking out and crossing and recrossing America, Julia came home to Britain and married Ian Hubbard, now a Consultant in Ophthalmology in the Lake District. Michael, our youngest, won a London County Council place at Dulwich College. After passing his A levels he decided – to my private delight – to try for a place at University College Cardiff, where he was accepted. While there he met Jenny Morris, a student from Gilfach Goch, a mining village in the Welsh valleys, and fell in love. She shared a flat with Glenys Parry, a student from Anglesey whose parents I had met some years before when speaking in North Wales. Glenys was a friendly girl with a ginger-haired, freckled, cheerful, argumentative companion by name of Neil Kinnock who was president of the Student's Union. He was an ardent socialist and born politician who enjoyed his college days, bringing an infectious enthusiasm to everything except study, always the leader in any enterprise.

In the 1964 general election all four came to work in the Cardiff South Committee Rooms, and I recall Neil drove a loudspeaker van around the constituency extolling the virtues of the Labour Party. Twenty years later he would lead the Labour Party and I would be a back-bench supporter.

To complete the story the Misses Morris and Parry in due course became Mrs Callaghan and Mrs Kinnock. Michael nowadays plans Ford's European corporate strategy, and like the other members of the family has never failed to spend part of every election in Cardiff.

As the children had grown up, Audrey was more free to use her abilities outside the home. She had always been attracted to working with children and when she became a Member of the London County Council in 1959 she made the care of children her special concern, becoming Chairman of the South-East London Children's Committee, which was responsible for the welfare of some three thousand children in the care of the LCC. Later, she became Chairman of the world-famous Great Ormond Street Hospital for Sick Children, and made this work her major contribution to public service. Even today she remains Chairman of the Trustees of the Hospital as well as Vice-Chairman of the National Children's Bureau. Yet notwithstanding these responsibilities, she has always given our children and myself the utmost support and understanding, affection and help, in our daily lives.

Together with the Foreign Office and the Treasury, the Home Office is regarded as one of the three senior Cabinet posts, and it may seem surprising that it has not been particularly sought-after by aspiring politicians. Rab Butler recalled that he 'accepted' the Home Office in 1957, but he would have preferred the Foreign Office. So would Roy Jenkins in 1974. David Maxwell-Fyfe wanted the Woolsack when he became Home Secretary, and Reginald Maudling hoped for the Exchequer in 1970. As for me, in 1967 I asked Harold Wilson to let me go to Education on resignation from the Exchequer. So the Home Office seems to have been a first choice much less often than one might expect. It is true that the path to No. 10 lies more frequently through the other two offices. In a period of forty years up to the end of the Second World War, every Prime Minister except one, Ramsay MacDonald, had served a term as Chancellor of the Exchequer. Since the war Foreign Secretaries have had more of a look in, but the previous Home Secretary to become Prime Minister was Winston Churchill, Home Secretary as long ago as 1910.

I found the Department an enormous contrast with the Treasury which, because of its control of public expenditure, knew what every Department was doing. Treasury officials and the Chancellor had a bird's eye view of all the activities of government, and were as well or better informed than the Prime Minister. The Treasury was the hub of the wheel, with the Home Office and other domestic Departments forming the spokes. The Foreign Office was a somewhat different case.

It came as rather a shock to discover that I no longer knew what was happening. At first I tried to remedy this by asking the Permanent Secretary Sir Philip Allen (later Lord Allen of Abbeydale), who had had experience in the Treasury, to allocate an additional Secretary to my office specifically for the purpose of keeping abreast of general government affairs, so that I could be well briefed for Cabinet Meetings, but the experiment did not succeed. However it had one fortunate outcome, for the official concerned became my Principal Private Secretary a little later and is now Sir Brian Cubbon, the Permanent Secretary.

Another marked contrast was the formality of the office. In the Treasury everyone called everyone by their Christian names from top to bottom, and in a Departmental meeting every official, no matter how junior, could have his say. The Home Office was much more hierarchical when I arrived and there was less of a collegiate style of management. Philip Allen made important changes and I believe the atmosphere is very different now.

A further contrast was the load of legislation. The annual Treasury Finance Bill was onerous enough, but there was a certain unity about its contents. In the Home Office I found in my first twelve months that I was piloting through Bills on subjects as diverse as gambling, race relations, the criminal law and immigration.

Perhaps the biggest contrast was the 'operational' nature of the Home Secretary's work, in which his decisions have a direct, visible, and sometimes fundamental effect on the individual citizen's liberties. As Chancellor I had been engaged in large discussions on major strategic issues – financial and economic. Suddenly I found myself immersed for some hours in reading the papers in a file an inch thick, knowing that on my decision depended the freedom of an individual prisoner, the dismissal of a police officer, or the deportation of an alien. In this lay the core of the Department. Its fascination was that its work was concerned with holding the balance between the state and the citizen, between law and justice and liberty and order. The balance is fundamental and the office must be held by a senior member of the Government.

His work is the stuff of newspaper headlines, the human story that will appear on the front pages: drugs, football hooligans, gambling, pornography, prison escapes, demonstrations, police behaviour, the treatment of immigrants. These are not abstract concepts like the Treasury's monetarism, or the Public Sector Borrowing Requirement, but are subjects about which every man knows that the opinion of the Home Secretary is no better than his own. The disputed territory is heavily mined and an unwatchful incumbent can easily be ambushed. Rab Butler said about the Home Office that he found it necessary to stay behind at night and 'poke around smelling for rats'. His verdict on one Home Secretary who fell into a number of difficulties: 'Poor man. No sense of smell.'

When I became Home Secretary the Home Office was responsible for the welfare of children in need of care and control, and I was influenced by Audrey's knowledge and experience. I decided to speed up schemes for reform of the existing system to make it more flexible and responsive to the varied needs of individual children. I was assisted in this by a growing recognition, even among staunch champions of the existing system of approved schools and remand homes, that they were too rigid to respond to the changing thinking about the penal custodial system at that time in force for juveniles.

There had been complaints about the ill-treatment of children in certain schools and, as Home Secretary, I found that Parliament expected me to intervene and account for what was taking place. The system worked badly. Two children out of three who came before the juvenile magistrates were recommitted to some institution at a later date. In many cases there was a distinct pattern of behaviour. The child would initially appear in a juvenile court, and this would often be the first step on the road to becoming an adult criminal, graduating via an approved school, followed by one or two spells in a borstal and after that a young offenders' establishment.

As a Member of Parliament I had observed that juvenile delinquency often ran in children of the same family and that in settled communities it occurred in successive generations of the same families. Moreover, what I had seen in my Cardiff constituency had convinced me that a number of young people who grow into adulthood are inadequate in their ability either to order their own lives or to guide and control their children. Some just drifted. Others went a stage further and engaged – usually unsuccessfully – in small-time crime. I was not soft-headed and I never believed that all juvenile delinquents were angels, but I had seen sufficient of them and their subsequent histories to know that the complete removal of a young boy (there were few girls) from his family and into custody, sometimes as a response to a series of comparatively trivial offences, would more often alienate than reform him.

Control of delinquency in children is not a separate process from social measures to help and protect them and their families: the aims are complementary. The Home Office had been working on these matters before my arrival, and with my encouragement and support they hurried matters on and produced a White Paper entitled 'Children in Trouble' which my Cabinet colleagues agreed I should publish in May 1968. It proposed that a child under fourteen years of age should not be taken to court automatically for an offence unless he was clearly beyond the control of his parents or they were not providing adequate support. Instead, a form of so-called 'intermediate' treatment was proposed for the under-four-teens which would not entail total removal from home, but which might entail short periods of absence, perhaps at weekends, for attendance at centres for disciplined training, care and recreation.

All the existing types of remand homes, reception centres, voluntary approved schools and local authority homes and hostels were to be brought together under the general name of Community Homes. These proposals were welcomed by professional workers and by both sides of the House and the next stage was to turn them into a Bill. But although the Opposition had generally approved of the idea of Community Homes, when the Bill came before the Commons they opposed it on the grounds that it took too much power away from the juvenile courts.

I was glad to have the help of Merlyn Rees in carrying the Bill through the House, and he bore the brunt of the attack. Merlyn was a longstanding friend who had been my Parliamentary Private Secretary when I became Chancellor of the Exchequer in 1964 but was quickly and rightly promoted to become a junior Minister in Defence. After three years in that office the Prime Minister agreed that he might join me as Parliamentary Secretary in the Home Office in 1968, just in time for the Children's Bill. Merlyn attracts such words as dependable, thoughtful, hardworking, but he is more than that. He is essentially a conciliator and this aspect of his character enabled him several years later to handle the problem of Northern Ireland with great aplomb. His obvious earnestness and sincerity appealed to both communities in that divided country and his goodwill won their confidence. Brought up in the valleys of South Wales, the Labour Party was in his bones and he had an instinctive politician's flair for detecting shifts in mood and opinion.

He is a very amusing raconteur who often lightened our proceedings, although he would fall into a typical celtic gloom from time to time. He had no side, whether as a back-bencher or as Home Secretary, and never pushed himself. If anything, he underrated his own strength. I have been fortunate to have him as a friend to whom I could always turn for advice and criticism, knowing that I had his understanding and support.

The Home Office was proud of its Children's Department, and was enthusiastic about the changes proposed in the Bill, and it was my hope that by combining welfare, discipline and care in the hands of one Ministry we would initiate a reform that would be more beneficial both to the children in trouble and to society. Unfortunately, this objective was threatened by a parallel set of reforms published at almost the same time by a Committee under the chairmanship of Sir Frederic Seebohm, recommending a rationalisation of all the personal welfare services of the local authorities, including children. Dick Crossman, Secretary of State for Social Services, naturally pressed for the Children's Department of the Home Office to become a part of his Department, a course which I resisted strongly and successfully. However, when the Conservative Government succeeded us in May 1970 the new Home Secretary, Reginald Maudling, agreed to the transfer despite my private representations. I believe this was a mistake, despite the bureaucratic tidiness of the arrangement.

The implementation of the Seebohm recommendations meant that social workers in the Department of Social Services found themselves coping with a huge reorganisation of their own Department while at the same time being saddled with the transferred Children's Department, which was itself absorbing its new responsibilities. Social Services had neither the time nor the knowledge to integrate this new Department, and there was a loss of momentum in the children's reforms we had steered through resulting in the old system being discarded without effective new methods of treatment being put in its place. There was an absence of liaison between the Local Authorities and the juvenile courts which would not have happened had the Home Office been allowed to continue its traditional role as linchpin between the two. Magistrates complained that juvenile offenders were not being brought before them, but were left at home without any apparent attention paid either to their offence or to its treatment, and there was substance in such complaints.

As I write the issue still has not been resolved and disagreement remains between magistrates, social workers and the police about their respective roles and responsibilities, about which it has been truly said that there is an 'uneasy coexistence of justice and welfare'.

The changing and more serious nature of offences nowadays committed by children only adds to the urgency of the situation. As I write, the present Home Secretary, Douglas Hurd, has suggested an experiment to confront juveniles more clearly with the responsibility for their actions, for example by making visible reparation to the victim. Those of us who have seen the effects of vandalism on housing estates and the distress which is caused to elderly people will agree that the experiment is worth a trial. But I fear that society is very little further forward in discovering the underlying causes of juvenile delinquency than it was twenty years earlier.

There seems to be a striking paradox in modern behaviour. There is as much, if not more, personal kindliness and good-hearted voluntary service to help the sick, elderly, handicapped or lonely as there was when I was young. I speak of those private actions outside the ambit of the social services, freely given by neighbours or men and women out of sheer good will. Yet this exists side by side with a heightened indifference, a lack of consideration and, in serious crime, even a brutalisation of attitudes to the victims. Why is this? A weakening of parental responsibility? A materialist society with changing values? A loss of faith? The daily reports of killing in Northern Ireland? The impact of violence on television? All make some contribution, although we cannot measure how much weight to give to each. There is no single cause of violence, and it would certainly be too simplistic to suggest that the deprivation caused by poverty is the single cause. But undoubtedly crime flourishes where social need is greatest.

I must add that I never accepted the words of those television producers who dismissed any argument that violence on the screen might have an impact on the increase in violence in society. It would be foolish to blame too much on television, but a medium that can turn a once obscure game like snooker into a national pastime with tens of thousands of new adherents cannot claim that it has no influence on other less desirable aspects of human behaviour.

Milton Shulman, a television critic of long experience, has written that 'the main thrust of the medium's message is that violence is not only normal but that it is an acceptable way to right an injustice or a moral wrong. The most admired heroes on the box, from sheriffs to special agents, are faster on the draw than villains, super efficient at mayhem, and totally indifferent to the ethical implications of killing and maiming as a way of life'. I go much of the way with him, although I do not believe that the greatest incitement to violence comes from watching make-believe Westerns which take place in a location and a period far removed from the experience of our children. There is more danger in watching violent scenes which are familiar because they appear to relate to our own neighbourhoods and our own daily lives. From them the impressionable may conclude that the violence shown on the screen is the norm and not the exception. This is not a plea that television news should omit to show us the horrors of violence when they occur in the Lebanon or Central America. It is important that we should know the truth, even if it carries the risk of desensitisation. But please spare us much of the fictional violence committed by people apparently like ourselves, which is a staple part of our TV diet.

While I was at the Home Office, I discovered that nearly fifty separate pieces of research were being carried out by universities and other bodies, directed mainly to evaluating what happened to offenders after they had fallen into the hands of authority. I asked that research should be stimulated in the direction of the earlier stages of offenders' lives. What caused them in the first place to become offenders – personality traits, social environment, what else?

We could not stop and do nothing whilst we waited for a definitive answer, especially as in another part of the Government an important discussion was taking place about how to give further assistance to towns and cities with social problems caused by the sudden concentration of large numbers of newly arrived coloured immigrants. But these areas were not alone in suffering serious deprivation. Other cities and towns without immigrant populations also had problems and Ministers ruled that the Government could not be seen to be giving help only to the former. I was therefore able to graft on to the draft proposals for helping these particular areas a wider scheme for assisting all deprived areas. It was given the title 'The Urban Programme', and its purpose was to assist with housing, health and education in all large cities with special needs. The Prime Minister announced the programme in a May Day Speech in Birmingham in 1968.

I had been struck by a remark made by Lord Simey about Liverpool's problems. 'Here we are, using our slender resources in an attempt to heave people up out of the swamp one by one. Why do we not try draining the swamp?' The Chancellor agreed to set aside £20 millions for my scheme, and a Cabinet Sub-Committee agreed that a number of Local Authorities should be invited to establish experimental Community Development Projects. The objective would be to encourage those who lived in the most poverty-stricken areas of inner cities to recognise that they

themselves possessed the capacity to manage the affairs of their neighbourhoods, to reduce their reliance on outside help and, in the process,
to achieve greater control over their own lives and more satisfaction from
them. We laid down the basic condition that the schemes must involve
the people directly concerned, by finding out their views of their needs,
and not by imposing ours; by encouraging them to draw up plans themselves; and finally by enlisting their cooperation in executing the plans.
All agencies, official and voluntary, local and national, were to be involved.
Above all, I reiterated that officialdom did not know the answers and that
we could find them out only with the active cooperation of the local people.

Much of this approach stemmed from the work of a brilliant and strong-
minded Home Office official, Derek Morrell, whose strong moral sense
derived from religious conviction. More physical resources were obviously
a first priority, but beyond these our purpose was to activate and infuse
the spirit of pride and self-respect in such areas; only the people living
there could do that.

The Labour Government launched the Community Development
Projects in four areas late in 1969, and the Conservative Government
which succeeded us added several others. They attracted the enthusiasm
of a number of recruits from the social science faculties of the universities
and polytechnics, which had expanded rapidly during the radical 1960s.
Entering into the lives of others even with the best of intentions to help,
demands maturity and sensitivity, and while many social science gradu-
ates were successful in this, a few students emerged from their courses
having apparently swallowed everything they had heard but having failed
to digest it. A group of them proceeded to misuse the infant Community
Development Projects to put their theories into practice, and used the new
sociological language with much gusto but less discretion. I still recall
watching a group of experienced local councillors and residents almost
visibly wincing as they listened to the jargon of 'social pathology' and
'the culture of poverty' employed to describe their neighbourhood.

The small radical element decided that they already knew the answers
which the Community Projects were set up to discover, and a few of them
had the gall to announce that their objective was to create confrontation
with the Home Office, force it to reveal itself as the chief state organ of
class oppression and compel officials to reveal their true repressive role.
This callow nonsense surfaced a year or two after I had ceased to be Home
Secretary, and perhaps a strong-minded and able official like Derek
Morrell would have been able to squash it. Unfortunately, he died too

soon, and from that moment the Community Development Projects drifted and lost their way. Home Office officials became thoroughly disillusioned, and by 1974 when the Labour Government again returned to office, the projects had foundered and were beyond saving. So died a worthwhile effort. Fortunately the much larger urban programme itself did not suffer the same fate, and although it never had sufficient resources much devoted work was done by local government officers, social workers and others.

But the 1960s were years of hope, belief and experiment. One of my major tasks as Home Secretary was to implement the provisions of the Criminal Justice Act of 1967 which had been carried through Parliament by Roy Jenkins, and represented the most fundamental change in the administration of justice and the treatment of offenders seen in this century. It was a new high water-mark in a process that began with the Gladstone Committee's Report in 1895, which had formulated the important principle 'that the purpose of prison was reformation as well as deterrence, and rehabilitation concurrently with punishment'. For many years governments had attempted to limit the number of people being sent to prison and the 1967 Act limited it still further. One major innovation gave the courts the option when passing a sentence of two years or less to suspend its operation, and in cases of a sentence of six months or less the court was required to suspend the sentence. This last provision was subject to certain exceptions, for example if the crime involved violence or the accused had previously received a prison sentence. The significance of this change can be gauged from the fact that in 1967 more than 60 per cent of those in prison were serving sentences of less than six months.

Another provision of lasting importance ensured that prisoners serving a sentence of over eighteen months could become eligible for parole when they had served a minimum of twelve months of their sentence. Each prisoner's case would be considered by an independent Parole Board which would make recommendations for release to the Home Secretary. These changes reflected the questioning that was going on in the minds of Home Office officials and others who studied these matters as to the usefulness of prison sentences as a blanket means of deterrence. One aim of the penal system, laid down by No. 1 of the Prison Rules, was 'to encourage and assist prisoners to lead a good and useful life', and this was the subject of a continuing debate on whether fines or probation and the use of half-way houses were alternatives to keeping offenders in custody. Despite the complexity of the task, there was a sentiment abroad that the new Criminal Justice Act gave opportunities for initiatives that had not been attempted previously.

These new initiatives were hampered by public concern about prison escapes. In the post-war years insufficient resources had been devoted to keeping prisons secure and in the early 1960s there was a series of spectacular escapes in comparatively quick succession: Frank Mitchell (the axe-man); Ronald Biggs and Charles Wilson (the train robbers); George Blake (the Soviet spy), and others. Roy Jenkins had asked Earl Mountbatten to investigate what should be done.

At the time of the Mountbatten Report the most dangerous prisoners had been concentrated in maximum-security blocks in Durham, Leicester, Parkhurst and Chelmsford prisons. I myself became conscious of the shortcomings of these maximum-security blocks when, three months after my arrival at the Home Office, a riot took place at Durham gaol.

The maximum security block at Durham, known as E Wing, was a separate part of the prison housing about twenty of the most dangerous prisoners. Ian Brady, the Moors murderer, was there, but was kept apart from the others; the two strongest characters were Charles Richardson and John McVicar. Richardson together with his brother had been leader of a gang convicted of a number of serious crimes of violence, assault and even torture. He was serving a twenty-five-year sentence. McVicar's sentence was twenty years for crimes of robbery with violence. He was described as an intelligent man in his late twenties whose record showed that the prison system had neither deterred nor rehabilitated him, though it had undoubtedly protected the public. He was sixteen when he was first sent to a remand home, and shortly after absconded. Later he was sent to borstal and on two occasions absconded. He had spent most of his adult life in prison; on one occasion he had escaped from the coach taking him to Winchester Prison, and his latest venture had been to lead an attempted escape from Chelmsford as a consequence of which he had been transferred to Durham.

E Wing had originally been prepared to house some of the train robbers and was equipped with closed-circuit television and electronic equipment to render it secure, cutting it off from the rest of the prison. Letters and visits from relations were restricted, and the main human contacts were the prison officers. When it was first established there was no workshop, few recreational activities and the prisoners lived a life of infinite tedium, waking up each morning to a fresh realisation that

many years of imprisonment stretched ahead of them without prospect
of relief. The length of sentences of some of this group ranged from
seventeen to twenty-five years, with one case of imprisonment for life.
Never was there more fertile soil for mutiny, and Mountbatten uttered
a harsh condemnation of the conditions. They were, he said, 'such as
no country in the world with a record for civilised behaviour ought to
tolerate'.

Mountbatten proposed as an alternative that a maximum-security
prison should be built in the Isle of Wight to house 120 of the country's
most dangerous prisoners in conditions that would be totally secure
against escape, but would permit a more relaxed regime inside the walls.
He also recommended a substantial increase in the resources devoted to
improving conditions in prison, where many men were sleeping three to
a small cell, the buildings were in a poor state of repair, and there were
few amenities. The practice of slopping out was particularly nauseating
but was maintained because men were locked in their cells at night.
Although Victorian prisons were reaching the end of their life, less than
five thousand purpose-built new places had been provided in the twenty
years since the Second World War. I had been dealt a good hand and I
used Mountbatten's proposals to persuade the Cabinet to agree to more
money and more staff; I was fortunate that Roy Jenkins as Chancellor
sympathised with the problem.

The Mountbatten Report resulted in some immediate interim improvements in the conditions of the high-security gaols. At Durham, a
workshop for fabricating wrought-iron was built and a proper exercise
yard was provided, but the adverse publicity that had been given to conditions in the gaols enabled the prisoners in E Wing to capitalise on the
public concern. After they had digested Mountbatten's Report they began
to regard themselves as an élite. Normal discipline was not for them, and
they perfected the art of 'dumb insolence' to express contempt, without
transgressing to the point where they exposed themselves to punishment.
Durham's reputation became widely known throughout the prison
service and in February 1968 a new Governor, Gordon Chambers,
arrived, determined to end a situation in which the prison staff were outraged by the prisoners' conduct, but were confused by public criticism
of the regime that they were supposed to operate. Towards the end of his
first four weeks at the gaol, the Governor assembled the E Wing prisoners
and informed them that the workshop was now ready and they would be
expected to work. They refused on the grounds that the work would be

uninteresting. He further told them that he expected them in future to wear proper prison shoes and trousers. They refused, they would continue to wear T-shirts, basketball boots and other informal dress. Nor would they agree to clean their wing; prisoners from other parts of the prison could do it for them. Finally, they threatened the Governor with a demonstration to attract the attention of the press. He was not deterred, and warned the Home Office that tension was rising.

Late on Sunday evening on 3 March 1968, three days after Governor Chambers had met with the prisoners and on the day before they were expected to begin work in the new shop, I received a telephone call at home to say that the expected demonstration had begun. Twenty-one prisoners from E Wing had seized a prison officer, taken his keys, unlocked the door to a corridor leading to the chapel and the Assistant Governor's office, and were erecting a substantial barricade. Once in the Assistant Governor's office they ransacked their personal files, and then enterprisingly telephoned the *Daily Mirror* giving an exclusive story to an astonished reporter. This ensured that they would get the publicity they were seeking. Their next step was to call their girlfriends; it was some time before the authorities realised what they were doing and cut off the telephone, the heating and the electric light. Incensed, the prisoners began to break up the furniture, shouted obscenities, and attempted to dig up the floor, while the more rational of them prepared a petition which they poked through the barricade to the Assistant Governor on the other side.

Fortunately, none of the remaining 730 prisoners in the gaol made any disturbance, so the Governor was able to concentrate all his attention on E Wing, and he and the Assistant Governor handled a difficult situation well. First the prison staff attempted to break through the barricade but it had been strongly erected and they had no success. The Governor adopted a relaxed approach, but was nearly thwarted when some prison officers, arguing that authority could be restored only by forcible removal of both barricade and prisoners, brought up hosepipes to flush out the prisoners. Others wanted to use tear gas and produced respirators but Governor Chambers rightly refused to take hurried action, and the position remained unchanged through the hours of darkness.

Very early the next morning Alan Bainton, one of the senior staff in the prison service, came to see me. I knew him as an experienced prison governor and after we had talked asked him to go to Durham to assist Governor Chambers. It was a lucky choice, for some of the prisoners in

E Wing had known Bainton earlier when they had served in other prisons, and trusted him.

He began by talking to the prison officers, a number of whom were in belligerent mood, and it took considerable argument to secure cooperation for his proposed line of action. With the Assistant Governor he approached the barricade and called to the prisoners, who were still loudly singing and shouting. When they realised that Bainton had come from the Home Office they quietened down long enough for him to explain that he had read their petition, and although he would make no bargains, he had authority from the Home Secretary to say that if they came out quietly, their requests would be given proper consideration. He would arrange for visiting magistrates to be present as they came out to ensure there would be no reprisals, and they would be given a bath, clean clothes and a meal. They must take down the barrier, and come our one by one. Bainton then retired, not certain what the response would be.

There was a fierce discussion amongst the prisoners, the more rational of them realising that they had achieved their objective of securing national publicity, and consideration of their complaints, and could hope for no further benefit from continuing their action. Eventually they prevailed over the hotheads, and in further parleys with Bainton demanded guarantees about no reprisals. These were successful, the prisoners took a vote, and a majority were in favour of giving up.

At the Home Office I was kept in touch with these events as they happened and eventually, to my relief, I was told the prisoners seemed to be removing the barrier. Several minutes later the first prisoner emerged, and gave himself up peacefully. Then, one by one, these tough, dangerous and daring men came out quietly at short intervals and without a struggle. There was no violence, and no one was hurt. A minute-by-minute diary had been kept during the twenty-seven-hour period of trouble. The final entry at 22.30 on Monday night, read, 'Mr Gibbon and extra officers leave – all quiet and incident over'. It was a laconic ending to a revolt that could have had extremely serious consequences if it had been mishandled.

This narrow escape alerted me to the dangers of putting all our bad eggs in one basket. Their combined presence forming an élite in an ordinary prison unsettled the rest of the inmates, and strengthened Mountbatten's case for separating them completely and imprisoning them in a secure, fortress-type gaol. On the other hand, there was a potential danger in aggregating the most dangerous of the prison population of young, vigorous professional criminals, some of whom had killed or attempted to do so in the course of ruthless robberies, and who were capable of further desperate acts, especially if they needed to prove themselves to their fellows. Eventually, the argument was settled in my mind by a report from the Home Office Advisory Council on the Penal System, although not in the way it intended.

Roy Jenkins had asked the Council to consider what kind of regime should be followed in a Mountbatten-type prison, and it came forward with a majority recommendation that to strengthen the security of the prison, watch-towers should be erected on the perimeter in American style and prison officers with guns should be stationed in them. Although it was not publicly known, this was not the first time that such a proposal had been made. When Frank Soskice was Home Secretary in 1964 he had also wished to issue arms to prevent a possible break-out from Durham, but his proposal had then been rejected by the Cabinet. On this occasion, the Advisory Council's advice was published and a public outcry immediately followed. Mountbatten publicly declared himself against the watch-towers, as did the prison governors and the Prison Officers Association, although the latter remained convinced of the need for a Mountbatten-type prison.

In April 1968 I paid visits to Durham, Parkhurst and Leicester in quick succession and saw for myself the living conditions of some of Britain's most dangerous prisoners in their security wings. I returned to the Home Office convinced that the best solution was not to build a special prison, but to disperse these particularly dangerous men in penny packets to a large number of gaols where their numbers would be too small to dominate the life of the institution. It was decided to act quickly and quietly in order to forestall demonstrations and protests in any of the gaols. The dispersal began early one morning in May 1968 and was completed within a short period without trouble from the prisoners or any publicity.

After two months had passed without incident I was glad to receive a letter from the Chairman of the visiting magistrates at Durham telling me that the prison was more settled, the atmosphere more relaxed, and there was a definite change for the better in every way. Similar reports arrived from other prisons.

Both McVicar and Richardson continued to be dominating personalities, wherever they happened to be. Many years later I received a letter from Charles Richardson in Wandsworth gaol. He was due to be released after serving eighteen years of his sentence and wrote to me: 'I wish only to earn the respect of my parents and children, to become an industrious member of society, and to live the rest of my life in peace.' I hope he will do so. Some time after the Durham prison revolt McVicar made a most daring escape and remained free for many months before he was eventually recaptured. During his subsequent period in gaol he passed the relevant O and A level examinations, and finally sat for and was awarded a BSc degree in Sociology at London University – naturally as an external student! Following his release he wrote a successful autobiography, and a film was made from the book which gave a telling picture of tensions in the life of a prisoner and also of the strain on his family.

After these episodes I turned thankfully from crisis management to a more hopeful prospect, namely the building of a new prison at Coldingly in Surrey to house three hundred prisoners. One welcome feature of its design enabled 'slopping out', hated by both prisoners and staff, to be eliminated. But its major purpose was to introduce a new regime for the inhabitants. It was the first 'industrial' prison in Britain, an institution planned so that the prisoners' lives would be centred as far as possible around a day spent in a normal working atmosphere. Both the buildings and the regime were designed to make this possible. The prison housed a modern up-to-date laundry, capable of executing orders from outside customers, and an engineering machine shop with a paint-dipping line for the manufacture of steel shelving and road-sign making. Many of the green motorway signs seen on our roads some years ago were produced at Coldingly.

Discipline officers were not present on the workshop floor during working hours. The instructors, called 'foremen', were responsible for discipline and security as well as training. The prisoners worked a forty-hour week, and clocked in and out as they would have done in outside industry.

The Minister of State at the Home Office was Lord Stonham, who before his elevation to the Lords had been MP for Taunton and a lifelong prison reformer. He undertook detailed discussions with the CBI and the TUC and secured their general support for the idea of Coldingly. Armed with this, Home Office officials were able to negotiate agreements with the Building Trade Workers Union, the TGWU and the Amalgamated Union of Engineering Workers to accept prisoners as full members of these unions immediately prior to their discharge, provided they had reached an acceptable standard. This meant they would have a much better chance of finding a job. Our hope was to offset the effect of the prison system in eroding a man's self confidence. When the prison gates close behind him he surrenders all responsibility. Coldingly's aim was that a prisoner be able to exercise a considerable degree of initiative and choice while inside. Our purpose was rehabilitation, to build a prisoner's confidence in his ability to get and keep a job once he had been discharged. Victor Feather, the General Secretary of the TUC, was a tower of strength in coping with the inevitable difficulties, and came with me, together with a senior member of the CBI, when I opened the prison on 8 October 1969.

Coldingly started with high expectations, and my intention was that if it proved successful, similar prisons would follow in due course. This has not happened, because of inadequate numbers of prison staff and instructors as well as the overcrowding to which the prison system is subject. We proposed that prisoners with a fair period ahead of them should be sent to Coldingly, but productivity was hampered by a rapid turnover of the work force which involved continuous retraining. More recently, in the early 1980s, the prison industry suffered from Britain's general mass unemployment which made unions and employers less willing to accept competition of the kind that Coldingly could offer.

Nevertheless, it survived, although without any great encouragement from above, and as I write it is the only industrial prison in the system. Most of the items it manufactures, produces or services are for use in other prison establishments and government departments. But there are also some sales to nationalised industries and to the private sector.

Some fashionable modern thinking has endeavoured to turn the tide against ideas of rehabilitation, and no detailed investigation has been carried out to show whether Coldingly has had a favourable impact. The National Association for the Care and Resettlement of Offenders (NACRO) reached a negative conclusion that 'it has not been demonstrated that a purely industrial regime is any more beneficial to offenders than any other in lowering re-conviction rates'. In an interim verdict the Home Office stated that Coldingly had shown the benefits of providing an outlet for the physical and mental energies of inmates, and 'aids the maintenance of good order and morale'.

I plunged with enthusiasm into a number of aspects of crime and penal policy. A management reorganisation of the prison service itself was overdue and I shared Mountbatten's belief that a decentralised service operating from a number of out-stations should have a recognisable head. Accordingly I created the post of Director-General of the Prison Service, and in 1969 William Pile, a Deputy Secretary, became the first holder of the office. By temperament, ability and character he was well fitted to hold such a position and I hoped he would occupy it for at least five years, in order that the prison staff would get to know him as the leader to whom they could turn, who would understand the difficulties of a widely scattered service and be able to make informed judgements and champion them when necessary. Unfortunately, shortly after the change of government in 1970, Pile was whisked off to the Department of Education to become Permanent Secretary. Home Office officials had not really approved of my concept, and the idea languished.

Another reform I worked hard at was to abolish the artificial 'class' barrier between the various grades in the prison service so that the basic prison officer when recruited would know that he would have the opportunity to become an assistant prison governor in due course, and rise higher if he were fitted. I have written earlier of the shortcomings of the 'class' system in the Civil Service and it had lingered on in the prison service. I made a little progress before I left.

One other task that fell to me was to introduce the new parole system which sprang from the Criminal Justice Act. We were lucky to persuade Lord Hunt, the mountaineer who led the first successful attempt to conquer Mount Everest, to be the first Chairman. He is a fine man – deeply conscientious, considerate of others and with a high sense of responsibility; a rare person who it is a privilege to know and to work with. Other members of the Parole Board were appointed on a voluntary basis, and all of them worked long hours in their own leisure time reviewing prisoners' history and the evidence submitted to them by the local review committees at the prisons. In the first two years of the Parole Board's existence I accepted their recommendations to release 2,500 prisoners on licence. All remained liable to recall if they breached the conditions of release, but by the time I left the Home Office it had been necessary to recall fewer than a hundred. In this connection, tribute should be paid to the earlier work of a Labour Party Study Group on Crime which had been the inspiration of much of the Criminal Justice Act itself.

The parole system contained some sensible safeguards; for example, the Home Secretary could not release a prisoner serving a life sentence, despite recommendation from the Parole Board, unless he also consulted the Lord Chief Justice and the trial judge. In later years, the overall parole rate increased from 8 per cent of eligible prisoners to 62 per cent but the system has had a varying effect on the prospects of reconviction. Its success seems to have been greater among medium-risk and low-risk prisoners serving sentences of between four and ten years, and in such cases the number of reconvictions within two years after release has halved. On the other hand, parole seems to have had little effect on 'high risk offenders' serving less than a four-year term.

There has been growing criticism of the system in recent years. For example, David Downes, in his Fabian pamphlet *Law and Order. Theft of an Issue*, asserted that the knowledge that parole might be granted had led judges to lengthen certain forms of sentence; in his view a refusal of parole is in itself a form of resentencing. He also criticised the absence of a right of appeal. There is force in some of his charges, and I would support changes to give a prisoner a right of appeal, in some cases a personal hearing, as well as the right to know the reasons for refusal of parole.

Parliament reviewed the system in 1983, and approved a further extension of the system. The original intention of Willie Whitelaw, the Home Secretary responsible for the review, had been that once prisoners had completed one-third of their sentence they should be automatically released on licence. Whether this was due to his belief in the value of parole or was a device to reduce overcrowding in prisons is a matter of speculation. I suspect it was a little of both. However, the judges and magistrates expressed strong objections to automatic release, and Willie Whitelaw withdrew the proposal and substituted instead a provision that the period which must elapse before a prisoner could be considered for parole should be reduced from twelve to six months. Parliament approved this amendment and it will no doubt cut down the numbers who would otherwise be held in prison, although it will not lessen the amount of crime.

Nothing that has been done by any government since the end of the Second World War has halted the inexorable rise in the number of offences. The figures speak for themselves. In 1950, 479,400 offences were recorded. When I became Home Secretary in 1967 the number had reached 1,316,000. By 1985, the total was 3,426,400. Within these figures, violence against the person rose from 6,249 offences (1950) to 29,000 (1967) and to 122,000 in 1982. This is a horrifying rate of increase of which an alarming element is the growing number of robberies by professional criminals ready to use weapons and violence against any who stand in their way.

The public demands and expects these offenders when convicted to be removed to prison for long periods, as a protection to the general public, as a punishment and a deterrent. Oscar Wilde wrote in 'The Ballad of Reading Gaol':

> 'All that we know who lie in gaol
> Is that the wall is strong
> And that each day is like a year
> A year whose days are long.'

Imprisonment with its denials of liberty is a punishment, but I am not certain that prison has as much value as a deterrent. Investigation about the subsequent careers of male prisoners discharged in 1974 showed that 53 per cent of those who served sentences of between three and eighteen months were reconvicted within two years of their release. For young offenders under twenty-one nearly two-thirds were reconvicted within two years of leaving a detention centre, borstal or prison.

Society must approach these questions without pretence or prejudice. There is an urgent need for more research into alternatives to prison. Little has been uncovered in my lifetime to bring society any nearer to solving the causes of crime or how best to deal with the persistent offender. Which is most efficacious? Custody, pure and simple, custody combined with treatment, or treatment without custody? We should not spare the effort to reach some valid conclusions.

8

The police and law and order – race relations and immigration –
Northern Ireland – 'In Place of Strife' leads to problems

One advantage I possessed when I arrived at the Home Office was a previous close acquaintance with police forces in many parts of the country. This had arisen because some twelve years earlier, in 1955, I had been approached out of the blue by Alec Hamilton, the then Secretary of the Police Federation. He had told me candidly that while the police service had serious grievances about their pay and conditions they were not as experienced at negotiation as the professionals employed by the Local Authorities, and they were convinced that they would continue to get the worst of any deal unless they could secure the help of someone who could negotiate with the police authorities on equal terms. Would I help? I accepted immediately because this kind of negotiation and representation was close to my earlier experience in the Inland Revenue Staff Federation, and it enabled me to practise my belief in the values of trade union activity in creating healthy industrial relations.

I visited the Police Federation office which at the time comprised two rooms over a shop next to Camden Town tube station, with a staff of Alec Hamilton himself, a shorthand typist and an elderly cleaning lady who polished the linoleum on the floor until it was highly dangerous. Alec was a shrewd and level-headed Metropolitan constable who weighed at least eighteen stone and whose deliberate slowness of speech concealed deep insight into the minds of his colleagues. The office contained a minimum of records and equipment and the two of us started almost from scratch. During the late 1950s I became the principal negotiator for the police force, with Alec Hamilton's practical experience and knowledge to back me up. We decided that our best tactic was to begin at the bottom and win a square deal for the police constable, believing that the higher ranks could subsequently build on such a foundation.

Within five years we had succeeded almost beyond our wildest expectations. We wrote detailed statements of the constable's duties and responsibilities; outlined the increasing difficulty of his work; researched the past history of police pay as far back as the First World War. In this work we were helped by a number of trade unions, and the Local Authorities were somewhat shocked at our aggression. They refused the claims, and we had to use the machinery of the Independent Police Arbitration Tribunal. At the first hearing, the Local Authorities conducted their own case and, to tell the truth, were not very impressive. The arbitrators awarded the police a substantial increase. The Local Authorities learned their lesson, and prior to the second case, the whisper reached us that they were to be represented by a barrister. I was not over worried, believing that an advocate who had been handed a brief could not know the background as well as someone who believed (as I did) wholeheartedly in the justice of his case, and had immersed himself in it for many months.

When the tribunal met I found that my opponent was no ordinary barrister, but Gerald Gardiner, perhaps the leading QC of the day. This was the first occasion I had witnessed a first-class lawyer presenting a case, and he was truly formidable, arguing with a subtlety and sophistication that I had not previously encountered. He switched unexpectedly from one track to another, and I was left unwillingly impressed. The arbitrators must have felt the same, because although they awarded a greater increase of pay than that offered by the Local Authorities, it was not as big as I had hoped for. I was certain the Local Authorities could thank Gerald Gardiner for that. Later, of course, Harold Wilson appointed him as Lord Chancellor in the 1964 Labour Government and as colleagues in Cabinet I never ceased to respect his acuity and directness in penetrating to the heart of an argument, although he had a certain innocence about political realities.

The biggest success of the Police Federation during the years 1955 to 1964 was to make use of Sir Henry Willink's Royal Commission of Enquiry into the Police to secure redress of their deeply felt grievances about inadequate rates of pay. The Home Secretary Rab Butler had established the Royal Commission for the purpose of enquiring into public dissatisfaction with police behaviour, and Sir Henry Willink's remit was to enquire into their constitutional position, and to recommend improved arrangements for their control and administration and for the handling of complaints. There was no reference to the grievances that the police themselves felt, and I approached Rab Butler both privately and publicly and persuaded him that these other issues should not be considered in isolation from police pay. He agreed to add to the terms of enquiry 'the principles which should govern the remuneration of the constable'. Armed with this, the next step was to ask the Commission to consider pay as the first subject for their enquiry. I lobbied successfully for this in a number of quarters, and then persuaded the Home Secretary to ask the Commission not to wait until they had considered every problem but to issue an interim report on pay as soon as they had examined the issue. Rab was once again very helpful. I was persuaded that low rates of pay were not only damaging police work but were also lowering the standard of recruits.

I knew the police had an unanswerable case for an improvement which had remained unremedied for too long. I recommended that the Federation should put forward a claim for a constable to be paid £1,000 a year – an increase of about 40 per cent, which seemed to the Federation leaders utterly beyond their reach. However, I managed to persuade them that this was a realistic target, and we went to work with a will to prepare written evidence. Tremendous enthusiasm carried everyone forward, despite the difficulties and the lack of time to prepare the case. We worked hard and late, and primed ourselves with every possible statistic, comparison and argument.

We appeared before the Royal Commission with some trepidation, but in the event the occasion turned out to be less taxing than tangling with Gerald Gardiner. Sir Henry Willink, who had been a Member of Parliament before becoming a judge, gave us every opportunity to present our case, and was indulgent to me as an erstwhile junior colleague in the House of Commons.

In due course in 1960 the report we had waited for so anxiously was published. The Royal Commission recommended that the maximum pay of the constable should be increased to £970 per annum, not quite the £1,000 target we had aimed for, but close enough. I was exultant. Police morale and recruitment improved at once, and remained high for a number of years. This achievement was the high watermark of my nine years of work with the Police Federation.

When the Federation had first approached me in 1955 I told them that I regarded myself as having a role for a limited time in helping them build up an efficient office and gain negotiating experience, so that they could conduct their affairs without outside assistance. By the time we parted company, as a result of the general election of 1964, they possessed both the men and the knowledge to do so.

I laid down three basic principles in industrial matters which had been drilled into me many years earlier as a young trade union official. First, once an agreement has been freely negotiated it should be strictly adhered to by both parties during the whole period of its currency. This was a firm dictum of Ernest Bevin's. Second, where arbitration is a formal part of agreed industrial relations procedure, recourse to it should be the next step once negotiations break down. Go-slow tactics and other practices should not precede arbitration. Third, by agreeing to go to arbitration, both sides morally bind themselves to accept the arbitrator's award. In the Civil Service, these practices were commonplace before the war and had a beneficial effect. More recently they have been set aside – and not exclusively by the unions. Government itself has been at fault.

I arrived at the Home Office in November 1967 with a certain background knowledge to find great changes taking place within the police service. Roy Jenkins had set in hand the amalgamation of several smaller and large forces. Panda cars were being used as a substitute for the man on the beat – a policy I did not care for – and new equipment such as personal radios was being issued. A number of forces were striving to get rid of the petty and irksome restrictions imposed on the official and private life of the constable by some short-sighted chief officers.

After 1960 the rate of pay of the experienced constable had once more fallen behind, and there was considerable pressure to make up a shortage of constables by recruiting young police cadets from school-leavers. The system produced many fine young policemen whose ability gained them rapid promotion, but I was keen to ensure that the police service should not depart from the tradition of being a civilian force, drawn from the people and remaining a part of the people. One of the most valuable elements in maintaining this tradition was the practice of recruiting a number of mature men who had spent some years in factory or office and had experienced life as civilians. These men bring to the police an understanding of the public that is different from the experience of the cadet who joined in his youth. For this reason, it was my policy that the cadet element should not exceed more than 50 per cent of all recruits.

The Home Secretary has a special responsibility for the Metropolitan Police, including the appointment of the Commissioner, and when the existing incumbent died in office it fell to me to choose his successor. I consulted a small group of provincial chief constables whose opinion I valued, and eventually appointed the Deputy Commissioner, Sir John Waldron, a rather stiff man but very popular in the force, with a genuine care and concern for its welfare, and a high standard of personal integrity.

His fault was to be too loyal to some serving under him who were undeserving of his confidence. He was immensely steady and unflappable during the large and sometimes violent demonstrations against the Vietnam War in 1968, and was a voice for sanity when other police officers overreacted. But in the following year he and I had a serious difference of opinion. In November 1969 *The Times* published a dramatic story on its front page directly accusing three officers of the Criminal Investigation Department of demanding money from a criminal in order to drop a prosecution. The newspaper named the three officers, said that its reporters held tapes of conversations to prove the offence, and backed the story with a photograph that appeared to show some financial transaction taking place between the officers and the criminal.

It was an alarming report which *The Times* obviously would not have dared to print unless they were satisfied it was true. Sir John Waldron came to see me immediately. He was devastated at the discredit that would be brought on the Metropolitan Police if the crime was proved, and vented his anger on the newspaper for not giving Scotland Yard prior warning, complaining that publication had given the police officers concerned time to cover their tracks and destroy any evidence.

I did not know until later that *The Times* had decided to publish because they feared that unless they did so the Yard would cover up a crime committed by their own men.

Events were to show that *The Times* was, I regret to say, only too correct in making such an assumption – which was more damning to the reputation of the Met. than the original crime had been. Sir John Waldron assured me that the matter would be rigorously investigated and appointed a Detective Chief Superintendent to take charge, while I consulted Frank Williamson, one of the Inspectors of Constabulary attached to the Home Office whose special responsibility was the oversight of criminal investigation.

In the light of our conversation I asked the Commissioner to see me again. He told me that he had no progress to report, upon which I said that it was a considered judgement that his enquiry team needed strengthening, and I wanted his agreement to add Frank Williamson to it to advise on the nature of the investigation. Inspectors of Constabulary are very senior officers who come to the Home Office after much experience in the field, and Williamson, a former Chief Constable of Cumbria, was a man whose professional ability was widely respected. Sir John Waldron bridled at my proposal, saying that Williamson's appointment would cast a slur on the efficiency of his team, but I insisted and a few days later Williamson joined the team at the Yard, having been told that he would be given personal access to me whenever he thought it necessary.

Six weeks later, early in 1970, Williamson came to see me. His report was disquieting. The Chief Superintendent in charge of the enquiry team seemed ready to work with him but he was receiving little coopera- tion from the other investigating officers and felt they were closing ranks against him. He put this down to his having been Chief Constable of a provincial force, and asked me to give him a little more time to work matters out. But he did not succeed, and decided to recruit a team of provincial police officers to support him. The next occasion on which he reported to me personally was shortly before the general election of 1970 and his news was even worse than before. There had been a total break- down of cooperation between him and the Metropolitan enquiry team and he had removed his own team from Scotland Yard to another build- ing to prevent this obstruction.

He said that he now believed there was more to the hostility than a mere dislike of him and his provincial team. He told me he suspected that corruption went deeper than the three officers who were still being investigated and that he intended to extend the scope of his enquiry. By this time the 1970 election was upon us so I asked Williamson to continue to do what he could, and said I would thrash the matter out with the Commissioner when we returned.

We were defeated, however, and Reginald Maudling took my place as Home Secretary. Before leaving the Home Office I sent a personal hand- written note to him. I did not retain a copy but remember its contents clearly. It contained two points: first, he should clean up the Criminal Investigation Department at Scotland Yard and rid it of any taint of corruption; second, as Waldron was due to retire within a few months, the best man to succeed him was Robert Mark, the Deputy Commissioner, who had been thrust upon a reluctant Metropolitan Force by Roy Jenkins when he persuaded him to leave his post as Chief Constable of Leicester. He was another provincial policeman who had served much earlier with Frank Williamson.

I lost track of events after my departure from the Home Office until one day I received a message from Williamson asking to meet me. This was unexpected but I agreed, and he had a sorry story to tell. Within a fortnight of my departure the Detective Chief Superintendent who headed the Metropolitan enquiry team, and in whom Williamson had great confidence, had been removed with the excuse that some extra-marital problem rendered him unfit to continue the investigation. He had been replaced by another Chief Superintendent who, said Williamson, was showing very little interest in the *Times* case.

Williamson had reported that there was a serious problem in the Met.'s conduct of affairs but had been told that he was wrong. He did not tell me to whom his report had gone. He wanted me to know that he was thoroughly disillusioned and frustrated. He had disbanded his provincial team of officers for they could get no further, and he himself intended to retire because he was certain that the truth was being concealed.

I asked whether he still had personal access to the Home Secretary, and if so had he told him this? He replied that he had submitted a written report which had been returned to him with the comment that the Home Secretary had seen it, but he had not seen Maudling personally. I asked him if he would have any objection if I were to see the Home Secretary, and he had none.

When I saw Reggie Maudling he told me frankly that he was unable to reach a conclusion about the extent of wrongdoing in the CID, but the Commissioner would shortly retire; Maudling shared my opinion of Robert Mark and intended to appoint him to succeed. Mark had strong opinions about the CID, and Maudling asked me to hold my hand and give Mark the opportunity to clear up the issue once and for all.

The rest of the story is public knowledge. Mark had no sooner taken over than he announced that the CID, which regarded itself as an élite force in the Met., was to be placed under the control of the uniformed branch. Further, a new unit would be set up, separate from the rest of the Met., to investigate all allegations of crime and other complaints against the force. These drastic changes caused consternation and some unrest in the CID but Mark did not waver and he got results. Two of the three police officers accused by *The Times* were tried and found guilty of taking bribes. And, crowning irony, the Detective Chief Superintendent whose disinterest when put in charge of the *Times* case had aroused Williamson's suspicions was charged with taking substantial bribes amounting to several thousands of pounds from a dealer in pornography and was sentenced to twelve years' imprisonment to mark the extreme gravity of his crime.

Williamson had been right and so had *The Times*. Corruption in the Metropolitan CID had spread from the highest rank of officer to the lowest. They formed a 'firm', but with the new Commissioner setting the tone, it was rooted out. More than four hundred officers were dismissed or retired and this marked the end of systematic corruption in the force.

The revelations sullied the public regard for the Met. and left the large majority of good men in the force aghast at the disrepute into which it had been brought. But the new Commissioner set about re-building both the morale of the force and the trust of the public, with the support of the overwhelming number of men and women in the Met. who were only too relieved to see the stable cleaned. We owe him a debt of gratitude.

The great majority of police officers have a high sense of public honesty and duty. But mixing regularly with criminals to get information, as some must do, puts them in the way of temptation, and a small number will tend to succumb. It will never be possible to root out dishonesty completely, and police and public must be constantly vigilant, for an incorruptible police service is a major pillar of a healthy society. As for Frank Williamson, who did his utmost to ensure this, he returned to his native north country a disheartened and frustrated man, but he should take comfort from the fact that events after he left the Home Office have entirely justified what he tried to do in upholding the standards of integrity that he believed in.

Young people in many countries chafed under the materialism and social norms of their elders, searching for new values and standards in questions such as racialism, civil rights, nationalism and sex. There was a fear of nuclear war – that this might be the last generation in history. Fortified by gurus such as Professor Herbert Marcuse, German students declared that they had no confidence in parliamentary democracy and were 'taking democracy into the streets'. In France a long build-up of student unrest led them to boycott their examinations and to occupy the Sorbonne with a defiant declaration that it was open to all workers. A general strike was called, there was disorder and violence over a period of several days. President de Gaulle, fearing for the Republic, left Paris. He had been so alarmed by the revolt that he paid a secret visit to the commanders of the French Army in Germany, presumably to reassure himself that he could rely on its support. The French Minister of Education was forced to resign and his successor promised far-reaching university reforms. It was an ugly period but eventually the violence burned itself out. In America, too, there were violent scenes at universities in opposition to the Vietnam War. The Civil Guard was called out on occasion, and in one terrible case students demonstrating at Kent State University were shot dead. It was unlikely that Britain would escape the general malaise.

The first serious disturbance in Britain took place in July 1968, when three thousand demonstrators marched to the United States Embassy in Grosvenor Square where they threw bottles and bricks, smashing windows and starting small fires. The police had not been well prepared and there were ugly scenes. As a result I urged the Commissioner to review police practice and training to ensure a well thought-out, disciplined approach. During August an appreciation was prepared of the prospects of student trouble in the forthcoming university year and of the action the police might need to take. My stance was that it was their responsibility and mine as Home Secretary to preserve 'freedom under the law', an attitude I much preferred to the slogan 'law and order'. It was reported that the July march had been intended as a trial run for a much larger demonstration planned for the autumn of 1968 in protest at the Vietnam War and its organisers were busy during the summer, their advance publicity claiming that the 'autumn offensive' was to be a massive affair.

The *London Evening News* and *The Times* published accounts of what they called 'startling plots' to use home-made bombs and of plans to seize sensitive installations and government buildings on the path of the march. Tariq Ali, one of the principal organisers, threatened that the planned demonstrations could be as violent as those of Paris and Berlin, but kindly promised no violence if the police stayed away. It was not possible to gauge how serious all this was, but an agitated atmosphere built up based on very little reliable information, with newspaper reports making the ordinary citizen's blood curdle about the horrors to expect.

This brought many demands that I should ban the march, and Quintin Hogg, the Shadow Home Secretary, came to see me in a state of great excitement. I should close the main line London stations on the day of the march, turn back all buses heading for London, and hold the Guards regiments ready in their barracks to deal with riots. I was not so alarmed. I had maintained contact with one or two political friends on the fringes of the preparation, and they told me that the main groups organising the demonstration were anxious that it should be non-violent. On the other hand, they knew that a Maoist group intended to try to lead a breakaway march to the US Embassy hoping for a punch-up, while some excitable young people at the LSE announced that they were prepared for a confrontation with the police and would take over their buildings as a base and a hospital for the wounded. Naturally, much of this reached the newspapers and added fuel to the flames.

I consulted carefully with the Commissioner. He agreed with me that it would be a victory for the extremists if the march was banned, for it would be represented as a denial of a democratic right. He added that as a result of the review of practice after July, he was reasonably satisfied that the Metropolitan Police could contain it, including the planned breakaway if it took place.

The Cabinet discussed the matter and I recommended that the demonstration should take place. This was what most of the Cabinet hoped to hear and they agreed. I was somewhat comforted by reports of violent quarrels between the organisers and the group planning confrontation. One of those who attended a planning meeting told me that at one point, when the quarrel became fierce, the Maoist group had climbed on their chairs, reciting in unison from their Little Red Book, *The Thoughts of Chairman Mao*, whilst the rest of the planners countered with a brave chorus from the 'Internationale'.

Daniel Cohn-Bendit (Danny the Red), who had played a major part in organising violent student revolts on the Continent, applied for a permit to enter the country in order to visit Scotland for a holiday. This seemed an unlikely tale and I authorised the immigration officials to refuse, stating that my policy would be to admit only those foreign students who had no proven record of violence. Cohn-Bendit was told that he would be free to tramp the Highlands after the demonstration was over, but for some reason the hills and lochs lost their attraction and he did not come. I answered many apprehensive questions in Parliament, and a delegation of newspaper proprietors whose buildings were on the route came to see me, asking what protection they could expect to defend their buildings from invasion.

The French example was in their minds, but they themselves had done much to create public fear. I told them that I did not intend to ban the march, upon which a storm broke over my head. The Home Office was inundated with hundreds of telegrams and letters of protest from members of the public, and Sir Gerald Nabarro, the colourful Member for Worcestershire South who was always good for a headline, summed up the mood when he announced on the day of the march: 'If there is disorder, arson and bloodshed, Mr Callaghan has only himself to blame.'

Throughout the period of waiting I was fortified by the calm confidence of the Commissioner and of Commander Lawlor, who had been newly

placed in charge of crowd control and who had been planning his dispositions since the summer. He called in the leaders of the proposed breakaway group to warn them formally of his preparations and tell them that
violence would not be tolerated in Grosvenor Square. They gave no
undertakings, but let it be known that they thought Tariq Ali, who was
in the forefront of the non-violent group, was a bourgeois reactionary. It
was the biter bit.

When the day arrived, I walked along the Embankment where the
demonstrators were assembling and was greeted with some good-
humoured booing; my escorts were relieved when I returned to the
Home Office in which a closed circuit television set had been installed,
taking the same pictures as were reaching the police crowd control centre.
Throughout the afternoon I was able to watch the whole gigantic procession as it snaked along the agreed route, peacefully and without disturbance of any major kind. The Maoists and a section of the crowd broke
away as they had threatened to do, and after reaching Grosvenor Square
adopted fierce tactics to try to reach the front door of the American
Embassy. There were some incidents and a number of policemen were
deliberately kicked and hurt, but they had prepared their tactics well and
the attacks were repulsed. The Commissioner had extracted a promise
from me that I would stay away from Grosvenor Square, but in the evening, when the tension eased, he relented and I was able to visit the police
and thank them for upholding 'freedom under the law' with such admirable coolness. I also talked to a number of demonstrators, who by this
time were dispersing. The hard men had already gone and those I spoke
to were genuinely concerned to make their protest against American
policy. I upheld their right to do so. The atmosphere improved and later
that night the proceedings concluded with the police and the remaining
demonstrators linking arms and singing 'Auld Lang Syne'. I was particularly pleased that the experience gained by the police in the July 1968
demonstration had prevented such ugly scenes on this occasion.

The Government, having come under heavy attack for not banning
the march, now found itself receiving plaudits for the way the march had
gone. The anticipated horrors of the day had been widely reported beforehand in overseas newspapers, and now congratulations flooded in
from a number of countries. Newspapers in America, France, Italy and
Holland all had kind things to say about Britain's way of handling the
affair, and contrasted it with their own experience. Perhaps in view of
the heavy criticism which was directed at me before the march, I may

be permitted to quote from a report in *The Times* of the following day from their Home Affairs correspondent, Norman Fowler, who later became Secretary of State for Social Services in the Conservative Government: 'There is no doubt that the biggest success belongs to Mr Callaghan. The Home Secretary refused to be stampeded into banning the march on the basis of some forecasts of violence, and his judgement proved correct.' In fact it had been my view throughout that the situation had never been as dangerous as the press made out, but that their reports, together with those on television, created much of the public fear and semi-hysteria.

Even so, I was not confident of the future. It was possible that we were entering an era of deliberate confrontation and I voiced my doubts when I addressed the Police Federation shortly afterwards:

> There are some people who feel that the increased violence which exists throughout the world could spread to Britain. It could be argued that in the end we might have to step up our preventive measures, but we should be reluctant to do so. By your success and self-control on this occasion you have put back by a very considerable period the moment when it might be necessary to take such steps . . . I must say despite the self-control of the majority that there was a minority that was willing to provoke violence. There is a move among a relatively small faction which is anxious to prove, by some inversion of argument, that our tolerance is really repressive. They are determined to show that you are the instruments of repression by provoking you to repress them when they attack you. It is a queer and twisted sense of logic.

To my regret, these forebodings have proved accurate.

Another issue which came to the fore during my term of office was racialism in sport. It came into public prominence through the affair of Basil D'Oliveira, an outstanding coloured cricketer born in South Africa who had settled in England some years earlier. He played in the Lancashire league before joining Worcestershire, and was selected to play for England in the series in the West Indies. In the final Test in 1968 he ran into his best form at the right time, making a century against Australia at the Oval. There is no doubt that he should have been included in the England team to visit South Africa, yet when it was announced a few weeks later, his name was missing. The MCC had apparently been told by the South African Government that a coloured cricketer was not acceptable. When this became known there was an outburst of indignation at D'Oliveira's omission, headed by David Sheppard, a former England Captain who later became Bishop of Liverpool. Some members of the MCC threatened to resign and called a special meeting, while the *News of the World* enterprisingly and mischievously jumped in with a financial offer to D'Oliveira to visit South Africa on their behalf as a commentator on the Test series.

Mr Vorster, South Africa's Prime Minister, arrogantly responded, 'Guests who have ulterior motives usually find that they are not invited', which added fuel to the flames. The MCC bowed to the storm of criticism and tried to mend matters by announcing that because of an injury to one of the team, D'Oliveira would, after all, be included in the side. Mr Vorster exploded. In a speech at Bloemfontein he said, 'It is not the MCC team. It is the team of the Anti-Apartheid Movement. It is the team of political opponents of South Africa.' Billy Griffith, the Secretary of the MCC, was having no more of this: 'If the chosen team is not acceptable to South Africa, the MCC will call off the tour.' Mr Vorster was unrepentant, and in the end the tour did not take place. I applauded this, and accordingly was surprised when, despite what had happened, the MCC announced that they had invited South Africa to play twenty-seven matches in England in the 1970 season. This decision showed a total insensitivity to the treatment of black and coloured people, and I was not surprised when agitation arose to 'Stop the Tour'.

The Chief Constables in whose areas the games were to be played took the prospects of disorder seriously, and met at the Home Office to make preparations to face it. They were concerned about the prospects of success in trying to guard the wide-open areas of turf on the cricket ground against determined efforts to interrupt play. Quintin Hogg, who was the Member for St Marylebone, added his ha'porth by seeking assurances that those of his constituents who lived near Lords would be given adequate police protection.

Agitation built up, and MCC officials asked to see me to say that they had decided to reduce the tour from twenty-seven matches to twelve, giving as their reason the cost to the counties of policing the grounds. But this did not make things much better, and people as diverse as Mike Brearley, Sir Edward Boyle, John Arlott and the editor of the *Sun* joined in with demands that the tour be cancelled. On 19 May 1970 the Cricket Council finally decided that there would be no further Test tours with South Africa until teams were selected on a non-racial basis. Two days later M. J. C. Allom and Billy Griffith, the Chairman and Secretary of the MCC, came to see me. Both said they were ready to go ahead with the restricted tour but they realised that it could have wider implications for such issues as race relations in Britain and the possible cancellation of the forthcoming Commonwealth Games. They said that they were not competent to judge such matters, and they asked for my views as to the effect if the tour went ahead.

I interpreted this as a willingness to cancel the tour provided the Government would accept the responsibility for them doing so. The first match was due to be played at Lords only a fortnight later, on 6 June. I told Allom and Griffith that while, as Home Secretary, I had no power to prohibit the tour, the Government certainly accepted responsibility for expressing a view about the consequences, and I believed that the tour would have a serious and adverse impact. On the grounds of broad public policy the Government would prefer the MCC to withdraw the invitation. Messrs Allom and Griffith, who were always cooperative and helpful during our meetings, told me that the MCC would almost certainly agree to such a request, and shortly afterwards I was glad to hear that they had cancelled the tour.

Several years later I was brought into the sporting arena again when as Prime Minister I presided at the Commonwealth Heads of Government Meeting held in London in 1977, and took part in negotiating the Gleneagles Agreement, which has been the basis of the Commonwealth attitude towards sporting contacts with South Africa ever since and which at that time prevented a serious rupture of the Commonwealth Games.

The Home Office is the focus of the anxieties and controversy surrounding the immigration of Commonwealth citizens, and the consequential issue of racial equality. Both topics are a challenge to principle and to conscience and evoke seemingly invincible prejudices that only time and knowledge will remove. The immigration of large numbers of coloured people arouses particular passion, and every Home Secretary since Rab Butler has been scorched by the flame. It was he, no less, despite his childhood in India, who decided with great reluctance in 1961 that he must bring forward the first Act in our history to control immigration from the Commonwealth. Before that time all citizens of the United Kingdom and colonies or citizens of other Commonwealth countries had enjoyed an uncontrolled right to enter and settle in Britain. Despite Rab's new controls, Commonwealth citizens and their families continued legally to arrive in large numbers, attracted by prospects of work for

264 TIME AND CHANCE

themselves in a full-employment economy, and hoping for better opportunities for their children.

During the mid 1960s, this form of immigration was given further impetus by the policy of Africanisation adopted by the new governments of Kenya and Uganda following their grant of independence. Their policy of giving more opportunities to the Africans was partially done by taking over the businesses and livelihoods of a large number of Asians living in East Africa and handing them to Africans. This caused great hardship, and there was further deep anxiety when the Kenyan Government announced that from December 1967 residents in Kenya who were not citizens would need to apply for so-called 'entry certificates' if they wished to remain in the country. This ignored the fact that most of the Asians affected had been born in East Africa, regarded it as their only home and had never resided in or even visited India or Pakistan from where their forebears had originally come.

George Thomson, the Commonwealth Secretary, took the matter up with Jomo Kenyatta, who justified the policy on the grounds that the Asians had been given the opportunity to become Kenyan citizens at the time of independence but had failed to take it. Therefore, said Kenyatta, he had no obligation to them and they should go. Naturally, there was widespread alarm among the Asians that they might be deported from the country of their birth without ceremony. What were they to do? They discovered a loophole. The Westminster Statute granting Kenya and Uganda their independence contained a provision that inhabitants of the territories who so wished would be entitled to a British passport on request. This had been inserted into the act by Duncan Sandys, the then Commonwealth Secretary, who wanted to safeguard the rights of British settlers, but the provision had been drafted in general terms and thousands of Asians who had not previously considered obtaining a British passport now rushed to do so as an insurance policy. Who could blame them?

The number of Asians leaving Kenya for Britain was two thousand a month when I arrived at the Home Office. I asked how many similar people possessed the right to come to Britain but officials had no reliable figures, although according to Dick Crossman, my predecessor Roy Jenkins had worked on the basis that it might be 200,000. Later estimates produced a possible maximum of 360,000, not taking into account a million Chinese living in Malaysia and elsewhere.

Before my arrival discussions had taken place between Roy Jenkins and Crossman, the Leader of the House, about the likely need for a Bill to limit entry, and the matter was still under discussion when Roy and I exchanged offices. A Cabinet Committee was in existence and had decided to consider the matter in January 1968 hoping that in the interval immigration would lessen, while the Commonwealth Office held talks with India and Pakistan. Mrs Gandhi, the Prime Minister of India, was helpful and said that India would have no objection to accepting Asians of Indian origin if Kenya actually deported them, but she would not say so publicly as this would make it easier for East African governments to discriminate against the Asians. I thought this was very reasonable and that our policy should also point in the same direction.

I did not know President Kenyatta well, although I had been allowed to visit him when he had been held in detention by the British Government in Kenya, and had corresponded with him at irregular intervals. I had some reason for hoping that if we put up a firm front, he would not proceed with mass expulsions. But he proved intransigent and, despite urgings from leaders of other Commonwealth countries, refused to give any assurances that would quieten the fears of the Asians. As a result, the number of immigrants from Kenya rose steadily month by month throughout the winter of 1967/8. Thirteen thousand arrived in the first two months of 1968 – twice as many as in the whole of 1965 – and as pressure increased on the Asians from the Kenyan Government signs of panic began to appear. The number of immigrants arriving at London airport reached 2–300 every day, with no homes or jobs to go to and sometimes with very little money. The newspapers carried large pictures and lurid and exaggerated accounts of how homeless families were drawing lavish assistance from the Social Services; and followed these up with descriptions of boatloads of illegal immigrants being smuggled ashore on isolated south coast beaches, where they were left stranded. Bradford and Southall rapidly became centres of immigration as the newcomers congregated in areas where their fellow-countrymen had already settled. Alarm was spread by reports that housing and education authorities were quite unable to cope with the influx. Everything conspired to build up an atmosphere of alarm, resentment and panic, both in Britain and in Kenya.

Enoch Powell fanned prejudice to fever heat with his speech in April 1968 about the personal habits, housing and education of the coloured immigrants, and dockers marched to Parliament to support his attacks. There was danger of a serious deterioration in race relations unless the Government acted to reassure the country that the situation would not get out of hand. I put it to Ministers that 'we shall remain subject to these risks of continuing tensions and stimulation of prejudice unless we amend the law so that the public in this country are confident that immigration is being effectively controlled. Only in such an atmosphere can good race relations be fostered.' I put forward two proposals: first, we should state clearly and unequivocally that we would fulfil our obligations to everyone who was entitled to come to Britain; second, we should establish a register of all those who wished to come and issue a number of entry vouchers year by year so that they would be admitted in an orderly queue, and so dispel the allegations that the country was being swamped by a tidal wave of immigrants.

It never was, of course, and some of my colleagues were uneasy; I could not entirely blame them, for the latter proposal took away the right of the immigrants concerned to come at any time of their own choosing. The great majority of the Cabinet accepted the proposal as a distasteful necessity, but it was suggested that before we took action, Malcolm MacDonald, our Special Representative in East Africa, should make a last effort to avoid legislation by making a personal approach to President Kenyatta, with whom he had been on very friendly terms. If anyone could soften Kenyatta, it was he. But Kenyatta remained adamant that the Asians must leave and on hearing this, the Cabinet reluctantly gave me permission to bring forward the Bill.

None of my junior Ministers liked it any better than the Cabinet, or I. David Ennals, who was responsible for carrying the legislation through the House, took it on the chin and the Bill passed through all its stages with a large majority in both Houses of Parliament in seven days and became law on 1 March 1968. While the Bill was going through Parliament I was given a difficult time, and was upset at the harsh tone of some of the personal criticism, which was extremely bitter. But although this was an unwelcome task, I do not regret the decision we took.

Harold Wilson and most of my Cabinet colleagues stood by me throughout the period, as did a great many of my parliamentary colleagues on both the right and left of the Labour Party. This was especially true of Members of Parliament from the Midlands, who told me at a meeting to discuss the problem that the public had resented the reluctance of politicians to face the issue, and welcomed the fact that I was dealing with it 'in a way that was humane and practical'. With all the bitter charges that were hurled at me, I could never understand why President Kenyatta should have escaped criticism for precipitating the problem by depriving

Kenyan-born Asians of their livelihoods and then expelling them with practically no resources.

Five thousand five hundred vouchers were allocated to heads of families for the first year, and by adding on surplus vouchers not taken up by other parts of the Commonwealth I expected in practice that there would be enough vouchers to allow the immigration of about thirty thousand Asians in the first twelve months. I hoped that when President Kenyatta saw we were in earnest in fulfilling our obligations, he too would accept some share of responsibility in preventing a wave of homelessness. It is possible that our actions had some impact, for towards the end of 1968 his office notified the British High Commissioner that they intended to withdraw work permits for no more than nine thousand Asians when they expired, and this might mean that twenty-seven thousand people would be expected to leave Kenya. This was a total that we could accommodate under the voucher system, and as many of them decided to go to India this eased the problem further.

If one task of a Home Secretary is to keep a sense of proportion during waves of public panic then I can claim that the 1968 legislation achieved its purpose. Thereafter, except for the zealots, there has been a growing acceptance that immigration is not out of control or 'swamping' the country. Mrs Thatcher tried to revive the word and the charge several years later in a television interview, but she had no lasting success and she did not return to the matter.

There was a postscript to these events at the ensuing Commonwealth Heads of Government Conference held in London in January 1969. I was eager for the future of the East African Asians to be discussed, as this was the appropriate forum in which to reach an agreed Commonwealth position, especially in view of the possibility that Britain might be faced in the future with a similar situation arising in some other Commonwealth country. Harold Wilson, who was to preside at the conference, proposed to inscribe an item on the agenda under the heading 'Citizenship and Immigration', but President Kenyatta and President Obote of Uganda, joined by some other Commonwealth Heads of Government, would not agree. There were some informal talks and a working party was set up but all four East African countries absented themselves from its meetings. They excused themselves privately on the grounds that had they attended they would have been embarrassed by the attentions of their own press.

The working party achieved little and the conference issued a meaningless statement directing the Secretary General of the Commonwealth to examine the general principles governing migration and citizenship and 'if necessary, to explore ways and means of studying the subject on a continuing basis with a view to providing relevant information to the governments concerned'. The truth is that some of those governments copped out and Britain took the flak. I did not regard this as the highest form of statesmanship.

Whatever views may be taken about the right of a nation to admit whom it chooses subject to the general interest, there can be no doubt that if a society is to remain healthy then once a person has been allowed to settle he or she must be treated in law, in employment, in housing, in education and health and in every other way without discrimination of any kind. Even now, thirty years after the first wave of coloured immigrants arrived, Britain is still far from attaining this ideal, as the Scarman Report on the 1981 Brixton riots showed. Equality of treatment and opportunity must remain our overriding aim, and we must work towards it positively and ceaselessly, not only because to do otherwise is to lower the status and dignity of the individual, but also because failure will coarsen our society and make a true long-term unity of the nation impossible. Such a social contract includes all citizens of whatever colour. Wherever there are concentrated, run-down city areas, wherever the virus of long-term unemployment exists, or poor housing conditions, there is to be found clear evidence of unequal treatment suffered by black and white alike. The race issue cannot be divorced from our wider socio-economic problems. Whilst all who are poor will suffer deprivation it is our responsibility to ensure that those who are coloured do not suffer additionally merely because of their colour.

The Labour Party manifesto in 1964 had contained a pledge to legislate against this kind of discrimination and Roy Jenkins began the process of discussion with various interested parties. When I arrived at the Home Office many issues still remained to be settled, but with Dick Crossman's help we made rapid progress and in April 1968 I was able to introduce a Bill into the House of Commons to make discrimination unlawful in matters of employment, housing, the provision of all kinds of services and also in the publication of advertisements. The purpose of the Bill was to make a declaration of public policy, to create a climate of public opinion, to seek a consensus, and to create a framework in which conciliation would be the first tool to be used to resolve disputes, backed at a later stage by legal proceedings if they became necessary. The Act was passed by Parliament and marked an important stage in the development of Britain's anti-racial public policy.

In the first two years of its operations, the Race Relations Board dealt with 2,800 complaints, over half of which were about discrimination in employment. The Act was successful in putting an end to discrimination in public houses, restaurants and other public places and in preventing the display of offensive racial advertisements. It had an important educative effect, but it was no more than an interim measure, and seven years later was replaced by one which shifted the balance towards stronger legal rights and enforcement. This is as it should be. I have always held that a reforming socialist Government which brings changes into force that fundamentally affect the economy or the social habits of a century or more must proceed with the maximum of agreement if its changes are to be lasting and permanent. Too much of our legislation has been bedevilled by a tit-for-tat approach in which an incoming Government has felt it obligatory to repeal the legislation of its predecessor. This is because we have not sufficiently sought for consensus. Yet radical change is necessary, and the task of government is to make the march forward as palatable as it can. A socialist Government must lead, but if those marching in the vanguard are so far ahead of their followers that they are out of sight, then the general body of the army will lose touch and stray off in different directions. This has always been a source of disagreement between myself and my left-wing colleagues.

In the matter of race relations, we got it right. We were ahead of public opinion when Parliament passed the 1968 Act, especially in the case of employers and trade unions, but its provisions were not so extreme that these bodies were outraged. Accordingly they acquiesced, although they did not like the legislation, and as the years went by came to see that it had been necessary. Enoch Powell in his speech of April 1968 quoted the remarks of a constituent that the black man would have the whip hand over the white man in Britain within fifteen to twenty years. That period has now elapsed and I note that there is not yet a single black Member of Parliament, that they are absent from the higher ranks of the law, the Civil Service, the police and the Armed Forces, and that the election of a black mayor is still regarded as newsworthy. It is mainly in the more open fields of the arts and of sport that the achievements and the reputation of coloured people match or exceed those of whites.

In the docks area of Cardiff a coloured lady, a friend of mine for many years, is Headmistress of our local school. She was born, brought up and educated in Cardiff, an understanding and tolerant person. Some time ago she conducted a party of her pupils on a holiday to the Continent; when they returned to Britain she alone was forced to halt for examination by immigration officials while the other teachers and her own pupils were allowed through. Mr Powell's constituent will have to wait for many more years before coloured people reach the heights which so alarmed him, and by that time I trust that he will have discovered that we all share a common humanity.

It goes without saying that Northern Ireland was an ever-present concern throughout my years at the Home Office, but I have not mentioned it so far because I wrote a detailed account of those years in an earlier book, *A House Divided.* By way of postscript, however, and to accord the matter the importance it deserves, I should make it clear that there were certain periods when the problems of the province almost totally absorbed the energies of the Home Office, and especially of Lord Stonham, the Minister of State, to the exclusion of other matters. At such times, I delegated wide responsibilities to the other Ministers, notably Merlyn Rees, David Ennals, Shirley Williams and Elystan Morgan, all of whom were my colleagues at the Home Office at different times. Harold Wilson very kindly gave me an almost completely free hand in choosing my colleagues, and we always had a strong team. Three of them went on to serve in Labour Cabinets in the 1970s. Merlyn Rees, who became Home Secretary, had the right touch for dealing with Northern Ireland, and was highly respected by all parties for his defence of freedom under the law, his integrity and fair-mindedness, and his commonsense approach. I am fortunate to have had him as a friend and counsellor.

Looking back, I would fix the short period from 1963 to 1966 as the three years when Northern Ireland had its best chance to prevent the bombings and shootings of the 1970s and 1980s. But the chance was lost. I offer some reasons. First, a six-year campaign of violence by the IRA during the 1950s had faded out by 1962 because the Catholic minority largely withheld support or shelter from the terrorists. The Protestants did not grasp the opportunity to turn this to the benefit of both communities, but continued to show bias, and discriminated against the Catholics in employment, in housing and in civil rights. This defeat of the IRA had coincided with the retirement of Lord Brookeborough who had been Prime Minister of the province for twenty years and was one of the old school, steeped in the traditions of the Six Counties. He was replaced by Captain Terence O'Neill, a younger politician who took a more realistic view of relations between Northern Ireland and the Republic. Indeed, he took the unprecedented step of inviting Sean Lemass, the Prime Minister of the Republic, to visit him in Belfast. O'Neill made genuine efforts to lessen sectarian bitterness caused by feelings of injustice on the one side and fear of absorption into a united Ireland by the other. He won a handsome majority for his policies in the Stormont election of 1965, but his good intentions were frustrated by growing opposition from within the Unionist Party. Discrimination in the allocation of houses, public appointments and jobs continued, as well as the gerrymandering of ward boundaries to ensure the election of Protestants. It was hard to see that O'Neill's policies were bringing much improvement to the minority and they formed a Civil Rights Association with a militant platform. This brought the Reverend Ian Paisley out in fierce opposition, and as sectarian feelings began to rise, so O'Neill's hoped-for changes were submerged. I have recounted elsewhere that it was not until April 1969 that the Ulster Unionists could bring themselves to concede the elementary right of universal adult suffrage. Even so, as a result Captain O'Neill was forced by his own party to resign and from that time forward events moved towards the disasters of the 1970s and 1980s.

It is possible that if the Unionist Party had been more far-sighted and generous, and had allowed Terence O'Neill to bring forward the reforms that simple justice demanded, the IRA might not have been able in later years to misuse and pervert the genuine anger of the minority. The agitation for a United Ireland would never have been stilled, but the IRA would have found the ground harder to cultivate.

Although the reforms that were prevented in the middle 1960s and only later implemented have been in effect for some years, it cannot be said that discrimination has disappeared. It still exists, but in some fields, of which housing is an example, considerable progress has been made. I had a particular interest in this, arising from an earlier visit I had paid to Northern Ireland in 1954 in company with Alfred Robens and Arthur Bottomley. The three of us formed a small delegation from the Parliamentary Labour Party, and we had been particularly incensed by the blatant discrimination shown in the building and letting of houses by Local Authorities. Some of them hardly troubled to deny that they built new housing estates only in Protestant areas, and had little or no intention of relieving overcrowded slum conditions for Catholic families. When I became Home Secretary several years later the position had improved very little and I applied strong pressure to the Stormont Government to remove their housing powers from the Local Authorities. Although they were reluctant to act, eventually the Northern Ireland Cabinet agreed. They substituted a Housing Executive whose role extended to the whole of the province. The new Housing Executive sensibly comprised both Protestants and Catholics, and staff were recruited at all levels on the same mixed basis. As a result, the situation – although still not perfect – has improved out of all knowledge, and Charles Brett, the Chairman for many years, has told me that since 1970 they have completed and allocated more than fifty thousand houses on a non-denominational basis. This was one success story in the deepening gloom.

I do not number the years 1968 and 1969 among my happiest political memories since for part of that period I was at odds semi-publicly with the Prime Minister about Barbara Castle's proposals for handling industrial relations in response to a plague of unofficial strikes.

These differences led to my removal in May 1969 from the small inner Cabinet that Harold had established. Dick Crossman told me at the time that in an autumn reshuffle I would be dismissed from the Cabinet itself, but before this could happen a serious outbreak of sectarian violence took place in Northern Ireland, and my handling of this won the Prime Minister's approval. I therefore considered myself reprieved – although I doubt whether the intention to dismiss me ever existed in other than Crossman's imagination.

The differences had arisen following the publication of the Report of the Royal Commission on Trade Unions and Employers' Associations set up in 1965 with Lord Donovan as Chairman. Its central theme was that Britain's system of collective bargaining was outmoded and primitive, required complete modernisation, and that this should be undertaken at once by industry itself – employers and trade unions sitting down together to reform their procedures for handling disputes, making changes in work-shop practices and instituting up-to-date negotiating methods.

The majority of the Commission specifically rejected using the law to coerce unofficial strikers or to make collective bargaining agreements enforceable through the courts. But it was strongly in favour of giving greater precision and significance to such agreements, and as a step in this direction recommended that they be required to be registered with the Department of Employment. Donovan's emphasis on industrial self-improvement by voluntary cooperation and his rejection of legal intervention was very much in line with my own thinking. I had been brought up on the iniquity of the Taff Vale Railway Judgement of 1902; in that case the Amalgamated Society of Railway Servants had had to pay out £23,000 in damages when an action was brought against it by the Railway Company in respect of a strike it had not authorised, but which later it sought to bring to a successful conclusion. This judgement had passed into trade union mythology, and I for one had grown up determined that the courts should be kept out of our affairs.

On the other hand I was under no illusion about the need for trade union reform, and a month before the Donovan Report was published had addressed the Fire Brigades Union, calling on the trade unions to do what was necessary to reform their relations with their own members and with the TUC. I said that the influence of the TUC with the Government had increased at a faster pace than its influence with its own member unions, and that it must be in a position where it could not only speak on their behalf but could act and deliver. I continued: 'Self-government is always better than government from above and I have no doubt that solutions to industrial and economic problems which are propounded by the unions themselves and accepted by the democratic decision of its individual members will be more lasting than government intervention.'

I forecast that when the Royal Commission reported there would be a demand for the Government to step into the industrial relations arena. 'I have no idea what the report will contain, but speaking as a fervent believer in the trade union movement, the unions themselves should now take a hand in initiating the necessary discussions . . . The unions themselves know what is necessary to be done and they can, if they choose, forestall the clamour that may be set up following the Royal Commission's Report.'

Although when the report appeared I was satisfied that Donovan had understood the nature of industrial relations, the First Secretary, Barbara Castle, was not, and she at once set about seeking remedies for unofficial strike action which the Commission had failed to find. With the Prime Minister's consent she by-passed the Industrial Relations Committee of the Cabinet of which I was a member, and established a small group of four to assist her in drafting her own remedies. It consisted, I understand, of Harold Walker, who was Barbara's junior Minister, Tony Benn, Peter Shore and Hugh Clegg, who was Professor of Industrial Relations at

Warwick University. This group went off to Sunningdale and produced a White Paper, 'In Place of Strife', much of which was based on the Donovan Report and contained excellent ideas. But the paper was flawed by ineffective proposals for legal sanctions as a solution to the problem. of unofficial strikes. Both industrial strikers and unions would be made liable to fines, but it would not be the employers who would take the strikers to court. The Government itself would make an order having legal effect, thereby bringing the state directly into conflict with the men concerned.

From the moment I set eyes on it I knew that such a proposal, which ran counter to the whole history of the trade union movement and to the ethos of the Donovan Report, could not succeed. Barbara galloped ahead with all the reckless gallantry of the Light Brigade at Balaclava, and tried to rush the Cabinet into publishing the White Paper only nine days after Ministers had first seen it. The issue had not been considered in the usual manner by a Cabinet committee so there were many rough edges and unanswered questions. Ministers revolted, even Dick Crossman declaring that the time allowed for consideration was unreasonable, and a further eight days grace was conceded.

From that moment on I declared my opposition to the legal sanctions in the White Paper on three grounds, which I repeated *ad nauseam*. The legal sanctions would not stop unofficial strikes. The legal sanctions would not pass through Parliament. The proposals would create tension between government and unions at a time when morale was low, to no real effective purpose. In the light of these and the criticisms of other Ministers, a concession was offered to the Cabinet: when the White Paper was issued on 17 January 1969, there would be a full summer for discussion and amendment and a Bill would not be introduced until the next Parliamentary Session, which was then ten months away. The proposals, when published, found a lot of support among the general public who did not realise that they would have failed to prevent unofficial strikes, and I hoped that this reaction would persuade the unions to put their house in order. But the promise of several months of discussion was broken and on 14 April 1969 Barbara returned to Cabinet with a demand for a Bill to be passed during the remaining months of the current Session. The Chancellor, Roy Jenkins, backed her proposal as a fallback position when the Prices and Incomes legislation should expire later in the year, as did the Prime Minister. 'In Place of Strife' was suddenly to be turned into instant government.

When the decision to speed up legislation became known, opposition flared. The TUC, as I had hoped, produced its own 'Programme for Action' on 12 May, but Harold Wilson and Barbara were dissatisfied with its provisions which they wanted strengthened. The TUC resisted; Barbara persisted; and deadlock resulted. Successive meetings failed to produce a compromise, and with each failure the atmosphere in the Cabinet and the Party grew worse. Barbara seemed to be heading for a showdown which she would lose. Because my opposition to the proposals was known, a number of approaches were made to me by members of the Government and others. One was from a member of the Sunningdale drafting team who came to me in the Tea Room of the House to tell me that Barbara had stopped listening and that he was thinking carefully about his future in the Government, if she insisted on going ahead. Another was from John Mackintosh, an able young right-wing Scots Member who came to ask if I would be willing to stand for the leadership and displace Harold as Prime Minister. He and a group of other Members were shortly to hold a meeting for the purpose of discussing such a plan and it would influence their decision if I was willing to agree. My answer was that no solid body of the Party was in favour of a change of leadership. I advised him not to go ahead. It seemed to me that when I said this that he was rather relieved, which was odd for a would-be assassin. George Lawson, a Scottish Whip, who was a friend of mine, came to me with a similar enquiry, and received the same answer.

It was at this point that the Prime Minister told me that it was the wish of my colleagues (I suspected he meant Dick Crossman and Barbara Castle) that I should be excluded from the small inner Cabinet. The Parliamentary Party was undoubtedly restless, and it seems that Mackintosh was using me as a stalking horse. Although he wanted Harold to go, it did not follow that Mackintosh and his friends wanted me to succeed him. In such an event they would have turned their eyes elsewhere, probably to Roy Jenkins, but I would have been useful in opening up a contest. I do not know what mischief was being poured into the Prime Minister's ears but in some notes I made at the time I wrote,

> It is put around that I am taking this line [of opposition] on the legislation because I want to challenge Wilson for the leadership. That is simply not true. I have taken this line from the beginning because I believe it to be right and in the best interests of the Party. I have never thought that the penalty clauses would ruin the unions and have consistently said that 90 per cent of the White Paper is not only acceptable but welcome, but I

object very strongly to the shabby and squalid intellectual dishonesty which pretends that these clauses are going to solve unofficial strikes and, therefore, are vital for our balance of payments problems; and I am astonished to hear people use this kind of argument. Barbara is a different case; she believes passionately in any job she is doing at the time, whether it is overseas aid or transport, and she is absolutely convinced, but there is no reason why the rest of us should be.

As the days went by, fewer and fewer people remained convinced. A crucial part was played by Douglas Houghton, the elected Chairman of the Parliamentary Labour Party. He and I were old friends and colleagues from the days when I was his Assistant Secretary at the Inland Revenue Staff Federation and we both thought alike on the issue. I talked over with him what I should do if the Cabinet went ahead with the Bill containing the penalty clauses and we both agreed that I would have to resign. I drafted my notes for the final appeal I would make to Cabinet, and read them to Douglas who made two or three additions. He himself spoke out publicly at the Party meeting and received a lot of support. I tried to convince Barbara that to give up the penalty clauses would not be a shameful retreat:

We were in the position of an army which had conquered a lot of fresh ground, some unexpectedly, and much more than we thought we would win. But the penal clauses represented an exposed salient in our front line that we could not defend, and it was surely far better to retreat from that exposed salient in order to hold all the other ground that we had won. . . If we did not withdraw from the salient, we would find ourselves driven right back and losing ground that we had won and which we could still hold.

Gradually, under pressure from many quarters, this view began to take hold in the Cabinet. The small group which had always been opposed, Tony Crosland, Roy Mason, Dick Marsh, Fred Lee and myself found ourselves joined by others. Barbara herself apparently told her colleagues in the inner Cabinet that under the threat of legislation the TUC had moved farther and faster in the previous two weeks than in all the past forty years. If she had been conducting an exercise in brinkmanship, I must congratulate her on a brilliant success, but it would have saved a lot of nervous energy had I known this at the time.

In his book *A Personal Record of the Labour Government*, Harold Wilson has described how his final negotiations with the TUC produced an agreement on the manner in which it would operate its rules when unofficial strikes and inter-union disputes took place, and how this enabled the penalty clauses to be withdrawn, to the great relief of us all. Harold records some of the favourable consequences that ensued, but concludes that the period between the agreement and the general election was too short to show what the TUC could have achieved.

This whole episode was a venture bound to end in tears. The favourable initial reaction by the public had revealed a widespread dissatisfaction with the unions, a sentiment which was shared by many union members themselves. But the unions failed to take heed, and the fact that Barbara's proposals were of such a character that the trade unions could not support them was bound to prove fatal to the Government's position in the long run.

The unions were blameworthy for failing, despite Barbara Castle's warning, to make their own programme of reforms effective. In 1969 they still had the opportunity to demonstrate that autonomous self-governing institutions could respond to adverse public opinion and reform themselves. They failed to do so, and this, coupled with the excesses of some activists in the 1970s, led inexorably to the Parliamentary legislation and the intervention by the courts in their affairs, a development I had always resisted.

There were many other issues which demanded attention during my stay at the Home Office: control of gaming; misuse of drugs; reform of the House of Lords; the final stages of the abolition of capital punishment; redistribution of parliamentary seats, and others. Some of these have a familiar ring even today, and I learned the lesson that certain issues are never finally settled but pop up again several years later in a different form. Perhaps all political memoirs should be entitled *Unfinished Business*.

The Home Office is often accused of being temperamentally reactionary, slow and inhuman. (Slow I would concede at once, and have spent years complaining about it.) Hugo Young in his 1982 Bicentenary lecture made the accusation: 'Given a choice between enlarging rights and liberties and restricting them, the Department's instinct leads it towards restriction.' It is of course a Department with a certain view of its responsibilities, especially as regards civil peace, but as to the rest, much depends on the tone of the Home Secretary. The complaint that it was reactionary was not heard when Roy Jenkins held that office – the criticism then was that it was 'permissive'.

It is for the Home Secretary to infuse in his officials the attitudes he wishes the Department to adopt, and the temper of the Government can frequently be read in the reaction of the Home Office to social and other problems. Of course, there are always some hard-hearted uncaring officials, but it was my experience that within the rules they had to apply, and for which they were not responsible, the great majority showed sensitivity in dealing with poignant human problems, as I have said. Nor were senior officials eager to trespass in the fields of individual liberty. As Sir Brian Cubbon, the Permanent Under Secretary at the Home Office put it, the object of the Civil Service is to marry 'the professionalism and experience of its individual officials with the policy objectives and political skills of the Home Secretary'. And I would add that it is a Department where the social attitudes of its ministers can have an effect on policy more surely and more quickly than in many other Departments.

PART FOUR

———◆———

FOREIGN
SECRETARY

9

The years of Opposition from 1970 to 1974 pulled me in different directions. I had reached the age of sixty and found the enjoyment and satisfaction of family life increasingly attractive. Politically, changes in the organisation of the Labour Party had resulted in the influx of a number of extreme left-wing very active Militants, whose separate organisation had failed to make any progress with the British people, and who therefore decided to batten on the Labour Party and use it for their own ends. The rancour between them and traditional Labour Party activists was well-publicised and there were doubts as to whether Labour could win an election with such an encumbrance.

During this period, Tony Barber, the Chancellor of the Exchequer, approached me with a suggestion that I might become the British candidate for Managing Director of the International Monetary Fund, which was about to become vacant. Because of my belief in the importance of international monetary cooperation, I allowed my name to be put forward, but Audrey was not keen to live in Washington and I was rather relieved when a French government veto put an end to the idea before it reached the formal stage. Among my colleagues I was very glad to strike up once again with Harold Wilson the friendly and confident relationship that had existed between us during my term as Chancellor of the Exchequer, but which had been ruptured in 1969 by what I considered was a misplaced intention to bring in new laws concerning industrial relations. Another positive factor was that despite the growing antagonism of the extreme left, the Party Conference had elected me as Party Treasurer annually from 1967 onwards. This was a particular satisfaction because, until the changes of the early 1980s, the post of Treasurer was the only office filled by election from all sections of the annual Conference. Every year I secured the support of the great majority of the trade unions, especially the medium and small unions, and also the votes of more than half of the constituency parties. In the light of these results, I could fairly claim that I had the confidence of the whole Party, especially as I was also regularly elected to the Shadow Cabinet by my colleagues in the House of Commons.

In April 1972 Jack Jones, the General Secretary of the Transport and General Workers Union, urged me to stand for election as Deputy Leader of the Party at the time of Roy Jenkins' resignation from that office. The Deputy Leader was elected on the votes of Members of Parliament alone, and I declined his suggestion not only because I was happy in the post of Treasurer but because I preferred my membership of the National Executive Committee to be the result of election by the whole Conference. In the end Ted Short was the choice acceptable to all, and as Deputy Leader he gave Harold Wilson steady support.

Roy Jenkins' resignation brought other changes. As a former Chancellor of the Exchequer, he had been the Opposition spokesman on Treasury matters. Harold Wilson asked Denis Healey to take over from him, and me to take over Denis's responsibilities for Foreign Affairs. I was very ready to do so and used the next two years to travel extensively, to the United States, the Soviet Union, the Eastern Bloc, and a number of other European countries, as well as the Middle East and the Far East, to prepare myself if we should win the election. I renewed many former friendships and acquaintanceships and learned a great deal.

Of all the visits I made at that time it is of Vietnam, North and South, that the most vivid impressions remain. The war between the two halves of the country was fought with the intense ferocity of all civil wars. North Vietnam was backed heavily, but indirectly, by Soviet and Chinese advisers and arms; the South had the direct support and intervention of American troops and arms. The Soviet Union was wiser than the United States, for by her direct involvement America had committed her prestige in a way that the Soviet Union had not. As the war dragged on with no sign of an eventual victory, the struggle rent a distracted America, troubled about both the morality of the enterprise and the possibility of victory. The South Vietnam Administration was widely and correctly seen to be corrupt and guilty of excesses against its own people, while America's television screens were filled nightly with pictures from the fighting, bringing home to the American people the destructiveness of modern warfare, on behalf of a cause about which many Americans were half-hearted and which grew increasingly unpopular.

Henry Kissinger eventually found himself saddled with the task of extracting the United States from the conflict on the best terms available.

He aimed to leave South Vietnam in a position where it could maintain its independence without giving North Vietnam the chance to claim a victory over the United States. Kissinger undertook the protracted negotiations with great skill, but he had an impossible hand to play, made all the more difficult by President Thieu's open opposition in Saigon to American policy, and also by the inflexible attitude of the North Vietnamese negotiators who, although ready enough to acknowledge their military inferiority to the United States, were also confident they would outlast them. I heard an echo of their attitude in a military museum I visited in Hanoi early in 1973. I tagged along behind a group of North Vietnamese soldiers and listened to a thumbnail sketch of Vietnam's long history from the young woman guide. This was the burden of her message: 'In our long history, we Vietnamese people always win our wars. We repulsed Chinese invaders; we defeated Japanese fascists; we expelled the French colonialists; and now we shall drive out the American imperialists'. I heard the same message in many different forms during my stay in North Vietnam.

The stubbornness of the North Vietnamese negotiators caused a short breakdown in the peace talks with America in December 1972 and in frustration the United States Government resumed massive air attacks by B52 bombers on Hanoi and Haiphong. This so-called 'Christmas bombing' led to feelings of violent revulsion in the United States, as well as in other countries throughout the world, and if it had continued would undoubtedly have caused Congress to cut off further funds with which to prosecute the war.

Both President Nixon and Henry Kissinger have since revealed that even while the bombing was going on, the two sides continued to exchange messages privately; Nixon justified the bombing on the grounds that it brought North Vietnam back to the negotiating table, and that when talks were resumed Henry Kissinger extracted a peace agreement on essentially the same terms as Hanoi could have obtained before the bombing. In Britain the Labour Party led the widespread opposition to the 'Christmas bombing', and a month later the National Executive Committee decided to send a three-man delegation of Ian Mikardo and myself, together with Tom McNally, the Secretary of the Party's International Department, to visit both South and North Vietnam. Mikardo and I both happened to have been born in Portsmouth, and although we frequently disagreed on politics and tactics, our personal relations were good. Tom McNally was a young, able and cheerful travelling companion, who looked after our needs and who could be kept content provided he was served with a constant diet of fresh newspapers. Never was there such an omnivorous reader. His knowledge and a mature judgement beyond his years impressed me and a year later in March 1974, after we had won the election and I became Foreign Secretary, I asked the Labour Party to release him to serve as my adviser, a role in which he was invaluable for the following five years, first at the Foreign Office and later when I became Prime Minister.

The peace agreement negotiated by Henry Kissinger had come into force on 27 January 1973, less than a fortnight before our party arrived in Saigon, but it was obvious that the cease-fire was not being observed. In Saigon at night we could hear the occasional 'crump' of a distant shell but as the cease-fire was only a fortnight old, we did not know whether this was the dying embers of the conflict or a deliberate intention to flout the agreement. The 'leopard spot' nature of the conflict confused the situation, for at the time of the cease-fire Vietcong guerillas effectively controlled many small areas dotted around in the South, with no marked frontier between their villages and those held by the Government. The peace agreement had laid down that Hanoi should not infiltrate troops or supplies into South Vietnam, but observing this would have meant their abandoning the reinforcement of the Vietcong guerillas along the Ho Chi Minh Trail through Laos, and it seemed unlikely that they would do this.

When we saw South Vietnam's President Thieu we sought his opinion on the peace treaty, and especially the provisions for the withdrawal of American troops and the re-unification of North and South Vietnam by negotiation. Thieu responded cordially and showed considerable interest in hearing how the situation appeared through the eyes of European socialists. He was a small, dapper man, with a ready smile, slicked-down hair, an open manner and air of technical competence and self-confidence. No stooge he, whatever the propaganda might say. In our presence he uttered no criticism of the United States, although he made clear his profound opposition to the decision to withdraw their troops; instead, he concentrated his remarks on his readiness 'to take a risk for peace', as he described it. He told us that he was willing to permit all Opposition groups in South Vietnam to campaign in an election to be held in the near future.

His manner was convincing, but it would have had more effect if we had not previously talked with several non-communist Opposition groups who were opposed both to Thieu and to the Vietcong, and who had produced irrefutable evidence of the imprisonment of their members. Their attitude could be summed up as one of believing Thieu when they saw his promises come into effect. In response to our questions, the President did admit that the Government held forty-one thousand political prisoners, of whom a few thousand had not been tried. We asked if we could visit some of them but were refused and he riposted that we should ask the Vietcong when we reached the Northern capital of Hanoi to see the fifty thousand South Vietnamese whom they had kidnapped from their villages. We suggested both to him and to Hanoi, when we reached it, that a panel of independent international jurists under the auspices of the Commission to oversee the peace agreement should be allowed to investigate the question of political prisoners and make recommendations. In both capitals we were listened to without enthusiasm.

I was surprised to find close personal links existed between leaders in the North and the South. Thieu told us that he himself was a Northener and I understood him to say that he had been at school with at least one member of the Politburo in Hanoi; another South Vietnamese Minister asked us to convey his greetings to a senior figure in the North who had been a near neighbour before the war. It was truly a fratricidal struggle.

During our visit we flew by helicopter to An Loc. While we were in the air the door remained open with a machine-gunner posted at the entrance, and we were accompanied by a more heavily armed gunship. The town was only sixty miles north of Saigon, the South Vietnam capital, but South Vietnamese troops had been surrounded and besieged by North Vietnamese forces for nine months, and helicopters were the only means of communication. We were told that the airstrip on which we were due to land was regarded as too near to North Vietnamese lines and we put down on a road on the outskirts of the town, where we hurried to waiting jeeps to get out of gunshot. The town itself was a scene of desolation almost as severe as Stalingrad, but not on the same scale. Life went on and small boys clambered over burnt-out Russian T52 tanks, standing on the turrets in order to get a better view. There were occasional small explosions but the morale of the defenders seemed good, despite being cut off by thousands of guerillas and North Vietnamese troops. The British Military Attaché who accompanied us was less than impressed by the North Vietnamese tank tactics as he deduced the manner of their attack from where the burnt-out hulls lay. We spent several hours in the town and were happy to return to Saigon without mishap, especially as two days later another helicopter attempting the same flight was shot down by a North Vietnamese missile.

We were advised that the only way for us to get from South Vietnam to North Vietnam was to fly by way of the neutral country of Laos. Once in the capital, Vientiane, we might find it possible to transfer to an International Control Commission plane that made irregular flights from there to the Northern capital. The Royal Laotian Airlines aircraft turned out to be an elderly Dakota, the much-used wartime DC3. Boarding was very informal and I enquired about several red ribbons hanging from the wings. I was told that these were prayer tapes to ensure a safe journey, but even prayer tapes could not increase our confidence when, during the flight, the pilot announced that he would have to come down as an air battle was imminent and fighter aircraft were about to take off from an airfield below us. We watched the air battle over our heads until it was safe to take off again, and eventually arrived at Vientiane, where John Lloyd, the British Ambassador, took us in hand.

Poor Laos. Its neutrality was totally abused. In the east of its territory the North Vietnamese came and went as they pleased up and down the Ho Chi Minh Trail. In the south of the country, irregulars from Thailand were fighting. In the north-west the Chinese built military roads with impunity and without regard to frontiers, while throughout the country American bombers rained down tons of high explosives in support of official Laotian forces which were struggling to maintain a semblance of independence. Meanwhile, in Vientiane, government and communist leaders met each other at cocktail parties. This was a country of subsistence farmers torn apart by invaders, yet the principal items in its foreign aid programme were a television service, a Coca-Cola plant and a brewery. We were glad to hear that the British contribution was an experimental unit for improving strains of rice. Corruption was on a mammoth scale, with a ruling élite profiting handsomely from the war, and a large batch of CIA agents who scarcely bothered to conceal their presence. Gentle, passive people, corrupt leaders and alien intruders all formed a mixture that made us sad and angry that a small, inoffensive country should be subjected to such barbarities.

The Prime Minister, Souvanna Phouma, lived in a simple, almost unguarded one-storey villa. He received us with a resigned dignity. As Prime Minister he presided over a coalition Cabinet, 50 per cent of which was communist and 50 per cent non-communist, depending upon American support. He told us, without conviction, of his hopes for a genuinely neutral Laos, free from foreign intervention, but under questioning admitted that he believed the communist Pathet Lao Party would play an influential and perhaps the dominant role. Although the Vietnam peace agreement negotiated by Kissinger had provided for the withdrawal of foreign troops from his country, he did not doubt that the North Vietnamese would retain at least ten thousand men in Laos to safeguard the Ho Chi Minh Trail. At a later meeting, we asked the Control Commission representatives how such a clear infringement could be reconciled with a peace agreement on which the ink was scarcely dry, only to receive the reply, 'This is not a peace-keeping force, but a peace-observing force.' True enough, but this offered no comfort for the future and as there was no goodwill on North Vietnam's part, the agreement that Henry Kissinger had painfully hammered out in Paris was a dead letter in Laos even at the moment it was signed.

The Laotians retained their sense of humour, however. In the centre of Vientiane stood a massive concrete column, somewhat resembling the Arc de Triomphe. I enquired what historic event was commemorated and was told it was quite new. Apparently, the CIA had decided that Vientiane needed a new airstrip, and the United States had transported many tons of cement to build it, but the Laotians, who are as stubborn as they are gentle, decided they neither wanted nor needed another airstrip. Instead, they used the concrete to build a useless column in the city centre and, in deference to the Americans, christened it 'The Vertical Runway'.

Hanoi could hardly have offered a greater contrast to Saigon. The public face of the South's capital had worn a hectic, feverish flush. Hanoi's visage by contrast was grim and grey. Saigon was bustling and Americanised, with small restaurants outside which ill-clad beggars asked for food. It was 'Hondaville', with well dressed girls riding dangerously side-saddle on motorcycle pillions, and well pressed military uniforms much in evidence. Hanoi was a city of grey tunics, black trousers and bicycles. The bridges over the Red River leading from the main airport to Hanoi had been destroyed by bombing, and as our car crossed the dangerous temporary pontoon bridge one of our first sights was of groups of young girls, looking very different from their sisters in Saigon, laboriously trundling huge barrels of black tar across the bridge for road-making.

Hanoi itself was a faded and neglected copy of a pre-war French provincial town which had retained its broad streets and tree-lined avenues, but where non-essentials such as a coat of paint on the deteriorating buildings enjoyed a very low priority. The military were far less in evidence than in Saigon, although the outward signs of war were plentiful with numerous air-raid shelters and streets pock-marked with one-man bolt holes sunk into the pavements, each with a concrete lid for the occupant to pull over his head as he jumped in during an air-raid.

The inner city of Hanoi had been little damaged, but industrial areas were devastated and we visited one densely-populated housing area that had been completely flattened during the 'Christmas bombing'. Large bomb craters existed where houses had formerly stood, but already the people were busy marking out afresh the obliterated boundaries of their homes and stacking piles of bricks to rebuild. Civilian casualties here had been very heavy.

We asked to visit the port of Haiphong since we had been told before leaving Britain that some British ships had been tied up unable to leave because the Americans had heavily mined the channel to the sea. Along each side of the road between Hanoi and Haiphong were long lines of crates, each neatly stencilled with its contents. The numbers were so great that we lost count and I assumed they were supplies from the Soviet Union that had never been unpacked. Our hosts offered a different explanation, namely that when the 'Christmas bombing' had begun, factories had hurriedly dismantled their machines, crated them and removed them from the industrial areas in the city.

We found two British ships and introduced ourselves to the astonished crews, who received us like visitors from another planet. They had been in considerable danger when the docks were bombed, but had not been hit. They entertained us royally and we were able to carry home a number of hastily written letters to their families, and promised to press the authorities to speed up the clearance of mines in the navigating channel.

Our next meeting was with Pham Van Dong, who had been Prime Minister of North Vietnam for twenty years, during the whole of which period his country had been at war. Thieu had appeared briskly competent; Souvanna Phouma in Laos gently powerless; Pham Van Dong was composed but slightly diffident until the conversation warmed up, when he demonstrated the total self-confidence of the Marxist who is certain that history is on his side. He was evidently relieved that the war against America had ended, but made clear that he would not shrink from further conflict with South Vietnam, although for the time being he was ready to wait, believing that what he called 'the inner contradictions' in the Southern regime would lead to its eventual collapse. He said with great emphasis that the future of Vietnam must be settled by the Vietnamese themselves, and he was utterly confident that the dedication and self-discipline which had already won a great victory over the 'foreigner' would prove equally effective in the forthcoming political battle.

Pham Van Dong was equally dogmatic when we discussed the question of aid to enable the country to recover from the ravages of war. He dismissed our proposals that aid should be channelled through United Nations agencies, or through an international consortium. He said, rather loftily, that he would be ready to discuss aid from abroad if it was offered on a purely bilateral basis. As to the United States, they were under an obligation to pay full compensation to his country for the losses it had suffered. His diffidence had vanished and was replaced by a single-minded determination that had no regard for the sensitivities of others.

I did not give much for the future of South Vietnam when we came away. Nevertheless, it remained militarily stronger than the North, and in our subsequent report to the Labour Party the three of us agreed that if economic, social, political and military capacity were taken together, President Thieu had 'the capacity to survive on all fronts for at least two years, but beyond that period, speculation is worthless'. It was not a bad judgement for in fact the final crisis and defeat for Saigon came just two years later, in April 1975.

The United States still seems unwilling to draw the lesson of the tragic story of Vietnam, namely that in a confrontation between two dictatorships, one of which is a society that lives by corruption and tolerates great extremes of wealth and poverty, and the other a body of inflexible, single-minded, self-confident Marxists, the rigid discipline of the communist will eventually triumph. The West should be careful whom it backs. It has been a mistaken policy to proceed on the assumption that a regime is entitled to aid and support no matter how corrupt or dictator-ridden, provided it is sufficiently anti-communist. This attitude is not only morally dubious, but usually a profound policy error.

Another visit during my period in Opposition was to the Middle East in January 1974. I have recalled it especially because it marked the beginning of a close relationship between President Sadat of Egypt and myself. I had known the leaders of Israel well for many years, but had never previously met Sadat and was anxious to do so before the British general election, which seemed likely to take place during 1974. My visit had a dual purpose, namely to mend fences with the Arab leaders in order to avoid any remote possibility that the Labour Party's close links with Israel might lead to an oil embargo against Britain if we won the election, and at the same time to reassure Israel that we would not depart from the Party's historic friendship for that country. There was of course little likelihood of our doing so with Harold Wilson as our leader. Indeed, when we won the election and I became Foreign Secretary he told me that he would not want a meticulous account of my handling of foreign policy with the exception of two areas – Israel and South Africa, the latter because of his honourable detestation of apartheid.

I explained to the Arab States that, whilst the Labour Party would not perform a 'U-turn' in its relations with Israel, nevertheless it was my intention to increase our contacts with and our understanding of the Arab world, and to emphasise that the Party recognised that the Palestinian people had legitimate aspirations. These should be settled by negotiation as a priority issue before a real peace could ensue.

I met President Sadat on 2 February 1974, and immediately felt at ease. He possessed a natural charm and friendly courtesy, and was a man with whom one could talk at first meeting as though one had known him for years. Sadat was clearly pleased that I had visited him as a representative of the Labour Party, and remarked that it was a sadness to him that he had received greater support in the past from the Conservatives despite the fact that his domestic aims and ideals were nearer to our own. As Israel was to be my next port of call, he asked if I would convey a number of personal messages directly to Golda Meir, the Prime Minister. He wanted her to understand that his plans to re-open the Suez Canal and to rebuild the cities of the Canal Zone were not the actions of a country planning for war. He asked me further to emphasise that he had already demobilised seventy thousand troops, intended to go further and was willing to give Israel security guarantees. He added, 'Tell Mrs Meir, do not ask for one inch of my territory, but remind her that I am the first Arab leader to declare my willingness to recognise Israel.' Could there not then be some formal link with the Israelis to discuss directly the prospects for peace, I wondered, and asked: 'Is there any chance of Mrs Meir coming to Cairo, or of you both talking in Tel Aviv?' His reply was sharp and interesting because it showed how his ideas had developed later on when he took his courageous decision to visit Jerusalem. 'If you mean that such a visit is what peace is about, you are unrealistic. My people would stone me. The Arab world would condemn me. That kind of peace is impossible.' Despite this, three years later, in November 1977, he felt strong enough to undertake his historic journey.

As to the Palestinians, he wanted the Palestine Liberation Organisation to join the international negotiations in Geneva, and would work to influence Syria and Jordan to his preferred solution, namely that the Palestinians should establish a national identity on the West Bank and in Gaza with the Israelis providing and safeguarding a corridor between the two areas. This would not threaten Israel as long as they dominated such a corridor, and in any case, he said, the Palestinians had already shown that they could co-exist with Israel. It was at this meeting that I encountered for the first time Sadat's dismissive attitude towards King Hussein. He was both unfair and unjust towards a courageous ruler who steered his country skilfully through the Middle East labyrinth.

Sadat's criticism was that the King had made grave mistakes. Sadat said he offered, prior to the war in October 1973, to send Egyptian officers to take charge of Palestinian units on the West Bank, so that Jordan's army would not have been involved. But King Hussein had refused and, in consequence, had lost everything. He added that it was untrue to suggest that he would work or plot against Jordan, but that at some time in the future the King would be forced to accept the Palestinians as negotiating partners. He was concerned about the security of Britain's supply of arms to Egypt and asked for an assurance that an incoming Labour Government would not cancel weapons contracts with British firms. I replied that we intended to review overseas arms sales, but that such a review would not be applied to contracts which had been already entered into. This was important, for I had been made aware before I left Britain that Westland Helicopters, Marconi and Plessey were all in negotiation with Egypt, and the first contract might be ready within a month.

President Sadat's final words were to ask me to assure Mrs Meir that he would 'work vehemently for peace'. This first meeting, held shortly before I became Foreign and Commonwealth Secretary, set the pattern for future visits. His favourite venue was an alcove in a room in his home overlooking the Nile, where he would sit and speak with great frankness on every topic. He had a slow, thoughtful manner of speech (except on the occasions when he denounced other Arab leaders), a cheerful laugh, constant pipe-smoking, a reflective attitude, all combining to give an impression of a serious and sensible far-seeing man. In one respect he held a resemblance to Indira Gandhi, being given to long reflective but not unfriendly silences. In company, he would sometimes sit and equally smoke his pipe while the conversation flowed around him. At meals he ate and drank very little and seemed to have no need to dominate the table, as some leaders did. I kept my counsel about his occasional far-fetched outbursts abusing other Arab leaders, in the hope that if Britain was to have any influence it would be because he and others could rely on my discretion, and know that my views and advice were wholly disinterested.

During the Camp David peace talks conducted by President Carter, Sadat personally kept me in touch with progress, on occasions telephoning from the United States to inform me of what had taken place and to seek a reaction. Prime Minister Begin, too, kept in close contact during these negotiations and I felt gratified that Britain's viewpoint should be valued by both parties. There have always been plenty of people on the fringe of Middle East problems ready to invent difficulties and create misunderstandings. Such a role was not for Britain.

Sadat never went back on any undertaking he gave me and, whether I was in office or out, he always extended the same personal consideration right up to the time of his death. He followed British politics closely and at our last talk in Cairo, shortly before his assassination, he gave me a detailed analysis of the way he saw the state of British political parties and the effect of the breakaway and formation of the Social Democratic Party. His forecast turned out to be not very far off the mark when the 1983 election took place. Like all of us, Anwar Sadat undoubtedly had his faults, but he was a man who thought on a large scale and his historic and courageous decision to visit Jerusalem was the most significant event that had happened since the establishment of the state of Israel. It set relations between Egypt and Israel on a new and more hopeful course.

As in Vietnam, so in the Middle East, there was no direct air-link between Egypt and Israel, and we were forced to travel from Cairo to Tel Aviv via Cyprus. We arrived in Israel to find reports from London that Mr Heath was about to call a general election, and I was rather distracted when I delivered President Sadat's messages to Golda Meir, amid her expressions of hope that if Labour won the general election, Israel would receive more sympathetic treatment than it had from the Conservative Government.

In addition to being Shadow Foreign Secretary I was Chairman of the Party, and was anxious to get home in case an election was called, although we would not have been caught napping as the Party had published a campaign document shortly before I left Britain, which could easily be adopted as an election manifesto. Since the previous November the country had been living under a state of emergency, with serious power cuts and a three-day working week in operation from the beginning of January. The miners were in dispute over pay and when they held a ballot 81 per cent voted for a strike, to begin on 10 February 1974. That seemed to have decided Mr Heath and on 6 February, as I stepped from the aircraft at Heathrow at 12.50 p.m. on my return from Israel, a reporter told me that the Prime Minister had announced a general election only five minutes earlier, and a BBC microphone was thrust at me with the demand that, as Chairman of the Party, would I please make some comments for the one o'clock news.

Labour morale was high during the election, although privately neither Harold Wilson nor I were at all certain we would win. But Heath's slogan 'Who Governs Britain?' was misplaced. The answer was surely obvious – it must be the elected government and no one else. Asking this question did not fully satisfy the electorate. Instead, people continued to ask what a new election would settle when the Government already had a working majority and still had eighteen months of its term to complete. Ted Heath's response was that victory would give his Government renewed authority, but a number of issues developed during the campaign which showed the Government in a confused state. When the result was declared we found, somewhat to our surprise, that Labour had won more seats than the Conservatives – 301 to their 297. Another thirty-seven seats were divided between Liberals, Scottish and Welsh Nationalists, Northern Ireland Members and others. We thought Mr Heath should have resigned forthwith, but he began negotiations with the Liberals. However, these failed and Harold Wilson had no hesitation in taking office with Labour as a minority government, knowing that another election must follow within a matter of months.

IO

Foreign Secretary – EEC renegotiations – a divided Cabinet –
relations with France and Germany

As we had previously arranged, the Prime Minister asked me to go to the Foreign and Commonwealth Office, and I spent two happy years in this Rolls Royce of Departments, making many lasting friends at home and abroad. The Prime Minister gave me a free hand in choosing the other Foreign Office Ministers. It had always been my intention to ask for Goronwy Roberts, the Member of Parliament for Caernarvon, who had served as Minister of State in the previous Labour Government. He was a gentle Welsh scholar who had entered the House when I did, in 1945, but in 1974 he was unexpectedly defeated by Dafydd Wigley, the Plaid Cymru candidate. Harold told me that if I still wanted him he would nominate him for the House of Lords and so enable him to become a Minister. A day or two after the election I had the pleasure of telephoning Goronwy as he sat gloomily at home, wondering what to do with himself now, and offered him in the same conversation both a post in the Government and a peerage. He cheered up immensely.

I also asked Harold for Joan Lester, a great-hearted soul with a following on the left of the Party, who would never fail to be my conscience. David Ennals, a former head of the International Department of the Labour Party, vastly experienced and knowledgeable, became the Minister of State. It was a good team. Later, to my regret, Joan resigned and Harold asked me to release David Ennals to become a full Minister. In Joan's place came Ted Rowlands, Member for Merthyr Tydfil and a former colleague in Cardiff, whose capacity for hard work and cheerful pertinacity I had always admired. He had little previous experience of overseas problems, but as I expected, refused to be overawed and did invaluable service both to the country and to the Party by the skill he showed in handling the problems of some of the smaller territories, such as the Falklands and Belize. Under his eye, I am sure the Falklands issue would not have been allowed to slip out of mind with such disastrous consequences as it did between 1979 and 1982.

I was glad to have Roy Hattersley to replace David Ennals for he was obviously of Cabinet calibre, as well as being a good team member and a most versatile colleague to put into bat at the Dispatch Box on a sticky wicket. He scored runs against the Opposition much more quickly than his great hero, Geoffrey Boycott, did on the cricket field. John Cunningham was another high flyer who had been my Parliamentary Private Secretary in Opposition and continued in that role now we were in office. He is cool, shrewd at assessing a situation, knows the Labour Party well for he and his family have grown up in it, and comes from Durham, one of my favourite areas. I was not at all surprised when some years later his Parliamentary colleagues elected him to the Shadow Cabinet, and he became one of Labour's most effective front-bench speakers. Altogether it was a team with conviction and ability.

There was a small, amusing domestic incident. The Prime Minister had not disturbed the allocation of No. 2 Carlton Gardens for the use of the Foreign Secretary of the day. It was a grand address and the house contains some elegant rooms, in which the Foreign Secretary may entertain visiting foreign ministers and other dignitaries, with a flat at the top of the house overlooking St James's Park. Alec Douglas-Home, my predecessor, had lived in the flat, but when he moved out his wife Elizabeth warned Audrey that it had its drawbacks. The roof leaked so badly that she had been forced to place a bucket at the right spot in the bedroom to catch the drips when it rained; the house was infested by dry rot and the external stone parapets were dangerous. The Government's Property Service Agency had been waiting for the changeover and sent a message saying that they had decided they must repair the roof and the house. This process lasted for the whole of my period as Foreign and Commonwealth Secretary, so we never lived there and I missed the prospect of having the Queen Mother as a near neighbour.

As to more serious matters, I went to the Foreign Office with fixed objectives, some of which arose from Party commitments and others from my own sense of priorities. Mr Heath's deep and lasting commitment to Europe had weakened our relations with the United States, and as a strong believer in the Atlantic Alliance, I was determined that these must be strengthened. Likewise, our relations with the Soviet Union were certainly worse than those of Germany and France, or even of the United States. The Federal Republic enjoyed an advantage over us because her proximity to the Soviet Union led naturally to a strong trading relationship. The Ostpolitick policy of Willy Brandt, the Chancellor, had valuable political consequences for the stability of Berlin. France too had deliberately cultivated relations with the Soviet Union during and since the days of de Gaulle. These had done her no harm and there was little doubt that political frostiness between the Soviet Union and ourselves had put our manufacturers and businessmen at a disadvantage.

It also appeared to me that the Conservative Government's concentration on the negotiations to enter the European Community had given the impression of a diminished concern about the Commonwealth, and I was anxious to repair that. I said during the general election that the Conservative Government had 'banked everything on our relations with Europe. The time has come to cultivate the rest of the world once more.' I called the Commonwealth High Commissioners en bloc to the Foreign and Commonwealth Office and informed them of my desire to give priority to Commonwealth consultation. Harold Wilson was keen to strengthen our political representation at the United Nations and we discussed how it should be done. He decided to appoint Ivor Richards as our Ambassador, and he set about his task with vigour. Ivor began regular and continuous consultations with other Commonwealth representatives at the United Nations, to secure a more coordinated Commonwealth policy there. The newly independent Commonwealth countries had a natural desire to work with other Third World countries, but Ivor Richards' efforts together with our greater activity in London and in Commonwealth capitals did much to create greater understanding of Britain's position and ease the fashionable tendency to make Britain a whipping boy at the United Nations. It also cleared the way for Harold Wilson to propose initiatives to meet the growing trade and financial problems of the Third World countries at the Commonwealth Conference, held in Jamaica during the following year. Our efforts ensured that the British Government's ideas met with a more sympathetic response than they would have done otherwise.

A Labour Foreign Secretary cannot tilt at every windmill but he must seek to apply principles to foreign policy – peace, justice, human rights and human dignity, opposition to racial discrimination and support for the principles of the United Nations Charter. He must recognise Britain's diminished international power, and exert his influence in those areas and organisations where such principles can best be furthered, while being ready to take such other initiatives as he can construct. He must use foreign policy to bolster Britain's economic strength, and in turn that will increase Britain's influence in international affairs. These considerations influenced a number of my early decisions and attitudes towards, for example, the imposition of an arms embargo in South Africa, the Greek Army dictatorship and the rebel Rhodesian regime.

But with all my concern for these questions, the first difficult task I had to undertake was the re-negotiation of our terms of entry into Europe. I had previously used the word 're-negotiation' to define our objective, and on the day I arrived at the Foreign Office I was told that Foreign Ministers of the Community were due to meet on 1 April 1974, only four weeks later, and were already asking that I should use that occasion to outline Britain's intentions. I agreed to do so. But, to start with, I needed to clear my approach with a newly formed Cabinet, all of whose members were intent on their own freshly discovered problems. However, we had talked about our approach so often that I did not at that stage encounter much difficulty from my colleagues. The election result had given us an opportunity to bring to an end the long-running and debilitating dispute about whether or not Britain should enter the Community or remain a non-member. These issues had divided the nation and the Labour Party. Joe Gormley, the miners' leader, said in his usual blunt fashion to the Labour Party Conference, 'Get this damn thing out of the way. We have been destroying ourselves for the last eight years with disunity, personalities and ill-feeling.'

Rifts had in fact existed for much longer. Within my own experience the Labour Party's attitude to Europe had been a matter of dissent from the time I was sent to the newly formed Council of Europe in 1949, with instructions from Herbert Morrison to ensure that the other member nations adopted the British Parliamentary procedures and took Erskine May as their Bible for the Council's proceedings. This was a task quite beyond me or anyone else, and I had to report back that I had failed and that all the other members of the Council of Europe were insistent on adopting their more familiar Continental practice.

The Council of Europe itself became the first step leading to the formation of a tightly-knit European Economic Community of six nations in 1957. The Conservative Government declined an invitation to assist in the formation, and from that time the dispute about Britain's attitude loomed larger every year.

In the Labour Party it was not a classic left versus right issue. Hugh Gaitskell had been influenced by his strong feelings for the unity of the Commonwealth and his belief in the Atlantic Alliance and had been opposed to membership right up to his death. So were others, such as

Douglas Jay, who in conventional terms were labelled 'right-wingers'. But during the 1960s advocates of membership grew stronger in both major Parties and General de Gaulle's veto on Britain's membership in 1963 served only to redouble their determination. In 1967 the Labour Party Conference had declared itself in favour of the principle of membership, and with George Brown as Foreign Secretary the Labour Government made determined efforts to secure membership, but came up against the same stumbling block.

It was not until de Gaulle was removed from office, and Mr Heath and President Pompidou, both of whom were convinced Europeans, were the leaders of Britain and France that terms were agreed. Mr Heath proposed to Parliament in October 1971 that the House should approve membership on the terms he had negotiated and this led to the first open split in the ranks of the Parliamentary Labour Party. Sixty-seven Labour Members voted with the Conservative Government and a further twenty abstained from voting. This resulted in much ill-feeling. The Labour Shadow Cabinet itself was divided, and a deep rift was opened as leading members such as Roy Jenkins, Harold Lever and Shirley Williams went into the Yes Lobby with the Government whilst the great majority of the Party marched with the rest of the Shadow Cabinet into the No Lobby, declaring that they were not against the principle of membership but were dissatisfied with the terms. The Heath Government won. The die was cast and on 1 January 1973 Britain became a full member of the Community.

The action of the sixty-seven in voting with the Government continued to rankle, and Harold Wilson had a difficult time holding the Party together. He performed this task with great skill and kept both opponents and supporters occupied by setting up special Party Committees to examine the matter, holding consultations with other socialist Parties in Europe and so on, demonstrating his belief that the best way to prevent the Party from becoming introspective was to keep it in a state of perpetual motion.

One result of this activity was the renewal of our earlier proposal that a future Labour Government should ask the British people themselves to decide the question of membership through voting in a referendum. The majority of those both in favour and against membership were ready to accept this proposal, but to Roy Jenkins it was the last straw. In his view a referendum would be an abdication by the Government of its responsibility and he therefore resigned his office as Deputy Leader. Harold Lever and George Thomson also both resigned from the Shadow Cabinet, to my regret.

At the next Annual Conference the Party once again declared that it was not against the principle of membership, but believed that the terms negotiated by the Conservative Government were not good enough. The Conference adopted as a policy the re-negotiation of the terms, to be followed by a referendum to put the result to the British people for a final verdict. Harold Wilson in his speech to Conference played it straight down the middle in an effort to keep the Party united. He aligned himself neither with those who, he said, would accept almost any terms of membership nor with those who would refuse membership however favourable the terms. He defined this position as being prepared to accept membership given the right terms, but ready to reject it if the terms crippled Britain's economy, Britain's independence or Britain's social welfare. He asked the Conference's support for negotiation by an incoming Labour Government in an attempt to improve the access of agricultural products from countries like New Zealand: to reduce Britain's contribution to the EEC Budget; to secure freedom to fix our own exchange rate; to ensure that we need not levy VAT on necessities; to retain powers to pursue Britain's fiscal, regional and industrial policies; and to encourage the initiation of policies to assist the developing countries. When this was concluded the British people would be given the opportunity to decide the future either through a general election or by means of a referendum. Harold Wilson's speech was masterly and carried the support of the delegates by 3,407,000 votes to 1,802,000. There were two other diametrically opposed resolutions in front of the delegates. The first called for full support for the EEC membership; the second for outright opposition to membership. Both were defeated.

The Party Leader's efforts at this period and during the following twelve months undoubtedly enabled the Party to approach the general election of 1974 with a viable policy and an appearance of unity. Nevertheless, Party opinion was not static and it was clear to me that the pro-Marketeers had lost ground since the 1960s and that anti-Market sentiment in the Party had increased.

It was against the unpromising background of directly conflicting views that, as Foreign Secretary, I began the task of re-negotiation in 1974 in the knowledge that such powerful and prominent members of the Cabinet as Roy Jenkins, Harold Lever, Michael Foot, Tony Benn and Peter Shore were already lined up on opposite sides. Without actually saying so to each other, the Prime Minister and I implicitly seemed to understand that we must both work in the closest unity if we were to bring the Government and the country successfully through this divisive issue – whichever way the decision might go.

Jean Monnet reports in his memoirs that when he called on the Prime Minister three weeks after the general election of 1974, Harold Wilson told him, 'I shall give Callaghan a free hand', and it was true that in the months ahead he gave me the fullest support at all times and our relationship was never closer. This was assisted by the fact that the Prime Minister knew that I had no intention of challenging his leadership – on the contrary, I did all I could to strengthen it. At that time in 1974 I was sixty-two years of age, and as Harold was four years younger than I, there was little expectation that I would become Prime Minister. I hoped to remain as Foreign Secretary for two or three years and insofar as I had thoughts about the matter, I assumed the day would come when Harold might say nicely to me that he would like a younger man to take over. I was reconciled to that. The fact that I became Prime Minister two years later was one more illustration of how great a part time and chance plays in political life. My expectation that not I but someone younger would succeed Harold in due dourse meant that our relations were extremely relaxed and cordial. During the whole of his premiership our conversations were frank and unguarded and we developed a partnership that was of great value in conducting the Government's affairs.

Harold held a regular meeting with Ted Short, the Leader of the House, and Bob Mellish, the Chief Whip, every Friday morning to discuss House of Commons affairs, and I was called in as an extra hand. When the meeting broke up it was my custom to remain behind to discuss progress on particular Foreign Affairs issues and from these our conversations would move to Parliamentary, Party, industrial and other political affairs which were current at the time. We aimed to reach preliminary conclusions on how such issues should be tackled, and Harold's confidence kept me fully in the domestic picture.

I decided that Germany should be the first country I would visit to sound out the prospects of re-negotiation. The SPD under Chancellor Brandt was the leading partner in the Government Coalition and as a fellow member of the Socialist International was keen that the Labour Party should play its full part in the Community.

In Bonn the weather was springlike. I felt full of energy and my reception was very cordial. I talked with Willy Brandt, Hans Apel and Helmut

Schmidt, as well as with Walter Scheel, the Leader of the Free Democratic Party, the junior partner in the Coalition, and Foreign Minister.

Brandt was tired and dispirited for reasons which became apparent a few weeks later. He was disinclined to talk about the detail of re-negotiation, and after a while our conversation became more general. I asked for his full support for the Labour Government's sanctions against Rhodesia; that Germany should not support any attempts by their businessmen to fill the vacuum that would result. I told him that the Government would shortly announce a strict policy against the Chile dictatorship, suspending our arms supply in view of its human rights record. As to the Soviet Union, I said that I intended to work at improving relations. Our meeting was friendly but I came away with the impression that I had not sufficiently impressed him with the significance of re-negotiation to the very existence of the Labour Government.

My exchanges with Apel and Scheel were much more lively. Apel was insistent that the principles of the Common Agricultural Policy were immutable, and I replied that they were not inscribed on tablets of stone to be handed down from generation to generation. Already they had been infringed in practice by the artificial creation of the green pound. In any case, I asked, what would he do when the cost of agricultural financial support bumped up against the limitation of available budget resources? There were no answers.

With Helmut Schmidt I found an immediate rapport which lasted throughout the period we both held office and continues today. He received me with the utmost friendliness and almost immediately settled into a frank and open conversation. His quick intelligence, mastery of economic thinking, practical mind and breadth of outlook meant that every conversation was stimulating. Helmut's bark is worse than his bite, and beneath the hard carapace he is a generous and basically modest man. We were both firm believers in the Atlantic Alliance, although even then he was impatient with American shortcomings. In the early days of our relationship he seemed reluctant to give the lead in political discussion that Germany's economic strength would have warranted. In private conversation I would urge him to do so, but he told me that he felt inhibited in certain political discussions in larger company because of his awareness of Germany's Nazi past. As time went by, he overcame this reluctance and his passionate approach, allied to Giscard D'Estaing's cool detachment, gave Europe valuable leadership during the difficult years of the 1970s.

When I returned from Bonn I told the Prime Minister that, while I had found sympathy for Britain's difficulties, there was no enthusiasm for re-negotiation, if only because the Germans, who were already the largest contributor to the Community, understood they would have to pay even more if Britain was to pay less. I recommended that we should not leave an empty chair at meetings of Ministers as de Gaulle had done on an earlier occasion, for I could see no way in which our absence would force the issue. We were, in Community jargon, the 'demandeurs' and must make the running. I also reported that I had agreed that I should make a preliminary statement on Britain's position at the next meeting of Foreign Ministers, which was to be held only one month after we had assumed office. I had told Willy Brandt that we would negotiate in good faith. By that I meant that if the Community was willing to agree to arrangements that broadly met our objectives, we would recommend the result to the British people either in a general election or through a referendum. I recognised that in negotiation there must always be some compromise but they must also realise that if they wished us to remain members of the Community we could not depart too far from our election manifesto.

There was naturally great interest in the Parliamentary Labour Party and in a much wider circle about the attitude we would take, and Douglas Jay brought an all-Party delegation to see me. Douglas is an English eccentric with a penetrating analytical intelligence and a well-stocked mind. For him abroad is 'bloody' and he fought passionately against England's entry into the Common Market, pressing me to do the same. He was probably right when he said that he cared more about issues and I more about people. The ideal politician would combine both. He was particularly effective as a back-bencher. Many Members when they ask a question of a Minister deliver themselves of a four-part blockbuster (or so they hope) which is too long and gives the Minister a chance to avoid the bits that are hard to answer. Douglas never did that. He knew that it was the short, sharp, one-sentence question which most often gets under the Minister's guard and he used it to devastating effect.

The Prime Minister decided to establish a major Cabinet Committee on European Strategy with himself as Chairman. Under this was a second committee of Cabinet Ministers to deal with tactical questions and decide on negotiating positions, of which he appointed me as Chairman. He and I were confident we could reconcile any differences that might arise between the committees. Different questions such as agriculture, access for New Zealand's lamb and dairy products, aid to developing countries, the Budget and so on were handled by different groups of European Ministers according to the subject, and the Prime Minister instructed that our attitude towards each issue must be determined separately as it came up for negotiation, with particular reference to the objectives of the manifesto; where Ministers were in any doubt during the course of the re-negotiations they should refer back to me. By this means my committee was firmly in charge of settling our policy and tactics in each subject and took the lead in coordinating overlapping problems at regular meetings held in my room at the Foreign Office.

In the intervals between meetings, minutes were showered on me like confetti at a wedding: my most prolific correspondents were Peter Shore, Tony Benn and Shirley Williams. Peter Shore, in his capacity as Secretary of State for Trade, wished to accompany me to meetings of Foreign Ministers in Brussels for negotiating sessions. I was unenthusiastic because I thought his hard-line opposition to membership would make the process more difficult, but I could not resist and so I counterbalanced his presence by the attendance of Roy Hattersley who, although not a fanatical pro-Marketeer, was nevertheless in favour of Britain's membership. I should add that Peter's opposition to Common Market membership was one of the few political differences we had. In later years we usually found ourselves on the same side, and I admired greatly his dislike of cant and humbug, his scorn for the impractical, and his eloquence, which at its best was as grandiloquent as Churchill's.

I aimed to steer a steady course in interpreting the manifesto. There was a difference in negotiating approach. Tony Benn would have had me adopt an all-or-nothing attitude – the manifesto, the whole manifesto and nothing but the manifesto. On that basis we were bound to fail and there would have been no point in beginning discussions, for the very act of negotiation must always imply an element of compromise, followed by a decision at the end of the process as to whether the final package meets the negotiator's broad objectives.

I recall that Tony remonstrated with me for agreeing to a resolution in the Foreign Ministers Council about the construction of a European policy for the aircraft industry. I replied that the wording was so anodyne as to be almost meaningless, and that I saw no need to have an unnecessary dispute when the remainder of the Council was unanimous, and the only result would be to sour the atmosphere for the issues that really mattered. Tony would not have it. 'We ought not to agree even to anodyne resolutions simply to avoid the charge that we were obstructive.' He believed that the aircraft resolution held potential dangers for the future of Britain's aircraft industry because the bureaucracy of the Commission would feed off it. The passage of time has answered him and writing now, many years later, there is no evidence that our national aircraft policy has suffered from that particular resolution.

I was faced with the hard task of yoking together horses which were pulling in opposite directions and this might have resulted in the carriage lurching so uncontrollably from side to side that it overturned the Government. My task was to keep the carriage on the road and to drive it to a vantage point from which Ministers could view the landscape as a whole, and then invite the passengers to reach a decision on their chosen direction. It was not easy, nor did the subject matter often lend itself to serious debate on great issues of principle. Instead, I found myself corresponding with the Chancellor, Denis Healey, about import levels of apricot halves and canned fruit salad, and with Peter Shore about mutton and lamb. I recall one low point when nine Foreign Ministers from the major countries of Europe solemnly assembled in Brussels to spend several hours discussing how to resolve our differences on standardising a fixed position of rear-view mirrors on agricultural tractors. I wondered what Palmerston, Salisbury or Bevin would have made of it, and sometimes I grumbled to my officials that I felt not so much a Foreign Secretary as a multiple grocer.

Some of my colleagues felt the same frustration. The differences between Cabinet Ministers on both objectives and tactics soon became publicly known and the Opposition naturally took full advantage of them to tweak the Government's tail and imply that we were being unreasonable and too demanding. This was inevitable but it aggravated the difficulties of our negotiating position with the Community because we had no Parliamentary majority. The other countries quickly realised that a second general election would be needed to elect a more stable Government and one or two of them were disinclined to begin serious discussions about re-negotiation until this uncertainty had been removed, and they knew whether they would be dealing with a Labour or a Conservative Government. Discussions on some of the more important matters were effectively stymied during the summer months of 1974 and this reinforced the Prime Minister's determination to call a second election in the autumn.

Other happenings also slowed us down. President Pompidou, who had probably been more favourable to Britain's membership of the Community than any of his Ministers, died in Paris just a month after Harold Wilson formed his Government, and a few weeks later, in May 1974, Willy Brandt, the German Chancellor, resigned. In due course Valery Giscard d'Estaing was elected in Pompidou's place and Helmut Schmidt became Chancellor of Germany, but these changes, although beneficial to Europe in the longer run, naturally led to a certain hiatus.

1974 turned out to be a year for the changing of the Guard both at home and abroad. Britain, France and Germany all had new Heads of Government. Golda Meir, the Prime Minister of Israel, resigned; President Nixon was replaced in America by Gerald Ford, who was much underrated as a President, whilst a coup in Portugal overturned the dictatorship.

Despite the uncertainty caused by changes in Community Governments, the summer was not entirely fruitless for my attendance at the frequent meetings of Foreign Ministers and discussions with the Commission enabled me to gauge how the Community worked in practice, and helped to firm up my views. At the beginning of re-negotiation I could not see what the outcome would be, nor whether I would be able to make a favourable recommendation to the Cabinet, but I knew it would be necessary, if the Government was to survive intact, to test all we did against the manifesto on which we had fought the election. My basic view of the effect of Community membership on Britain's economic prospects had hardly shifted since I had been Chancellor ten years earlier. That is to say I shared neither the conviction of the pro-Marketeers that it would result in a vast improvement in our economic performance nor the deep despair of the anti-Marketeers that membership would ruin Britain. I continued to affirm publicly and privately, as I had done in the 1960s, that Britain's economic salvation depended upon ourselves; whether we were in or out of the Community was marginal to the result.

On political issues I was sympathetic to closer cooperation with our European neighbours. I was of course a firm believer in the Atlantic Alliance, but as the years went by, it seemed that the strength of the Superpowers was so much greater than other individual nations that the voice of Europe was in danger of being lost in world affairs. It was my experience in my travels that this was an unwelcome development to many countries in Asia and Africa and even in the Far East, despite their experiences of European colonial rule. Indeed it was perhaps the residue of this outmoded imperial relationship that led them to say to visitors like myself that Britain understood them better than the Superpowers, and they hoped we would exert ourselves to influence world developments by a stronger European voice. My instinct was to agree, but we were handicapped by a resumption of the long-running and tiresome argument between European Federalists and the rest. The Federalists argued that it was first necessary for the members of the Community to unite in an economic, monetary and political union by the year 1980. It was obvious that this would not happen but some countries paid lip service to the idea. Attempts were made to commit Britain to such principles not as long-range ideals, but as objectives to be reached by the end of the decade.

Two months after I became Foreign Secretary, a weekend discussion on the subject took place among Foreign Ministers at a German Schloss, and this quickly confirmed my scepticism that none of the advocates were serious about working out the details of a European Union or of how it could be achieved politically. Nevertheless, they seemed ready to pay lip service to the idea and pressed for a declaration of faith by Britain, which I resolutely refused to give. For me to have done so would have achieved nothing practical but would have enraged the anti-Marketeers at home, who were on the watch to exploit any scintilla of derogation from Britain's sovereignty. I had little sympathy with this attitude as there were many precedents for Britain yielding up exclusive control of particular issues when it had been in our interest and the common advantage for us to do so. But I could not hand them this big stick with which to beat the Government. Sometimes I thought I detected a sardonic smile on the face of M. Jobert, the French Foreign Minister, as he listened to the others exerting pressure on Britain to recite the catechism of European Union, for France, one of the oldest and most nationalistic of countries, could not have agreed to take meaningful steps in that direction. As a founder member of the Community, however, France was exempt from the pressure applied to the new members. Of the other two new members, Ireland seemed ready to go along with the majority, but the Danes were as forthright as I was and remained unconvinced.

In due course the advent of the realistic Helmut Schmidt as Chancellor of Germany brought such unreal talk of early European political union to an end, and I was able to report to the Prime Minister that the Community had departed from theoretical discussion and was more flexible and adaptable to the needs of its individual members than I had imagined when we began. During the late summer of 1974 this new spirit influenced me to move more towards support for Britain's continued membership, always provided we could broadly satisfy our negotiating objectives.

The European Commission, although not directly involved in the re-negotiation, naturally took great interest in it, but was not always helpful as its members seemed more keen on preserving the letter of the Treaty of Rome than in recognising the practical problems of a sovereign state. One exception was François Ortoli, the Chairman, who seemed genuinely anxious to help. He suggested that he and I should meet, which we did on the 13 May 1974.

Knowing that there would shortly be a further general election, I told him that, come the autumn, the British Government would expect to have a good idea of the Community's response to four of our major problems – Britain's contribution to the Budget, the Common Agricultural Policy, the prospects for improved access to the Community for the produce of Commonwealth countries, especially sugar and processed foods, and our requirement that we should be able to continue our national policies of financial aid to development areas in Britain. He took full note of what I said and undertook to do some work on all these matters so that the other Governments of the Community would be able to assess what was involved.

Our conversation showed how much hard work lay ahead. Ortoli's view was that the Community would be able to make adjustments on some of the issues I had raised, but he was adamant that they could not alter the existing settlement on Britain's Budget contribution. The British Treasury had estimated that Germany was the largest net contributor to the Budget, Britain the second largest, France made a small net contribution, and Denmark, Holland and Ireland were big net gainers.

Britain was currently paying 10 to 12 per cent of the Budget and receiving in return no more than 8 per cent. By 1980 our estimate was that Britain's net contribution could rise as high as 24 per cent and although we could not forecast what receipts would offset this, the calculation was that Britain's Gross National Product by that time would be no more than 14 per cent of the Community total. There would be a big gap. Ortoli disputed both the methodology and the arithmetic. His view was that the situation was not adverse to us at the time and the situation we foresaw could not arise for some years, because the transitional financial arrangements that phased Britain's contribution on an upward course over a number of years provided a cushion. But, he went on, even if that were not the case, there could be no tampering with the principle that the financial resources of the Community were its own property and were inviolable. We should wait for some years to see if matters turned out as badly as we feared. If by then Britain had accepted the principle that the Community's resources were its own, we would stand a better chance of improving our financial relationship because any unfairness would be obvious to the other member states. I would not accept this delay and told him that it was both a practical and political necessity for the British Government to pursue the matter forthwith.

This was only the first of many similar bilateral discussions with the Commission's Chairman and with other Foreign Ministers, in addition to our formal collective discussions at meetings of the Foreign Ministers Council. I could understand their unwillingness to address the issue. Any new agreements by them that Britain should pay less meant that they would pay more and just as important, it was not so long since the previous Conservative Government had agreed to the existing financial arrangements. The other Community members were somewhat aggrieved that a newly elected Government should so swiftly seek to change the terms.

This sentiment was probably our biggest obstacle. At our meetings the other countries' objections took the form of constantly disputing our arithmetic as their best means of preventing a discussion on the merits of the case. Our officials found they had to fight a running battle for several months before they could win even a grudging acknowledgement that there might be something in Britain's arguments.

The summer months went by quickly, especially as I was distracted by events in Cyprus, and we made little progress on the Budget dispute. On 14 September 1974 the Prime Minister visited Paris at the invitation of the French President, Giscard d'Estaing, for a meeting of Heads of Government. Whilst there, he used his authority to restate our objections to the budgetary arrangements and to reject European Union as a practical concept. The French President's response was to propose a further summit meeting to be held in December 1974, by which time it was implicitly assumed that Britain's second general election of 1974 would have been decided. Harold accepted the proposal and on the day after he returned we published our election manifesto.

Parliament was dissolved on 20 September and brought to an end the shortest Parliament of the century; on only one previous occasion had there been two general elections in the same year. The minority Labour Government had been defeated no fewer than twenty-nine times in the two months prior to the summer recess, and it was obvious that a more settled verdict was needed. During the campaign the opinion polls gave Labour a big lead, but when the real poll took place on 10 October, this was not borne out. Our vote had fallen by 200,000, though fortunately this was more than offset by the collapse of the Conservative Party's vote, which was the lowest since 1945. The consequence was that the Labour Party ceased to be in a minority in the House of Commons and enjoyed a narrow majority of three – 319 to 316. We were disappointed, although Harold Wilson was characteristically undaunted, believing that various Opposition groups would not be able to unite. He forecast that we would be able to govern for a period of two to three years before another election must become inevitable and sent a sharp note to one Minister, rebuking him for an incautious remark that the Parliamentary situation could not last for more than twelve months.

In the end we bettered Harold's forecast. He was himself Prime Minister for the first eighteen months and I then succeeded him for a further period of three years making four and a half years in all, something little short of a miracle. The short election campaign had hardly interrupted the flow of Government business, and within a week I was making proposals to the Prime Minister on the next steps for re-negotiation.

We had included in our election manifesto the proposal to hold a referendum at the end of the re-negotiation period to enable the electorate to declare their view. I proposed to the Prime Minister that the Cabinet should at once establish an official committee to prepare the necessary Bill to enable a referendum to be held and he appointed the Lord President Ted Short, who possessed the additional advantage of being Deputy Leader of the Labour Party, to take charge of the preparations. Ted very sensibly consulted the other Parties in an effort to produce an agreed Bill, but despite his efforts the Tory Party voted against it, although there was little genuine sting in their opposition. Things went better for the Government as both pro- and anti-Marketeers in our ranks joined together to vote in the Bill's favour.

In general I am not myself a lover of referenda, believing that the task of an elected Parliament is to decide. A referendum places much opportunity for influence in the hands of a partisan press which may not scruple to angle public issues to fit its proprietors' prejudices. Nevertheless, as leading members of the Government and the Party were locked in irrevocable opposition to one another on the issue, a referendum seemed the best way to resolve it without too much loss of face for the losers. Tony Benn had first suggested the idea four years earlier when we were in Opposition, at a time when he was in favour of Britain's membership. I had said at the time that it might turn out to be a life-raft that both sides in the Party would one day be happy to scramble aboard. And so it turned out.

With the election won, the other members of the Community recognised that a Labour Government was in office for a longish period, and a more businesslike attitude began to prevail among the Foreign Ministers as well as within the Commission. Our election manifesto had promised a referendum within a year, and because of its divisive nature I was anxious to get re-negotiation completed by early summer of 1975. The matter took up much of my energies and the constant journeys and meetings left too little time for other important problems that I cared about, especially the situation in Rhodesia. Visits to Brussels were usually fraught. Frequently a morning meeting would be preceded by a late night at the House because our tiny majority demanded that I be present to vote. The morning start was very early because Continental time is one hour ahead of ours: a hurried car journey to Northolt RAF Airport during the rush hour, and a swift flight to Brussels, where my small team would be met by the Ambassador's car drawn up on the apron. We would speed to the meeting; on the journey the resident Ambassador would brief me on recent happenings and such intelligence as he had gleaned.

Then would follow a day of talks and discussions in which I was frequently in a minority of one, interspersed with telephone calls to and from the Foreign Office or other Ministries, followed by a late-night return journey to be met at Northolt, perhaps at midnight, by a Private Secretary with urgent telegrams and messages to be dealt with, or with Party business that required my attention as Party Chairman. It demanded considerable stamina, an ability to switch rapidly from one problem to another, and a capacity to survive on unending cups of coffee and sandwiches. I was helped very much by my previous experience as Chancellor and as Home Secretary in gauging the reactions of the Cabinet.

The quickened pace of re-negotiation following the Government's October election success was assisted by a proposal from Giscard d'Estaing that European Heads of Government should meet in Paris during the six months of France's Presidency of the European Community. He was concerned less with British re-negotiation than with the deteriorating economic situation in the Community, following the dramatic increase in world oil prices in 1973 and the growth of inflation. His aim was to achieve some common action amongst the Community Members to offset the effects of these. The Prime Minister and I were very ready to agree, as we could also use the occasion to advance our re-negotiation objectives. We were making some progress but our Foreign Ministers meetings had become bogged down in Britain's claim for a new financial settlement, and we seemed increasingly incapable of reaching a satisfactory conclusion. The item was inscribed on the agenda of every meeting, but when it was reached we rarely discussed it as a single issue, as other Foreign Ministers took the opportunity to air their own financial grievances. Garret Fitzgerald, the Foreign Minister of Ireland, was vocal about his need for a bigger share in the money allocated to regional aid. Italy's Foreign Minister took the same line with claims on behalf of southern Italy. Hans-Dietrich Genscher, the German Foreign Minister, while not unsympathetic to our case, claimed that Germany could pay no more.

The French Foreign Minister put forward a wide range of proposed institutional reforms that would have postponed decisions on our re-negotiation objectives until the Greek Kalends. The Foreign Ministers' Council was stalled and a meeting of Heads of Governments would be necessary to break the log-jam and issue some clear-cut decisions and instructions. Harold Wilson accordingly encouraged the French President to press ahead with his proposals, and I instructed our Ambassadors to lobby vigorously in their various capitals. Helmut Schmidt was favourable to Giscard's proposal, but obstruction was caused by some of the smaller countries which sought to bargain their willingness to come to a meeting against prior agreement that their various claims would be conceded. The prospects of a summit meeting remained in doubt until the last moment, but as often happens in Community matters, the obstacles were eventually overcome and a meeting was called in Paris for 9 December 1974.

The Prime Minister and I prepared for it carefully. The annual Labour Party Conference had been delayed by the election and was due to be held in London at the end of November, and I suggested to the Executive Committee that as I was the Chairman I should invite Helmut Schmidt to address the delegates. They agreed. The newspapers, always hopeful that a Labour Party row would enliven their reports, speculated that he would come with a big stick to belabour the Conference for our lack of European spirit and some of the left-wing delegates at once swallowed the bait and announced their intention to walk out during the speech. Helmut and I discussed the theme of the speech carefully. I made several suggestions and he sent me the draft for my comments.

As I had hoped, the speech turned out to be a considerable triumph. He addressed us in English, emphasising the solidarity of our two Parties, commented disparagingly on the Common Agricultural Policy, called for a common effort to overcome the twin evils of inflation and unemployment, making clear that while he would not try to influence the Labour Party's decision, nevertheless in his view the advantages of a European Community outweighed the burdens. He made some good jokes, quoted Shakespeare, spoke flatteringly of the Labour Party's historic contributions to trade unionism and the welfare state, and in general cut the ground from under the feet of some of the most insular of our comrades by appealing to the Labour Party's traditional internationalism. The threatened walk-out did not materialise and he was very warmly received and applauded.

At the end of the Conference, Harold entertained him at Chequers, where we had a fuller opportunity to explain at length our need for a decision in principle that the Community recognised that Britain had a legitimate Budgetary problem and would be willing to remedy it. If the forthcoming Paris Summit was willing to do this, then the following weeks could be devoted to finding an acceptable formula.

The German Chancellor was concerned about his country's own budgetary problems, but nevertheless seemed ready to back us. He had frequently said that Britain would bring added stability to the Community but he now raised a personal question. He enquired what would be the personal attitude of the Prime Minister and of myself if the Community made concessions which were satisfactory to us. Would we make a neutral report to Parliament on the negotiations or would we be prepared to make a positive recommendation? I replied at once that from the beginning of the process I had said that I was negotiating in good faith, by which I meant that if in my judgement that outcome met Britain's requirements, I would say so publicly and make a positive recommendation. Harold was just as firm, to which Helmut replied that our replies would encourage Germany to make concessions which she might not have been willing to do otherwise. He reverted to this matter on several occasions during the ensuing months and always received the same answer.

Helmut Schmidt returned to Bonn and a few days later on 5 December 1974 Harold and I continued our preparations by visiting the French President. His attitude was important for not only was he the Chairman of the Summit, but his intellectual authority could set the tone of the discussions. As always, we were received with typical French courtesy and style. Giscard was more friendly, helpful and forthcoming than his officials, who seemed to regard the re-negotiations as a game in which they were required to score as many points as possible. The President emphasised his desire that Britain should remain a member of the Community but argued strongly that there could be no weakening of the principle that the Community's income was inviolable. There was no way in which Britain could be allowed to pay less into the Community's budget.

Once again we explained, as on so many previous occasions and as we were to do many more times in the future, that meeting our aims did not necessarily require any diminution of total payments into the Budget; they could be satisfied by making a repayment from the Budget to offset Britain's unfairly high payments. Giscard said that this would amount to much the same thing, and in a practical sense he was of course correct. But, we argued, as the Community paid such attention to principle, our solution would not breach the principle that the Community's 'own resources' were its own and it was therefore entitled to make payments from the Budget by its own decision. Harold Wilson and I spent a lot of time elucidating the special difficulties of New Zealand, whose traditional market in Britain had been adversely affected by our membership. The Community countries did not understand the nature of the relationship between Britain and the Commonwealth and we had to work long and hard before they would admit that there was a problem. Both the Prime Minister and I viewed it as a moral obligation. On this occasion Giscard was noncommittal, and the issues were the subject of great argument in the ensuing months. I doubt that the toughness of our battle on their behalf was always appreciated by some Commonwealth members.

Not all of the meeting with Giscard was devoted to re-negotiation. On other matters we found, as we expected, that Giscard continued to support the practice of reaching Community decisions by consensus and was opposed to taking decisions in the Foreign Ministers Council by a majority vote. This was much favoured by the smaller nations and Giscard suggested as an alternative that three or four meetings be held each year of Heads of Government, who would not necessarily reach decisions, but would review the progress made at the meetings of Foreign Ministers. He suggested the Heads of Governments should be assisted by a small Secretariat. The Prime Minister agreed to support this, the proposal was accepted by the other countries and in due course meetings of Heads of Governments became a regular part of the calendar and have continued until now, though without the assistance of a permanent Secretariat.

As always, we were entertained to a delicious but not ostentatious dinner. Madame Giscard had secured the services of a chef who did full credit to the traditional excellence of French cuisine. I was told that Giscard himself took personal care of the preparation of the menu cards, which were themselves things of beauty, with reproductions of French paintings as their frontispiece. They were so outstanding that I would bring mine away to be admired as an ornament in its own right. The French display a natural style in these matters that far exceeds our own.

We returned from Paris on this occasion reasonably encouraged by Giscard's attitude, which had been markedly more flexible than that shown by French officials during previous discussions, when they had always taken the most severely legalistic line of all the Community countries.

We could not be certain what the French line would be when it came to practical negotiations at the Summit meeting itself. Giscard would be in the Chair, and could therefore exert considerable influence on the way the discussion would go, but where would he direct it? We therefore planned a dual approach. Our proposed course would be to secure acknowledgement by all Heads of Governments, including the French President, that Britain had a genuine budgetary problem and that a method should be sought to resolve it as a matter of urgency. If, however, France should prove obdurate, we would then fall back on a formula that would unite everyone except the French, in the hope that if the President found himself isolated he would feel bound to fall into line. There would be a special reason for him to do so as Chairman, for having taken the initiative in calling the Summit, he would naturally wish it to be a success and so pave the way for further gatherings.

To bolster this dual approach, we began to switch the emphasis from the British case to a more general proposal that any member country whose Gross Domestic Product was below that of the average of the Community should not bear an unfair share of the burden of financing the Community's Budget. The advantage of such a formula was that it effectively linked Britain's requirement to one of the major objectives of the Treaty of Rome, namely the intention to promote convergence in the performance of the Community's economies. This would take the wind out of the sails of objections that our proposition was not 'Communitaire' in spirit. The fact that Britain was the only country that could expect to benefit at the time was no disadvantage.

Our enquiries in Brussels showed that the Belgians would be helpful, although they wished to couple their assistance with some theological reference to the aim of achieving economic and monetary union. This would have made my life more difficult in rebutting the arguments of the hard-line anti-Marketeers at home.

The Dutch too were ready to go down this road, although they suggested that the formula be limited to our balance of payments position. I was chary of accepting this because we were looking for a substantial bonus from North Sea oil by 1980. We found Luxembourg in our support, ready to argue that our proposals did not offend the principles of the Treaty of Rome. Apart from our uncertainty about the French, it seemed that the Germans might cause us most trouble. Hans-Dietrich Genscher, the German Foreign Minister, although by no means hostile, was arguing that because the adverse situation we foresaw would not arise for some years, the Heads of Governments could put off devising a solution until 1978 (to take effect from 1980). If his view prevailed I could see no prospect of a successful re-negotiation.

The Prime Minister and I set off for the Paris Summit on 9 December, hopeful but by no means confident of the outcome. We had done all we could to prepare the ground through our preliminary meetings and the efforts of our Ambassadors. Throughout this period, I was much indebted to the ingenuity and hard work of the officials of the Foreign Office. I was in no doubt that most of them believed that it was in Britain's long-term interest to remain in the Community, but this made them all the more keen to achieve the objectives set out in the Labour Party's election manifesto, and they worked with a will.

Harold was experiencing a number of minor indispositions at the time and was not wholly well during the Paris Summit. He always pooh-poohed references to his state of health and disliked making a fuss, but although these minor ailments must have sapped his strength, he fought like a tiger to secure agreement to our preferred formula. The exchanges were long, argumentative and tense at times. Giscard, in his capacity as President, was very fair and did nothing to make our task more difficult, although the French Foreign Minister argued the case for the inviolability of the Community's revenues, as did the Chairman of the Commission. But I could feel the tide flowing in our direction and at the end of the discussion we agreed 'to set up as soon as possible a correcting mechanism of a general application' and invited the Commission to prepare proposals for this purpose.

We left Paris satisfied at having achieved our immediate objective, although we knew we would have a hard fight on our hands when the time came to translate the formula into a sum of money. Giscard's proposal for Heads of Governments and Foreign Ministers to meet jointly three times a year was also accepted, as was a proposal that the Prime Minister of Belgium, Leo Tindemans, should prepare a comprehensive report on what would be involved in a European Union. This was a question that I had frequently addressed to the other Foreign Ministers, some of whom used the term as an incantation whose meaning was both cloudy and obscure.

A more practical approach began to develop, Helmut Schmidt, for example, referring to the concept of economic monetary union as 'created by idealists who simply did not understand the subject', and there was little doubt that the change of guard at the top in France, Germany and Britain in 1974 had done much to create a more realistic attitude. Among the other decisions, a special fund was created to assist the industrial development of hard-hit regions in southern Italy, Wales, Scotland and the Republic of Ireland, and Germany and Belgium undertook to stimulate their public and private investment in order to support high levels of employment, not only in their own countries but also in the belief that this would have a beneficial effect throughout the Community. These were early examples of a growing tendency during the 1970s to recognise the interdependence of our economic policies. Unfortunately, this was abandoned when the Thatcher/Reagan ideology became fashionable.

Another welcome aspect of the Heads of Governments meetings was the growth of a 'collegiate' atmosphere on issues that lay outside the competence of the Treaty of Rome. These became known as 'political cooperation' to distinguish them from the economic provisions of the Rome Treaty. At formal meetings the agenda was strictly prepared to include only those matters which fell within the provisions of the Treaty, but when the formal day's business was completed and the meeting ended, an 'ad hoc' arrangement grew up in which the participants adjourned for dinner as a group and then, at the coffee stage, would move without any semblance of protocol to another room more comfortably furnished. The early-comers seized the best armchairs and settees, others would perch where they could – a Head of Government even on occasion squatting on the floor. We would then launch into an after-dinner discussion on those political problems which did not fall within the Treaty.

The talk might be about any subject; perhaps a review of the Middle East situation or a discussion about Western defence – although on this latter issue, Garret Fitzgerald and Liam Cosgrave were always careful to indicate the neutrality of the Republic of Ireland. At the first Paris meeting Helmut Schmidt began our after-dinner exchanges by giving the other Heads of Government a colloquial account of his talks in Washington with President Ford, together with his impressions of the American scene. His comments were more revealing than any official account would have been and enabled the company to focus on the line that the French President should adopt on a visit he was about to undertake to the United States.

A consensus began to emerge: Giscard should encourage President Ford to coordinate the economic policies of America with the Community in a common effort to offset the adverse effects of the recent drastic oil price increases on inflation and unemployment. Obviously, there was no attempt to instruct the President of France about his conversations, but knowing the views of his European allies, he would be more strongly armed in his discussions.

I cannot overemphasise the informality of these after-dinner talks. There was no chairman, no agenda and no formal decisions. Drinks would be brought round at intervals, and it was not unknown for someone to nod off if we had held a particularly long and tiring session. The exchanges enabled all of us to gain insight into the views of the other leaders and to profit from their experience and their contacts.

It was an arena in which Harold Wilson and I could participate without any of the reserve or inhibitions caused by our re-negotiation, and I found it of assistance in the formation of British foreign policy. This political cooperation was another factor influencing me to support Britain's membership of the Community, provided we could satisfy our negotiating objectives.

The Prime Minister's mind was moving in the same direction and he made an important speech to London's Labour mayors, in which he followed up his earlier undertaking to Helmut Schmidt and stated publicly that provided the re-negotiation process turned out successfully, he would recommend that Britain remain in the Community. This alarmed the 'all out' opponents of membership and Michael Foot, Peter Shore and Tony Benn jointly wrote an unpublicised letter to Harold Wilson urging that they should be as free to express their views publicly as the Prime Minister was.

Harold Wilson put the matter to a Cabinet meeting in December. The discussion was temperate and a decision was reached that until negotiations were completed and the whole package could be seen in its entirety, the doctrine of collective responsibility for Government policy should apply, but that at the end of the process a further decision would be taken on how Ministers should conduct themselves during the referendum. Notwithstanding this, Tony Benn began the New Year of 1975 by sending an open letter to his constituents which he intended should convey his continued opposition to membership, no matter what the terms of our re-negotiation. When asked how he reconciled this with the Cabinet decision, he explained that he had written to his electors not as a Cabinet Minister but as their MP, so that they should understand that continued EEC membership would weaken the bond between an MP and his constituents. Such dissembling cut no ice with Harold, and he curtly told Tony Benn that his letter was not within the spirit of the Cabinet's December conclusion, adding that if any individual member of the Cabinet jumped the gun, others would do the same. Tony Benn's action made it more difficult for the Prime Minister to restrain the pro-Marketeers in the Cabinet from also stating their views publicly, and he feared the Cabinet would be thrown into public dispute and the Party into turmoil even before we knew the result of the re-negotiations. He therefore told Benn to refrain from any further public pronouncements of his own views and to remain within the terms of the Cabinet's decision. One of Tony's blind spots was his inability to understand that for him to argue that he was keeping within the letter of the law, when he clearly offended against its spirit, aroused hostility even among those of his colleagues who shared his opinions on the merits of the issue.

Michael Foot and Peter Shore pursued their opposition strongly within the Cabinet itself and in letters to the Prime Minister, concentrating especially on some sentences in the Paris agreement which they believed weakened the right of a nation to use its veto to prevent a Community decision from becoming effective. They objected also to the move towards electing members of the European Assembly by direct universal suffrage. I had no real difficulty on either score, and once again I do not believe that experience has borne out their fears. Michael and Peter are both men of integrity, who behaved with total loyalty and in a spirit of comradeship during a period which was difficult for all of us.

The strains were telling, and it was clear that the time would come when it would be impossible to hold a divided Cabinet together any longer; in

Harold's words, its members would have to be let off the lead and be free to express their own views. We were agreed that we must make this period as short as possible, if the Government's authority in other areas was not to be fatally weakened. Accordingly, he and I decided that we would do our best to bring the re-negotiations to a conclusion at the next Summit meeting, which was to be held in Dublin in March 1975, with Garret Fitzgerald, the Prime Minister of Ireland, in the Chair.

We intensified our negotiations in Brussels and my colleagues and I paid even more frequent visits. So great was their wariness that it had been my practice to circulate a record of every conversation I held in Brussels to all Cabinet Ministers, irrespective of whether or not their Departments were directly affected. I had begun this in the hope of disarming suspicions that I might be exceeding my instructions, but the consequence was that both sides in the Cabinet examined minutely each nuance in my hurriedly dictated reports, and then shouted or whispered contradictory advice on the next step.

I found this somewhat irksome and on one occasion unwisely circulated a minute to the effect that I would no longer send every communication to everyone, although I would maintain the closest consultation with those particular Cabinet Ministers whose Departmental interests were under discussion. My intention was that the Cabinet should judge the result of each separate set of negotiations as each item was completed. This was a mistake, and brought indignant complaints from some Ministers. Harold backed me, saying that I was not getting the help and support I was entitled to, but promised that the Cabinet would be kept informed of every significant development. This was accepted and I was very grateful to him for getting me off the hook for an initiative that could have been better phrased.

As a result of the efforts of my Cabinet colleagues, rapid progress was made in the early months of 1975. Henry Kissinger, the United States Secretary of State, visited me in February and during the course of a long talk, I described the state of our negotiations. The United States rightly did not express any formal view on the British Government's attitude, but Henry Kissinger and I had struck up a good relationship and I always treated with him on a basis of frankness. He responded with generosity and I took advantage of this to get his own views 'off the record'. As I expected, he favoured Britain's continued membership, but said significantly that if the decision went the other way, we could be sure that the United States would do all it could to help Britain and to sustain the relationship between our two countries. It might mean that we would work together even more closely than before, taking into account Britain's economic problems, but in any event Britain need not fear that she would be cold-shouldered. This was genuinely meant and it was reassuring to know, but neither he nor I was under any illusion that a withdrawal could be painless or that a closer relationship with the United States would not involve Britain paying a price for such support.

This talk with Henry Kissinger was part of a regular system of consultation and information which included Commonwealth Governments and bodies such as the TUC International Committee, the Labour Party and the CBI. The meetings with the TUC were particularly interesting. There was no precedent for such occasions – that organisation and the Foreign Office lived in different worlds. But the world of labour is international and trade union leaders have many overseas links, which sometimes gives them a slant on issues different from the experience of our Ambassadors. Jack Jones was Chairman of the TUC Committee and he and I agreed to hold meetings at fairly regular intervals in which we would discuss any issue they wished. I found these occasions very helpful and used them to explain the reasons for the Government's actions on such issues as Greece, Cyprus, Chile, South Africa, Rhodesia and Portugal. One result was that despite the opposition of Congress to Britain's membership of the EEC, we experienced little hostility on other questions.

I encouraged our Embassies to create opportunities to meet with British trade union leaders when they travelled overseas to attend international conferences. Our people were often too modest to use the resources of the Embassies in the proprietorial manner of some I know, but they had contacts and sources of information which threw valuable light on the work of the Embassies. It was also helpful for officials serving overseas to meet trade union leaders fresh from home and hear at first-hand their views, especially as industrial relations are given such partisan treatment by the press. I found that most Embassies welcomed this.

In preparation for the Dublin meeting of the Heads of Government of European Community members on 10 March 1975, I drew up a minute in the form of a balance sheet, and sent it to the Prime Minister. On the credit side, there would be no practical difficulties for us about economic and monetary union or our ability to control capital movements, about harmonisation of VAT or our regional policy; no one would make waves about these. We had secured a substantial improvement in the Commonwealth Sugar Agreements, and the new Lome Convention, which offered technical cooperation to Africa and to the Commonwealth countries of the Caribbean and the Pacific, was now ready to be signed. On the debit side, we had not secured adequate safeguards for New Zealand, and although good progress had been made since December 1974 in devising a budget mechanism to reduce Britain's net financial burden, its adoption would be a political decision and not merely a technical solution. Hence we could run into difficulties, which might cause us to say that re-negotiation had failed.

We were already in difficulty about the Common Agriculture Policy, for I could not claim any fundamental re-negotiation of its principles. On the other hand, the German Chancellor and other Heads of Government had expressed their strong dissatisfaction with its operation and acknowledged that changes would have to be made. It was not the strongest moment to press our objections for at that time world prices for grain were (unusually as it turned out) higher than the internal Community price, so I could hardly argue that the British housewife was being denied cheap food. And I was in no doubt that if the member states dallied over reform, it would be forced upon them eventually because expenditure would grow faster than revenue. The inevitable deficit would force a fundamental reform of the Common Agricultural Policy, but I could not forecast how soon it would come. It was clear that Dublin would be a tough meeting. We knew that some Heads of Government would try to play off concessions by them on New Zealand's dairy products in exchange for concessions by us on the Budget. Helmut Schmidt's attitude to our claims would be influenced by whether or not the Prime Minister would state once again his intention positively to recommend and support a satisfactory new settlement. The French would want to hear a positive statement from us on European unity however remote this might be in practice.

The press of Europe and the world, knowing that the re-negotiations were approaching a climax, arrived in Dublin in force and heightened the drama. Hans-Dietrich Genscher took me on one side before the first session began. He was an ardent believer in European unity, a man who endeavoured to build bridges whenever difficulties arose between the member states, and a hard worker who kept his finger on the pulse of the Community. He radiated an air of solid judgement and I listened carefully as he told me that the Dutch and the Danes would be very difficult about importing New Zealand butter and cheese, and the Germans too had similar difficulties, but he believed they would make concessions in the end because he sensed a general feeling that everyone wished to bring the year-long negotiations to a conclusion. I thanked him and said that I agreed that we could not carry on discussions beyond the Dublin meeting. This meeting would be make or break. I told him that the Government would be presenting the Referendum Bill to Parliament within a few days and this meant that the time was fast approaching when the British people as a whole would express their opinions, hence the supreme importance of what we were about to do in Dublin. Genscher encouraged me by saying that if certain matters were unresolved the Foreign Ministers' monthly meetings would enable us to iron out the difficulties that might remain.

Genscher's forecasts were correct. Harold Wilson began with a strong appeal on New Zealand's behalf for greater access for their dairy products, only to be met with strong opposition from the Prime Ministers of Denmark and Holland. Giscard too was unenthusiastic. We were not able to reach agreement and so branched into the problems of the Budget. The Commission Chairman explained that the Commission had devised a financial formula which he believed met the objective agreed at the previous meeting and he recommended it. I was disconcerted when he was immediately attacked by Helmut Schmidt. The Chancellor argued with some asperity that Germany was already the largest net contributor to the Community Budget and he had his own domestic budgetary difficulties. Germany was ready to agree to some change, but the magnitude of possible refunds to Britain under the Commission's formula was too large for Germany to accept. Giscard took up the theme of economic and monetary union. Would Britain agree to it or not? Harold and I were playing as a team and he handed the baton to me. I asked why France was raising this matter at such a late stage. There had been a full discussion earlier and Britain had been party to the statement that had been issued when he was in the Chair at the Paris Summit. We had nothing to add or to subtract from what had been published. When I finished it seemed that the other Heads of Government did not wish to follow Giscard into this minefield, and he pursued the matter no further. I came to the conclusion that it had been a diversionary tactic to steer the discussion away from the Budget.

This was confirmed in informal talks I had with other Ministers during the evening. Genscher was once more reassuring that an opening would come, and with the knowledge gained from experience of Foreign Ministers' meetings I was inclined to believe him. Only too often I had seen the Council drive up to the very edge of the cliff and then go into reverse just before they drove over. The question was how could we convince them that they were at the edge. The Prime Minister and I were both aware of the overriding importance the Community attached to the doctrine that the 'financial resources' of the Community belonged to it and to it alone, and could not be tampered with by reducing any nation's contribution. This had been one of the points raised by the German Chancellor during the previous day and by agreement with Harold, I opened the discussion when we resumed the following morning. I repeated once more that Britain had no intention of dismantling the Community's revenue system; we did not challenge the VAT contribution; our difficulties could be met by the Community agreeing to repay part of our contribution. This method would ensure that it was regarded as Community expenditure. I had made this speech many times before to sundry audiences and it contained nothing that was new, but as I spoke the atmosphere seemed to change as though those present recognised that the time for decision had come. Helmut Schmidt's tone was different from the previous day as he set the ball rolling.

He said he had listened carefully to my remarks and had come to the conclusion that Britain had made out a case for the Community to meet. Britain's net contribution should be modified and Germany was ready to support the formula drawn up by the Commission. We had found a Community solution, as this formula would also apply to any other member of the Community which found itself in a similar position in the future. It provided for a revision if the country concerned was contributing more to the total Budget than its appropriate percentage of its total Gross Domestic Product. Schmidt said he agreed that this was fair, but Germany had her own budgetary problems and he proposed a maximum refund of 250 million units of account, equivalent to about £125 millions in any one year.

This seemed a very reasonable offer for we had calculated that our net contribution for 1974 would be about £70 millions, but we also had to cater for the position in later years, when our gross contribution was scheduled to increase rapidly. The other Heads of Government joined in and confirmed that they too would be willing to accept the Commission's formula subject to the German amendment, and it became obvious that François Ortoli, the Commission Chairman, and the German Chancellor had both been hard at work since the previous day.

The Prime Minister and I conferred while the others waited. We both took the view that there was no better financial bargain to be struck at that time, but we or our successors would need to see how the formula would apply in the changing circumstances of later years, and we must reserve our right to raise the matter again if events did not turn out as the formula intended.

We returned and Harold intimated this to the assembled Heads of Government around the table. There was no visible dissent, although clearly they hoped the issue would not be resurrected. The atmosphere in the room lightened immediately. There was no doubting the genuine desire of the countries present that Britain should remain a member of the Community, and they took this financial settlement to mean that the Prime Minister and I would recommend continued membership to the country. The meeting ended almost light-heartedly with another crisis point having been surmounted, and Irish hospitality cemented (or more correctly, liquefied) the deal.

For Britain the importance of the Dublin agreement was that the other members had accepted the principle that Britain had established her financial case and had devised a formula to correct the unfairness. This was more important than the actual figure of £125 millions, as that could be discussed again when time showed how it worked. It meant that when my successor, Mrs Thatcher, raised the matter again in the early 1980s she did not have to argue the principle or the need for a formula. We had won that ground. Her task was to secure a different formula that would produce a better result. This was certainly difficult and she had to work hard, but no harder than the Labour Government had done to make the initial breakthrough. She was less than just in her constant iteration that she had secured a victory that the Labour Government had not.

Harold Wilson called a press conference in Dublin Castle, and the room overflowed. The journalists were anxious to know his attitude to continued membership. The Prime Minister was cautious. The negotiations had resulted in a great improvement, he said, and he was satisfied that no more could be got at that time, but it would be for Parliament and the people to decide whether they were good enough. I told the press I would recommend to the Cabinet that Britain should accept the new terms as a package. Harold was generous in sharing any credit there was. 'We have the great advantage that Jim and I are a complete partnership,' he said with his eye on the forthcoming Rugby International. 'We pass the ball from one to the other and break through the opposition.'

A Cabinet Meeting held a few days later voted by a majority to accept the terms, but the differences between Ministers were fundamental. The Prime Minister handled them with great tact for it was an issue which could have broken up the Cabinet. He issued his judgement of Solomon. Ministers who opposed the decision were free to speak against the Cabinet decision and to vote 'No' in Parliament and also in the referendum, but those Ministers who were elected to the National Executive Committee of the Labour party enjoyed in this unique instance a personal freedom only, and did not have a licence to organise a coordinated campaign within the National Executive Committee against the Government.

The rest of the story is well known. The Prime Minister gave a detailed report to Parliament. He avoided nothing, setting out each and every point in Labour's manifesto one by one, and then explaining in each case how far we had attained our objective. He was totally frank when he reached his conclusion:

> The Government cannot claim to have achieved in full all the objectives that were set out in the manifesto on which Labour fought. It is thus for the judgement now of the Government, shortly of Parliament, and in due course of the British people, whether or not we should stay in the European Community on the basis of the terms as they have now been re-negotiated.

The Prime Minister and I continued to work together and although we were faced by such powerful dissenting Ministers as Barbara Castle, Michael Foot, Peter Shore, and Tony Benn, this did not disturb the other business of the Government. Parliament voted by a large majority to accept the terms, with Labour Members almost equally divided, a small majority voting against acceptance. A special Labour Party Conference was called and despite speeches from Harold and myself, this voted against acceptance by a substantial majority. However, the die was cast and we had promised a referendum in advance of which the Government financed the printing and circulation of leaflets to every household, setting out both the pro-Market and the anti-Market case, together with the Government's own recommendation. The Government also provided grants of £125,000 to both pro- and anti- campaigning organisations. Despite this, the pro-Marketeers held the advantage in money, organisation and press sympathy, as well as the prestige conveyed by a recommendation from the Government, backed by the Conservative and Liberal Parties. Several Commonwealth countries also made statements supporting Britain's continued membership on the basis of the results of the re-negotiated settlement.

The referendum was held on 5 June 1975, and gave a clear mandate in favour of Britain continuing its membership of the Community by 17,378,581 votes to 8,470,073, a massive majority of nearly nine millions.

It is an interesting footnote that when, four months later, the annual Labour Party Conference was held, there was not a single reference to the bitter dispute that had split and divided the Party for fifteen years. That in itself was a tribute to the skilful way in which Harold Wilson had managed apparently unbridgeable differences in the Party and kept his Government intact. By this time few members of the Cabinet, if any, believed that the decision itself would solve Britain's economic problems. That easy view might have been held by some pro-Marketeers in earlier years, but such euphoria had long since evaporated. There were one or two Cabinet Ministers who believed that Britain's problems could only be solved by withdrawing into a siege economy, in which we surrounded these islands with a mighty panoply of controls and tariffs. These Ministers were of the opinion that Community membership would positively prevent the Government from doing what was necessary to rebuild the economy.

Such views were openly expressed in the winter of 1974 at one of the weekend discussions at Chequers that the Prime Minister called from time to time. These exchanges were not Cabinet Meetings in the formal sense, but a form of seminar at which everyone was free to express his views on the medium term outlook and the Government's strategy. I was feeling particularly gloomy: 'Our place in the world is shrinking: our economic comparisons grow worse, long-term political influence depends on economic strength – and that is running out. The country expects both full employment and an end to inflation. We cannot have both unless people restrain their demands. If the TUC guidelines [on pay] are not observed, we shall end up with wage controls once more and even a breakdown of democracy.'

After this apocalyptic vision I cracked a joke: 'Sometimes when I go to bed at night, I think that if I were a young man I would emigrate. But when I wake up in the morning, I ask myself whether there is any place else I would prefer to go.' This summarised my long-held view that Britain's economic destiny was in our own hands but even if we were not doing well, Britain was still the best country in which to live. Membership of the Community was only marginal to our economic success or failure.

But membership did offer important opportunities. The anti-Marketeers in the Cabinet continued to emphasise the difficulties of marrying their Departmental policies with those of the Community and sometimes, but by no means always, their complaints were justified. To offset this and to present a more balanced picture I was looking for some incontrovertible and tangible proof that Community membership could provide Britain with a benefit that would not otherwise have accrued to us. By chance I found it in September 1975 when I came across a report that the Commission was proposing a European research programme into thermo-nuclear fusion (not fission) to include the construction phase of a major experiment that was christened the Joint European TORUS (JET for short). Torus is a word derived from geometry and describes a solid ring or circle, whose revolution is the basis of the energy to be produced. JET would attempt to harness a clean source of power by trying to build machines that would generate energy by fusion, leaving no nuclear waste for disposal. Both Russia, whose venture is called TOKAMUK, and the United States were already in the field but the sheer scale of research meant that no single European country could compete. However, Britain did possess one of the leading fusion laboratories at Culham in Oxfordshire, whose work had won our scientists world renown. It meant that this country was ideally placed to become the European centre of an exciting project for the future. The Treasury was arguing that this was an experiment we could not afford and I fired off a minute to the Chancellor, Denis Healey, asking that Treasury opposition be withdrawn. 'If JET is successful it could be of the greatest significance to the lives of future generations. We should mount as soon as possible a vigorous and determined campaign at a high level for JET to be sited in the United Kingdom.'

As a result Treasury opposition softened, but I then discovered that Culham had two serious rivals, Ispra in Italy and Garching in Bavaria. Both institutions had first-class reputations, although Ispra suffered from having no experience in this particular field. It was probable that however high the merits of Culham, the decision would be taken largely on political grounds, and I threw myself into the fight. I tackled Helmut Schmidt first, in view of his known desire to make Britain's membership of the Community a success. He had not followed the issue and I explained to him my personal concern that Britain should become the home of a European institution. I told him about Culham's work and the fact that it possessed a first-class scientific team which was in danger of being lured to the United States to undertake work for that country and would consequently be lost to Europe. Helmut promised to help.

By this time I had become Prime Minister and I approached Giscard next, saying that I would prefer a European solution, but I was in no circumstances ready to see our British team dispersed (as the United Kingdom was a leading nation in this research), and if necessary I would make cooperative arrangements with some other country, although when I said this I had no idea with whom. Giscard was by no means hostile but said he was not well informed and promised to make enquiries. Meanwhile, the Italians, who had had strong hopes for Ispra, seeing that matters might not turn out as they wished, had placed a block on the whole programme so that no progress of any sort was taking place.

Knowing that the staff at Culham were frustrated and the team in danger of breaking up, I asked Sir Douglas Allen, the Head of the Civil Service, to give them a personal message from me. He should make known that I was determined to see the British capability continued. They should be patient for a little while longer. He did so and the message had the effect of halting the likely drain to the United States.

I then wrote to Helmut Schmidt saying that the delay in getting ahead was a discredit to Europe, and that a quick decision must be reached. He replied with bad news. Garching in Bavaria, which had always been a competitor, although not as active as Ispra, had now re-entered the fray, its cause having been taken up by no less a person than Franz-Josef Strauss. This changed the balance of forces. German officials withdrew support from Britain, although privately Helmut Schmidt was still sympathetic, especially in view of the help Britain had given him recently over the hi-jack of a Lufthansa plane. We redoubled our efforts. Tony Benn, the Secretary for Energy, was enthusiastic again, having cooled off at an earlier stage, and went to work to convince the Germans that they would have a large share of the research when they joined us at Culham. I put our Ambassadors in to bat in every capital in the Community (except Rome), asking them to make an exceptional effort to win support.

The propaganda battle swayed to and fro but at last in October 1977, two years after the struggle had begun, the Council met at Luxembourg and decided that JET should proceed, that it would be properly financed and above all that it should be based at Culham. Work has gone ahead in Oxfordshire since that time and the European team remains well abreast of similar research being undertaken in the Soviet Union, the United States and more recently, Japan.

The scientists have set themselves a target of 1989 to demonstrate the feasibility of a JET-type machine for use in a power station. This is a project for the twenty-first century but already some valuable results are beginning to emerge, and Europe has retained a capacity in a pioneering scientific area that would otherwise have been lost.

The Community's existence created the mechanism for close Franco-German cooperation and this was deepened by the understanding between Giscard d'Estaing and Helmut Schmidt. For those who do not recall the bitter Franco-German hostility which characterised so much of the first half of the twentieth century, it is difficult to appreciate the significance of this change. The Franco-Prussian War of 1870, the First World War and the Second World War had fuelled French fears of German power and German politics, but after 1945 France's relations with the Federal Republic were to develop along different lines; cooperation replaced antagonism to the point where even West Germany's emergence as the dominant economic power in Europe could be accepted. With every year that elapsed, a younger generation emerged in Europe which had been nurtured on the fruits of greater understanding. War between the states of Western Europe became unthinkable.

Franco-German friendship has become the linch-pin of the Community. Undoubtedly Giscard d'Estaing and Helmut Schmidt helped in the transition. They steadied Europe at a period when the recession of the 1970s could easily have led to a whole range of protectionist measures being adopted haphazardly by European countries acting in isolation and without regard to the general interest. Giscard was more inclined to protectionism than Schmidt, but their different approaches modified and complemented one another. Despite the rhetoric, they set the tone by recognising that Europe could not act as one in economic matters until the level of economic development in every country became more equal. We are still a long way from that, and the advent of Greece, Spain and Portugal, despite its political merits, sets back even further the founding fathers' ideal of economic integration. Their high aspiration has given way to a more humdrum outlook, and to Europessimism – a combination of resigned regret at the loss of control over Europe's destiny and a submerging of the ambition to erase Europe's economic frontiers which inspired so many post-war idealists.

European unity is still too big a step for Europe to take in the short term, but there are other measures which could make Europe both a viable economic entity and a powerful voice and influence in world affairs – liberalisation of the internal market, cooperative research and development, standardisation and the proper utilisation of economies of scale, cooperation not duplication. Latterly we have seen a United States administration manifest an increasing tendency to go it alone, with small regard to the views of her allies. This has encouraged the Soviet Union to deal directly with the United States, while dealing separately with European countries on a bilateral basis as far as possible. This carries a danger of splitting the West, and of exacerbating tensions in the longer term. Western Europe should make a threefold reply. We must work together more closely in order to speak as one whenever possible, so bringing a European influence to bear in Superpower relations; we must deepen relations with the countries of Eastern Europe; and we must sustain the strength of the Atlantic Alliance through greater consultation and the harmonisation of mutual interests. In this way, both the United States and the Soviet Union will be compelled to pay more attention to the views of Europe as a whole. Instead of our being little more than the subject matter of American–Soviet relations, we must aim to become an equal determinant in our own future.

The European Community has an important role to play in this: the Assembly for example could take the lead in cultivating relations with Eastern Europe. But the main thrust must come from the governments of the member countries, whose Ministers could agree to set aside the need for unanimous voting on certain issues. They could also strengthen their political cooperation through a small, permanent secretariat to service the European Council and coordinate decision-making. Provided we keep our goals clearly in mind, there will always be an incentive to reach them, although we must not be disillusioned when progress comes only step by step and is piecemeal.

II

---

*Cyprus – background to the Turkish invasion – negotiations at
Geneva – President Nixon's resignation*

Foreign policy is a mixture of the old and the new. We may initiate but
we also inherit; we may vote at the ballot box for changes in policy and
personalities, but on acquiring office governments inherit an international
situation on which the footprints of the past are heavily marked. We
cannot legislate about the actions of other nations, we cannot wipe the
slate completely clean. We become at once both instigator and recipient,
actor and stage manager. With the EEC, Ministers were dealing with
relatively new institutions, attitudes and policies in areas where there was
little precedent; with Cyprus we were to confront a situation where the
past limited and defined the possibilities of the present.

In 1878, after three centuries of Ottoman rule, Britain took possession
of Cyprus. With it we at once inherited the problem of Enosis, the demand
by Greece for union of the island with the mainland, a demand which had
become a rallying cry throughout the century that followed the Greek
War of Independence in 1821. But the call for Enosis aroused the hostility of Turkey and of the 20 per cent Turkish minority living in the island,
and was a source of constant tension with Greece.

Everywhere the break-up of the colonial empires after the end of the
Second World War brought about a demand for the right to self-determination and Cyprus was no exception. But in Cyprus there was a twist, for
to grant the right would mean not only independence, but also the right
to vote for union with Greece. One of the strongest advocates was Michael
Christodoulos Monakos, a priest from a poor shepherd home whose
ability had won him scholarships to universities in the United States.

He returned home from America as a churchman with political aspirations and with an organising ability out of the ordinary. In due course he
became a bishop, owing his advancement and his popularity to his
advocacy of Enosis, and when the incumbent Archbishop of Cyprus died,
Michael Monakos was enthroned in his place as Archbishop Makarios III
at the youthful age of thirty-seven, the youngest Archbishop in the island

of all time. He set out to travel the world and took advantage of the flowing tide of anti-colonialism to gain recognition of the cause of Enosis. The British Government were slow to point to the international difficulties this would cause, and made matters worse by refusing to have any dealings with him, although he had become the undoubted leader of the Greek Cypriots. It was not until after violence had broken out between Greek and Turkish Cypriots that the British Governor of the island for the first time called in the Archbishop for talks.

The issue which pitchforked the question of Enosis into the forefront of post-war international affairs and cost many lives and much misery was the announcement on 28 July 1954 by the British Government of their intention to withdraw British troops from Egypt, where our position had become increasingly untenable. As a substitute for the Suez Canal, Britain's Middle East base was henceforth to be Cyprus. The decision to withdraw from Egypt caused uproar among many of the Government's supporters. In the House Conservative back-benchers went round uttering open cries of mutiny even to Labour Members. They used words like 'feeble', 'disastrous' and 'scuttle' to describe their Government's actions. They asked how, with such a pusillanimous attitude, they could place any reliance on their holding fast in Cyprus if serious opposition arose in that island? There was no doubt about the fierce temper against the Cabinet and the Minister of State for the Colonies was put up to reassure the rebels. The Government, he said 'wish to make it clear once again that they cannot contemplate a change of sovereignty in Cyprus'. I sat listening on the front bench to this flat-footed declaration which flew in the face of the whole post-war direction of Britain's colonial policy from the independence of India onwards. Jim Griffiths, Labour's Spokesman on Colonial Affairs, immediately challenged the Minister. Did his statement mean that Cyprus would not at any stage have the right to decide its own future? The Minister's reply was even more dogmatic. 'There are certain territories which . . . can never expect to be fully independent.' He was challenged yet again and once again refused to qualify his answer. Altogether he repeated his unequivocal message in similar language five times that afternoon.

On the Opposition front bench we sat aghast as he proceeded not only to slam the door on self-determination, but proceeded to bolt and bar it apparently for ever. A number of us, including myself, tried to secure an immediate debate, but Mr Speaker refused, although later in the day Tom Driberg succeeded in raising the matter. The uproar was such that

Oliver Lyttelton, the Secretary for the Colonies, appeared in the Chamber in an attempt to retrieve the situation and tried to back-track a little. 'I never used the term "never" and neither did my Right Honourable Friend.' But next day the Hansard Report showed that the fatal word had been uttered and this spark set the island on fire.

A Greek Cypriot terrorist organisation under the command of Grivas, a former Colonel in the Greek Army, had been secretly coming together for some time, and under the name of EOKA it now came into the open and carried on during the next five years a violent guerrilla campaign of sabotage and murder against the occupying British troops. Makarios neither controlled Grivas nor disowned him, and the guerrilla success grew, until in 1959 Harold Macmillan wisely changed course and decided that Britain did not need to occupy the whole island as a base. Our purposes could be satisfied if we were assured of a secure base on the island.

This decision opened the door to self-determination, but as it brought the prospect of Enosis nearer, it also raised the tension between the Greek and Turkish communities, with further outbreaks of violence. These had grown since Field Marshal Sir John Harding, the island's Governor, had recruited auxiliary police units from the Turkish minority to fight the EOKA guerrillas. Greeks and Turks who had lived in mixed communities moved into separate enclaves and British troops erected barricades to separate them. As the atmosphere deteriorated, the leaders of the two communities found it impossible to work together to produce an agreed independence constitution, and with the British Government standing on one side, the Greek and Turkish Governments took over the negotiations on behalf of both communities, deliberately excluding them from the discussions.

In due course Greece and Turkey produced a constitution to bring Cyprus to independence. It provided, sensibly enough, for a Greek Cypriot President and a Turkish Cypriot Vice-President, but its detailed provisions were drawn in such a way as to ensure the maximum possible separation between the two communities at all levels, and rendered remote the possibility of a genuinely united island. The leaders of the two communities were peremptorily told to sign on the dotted line if they wanted their independence, and Makarios eventually agreed to do so, reluctantly putting aside his demand for Enosis as the price to be paid.

With such an unpromising beginning, the constitutional balance, which had recognised the predominance of the Greek Cypriots while safeguarding the rights of the Turkish minority, never had a chance of success.

Neither Greek nor Turkish Cypriots fully accepted the imposed constitution; neither community felt any moral responsibility for it, and both parties twisted it to their own advantage, or ignored it if they could do so. Archbishop Makarios became President. He had been forced to yield on his demand for Enosis, and now he found himself thwarted in his plan for a truly united Cyprus. In 1963 he put forward certain proposals to establish majority rule but the Turkish minority rejected them.

Tension grew and both sides reached for their guns. Grivas, who had left the island after it secured independence, returned in 1964 and took over supreme command of the newly formed National Guard. He was well versed in the arts of terrorism and there were brutal shootings of civilians, to which the Turks responded with equal ferocity.

In an attempt to keep the peace between the communities, the Security Council of the United Nations sent a mixed force (UNFICYP) to the island. On more than one occasion Turkey threatened to invade the island to safeguard the Turkish minority, and hostility grew in 1967 when a coup in Athens by a group of Army Colonels established a military dictatorship which revived the call for Enosis. But Makarios had tasted independence and had gone cool on union with Greece. He began to make attempts to improve relations with the Turkish minority but this was bitterly resented as treachery by Grivas and his EOKA guerrillas, who turned against Makarios and made two unsuccessful attempts on his life – the second in 1973.

While the cauldron bubbled Britain's general posture was to detach herself from the internal difficulties of the now independent island and confine her interests to the Sovereign bases. Cyprus joined the Commonwealth; Makarios became a regular attender at Commonwealth Conferences and relations between him and Britain became warmer, while Britain supplied troops to bolster the United Nations Peace Keeping Force.

The settlement of 1960 had left Britain with residual responsibilities. The intended effect of independence and of the 1960 constitution was that Britain should abandon sovereignty, Greece should abandon Enosis, and Turkey should abandon her demand for partition of the island. This arrangement was buttressed by a separate Treaty of Guarantee, under which the three nations became guarantors of the island's new status, and undertook to prohibit either the union of Cyprus with another state or its partition. Article IV provided for the three nations to consult together in the event of the Treaty being violated, and if concerted action was not possible 'each of the three Powers reserved the right to take action with the sole aim of re-establishing the state of affairs created by the present Treaty'.

The treaty also permitted Greece and Turkey to station contingents in Cyprus and in 1974 Greek army officers acting under orders from the Greek Military Government began to fan the Enosis flames and attempted to undermine Makarios. By this time he was openly at odds with Athens and on 2 July 1974 called on the Greek Military Government to withdraw all Greek officers from the island and to cease to give active support and arms to Grivas and EOKA. This demand set in train a series of events which in the course of the next four years were to lead to the overthrow of Makarios, the downfall of the Greek military dictatorship in Athens, the invasion of Cyprus by Turkey, the prospect of war between two NATO members, Greece and Turkey, and the effective partition of Cyprus. The call made by Makarios to Greece coincided with a visit to London by Henry Kissinger, the United States Secretary of State. He was returning to America following a summit meeting between Nixon and Brezhnev in Moscow – the last they were to have before Nixon's resignation on 9 August 1974.

Kissinger was somewhat weary from a succession of visits to other European capitals to brief the NATO allies on the Moscow talks, but this did not prevent him from giving me a most comprehensive account of the SALT talks, which were of stupefying complexity and now seemed likely to end in deadlock. We discussed our response to the Soviet demand for the inclusion of French and British nuclear deterrants in the talks, which both Governments opposed, the possible political developments in Spain and her future relationship with NATO, the situation in the Middle East, the prospects for oil supplies, and touched on a number of other issues. I mention these because at no time in our long discussions did either of us speak of the Cyprus situation, and I can only conclude that we had no inkling that the ten thousand-strong Greek National Guard would launch a *coup d'état* against their own President within the next seven days. Over the years I had come to regard Cyprus as the villagers who continue to cultivate their vines on its slopes regard Mount Etna: knowing that it is always likely to erupt but not expecting every subterranean rumble to lead to disaster. So Makarios's demand on 2 July for the withdrawal of the Greek officers might be no more than another rumble deep in the heart of the volcano.

We were soon enlightened. Early in the morning of 15 July I received an immediate 'flash' message, reporting that a coup had been launched by the Greek National Guard under the pretence that they were intervening to stop fighting between different Greek factions on the island. In truth they were themselves responsible for the fighting by their attacks on Makarios's supporters. The report added that they had attacked and occupied the Presidential Palace and claimed to have killed Archbishop Makarios. The airport had been seized and was closed, and the leaders of the coup had installed one Nicos Sampson as President in place of Makarios. My first thought was 'Nicos who?' as the name was totally unknown. He turned out to be an unsavoury adventurer who was one of the leaders of the terrorist EOKA guerrillas.

The news pushed other problems off my desk and during the morning I sent urgent messages to the Greek and Turkish Governments, calling attention to provisions of the Treaty of Guarantee for the territorial integrity and security of the island, and asking for their reaction. We urged the need for restraint by both countries.

It was the height of the holiday season and one source of great concern was that many thousands of British holiday-makers were on the island and could easily become involved in the fighting. The British High Commissioner, Stephen Olver, at once made their welfare and safety his first responsibility, and during the period of the emergency, both in this matter and many others, I had the utmost regard for his energy, determination, stamina and coolness.

Foreign Office officials are the butt of many jokes, but whatever their shortcomings, it has been my happy experience that whenever a real emergency does arise they will accept any challenge, however remote from their daily experience, assume great responsibilities and work tirelessly and with skill. On that first morning I sat down with the Foreign Office Ministers, Sir Thomas Brimelow, the Permanent Under-Secretary, and other officials to identify the general lines on which we should proceed. I had no hesitation in accepting that it was for Britain to take the initiative with Greece and Turkey. Quite apart from the safety of British dependents and holiday-makers, we had a prime interest in the safety of our sovereign base areas, and as a party to the Treaty of Guarantee, we were concerned that the *coup d'état* should not escalate tension between Greece and Turkey. In those first hours we were unaware of the degree of culpability of the Greek Colonels' regime itself in precipitating these events.

It was Napoleon who said that international incidents should not govern foreign policy, but foreign policy, incidents. In Cyprus the two were inextricably bound. There was a multiplicity of interests and concerns whose impact and implications defied the exactitude of predetermined solutions. The groundwork that had been laid for the island's future in the constitution of 1960 had been undermined from the beginning by both communities, aided and abetted by elements in the two countries which had devised the constitution. Sir Thomas Brimelow summed up the position: 'We have become familiar with deaf ears in Cyprus. For eleven years Britain had urged negotiations between the communities – nobody listened.'

The conclusions we reached on the morning of the coup were as follows: We should aim to avoid an armed response by Turkey. The Greek Military Government was probably culpable. Despite this, Britain should proceed at once to consult with both Greece and Turkey as laid down by the Treaty of Guarantee, and thereafter with Cypriot representatives. Even if Makarios was dead, we should not recognise any other government of Cyprus for the time being. On the other hand, the Cyprus Government had serious defects in its treatment of the Turks and we need not aim at a restoration of the *status quo ante*. For years, the Turkish Cypriots had either been denied or had not practised their rights under the 1960 constitution. We should endeavour to remedy their position and even establish a better relationship with the Greek Cypriots.

I went down to the House and reported. Alec Douglas-Home, who was acting as the Shadow Foreign Secretary, was helpful and urged that we should not hesitate to defend the British bases if attacked. A few hours later, news arrived that the Greek National Guard had lied in reporting that Makarios had been captured and executed. In fact, he had escaped, was in hiding and had sent a message secretly requesting that he be given refuge in one of the British sovereign bases. These are not legally part of the territory of Cyprus and, after consulting the Prime Minister, I at once gave permission and an RAF helicopter was sent to collect him from his hiding place near Paphos, in the extreme south-west corner of the island. This was accomplished safely and he was flown to the British base at Akrotiri. Fighting was still going on and if his presence there had become known it might have prompted disturbances or even an attack. Our apprehension coincided with his wishes and an RAF aircraft therefore flew him to Malta and onwards to London as his main concern was to present his country's case as quickly as possible to the Security Council in New York.

He told me that following the two previous unsuccessful attempts on his life, he had expected that the palace might be attacked at some time and so was not wholly unprepared. When the shelling started, he made his way to a little-known exit from the palace, threw off his ecclesiastical robes, scrambled along a ditch and, helped by friends, made his way to a waiting car which carried him unrecognised away. Dom Mintoff had earlier telephoned me from Malta to say that the Archbishop had no money or clothes, but by the time we met he was again fully clad in his regalia, dignified, composed, philosophical, and grateful to the RAF for his rescue. However, he was critical of the Americans, whom he felt had been too lenient with the Greek Colonels' regime. He said bitterly that it had only been necessary for the Colonels to declare themselves anti-communist to win a measure of understanding. I was able to tell him that the Prime Minister of Turkey would arrive in London for consultations on that very evening of 17 July, but I had not yet received a reply from the Greeks.

Both British and Turkish Governments refused to have any dealings with Nicos Sampson, and I dispatched a firm note to the Greek Government calling on them to withdraw their officers from the Cyprus National Guard and recall them to Greece. In doing this I was backed by the Archbishop's opinion that if the Greek officers were withdrawn the Sampson regime would at once collapse and open the way for a more representative Administration. He added realistically that he himself might not be able to return personally for some time to come. Makarios's criticism of America was understandable. They had objected strongly to his declaration that he would take help from anywhere – even the Soviet Union – to maintain the independence of Cyprus, believing that such a course would have undermined the south-eastern flank of NATO, about which the West was rightly sensitive. I had no doubt that Makarios was genuine in his desire for Cypriot independence – indeed that was the reason for his break with EOKA – and by openly supporting him, we could avoid him turning to Moscow. This I did. Like him, I did not believe there was any long-term prospect of the survival of the Greek Military Government. The proud independent spirit of the Greek people would break through in due course, and in the meantime, the regime should be made to feel the weight of the West's dislike.

One of my earliest steps as Foreign Secretary had been to demonstrate Britain's disapproval of the regime by authorising the cancellation of a flag-flying visit by Royal Navy ships to Greek ports. The difference in emphasis between the United States and Britain about the attitude that should be adopted towards the Archbishop extended to other matters, and although our two countries were agreed on broad objectives, we differed on procedures and tactics. This persisted throughout the ensuing weeks and we did not succeed in establishing the coordination of policy that I had hoped for and which was necessary.

The failure was not merely caused by our different perceptions. It was another malign consequence of the Watergate affair, which at that time was rapidly approaching its climax and engaged so much of Henry Kissinger's attention that on occasion he and I lost contact during critical hours. In discussion I have never found Henry impervious to reason or argument. He has the power of understanding and imaginatively entering into the feelings of his interlocutor and transmuting them into a constructive course. But it is hard to do this over the trans-Atlantic telephone, and his preoccupation with the consequences of Richard Nixon's final days as President prevented us from having that continuous face-to-face personal contact that would have settled differences and enabled Britain and America to march together.

Britain felt a special obligation to Cyprus as a member of the Commonwealth, and to her people because of our past links, as well as our responsibility under the 1960 Treaty. The United States had neither a similar background of history nor a similar treaty relationship. Their principal concern was to avoid an extension of Soviet influence in the Middle East, and to the extent that this meant preventing Turkey and Greece from getting at each other's throats, British and American policy coincided. But it also resulted in the United States being less willing to antagonise either the Greek Colonels in the early stages of the conflict or the Turks after their invasion. I felt fewer inhibitions.

Prime Minister Bulent Ecevit of Turkey arrived at No. 10 Downing Street on the evening of 17 July, accompanied by some of his Ministers' and two Generals. On our side were the Prime Minister, Minister of Defence Roy Mason, and myself. Ecevit was very direct. In view of the coup he no longer recognised Greece as a Guarantor of Cyprus and he would not therefore meet them for the consultations among the three powers, as laid down in Article IV of the 1960 Treaty. There must be immediate action to bring about an effective Turkish presence on the island to save Turkish lives. This could be achieved if we would allow the British sovereign bases to be used by Turkey for the purpose of landing troops in Cyprus. If Turkey was permitted to use these facilities she would minimise any embarrassment that might arise between the Greeks and ourselves. In future it would be necessary for Turkey to have secure access across the sea at a point somewhere close to Turkey. In an interesting aside which showed how much relations had improved between Makarios and the Turks Ecevit added that he was 'almost weeping' over the departure of the Archbishop, and hoped that one day a dialogue with him might create a sense of nationhood on the island.

I had not been prepared for this direct request to use British bases, but it was an impossible proposition. The island needed fewer Greek troops, not more Turkish troops, and we had called on the Greek Government to withdraw their National Guard officers. Both the Prime Minister and I emphasised that the legal status of the bases was different from the rest of the island and that to permit them to be used for a third country's troops to enter Cyprus would certainly give rise at some stage to a direct challenge to their status by the Government of Cyprus. Harold Wilson then suggested an alternative way forward. Despite Ecevit's declaration, Turkey and Britain had a responsibility to set the Treaty of Guarantee in motion and both countries should jointly invite the Greeks to join us in London for the consultation provided by Article IV. I added that the Turkish Government should not confuse our objective of restoring democracy and constitutional legitimacy in Cyprus with restoring the *status quo ante*, for Britain recognised that the Turkish Cypriots had legitimate grievances that needed remedy.

After an adjournment for dinner together, both sides returned to the Cabinet Room where we went over the same ground again. Despite all our efforts, Ecevit adamantly refused to send a joint message to the Greek Government inviting them to a meeting, although he saw no objection to Britain meeting the Greeks separately. Early on the following morning, I tried to restart conversations with the Turkish Foreign Minister, but although he came to see me, he was under instructions and we could make no progress. My final message was that Britain expected Turkey not to resort to unilateral military action and so worsen an already bad situation. The Foreign Minister gave me no assurance on the point and when the Turkish Prime Minister and his party left London later that day, we did not know what action they would take. On 18 July we at last received a reply from the Greek Military Government. Brigadier Ioannidis was as uncompromising as Ecevit had been. He told our Ambassador that Greece would not come to London for talks, either between the three Guarantor Powers under the Treaty or bilaterally with Britain.

Britain was faced with a situation in which two of the three Guarantor Powers had declined to play the part they had undertaken to do in the Treaty of 1960, but the matter could not be left where it was. We needed to remove any pretext for a Turkish invasion and our policy became one of securing the overthrow of Sampson and the return of Makarios, with new safeguards for the Turkish minority. The Sampson regime was no more than surface deep and the Military Government in Athens was running into difficulty. I therefore worked to increase converging pressure on Athens by Britain, by the European Community of which France held the Presidency, and by NATO. Above all, we would need the utmost United States pressure on the Military Government in Athens, for America had more influence than any other country.

My belief was that prompt withdrawal of the Greek National Guard officers who had initiated the coup might persuade Turkey to stay her hand. I urged the United States on 17 July to use their influence with the Greeks to procure the downfall of Sampson, and Henry Kissinger sent Joseph Sisco, Assistant Under-Secretary of State, to London overnight, with the intention that he should travel on to Athens. Sisco arrived in London before Ecevit had left for home and he offered to travel to Ankara for talks on 20 July, after he had seen the Greek regime. Ecevit was clearly determined to keep the United States at arm's length and rebuffed him, saying that his visit would not be convenient. Sisco and I reviewed the situation and both of us shared the view that, despite Ecevit's tactics, military action by the Turks was not imminent.

I urged on Sisco the need to evolve a joint Anglo-American policy as the only way of containing the serious Turkish-Greek differences. Not only did the United States have much more influence with both countries than Britain, but our experiences in the Second World War led me to be a strong advocate of Anglo-American cooperation when crises developed. I had no intention of exposing Britain to the kind of differences with the United States which existed at the time of the Suez invasion and which had resulted in a terrible setback for British arms and influence. During that contest the radar of the American fleet had deliberately interfered with and confused the signals of the British and French ships. Further, American destroyers had moored themselves alongside Egyptian ships in harbour so that the Royal Navy could not fire. I was determined that if military force had to be used in Cyprus, there must be a clear understanding with the United States, with their support fully guaranteed.

I admired very much the diplomatic skills which Henry Kissinger had demonstrated after the Arab-Israeli War. No one could handle the Greeks and Turks better if he were so minded, and I therefore sent him a detailed personal message on 19 July urging the need to coordinate British and American views on the best way to bring the situation under control. I made certain proposals on lines of policy. These were: to assert the legitimacy of Makarios; to work for the disappearance of Sampson; to use the constitution for the legal appointment of a successor to Makarios if he was unable to act; to revise the military agreements under which Greek and Turkish armed forces were present on the island; and to consider constitutional changes which would give better protection to the Turkish minority. Procedurally we should work bilaterally, aiming to bring the parties together, but also using the United Nations for this purpose.

In short, at that stage very great pressure was needed on the Greeks in order to remove any excuse for a Turkish invasion. To this end I asked that America should redouble its efforts. Because of President Nixon's preoccupation with Watergate, it seems to me that Henry Kissinger was unable to get any clear guidance from him. He telephoned our Ambassador in Washington with his reply, saying that the United States would certainly not work to keep Sampson in office and agreeing that this was the least desirable outcome. On the other hand, he was cool about Makarios's return, although he would go along with my efforts – perhaps one step behind. The United States would not be hurried into committed positions on constitutional change, and as to putting pressure on the Greeks, he would be ready to do so only once it was clear what our goals were in the matter of constitutional change. This was of no immediate assistance to me, for constitutional discussions would obviously stretch into the future, whereas pressure on the Greek Government to withdraw their officers was needed without a moment's delay if the Turks were to be denied an excuse for acting.

Whilst this exchange was taking place we became aware that Turkish troops and ships were on the move, and some time after midnight Turkish forces landed on the island. I was awakened with the news at 4.20 a.m. on the morning of Saturday 20 July as a result of a telephone call from Henry Kissinger to my home. I telephoned at once to the Resident Clerk at the Foreign Office to alert the Private Office staff to send a ear to collect me, but it had not arrived in the few minutes it took me to get dressed. I went into the street, but there were no taxis at that early hour and very little other traffic. A van was approaching, which I flagged down and asked the driver if he would be good enough to take me urgently to Downing Street.

He looked somewhat suspicious and said he was on his way to start his delivery round (milk or bread – I forget which), but fortunately he recognised me and a few minutes later the delivery van and I drove in style down Whitehall.

Now that the crisis had burst, my spirits rose and my energies redoubled. First I awakened both Greek and Turkish Ambassadors, who came at once. I saw them separately and reminded both that their countries had by Treaty guaranteed the territorial integrity of Cyprus and had further agreed to prohibit either Enosis or partition. The provisions of the Treaty were now being violated by both countries and we had a joint responsibility under Article IV to consult together to bring this state of affairs to an end. I therefore formally called on the Greek and Turkish Governments to meet with the British Government immediately, either in London or at any other agreed location, and asked the Ambassadors to convey this at once to Athens and Ankara.

On this occasion it did not take long for the Greek Junta to respond. By eight o'clock the Greek Chargé d'Affaires informed us that his Government was not willing to meet with the other Guarantors and that unless Turkish troops were withdrawn from Cyprus, Greece would declare war on Turkey and declare a state of Enosis that would permanently unite Cyprus with Greece. The Turks made no reply during that day.

My next step was to call in the Soviet Ambassador. It was still very early in the morning and he was unaware of the invasion until I explained to him what had taken place and what I proposed. I told him he would be kept closely informed of developments for, although I certainly did not expect Soviet assistance, I did not want Soviet misunderstandings to complicate further a tangled situation. Foreign Office officials continued to brief Soviet representatives privately whilst the tension was at its height, with some advantage to the general situation. The Russians were watchful and questioned us closely throughout the period about our actions and our intentions, and my policy was to respond as frankly as possible. As was to be expected, they made propaganda about our supposed intention to convert Cyprus into a NATO base, but their heart was not really in it for they knew we were being candid with them. There was only one occasion on which I had a major grievance against them, namely when the Soviet Union vetoed a Security Council Resolution to expand the United Nations Force on the island. I complained strongly but privately and twenty-four hours later they abandoned their veto, allowing the force to be strengthened.

I am told that the use of the international telephone as a method of dealing with crisis diplomacy hampers professional historians who are hungry for written evidence in their search for truth. No doubt it also frustrates the man on the spot and is probably little improvement on the more sedate exchanges of earlier times. The belief that personal contact leads to more accurate understanding is often true of face-to-face contacts, but much more doubtful when the telephone is used.

The weekend of 20 July was a period of heavy, unrelieved pressure on the energies of the American Secretary of State. Pressure had been growing week by week for the impeachment of the American President and on the day of the Turkish invasion, Nixon had called Kissinger to California for consultations. During the following week Congress was to begin televised proceedings and these could lead to a vote on whether to impeach. Nixon was desperate to construct a majority to prevent this. Kissinger flew from Washington to San Clemente in California with the result that he and I were out of touch for all of Saturday. He has subsequently written that so many documents relating to Watergate were being sent over the circuits to President Nixon that he had to secure special priority for cables about the Cyprus crisis.

Sunday 21 July was a mad day of activity. Henry and I spoke on the telephone about nine or ten times, and it may be of interest to those who wonder how such matters are conducted if I set down some of the telephone conversations that were held that day.

12.45 I telephoned Ecevit and urged an immediate cease-fire in accordance with a Security Council Resolution of the United Nations. He promised to put the proposal to his National Security Council later today. Would he be ready to meet me? Says he can't afford to be too far from Ankara, but suggests Switzerland as the venue. I tell him Greeks have demanded that Turkish Air Force should not bomb a convoy of Greek ships en route to Cyprus and urge compliance. He agrees provided the warships accompanying these ships turn away. (We telephone Greeks to tell them of this exchange.)

13.20 I telephone Bruno Kreisky (Chancellor of Austria). If Switzerland is not available as a meeting place, could Ecevit and I (and perhaps Greeks) meet in Vienna? He agrees.

13.30 Kissinger telephones. Arrangements for cease-fire are making progress. Greeks accept without conditions. Two Governments will announce and subsequently I can announce further talks between the three Guarantor Powers.

13.45 Kissinger telephones. Greek Government is very weak. Athens should not be asked to make more decisions than it can handle. This may slow down the timetable for talks. Kissinger says Turks are not now ready to cease-fire.

15.55 Kissinger calls. He says if cease-fire is not agreed he has authority from President to threaten removal of United States nuclear weapons from Turkey. Also, if war breaks out between the two countries, nuclear weapons will be removed.

16.25 Kypraios, Greek Foreign Minister, telephones in highly emotional state. Turkish Air Force is bombing Greek Cypriots, cannot wait three days for cease-fire. If cease-fire is not agreed immediately, the Greek Army will launch an attack on Turkey.

16.50 I reach Kissinger, and tell him the Greek Government will decide at 19.00 today on beginning hostilities. Kissinger says United States supports removal of Sampson. Kissinger says he has told Ecevit that the United States will proceed to remove nuclear weapons from Thrace and Anatolia if there is no cease-fire. This has made Ecevit think again and he has promised a further answer within thirty minutes.

16.55 During my call to Kissinger am told that Ecevit is waiting to speak to me (presumably as a result of Kissinger's ultimatum). He says he wants to postpone a cease-fire because the Greek Colonels may resign and there may be a Moscow-inclined Administration in Greece by tomorrow. I reply 'no dice' unless he also wants war and tell him what I know of Junta's intentions. His best course is to accept Security Council's Resolution. He says he intends to tell Kissinger he accepts cease-fire 'in principle', but will not implement completely until Tuesday 22 July. He complains that Greek ships are landing troops in Cyprus under cover of flying the Turkish flag and Greek planes have Turkish-speaking pilots on board to confuse. I propose that the three Powers meet in Vienna at 08.00 on Tuesday 22 as soon as cease-fire is in place. He will let me know.

17.20 I telephone Kissinger and tell him of Ecevit's response. I say I believe he will come to talks. Now Turkey accepts cease-fire in principle, I suggest he pressures Greeks to come to Vienna.

17.55 Kissinger calls. Joe Sisco is going to see the Greek Junta now. They want a cease-fire tonight and a meeting on Tuesday morning. If they won't buy a cease-fire 'in principle' effective Tuesday, he and I must both tackle Ecevit again.

20.40 I tell Kissinger there must be a definite cease-fire by 14.00 on 22 July so that the three Powers can meet. He asks me to telephone Ecevit and he will do the same. We should both send notes on the same lines to Athens. Would I approach the Nine to do the same?

21.00 I speak to Sauvagnargues (French Foreign Minister) who is acting for the Community. He agrees to take action in both capitals at once.

21.40 Kissinger calls. Sisco is still with Greeks. They are naturally more interested in assurances from the United States than Britain. He says the Junta don't love Britain. Turks now promise effective cease-fire tomorrow. He will propose noon Washington time. I suggest noon local time. I say we are getting reports that Turks have bombed and sunk some of their own vessels. This will not improve their mood.

22.25 I speak to Kyraios about proposed cease-fire and urge him to come to Vienna on 22 July. He says he will not meet Turks until they adhere to the terms of the Resolution passed by the Security Council.

23.00 Sauvagnargues calls to say that French Government will despatch note on behalf of Nine tonight.

23.10 Kissinger telephones. Ecevit has now finally agreed to recommend acceptance of cease-fire for 14.00 tomorrow.

These almost continuous telephone exchanges were slotted into many other activities that day. It was necessary to keep the Prime Minister thoroughly up to date as well as remaining in close touch with the Minister of Defence. Broadcasts had to be made to our own people, and emergency evacuation arrangements for the many thousands of British tourists and holiday-makers. Roy Hattersley took charge of this aspect and like everyone he turned to the task with tremendous zest, unafraid to take decisions.

Thousands of Greek Cypriots were fleeing from the area where the Turkish Army was fanning out whilst other thousands of Turkish Cypriots living in Greek Cypriot areas were taking refuge in Turkish strongholds to escape the wrath of the Greeks. Our first step was to advise the seventeen thousand British residents and dependents of servicemen who lived among the civilian population to withdraw to the sovereign base areas, where they would have protection from the inter-communal hatred. Stephen Olver, sometimes telephoning London from the basement of his office in Nicosia whilst a violent battle raged around it, speedily organised a convoy of a thousand cars to take British evacuees to the nearest British base. A British armed convoy was sent from Dhekelia to escort them and 4,500 passengers drove perilously from Nicosia to the southern base. All arrived safely. It was a successful mixture of improvisation and planning. Britain had undertaken to help the nationals of other European countries as well as Americans, and they and some other British residents and holiday-makers grouped together to make their way north to Kyrenia, hoping to be evacuated by sea. Turkish tanks were already in the town and our High Commissioner engaged in some delicate negotiations.

Large crowds of evacuees gathered on the beaches and the Royal Navy, with crews at action stations, came close in to the shore, despite some slight attempted harassment by the Turkish Navy. I called Bulent Ecevit to complain about this and he admitted that the Turkish Navy had orders to keep the Royal Navy ten kilometres from the coastline. I warned him that our ships were going in and that we would hold Turkey responsible if there were any incidents. Fortunately for the Turkish ships they did not attempt to enforce their orders, and by 9.15 a.m. on Tuesday morning 22 July, with Turkish ships watching, HMS *Devonshire* and HMS *Andromeda* had safely embarked every single person who wished to leave.

I believe Ecevit himself was anxious to avoid any action that might have led to an armed clash with the United Nations Forces or with Britain, but some fire-eating Turkish Generals were at large in Cyprus, backed by a belligerent Turkish Ambassador. At one stage Turkish tanks began to mass around Nicosia and the Commander of the United Nations Force reported that they feared an attack on their positions at the airport. They possessed only side-arms for protection. We at once offered reinforcements to the United Nations forces and flew 1,300 extra troops from Britain to Cyprus. Their arrival had a steadying effect.

The Turkish Government had given an undertaking not to take over the airport at Nicosia, but despite this they continued to inch forward, slowly edging the United Nations forces back. As soon as the British 16/5th Lancers reinforcements were in position I asked that they be given orders to stand fast and not give further ground. At the same time Phantom aircraft were flown out from Britain to give them air cover. I telephoned Ecevit personally and told him of the orders the 16/5th Lancers had received, that they would hold their ground and resist any further encroachment. If they were fired on they would respond. We held an acrimonious conversation, at the end of which Ecevit undertook to look into the matter personally, saying that Ankara did not always know what was taking place on the island. The upshot was satisfactory, for the Turks halted their gradual push forward and the airport did not pass into their hands although it remained closed.

The cease-fire finally came into force on 22 July and on the following day the humiliated Greek Junta resigned, while in Cyprus Nicos Sampson was replaced by a respected Greek Cypriot leader, Glafkos Clerides, as Acting President. In Athens Constantine Karamanlis, a statesman of wide experience, formed a new Government committed to democracy and at once reversed the Junta's position by agreeing to take part in three-party talks under the Treaty of Guarantee. The Turks also changed their position and assented. By agreement we switched the venue from Vienna to Geneva; I met the other two Foreign Ministers there on 25 July in the Palais des Nations.

With the arrival of a democratic government in Greece, British policy acquired a new element. It was important for the Greek people and for international relations that Greek democracy should be strengthened. The new civilian Government must not be brought down by the folly of its predecessor, nor humiliated in the forthcoming talks with Turkey. George Mavros, the newly appointed Foreign Minister, had been arrested by the Greek Junta for applauding my decision in the previous spring to cancel the British naval visit to Greece, and was exiled to the island of Cos. He said with a smile when we met at Geneva, 'You took the action. I paid the price.' But as he also attributed his later release to the efforts I had made on his behalf, we began (and remained) on good terms. He was a convinced democrat and a leading liberal politician, very conscious of the dignity of Greece, sometimes irascible when under strain (he occasionally threatened to walk out), but anxious to reach an agreement with Turkey.

Turan Gunes, the Turkish Foreign Minister, was a dark, loquacious character who looked somewhat like Groucho Marx but without the humour. He was capable of repeating the same interminable argument time after time until the words lost their meaning. He was moved neither by passion nor patience. He was an expert at obstruction, once holding up one of our meetings for several hours as he elaborated his objections to the name-plates that identified us at table. He sometimes disappeared without trace at critical moments and was said to be visiting the casino. It was typical of Gunes that a few hours before the Turkish invasion he had on my instructions been asked by our Ambassador in Ankara, Sir Horace Phillips, to confirm categorically that the Turkish sea-borne force was not about to land. He gave what Phillips later described as a 'duplicitous assurance' that they had been given no instructions to attack. Despite this I at first gave him the benefit of the doubt, but soon was convinced that he used stalling tactics merely to gain time and prevent progress.

The Turkish delegation became little more than a cypher, and on one occasion this resulted in Ankara repudiating a rare agreement that had been hammered out between Mavros, Gunes and myself. It seemed to us that Gunes had little or no authority. Behind him stood the Turkish Cabinet, and behind the Cabinet stood the Turkish Generals. I told him that I was negotiating with a highly random telephone wire, the British role being that of patient referee and mediator, with my officials continuously bringing forward new initiatives and proposals.

The talks developed into a gruelling cliff-hanger with the Turks as well as the Greeks at times inclined to say that they were prepared to face war rather than 'retreat' or 'humiliation'. With up to fifteen thousand fighting troops landed on the island the Turks held most of the cards, and as our formal sessions were rarely productive, I spent much of my time bilaterally with one or the other in an endeavour to secure two major objectives: first, to make the cease-fire stick; and second, to prepare the ground for a new settlement between Greek and Turkish Cypriots that would strip the Turkish Army of any excuse for remaining in the field. Henry Kissinger continued his diplomatic pressure from afar and ten days after the invasion had begun, on 30 July, both parties were ready to sign a declaration committing themselves to a standfast cease-fire, acceptance of the principle of a buffer zone between the two sides to be patrolled by United Nations forces, and agreement to meet again on 9 August with the addition of representatives of Greek and Turkist Cypriots to consider the wider issues involved in a lasting solution.

These were important gains, provided both sides adhered to them, although the size and shape of the buffer zone and the precise functions of the United Nations Force remained to be delineated. But within a day of my return to London, the new Acting President of Cyprus was complaining of violations of the cease-fire by the Turks and mutual accusations of infringements grew as a team of British, Greek, Turkish and UNFICYP representatives began demarcating the buffer zone. The second round of talks therefore began on 9 August in an atmosphere of charge and counter-charge. The Turks were flushed with success and their Government enjoyed a new-found popularity at home, while the Greek Government was too weak to be able to compromise.

It would be tedious to recount the wearisome exchanges of the following days: their flavour can be gathered from the account I sent to the Prime Minister at the end of our very first meeting. 'I am fairly satisfied at having prevented the meeting from breaking up in disorder . . . At least they managed to [put their case] without anyone walking out and we are to meet again tomorrow. I did not hope for much more.'

From the beginning Gunes was adamant. His position was as follows: the Greeks themselves had overthrown the 1960 constitution and the island would not return to it. Our declaration of 30 July had failed because thousands of Turkish Cypriots were refugees. Their permanent safety must be assured and this required a geographic division into two separate zones, autonomous in internal law and administration, but unified within a federal state. He demanded an answer from the Greek Foreign Minister and the Acting President. Clerides was firm but patient. He agreed that the 1960 constitution was unsatisfactory and required substantial change, but he was not prepared to accept a new constitution at the hands of the Guarantor Powers. Cyprus was an independent sovereign state and the communities themselves must work out the necessary amendments. He accepted that a degree of internal autonomy was required for the protection of both Turkish and Greek communities, but neither he nor Archbishop Makarios, who had remained in New York, could accept federation based on a geographical division.

Mavros reinforced this, adding that the Greek Government would be humiliated by such a solution. We adjourned and the British team spent some time trying to discover by bilateral talks with each side whether there was any room for accommodation. As the days went by, we were forced to conclude that there was no 'give' of any kind in the Turkish position, although the Greeks might have been willing to concede some kind of autonomous administration in separate regions.

I must also place on record that during these talks Gunes reassured me on two occasions that Turkey had no intention of her troops advancing nor of them remaining on the island. But my doubts increased, especially in the light of a talk I had with Dr Waldheim, the Secretary General of the United Nations, who called on me in Geneva. He was deeply concerned that the Turkish Prime Minister had brusquely informed him that the United Nations Force had no judicial right to take action in any area controlled by a Guarantor Power, and he should therefore withdraw the Force from the Kyrenia–Nicosia Turkish enclave. Kurt Waldheim said he was haunted by memories of U Thant's disastrous decision to withdraw United Nations forces from Sinai in 1967. I agreed and encouraged him to make a robust response.

The next day we met again. I told him of my growing belief that the conference would end in deadlock and if so, the Turks might resume their advance, perhaps in the week of 18 August. This would be bound to carry them through areas patrolled by the United Nations Force. On the previous occasion Britain had provided reinforcements to the United Nations very rapidly and if the occasion arose we would once again supply troops, equipped with anti-tank guns and heavy artillery. If we did so would the Secretary General seek authority for United Nations Forces to stand astride any Turkish line of advance, thus placing the onus on the Turks to decide whether to advance in the knowledge that the British troops, acting under the authority of the United Nations, would not be pushed aside?

Waldheim said that UNFICYP's original mandate did not extend to resisting the forces of a member state, but in the prevailing circumstances he did not believe that the Security Council would be an impediment to this. The Soviet Union would probably not oppose and the Chinese would absent themselves. He was very ready to cooperate, and I was heartened by his staunchness. Although I was in no doubt that the Soviet Union would not be unhappy if we all became embroiled in Cyprus, there was a balance of risks and my assessment was that if we showed ourselves sufficiently resolute the Turks would at the last moment back off. They had done this in earlier years and once again within the previous few days, when they had been faced by the 16/5th Lancers at Nicosia Airport.

I gave a private briefing to the British press and, as I had intended, it soon became public knowledge that in view of the uncertain situation the British Phantom aircraft, together with the added British troops sent to the island, would not be withdrawn and would be reinforced if necessary. I reported to the Prime Minister and also explained my thinking to Arthur Hartman, the American Assistant Secretary of State, who had accompanied me to Geneva at Henry Kissinger's request, adding that I feared that the still-fragile Greek Government of Karamanlis might be driven from office if the Turks broke the cease-fire. Hartman responded that there was no longer an odious regime in Athens, no illegal regime in Cyprus, the Turkish Cypriots were protected, and there was a strong United Nations Resolution. These were rational arguments that should appeal to Turkish intelligence, and restrain them from action. I replied that I could not agree with the assumption that we were in a rational situation and I asked Arthur Hartman to convey to Washington my misgivings and proposals, and ask that prudent forethought be given to possible Turkish military intentions so' that the attitude of both our countries could be decided before a response was needed.

At noon on Sunday 11 August 1974 he returned with the Administration's reply. Hartman is an able career diplomat, a European and Soviet expert, courteous, quiet but firm in manner and an excellent analyst. On this occasion he abandoned the relaxed informality we had become accustomed to as he informed me stiffly that the United States was not happy with Her Majesty's Government's approach. Dr Kissinger had spoken to Prime Minister Ecevit following the receipt of the British assessment urging him to refrain from military action and making clear that Turkey would get no support from the United States if they made any further advance. As a result of this conversation he was convinced that Ecevit understood that further action would have serious consequences and Kissinger had asked Hartman to tell me that he had received assurances from Ecevit on this score with which he was content.

Hartman added that the Secretary of State would react very strongly against any further announcement of British military activities, because it would have an adverse effect on his tactics with Ecevit. He said that the best course was to keep the diplomatic talks going, and he hoped I would be prepared to listen and wait. The Turkish Foreign Minister should be receiving fresh instructions from Ankara allowing him to be more flexible. I responded that I was doing my best to keep discussions alive, despite the fact that the Turkish Foreign Minister was preventing us from meeting by absenting himself from arranged sessions, but I asked him to tell the Secretary of State of my anxiety that the Turks were not being handled effectively, nor were we preparing our response in the event of further Turkish military action. I believed the worst interpretation should be put on Turkish future intentions and there were sufficient pointers in this direction for us to prepare contingency plans. What was the United States prepared to do if the Turks enlarged their bridgehead? Hartman replied that Kissinger would not get himself boxed in on this question – even to focus on this eventuality would influence events to move on to a military plane. The Secretary of State had the same objective as I had but reached a different assessment on how they could be achieved. My response was that Dr Kissinger was mistaken. The Turks had backed off at Nicosia Airport, but it was highly likely they would try again.

I told Hartman that I had earlier made clear to Ecevit that although the British troops facing them were wearing United Nations berets, they would stand their ground in face of a Turkish Army encroachment and my country would not be prepared to see them pushed aside. Since that conversation the Turks had been heavily reinforced, but Britain was ready to strengthen a static defence against possible lines of Turkish advance by moving in more reinforcements and flying in further Phantoms. I would repeat the warning to the Turks on whom would fall the onus of challenging the United Nations, but I must be assured of American support if I were to do so, and in the light of our conversation this would apparently not be forthcoming. I continued that I understood American concern with the broad issues of the south-east flank of NATO but the United States was ignoring other perspectives, including Britain's role as a Guarantor Power and the safeguarding of the lives of thousands of British citizens.

As soon as Arthur Hartman had left, I fired off a telegram to Henry Kissinger, saying that these important differences were impairing our mutual confidence. I reiterated that it was not sufficient to approach the Turks solely through the medium of diplomacy. The correct policy was to tackle them on parallel lines, namely to convince them that we were in earnest on both the diplomatic and the military level. This was the most likely way to achieve results. As to his complaint that the British had introduced a military dimension, I reminded him that the reality was that this dimension was constantly hanging over the heads of the British troops who were heavily outnumbered by up to twenty-five thousand Turkish soldiers.

Kissinger's response was to telephone Ecevit once more to renew his personal plea that Turkey should adhere to a political solution, telling him that he could expect no support if the Turks made a military move and that the United States would mount a major diplomatic effort to halt them. Kissinger told me that he would give every support to British efforts to save the crisis by diplomatic means, but he did not consider threats of military action either helpful or appropriate, as they distracted attention from the political options. I recognised both Henry's ability and the influence of America, which had been very considerable in securing the cease-fire on 22 July, but I was convinced that more would be needed on this occasion. The only thing that might deter the Turks was the conviction that they would face military opposition if they attempted to advance further.

I continued with our diplomatic efforts, but with every hour that passed our team became more gloomy. There were flashes of common sense. Acting President Glafkos Clerides and Rauf Denktash, the leader of the Turkish Committee, both brought intelligence and genuine concern to the discussion on the future of their country. If it had been left to them it is conceivable that they might have hammered out an understanding. But Denktash was not a free agent, and confessed to me that in the last resort he was obliged to obey his masters on the Turkish mainland.

By the evening of 12 August matters had reached an impasse. Clerides was near despair when I told him that there was no prospect of a determined stand by the United Nations, the United States and Britain of the kind I had worked for. Despite Waldheim's earlier optimism, the United Nations forces were ready to withdraw if the Turks advanced, while the United States was not prepared to put military pressure on the Turks. In these circumstances I suggested he should work for the best possible accommodation. Both he and Denktash had already agreed on the need for constitutional revision, the creation of a federal system which would accord with the bicommunal character of the island, and both of them were keen to preserve the independence and sovereignty of the island. He had hinted earlier that he might be ready to consider two internal zones and I urged him to consider very seriously the establishment of two autonomous Administrations with defined geographical boundaries within a federal state. I read out a draft prepared by my staff that covered these points, and which proposed that further discussions should take place in Nicosia immediately between him and Denktash, followed by a report to the three Foreign Ministers in Geneva on a later date in September.

Clerides promised to consider these proposals subject to the reasonable condition that his acceptance of such a framework would be conditional on all Turkish forces withdrawing from Cyprus. We agreed to call in the Greek Foreign Minister, and at the end of our talk both Clerides and Mavros said that they were willing to return to Athens and Nicosia to consult their colleagues and secure their reaction to the proposal for two zones. They would leave at once and would return to Geneva the following evening with their answer.

As the Turks and Greeks had both given up tripartite meetings I at once took this proposition personally to Gunes. He responded angrily. Unless Clerides was willing to state in advance of his departure that he accepted the principle of a single geographical zone for the Turks he, Gunes, would also leave Geneva and bring the conference to an end. I urged patience, saying that in my opinion Clerides would in fact advocate such a single zone when he met his colleagues but would probably argue for a smaller area to be allotted to the Turkish minority than they claimed. Gunes remained adamant and also declined to attend a further joint session unless he was assured beforehand of Clerides' agreement. When we parted I enlisted Henry Kissinger's aid and we both telephoned the Turkish Prime Minister. He may subsequently have instructed Gunes to attend a further meeting and accordingly we met for a final gruelling but pointless session in the company of observers from the United Nations.

Gunes repeated his demands, putting them in the form of an ultimatum. Did the Acting President and the Greek Foreign Minister accept here and now that there should be a Turkish region extending from the Turkish sector of Famagusta to the Turkish sector of Nicosia, continuing on a line that would extend to 34 per cent of the area of Cyprus? Further, that this new zone must be established within the next three or four days? He must have a reply that very evening and if Clerides and Mavros were unable to indicate their acceptance there would be no point in continuing the conference. He would have no more to say.

Despite this, the death throes of the conference continued for several hours. Clerides and Mavros repeated once again that they must have time for consultations in Nicosia and Athens. They were ready to return to Geneva within thirty-six hours. I asked Denktash if he would agree but he replied that he was bound by the Turkish Government; he would attend a further meeting only if the Turkish Foreign Minister would do so. I appealed to Gunes to accept the time that Clerides and Mavros had asked for. Once more Gunes refused. There was no formal end to the proceedings. Gunes rose from the table at which we sat, ungracious as ever, and departed, followed by his aides. The time was 2.25 a.m. on the morning of 14 August. The rest of us shook hands and filed out wearily. I gave a press conference in which I did not spare the Turkish tactics. Even while I was speaking, the Turkish Army was advancing once more, breaking the cease-fire. Gunes had played out time.

At 5.00 a.m. on the same morning the Greek Cabinet met in the Ministry of Defence. With the exception of the Prime Minister, Constantine Karamanlis, those who were present demanded that Greece declare war on Turkey forthwith. The Prime Minister, who kept a cool head throughout, proposed as an alternative that Greece should request NATO's immediate assistance in accordance with the dictum that an attack on one is an attack on all. The Greek Cabinet agreed but Joseph Luns, the Secretary General of NATO, was told by the Turks on the next day that 'a visit from him would not serve any useful purpose and might be counter-productive'. Luns withdrew. Karamanlis saw there was nothing more he could do to save Cypriot unity. He withdrew Greece from NATO and, unwelcome though that was, by doing so he saved his country from a war that would have been disastrous for the future of the new domacracy.

More than a decade has passed and Turkish troops are still on the its own and held elections which have consolidated the island's division. The prospects of unity within a federal Cyprus grow more dim, especially with the heightened tension arising from the legitimate security concerns of both Greece and Turkey in the Aegean Sea.

In August 1974 there was a fleeting opportunity to remove the problem from the world's agenda, and we failed. Nevertheless, when I look back on that fateful and absorbing period there were some rewards. Democratic government in Greece was an uncovenanted bonus and I believe Britain did a great deal to assist its consolidation in those first days of uncertainty. The British Armed Forces did wonders in evacuating both British and other nationals from Cyprus unharmed and have never received sufficient thanks. Archbishop Makarios survived and lived to render valuable service when he later returned to Cyprus.

Ten years after the events *The Times* argued in an editorial that it was 'a grave, unforgiveable error of omission' for Britain not to have delivered an ultimatum to Turkey when the second Geneva conference broke down. *The Times* believed that the Turkish Generals might have been dissuaded from resuming hostilities. A contrary view is held by Henry Kissinger, who has written that no pressure by the United States at the time would have succeeded. All opinions are speculative but I am convinced that Britain would have been courting military disaster if heavily outnumbered British troops, trained to guard a base, had taken the offensive in the face of opposition from the United States. The subsequent failure would have resembled a second Suez.

The direct converse of this argument has also been advanced, namely that Britain should have cooperated with the Turks and allowed them to use the sovereign bases in order to be able to control their invasion. This was neither a feasible short-term option nor the basis of a long-term solution, and we would have been utterly friendless. There is no question that the Turkish Cypriots had for many years been denied their political rights under the 1960 constitution, and their basic human rights. My proposal for trilateral negotiations to pave the way for effective amendments to improve the minority's position under the constitution could have remedied that, but for Britain to have cooperated with the Turks to impose a Turkish regime in the north of the island was unthinkable.

Neither of these courses was suggested at the time and I dismiss them now. Britain behaved honourably and fulfilled her obligations to the limit of the possibilities open to us. This was widely acknowledged at the United Nations General Assembly in the autumn of 1974 and subsequently by Prime Minister Karamanlis. We must deeply regret the failure. Others may distribute the blame but I do not feel ashamed of what we tried to do.

12

---

*Portugal's return to democracy – Anglo-Soviet relations – the
Falklands – Southern Rhodesia*

After the second Turkish invasion a month passed before Henry Kissinger
and I could meet and discuss, as between friends, our differences over
Cyprus. With time to reflect I realised how difficult his situation had been
during those fateful days in August when the vice-like pressure on
President Nixon to resign office had overlapped the crisis in Cyprus.

Kissinger had been caught up in the drama and strain of Nixon's last
days, during which time disasters had followed closely upon one another.
Terms of imprisonment were passed on his principal aides for conspiracy
and perjury, and three successive votes by the House Committee im-
peached the President himself. The drain on energy and nerve must
have been almost unbearable at a time when every moment of our attention was needed to avert the invasion of a sovereign country and the
possibility of war between two NATO allies.

Henry Kissinger had told Sir Peter Ramsbotham, our Ambassador in
Washington, that there were days at a time when he had been out of touch
with Cyprus developments, and this was an undoubted handicap in
coordinating our approach. In Washington in the autumn of 1974 criticism was directed at America's role during the Cyprus crisis, and the
Secretary of State bore the brunt. When we met he was obviously angry
about the criticism, but we discussed the issues in a way that was appropriate to what I referred to as 'a difference of opinion in the family'. At the
end he said with a charm and warmth I could not resist, 'Jim, you and I
have a trusting relationship, and I shall always open my mind to you
knowing you will understand, even when we have differences.'

We shared this sense of trust and I never hid my views from him,
whether about Vietnam, Rhodesia, European-American relations or
much else. Beneath his outer certainty there lurked a basic anxiety which,
with the passing of the years, has now vanished as a result of his happy
marriage to Nancy Maginnes in 1974. He possesses the perception and
insight of a deeply sensitive person and bleeds freely when criticised. Yet

despite his own sensitivity he can be scathing about those he works with.

He was born in Germany and did not leave for the United States until he was fifteen; he had lived under Hitler for five years, but I have always heard him speak of the country of his birth with great understanding and affection. He is very proud of having achieved the office of Secretary of State, 'an office I have never imagined within my reach', and was determined to uplift it and make America an effective leader of the Western World. His strategic sense, a feeling for history, coupled with great negotiating skill and persuasive powers made him the most outstanding figure to operate in the foreign affairs scene for many years. Yet until his marriage, even in moments of triumph he seemed to have a distrust of success. When he had moments of self-doubt I believed it was in all our interests that he should be reassured and I made it my task to do so. The flexibility and quickness of his mind gained him a reputation in some quarters for deviousness, and I therefore place on record that he never misled me in any of our joint enterprises.

He is intensely curious, always anxious to learn, and a man of great personal kindness. When he learned that my city of Cardiff was conferring its Honorary Freedom on George Thomas and myself, he insisted on flying the Atlantic at considerable inconvenience to his schedule to be present with Nancy, and they spent a whole day at the festivities. The advance news of his intention created considerable interest. On the day itself it seemed that every demonstrator in the United Kingdom had descended on Cardiff from afar, waving protest banners about Kissinger's various alleged misdemeanours. This view was not shared by the ordinary people of Cardiff, who greeted him enthusiastically. As we entered the City Hall, I noticed among the forest of banners attacking Kissinger a small group of placards held aloft proclaiming 'Callaghan, Murderer of Cyprus'. I pointed these out to Henry to prove he was not alone in the dog-house. He turned to me in mock fury. 'I resent those placards,' he said. 'I demand star billing wherever I may be.'

He is a true American in his approach to problems: they exist to be settled, not lived with, and solutions can be found. But he is also European in his anxious awareness that mankind is fallible and that age-old problems have their own momentum and may in the end prove intractable. It was a rewarding experience to have served with him.

Despite the setback in Cyprus, 1974 registered some important gains. At one end of the Mediterranean the Greek Colonels were overthrown, while at the other, the Portuguese people experienced a 'bloodless' revolution that ended fifty years of a species of Fascist rule and took the first steps towards rejoining the democracies of Western Europe. Prime Minister Salazar had ruled Portugal for thirty-six years until his death in 1970 and had long made it clear that decolonisation would form no part of his policy. But after his death discontent had grown in army circles at the prospect of having to continue to fight to hold Angola and Mozambique with a continuing loss of life and no prospect of victory. His successor lasted for four years but on 25 April 1974 the Portuguese President and Prime Minister were removed by a military coup; a Junta of seven officers from the Armed Forces Movement (AFM) was installed in Lisbon.

Though not wholly Marxist, it soon became clear that the AFM was Marxist dominated. Close liaison was established between the military Marxists and the hitherto exiled Portuguese Communist Party. Together these two groups enjoyed a commanding position, the Communist Party drawing on the clandestine cells established during the days of Salazar to seize control of the press, radio and trade unions. Initially these two groups were perhaps the only bodies sufficiently well organised to be able to step into the power vacuum. In a country starved of political, social and cultural freedom since the 1930s the coup was greeted enthusiastically. Various democratic parties long suppressed began to spring up and organise. The Labour Government's policy was to ensure that these democratic groups were given a fair opportunity to appeal to the Portuguese people without being shut out or dominated by the Portuguese Communist Party.

Foremost among the democratic parties was the Portuguese Socialist Party, which the British Labour Party had recognised and supported throughout its years in exile. Mario Soares, its Leader, was undoubtedly the best known Portuguese political figure, and though exiled was the nearest approximation to a national leader. I had come to know Soares while in Opposition and was in no doubt that though he used Paris as the base for his exiled party, it was to the British Labour Party that he looked for support. Immediately after the coup I invited him to London, the first of many visits over the next few months when we would discuss the help that Portugal needed to establish democracy. While Soares visited London, Cunhal, the Communist Party Leader, went to Moscow for support.

Some believed our efforts would be in vain. The view was even expressed that a communist dictatorship might not be altogether without redeeming features since it might serve to 'vaccinate' the rest of Western Europe, and especially Italy (and possibly Spain), against following suit. This was nonsense, but Soares needed all the help he could muster if those who said that a communist dictatorship was inevitable were to be proved wrong. At a time when the Communist Party had more than two hundred full-time workers, the Portuguese Socialist Party had no more than two, backed by a group of enthusiastic but wholly inexperienced young volunteers. I asked the British Labour Party and the trade unions to help, and Tom McNally contacted the Tory Party Central Office at my request to encourage it to establish links with other democratic politicians in Portugal.

Other member countries of the Socialist International also gave assistance. When Olof Palme, the Prime Minister of Sweden, was asked whether such actions constituted an interference in the internal affairs of another country he was particularly robust, replying that it was the duty of every European Socialist Democratic Party to make every effort to prevent Portugal from falling victim either to Fascism or to Communism, so that basic human rights might be protected. The political Parties were jostling for position and the AFM, which was still in control of the country, insisted that a Government be drawn from all Parties. Mario Soares chose to become Foreign Secretary, a position from which he could rally international support for a democratic Portugal. Cracks had begun to develop in the AFM itself, with the Marxist members demanding more extreme policies while the less political soldiers wanted nothing more than to get back to barracks.

Soares and I met at regular intervals. We shared the view that the Portuguese situation bore some resemblance to that of Prague after the Second World War, where a Government similarly made up of Catholics, communists and socialists had been ousted in 1947 by a Communist Party take-over backed by the Soviet Union, with the result that democratic Parties were subsequently forced out of existence.

Soares feared that history might repeat itself in Portugal, especially as some Army divisions stationed close to Lisbon were commanded by officers who seemed to owe allegiance to the Communist Party. However, the Army in general was inclined to support the democratic parties, as did the Air Force and some naval units, although others were pro-Communist. It was a tangled situation, and there were times when Soares feared he and others might be forced to leave the capital and regroup in the north, where democratic support was strong. For many months he dared not sleep in the same place on consecutive nights.

I made use of all the facilities at the disposal of the Foreign Office to support Portugal's struggling democracy and in conjunction with Mario Soares and a handful of others, we laid plans against the worst-case scenario of an attempted Communist coup, but it would not be appropriate to detail them here. The situation continued to deteriorate during the winter of 1974, with the Communist Party strengthening its control over a number of Government Departments and taking over the former Fascist trade unions. There was public disorder, unlawful expropriation and the dismissal and replacement of officials by communist sympathisers. Nevertheless, there were signs of hope; resistance was gradually building up especially in the countryside, and the AFM, whose writ still ran, gave the Socialist Party a firm guarantee that national elections would be held to elect a constitutional Assembly. Soares and I discussed how to avoid the danger of the Communist Party taking sole control of the election procedures and machinery.

Although the Armed Forces were split, the Marxist element was sufficiently strong for the communists to believe in the prospect of a Marxist military dictatorship emerging from the current disorder, with the Communist Party acting as its disciplined civilian army. For such a plan to succeed, the support of the Soviet Union would be essential and Harold Wilson and I decided we would raise the matter during a visit we paid to Moscow in February 1975. We had been received with great friendliness and I had no hesitation in tackling Prime Minister Kosygin. I told him of the alarm we felt about Portugal's situation; that I knew this was shared by other European countries; and I made a strong request to him to use his undoubted influence to 'call off' the Portuguese Communist Party. I continued, saying that I understood that detente was the first priority of the Soviet Union and that they desired a European Summit to put the seal on greater East–West cooperation; the Soviet Union would surely understand that these prospects would be blighted if a communist coup in Portugal took place against the wishes of its people.

In reply Kosygin made the usual disclaimers, denying either Soviet intervention or Soviet influence, but went on to say that he wanted the role of the Communist Party in Portugal to be that of a responsible partner with the other parties; he hoped their participation in government would continue. From these and his other comments, together with his calm response, his lack of resentment at our remarks and the tone of his replies, we concluded that the Kremlin was not seeking a new adventure in

Portugal and regarded the success of their detente policy as more important than the success of the Portuguese Communist Party.

The next step came not long after our return from Moscow, when the National Assembly elections promised by the AFM resulted in the Socialist Party coming top of the poll, and the communists bottom. This result made it doubtful whether the Marxists in the AFM and the Communist Party could hold on to power even if they seized it. But we could not afford to relax, for in the Government Coalition the new Prime Minister, Vasco das Santos Goncalves, was a theoretical Marxist army General, and as 1975 wore on it was obvious that the Communist Party was once again gaining control. The socialist daily newspaper was suppressed, and the Socialist Party itself, together with the smaller centre Parties, left the Government.

I asked Major Melo Antunes, the new Foreign Minister and a member of the Revolutionary Council of the AFM, to come to London in June 1975 and told him of Britain's concern that anti-democratic elements in the AFM seemed to be getting the upper hand; the Communist Party was gaining ground and there was an obvious slide towards totalitarianism. He said that the totalitarians made the most noise but there was a majority in the AFM which would not accept a communist regime; that in fact the AFM supported a socialist policy within a pluralistic Party System, with an important role for the private sector. He asked for Britain's continued support and understanding, and pledged that the Armed Forces would do everything within their power to ensure that the people's will prevailed.

Major Atunes' straightforward approach made a good impression both in London and later when he visited Bonn, but the situation continued to be alarming, and Harold Wilson raised the matter once again when we met President Brezhnev at Helsinki on 1 August 1975 to sign the Detente Agreement. The Prime Minister said that in our view Portugal was a practical test of detente in Europe. He asked Brezhnev to use his influence to ensure that the political uncertainty was resolved in a way that could accord with the people's wishes, to which Brezhnev replied mildly that Portugal was an independent state. The Soviet Union was not sending arms as they recognised that it was a complicated situation; other countries had approached him on the matter during the Helsinki meetings and he recognised our concern; he would think the matter over and he and his colleagues in the Politburo would discuss it when they returned to Moscow. I in turn undertook to prepare a memorandum on the situation as we saw it and send it to Brezhnev.

No one knows the result of the Politburo's deliberations but after Helsinki we observed that the political situation in Portugal began to improve slowly, although the same could not be said of its economic prospects. Prime Minister Goncalves, who for some time had seemed either exhausted or afraid of his Marxist military guards, was obliged to resign. General Antonio Ramalho Eanes was appointed Chief of Staff and began to restore a semblance of military discipline. In 1976 he was elected President with a clear majority in a nation-wide ballot, while a general election led to Mario Soares forming the first Constitutional government at the head of the largest party in Parliament but without an overall majority.

The Portuguese people themselves had played the biggest part in ensuring the survival of their 'young democracy', but I believe it can be claimed with truth that the determined attitude and help of a number of European Governments, with Britain in the lead, materially assisted. At a critical period a collapse into anarchy or into rule by the Communist Party, in conjunction with elements of the Armed Forces, was averted. Throughout this period it was fortunate that these events coincided with the final stages of the negotiations for a treaty on security and cooperation in Europe. A prime objective of Soviet policy was its successful conclusion and when the leadership realised that an attempted Communist take-over in Portugal would jeopardise both the Helsinki Agreement and detente itself, Brezhnev refused to pick up the bill.

The Prime Minister and I met Brezhnev, Kosygin and other Soviet leaders twice during 1975 – the first occasion being the official visit I have referred to in February, and again a few months later at the Helsinki Conference. Harold Wilson had visited the Soviet Union more frequently than any other leading British politician since the Second World War and always looked forward to such occasions. Accordingly he needed no urging from me to return once again as Prime Minister. For my part I was anxious to restore high level Anglo-Soviet contacts following a three-year interval during which relations between the Heath Government and the Soviet Union had been entirely frozen as a result of Alec Douglas-Home's expulsion of 105 Russian spies from London in 1971. I had no quarrel with his decision, for it was generally known that the Soviet Union made Britain a particular target for their intelligence work. But the expulsion of such a large number had undoubtedly hindered legitimate trade relations, and it seemed to me that a change of government was a suitable occasion to mend fences, to explore prospects for increasing our stagnant trade and to get to understand current Soviet thinking and objectives. Accordingly soon after becoming Foreign Secretary I issued an invitation to Foreign Minister Andrei Gromyko to visit London, hinting that an invitation from the Soviets to the Prime Minister to visit Moscow would not be unwelcome.

Before I leave the subject of spies, I may add that the Soviet Union made some attempt to insert KGB officials into their London offices during my period as Foreign Secretary. We became aware of this and the Soviet Ambassador in London was informed that certain named officials for whom they had requested visas could not be admitted. As a next step our Ambassador in Moscow, Sir Terence Garvey, was called to the Soviet Foreign Ministry where the Deputy Foreign Minister informed him that the Soviet Union could not understand our decision. He asked us to reconsider the matter in the interests of good Anglo-Soviet relations and gave the impression of possible retaliation against British Embassy officials in Moscow. I secured the Prime Minister's endorsement of my view that we should not budge, for the evidence was plain, and to accept the officials would have been to acquiesce in the gradual reconstruction of the KGB apparatus in London. The Soviets did not press the issue further and we emerged with our relations unimpaired. These exchanges took place without publicity on either side, which is usually the best way to handle such matters unless one or other country is anxious to stir the pot, and in the mid-1970s this was not the desire of either side.

The Russians understood that the Labour Government's policy was firmly grounded in NATO, and although Brezhnev enquired in private conversation whether we intended to close the American bases in Britain, he could guess the answer before he asked and did not raise the subject in our official exchanges. He and Kosygin were aware that we genuinely wished to build a more productive Anglo-Soviet relationship and they responded accordingly. In this context I proposed that we establish an Anglo-Soviet Round Table, comprised of people in different walks of life – academics, scientists, trade unionists, businessmen and journalists. They would meet for a few days once a year to exchange ideas, and by becoming better informed about each other's countries, would correct some of the myths that flourished. Gromyko agreed, and on the British side I placed the arrangements in the hands of the Royal Institute of International Affairs. The first meeting took place in 1975 and has been held alternately in London and Moscow every year since. There is no shortage of would-be British participants and the annual exchange of views makes a modest contribution to a fuller understanding.

I have always believed that despite our differences in ideology and philosophy, and notwithstanding the harsh Soviet position on human rights, we should hold a steady course in dealing with the Soviet Union. That great country will not disappear. We must live in the world as it is, while we work for the world we would like to see, in the belief that our concepts of freedom and democracy will eventually prevail. We should take every opportunity to state our views plainly without using offensive or provocative rhetoric, but at the same time seek to gain Soviet cooperation in areas in which East and West share a common concern. I refer to problems which need to be handled globally such as the environment, health and medicine and nuclear proliferation. During recent years I have found a growing Soviet interest in such cooperation, which shows signs of developing further under General Secretary Gorbachev.

Back in Moscow in 1975, amidst our discussions on trade, industrial cooperation, the Conference on Security and Cooperation in Europe, Portugal and other matters, one session stands out in my memory. As our meeting drew to a close, Brezhnev suddenly launched into a passionate harangue on the evils of nuclear war. It was his constant preoccupation, he said, for such a terrible catastrophe would bring death to hundreds of millions, and the entire 'white race' could perish. From his own experience he knew how dreadful war could be and this was why he dedicated himself to strengthening peace – a policy handed down by Lenin; it was peace that mattered, not digging around in Basket III of the Security and Cooperation negotiations, discussing extensions of tourism or whether we could open up a bar or café in someone else's country. With a stable peace we could all have fewer submarines and bombers – and not ten thousand nuclear warheads apiece. That was no small consideration. If the United States would remove all their nuclear weapons from West Germany, he would undertake to notify us of the movement of every Soviet military unit – even of a single regiment – right up to the Urals. He could cooperate with Chancellor Schmidt and President Giscard d'Estaing and he had liked the new President Ford, who had taken over after Nixon's resignation. He believed Ford was having a hard time on inflation and rising military expenditure and there was no easy way out for him except peace. He concluded his vigorous and lengthy monologue and sank back in his chair. Our talks had continued long after the time set for them and Gromyko whispered to him. Brezhnev resumed on a different tack.

His mood lightened. He said it was getting late and perhaps we should adjourn, but before we did so he might persuade me, as Treasurer of the Labour Party, to sign a cheque for an extended trade credit to the Soviet Union; an appropriate sum would be $4.5 millions and if I was willing, he would be ready to sign such an agreement there and then and we could all enjoy our dinner. There was some banter which Harold swiftly concluded by saying that unfortunately I had not brought the Labour Party's cheque book with me. I had no doubt we had listened to the real Brezhnev, and I was convinced of the sincerity of his horror of total war, a sentiment shared by all of us who had experienced the Second World War. During his discourse on the evils of war there were moments when he seemed to be talking as much to himself as to his hearers, and different expressions chased across his lively face. In appearance he was of medium height, broad-shouldered, giving an impression of great physical energy as he hit the table to emphasise his points or lunged forward to grab a handful of sweets from a bowl and push them across the table to us. His animal spirits and his obvious command as he sat in the centre with Kosygin and Gromyko on each side made Brezhnev's later deterioration the more painful to watch.

When the session was over he grabbed my red Dispatch Box, pretending I had nuclear secrets in it and was taking away details of the very large and impressive Guard of Honour that had greeted us at the airport – 'all intended for an attack on Western Europe', he said. He was obviously attracted by the Box so before our next visit I had one specially made, with his name and office inscribed in gilt letters. For obvious reasons they are very soundly constructed and I wondered later if someone in Soviet military intelligence had spent a hard day trying to dismantle it to make sure nothing was concealed within.

Personal contacts are an indispensable element of politics. Politicians meet and discuss, perhaps not always with as much antagonism as political scientists, schooled in the disciplines of political confrontation, expect. East–West relations need such contacts. They do not need mean seduction or appeasement, nor will they always lead to agreement, but though we live in an increasingly complex and technological world where information can be transmitted around the globe in seconds, we have developed no substitute for the personal meeting. To meet is to acquire a broader frame of reference, a better understanding of one another's perceptions, a sharper focus. Those who argue that such contacts are dangerous mistake the point. We will not learn to live together by mentally or physically isolating ourselves.

My last major engagement as Foreign Secretary was to receive Andrei Gromyko in London in March 1976 for three days of talks covering bilateral and European topics, Middle Eastern problems, and a smattering of domestic politics. Harold Wilson had announced his intention to resign as Prime Minister shortly before the visit and Gromyko was keenly interested in the Labour Party's method of electing a new leader. He told me he was confident that on the next occasion we met I would be the Prime Minister, and this excursion into an area that was not normally discussed prompted me to ask a similar question about the Soviet system. Romanov's name had been much mentioned in the press as a possible successor if Brezhnev stepped down, and I enquired whether he was in fact the leading contender. Gromyko replied that he was a very able man, but (with an expressive shrug) the recent publicity would be of no significance when it came to the question of succession. Romanov was but one of a group of younger men which was rapidly coming to the fore and it was impossible to tell whether the next leader would be one of the older or younger members of the Politburo. It could be either, he claimed, because in the USSR a new leader 'tended to emerge'. I told him that this was the formula the Conservative Party had formerly used to find their leaders, but they had now joined the modern world. When would the Soviet Union do the same?

He smiled and passed to the position in Yugoslavia, where Tito's age had given rise to speculation about the future. Gromyko volunteered that in the post-Tito era the Soviet Union would have no desire or intention to try to reincorporate Yugoslavia into the Warsaw Pact sphere of influence. Although this was no more than I had expected it was interesting that he had been thinking about the matter as Henry Kissinger, the French Foreign Minister Sauvagnargues, Hans-Dietrich Genscher of Germany and I had recently discussed the same thing and reached similar conclusions about Yugoslavia's relations with the West. I was therefore able to tell him with confidence that the West, including the United States, would likewise do nothing to disturb the *status quo*. Gromyko later asked me to confirm again that this was what we intended and I did so, adding that we feared the complications that might ensue between East and West if Yugoslavia were to break apart and its component parts move in different political directions. Gromyko agreed that this would be dangerous and the

Soviet Union would not want it to happen. Helsinki had brought, in his words, 'a warmer breath' to Europe, and the Soviet Union would not seek unilateral advantage.

Gromyko was very firm in ruling out German reunification. 'Never, never, never,' he repeated. I said that the imprisonment of the aged Rudolph Hess in Spandau had become ludicrous and that the four powers should make other plans for his future that would replace the existing elaborate arrangements. Gromyko rejected this. There could be no change. Hess, he said, was a living symbol of German Fascism, and no personal consideration could outweigh the terrible fate of the innumerable victims of the Second World War.

We exchanged views about the Middle East, arms control and bilateral issues such as trade, and a request I had made that the Soviet Union should afford overflying facilities for Concorde flights to Tokyo. Gromyko replied that he was not offering a negative response, but domestic aspects of the matter in the USSR had not yet been resolved. There were environmental problems of noise and they needed more time.

On family reunification and the question of giving exit permits to Soviet citizens, I repeated a tactic that had produced results in our previous meetings. I handed over a list of persons with a request for consideration, but without entering into a long discussion, which I had found only produced the standard defence of the principle of non-interference in each other's internal affairs. It was my experience that if we did not make huge publicity about certain cases, dissidents and Jews were often quietly allowed to leave, especially during the period of detente. Gromyko left the list lying on the table between us, as he had done on earlier occasions, but then departed from our usual practice by saying that he wished to make some informal remarks. He had noted the appearance of certain demonstrators when he had visited the Tate Gallery with Mrs Gromyko, accompanied by my wife. There had been nothing insulting in their behaviour and he would have liked to talk with them and explain the reasons for Soviet policy, as the mass media did not take an objective line. I replied that if he had time this could be arranged and added that for my part I felt the same objections to the reporting of Northern Ireland by the Soviet media. They failed to project any of the complexities of the problem. Gromyko did not follow the matter up.

As I expected, there was no official response to the list of would-be emigrants I left with Gromyko, but during the ensuing months we heard from time to time of exit permits being given to certain of those on our list, and this quiet diplomacy was undoubtedly effective.

Both Gromyko and his wife, a bustling cheerful lady, have a keen appreciation of art, and Gromyko likes to visit the galleries when he is in a foreign city. I have hanging in my home a fine painting of the Russian countryside in winter, depicting snow-covered fields, haystacks and a distant church, which he kindly gave me. Despite this agreeable side, in his professional demeanour he was as tough as they come. He could be extremely charming and speak English to his guest, or become cold and distant, reverting to Russian and speaking through an interpreter. This gave him the advantage of extra time to think as he waited for the interpreter to translate English into Russian. He was a master negotiator, never yielding an inch or a comma until the last possible moment. With experience of trade union negotiations I enjoyed such encounters. In negotiating with the Russians it is important to know before you begin where you intend to draw the bottom line. You can be certain that they will know what their objectives are, and will have decided beforehand whether they are ready to depart from them, and if so by how much. Unless you are equally clear you will be in danger of being overwhelmed by a mixture of arguments, bluff, anger, jokes, sunshine and storm.

The Labour Government of 1974–9 and the Conservative Government of 1979–83 both faced the same problems in their relations with Argentina over the Falkland Islands. The verdict of history must be that the Labour Government kept the peace and the Conservative Government won the war. There is no doubt that the Conservative Government basked in greater popularity, for as Lord Salisbury once remarked, 'There is nothing dramatic in the success of a diplomatist.' But keeping the peace is infinitely less costly in resources and money, nor does peace involve the sacrifice of young lives or the mourning of the mothers, the wives and the families who are left behind.

Were then the difficulties our successors faced greater, or was the Labour Government more fortunate in its timing? I do not believe either is true.

1 Both Labour and Conservative Governments had to grapple with an almost intractable conflict. On the one hand stood the historic claim of Argentina to the Islands and the readiness of many members of the United Nations to regard the Falklands as a colonial problem. On the other, the Islanders claimed the right to self-determination as enshrined in the United Nations Charter.

2 Both the Tories and ourselves recognised that the Islands were suffering from a slow and debilitating economic decline with a net loss of population by emigration.

3 Both of us faced a total disinterest by the British public in the problem, with the exception of a small but powerful pressure group known as the 'Falkland Islands Lobby', which raised an almighty shout whenever it seemed that the interests of the Falklands Islands Company (which owned much of the land) might be affected.

4 Both Governments faced a military junta in Argentina for at least part of the time, and unstable government throughout the whole period.

5 Both Governments were ready to reach an agreement with Argentina. Yet the results were quite different. The Conservative Government failed to watch the situation carefully enough, failed to make clear its readiness to fight until it was too late for the Argentinians to withdraw, and sent out misleading signals, such as the withdrawal of HMS *Endurance*, that led the Argentinians to conclude that they could embark upon invasion without fear of a serious reprisal. I remain deeply critical of the Government's failures in these respects, which I believe led to an unnecessary war.

That the war could have been avoided without the loss of any vital interest must not be allowed to detract in the slightest from the courage, skill and determination with which it was fought by our Armed Forces, nor the almost incredible logistical feat of assembling, supplying and supporting the ships, men and reinforcements that were needed. Britain took an almighty gamble and it came off. But that gamble would not have been needed if the situation had been handled differently by the Conservative Government in the months that preceded invasion.

Consider the background and the lessons which should have been learnt. For some years prior to 1982, Argentina's political instability had led to threats against Chile as well as the Falklands. At one stage during the period of Labour government it seemed quite possible that the Argentine Junta would use force to occupy the Chilean territory of Tierra del Fuego and the islands in the Beagle Channel. The constant political manoeuvring among the leaders of Argentina's Armed Forces heightened the possibility that an ambitious Service Chief might lash out at the Falklands in frustration at Argentina's lack of success over the Beagle Channel dispute. In September 1977 Admiral Massera, the Commander-in-Chief of the Navy, a man himself heavily involved in manoeuvring for power, ordered the Argentine Navy to fire on Bulgarian fishing boats and arrested seven Soviet trawlers. We knew that the Army was less emotional, but the Navy controlled the Foreign Office; we could not afford to ignore the possibility that plans were being drawn up for the Argentine Navy and Air Force to occupy the Falklands. But we assessed, rightly I believe, that a decision to invade would need the agreement of the Army and that this would not be forthcoming if it was made quite clear that Britain would fight.

The fact that the threat of invasion was never constant but rather waxed and waned according to the composition of Argentine Governments, the degree of their domestic difficulties and the adventurism of the Armed Forces meant that Britain did not maintain a force either on the Islands or at sea capable of repelling an all-out Argentinian attack. This made it all the more vital that the Foreign Office should always have up-to-date knowledge of the state of Argentine politics, and they did. Above all, the Argentinians themselves should never be left in doubt that an invasion or an attack would precipitate hostilities with Britain. Ours in essence would be a policy of deterrence, of preventive diplomacy; the Junta would know that force would be met by force. In April 1975 the Embassy informed me that Señor Vignes, the Argentine Foreign Minister, had declared that if Britain were not prepared to negotiate 'the only other option open to the Argentine Government is a resort to force'. This could not be left unanswered, particularly since there was a tendency, quite mistakenly, to equate the Labour Government's preference for the peaceful resolution of disputes with weakness. The British Ambassador had but newly arrived in Buenos Aires, but I instructed him to call at once on the Argentine Foreign Secretary. He was to inform him that Her Majesty's Government were determined to defend the Falkland Islands and the Argentine Government must clearly understand that an attack would meet with a military response and would precipitate armed conflict between our two countries. It was a difficult task for a new Ambassador but he left Señor Vignes in no doubt of the seriousness of his message and the matter quietened for a time.

On a later occasion I received reports of a possible occupation of South Georgia and once again the Argentine Government was given a clear warning that they would face military action if they did so.

I sought the acquaintance of Señor Robledo, who had succeeded Vignes as Foreign Minister, and we met at the United Nations Assembly in New York. I was ready to put our relations on a constructive footing and I enquired of him whether Argentina would be willing to join Britain in a high-level economic survey of the area around the Falklands, to be led by Lord Shackleton, which could explore the possibility of joint ventures by our two nations, especially in exploration for oil.

We had received a report prepared by Professor Griffiths on the oil deposits in the Falklands area and had made our own evaluation. Although exploring for oil in that area was not a top priority for Britain (we expected oil from the North Sea to come on stream within a year or two), I hoped that if we could interest Argentina in a joint venture, especially in view of her precarious economic situation, it could also strengthen political ties between us. Moreover, in the future it would obviously be much easier to carry out exploration and exploitation jointly than for Britain to face an uncooperative and perhaps hostile Argentina.

Robledo was receptive and I offered to send him the Griffiths Report and our evaluation. He said he was very ready to examine prospects of cooperation; Argentina would welcome an active British presence in the area which would assist stability. As it was our first meeting, I took the opportunity once again to make Britain's position clear on the sovereignty of the Islands, reiterating that an attack on them would lead to hostilities. Robledo gave an assurance that the Argentine Government had no intention of trying to solve the problem by force.

I had sent a seventeen-page memorandum about the Falklands to the Prime Minister in May 1975 (with apologies for its length), saying that if we were ever obliged to liberate the Islands from an Argentine occupation our political task at the United Nations, in Washington and in Latin America would be formidable. The memorandum said that since our tiny force on the Islands would not be able to repel an attack it was imperative that Argentina should never be misled, even for a moment, into believing that Britain had lost either her interest or her resolve. We would be risking an invasion if Argentina concluded that there was a moment when she could take action without overmuch response from Britain. I recount this to show that the invasion of 1982 was no bolt from the blue. The possibility and the consequences had been foreseen, but the risk was one that past experience had shown could be averted, always provided Argentina was in no doubt about Britain's resolve.

The charge against the Thatcher Government is that in the years following 1979 they gave the impression that their interest had waned. If they had signalled their determination more clearly at an earlier stage, they might never have needed to prove it by fighting and winning a costly war.

I had reported my conversation with Señor Robledo and the interest he had shown to the Cabinet, who agreed that we should promote Anglo-Argentine cooperation in jointly exploring and exploiting resources of the south-west Atlantic, using theprospect of oil as a constructive input to the dialogue. But Señor Robledo resigned and was replaced by Señor Araug Castex, who carried the idea further by suggesting that Argentina send two or three scientific experts to accompany Lord Shackleton's mission. I agreed but when Castex took the proposal to President Perón, he was rebuffed and the proposal was dropped. I was under no illusion that this policy would square the circle and satisfy Argentina's demand for sovereignty over the Falklands. On the other hand, joint ventures would concede some of the facts of sovereignty over the continental shelf and the uninhabited dependencies such as Thule more than a thousand miles away without giving up the legalities.

However imperfect, it was a means of keeping the negotiating path open and it also helped to satisfy the United Nations, which regularly called for negotiations and tended to lean to Argentina's side. I hoped that if we could develop the habit of cooperation and associate the Islanders fully with the process, it would be possible for both sides to live together even though the problems remained. The consent of the Islanders continued to be paramount, as it had been for many years, and they possessed an effective veto on any policy they disliked. Nevertheless, during the early 1970s relations between them and Argentina had grown closer in a number of areas. The Heath Government had signed an agreement in 1971 on communications which improved the Islands' links with the outside world; Argentina had provided scholarships for study in Buenos Aires for some of the Islanders' children; the Argentine National Oil Company supplied the Islands' fuel; there were improved postal, telephone and medical services via Argentina; and a weekly air and sea freight service was operating.

The Islanders valued these facilities but there was no meeting of minds on sovereignty and it was necessary to repeat to successive Argentine Ministers (they seemed to change rather quickly) that whilst I was ready for close economic cooperation, on the question of sovereignty I was empowered by the Cabinet only to listen to what they had to say. I could not expect them to be satisfied, but our willingness to cooperate on other aspects plus our firm demeanour on defence proved successful. There was no invasion and the door was kept open to the future.

The constant presence of HMS *Endurance* flying the white ensign and patrolling the waters around the Islands was a visible symbol of the latent power of the Royal Navy and of Britain's determination. In 1976 the Ministry of Defence reinforced this by improving the ship's capability, fitting her with two Wasp helicopters and air-to-sea missiles. But I had to fight a constant battle against the Ministry of Defence because certain short-sighted elements wished to scrap her on grounds of costs and increasing age. Every year from 1975 onwards the Defence Ministry announced that they wished to withdraw her from service. Every year I replied in the same manner, namely that their proposal would have serious consequences for our policy of sustaining the Islands, and I would consent only if she were replaced by a ship of similar or improved capabilities. This was never forthcoming and after I became Prime Minister, the Ministry of Defence came to realise that they would not get their way.

When I left Downing Street in May 1979, the Ministry of Defence were under instructions to keep *Endurance* in service during the years up to 1981, which gave our successors enough time to decide what they should do. From time to time, when uncertainties about Argentina's intentions made it desirable to show the flag, we reinforced the presence of *Endurance* by sending a frigate to the Falklands area, and in December 1977, when it seemed possible that our next round of talks might result in considerable tension, a force was despatched even before the negotiations began, backed by a nuclear-powered submarine with orders to remain submerged and exercise surveillance over the seaward approaches to the Islands. This submarine carried out a very valuable function in observing ship movements in order to assess any build-up that might point to an invasion.

Fortunately the talks which were held between Ted Rowlands, the Junior Minister at the Foreign Office, and Argentine Ministers ended in an agreement to examine certain matters further. The force was able to return, the only misfortune being that the ships' companies missed Christmas with their families. We made no formal communication to Argentina of these precautionary moves, but I informed the Head of MI6 of our plans before the ships sailed and it is possible that, as I hoped, some information reached the Argentinian Armed Forces.

According to the Franks Report on the Falklands dispute, the Ministry of Defence returned to the charge in a further attempt to scrap *Endurance* in 1981. Lord Carrington apparently put up resistance but obviously did not fight hard enough, nor did he have the Prime Minister's backing. In June the Defence Secretary, Sir John Nott, announced that *Endurance* would be withdrawn. The Ministry of Defence had won at last – but it was to prove a costly victory. Not only was it a major psychological blunder but the decision coincided with other policy changes – the refusal to grant British citizenship to Falkland Islanders in a new Nationality Bill, and a further statement of the Government's intention to close a British Survey Base in South Georgia on financial grounds. When these moves, all taken within a short interval, were assessed by military intelligence in Buenos Aires they must have fuelled their hopes that Britain was indeed losing interest in the Falklands. Indeed the Franks Report reveals that the British Embassy in Buenos Aires informed the Foreign Office that Argentine newspaper articles highlighted them under the theme that 'Britain was abandoning the protection of the Falklands base'. Ministers took no notice of this nor did they respond to the many private and public representations of anxiety voiced by members on both sides of the House. For example on 9 February 1982, shortly before the invasion, I made a public appeal to the Prime Minister at Question Time:

> MR JAMES CALLAGHAN: Is the Prime Minister aware that the Government's decision to withdraw and pay off HMS *Endurance* when she returns from the South Atlantic is an error that could have serious consequences? Is she further aware that this stale old proposition was put to me on more than one occasion when I was Prime Minister and after considering it I turned it down flat? Will she please do the same?
> THE PRIME MINISTER: I recognise that this was a very difficult decision for my Right Honourable Friend the Secretary of State for Defence. The Right Honourable Gentleman will appreciate that there are many competing claims on the defence budget, even though we are increasing it substantially. He will also know that the defence capability of that ship is extremely limited. My Right Honourable Friend therefore felt that other claims on the defence budget should have greater priority.

Mrs Thatcher's reference to the ship's limited defence capability showed that she did not grasp that the value of HMS *Endurance* was as a deterrent, a symbol that Britain would resist an armed attack, and a visible sign of British sovereignty.

Paragraph 116 of the Franks Report confirms this. Six months prior to the invasion Ministers received an intelligence report quoting an Argentine diplomat that the withdrawal of *Endurance* had been construed by Argentina as a deliberate political gesture, 'since the implications for the Islands and for Britain's position in the South Atlantic were fundamental'.

It shows an unforgiveable lack of grip that the British Government took no steps following this report to warn Argentina that the withdrawal of *Endurance* did not lessen Britain's determination to defend the Islands by force if necessary. Yet the Franks Report contains no indication that this was done. Indeed it seems that it was not until a further five months had elapsed that the British Government got around to sending a note reasserting Britain's continued sovereignty; even as late as a month before the invasion, Lord Carrington decided not to send a force to the South Atlantic on the grounds that it would have jeopardised the prospects of negotiations. The Franks Report says about this incident, 'The evidence we received suggested to us that Foreign and Commonwealth officials did not press Ministers to consider deterrent rather than diplomatic counter measures.'

This sentence is both illuminating and alarming. It confirms that the Government had no understanding of the purpose and uses of sea power and that the Foreign Office had obviously forgotten. Let me repeat the age-old lesson. Warships are flexible instruments. They can transit the empty expanses of ocean, move towards potential trouble spots in an unimpeded manner without causing alarm unless they so intend. They can hold station while events develop and position themselves close enough so that when the situation clears, they are able to move in quickly or to withdraw as unobtrusively as they came. The whole operation can be conducted without loss of face. There is evidence that on more than one occasion when Buenos Aires discussed harassment or invasion, a major factor in deciding not to take action was the belief that there would be a determined and fierce reaction by Britain. But in 1982 the Junta misjudged this and the Conservative Government's major errors contributed to their decision to embark upon a war that was disastrous for Argentina and won at a heavy price by us.

The conclusions of the Franks Report on this matter are perverse in the light of the evidence the committee heard. They conclude that because it was impossible to judge whether any alternative course would have prevented an attack, 'we would not be justified in attaching any criticism or blame to the present Government for the Argentine Junta's decision to commit an act of unprovoked aggression'. Of course we can agree that no failure by the Government to make its attitude clear, nor its lack of preparation to deter an invasion, could justify an armed attack by Argentina. But that is not a sufficient test. Errors of omission and commission made by Ministers in administering routine matters can be shrugged off, but sterner standards apply when Ministers face great issues of public policy that result in war.

Sir Francis Drake understood these matters better than the Franks Committee. When these Islands were threatened with invasion by the Spanish Armada three hundred years ago, Drake wrote, 'The advantage of time and place in all martial actions is half a victory, which being lost is irrevocable.' Ministers who are confronted by evidence that is unclear, or officials who are uncertain, must be guided by their own judgement and act with foresight and despatch. That is the ultimate test of leadership and on that count the Prime Minister and the Conservative Government is guilty.

Many events other than those I have described took place during my crowded two years as Foreign Secretary. There was an important Commonwealth Heads of Government Conference in Jamaica at which a principal topic was the future of Rhodesia. I paid visits to six African countries including South Africa, to the Gulf States and Iran, to Washington and Ottawa, and a risky but successful adventure to Zaire and Uganda to recover Denis Hills, an English resident who had fallen into the clutches of Idi Amin. This was an occasion on which Colonel Gadaffi of Libya was helpful to us.

We were caught up in the wretched Cod War with Iceland; and there was a difficult dispute with Guatemala about our intention to bring Belize to independence, where Prime Minister Pierre Trudeau of Canada was of great assistance in allowing our aircraft to transit through Newfoundland in order to reinforce Belize quickly when Guatemala threatened that small territory. I have many recollections of my visits to the United Nations Assembly in New York, including an occasion in September 1975 when I was mystified to hear Lin Chiang, the Chinese Minister of Trade, begin his speech with the words, 'The current international situation is characterised by great disorder under heaven and the situation is excellent.' I am still wondering what he meant.

But these memoirs are not an exhaustive history and there is no space for everything. The future of Rhodesia, however, was a constant preoccupation and I conclude with an account of an incident which gives substance to the text-book principle that the function of a constitutional Monarch is to warn, advise and encourage her Ministers. I had received a visit on 13 February 1976 from Lord Robens, who had been a colleague and friend in the Labour Shadow Cabinet during the 1950s. He had recently returned from Rhodesia, and reported on a conversation he had had with the rebel leader Ian Smith in Salisbury. Smith said he realised that he could not hold out indefinitely and wouldhave to compromise with the Africans, but predicted that this would cause great trouble with the right wing of his party. Smith had said that Joshua Nkomo, the African leader, also recognised the need for compromise if he too was not to be swept away by the guerrilla forces. Smith had added that Nkomo could not have majority rule 'tomorrow': both sides must move their present position and if a compromise backed by the United Kingdom could be reached it would have every chance of success, even if it meant that he would have to split his Party.

I asked Robens what period Smith had in mind before majority rule was conceded, saying that I thought the African leaders would do business if the period was as short as eighteen months. Smith had not stated any period, but Vorster, the South African Prime Minister, who had great influence with him and whom Robens had also visited, had told him that in his opinion, white Rhodesians would settle for an interim period of five years. This seemed too long, but Alf Robens urged me to send someone to test out Ian Smith. After thinking the matter over, I decided we should not let the opportunity slip, although I was well aware that Smith was an elusive, not to say slippery, negotiator who could rarely be pinned down to precise commitments.

I asked Lord Greenhill to undertake a secret mission to Salisbury. He was well qualified to do so. As Sir Denis Greenhill, he had been Head of the Diplomatic Service and knew Smith's characteristics. He returned saying that Smith had confirmed that he wanted a compromise even at the expense of splitting his Party; a period of three years before majority rule had been mentioned (but as usual without any true commitment from Smith), and the Chiefs of Staff in Rhodesia were confident that this would so change the political atmosphere that the armed forces would be able to handle any ensuing guerrilla threat. It seemed that Smith wished Britain to 'arbitrate' between himself and the African leaders but was not ready to make any public statement to this effect.

My advisers at the Foreign Office examined Greenhill's report and submitted their conclusion to me on 28 February 1976. Their view was that while Smith was aware that guerrilla war held dangers for him, he did not yet understand how serious its consequences would be, nor how deeply his position was being undermined. Their opinion was that he was probably playing for time and they had no confidence that a settlement could be reached at this stage. Although I was bound to agree that the official assessment was probably correct, it seemed to me that sufficient had emerged from the visit to warrant following up. It was at this juncture, while I was considering what to do next, that by chance I had an opportunity of talking with the Queen.

She had been present at a performance at Covent Garden of Rossini's opera *La Cenerentola*, conducted by La Scala's principal conductor, Claudio Abbado. The occasion was a visit to London by Signora Leone, the wife of the President of Italy, and I was among the guests. The Italian Ambassador invited us to supper at his residence in Grosvenor Square when the performance was over and kindly placed me next to the Queen. During supper I described to her Lord Greenhill's visit to Rhodesia and the aftermath, and discussed the alternative courses of following the matter up, or of letting it simmer for the time being, adding that I had not yet decided which would be better. After supper we met other guests among whom I was particularly glad to make the acquaintance of Toscanini's daughter, as Audrey and I had followed this great conductor with rapt attention during the late 1930s when he conducted the BBC Orchestra in a series of Beethoven's symphonies in the old Queen's Hall in London. The Queen departed at about midnight and the rest left shortly afterwards.

The next afternoon a letter was handed to me from Sir Martin Charteris, the Queen's Private Secretary. He said that the Queen had told him how much she enjoyed our conversation about Rhodesia. She had reflected on our talk and 'she recognises that any initiative you take may prove ineffective, but none the less believes it would be worthwhile to make the effort. Her Majesty sends you her best wishes for your efforts in dealing with this intractable problem.'

Inevitably the Queen's opinion was enough to tip the scales, for she is an authority on the Commonwealth and I respected her opinion: I decided to go ahead. Two years before, when I became Foreign and Commonwealth Secretary, I had told the Queen's Private Secretary of my hope to build stronger links with the Commonwealth and his reply at the time, as well as the Queen's comments on other occasions, left me in no doubt of the keenness with which she followed Commonwealth affairs and of her genuine concern for its well-being. Her very perceptive understanding comes not only from many years spent reading Foreign Office documents, but also from her numerous meetings with successive Commonwealth leaders and her regular overseas tours. These have given her a knowledge of Commonwealth politicians and politics unequalled by any member of the Diplomatic Service or any British politician. I should also add that she is extremely careful to separate her duty as Queen of the United Kingdom from her responsibility to individual Commonwealth countries and to the Commonwealth as a whole, and long experience enables her to reconcile her various roles with wisdom and tact.

On receipt of the Queen's letter, I called a meeting with the other Ministers at the Foreign Office, Roy Hattersley and Ted Rowlands without telling them of the Private Secretary's communication. We agreed that I should send a message to Smith, telling him that in the view of Her Majesty's Government the spread of guerrilla activity meant that if he was willing to give a public commitment to majority rule and to hold elections on this basis within the next eighteen months to two years, Her Majesty's Government would be willing to play a constructive part in negotiations between him and the African leaders in order to prevent chaos and loss of life, and to reach a settlement satisfactory to both Europeans and Africans. As part of a settlement Britain would be ready to contribute towards compensation for those adversely affected, and to give financial aid for development and African education. We would also recommend that sanctions be lifted by the United Nations.

At this point the negotiations which had been taking place between Smith and Nkomo broke down, leaving a political vacuum that was filled by increasing guerrilla activity. I decided that in view of the deteriorating situation I should convey our proposals not only to Smith but also to Parliament and this I did on 22 March 1976. Reggie Maudling, the Shadow Foreign Secretary, and members on both sides of the House urged Smith to accept the broad principle of my approach; the level of approval was so high that I said that I hoped 'the several expressions of view of the Opposition benches will convince Mr Smith that in this approach there is a great deal of unity in the House of Commons'.

Shortly after this I left the Foreign Office and as history records, Smith did not agree. In later years, while he clung to power, the prospects of any settlement were undermined by visits to Salisbury by right-wing Conservative MPs who encouraged him to believe that if he hung on, the eventual return of a Conservative Government would improve his prospects. Again, history shows that they were wrong.

Harold Wilson had announced his resignation only a few days before my statement to the House and a handful of cynics scornfully claimed that I made the intervention only as a play to assist my campaign to be-

come Leader of the Party and Prime Minister. They were not aware of
the events that led up to it, but I do not suppose it would have made any
difference had they known.

I have always thought since that the Queen's initiative on Rhodesia
was a perfect illustration of how and when the Monarch could effectively
intervene to advise and encourage her Ministers from her own wide
experience and with complete constitutional propriety.

PART FIVE

PRIME MINISTER

13

*Harold Wilson's resignation – the office of Prime Minister –
Cabinet colleagues – the Great Debate on Education*

When I was a Minister I looked forward especially to the twelve days of
Christmas as a period when it was possible to lead a rational life. Parliament was up; members and their constituents were enjoying the post-
Christmas festivities which in recent years have extended into the New
Year; Cabinet business slowed down to a trickle; London seemed half
empty, and there was time to enjoy a leisurely lunch and still go home at
a reasonable hour.

The post-Christmas period at the end of 1975 was about average for
the Foreign Secretary, although there were two matters that needed close
attention at the end of the year. The skippers of the Icelandic gun-boats
were pursuing aggressive and dangerous tactics in their dispute with
Britain over fishing-ground limits. First, on 28 December they deliberately involved HMS *Andromeda*, one of our frigates, in a collision at sea.
Fortunately no one was injured. This was one of a series of such incidents
in which our ships were provoked but where retaliation would have called
down cries of bullying. I said as much to Henry Kissinger and he replied
with a quotation from Bismarck, 'The weak are strong because they are
reckless. The strong are weak because they have scruples.' Unfortunately,
we could gain very little sympathy in international circles.

The second matter concerned Dr Shirley Cassidy, a medical missionary
working in Chile who had been arrested by the Chilean secret police for
giving medical attention to a wounded guerrilla fighter. She had strayed
into the dark undergrowth of Chilean repression when she was asked by
a Chilean priest to go to a convent to treat a man with a bullet in his leg.
She paid several visits, and became aware that he was a guerrilla fighter
who had been given sanctuary. Despite her attention his condition deteriorated in the absence of proper medical facilities, and he was removed
secretly to the residence of the Papal Nuncio in Chile. She was asked to
continue her treatment but following one of her visits she was arrested by
the Chilean secret police and questioned to discover what she knew.

Sheila Cassidy refused to give details that would lead the police to the nuns, and as a result was subjected to torture by the application of electric shocks to parts of her body. The British Ambassador, who was not aware of this treatment, had made several urgent representations for her release, all of which the Chilean authorities rebuffed. But on Boxing Day 1975 signs of a softening of the Chilean attitude came when our Consul and his wife were permitted to visit her, and three days later the Ambassador was suddenly informed that she was to be released. I had been following the matter closely and felt some belated satisfaction at the outcome, but this vanished when I was given an account of the torture to which she had been subjected. I instructed the Ambassador to express Her Majesty's Government's outrage, and then to return to London at once to report to me personally as a public sign of Britain's indignation.

While I was occupied with these matters, Harold Lever telephoned to say he wanted to talk. He was an old friend of many years' standing, always cheerful and bubbling with new and fertile ideas, generous with his friendship, ingenious in finding new solutions to old problems. A splendid raconteur, he possesses much worldly common sense. Harold Wilson had given him a roving commission as a Cabinet Minister. When he arrived at the Foreign Office late in the afternoon, followed by the Foreign Office messenger bearing the best Foreign Office teapot in honour of the Chancellor of the Duchy of Lancaster, I settled down to spend an enjoyable hour, but immediately discovered that he was bent on serious business.

He emphasised that what he was about to tell me must be treated in the strictest confidence. His news was both dramatic and unexpected. The Prime Minister had made a firm decision to resign in March 1976, and I must prepare myself to take over. That was his message. I was initially disbelieving. I knew that Harold Wilson had felt unwell before Christmas and I had successfully urged him to postpone a proposed New Year's visit to Egypt at Sadat's invitation in order to give himself a chance to get better. I did not for a moment believe he was likely to or needed to resign. Sceptically I probed Harold Lever about the reliability of his sources, but always totally discreet, he refused to give me any clue that would enable me to verify what he had said. He would only repeat that I could rely on his information, and as I had previous experience of the accuracy of his intelligence I slowly became convinced.

But, I argued, even if this was Harold's present turn of mind, there would be plenty of time before March in which the Prime Minister could change his opinion. Not so, said Harold Lever, the decision was firm and I must make ready. He then became his usual bantering cheerful self and with expressions of good wishes for the New Year, departed.

I sat gazing out at the shadows cast by the lights in St James's Park, the people hurrying home from their offices and the dim outline of the lake, and wondered what 1976 would bring. Ten years earlier I would have been avid for the Party leadership, and the prospect of leading the nation, but now I was almost sixty-four years of age. For nearly thirty years I had served continuously either in Government or in the Shadow Cabinet, and for twenty years on the Party's Executive Committee or as its Treasurer. I had been at the centre of all the controversies, but since becoming Foreign Secretary two years earlier I had begun to feel a little detached, especially as my visits abroad prevented me from attending Cabinet and Party meetings as frequently as before. I had assumed, as I have said, that the time would come before long when the Prime Minister would tell me in a kindly way that he would like me to make way for a younger man. Now everything would be in the melting pot.

I decided to talk only to my closest friend, Merlyn Rees. He was discreet, knew the Party, in which he had deep roots, had sound judgement and would not spare himself to give me the best advice. He had no hesitation. In the event of Harold's resignation, I must stand and I would win. If I had any doubts he swept them away. We both agreed that until any announcement was made there was little that could be done, and although my schedule for the early months of 1976 involved a lot of foreign travel, I decided to keep to it.

I was deeply convinced of the need to win the battle against inflation and of the need for a second year of pay restraint. So that there should be no doubt about my position in the event of a leadership contest, I took the opportunity to make a speech to the Woolwich Labour Party at the end of January 1976, strongly supporting the continuation of an incomes policy. Tom McCaffrey, the Chief Information Officer at the Foreign Office, was somewhat surprised at my insistence that the speech should get widespread publicity, as he did not know the underlying reason.

I travelled to Germany, visited Berlin once again and from there travelled to Helmut Schmidt's home town of Hamburg to speak to the Ubersee Club on the British attitude to the construction of Europe. Hamburg is a fine city which has made the most of its situation and environs and I was very impressed with the lay-out and efficiency of the Port. The kindness of my hosts made my visit a very enjoyable occasion.

There is an empathy between Hamburg and the British, which Helmut Schmidt illustrated by telling the local joke that when it rains in London the people of Hamburg put up their umbrellas.

I did not look forward nearly as much to visiting Iran. I did not care for the manner in which all the Western powers, including ourselves, felt that they must pay court to the Shah, and I had no sympathy with the brutal internal repression practised by the regime's secret police, of which the Foreign Office received evidence from refugees living in London. But I decided to make the best of it and in view of Iran's relations with South Africa, I proposed to carry the message that Iran could play a more active role in exerting influence indirectly on Rhodesia through the South African Government. There was some concern about the prospects for British Petroleum and Shell in Iran, since the Shah had complained that the international oil consortium was not lifting all the oil it had promised to take in June 1973. A contributory factor was the world's industrial recession, but a major reason was that Iran's heavy crude oil was over-priced and provided only ten to eleven cents a barrel profit, whereas Saudi Arabian oil offered twenty-five cents profit per barrel. The result was that the Shah was becoming short of money, and less able to meet the rising expectations of his people, while his pride made him reluctant to seek credit.

He received me in the ornate Golestan Palace in Teheran on 6 March 1976, accompanied by a number of Ministers who were deferential to the point of being obsequious, and I doubt ever told him any unpleasant truths.

I started at once on the topic of Iranian oil, in accordance with my usual negotiating technique of seeking to gain the confidence of the other side by showing them that you take their principal concerns seriously and give them priority in your discussions. On this occasion it seemed to bear fruit, for notwithstanding the worries in London, the Shah intimated that he fully understood the British oil companies' position. They had difficulties, but BP was doing its best to stand by the agreement. On the other hand, he said, the American companies were not. He then placed his need for additional revenues in a broader context, saying that if Iran was to assume its proper role in the Gulf, the sub-continent and the Indian Ocean, he must spend more on arms. He then drifted into a high-flown and un-realistic proposal, namely that the stability of the Indian Ocean could best be safeguarded by tripartite cooperation between Iran, Australia and South Africa.

It seemed in the highest degree unlikely to me that the Australia of Gough Whitlam or of Malcolm Fraser would take part in such a venture, and I interposed that Australia's priorities seemed to lie more in the Pacific and to developing her industrial relations with Japan and China. It was unlikely that she would be ready to spread her wings in the Indian Ocean in the near future. The Shah replied that perhaps the Australians would be too timid (at which I exclaimed) but he hoped not, for there was no resentment against Australia in south-west Asia, and they were a solid people with a tremendous future backed by new discoveries of natural resources.

At least I could agree with him about the last point. His reference to South Africa gave me an opening to ask for his help in bringing pressure on Rhodesia. He questioned me about South Africa's influence with Ian Smith and whether a collapse in Rhodesia would spread to South Africa. He remarked that his extensive links with that country were not only through oil supplies, but also in mining and nuclear development, especially in the use of South African uranium. He went no further than to promise that after his return from a forthcoming visit to Pakistan, he would consider what he could do. I heard no more.

The Shah showed a much surer touch on Indo-Pakistan relationships. Pakistan must give up any idea of revenge against India. They could not win a war and it was in their interest to improve collaboration with India. They should try to overcome their complex about their military inferiority, which was unhealthy, for the bigger their sense of military need, the stronger became the influence of the military. On the other hand, India should do nothing to encourage the disintegration of Pakistan, a view which, he said, Mrs Gandhi shared.

This led into a discussion about ideas for a greater Baluchistan, to which he was vehemently opposed. He argued that it would not only involve the incorporation of some Iranian territory, but it might be linked with Afghan plans for 'Pakhtoonistan', and give the Soviet Union the opportunity to realise its old Imperial dream of achieving an outlet to the Gulf. Soviet aims in the area, he said, were not so much ideological as traditional and imperial. He went on to describe how impressed his military observers had been a short while before when they attended manoeuvres by Soviet armed forces in the Caucasus. Their sophisticated operations had demonstrated that they had the numbers and the ability to move easily beyond their borders, and this appearance of Soviet power had an important effect on decision-making in all the neighbouring countries of the Middle East. His conclusion was correct and was borne out three years later when the Soviet Armed Forces crossed the border into Afghanistan.

As our lengthy discussion continued, the Shah's somewhat melancholy and withdrawn attitude was replaced by an air of near vivacity. He was more interested in discussing geo-political concepts than the economic or political issues of Iran and Britain, but when I turned the conversation to these affairs it was apparent that his aim of modernising his country was a genuine resolve to ensure a future for his people if and when Iran's oil reserves were depleted. Despite my prejudice against the wealth and corruption of the regime, I could not help being affected by his obvious earnestness, although I was unimpressed by his remoteness from everyday affairs. Before we parted, we had a family group photograph taken with the Shah and the Empress, Audrey and me. I cannot claim that I foresaw in 1976 that he would be overthrown only three years later, but we were all agreed that his refusal to share his power, the employment of draconian measures of modernisation, and the regime's dependence on repression to maintain its authority meant that in the long run it must prove unstable.

Yet I could not help but feel sorry for him at the end when, near death, he was shunted from country to country.

Audrey and I returned to England just in time for a dinner party given by George Weidenfeld at his home in honour of Harold Wilson's sixtieth birthday on 11 March. The thirty or so present spent a convivial evening but Harold and I had to leave shortly before ten o'clock to vote at the end of a debate on public expenditure, arranging to return later for Mary Wilson and Audrey. As if on impulse, Harold asked me to travel with him and as the car sped along the Embankment he told me in confidence the news that Harold Lever had forecast and which a few days later was to astonish the country. He would call a special Cabinet Meeting on the morning of 16 March to inform Ministers of his intention to resign, and meantime I should begin to make preparations for the inevitable contest. Despite Harold Lever's prior warning to me, the actuality still came as a shock, and I hardly had time to say much before we arrived in New Palace Yard. I walked through the Division Lobby in a bemused state, hardly grasping that the Government was actually in the throes of a crisis: a large group of Labour left-wing Members were deliberately abstaining from voting in support of the Government because of their opposition to the Cabinet's expenditure plans. Denis Healey had borne the brunt of the debate and was now engaged in a public row with them whilst the vote was going on, telling them with his combination of Yorkshire bluntness and Irish impetuosity exactly what he thought of them, to which some of them responded in kind. Thirty-seven Labour Members abstained from voting and the Government suffered a major defeat by twenty-eight votes.

It was not the happiest conclusion to the Prime Minister's birthday party, and as we drove back to Chelsea our conversation was raggedly divided between deciding to call for an immediate vote of confidence and my urging Harold not to resign at such a moment. He seemed less affected than I was, chuckling at what might have happened if the abstainers had known, and it was soon obvious that his mind was totally made up and he would not be deflected. From what he told me I could gather that he had already set the machinery for his departure in motion. I did not stay long after we returned to the party, and confided in Audrey as soon as we reached home. She took the news in her accustomed calm, competent manner and immediately made clear that she would expect me to be a candidate – indeed in her eyes the best candidate. It was yet one more example of her love and loyalty.

Harold's secret was well guarded and the Cabinet gathered at No. 10 on the following Tuesday without the slightest inkling of the dramatic news they were to hear. Whilst Ministers were assembling, Harold called Ted Short, the Deputy Leader, Denis Healey and me to his study and there broke the news to the three of us. I do not know whether the other two also had prior knowledge, but no one gave any indication to this effect as we all filed silently to the Cabinet Room.

The Prime Minister opened the meeting, Ministers had hardly settled themselves in their seats before the bombshell burst. It was several seconds before they recovered their breath. The purport of his remarks is already familiar. This was no sudden decision on his part, as he had never intended to stay longer than two years after the 1974 election. The task of the Prime Minister was unremitting, for he was on duty every minute of the day and night and must know all that was going on in the Government. That demanded constant attention, and yet the Prime Minister must also be able to stand back from the pressure of events and think about the future. He recalled that he had led the Party for thirteen years, nearly eight of them as Prime Minister. We were living in a period of change and he wanted to avoid the danger of rejecting courses of action merely because they had been considered and turned down on some earlier occasion during his leadership. He had stayed long enough to see the first stage of the counter-inflation policy accepted and the clash and confrontation of two years earlier replaced by a new partnership.

His next sentence unobtrusively removed an argument that might have been used against me in the leadership contest. He said the fact that he was leaving at the age of sixty should have no bearing on the choice of his successor. I was grateful for not only was I four years older than he but I would also be the oldest of the potential candidates.

It was a great regret to me that our partnership was to come to an end. Except for our differences over Barbara Castle's proposals for trade union reform, he and I had worked closely together since 1964, and during my early days as Chancellor of the Exchequer when sterling was under great strain he was a considerable strength and comfort.

When we were in difficulties his sagacity and sangfroid were beyond doubt, as was his kindliness to his colleagues. There had been a period when he allowed Barbara Castle, Dick Crossman and George Wigg, all of whom suffered from the belief that politics was a conspiracy, to influence him too much, but in later years he had broken free from them and I suddenly realised how much I had got used to him being there to shoulder the final responsibility, to feeling able to turn to him naturally for a second opinion and for well-informed advice. Now in a short time he would be gone, and the era that had begun in the 1960s with the triumvirate of Harold Wilson, George Brown and myself would be at an end. Only I would be left. Three weeks later, on the day I became Prime Minister, my first impulse was to sit down in the study which had been Harold's and write him a letter of appreciation and grateful thanks.

Strangely enough, at no time did I have real doubts that I would be elected, and this determined my public attitude during the three successive ballots that were necessary. Merlyn Rees, Gregor Mackenzie and John Cunningham, all of whom were friends who had served me as Parliamentary Private Secretaries, rallied at once and with Tom McNally, my Political Adviser, formed a small inner team to conduct the contest on my behalf.

I told them I would prefer to give no interviews to press or television. In my view our fellow Members, who lived with us cheek by jowl, were fully aware of my strengths and weaknesses and were unlikely to be impressed by pictures of me on their TV screens dressed in a striped apron and pretending to wash up in the kitchen, as had happened during the Tory leadership election. Coincidentally I had a very busy schedule as

Foreign Secretary at that time. During the ensuing three weeks the French Foreign Minister, M. Sauvagnargues, was due to visit me in London for talks, as was the Turkish Foreign Minister. There was to be a European Council Meeting in Luxembourg which required the attendance of both the Prime Minister and myself, and in an important improvement in Anglo-Soviet relations, Andrei Gromyko, the Soviet Foreign Minister, had accepted my invitation to pay an official visit to London – his first for some years – for discussions on East-West relations and bilateral affairs.

All of these meetings required careful preparation and I was relieved when my election team agreed with my general tactics, although they added that I must make myself available for private talks with any colleague who asked to see me. We further agreed that we would make no promises and twist no arms, and having decided on this general strategy, my friends urged me to leave the campaign to them. We expected Michael Foot, Roy Jenkins and Tony Wedgwood Benn to stand, but when Denis Healey and Tony Crosland also announced they were candidates, my team calculated that I would lose a number of votes to them, for the three of us were close in our thinking and attitudes. As far as I am aware, there was good feeling between the candidates during the election, and I was somewhat surprised to read in Susan Crosland's splendid biography of her husband that Roy Hattersley had told him I was angry that he was standing, and that he must give me his support before the first ballot or I would have no interest in him. If this happened, it was a piece of private enterprise and done without the agreement of my election team or myself.

Another factor that assisted in maintaining a good atmosphere was that Merlyn Rees was Secretary of State for Northern Ireland, and Stanley Orme, who acted as Michael Foot's campaign organiser, was his Minister of State. Not only were they colleagues but also friends, and relations were so good that they privately compared the names of those who had declared their support and enjoyed a quiet chuckle at a certain number of names which appeared on both lists. As the ballots proceeded on an exhaustive basis, matters turned out much as we anticipated. Michael Foot led on the first ballot and Tony Crosland, who always knew he would be defeated, had the least number of votes, automatically dropped out and thereafter supported me.

Roy Jenkins and Tony Wedgwood Benn also decided to withdraw before the second ballot, with Tony asking his supporters to vote for Michael. Three of us contested the second ballot in which Denis Healey was eliminated and this led to the final ballot on 5 April 1976. The result was 176 to me, 133 to Michael Foot. It seemed that Benn's votes had gone to Foot, and I had gained nearly all the votes initially given to Crosland, Jenkins and Healey.

My election team's confidence had been fully justified, and John Cunningham proudly claims that his final estimate was within one of the actual result, although he must share some of the credit with Andrei Gromyko who had told me before he left London, and when Michael was leading after the first ballot, that he fully expected that I would be the Prime Minister on the next occasion we met.

After the result I went to Labour Party Headquarters at Transport House to greet the Party officers, and also because I wished to make the symbolic gesture of linking the Party in the country with the Labour Members of Parliament who had elected me. I therefore intended in due course to set out from Transport House for Buckingham Palace. The expected telephone call soon came, and Sir Martin Charteris was enquiring, 'When would it be convenient for you to come to the Palace?'

Convenient! I am sure he enjoyed the delicate meiosis of the word. I got my own back a few years later when he retired after serving the Queen for several years, and was appointed the Provost of Eton. It was the Prime Minister's responsibility to sign the formal scroll submitting his appointment to the Queen for her approval. After the mediaeval language of the warrant, I added in manuscript, 'I can thoroughly recommend this promising young man to your Majesty.'

Audrey and I left the moment I received the summons and drove to the Palace together. There she waited in an ante-room while the Queen received me in audience and invited me to form a Government. This was a necessary step to conform with the well-established convention that when the Prime Minister resigns, the Government ceases to exist.

There is no formal ceremony for the appointment of a Prime Minister. That evening I took no oath and received no official communication. Although the term 'Prime Minister' has been used for two hundred years, it was not until the Treaty of Berlin in 1878 that the Prime Minister was so described in a public document, and the formal position today is that he is 'sworn First Lord of Her Majesty's Treasury'. I had already been Prime Minister for a week before that ceremony took place and I kissed hands. He would be an unfeeling man who could sit for the first time in the Prime Minister's seat at the centre of the Cabinet table in No. 10 and feel no emotion. For me, it was a boyhood dream come true.

At school nearly fifty years earlier I had been introduced to the history of the eighteenth and nineteenth centuries and had been enthused by the deeds and speeches of the statesmen of those days. At that time I had no expectation of following in their footsteps but now, on the morning of 6 April 1976, I was in the direct line of succession to such great names as Pitt, Gladstone, Disraeli and Lloyd George. Even the familiar furnishings of the Cabinet Room glowed more brightly, for I was sitting there as of right and not by invitation. I had no doubt of my capacity to run a Government, for I had watched Attlee and Harold Wilson operating in that very room and had observed five Conservative Prime Ministers in the House of Commons over a period of thirty years. If that sounds immodest then I appeal to Trollope's description in my defence. 'One wants in a Prime Minister a good many things, but not very great things. He should be clever yet need not be a genius; he should be conscientious but by no means strait-laced; he should be cautious but never timid, bold but never venturesome; he should have a good digestion, genial manners, and, above all, a thick skin.'

I knew it would not be easy for me to leave a distinctive stamp on the new Administration, for the broad outline of the Government's policy on major issues such as Devolution had been settled before my arrival and legislation such as the nationalisation of shipbuilding and aerospace industries was at that moment proceeding through Parliament and being heavily buffetted in the process. The Government at no time had an effective majority; there were heavy hints that I was a stopgap Prime Minister and the favourite forecast for the date of the next general election was September 1976. I was having none of that. I might not have been over-anxious to take over Harold Wilson's mantle when Harold Lever first broached the subject, but having donned it I was determined to keep it.

What did I want my Administration to stand for? It was of course, in Bagehot's words, at the head of our national business, but I needed some objectives over and beyond that. I had never accepted the dictum of one of my predecessors as Prime Minister who was reputed to have said, 'If it's morality you want, you must go to the Archbishop.' Central to the purpose of a Labour Government is responsibility for eliminating social wrongs and promoting social well-being. The class system had grown less rigid during my lifetime but it was still a millstone that hampered progress, as was gross inequality.

Men and women are not born equal in the sense of being equally endowed, but equal opportunity is a basic principle of social justice. It appeals particularly to those who know at first hand what its denial can mean in terms of frustrated hopes or unfulfilled achievement. Its purpose is to give to every man and woman the chance to develop his or her individual personality. Talent and creative ability are brimming over in the working class but too often in the past they remained undiscovered.

> Full many a gem of purest ray serene
> the dark, unfathomed caves of ocean bear:
> Full many a flower is born to blush unseen,
> and waste its sweetness on the desert air.

Our purpose is that men and women may be enabled to lead the fullest possible lives, not solely for their own satisfaction, but in order that they may contribute to the development of others – whether in this country or overseas.

In my youth we used words like 'fellowship' and 'solidarity' to express these concepts, and they were the ethical basis of our belief in socialism. Socialism should concern itself with the weak and underprivileged whoever they are – the poor, ill-educated, disabled, or coloured. We were always painfully conscious that the idealism of the Labour Movement could come into conflict with its materialistic aspect – but we claimed it was the aim of socialism to reconcile the two.

In 1945 we had nationalised the coal mines not only to improve their efficiency, but as a means of removing a burning social injustice that stemmed from years of harshness. The intervening years had shown that in the world of today, power is exercised by function as much as by the ownership of wealth. We had limited but by no means removed the power of wealth to exploit, but whilst we were engaged in doing this, new sources of power had grown up. The centralisation of function and policy-making in the name of efficiency, the diverse interests of the multinational corporation, the growth of bureaucracy, new inventions such as the microchip and the computer that confer the power of instant transnational communication, the post-war strength of the trade unions all led to the creation of other great sources of power that could and sometimes did exercise their veto against the national interest.

Society is in a permanent state of flux and I had learned that it is not enough to enforce changes in the economic structure to ensure the fulfilment of ideals. These require changes also in human attitudes and relationships which will only be both permanent and of benefit if they are attained through education, persuasion and understanding, not through coercion. There will be conflicts among such groups and between them and Government. I was not content that these should be resolved by the exercise of muscle alone. We should use rational means to reconcile differences between groups, to persuade them that they are all part of the common weal which determines the quality of our society as a whole. I tried to reflect something of this approach in my broadcast tò the nation on the evening of my appointment, while in an article in the *Daily Mirror* I explained something about the nation's business.

Both pieces reflected my keenness that people should believe that their Government would take them into its confidence. Cynicism in politics is a corrosive acid which will dissolve faith in democratic leadership and I was determined to try and avoid it. My first broadcast called for honesty and fair dealing in our relations with one another, and I appealed that we should face our problems not in a divided manner but as a community. I summed up my approach: 'Tell the people; trust the people; consult the people.' In the *Mirror* article I spelled out the nature of our problem, and said there was nothing complicated about it. Quite simply we were spending more than we produced and earned, and the enemy at the gate was inflation. Our common objective must be to bring it down to less than half of what it was at that time (in March 1976, it was 21.2 per cent) and thus increase employment. I emphasised the new Government's intention to continue with an incomes policy, to restrain pay increases and put more real money into people's pockets. 'No one can save us but ourselves', I wrote.

My first public engagement as Prime Minister came a day or two later in my own constituency where I had a long-standing engagement to open a newly built bridge in the docks area. John Morris, the Secretary of State for Wales, and Cledwyn Hughes, the Chairman of the Parliamentary Labour Party, both came up with the appropriate suggestion that I should adopt an old Welsh maxim as my motto, 'Bid ben: bed bont', which they freely translated as 'He who would lead must be a bridge.' Both of them had supported me during the leadership contest, and they knew that 'Bid ben: bed Bont' would represent my style of leadership. I used it on many occasions and it appealed to George Thomas also, for when he ceased to be a very successful Speaker of the House of Commons and took the title of Viscount Tonypandy, he inserted it in his coat of arms.

A month later, in May 1976, when the early demise of the Government was being freely forecast, I sat down in the Cabinet Room and boldly scribbled on a rough piece of paper my 'Objectives for 1980': 'Reduction of inflation below 5 per cent and unemployment below 3 per cent; a manageable balance of payments; Devolution within the United Kingdom, and the country to play a leading role in European, Commonwealth and world affairs; to resume our social aims in housing, education, health and welfare to build a cohesive society; and to win the general election for Labour.' We had a few successes, there were some near-misses and the rest were failures. The critics may be scornful but I would claim that although we were a Government without a majority, it was better for us to have some long-range objectives than to live from day to day.

While writing this I received a letter from a member of the public unknown to me, living in Hertfordshire. He had seen the notice of my birthday in the newspapers and wrote, 'Your administration will always be noted for the humanity that it brought to government.' If that were to be the final epitaph I should not be unhappy. My personal attitude to politics chimed well with the Government's Strategy for Industry. This had been devised under Harold Wilson and I carried it on and accentuated it. The main purpose was to order our priorities in such a way that we made abundant resources available to manufacturing industry to enable it to modernise itself and catch up with similar industries in other countries. The prime impetus must come from industry itself but to help it the Government offered direct financial assistance, tried to moderate the level of taxation, and assisted reorganisation through the use of executive instruments like the National Enterprise Board, a body made up of both employers and trade unionists. Devoting such priority resources to industry made it necessary to keep down increases in public expenditure for other purposes in the years ahead of us. This expenditure had been neither committed nor spent, but forecasts had been made and it was the downward adjustment of these that had led to the Chancellor's public dispute with our critics prior to Harold Wilson's resignation. These attacks continued throughout my own tenure of office.

The Government's second priority was to restore the confidence of the public at home and of investors, traders and customers abroad in Britain's ability to keep down the level of inflation.

Influential figures on the TUC General Council like Hugh Scanlon of the AUEW were pleased at the priority given to the modernisation of manufacturing industry and accepted the reduction of future expenditure plans as a necessary part of the process. Others were not as realistic but

Ministers established good relations with both sides of industry – the CBI as well as the TUC – in pursuing these two objectives.

It was not my intention when I became Prime Minister to over-involve myself in economic policy. The Chancellor, Denis Healey, had gained experience since he took over in 1974, and the clarity and force of argument he employed, his penetrating mind as well as his remarkable stamina, ensured his authority in Cabinet and Parliament, as well as in international finance circles. I had myself long been convinced of the necessity of international economic and monetary cooperation for the prosperity of the Western World and of Third World countries, and had paid annual visits to the World Bank and International Monetary Fund meetings.

Alas for my intention to devote my time to other issues. I found, as I suppose other Prime Ministers have done, that economic problems obtruded at every street corner, and despite my good intentions there were periods when they occupied large slices of my time. Denis was one of the sheet anchors of the Cabinet, and I was relieved to find when I took over and asked him about his future that he preferred to stay at the Treasury. The post of Foreign Secretary had to be filled and in other times Roy Jenkins would have been a natural successor. His keen historical sense gave him a wide-ranging geo-political viewpoint, and his experience as Chancellor would have fitted him well for the increasingly economic aspects of the Foreign Secretary's responsibilities. But the wounds had not healed since his resignation as Deputy Leader during the European Community battles, and as he had been the leading protagonist on one side, every action he would have taken as Foreign Secretary would have been regarded with deep suspicion by the anti-Marketeers on our benches. Often, in politics, who does it counts for as much as what is done, and I decided I could not risk the uneasy truce that then prevailed in the Party by appointing someone who would be accused of tilting the balance, however scrupulous he might be.

In any case there was another suitable candidate, in the person of Tony Crosland. He was not nearly as committed as Roy Jenkins to Community membership and would not arouse as much suspicion when he took the necessary decisions, as he must, that would link Britain more closely with the Community.

We had met shortly after the war when he entertained me in his rooms at Trinity, Oxford following a speech I had made to the Socialist Club. I was intrigued by his casual manner as he told me of his ambition to stand for Parliament. Looking around his attractive rooms I said I could not see why he thought that becoming an MP would be more worthwhile or more pleasant than what he was doing already. I should add that I was a back-bencher at the time. After that we met quite often, mostly at Fabian Society affairs at which he would turn up wearing his parachute regiment's red beret at a dashing angle while the girls flocked around.

I enjoyed his reckless devil-may-care attitude, and his teasing manner which made me laugh a great deal. He was good company and although some were put off by his apparent lofty arrogance, his friends quickly saw that it was a camouflage behind which lay a deeply serious intellect. The trade unionists sitting in the Tea Room at the House, who were used to judging their men, took no offence at his direct manner and made him more welcome than some of those who made an effort to play up to them.

I was very pleased that he chose to support me in the election for Party Leader following Hugh Gaitskell's death, and he did me a further service when I became Shadow Chancellor as he arranged for a distinguished group of economists at Oxford to meet with me every fortnight to discuss the economic problems that a Labour Government would face.

It was just as well that we remained good friends for we shared adjoining rooms in the House of Commons, and from time to time he would bang on the thin dividing wall complaining that he could hear every word I was saying on the telephone and that I was preventing him from sleeping. I was happy when the time came to ask him to succeed me at the Foreign Office. He liked the office, brought a bump of cheerful irreverence to it, got on well with his colleagues, and would have been a great success but for his untimely death less than a year later. His passing was both a personal and a political loss.

The decision to appoint Tony Crosland settled Roy Jenkins' thoughts about his own future. While I was still Foreign Secretary, Giscard d'Estaing and Helmut Schmidt had told me that the time was coming for someone from Britain to hold the office of President of the European Commission, and Giscard in particular had hinted that he would be happy if Roy Jenkins were to be nominated by Britain. Accordingly I was not altogether surprised when Roy Jenkins came to me a fortnight or so after I had appointed Tony Crosland as the new Foreign Secretary to intimate that he would welcome it if I would nominate him as the Commission's President. I was sorry he had so decided, but agreed without hesitation to put his name forward. I was sorry to lose him; one consequence was that within a year, one of the strongest and most experienced post-war Cabinet teams this country has seen was broken up, with the

19 Arriving at the Treasury for the first time
as Chancellor, October 1964.

20 LEFT: Harold Wilson looks apprehensive at what I am saying to the Party Conference.

21 CENTRE: 'Then raise the scarlet standard high' with Jenny Lee, Tony Benn, Dick Crossman and Barbara Castle.

22 BELOW: A collection of Chancellors.

23 RIGHT: The First Secretary and I launch the Labour Government's new economic policy, October 1964.

24 BELOW RIGHT: Congratulating the police for their handling of the breakaway anti-Vietman war demonstration which attempted to force its way into the American Embassy in October 1968.

25 ABOVE: President Sadat arriving in London, February 1978. President Carter would usually telephone me as Sadat left Washington and Sadat's London stop-overs gave us a chance to test his reactions to their conversations.

26 BELOW: Helmut Schmidt, Giscard d'Estaing, Jimmy Carter and I discuss cruise and Pershing missiles in a palm-fringed hut in Guadaloupe, January 1979.

27 ABOVE: Anne Armstrong, America's first woman Ambassador to London, accompanies Henry Kissinger to the Foreign Office.

28 CENTRE: Behind Jimmy Carter's famous smile was a man of great earnestness and principle.

29 BELOW: Audrey and I greet Foreign Minister Gromyko and Mrs Gromyko at Heathrow. Her first request was to visit the Tate Gallery.

30 LEFT: At the opening of the Henry Moore Exhibition in Kensington Gardens in October 1978. Helmut Schmidt is a great admirer of Henry Moore's work and one of his sculptures now stands in the garden of the German Chancellery in Bonn.

31 BELOW: Audrey receives gifts of toys for the Great Ormond Street Hospital for Sick Children, of which she was Chairman for fourteen years.

32 RIGHT: Cardiff South East Labour Party marching past Cardiff Castle in 1981 in a demonstration against unemployment. During my time as Member, the constituency party has produced seven Lord Mayors and six Chairmen of the County Council. Two of them, Gordon Houlston and Ken Hutchings, are in the photograph.

33 BELOW: Michael Foot and I, looking concerned at the Brighton Conference in 1979.

34 The family at Chequers on 28 July
    1978 for Audrey's birthday and
    our fortieth wedding anniversary.
    Front row: Margaret Jay, Tamsin Jay,
    Tobin Hubbard, me and Audrey,
    Sam Hubbard, Tom Hubbard and Julia
    Hubbard. Behind: Jennifer Callaghan,
    Kate Callaghan, Alice Jay,
    Ian Hubbard, Patrick Jay, Joanna
    Hubbard, Sarah Callaghan and
    Michael Callaghan. Our tenth
    grandchild, Joe Callaghan, was
    not born until 1981.

retirement of Harold Wilson, the departure of Roy Jenkins and the death of Tony Crosland.

I consulted Michael Foot, as runner-up in the leadership election, about his personal preferences for office. He has a deep affection for Parliament and I was happy to meet his request to become Leader of the House of Commons. Michael and I had never worked together before, but now it was essential that we should do so if our minority Government was to survive. Once you penetrate his shyness, his natural worth and lack of artifice make him an easy man to like. His absence of self-seeking is matched only by his optimistic belief that even the most unworthy colleague has some redeeming trait, a foible which sometimes renders his judgement fallible. His indifference to dress and form does not arise from lack of respect, for he is courteous and considerate of the personal feelings of others. Rather it springs from his unspoken assumption that these are but trappings and that a man should be judged by the sincerity and passion of his convictions. The vividness of his use of language is linked with a mischievous sense of humour and a wide literary knowledge, as he showed shortly after my appointment.

Some left-wing members of the National Executive Committee had been conducting a campaign to try and wrest from my control money that had been voted by Parliament for the use of the Parliamentary Labour Party. This was quite improper and I rejected the demand. While this was going on, Michael pushed a note across the table to me at a meeting where the subject had been raised once again. It was as follows:

P.S. Just recd. 2.35 p.m.

A COINCIDENCE

I have just (this second) read in the latest volume of *Byron's Letters* 1822, 'Your advertisement says, that Mr. L. CALLAGHAN (a queer name for a banker) hath been disposing of money in Ireland sans Authority of the Committee. I suppose it will end in Callaghan's calling out the Committee, the Chairman of which carries pistols in his pocket of course.' There; we wonder what you did with the money. Any further trouble and I'll pass this piece of authentic news on to Norman Atkinson [the Treasurer of the Labour Party].

But apart from his sense of fun, Michael extended to the Government and to me his protection and personal loyalty. There were occasions when he had to swallow his views in order to bolster our position but he never failed to do so. He was a true comrade. Supported as I was by the loyalty of Michael Foot, the ability of Denis Healey and the long-standing friendship of Merlyn Rees, I felt confident in 1976 that we could face the future. From the beginning, I took Michael into my confidence and in our first discussion told him of my objective that the Labour Government should remain in office as long as we could govern effectively and that we should make whatever ad hoc arrangements were necessary to ensure this. I was happy to find he was of the same mind.

There was a vacancy to fill in the Cabinet caused by the appointment of Tony Crosland to the Foreign Office, and this led to further changes. I took a deliberate decision to replace some Ministers in their sixties by younger people who would enjoy some experience of Cabinet even if we should be defeated in the near future. I was influenced by my recollection that in the Wilson Cabinet of 1964 only the Prime Minister himself and one other Minister had previously served in the Cabinet, plus a handful of us who had held junior Ministerial positions. Such a situation is not an insuperable obstacle for a new government but it is an unnecessary handicap to be avoided if at all possible. I therefore asked Willie Ross, Bob Mellish and Barbara Castle, all of whom were over sixty, to pass on the baton.

Only Barbara took it badly. She was a great propagandist for the Party, and I admired her courage and her daunting persistence in overcoming obstacles. She has great intelligence and is one of those rare people who can immediately go to the heart of an argument. But she and I were rarely on the same wave-length. She thought that I lacked ideology, and I thought she sometimes allowed ideology to prevail even when her commonsense and instinct should have told her otherwise. Nor did I think she would wish to be in a Cabinet led by me, but I was apparently mistaken for she made her willingness to stay only too clear. Michael Foot pleaded hard for her. He acknowledged that I had accepted a number of his suggestions for appointment, all of which were from the Tribune Group, but said that these newcomers were more than counterbalanced by my other new appointments. I did not see it in that way.

In my first speech to the Parliamentary Labour Party following my election as Leader I had called, vainly I fear, for organised Party groups to be wound up as I knew that many members of the Party believed that belonging to such a group was the best avenue to promotion. I was anxious to discourage this unhealthy belief and some of my junior Ministerial appointments were made to that end.

I did my work mainly in the Cabinet Room at No. 10, for I liked its

sense of history. It also has the asset of being more airy and less claustro-
phobic than the Prime Minister's study on the first floor, and as the Private
Secretaries live in the next room, it saves their legs. For the first day or
two while I was making governmental changes there was a constant
stream of Ministers coming and going, but once that was complete I sat
back and realised I had nothing to do. Ministers were busy with their
Departmental work; the telephone did not ring for, generally speaking,
people do not telephone the Prime Minister – the Prime Minister telephones them; replies to hundreds of letters of congratulations were being
drafted elsewhere; the Cabinet Secretariat was efficiently arranging the
meetings of Ministerial committees and my next appointment seemed to
be a meeting of the Cabinet in two days' time.

In all my previous Departments Private Secretaries would have arrived
in the room as soon as I set foot in the door, bearing piles of official papers
to read and files with urgent problems for immediate decision. For a brief
period as I sat in the Cabinet Room I savoured the suspicion that as everyone else was doing the Government's work, I could be the idlest member
of the Administration if I was so minded. It was of course an illusion,
although I never went to the other extreme and believed that a Prime
Minister must be a workaholic. There are several instruments at his hand
whose purpose is to ease the load, and provided he understands what can
safely be delegated, and has a politically sensitive network around him to
ring alarm bells before matters go too far wrong in Cabinet, Parliament
or Party, he need not be the hardest worked member of his Government.

In my experience the work-load was greater both as Chancellor and as
Foreign Secretary. To a large extent the Prime Minister makes his own
pace. It is the Prime Minister himself who takes the initiatives, who pokes
about where he chooses and creates his own waves. Ideally he should keep
enough time to stand back a little from the Cabinet's day-to-day work,
to keep in touch with Parliamentary and outside opinion, and to view the
scene as a whole, knowing full well that periods of crisis will occur when
this will be impossible.

The instruments I refer to exist not only to ease the Prime Minister's
load, but are also levers that can be pulled whenever he wishes to take a
decisive hand in events. During my administration they included the
Central Policy Review Staff (the Think Tank); the Policy Unit; the
Private Office; the Political Office; the Press Office; and at the centre,
the Cabinet Office acting as the hub of the wheel. The CPRS Think Tank
under Sir Kenneth Berrill worked closely with the Cabinet Office and

tended to be given long-range social and economic problems to study without a prior political thrust in any direction. It was in the Civil Service but not of it, and had no hesitation in producing well informed, unorthodox opinions and occasionally devastating comments on proposals put forward by the Treasury or some other Department. The Prime Minister had first call on its services and I used it to inform and advise me on current problems such as, for example, the controversy on the best choice of a civilian nuclear reactor.

One of the most successful occasions for its use was the help it gave me to unravel the differing interests of British Aerospace (manufacturing aircraft wings and body), Rolls Royce (aircraft engines) and British Airways (the customer) on whether these three great national enterprises should link up with the American aircraft companies or with the European airbus industry to build the next generation of aircraft. The wish of the three groups to go in different directions had important financial and industrial consequences, and in addition there were political dimensions involving the French, German and American Governments at the highest level. Because of the diverse interests involved, I handled the protracted, top-level negotiations personally, aided by Sir Kenneth Berrill and the Think Tank\which, together with the Departments, teased out the problems and the alternative choices. At the end there was agreement that Britain had secured an excellent all-round deal in this complicated affair and tribute is due to the Think Tank for its backroom work. To my regret, and I believe her loss, the unit was disbanded by Mrs Thatcher.

Another of the Prime Minister's levers was the Policy Unit headed by Dr Bernard Donoughue (now Lord Donoughue), who was my Senior Policy Adviser. This was one of Harold Wilson's effective creations which I was happy to inherit. It was staffed by specialists from outside the Civil Service and was more overtly political than the Think Tank. It provided me with systematic policy analysis distinct from that of the Departments, and thus supported by facts and figures, I was in a stronger position to challenge Departmental proposals – especially those from the Treasury, which usually fired the heaviest guns. I had considerable respect for the Treasury's intellectual fire-power, but I also knew how they could spread confusion in the fog of battle and disperse and destroy their opponents one by one. Bernard Donoughue's task was to clear away the fog. He has a keen political insight and employed his unit for the purpose of what the Americans call an 'overview' of the Government's progress. He helped me in my effort to stand back and view developments as a whole. The unit proposed new initiatives from time to time where gaps existed and would call my attention to inconsistencies in Government policies. Its thinking was unorthodox and refreshing and it had considerable influence when I launched the so-called Great Debate on education.

The Private Office, whose room is the only one that opens directly into the Cabinet Room, is in every sense closer to the Prime Minister than the Think Tank, the Policy Unit or even the Secretary to the Cabinet. It is small in numbers, staffed on secondment by civil servants drawn from a number of Departments, with the Treasury and the Foreign Office always supplying at least one apiece. Normally the Prime Minister is given a list of the high-fliers in the main Departments and he makes his own choice of Private Secretaries from this, often interviewing them personally before they join his staff. Their tasks are limitless, bounded only by the number of hours in the day and the curiosity and energy of the Prime Minister. But a prime task is to sort out essential items for him to consider from the flood of reading matter that reaches the office in the form of Cabinet memoranda, correspondence from colleagues, resolutions from the Party, letters from the public, pleas from industrialists, seekers of honours, foreign telegrams and so on, in a never-ending forest of paper.

The Private Secretaries are the focal point for the Prime Minister's activities: they coordinate his engagements; take responsibility for assembling material for his speeches and usually have an important hand in drafting them; ensure he is properly briefed before Cabinet and other meetings at home and when paying official visits overseas; act as eyes and ears by maintaining a close liaison with other Ministers' Private Offices; act as the link with the Queen's Private Secretary; and act as a filter through which those who wish to see the Prime Minister must pass. They need to be diplomatic enough to pacify the untimely visitor – once it was Earl Mountbatten who received the treatment when he called unannounced at No. 10, choosing a moment when it was impossible for me to see him.

The Private Secretaries are among the few who may walk in to the Prime Minister's room at any time, and if he is wise enough to strike up a trusting relationship with these young men and women, he will benefit greatly by being offered the frank opinions of three or four of the best and most intelligent members of their generation. They understand the mysterious ways of the Whitehall machine and how to make it respond, and are almost certainly destined to rise to the top of their profession. They act as though they share your successes and care about your failures, and as you all face the music together a corporate spirit develops. I place on record my debt to all my Private Secretaries, headed by Sir Kenneth Stowe who like the others has gone on to higher things and is Permanent Secretary at the Department of Health and Social Security. Perhaps the best illustration I can give of our close relationship is that although the No. 10 team has long been dispersed, some serving abroad as Ambassadors or in high positions at home, we still enjoy a regular reunion to renew our friendship and exchange our news. I may add in passing that because I had served in government at periods since 1947 there was a time while I was Prime Minister when no fewer than four Permanent Secretaries and a brace of Ambassadors had acted as my Private Secretary in one Department or another in the past.

Another lever at the Prime Minister's hand is his Political Office. This is made up entirely of non-civil servants recruited from among Party members and paid for by funds that the Prime Minister has to find for himself. This Office was headed by Tom McNally, at one time the Secretary of the International Department of the Labour Party, whom I had recruited while at the Foreign Office and took with me to Downing Street. His task was to maintain constant contact with the officers and National Executive Committee of the Labour Party. He dealt with local constituency parties, and kept in touch with the senior officers of the trade unions. He fulfilled an indispensable liaison role, and made sure I was informed about Party developments, alerted me to signs of dissatisfaction from the National Executive Committee, suggested visits to factories and different areas of the country and generally made certain that in carrying out the absorbing tasks of government I did not overlook the foundation upon which it all rested – namely, the support of the Party in the country.

Tom had a fertile mind, and was adept at ensuring that I was constantly reminded of the party political background against which Ministers' Departmental programmes should be judged. He was very ingenious in suggesting courses of action and then in carrying them through. Naturally the Political Office did not work in isolation either from the Policy Unit or the Private Office, and all of them had close links with the Press Office under Tom McCaffrey. There was much cross-fertilisation and through this we endeavoured to secure an integrated approach, though sometimes there was overlapping. Tom McCaffrey was also an old friend who had been the Press Officer at the Home Office several years earlier during my period there. When we won the election of 1974, I asked the Home Office if he could join me at the Foreign Office and they agreed. Later, he was to come with me to No. 10 and when I left No. 10 he too left and resigned from the public service. I admired his fierce Scottish integrity and his candour, of which I had been the victim when I had been at the Home Office for only a few weeks and he told me bluntly that I was not living up to the high expectations with which the Home Office had greeted me. These traits not only gained him my respect; the press and other media trusted him, for while he sometimes could not tell them the whole truth, he made it a point of principle never to mislead them or lay false trails. It was thanks to him that I enjoyed a less barbed relationship with the press than I might have done, for his patience and modesty were greater than mine. Like the Private Office staff, Tom McCaffrey could see me at all times.

All these levers are directly under the Prime Minister's eye and are very personal to him and his requirements, but there is another and more powerful lever at one stage removed. The conventional role of the Cabinet Office is to serve all members of the Cabinet, but if the Prime Minister chooses, as nearly all of them do, to work closely with the Secretary to the Cabinet, then it becomes an instrument to serve him above the others. Its work has been often described and I will not repeat it here, except to emphasise the importance of its central role in coordinating the work of the Cabinet, which in turn puts it in a powerful position to exert influence over the rest of the Civil Service. The Cabinet Secretary prepares the agenda for Cabinet meetings, so he is in a position to influence what shall be discussed and when, although the final decision rests with the Prime Minister. All papers prepared by Ministers for the Cabinet's considera-tion are first sent to the Cabinet Office for circulation, which in turn gives the Prime Minister the chance to defer it by asking a Minister to think again or alternatively to accelerate its discussion. At iner-Departmental meetings of Civil Servants it is the Cabinet Secretary or one of his assist-ants who will frequently take the Chair, with all the opportunities for in-fluence over the discussion that such a position bestows. And if, as in Mrs Thatcher's Administration, the Cabinet Secretary is also the Head of the Civil Service, the holder of the dual office is in a unique position to shape appointments as well as influence policy and so enables the Prime Minister to control the Government's actions with considerable economy of effort. It is not, however, an arrangement I recommend.

I have set out this catalogue of levers at the Prime Minister's hand because from time to time there is discussion about the need for a formal Prime Minister's Department and such talk frequently overlooks the instruments he already has. He is able to provide himself with his own sources of information; he can send up a trial balloon or fire a sighting shot across a Ministerial bow without directly involving his own authority or publicly undermining that of the Minister; and he has the necessary facilities to take a decisive hand in policy-making at any moment he chooses to intervene.

The establishment of a formal Prime Minister's Department, with the Prime Minister's representatives attending Cabinet Committees, would not only add an unnecessary layer of administration, but could have the political disadvantage, when contentious issues were under discussion, that his or her representatives would be forced to take a line too early and thus restrict room for manoeuvre later on. For, despite current fashion, reconciliation and compromise between contending groups in a well-ordered system of Cabinet Government will continue to be an important function of the Prime Minister, as well as the need to give a clear lead when the occasion demands.

It had been my experience that Ministers usually asked to see the Prime Minister only when they had a personal problem or had run into a difficulty, and I decided to reverse this. So during the early months after I took office, and in pursuit of my intention not to become over-immersed in the Chancellor's economic problems, I invited other Ministers to come to see me individually and without their officials, to tell me about their work. We sat informally in the study at No. 10 and I put to all of them two basic questions. What were they aiming to do in the Department? What was stopping them? I prepared for these chats by asking Bernard Donoughue and his Policy Unit, in conjunction with my Private Office, to prepare an overview of each Department's activities before I saw the Minister, and Bernard would also suggest certain areas for me to probe. I was told later that preparation for these occasions used to cause a flurry of activity in the Department. Officials were naturally anxious to put the best possible face on their work, and the fact that their Minister would be accounting *à deux* to the Prime Minister, who might ask awkward questions if he were well enough informed, added spice and a touch of danger to the meeting. Moreover, it gave Ministers the opportunity to bend my ear and create a favourable climate for their activities. I learned a lot and I believe it made busy Ministers immersed in never-ending Departmental activities pause and think.

One of my earliest visitors was Fred Mulley, the Secretary for Education, whom I asked to see me on 21 May, only a few weeks after my appointment. I have always been a convinced believer in the importance of education, as throughout my life I had seen how many doors it could unlock for working-class children who had begun with few other advantages, and I regretted my own lack of a university education. I was also aware of growing concerns among parents about the direction some schools were taking and I was anxious to probe this.

Many schools had developed experimental methods of learning, more centred on the child and less on the subject. When I visited I saw many happy, alert children far less repressed than I had been and occupying themselves with a wider range of activities. But were they also acquiring skill in handling the basic tools of knowledge they would need in later life? I raised four areas of concern with the Secretary for Education. Was he satisfied with the basic teaching of the three Rs; was the curriculum sufficiently relevant and penetrating for older children in comprehensive schools, especially in the teaching of science and mathematics; how did the examination system shape up as a test of achievement; and what was available for the further education of sixteen- to nineteen-year olds? I told Fred Mulley of my doubts and said that I was considering making a speech on these issues. He undertook to prepare a memorandum on these matters and this reached me in early July.

Meanwhile I had been asked by Billy Hughes, the Principal of Ruskin College, Oxford, to lay the foundation stone for new residential accommodation at the college. Ruskin's purpose is to give adult students who missed out educationally in their youth a second chance. It has left its mark on many men and women, and Jack Lawson's book *A Man's Life* gives a moving account of how he, a Durham miner, raised the funds to go directly from Boldon Colliery in the early years of the century to study at Ruskin for a year, and then returned at the end of that period to work once more in the pit. In due course Jack Lawson had entered Parliament and become Secretary of State for War in the post-war Attlee Government. There were five former Ruskin scholars in my Government, including one Cabinet Member.

Billy Hughes was an old friend of Fabian days. We had climbed together in Snowdonia but after a short period as the Member for Wolverhampton, he left Parliament and became a prominent figure in the adult education world. I wished to recognise his work by proposing him for an honour but he declined. By contrast many less worthy but more self-seeking gathered like wasps around that honey pot. Billy Hughes' invitation to Ruskin fitted well into my plan for a speech on education, and I at once accepted, asking my office to prepare a draft and reminding them that 'education has always been very dear to the Labour Movement, no doubt because of our backgrounds'.

My general guidance for the speech was that it should begin a debate about existing educational trends and should ask some controversial questions. It should avoid blandness and bring out the criticisms I had heard, whilst explaining the value of the teachers' work and the need for parents to be closely associated with their children's schools. It should ask why industry's status was so low in young people's choice of careers, and the reasons for the shortage of mathematics and science teachers.

At this stage I tripped over some appalling educational snobbery – the Secretary of State's memorandum to me had been given to the *Times Educational Supplement*, and they wrote an article that was both scornful and cynical about my intention. It complained that while I was a professional politician I was no more than an amateur educationalist, and doubted the propriety of my raising question on what should be taught and how it was to be taught. It said that I was falling a victim of an attempt by the schools inspectors to gain more control. The *Times Educational Supplement* did not object to a debate, but it should be conducted by those who knew what they were talking about and I should not trespass into this sensitive and professional field. The article concluded by 'suspecting selfish political motives and . . . political demagoguery'.

This article set off a chain reaction in other newspapers and the chalk-dust flew. Norman St John Stevas, the Conservative Education Spokesman, published a not unfriendly open letter to me with some party jibes to garnish it, while the National Union of Teachers issued a statement which combined flattery about my intentions with doubts about my capacity. It was obvious that there was much suppressed questioning which had only needed an accidental trigger to set it off. Part of my aim was already achieved, and the Great Debate I had hoped to launch had left the slipway and entered the water even before I had time to crash the bottle of champagne on its bows. When I went to Ruskin to deliver my speech I was met by a student demonstration against the Government's economic policy, and poor Billy Hughes felt rather embarrassed, but the speech itself had been distributed beforehand and was given wide national publicity by the media, not only in this country but also overseas.

Teachers, I said, must carry parents with them. Industry complained that some school-leavers did not have the basic tools to do the job and many of our best-trained students from university and polytechnics had no desire to join industry. Why was this? Why did so many girls abandon science before leaving school, and why were thirty thousand vacancies in science and engineering at universities and polytechnics not taken up, while the humanities courses were full? Were we sacrificing thoroughness and depth of courses in favour of range and diversity? I favoured a basic curriculum with universal standards. 'The essential tools are basic literacy and numeracy; the understanding of how to live and work together; respect for others; and respect for the individual. This means acquiring basic knowledge, skills and reasoning ability; developing lively inquiring minds and an appetite for further knowledge that will last a lifetime.' The goal of education was 'to equip children to the best of their ability for a lively constructive place in society and also to fit them to do a job of work' and, I emphasised, 'not one or the other, but both'. In today's world there would be fewer jobs for those without skill, and I concluded by asking for a positive response and not a defensive posture in the debate which I hoped would begin.

Since I had first raised the question with Fred Mulley, Shirley Williams had taken over as Secretary for Education in the reshuffle that became necessary following Roy Jenkins' departure to Brussels. She needed time to play herself in, but I suggested she should hold a series of regional conferences with teachers, employers, parents, trade unionists and others. It seemed to me that the Department of Education was pulling at her coat tails and it was spring 1977 before she finished the series of eight regional conferences.

Shirley submitted the first draft of a Green Paper giving her views in May. She was doubtful about including any references to the need for a basic core curriculum, but when I pressed, she agreed. With the active help of Bernard Donoughue and his Think Tank, the Department's rather introverted draft, which addressed itself mainly to educationalists, was broadened to appeal to a wider public. The Liberals, whom we had undertaken to consult, had no major comments, and Shirley personally undertook much of the redrafting and livened up the turgid language of the Green Paper. The Cabinet agreed to publication on 7 July 1977.

A decade later the echoes of the Great Debate can still be heard. It had its impact on the curriculum; it promoted a better understanding between schools and industry; and it affected the teaching of science and mathematics, and led to changes in teachers' training courses. More needs to be done and I regret the slowness of change, but the Ruskin Speech was successful in calling attention to a number of doubts and short-comings in both objectives and practice, and triggered a public interest which has intensified rather than flagged as the years have gone by.

14

The fight to beat inflation and protect sterling – the Cabinet debates the IMF loan – defeat on Devolution

The range of topics coming before a Prime Minister is so wide, his engagements so varied, and the number of interesting people he meets so many that the days pass with the speed of an express train and in recollection some periods are little more than a kaleidoscopic blur. Perhaps Aneurin Bevan had this in mind when he said, 'I never read autobiography: I prefer my fiction straight.' However, certain issues, especially if they are central to the life and morale of the Government and Party, remain vividly in the memory. One such was the state of the economy. It would be tedious to write, and even more to read, a blow-by-blow account of all that took place during my three years at No. 10, but an impressionistic account of how certain events looked from that vantage point may offer an additional dimension to the recorded history of the period.

First, then, the background against which I took office. During the previous two years disastrously high wage settlements of up to 30 per cent had been conceded, but as inflation approached the same level, the trade unions and the British people at last drew back in alarm. There was general understanding that a halt must be called, and Harold Wilson had sent for the unions and with the assistance of Michael Foot had reached a new understanding that excessive wage claims must be abandoned in exchange for a voluntary incomes policy giving a maximum increase of £6 per week for a period of twelve months. This had been widely accepted and there were few industrial disputes, with the result that by April 1976 the country had experienced a remission from the hyper-inflation of earlier years. When I arrived at No. 10 the duration of the agreement with the unions was coming to an end, and we needed a further period of pay restraint to consolidate the anti-inflationary gains and to keep down domestic manufacturing costs. I found that the Chancellor, Denis Healey and Michael Foot had already begun to engage the TUC in discussions for the year that would begin in August 1976.

The second major problem and one that was within the Government's control was the level of public expenditure, which according to Treasury forecasts would require the Government to borrow some £12 billions to finance its expenditure for the year 1976/7. This was too high and the Chancellor had brought the matter to the Cabinet during the winter of 1975. After tough discussion with some sceptical members the Cabinet had agreed to a reduction. It was this decision that led to the scene in the House on Harold Wilson's birthday referred to earlier, when several Labour Members refused to support the Government's expenditure plans.

A third problem was the shaky position of sterling. The Chancellor and the Bank of England had apparently agreed during February 1976 that the exchange rate of sterling, which was then about two dollars to the pound, was unrealistically high and the Bank set out to edge it down, but the manoeuvre got out of hand when foreign exchange dealers realised what was afoot, sterling fell faster and further than was intended, and the Bank of England was forced to spend substantial reserves to hold the exchange rate up.

Here then were the immediate problems: inflation, public expenditure, and sterling, and it is not surprising that my first three invitations to No. 10 were to the Chancellor, to Jack Jones, the Chairman of the TUC Economic Committee and General Secretary of the TGWU, and to Gordon Richardson, the Governor of the Bank of England. I saw the Chancellor first. He gave me a report on the prospects for a further pay agreement with the unions, which ideally he would have liked to be as low as 3 per cent per annum, warned me that inflation would (statistically) be increasing over the next twelve months, and forecast that he would need to restrain the proposed growth in expenditure for 1977/8. I was shocked when he told me how much had been spent by the Bank of England to support the sterling exchange rate since 1 January 1976. Denis added that we might need to make an approach to the IMF during the summer to replace the reserves we had spent, but I did not fully take on board how significant that comment was to become.

I began the conversation by making clear my intention that he and I should work in partnership if the Government, without an effective majority and given the seriousness of the economic situation, was to survive. I asked him to bring to me any major initiative he might wish to take before it went to the Cabinet, and if he and I could then agree, I would back him when such matters came before our colleagues. In proposing this, I had in mind that the Chancellor of the Exchequer is the loneliest man in the Cabinet and needs constant support, because the spending Ministers gang up together to protect their programmes. I also had in mind the Treasury's propensity to 'bounce' Cabinets with entirely new proposals put forward at very short notice, and I intended to protect both Cabinet and myself. Denis welcomed my suggestion and looking back I believe he and I implemented it on all major occasions. Naturally the arrangement had a built-in advantage for him, for he could be sure of having the Prime Minister on his side before the argument began in Cabinet. I also said to Denis that without any intention to interfere with his relations with the Bank of England, I would like to see the Governor at regular intervals to keep myself informed of his views, especially about the international monetary scene in which I had maintained my interest since my own period as Chancellor.

The Governor was my next visitor, on 15 April 1976, and Jack Jones followed him on the same day. It would not have done any of us any harm if they had come together. When I met Gordon Richardson it was uncannily like stepping back twelve years and listening to a record of one of my talks with Lord Cromer when he was Governor. The decline in the sterling rate (it stood at about $1.80) was a direct response to unparalleled uncertainty and loss of confidence. The United States was taking a gloomy view of sterling's future and industrialists were saying that all that appeared to be happening was that a bankrupt nation was selling off its stock. The Government's borrowing requirement was too high and in due course would crowd out investment by the private sector. There was more in the same dispassionate vein, for despite the resemblances in matter, the restrained style was in marked contrast to Roly Cromer's exuberant manner. I agreed with much of what he said, but regarded myself as having been vaccinated against the disease I had christened 'Governor's Gloom', for had I taken it all at face value the only thing to do would have been to throw myself out of an upper-floor window on to the Downing Street pavement.

I told the Governor that I had asked the Chancellor to prepare a detailed appraisal and come forward with any necessary proposals. Perhaps I exaggerate the Governor's pessimism a little, and in fairness I must add that I formed a great respect for Gordon Richardson's knowledge and judgement during our regular meetings, and never hesitated to rely upon him for an unprejudiced professional opinion, even if I did not always accept it.

Jack Jones arrived as the Governor departed. He consistently made it clear in all our contacts that whatever differences might exist on policy his overriding passion was to maintain a Labour Government, and until his retirement and that of Hugh Scanlon, which unfortunately came too close together, the TUC had two leaders of contrasting styles but forming in partnership an amalgam of gritty integrity, strength and subtlety. Jack Jones urged on me the need for simplicity in explaining the Government's anti-inflation programme to the shop floor, and was enthusiastic about my intention to visit a number of union conferences in order to speak directly to the delegates. He warned me that there was no possibility of the TUC agreeing to a wage increase as low as 3 per cent. I knew this was a correct reading but told him at the time and repeated on many occasions subsequently that Britain's competitive position, our capacity to sell our goods abroad and to maintain jobs at home, required the Government to bring down the inflation level to 5 per cent by the end of the Parliament, with all that would imply in increasing productivity and restricting wage increases.

A week or two later I had my first meeting with the TUC General Council and gave a solemn warning that failure to reach an agreement on another round of pay restraints would mean the immediate end of the Government's life. They took me seriously but it did not prevent Jack Jones, Hugh Scanlon and the others from engaging in fierce argument urging the Government to agree to a minimum increase of £3 per week or a 6 per cent increase, whichever was the greater, with a maximum increase of £5 per week.

I marvelled at the stamina and persistence of Michael Foot and Denis Healey in the prolonged discussions which followed and which persisted far into the night. From these they eventually emerged with an agreement for the 1977/8 year of a minimum increase of £2.50 per week or 5 per cent, whichever was the higher, and a maximum increase of £4 per week. The Treasury estimated that the final effect of the agreement would be an increase in the Retail Price Index of 7.5 per cent, which would seem a miracle by comparison with the summer of 1975 when it was as high as 26.5 per cent.

In the final stages both Government Ministers and the TUC were much indebted to Lionel Murray for his patient unravelling of the knots, which included questions raised by the trade unions on the Government's future policy on prices, specific measures to reduce unemployment and pension levels. I welcomed these wide-ranging discussions, which were an essential condition of the Social Contract which had formed the basis of Labour's election manifesto in 1974. It was founded on the idea of government by consent. By it, the trade unions acknowledged that they had a wider loyalty to the community and were not simply seeking to increase their members' wages irrespective of the consequences. The Labour Party in return undertook to consult the unions about social priorities and policies. It had great value for both the unions, the Party and the country.

I found it strange that the final package was better received by the workers directly affected than by some active members of the Labour Party. There were two opposing lines of criticism. The left complained that we had delivered an ultimatum to the TUC to which they had bowed, while on the right there was grumbling that we had handed the economy over to the unions. Neither group was correct. When the issue was put to the test, unions such as the Mineworkers and the TGWU voted strongly in support. In conjunction with other Ministers, I took the case personally to union conferences large and small, and in the process gained an encyclopaedic knowledge of the seaside hotels in which they were held. Finally, a specially convened Trade Union Congress set the seal of approval on the new package with a massive majority in favour.

In retrospect, it was always on the cards that the Government would get such an agreement in the early weeks of my Prime Ministership, so keen were the trade unions to maintain the Government's credibility in office, and also, as Lionel Murray has since said, because they did not doubt that I meant what I said about the Government's future. This was a trump card which I used sparingly and only when I believed it to be true, and the response of the unions was a continuation of loyalty and a hard-headed perception of where their members' true interests lay. It was not until the winter of 1978, by which time some trade union leaders of great experience had retired or died, that the new men who succeeded them opted out. In saying this, I do not underrate the new union leaders' difficulties, for with every year that elapsed the anomalies of a relatively simple incomes policy compounded the difficulty of wage differentials, leading to industrial difficulties. On the political front, the left, which had never subscribed to the Social Contract, blamed it for every ill and for every failure of the Government to respond favourably to impossible demands.

From my earliest experience of Stafford Cripps's attempts at an incomes policy in the late 1940s, I had never been under any illusion about the problem of operating a fair incomes policy in the longer term, and I minuted the Chancellor within weeks of reaching the new agreement in

May 1976, 'We cannot expect a third year of very severe restraint (i.e. August 1977), yet we cannot afford renewed wage inflation.' I asked him to undertake further talks with the TUC about the longer-term future. I cannot be accused of failing to recognise that an incomes policy is a wasting asset, but I can be faulted for not finding a viable alternative before its credibility expired. This problem will continue to haunt Governments, but I find it intolerable that Ministers should be sunk into the cynical complacency of relying on high levels of unemployment to take the edge off aggressive wage claims.

In 1976 it was the conscious decision of the trade unions to stand back which afforded the nation a respite from inflationary wage claims, despite the high level at which inflation was still running. The Government was given a breathing space for the ensuing fifteen months until August 1977, for which tribute is due to the TUC and to the good sense of ordinary trade unionists. As soon as the terms of our agreement had been reported overseas, I was cheered to receive a long telephone call from the German Chancellor in Bonn. I had been at No. 10 for little more than a month and the congratulations he expressed on the pay deal, together with his encouragement for the future, increased my self-confidence, gave me the sense that Helmut Schmidt understood Britain's problems and wanted our country to succeed and also cemented the intimacy that he and I had established whilst I was Foreign Secretary.

It was not unreasonable to suppose that the reduction in inflation which would result from the new pay arrangements would have done something to quieten the agitation about sterling on the foreign exchange markets, but nothing of the sort happened. Gavyn Davies, one of Bernard Donoughue's team who had good contacts in the City, had reported to me on the day I became Prime Minister that sterling holders believed a further devaluation of between 5 and 10 per cent in the value of sterling was inevitable. (Once more, echoes of 1964.) Sterling then stood at $1.84, so a 10 per cent fall would have taken it down to about $1.66 to the pound.

Throughout April and May 1976, despite the pay agreement, the rate continued to fall and by the end of May it stood at no more than $1.70. It seemed to have a self-perpetuating downwards momentum, and there were fears among the experts that the fall would not stop at any level. The Chancellor told me of his concern that the decline would have an adverse effect on costs and inflation, coming as it did so shortly after our agreement with the TUC. There was agreement among the Finance Ministers and central banks of other countries that the downward movement of sterling was a victim of 'the unreasonable exaggeration' of the foreign exchange markets, in the phrase used by Dr Witteveen, the Managing Director of the IMF.

This decline also had an unsettling effect on the currencies of other countries, and in June 1976, in an attempt to arrest the fall in sterling and to avoid their own positions being undermined, the Group of Ten industrial countries offered Britain a short-term loan of $5 billions. The Cabinet decided to accept but I warned them that it should not be represented as a triumph, for it was no more than a repetition of a well-known tactic of amassing a sum of immense magnitude in defence of a currency so that speculators are frightened and genuine holders reassured. For a time the tactic succeeded, but speculators and others soon grasped that the loan was only short-term and Britain would be required to repay it in December 1976. When they digested this, pressure on sterling reasserted itself.

The Chancellor and I were due to attend a meeting of the Industrial Seven called by President Ford in Puerto Rico, and remembering my hopes of a decade earlier when I had discussed with Joe Fowler, the American Secretary to the Treasury, the possibility of converting Britain's unstable short-term sterling liabilities into a stable long-term arrangement, I decided to revive the plan. My idea was to fund the existing short-term liabilities and to spread repayment of them over a longer period into the 1980s. I chose this period with an eye on Britain's future as an oil-rich country. In the summer of 1976 the Government was receiving no revenue from North Sea oil. On the contrary, Britain's balance of overseas payments was being badly affected by the purchase of installations and ships in readiness for its exploitation. It seemed reasonable to me that part of these expected revenues should be used to pay off the sterling debts. I discussed the matter with the Chancellor and suggested that we should use the forthcoming visit to Puerto Rico to explore the prospects with President Ford; Denis agreed with the general objective but preferred that he should first discuss the matter with his opposite number, the United States Secretary to the Treasury, before I took it up with the President and other Heads of Government.

We flew to Puerto Rico in style for I decided it was a good opportunity to show the flag by chartering Concorde to carry us there. The plane was still a novel sight and our flight was the first commercial charter of this magnificent aircraft. It aroused fantastic interest as it came in to land at San Juan. We looked down and saw the roads to the airport jammed with cars and excited onlookers, and the aircrew made certain that the Union Jack was flying prominently. This was the first occasion on which I noticed that flying Concorde results in an almost complete absence of jet lag, and considering the great pressure to which Heads of Government are subject and how they frequently embark on important talks within an hour or two of landing after travelling three or four thousand miles, it would probably be better for us all if they used Concorde whenever possible.

On the day after our arrival the Chancellor reported to me that he had engaged the American Secretary to the Treasury in talks about replacing the $5 billion loan with new long-term arrangements but had been rather discouraged. Exchanges that take place among officials of central banks and treasuries of various countries are sometimes as important and, on occasion, more important in creating a general climate of opinion than the discussions of their political chiefs. On this occasion I was not satified that at an official level in the Treasury or in the Bank my proposal was pursued with sufficient enthusiasm or ingenuity, although I must add that there was a further complication in that both President Ford and Chancellor Schmidt were shortly due to face elections, and at such times Governments are disinclined to undertake big new decisions.

Puerto Rico was not a memorable meeting and we left without making any progress on the long-term stabilisation plan. The psychological moment passed, and pressure on sterling continued spasmodically throughout the summer months. The Bank used the short-term $5 billion loan for its intended purpose of repelling these attacks, but it became clear that when the time for repayment arrived in December 1976 we would need a long-term credit from the IMF. However, I did not give up the idea of providing a firmer footing for Britain's sterling liabilities, and returned to it later at the time of the IMF negotiations, with some success.

We usually spend the month of August at the farm, helping to get the harvest. It is a combination of physically tiring work, long hours, frustration when it rains or the machinery breaks down, an atmosphere of expectation as the first cut arrives at the grain bins and is judged for quality and yield, a growing feeling of satisfaction as successive fields are cleared, and of immense fulfilment as the final trailer-load is tipped in the barn, marking the completion of twelve months' work. Then a short period to walk the stubble in empty fields before beginning the autumn cultivations for next year's harvest. The rhythm of the seasons meets a deep-felt need.

August 1976 was the year of the drought. The harvest was easy but light, some wheat and barley died in the ear, there was little fodder, the grass dried up, turned brown and even crackled underfoot in the baking heat. As this was my first few months as Prime Minister, I was quite content to stay near London to keep an eye on things while Ministers took a well-earned holiday. But it had been an ambition of mine to travel across Canada from coast to coast, inspired by boyhood reading of accounts of the building of the Canadian National Railway and the Canadian Pacific. I had mentioned this to Pierre Trudeau when we met at Puerto Rico and he had at once proposed that I use a Canadian Government plane so that we would have more time to see his vast country. I immediately accepted and set aside ten days in September, but unfortunately the start was delayed because of a seamen's strike accompanied by the inevitable press photographs reproduced around the world showing British ports with empty wharves and gaunt cranes unmoving against the sky. I was eventually able to set off but as the detailed programme could not be rearranged, we were forced to forego the first stage of the adventure and never reached Vancouver, which I particularly wanted to see.

We began our tour in Alberta where we were thrilled by the beauty of the incomparable Lake Louise, set against the background of the Rocky Mountains, and where, sitting on straw bales, we were served the largest and most tender barbecued steaks I have ever eaten. From there we flew across the apparently never-ending great plains to Regina, and then on again to resume old friendships in Toronto and Ottawa. We journeyed through the beauty of the autumnal reds and gold of Quebec and finally reached the rocky shores of Nova Scotia. On our journey we talked with oilmen in Alberta, with cattlemen and farmers, industrialists and politicians, and fishermen on the Atlantic coast.

In a friendly gesture, the Canadian Government kindly dedicated and named the Callaghan Trail to commemorate my visit, and I still have an unfulfilled ambition to walk its eight-kilometre length up the Gros Morne Mountain on the West Coast of Newfoundland. I may interpose here that some years later, shortly after I had left office, I undertook a similar visit to Australia. Malcolm Fraser, the Prime Minister, invited me to give a series of lectures which were arranged so that once again I visited every part of the Australian Continent from Perth to Sydney and Hobart to the Great Barrier Reef, as well as many places in between. This also was an unforgettable experience, and these two visits are among my happiest and permanent memories of what is called the 'Old Commonwealth'.

At about the time of my Canadian visit, the Bank of England, with the Chancellor's agreement, decided not to re-purchase further sterling in support of the exchange rate. Harold Wilson had agreed to do so at the Rambouillet Summit Conference of the Industrial Seven the previous November, as our contribution to international monetary cooperation, but despite massive intervention by the Bank since March 1976, pressure on sterling had continued spasmodically and at times very heavily indeed. The Bank's policy had been to hold the rate at about $1.77 and they succeeded in doing so for several months only by dint of using the $5 billion loan.

The Chancellor and the Governor of the Bank were both worried about the effects of stopping the support of sterling. They feared that the rate would fall heavily, and in the short run prices would increase (especially of imported raw materials and semi-manufactured goods) and give another upward twist to inflation.

The foreign exchange markets might become very disorderly once it became known that the Bank had ceased to support sterling, and sterling might settle at a much lower level, though no one could say how low. On the other hand, the reality was that as soon as the Bank repaid the $5 billion loan, it simply would not have the resources to sustain sterling at $1.77. This seemed to both the Chancellor and me to be conclusive, but the Governor was less certain and would have preferred to continue to support the rate, at the same time introducing a system of import deposits (which would have required legislation), and taking tough action to correct our underlying balance of payments deficit.

There was no disagreement between us about the last point. The Chancellor had produced new forecasts which showed a balance of payments deficit of about £3 billions for 1977, and given the size of our earlier borrowings, I had no doubt that the Government must take the necessary action to reduce this.

Another piece of bad news was that the forecasts now showed a Public Sector Borrowing requirement of some £10.5 billions for 1977/8, a substantial increase of £1.5 billions on the reduced figure of £9 billions that Denis had announced as recently as July. Such figures could not be disguised even if we had resolved to do so – and I did not, for the nation should not be allowed to live in blinkered ignorance. The only doubt in my mind, borne of previous experience, was how far to trust the figures.

They were, after all, no more than forecasts, and despite the care with which they were produced, were not nearly as reliable as the weather maps on our television screens. But Chancellors must have some landmarks to guide them and if there are none other then for better or worse, and with all due scepticism, forecasts must be treated as the best signposts they have. The Chancellor's conclusion earlier in the summer of 1976 had been that after taking into account all the factors, such as the levels of activity – savings, taxation, private investment and so on – the figure of £9 billions was about the right level for Government borrowing for the following year, and after some difficulty we had persuaded the Cabinet to accept the necessary reduction in their programmes to enable him to keep, as we had thought, within that figure.

He had acted on the best information available at the time, and it was particularly aggravating that only three months later he should need to go back to the Cabinet and tell Departmental Ministers that on the basis of the latest forecasts they would need to reduce their own future programmes once again by a further £1.5 billions. Nevertheless, with the experiences of the previous years in my mind my top priority was to continue to bring down inflation from the insupportably high and corrosive level of over 20 per cent in the spring of 1976, and I agreed with the Chancellor that if we were to succeed Government borrowings must not exceed £9 billions for the following year. Action was needed on two fronts.

First, as Denis had earlier foreseen, we would need to apply to the IMF in the late autumn for a standby credit sufficient to finance the expected deficit of £3 billions in Britain's trading and other accounts with overseas countries for 1977. Second, we must review the Government's own future expenditure once again, to reduce it by about £1.5 billions.

Recalling my own negotiations as Chancellor in 1964 with Pierre-Paul Schweitzer, the French Managing Director of the International Monetary Fund, I expected the Chancellor to have little difficulty with his successor. Schweitzer had told me then – in his charming Maurice Chevalier accent – that all he needed 'was a nice little letter'. But when Denis began his discussions in November 1976, he found that times had changed and the examination of our affairs was much more rigorous. On the other hand, neither of us was under any illusion about the adverse impact of further public expenditure reductions on the Cabinet and the Party. The Party argued that the country's social needs required a high level of expenditure, and I could not disagree. But it was necessary to cut back, even if we were embarking on an exercise fraught with pain, indeed one which the Government might not survive. I had no doubt that if the Labour Party was to fulfil its responsibilities as a Party of government, its leaders must not shrink from telling the truth as we saw it, and then act accordingly.

I took the first opportunity of doing so in my Annual Report to the Labour Party Conference at Blackpool on 28 September 1976. This was to be my first appearance before the Conference as Party Leader and I intended to put my views as clearly as possible. This might be my only chance to do so as Prime Minister if the Government did not survive the forthcoming debate on the Queen's Speech.

At the general election two years earlier, during the wretched three-day week, we had told the nation that it faced the most serious crisis since the end of the Second World War. Since then the Social Contract had brought a period of industrial peace, in place of the strife and strikes the Labour Government had inherited – but at a price. The autumn of 1976 was not the time for renewed confrontation between workers and employers, and nor could the Government continue to cash cheques at the existing rate. The TUC and the Labour Party were both impatient for results, and there was pressure to stimulate a consumption-led boom and for import controls. In a period of high unemployment I did not believe either would work except in the very short term. Previous experience showed that the action of stimulating consumption led to higher imports rather than to higher domestic production and would make the balance of payments even worse than the £3 billions deficit already forecast for 1977. The other remedy, of a general restriction of imports, would have been an even harsher policy than our existing course, for it would have meant cutting the standard of living. Selective import controls to combat subsidised and unfair competition were a different matter, and I was ready to consider them on their merits.

I had explained this to the TUC General Council when they came to see me in Downing Street before they went to their annual Congress at the beginning of September 1976. They had pressed me for a wide range of import controls and for an unemployment target of 600,000 by 1978 – a figure that was unrealistic. I knew they would have difficulty in explaining the position to the delegates, but I was very heartened by their private understanding and when the Congress itself met, it agreed that a wages free-for-all must be avoided, although this was qualified by saying that the wages round, beginning the following August 1977, should be regarded as part of a planned return to free collective bargaining. I knew that the Chancellor's unpublished view was that the Government's objective for that round was an increase of 5 per cent. However the Government could look forward to several months of cooperation on the wages front before difficulties would arise. As I saw it, the country needed action on two fronts.

First, long-term, intelligent cooperation between both sides of industry and the Government to build a modern manufacturing sector by enabling it to make sufficient profit to invest in new technology and plant with confidence, with back-up from the National Enterprise Board and the industrial strategy which had been agreed with the CBI and the TUC.

Second, in the short term, to harmonise the creation of wealth with the fair distribution of wealth. Public expenditure had increased to the point where it was being financed by overseas borrowing, a state of affairs that could not continue.

An enlightened industrial management was required which would take the workforce into its confidence and give them a real sense of joint responsibility for carrying through the things that needed to be done. We needed also to close the gap between education and industry. I was waiting for a report from the Committee on Industrial Democracy whose Chairman was Lord Bullock, and I hoped this would help create a framework of joint responsibility.

With all this as background, I asked my team to produce a speech for the Labour Party Conference along these lines and they succeeded. In particular Peter Jay, whom I consulted, produced one paragraph that made the fur fly. Here is an extract from what I said on Tuesday morning, 28 September 1976, at Blackpool.

> For too long, perhaps ever since the war, we postponed facing up to fundamental choices and fundamental changes in our society and in our economy. That is what I mean when I say we have been living on borrowed time. For too long this country – all of us, yes this Conference too – has been ready to settle for borrowing money abroad to maintain our standards of life, instead of grappling with the fundamental problem of British industry. Governments of both parties have failed to ignite the fires of industrial growth in the ways that countries with very different political and economic philosophies have done. Take Germany, France, Japan – different countries, different philosophies. We are, as you know, still borrowing money. But this time we are not borrowing – if the Government continues on its present course – to pay for yet another short-lived consumer boom of the kind which used to buy success at the polls (or so we are told), but which never bought success in the world's markets or at

the work place. We are borrowing now partly to pay for our high investment in the North Sea. We are borrowing, too, because other industrial
nations volunteer credits, so that our strategy and our proposals for re-
generating British industry need not be thwarted by short-term speculative movements of sterling balances – a load we have still been unable to
shed. We are determined that this borrowing will be used to act and to
press on with the task of rebuilding a regenerated manufacturing industry.
This time we are not going for a consumer boom on borrowed money:
we are going to invest it in our future.

The cosy world we were told would go on for ever, where full employment would be guaranteed by a stroke of the Chancellor's pen, cutting
taxes, deficit spending – that cosy world is gone. Yesterday, delegates
pointed to the first sorry fruits: a high rate of unemployment. The rate
of unemployment today – there is no need for me to say this to you –
cannot be justified on any grounds, least of all the human dignity of those
involved, but, Mr Chairman and Comrades, still less did I become the
Leader of our Party to propound shallow analyses and false remedies
for fundamental economic and social problems. When we reject unemployment as an economic instrument – as we do – and when we reject also
superficial remedies, as socialists must, then we must ask ourselves un-
flinchingly: what is the cause of high unemployment? Quite simply and
unequivocally it is caused by paying ourselves more than the value of
what we produce. There are no scapegoats. This is as true in a mixed
economy under a Labour Government as it is under capitalism or under
communism. It is an absolute fact of life which no Government, be it left
or right, can alter. Of course, in Eastern Europe you cannot price yourself
out of your job, because you cannot withdraw your labour. So those
Governments can at least guarantee the appearance of full employment.
But that is not the democratic way.

We used to think that you could spend your way out of a recession and
increase employment by cutting taxes and boosting Government spending. I tell you in all candour that that option no longer exists, and that
insofar as it ever did exist, it only worked on each occasion since the war
by injecting a bigger dose of inflation into the economy, followed by a
higher level of unemployment as the next step. Higher inflation followed
by higher unemployment. We have just escaped from the highest rate of
inflation this country has known; we have not yet escaped from the consequences: high unemployment. That is the history of the last twenty
years. Each time we did this, the twin evils of unemployment and inflation have hit hardest those least able to stand them. Not those with the
strongest bargaining power, no, it has not hit those. It has hit the poor,
the old and the sick. We have struggled, as a Party, to try to maintain

their standards, and indeed to improve them, against the strength of the
free collective bargaining power that we have seen exerted as some people
have tried to maintain their standards against this economic policy.

Now we must get back to fundamentals. First, overcoming unemployment now unambiguously depends on our labour costs being at least
comparable with those of our major competitors. Second, we can only
become competitive by having the right kind of investment at the right
kind of level, and by significantly improving the productivity of both
labour and capital. Third, we will fail – and I say this to those who have
been pressing about public expenditure, to which I will come back – if
we think we can buy our way out by printing what Denis Healey calls
'confetti money' to pay ourselves more than we produce.

My speech was quoted extensively and approvingly throughout Europe
and America, and more recently has been misused by Conservative
spokesmen to justify their malefactions in refusing to increase public
expenditure at a time of recession, of low investment and low inflation, and
of record levels of jobless. I see no reason to retract a single word of what
I then said. The passage I have quoted does not say that Governments
should never increase public expenditure or reduce taxation as methods
of boosting employment. My argument was that in the circumstances of
1976 these measures were not appropriate, nor were they an alternative
to facing up to the long-term changes that were required in our economy
and in our society. I am no theologian in monetary doctrines, but I was
always prudent in economic affairs, and agreed with a view expressed by
Bernard Donoughue that 'certain monetary disciplines were essential to
good economic management, and conversely that monetary laxity would
undermine the foundations of sustained economic growth'.

I had an unwelcome beginning to the day on which I was to make my
speech to the Party Conference. Sterling had been under attack for several
days as a bout of nerves hit the foreign exchange markets in anticipation
of what might happen at the annual gathering of the IMF, which was due
to take place in Hong Kong at the same time as the Labour Party Conference in Blackpool. The Chancellor had been due to leave for Hong
Kong on the morning of 28 September, but when he reached Heathrow
the news of the early morning's trading was so horrid that he thought I
should know and telephoned me just as I was about to leave the hotel to
deliver my speech to the Conference.

At the beginning of September, the sterling/dollar rate had stood at
about $1.77, but by 25 September it had fallen to $1.63. Denis told me

that Bank of England experts were forecasting gloomily that sterling would continue to fall at about one cent a day as low as $1.50 and no one could tell whether it would then stop. He said the Bank was considering selling a large number of dollars to support the sterling rate, and he was uncertain whether he and the Governor of the Bank should leave for the Far East at such a moment. My view was that if staying in London would make the situation easier, he should do so, but I said I was not in favour of spending a substantial sum from the reserve to bolster a falling rate. The Cabinet had already given authority for an application to be made to the IMF later in October for a stand-by credit, and I asked him whether a public announcement to this effect would help to steady sterling. If not, I would prefer to sweat it out. Denis was not keen to announce an application to the IMF whilst the Hong Kong meeting was in progress, but said he would think about it again. I should have encouraged the Chancellor to go to Hong Kong, for as soon as the City learned that he had decided not to go, hysterical panic set in for forty-eight hours. The markets behaved with all the restraint of a screaming crowd of schoolgirls at a rock concert. At such moments the wildest rumours are flashed around the world and gain credence with each repetition, every action by the authorities has the worst interpretation put on it, and normally sane individuals take leave of their senses.

I had lived through it before and by this time was case-hardened, and although concerned, I was not nearly as anxious as I would have been in the 1960s, for I knew the situation must stabilise in due course. My principal worry was the depression caused by the doom-laden headlines in the newspapers, and the effect of the funereal tones of the radio and television announcers on the public and on the nerves of some of my Cabinet colleagues, whilst the Opposition naturally had a field day. After reflection, Denis decided to announce the Government's decision to apply to the Fund for a stand-by credit of about £2.3 billions which would go some way towards financing the expected £3 billion deficit in Britain's 1977 balance of payments. His announcement had a steadying effect on the markets almost at once.

One unexpected result of the gloom and doom headlines was a most remarkable intervention by George Meany, the President of the AFL/CIO, the American Trade Union Movement, who in a letter to President Ford during the height of the storm called on the Government of the United States to assist 'America's oldest and most steadfast friend in the world'. In part, the letter read:

As the world's leading free and democratic power, the United States must move forcefully now, as it did when the United Kingdom stood alone in the face of military disaster in World War II and in the post-war period, and place our strength and resources in the balance on the side of Britain. I urge you to declare, as strongly as possible, that the full faith and credit of the United States stands behind the British people in this crisis. I further urge that you direct the appropriate agencies of your Administration to proceed at once in consultation with the British Government, to devise and initiate concrete measures in the form of whatever guarantees, loans, or other programs of aid that may be required to overcome this emergency and to restore confidence in the future of the British economy, so that the United Kingdom may resume its proper role as a great asset to the universal cause of human progress and freedom.

George Meany sent a copy of this letter to me and I was immensely moved by this spontaneous expression of goodwill. I decided to tell President Ford and Chancellor Schmidt how I saw the situation, and so whilst the delegates at the Party Conference were debating, I remained in my suite at the Imperial Hotel and made some international telephone calls. I did not detain Helmut for long, as he was in the midst of a general election, but he volunteered that if he won, he would come to London at once to talk things over – an offer I gratefully accepted. A fortnight later he spent the weekend of 10 October with me at Chequers.

President Ford's election was still several weeks away but he also had begun campaigning when I called him. He greeted me with, 'Jim, you made a helluva speech yesterday.' I was surprised that he had heard of it so quickly, but his later comments showed that he must at least have read a précis, which was an indication of the stir that events in the London foreign exchange markets were making in Washington, Paris, Bonn, Frankfurt and Tokyo. I explained that we needed two things. First, an early intimation that a stand-by loan would be forthcoming from the International Monetary Fund. Second, I reverted to my King Charles' head: sterling needed long-term protection against the volatility arising from the low ratio of our reserves compared with the much larger overseas holdings of sterling. In other words, we needed a safety net.

Gerald Ford readily undertook to do everything in his power to be helpful on both matters. He knew of the Chancellor's intention to take further action to improve our balance of payments and to reduce the public sector borrowing requirement, but he raised one more serious point.

PRESIDENT: 'Are you contemplating import restrictions?'

PRIME MINISTER: 'Not at the moment, but this is the alternative strategy that is being dangled in front of people.'

PRESIDENT: 'We would have reservations, and hopefully, Jim, you could avoid the trade limitation.'

PRIME MINISTER: 'If the alternative strategy were adopted it would call into question Britain's role as an Alliance partner which I am anxious to preserve.'

PRESIDENT: 'We certainly need you standing tall and strong, and I assure you, Jim, I will work with you on that.'

I never had cause to doubt Gerald Ford's word or his good faith. It may seem strange that a Republican President and a Labour Prime Minister could work so confidently with each other. The reason was that although the President was a quintessentially loyal member of his Party and I was of mine, we both accepted that the interests of our two countries and of the Alliance transcended political differences. Since those days our feelings of mutual respect have grown into friendship. Unfortunately, when he lost the Presidential Election to Jimmy Carter on 2 November, his influence quite naturally waned, at the time when we most needed his help.

I knew there would be renewed pressure from a sector of the Parliamentary Labour Party and also from the TUC for import controls, which were being peddled by some circles on the left as a specifically socialist alternative strategy. I attempted to counter this impression in my Conference speech, reminding the delegates that on a previous occasion when they had been introduced, in the 1930s, it was by a Government with an overwhelming Conservative majority. In short, there was nothing in their ideological pedigree; their introduction should be considered only on its merits.

This did not dispose of the argument which was to recur a number of times in Cabinet discussions during the negotiations with the IMF. We had to decide how to handle the IMF team, and the Chancellor began to prepare for this as soon as he returned from the Party Conference. He and I knew he would face a restive Cabinet. Ministers had agreed to reductions in their future public expenditure as recently as July, and they were 'justified' in assuming that what they had then agreed would put the Government back on course. In addition, another cause of pain was that although the incomes policy was working, it had not yet had time to slow down the rise in prices and there was dissatisfaction among our supporters in the country. There was also some grumbling to the effect that the Government was being pushed from pillar to post, that the economy was bleeding to death, and that protectionism was necessary to restore a coherent strategy for recovery. Although sterling had steadied after the Chancellor had announced his intention of negotiating a loan with the IMF, it was still in a fragile state and loose chatter abounded.

At that time I regret to say I received well authenticated reports that a prominent front-bench Conservative spokesman, who has since served in Mrs Thatcher's Cabinet, was in Washington trying to influence the Administration very strongly against the Labour Government. Despite this, however, Helmut Schmidt, who had recently returned from the States and knew of the incident, told me that both President Ford and Henry Kissinger were sympathetic to our efforts, but that William Simon, the Secretary to the Treasury, and Arthur Burns, the Governor of the Federal Reserve Bank, were unhelpful.

Helmut Schmidt had offered me his friendly advice from the outset. He believed the trade unions' restraint on pay had been a significant element in the right direction, but he also held the view that further steps were necessary in budgeting and currency policy. We talked the matter over together during his promised weekend visit to Chequers following his election victory. We sat together in the historic Long Gallery in front of a blazing log fire. Outside, the cattle were picking at the grass, and in the distance I could hear the plough at work.

I enquired what help Germany could give to assist the long-term stability of Britain's overseas sterling holdings, and in reply Helmut Schmidt unfolded the picture of the German currency reserves. They were largely held in dollars and financed the American deficit, a subject on which he was lengthily and disapprovingly vocal. If Germany were to recall part of her dollar reserves this, together with similar assistance from the United States and one or two other countries, would make it possible to devise a plan that would offset the instability of the sterling overseas balances, and bring much-needed relief. He promised to follow up this idea with the Americans, and did so, but once more we were foiled on the political front by the hiatus that arose following President Ford's defeat on 2 November. On the technical front, in the labyrinth of the Central Banks and the Treasury, there was never any real enthusiasm for such a solution. They used the excuse that they wished the completion of the IMF negotiations to take place first. These officials were so short-sighted that they were unable to understand that the announcement of such a scheme would have made these negotiations more acceptable and enabled us to conclude them with less political difficulty.

Three days after the American election result, when these matters had come to a complete halt, I had a long telephone conversation with the German Chancellor. From this emerged an unexpected offer that was to be of tremendous reassurance during the difficult weeks that followed. It was this. Without any request or prompting from me, Helmut Schmidt said he felt Germany must be ready to act when required, in order to make the British Government feel a little more secure. Therefore, on a personal basis, he undertook that if ever an acute danger of necessity should arise, Britain could draw upon Germany within twenty-four hours, and the German Government would make whatever improvised arrangements were necessary.

He explained that as he headed a Coalition Government he would find it necessary to clear this understanding with his partners, and he had already begun to explain something of the situation to them, so that there would be fuller understanding if such a step were ever required. Since he had asked me to regard this assurance as a personal one, I told only the Chancellor and then arranged for the Secretary to the Cabinet, Sir John Hunt, to pay a private visit to Bonn in order that both sides should be clear about what would be done if we ever needed his preferred assistance. During the weeks that followed, this tangible expression of his confidence and support was a tremendous reassurance.

One of our difficulties about securing a safety net for sterling was a suspicion in the IMF that if we acquired such a safety net, we would not reduce Public Sector Borrowing. I had met the leader of the IMF team at the Chancellor's request and informed him this was incorrect but I am not certain he believed me, although both Gerald Ford and Helmut Schmidt did. In an attempt to remove this impression, I asked Harold Lever to go to Washington to talk to the American Treasury, the IMF and the Federal Reserve Bank. I telephoned President Ford in Washington to ask him to receive Harold.

His voice was still a little husky, recovering from having lost it completely at the end of his gruelling election campaign. I enquired how he was feeling and he told me that he intended to leave Washington for good as soon as Jimmy Carter took over in the following January. He would move out to the West where the climate would improve Mrs Ford's health. I did not know it at the time but this was to lead to some happy consequences for Audrey and me. In due course Gerald Ford built a new home at Beaver Creek, high up in the beautiful Rocky Mountain state of Colorado, and every year since I ceased to be Party Leader Audrey and I have visited them, making new friends and strengthening our own friendship.

The President at once agreed to my request to receive Harold Lever, but his authority was inevitably waning and despite Harold's skill at presentation and his persuasiveness, supported by help from Henry Kissinger, he could not break down the opposition of the United States Treasury, nor of Arthur Burns who was adamant and refused point-blank to participate in any talks about a safety net until the IMF talks were completed.

During my own conversation with the IMF, I had indicated my idea of an appropriate settlement. I had previously agreed with the Chancellor that we could not sustain the most recent forecast of a borrowing require-ment of more than £10 billions for 1977/8, but I was not willing to go below the £9 billions that the Cabinet had agreed as recently as July, as that seemed a reasonable figure. But the health of the domestic economy and the confidence of foreign investors required that the Government should take the steps necessary to validate the figure of £9 billions, and this I was ready to do.

The Treasury had told us earlier that sticking to this target should enable the economy to move back into balance, and had even forecast a small surplus in the United Kingdom's overseas balance of payments in 1978, by which year North Sea oil would be flowing, with the prospect of a massive favourable turn-round in our balance of payments in the 1980s. In the meantime the incomes policy was about to bring down the rate of inflation, and in addition I had hopes that we would begin to see results from the cooperation of the CBI and TUC in working out the industrial strategy to which both sides had agreed, with beneficial effects on pro-ductivity and efficiency, supplemented by the work of the National Enterprise Board and the Scottish and Welsh Development Agencies. The seed had been planted, but the harvest was some way ahead and everyone was impatient for quick results. The country needed a breathing space, and I was ready to go with the IMF as far as was necessary to restore validity to our July estimate, but no lower.

The IMF took this badly and the Chancellor and I had to decide what to say to Cabinet. My aim was to keep the Government intact by prevent-ing any Ministerial resignations; second, to keep the Party together by making clear that as we had no Parliamentary majority, failure to support the conclusions the Cabinet would eventually reach would mean defeat in the House and a general election; and third, to avoid a break with the TUC which would have destroyed the Social Contract.

This was my first real test as Prime Minister and Leader of the Party. The Cabinet was divided and deeply suspicious of the IMF, and their doubts would speedily become known to the Parliamentary Party and the TUC. It would have been best if we could have reached a quick decision, but I knew this would not be possible if we were to remain together, so by instinct more than by rational judgement I decided not to bring matters to a head but to allow time to work and Ministers to become familiar with the problems, with the arguments and with the possible solutions.

There were many occasions in the lifetime of the Government when on particular issues I did not hesitate to express my views clearly and, some of my colleagues might think, too bluntly. But throughout the IMF negotiations I was determined to carry all my colleagues with me, and so although I knew how far I was ready to go to secure agreement with the IMF, I saw no advantage in making my position clear at an early stage. The best way to guide the Cabinet towards a united conclusion in the face of their deeply held opposing views was not to suppress Ministers' unhappiness or attempt to bludgeon them but to bring everything out into the open.

Accordingly I opened the Cabinet Meeting of 18 November 1976 by offering my view that the Government was at a critical phase in its life. The Chancellor had been given a tight mandate in his negotiations, and would enter into no agreement with the IMF unless he secured the approval of his colleagues. I had seen the leader of the IMF team to make sure they understood this political dimension. The Cabinet would receive regular reports of the negotiations as they progressed. I warned Ministers that they would need to be on call for as many meetings as might prove necessary, and must make these their first priority. I said that I knew different views were held by my colleagues and I was agreeable that any alternative strategy should be placed before the Cabinet, but I warned that while the negotiations proceeded, it was in all our interests that we should appear to remain united in public, or we might find ourselves arguing for our preferred alternatives from the Opposition benches when the Government was brought down.

Among the different views I referred to, some Ministers, like Shirley Williams at Education and David Ennals at Social Services, were obviously concerned to protect their cherished programmes. Tony Crosland, the

Foreign Secretary, an intellectual heavyweight with sufficient firepower
to take on the Chancellor, argued that there was no economic case for
cutting back on our forward plans. The Government's existing strategy
was working and should be given more time. He concluded that the IMF
could not risk denying us a loan, because to do so would push Britain
into a seige economy accompanied by protectionism.

Tony Benn, the Secretary for Energy, argued that we should voluntarily embrace some form of protection through import quotas, controlled
industrial investment and compulsory planning agreements with companies. He would seek the prior agreement of the IMF to this course in
the expectation that if it was forthcoming the International Monetary
Fund would then agree the loan, and so ensure the success of the Government's re-industrialisation plans.

I was personally unconvinced that either scenario would work, but it
was clear that one or other of these courses appealed to several Ministers,
and opinions began to crystallise around the alternatives. News reached
me that two groups were intending to hold separate meetings outside the
Cabinet to plan their next moves.

Neither group made its existence known to me directly, but it is surprising how much information filters through to Downing Street and
I had a fair idea of the state of play. The two groups were distinct, and
I am sure their motivations were good, but they were playing a dangerous
game which I determined to circumvent. It was apparent that if the two
groups were to coalesce the Chancellor would not have a majority in
support of his negotiating stance. He was very hard-pressed throughout
this period and I did not know what his reaction might be if the Cabinet
overturned him. At a pinch we could afford to lose the Secretary for
Energy, or in extremis even the Foreign Secretary, but the Government
would not have survived the resignation of the Chancellor.

The best possibility of avoiding this was to set aside other business and
bring the arguments into the heart of the Cabinet. I proposed to my
colleagues that those Ministers who had doubts about our present policy
should put their views and their alternative courses of action on paper
and send them to me. I would arrange for these to be circulated to all their
colleagues, and ensure that they were fully discussed. Several Ministers,
including those leading the two main dissenting groups, took me at my
word. I was grateful, for this action prevented the growth of any suspicion
that might have developed if rumours had continued to circulate that
cabals were plotting their own courses outside the Cabinet.

The strain on Ministers was considerable. In addition to running their Departments, visiting their constituencies and constant attendance on Parliament, I called them to nine long Cabinet Meetings in a period of three weeks. Every paper submitted by a Minister was placed on successive Cabinet agendas. I would begin by inviting the Chancellor to report on the present state of his negotiations, and after questions to him would call upon the Minister who had submitted a paper to speak on it. He would then be subjected to pretty severe questioning by his colleagues, as well as by the Chancellor and myself, and in answering would find himself forced to justify his arguments and rethink his position. At no stage did I disclose my own hand beyond reiterating that the Cabinet's international credibility depended on sticking to the July borrowing target of £9 billions, but it was noticeable how, under the force of prolonged questioning and argument, Ministers gradually began to adjust their positions.

Tony Crosland was brought to acknowledge that we were dealing partly with an issue of market confidence, but for some time he would not accept that we must act to shore it up. For me, the issue was not in doubt. We had to repay $1.6 billions on 9 December. We were running a large current account deficit on overseas transactions that we would need to finance in 1977, probably to the tune of a further £3 billions, and oil revenues from the North Sea would not begin to accrue until 1978 or 1979. I accepted the Chancellor's argument that while the IMF loan was necessary, it was less important than the favourable impact its existence would have on the market. If there was no loan, there would be no return of confidence. Therefore our task was to keep the IMF from driving us below the £9 billions target we had all agreed on the previous July, but we must also be ready to make the necessary reductions that were needed to keep to that figure.

At this time President Perez of Venezuela arrived in London for an official visit. Venezuela was a founder member of OPEC, and I was eager for talks with him, though I found it difficult to give him the full attention he deserved. The Queen readily agreed that he should be entertained at Buckingham Palace, and the Foreign Secretary and I were bidden to dinner with other guests. Away from the atmosphere of Whitehall I took the opportunity to have a further quiet word with Tony Crosland about the IMF, and after dinner we sat down together in the Picture Gallery. I said that although I had not fully shown my hand in Cabinet, I wanted him to know my views, which I then explained. I said I recognised his intellectual difficulty with our policy – indeed I shared some of his reservations, but supposing his tactics turned out to be wrong? He might think the Government would be in danger from our own supporters if we reduced the following year's expenditure, but did he believe the Government could survive without the loan? If so, how?

Tony seemed very depressed, but promised to think the matter over again, and the next day there was some slight modification in his attitude, when he intimated that with great reluctance he would be ready to go part of the way towards the £9 billions expenditure target for 1977/8. This was a small gain, but his basic approach still commanded support among his colleagues and I began to get the impression that in the last resort he would regard the break-up of the Government as the lesser evil. I used this in my conversations with President Ford and the German Chancellor to make sure that both knew the strength of feeling in the Cabinet. Giving myself a little margin, I told them that the Cabinet would agree to nothing less than £9.5 billions for 1977/8. There was strong objection to substantial deflation with higher unemployment, which would utterly destroy our hard-won agreement with the TUC on pay. Moreover, I would not be able to carry it in the House of Commons. I asked them to talk to their representatives in the IMF. Helmut Schmidt recognised our political difficulties and was fearful of the world moving down a protectionist path. He undertook to telephone President Ford, but in Washington Secretary Simon's influence was paramount, and the President could not deliver beyond repeating his assurance that the United States would move sympathetically on creating a sterling safety net as soon as we had reached substantial agreement with the IMF on the conditions for the loan.

It was important for the Government to have the understanding of the TUC on any agreement we might reach. I called in the General Secretary, Lionel Murray, who was a Privy Councillor, informed him of the state of our negotiations, and talked frankly about the prospects. He was a level-headed colleague, straight, with a firm grasp of the economic and public expenditure aspects of the Government's problems. He never failed to put the TUC's view with conviction but with courtesy and always in an attempt to build bridges and find solutions. He commanded the respect of the members of the General Council of the TUC, and I regarded him as a partner in a common enterprise to secure the best for our people. Like his colleagues, he was strongly in favour of the Labour Government continuing in office.

The Cabinet continued its marathon discussions on alternative strategies while the Chancellor pursued his negotiations, although I was not anxious for them to be hurried until the Cabinet as a whole had soaked themselves in the issue. Another opportunity came to sound out the Foreign Secretary when he and I attended the European Council at The Hague on 29 and 30 November 1976. I made a special point when talking with Helmut Schmidt to involve Tony Crosland in our conversations.

The German Chancellor again expressed his fear that the world was moving down a protectionist route, and that a decision by an important trading nation like Britain to take protectionist measures would set the ball rolling with adverse consequences for every country. Helmut Schmidt knew my views thoroughly from our conversations and my telegrams, but I took the opportunity, while Tony Crosland was there, to enquire if he would be willing to intervene with the IMF to secure better terms. He made a temporising reply, but it was obvious to Tony that he believed we should reduce our borrowing requirement and was politely saying 'No'. I was not surprised.

The return journey from The Hague in the eight-seater HS 125 jet takes less than an hour, but I made use of the time to press the Foreign Secretary once more. The Cabinet had had plenty of opportunity to walk all round the question, and I told him that at our next meeting I would indicate that Ministers must now reach a conclusion on their general strategy. I knew where I stood; what would he do? I reminded him that he had great influence with a section of the Cabinet and must decide where to throw his weight.

On my return to London, I asked Michael Foot to come for a talk. He too was deeply unhappy about the negotiations, and was in touch with Tony Benn's group. Michael's concerns were with the consequences for unemployment and the level of social benefits, but his overriding consideration was that there should be no whiff of a repetition of 1931, and I summed up his view as being that it would be better to stay together than to stay in government. Fortunately he understood that I was as determined not to split the Party as he was. I went to bed wondering whether we would still have a Labour Government in a week's time.

On the following day, Wednesday, I began to see some rays of light. I invited Jack Jones and Lionel Murray for a talk, but because of prior engagements, they came separately. I explained my views about a solution and told them how the negotiations stood. As I was talking with Lionel in his capacity of General Secretary of the TUC, I limited my conversation to the financial and economic implications of the alternative courses, and sought his advice on the reactions of the TUC. As ever, he was extremely helpful, enabling me to gauge the severity of the unions' response. With Jack Jones I went further, for he had a dual role not only as a member of the TUC General Council but as General Secretary of a trade union affiliated to the Labour Party. I spoke very frankly about my determination to avoid another 1931; that the Cabinet and the Parliamentary Party must remain united on whatever course was finally decided. Jack Jones warned me strongly about the consequences to the Social Contract if there was a large increase in unemployment or reductions in social benefits, but he gave me every encouragement to maintain a Labour Government, even if it meant taking some decisions the TUC would not like and would oppose.

My next caller was Tony Crosland. He did not beat about the bush. He remained unconvinced about the policy but the new factor (he said) was my clear intention to support the Chancellor in Cabinet, and he recognised the Government could not survive on such an important issue unless it backed me. He would make all this clear at the next day's Cabinet Meeting. He said this very coolly but I knew it cost him a lot. I was both grateful and relieved; without his advocacy the little group of Ministers who had gone along with him would break up; I would be able to secure a majority in Cabinet for the Chancellor's approach. I could therefore declare my hand without the necessity of delivering an ultimatum to the Cabinet, for although I would not have been prepared to continue if the Cabinet had failed to back me, no one except Tony Crosland knew this.

My last caller of the day was the Chief Whip, Michael Cocks. I asked him for an assessment of the mood of the Party. He said there was pretty general despondency with a left-wing group almost certain to vote against any particular piece of legislation which involved a reduction in public expenditure. They might however sit on their hands in a vote on the package as a whole, if it was an issue of confidence in the Government; they did not want the Government to fall.

Cabinet on the following morning, Thursday 2 December, was the moment of decision. The Chancellor's statement was clear and firm. The Government must borrow less in the following year, not because of the demands of the IMF, but because the latest forecast rate of borrowing at £10.2 billions would prove severely inflationary, was inconsistent with the Government's creditworthiness and would cause a further collapse of sterling. He recommended a reduction to £8.7 billions, which would have the effect of increasing unemployment by thirty thousand and would be met by selling £500 millions of British Petroleum shares and by reducing public expenditure by £1 billions. He was ready to put this to the IMF negotiators, although at that stage he did Wot know what their reaction would be.

The Chancellor's proposed figure was £300 millions below my own target of £9 billions, but on the other hand it included the British Petroleum shares sale which other than in the convoluted mysteries of 'creative' Government accounting would not normally be accepted as reducing expenditure. I had no hesitation in accepting his proposal and said so at once to my colleagues, adding that everyone should now speak his mind because the time had come to make a decision.

I asked each Minister to express his or her agreement only if they were prepared individually to carry through the difficult decisions that would subsequently be necessary on their own programmes, in reducing either capital or current expenditure or even both. I said that when the time came to submit a package to the House of Commons we should be putting the Government's life at risk, but in my view there was an even greater risk if we did nothing.

I recognised the package would have an adverse effect on some of the Government's supporters in the House, but not nearly as much on the public at large. I then went around the table one by one, inviting the opinion of every member of the Cabinet. When the last Minister was reached, it was obvious that there was a substantial majority for the Chancellor's proposal, although a minority found it unacceptable. I summed up that the Chancellor was authorised to tell the IMF how far the Cabinet was ready to go, but that a final decision would be taken by the Cabinet.

The unanswered question was whether Denis could get the IMF on board on the basis of the Cabinet's figure, and he arranged to meet their team at noon on Friday 3 December.

I left for Yorkshire to visit textile factories and engineering works, and when I returned to my hotel in Leeds late in the afternoon, my Private Secretary was waiting with a cryptic message from the Chancellor, the gist of which, in typical robust Healey style, was that he had told the IMF team to go and jump in the lake. Apparently they had been given written instructions by the Managing Director of the IMF in Washington that in the opinion of the Fund, our expenditure would need to be cut by £2 billions in 1977/8 and by up to £3 billions in 1978/9. I could get no more information because Denis was already on his way to his constituency in

Leeds, and it was not until nearly midnight that we could meet at my hotel to discuss the breakdown.

It seemed that the Chancellor had delivered a brisk homily to the IMF indicating how far the Cabinet thought it right to reduce expenditure, emphasising that they would go no further than they believed to be necessary to get the economy into balance. If the IMF then refused a loan, the Government would ask the Queen to dissolve Parliament and we would call a general election on the issue of the IMF versus the people. With this message ringing in their ears, the IMF negotiators had made a hurried departure for Washington. I had not given the Chancellor any authority to threaten a general election but I was quite happy that he should have done so. He and I sat for some time in my bedroom talking over the various drastic policy changes that would be needed if a loan was not forthcoming. They would have meant a bumpy ride not just for the British people but also for the international community, with serious implications for our relations with the GATT, the European Community and NATO, as well as the United States. On that night anything seemed possible.

The next morning we parted and I travelled to Chequers for the weekend, and on arrival was handed a message I had not expected. It contained the news that the IMF negotiators had reported back in Washington and had shortly afterwards telephoned London, suggesting a renewal of contacts between them and our Treasury officials. I was of course agreeable. I assumed that the Chancellor's bluntness had led them to conclude correctly that the Government would not be pushed further than we believed the economic situation warranted. The negotiators flew back and further talks began almost at once; as often happens following a breakdown, they proceeded much more easily than before. Indeed, only forty-eight hours elapsed before the Chancellor was able to tell the Cabinet that he had reached an agreement that he was ready to recommend to his colleagues. Put simply, he would limit borrowing by the Public Sector to £8.7 billions in 1977/8 (plus £500 millions from the sale of British Petroleum shares) and to £8.6 billions in 1978/9, although there was no conclusion on how the latter figure would be arrived at. This was good enough and the Cabinet accepted it.

Looking back on that period, it seems to me that the strength of the position taken by the Chancellor and myself was that we knew how far we were ready to go, and did not intend to be pushed further. We shared one thing in common with the IMF, namely that both parties were agreed that the total borrowing requirement of £9 billions for 1977/8 which the Cabinet itself had agreed in the previous July must not be exceeded. On the other hand, I had no intention of being pushed seriously below that figure. I did not need to be convinced by the IMF that we ought to bring the growth in public expenditure closer to the growth in industrial output which supported it in order to avert a further rise in interest rates and restore confidence in sterling.

During the week of 6 December I called a series of dreary Cabinet meetings to wring programme reductions out of the Ministers in order to keep within the £8.7 billions maximum. For Ministers such occasions, which all Cabinets go through during their lifetime, are like teeth extractions, with the Chancellor and the Chief Secretary to the Treasury as the dentists. My role was to encourage the victim to believe that it would not hurt as much as he had thought, and to stop the drill when the pain was too great. Nor was all expenditure reduced by mechanical cuts across the board. The Cabinet agreed to increase the resources of the National Enterprise Board and the Scottish and Welsh Development Agencies, as well as of schemes for encouraging industrial investment and training for employment. The main social security benefits were not reduced. The effects of these measures together did much to mollify the minority of Ministers who had been opposed to the package as a whole. I began to grow more confident that I could avoid resignation.

The next step was to call in the sixteen Whips, led by Michael Cocks and Walter Harrison. They not only reflect the mood of the Parliamentary Party, but can do much to influence it, and during the period of 1976 to 1979 they performed heroically. It should be put on record that it was the Whips acting in conjunction with Michael Foot, as Leader of the House, who between them ensured the miraculous survival of the Government for a period of more than three years when we did not have an overall majority in the Commons. Our critics in the Labour Party usually ignore that. How much easier it would have been if we could have sailed along with an overall majority of fifty or one hundred.

When the Whips arrived in the Cabinet Room, I was able to tell them they were facing neither another 1931 nor 1951. The Cabinet had reached a decision and, unlike 1931, would stay together. We were ready to fight for the Government's life and, unlike 1951, I had no intention of calling an election. It was now for the Whips to assess whether the Parliamentary Party would remain united. What was their view? They told me that it was demoralising for the Party to have agreed to a set of measures in July, and then to learn that more was required in December, and a group of those they called 'kamikaze' members might vote against the Government on specific issues. Nevertheless, the Government would win if it came to an issue of confidence, but they advised me, if possible, to avoid reductions in expenditure that would require legislation, for they could not guarantee a majority. If a choice had to be made they would prefer that our measures should reduce unemployment rather than increase social expenditure, and they believed this represented the view of the Party in the country who, they said, understood the Government's problems and the absolute priority of avoiding a Conservative Government.

There was an encouraging degree of unanimity and helpfulness in their comments and, once again, their report on the constituencies reminded me how often we forget the basic commonsense and loyalty of our supporters, and mistake the shrill cries of an unrepresentative handful for the views of the people. The Whips left Downing Street to prepare the Parliamentary Party for a meeting in due course, while I had a talk with Cledwyn Hughes, the Chairman, to put him in the picture. He too was unfailingly helpful to the Government throughout the whole period, and added a large mixture of wisdom to a capacity for manoeuvre and understanding in handling his flock. Never underrate the subtlety of the Welsh mind, especially if it has been legally trained. When Cledwyn was working in partnership with Elwyn Jones, the Lord Chancellor, and John Morris, a Queen's Counsel who was Secretary for Wales, it was a formidable combination for which I was grateful more than once. At the Parliamentary Party Meeting there was a lot of criticism from left-wing members. I replied with the question, 'Do you want us to go on?' Faced with that, there was no doubt about their answer.

During this period the Chancellor kept Lionel Murray informed of the way things were going. In due course when he made his announcement to Parliament on 15 December, the TUC General Council responded with a markedly understanding public statement to the effect that there was no real alternative to seeking financial support, although they were concerned with the effects on unemployment, the construction industry, and called for some import controls of a selective nature. More ominously, they emphasised their belief in the need for 'an orderly return to collective bargaining', but the general tone of their comments was supportive. Denis had a rougher time in the House, and not only from the Opposition. Eric Heffer aggressively told him he should resign, although this attitude was unrepresentative of the general body of our supporters, who were dispirited but not hostile. I was unduly irritated by the remark because the Cabinet as a whole had taken the decision and I knew from my own experience the strain which the Chancellor had been under in the preceding weeks, and I regarded him as an indispensable member of the Cabinet.

There was one more Cabinet Meeting before we dispersed for Christmas, and it was noticeable that the tension had disappeared and the atmosphere lightened. When we finished our business we enjoyed some modest refreshment together in the Cabinet Room in light-hearted mood. I was very grateful to all my colleagues, without exception, for the tolerance they had displayed in the preceding three months. Once they had absorbed the initial shock there was a feeling of common purpose to surmount the problem, and with some difficult moments relieved by a sense of humour, we emerged scarred but unshaken. In the plan of Cabinet seating I had placed Shirley Williams, who is a warm-hearted soul, next to Tony Benn, and their personal relations were very good. Tony can be extremely amusing and he sometimes enlivened Cabinet with genuine flashes of wit. Tom McNally, who sat in an adjoining room, used to say that he could tell how well our meetings were going by the amount of laughter he heard during the morning.

It was always my aim to keep down the temperature of our discussions and not to allow the atmosphere to become too offensive. I usually succeeded, despite breaking my own rule now and again, and I would claim that the Labour Cabinet of 1976 to 1979 would stand comparison with most as a good-tempered body, with a minimum of personal backbiting, very little malicious leaking and a strong feeling of solidarity. Perhaps this was helped by the absence of a Parliamentary majority, the knowledge that our collective life usually hung by a thread and that we ourselves could end it.

I left to spend Christmas at Chequers. Our family has always foregathered whenever we can, and children and grandchildren arrived on Christmas Eve. That large country house, set in its own grounds, is a wonderful place in which to hold a family party, especially as the staff enter into the spirit of the occasion. They created an almost lifesize snow-covered cardboard reindeer and sledge outside the grandchildren's bedrooms, while in the towering Great Hall with its huge log fire stood the tallest decorated Christmas tree they had ever seen indoors – twenty feet high at least.

The pace of office work slowed to a crawl, but even on Christmas Day it never completely stopped and a trickle of incoming messages and telegrams continued to arrive for me in the communications room, where the duty clerks handled them amid mince pies and turkey. The battery of modern telecommunications equipment contrasted markedly with that existing at the beginning of the Second World War when there was only one telephone installed at Chequers and the Prime Minister had to visit the butler's pantry if he wished to use it. The pressure of events must have been relatively slight during that first winter of the war for Neville Chamberlain has left at Chequers an interesting portfolio containing photographs that he took himself of all the major trees on the estate, identified and labelled by him.

Chequers is a relaxing place, with walks through farmland to the beech-woods by hedges in which grow large quantities of box wood; in spring the grassland is smothered in cowslips, and a vast collection of old and new roses blooms in the summer. Lord Lee of Fareham, who bequeathed it for the use of the Prime Minister of the day at the end of the First World War, could not have made a more imaginative gift than this lovely old house. Some agreeable customs have grown up during the years. One is that every Prime Minister plants a tree of his own choosing in the grounds. Stanley Baldwin's oak and Clement Attlee's hornbeam are two of the most sturdy. One only has died and this was later replaced. I chose for my own tree a South American beech (*Nothofagus*) and Audrey, who was encouraged to do the same, planted a catalpa.

The Long Gallery at Chequers where I took part in many discussions must be between eighty and ninety feet in length and its walls are pierced at regular intervals by a series of long, narrow windows. When a Prime Minister leaves office, a panel in painted glass is inserted in one of the windows with his name, date, and his coat of arms. I did not possess one and the Trustees of the Chequers Estate commissioned an artist to create a design that would not disgrace the rest. He produced a sailing ship for the place of my birth, Portsmouth, a Red Dragon to signify my long connection with Wales, with a mediaeval chequer-board, the Tudor Rose and a representation of the globe for the three offices of Chancellor of the Exchequer, Home Secretary and Foreign Secretary. I am very happy to think that this window panel now marks a small footnote in our national history. The Long Gallery might have been created with family games in mind and our grandchildren never tired of rushing through the series of connecting rooms and rediscovering the secret door amid the bookshelves.

With Christmas over, the family dispersed and I returned to Downing Street, refreshed to find that the Chancellor had already been at work and was on the way to resolving the problem of securing a safety net for sterling. He had taken this up again now that the traumas of the previous autumn had subsided, in the light of the undertaking that we should revert to it once the International Monetary Fund negotiations had been completed. Gordon Richardson, the Governor of the Bank, conducted a series of negotiations with his colleagues in Basle and by the middle of February was able to report that he had concluded a very satisfactory agreement which held three advantages for us. The new arrangements shielded the sterling exchange rate from the adverse effect of further running down of sterling balances by overseas Governments. Secondly, it thereby protected our domestic economy from undue increase in interest rates. And thirdly, it fulfilled my long-held objective of securing an orderly reduction in the role of sterling as a reserve currency. This was done by offering overseas Governments an option to convert any part of their sterling holdings into longer-term bonds which were negotiable, and for this purpose the central banks of eleven countries provided the Bank of England with backing finance directly related to the total of the overseas official holdings of sterling.

This was eminently satisfactory – just what I had hoped for – and I was very grateful to the Governor for his skill and inventiveness, although I could not help thinking that some of the instability on the world's exchanges might have been avoided in the intervening years if the ideas I had floated as long ago as the mid-1960s had found international acceptance at the time.

Still, better late than never, and twelve months later the Bank of England was able to report that it had been successful in reducing the short-term sterling holdings of overseas Governments, so lessening a serious potential cause of instability. In due course it was possible to wind up the scheme, which had proved itself an instrument of international cooperation to reduce the prospects of disruption in both Britain's domestic economy and the international monetary world.

Once the sterling exchange rate was stabilised, interest rates at home rapidly declined during 1977 with corresponding benefit for industry and home borrowers, and this engendered a feeling that the economy was reviving. The upshot was that the Government needed to draw less than one half of the total IMF loan and by the winter of 1977/8 it was possible for us to repay even that half at any time the IMF should ask for it. But we did not hurry to do so, for it was cheap money – cheaper than the Government could have got anywhere else. There was a second reason too. Unlike a year earlier, foreign traders and others were now anxious to buy sterling and if we had repaid the IMF, they might have concluded that our recovery was better than we knew it to be and perhaps pushed the value of sterling higher to the detriment of our exports. This did in fact happen when at a later date we repaid about a billion dollars.

Not for the first time as overseas confidence grew in our ability to pull Britain round, so we began to lose the support of the electorate. Committed Labour Party supporters and the trade unions stood remarkably firm. They accepted that in selecting what economies must be made the Government had, as a deliberate matter of policy, maintained the living standards of the sick, the poorest, the unemployed and the pensioners. Nevertheless, our stock was falling, especially among women and skilled workers and I could understand why. Every time the housewife went to shop, she found that prices were still rising fast, mainly because the measures the Government had taken had not had time to slow down the inflation rate. I knew the benefits would be felt in due course but meantime the Local Authority elections were due, and in May 1977 the women in particular punished us savagely. Many good Labour Councillors lost their seats for reasons that had little do do with their stewardship.

Another source of discontent was that the flat-rate pay increases of earlier years were compressing the skilled workers' differentials. But without doubt the most important cause of discontent was a fall in real take-home pay of as much as 5 per cent during the preceding twelve months. This had to take place for it was an overdue, delayed adjustment to the 5 per cent reduction in the national income caused by the dramatic oil price increases in 1973. But as every politician knows, however unassailable a Government's logic and however virtuous its policies, it will not be spared the wrath of the electors if their standard of life has been tampered with.

It was during this period that in February 1977 I was faced with the unwelcome task of filling the gap as Foreign Secretary caused by Tony Crosland's untimely death. Denis Healey could have filled the office with ease, but he was at that moment deep in preparation for his Budget which was only one month away, and was in any case indispensable at the Treasury to reassure opinion, especially overseas, that there would be no departure from the policy the Government had adopted only three months earlier. Roy Jenkins too would have been a strong runner, as the Common

Market controversy had begun to lose its heat, but he had departed to become President of the European Commission.

Other members of the Government could of course have taken over, but this would have meant a Cabinet reshuffle of the same faces. We were going through a difficult time electorally, and the thought came into my mind that it would do the Government no harm if I surprised the press and others who were already picking Tony's successor by bringing in someone entirely fresh and young whom they had not thought of. Anthony Eden had after all become Foreign Secretary at the early age of thirty-eight, and had rapidly become a senior figure in the Cabinet. To do something similar would have the additional advantage of strengthening the group of younger Cabinet Ministers who would be restless, with new ideas, and prevent a feeling of staleness.

There was more than one to choose from but an obvious solution appeared at once. David Owen was already serving as Minister of State at the Foreign Office, and earlier had been at the Ministry of Defence. He was thirty-eight years of age, of striking appearance, and I had heard good accounts of his work at the Foreign Office. I did not think it would take him long to gain confidence, and I would back him up with my background knowledge of the problems he would face.

It is a cliché to say that when someone is given unexpected news he goes as white as a sheet, but I can only say that I watched David Owen visibly pale as he sat beside me in the Cabinet room and I told him what was in my mind. I wanted to safeguard Denis Healey's claims to the post at a later date, so I added that he should not think that he possessed a freehold tenure: it might be necessary for him to move elsewhere after eighteen months to gain different experience.

The new Foreign Secretary was energetic and ready to adopt new ideas, and threw himself into the problem of solving Rhodesia's Unilateral Declaration of Independence and achieving African majority rule.

A few months later he came to tell me that he wished to make a change at the Washington Embassy. Jimmy Carter had become President as recently as January 1977 and with the advent of a new Democratic Administration in America the Foreign Secretary believed this would be an appropriate moment to appoint a younger Ambassador, and one more in tune with David Owen's own ideas. It was then his turn to surprise me. The man he wanted was Peter Jay. I at once reacted negatively. Everyone knew Peter's great ability, but he was my son-in-law and I could imagine how malicious tongues would wag.

I told the Foreign Secretary I could not agree and he should find somebody else. He went away and I dismissed the matter from my mind, but perhaps a month or six weeks later he returned. He said he had looked elsewhere, but had reached the same conclusion. He still wanted Peter Jay. I thought about it, recalling that when I became Chancellor I had been the cause of an interruption in his career simply because he was my son-in-law. That had cost him one of the best postings in the Treasury. Was he to be disadvantaged a second time when David Owen clearly wanted him on his merits, which were undoubted? So I agreed.

Until 1976 Harold Wilson's administration had survived precariously, with a majority of three in the House of Commons, later reduced to two, suffering several defeats along the way. Soon after I became Prime Minister even this miniscule majority was finally whittled away when John Stonehouse decided to sit as an Independent and two of our Scottish members defected because of the slow progress we were making on Scottish Devolution. From that time on, for the remaining three years of the Government's life, at no time could I command a majority in the House of Commons from among Labour Members of Parliament acting as a single Party.

We always needed the support of other Parties for our legislation or on occasion our very existence. This made for an exciting ride on the Parliamentary switchback, which the Opposition and the onlookers enjoyed more than the Government, and the ride became even more bumpy as Labour Members tumbled to the fact that they too could threaten to abstain or vote against their Government unless they got their way. It needed only a handful to threaten us and we were sunk. One such occasion arose on the Bill to provide for the setting up of elected Assemblies in Scotland and Wales. This was not only a major item in the Government's legislative programme but had been a commitment in the Manifesto on which Labour had fought the election, and was Party policy approved by the annual Party Conference. When the issue was debated in the Commons, it soon became clear that the Bill's opponents in all Parties would use every delaying tactic to prevent its completion. The Government brought forward a proposal for a timetable that would have allowed a total of thirty-five days for the Bill's consideration. This was ample time but the opponents were intractable; when the timetable was put to the vote, no fewer than twenty-two Labour Members voted with the Conservatives and a further twenty abstained. This was decisive in ensuring the Government's defeat and I noted that among the Labour dissidents were some who were most self-righteous in condemning the Government if it ever failed to regard Party Conference decisions as immutable. I never succeeded in getting any left-wing purist to explain why he should have a dispensation to ignore Conference decisions while he denied the Government, with its greater responsibilities, the right ever to do so.

15

*The Liberal Pact – Summits at Rambouillet, London and Bonn – the
European Monetary System – Northern Ireland*

Three weeks after this serious defeat on the major item in the Government's legislative year, the Chief Whip visited me on 16 March 1977 with more bad news. He reported that a number of left-wing Members intended to abstain in a debate on the following day about the Cabinet's public expenditure plans for 1977/8. The Whips were usually extremely accurate in their forecasts of how a vote would go and I had no hesitation in accepting the Chief Whip's estimate that the Government would lose.

It would have been insupportable to lose this vote immediately after the defeat on Devolution, especially as the public expenditure proposals were an essential ingredient of the plan to keep the Government's borrowing requirement in line with our target of £8.7 billions. The Chief Whip suggested a procedural device which would enable the Government to avoid a vote at the end of the debate. It was not a very glorious posture but glory is relative and defeat would have been even worse; it could unsettle sterling and undermine the confidence that was slowly returning.

I agreed to the Chief Whip's suggestion but suspected that such devices could not sustain the Government for long. According to the public opinion polls, the Conservative Party enjoyed a lead of over 16 per cent and both we and the Liberal Party would face heavy defeat in a general election.

I had discussed the alternatives with Cledwyn Hughes, the Chairman of the Parliamentary Party, more than once and when, a week or so earlier, Cyril Smith, the Liberal Member, had asked to see me about some proposal of his for making a political arrangement between the two Parties, I had replied suggesting he should first meet Cledwyn. Cyril Smith apparently took umbrage at this and refused to see Cledwyn – a rather silly attitude for he must surely have understood that such matters are best begun by go-betweens who can explore whether any common ground exists before the principals emerge on to the stage with the resulting inevitable publicity. I did not even know when he made his approach whether he was acting with David Steel's knowledge, although much later I discovered that this was so. His request to see me had been so informal that apart from telling Cledwyn about it, I did not think it necessary to inform any of my other colleagues, but my thoughts reverted to it after the Chief Whip had left and I sent a message to Cledwyn asking him to see me urgently. When he arrived I gave him the Chief Whip's gloomy forecast, and suggested that the Government's situation was so unstable that he should make an immediate opportunity to see David Steel, apprise him of the position and discover what he could about the Liberal Party's attitude, and particularly their reaction to having to fight a general election at such an unpromising moment.

Cledwyn acted quickly and talked with David Steel while the public expenditure debate was taking place. Naturally David Steel did not disclose his full hand. He tried to bluff Cledwyn into believing that he did not mind fighting a general election, but this was so transparent that Cledwyn was not taken in, nor did David Steel expect him to be. From the other exchanges that followed, he came away believing that it would be worthwhile to keep in contact with Steel. Unfortunately for us, despite the Chief Whip's procedural device, when the vote was called at ten o'clock he was foiled by the Scottish Nationalists, who pressed for a vote and were then followed into the Lobby by a rather sheepish Conservative Party. We were in an even worse case for our decision meant that Ministers sat on the front bench during the vote looking embarrassed and marooned. Technically the Government avoided a defeat but I was not comforted by the result nor surprised when the Tory spokesman gloated that 'the shades are closing in on the Government. We must be very near the end.'

This was far from my mood. I had not lived through the previous autumn to surrender to the Conservatives at the moment when we were beginning to see the first glimmering of improvement in our economic and financial situation. As soon as I could leave the Chamber, I called the Chief Whip to the Prime Minister's Room behind the Speaker's Chair, together with his Deputy, Walter Harrison (who was always full of ingenious ploys), Michael Foot and Cledwyn Hughes. They were all in fighting mood and we sat until after midnight discussing how to retrieve our position. The next morning, with the addition of Merlyn Rees, we met again and learned that Mrs Thatcher had moved in for the kill: she was tabling a motion of 'No Confidence' in the Government. At this stage the Opposition believed they had us on the ropes, as did much of the press, but they did not know how determined all of us were to avoid defeat, nor were they aware of the steps we were taking or the tasks we had allocated to each Minister. Merlyn Rees was the mediator with Gerry Fitt and Roy Mason with the Ulster Unionists. Cledwyn Hughes was the principal contact with the Liberals, with Bill Rodgers also playing a subsidiary role. The Whips played their part with other minor Parties. Altogether it was a coordinated effort and I left for Cardiff on Friday afternoon, 18 March, not knowing whether we would avoid defeat but confident that we were doing all that could be done. Perhaps that is why the weekend press reports described me as appearing very relaxed.

I returned to Chequers on Saturday night and spent much of Sunday telephoning, although I managed to find time for a walk to the top of Beacon Hill with Audrey, breathing the air and enjoying the lovely views of the neighbouring counties. We then set off to No. 10 Downing Street, where I had called an evening meeting with the Lord President, the Home Secretary, the Secretary for Northern Ireland and the Chief Whip.

Cledwyn had already told me over the telephone that David Steel intended to hold a meeting of Liberal Members on Tuesday 22 March – the day before the 'No Confidence' motion – and he strongly urged me to see Steel before the Liberals met. I reported this to my colleagues who agreed that the time was ripe, and arrangements were then made for a meeting on Monday 21 March.

Michael Foot and Roy Mason reported on their conversation with Jim Molyneaux. Both recommended that I should see him and this was also agreed. On Monday, Molyneaux came first, accompanied by Enoch Powell, with Michael Foot also present. I opened the discussion. I said I gathered there had been talk of an arrangement between us, and I was ready to consider it. But I was not ready to forfeit the Government's self-respect: if that was the price of an agreement, then reluctantly I would prefer to go to the country and hold a general election. I would also do the same if I felt that such was the country's wish, as it had been in 1951, when there was a widespread feeling that it was time for a change in direction. But although the Government was unpopular, that was not my interpretation of the country's present mood.

The Government's economic line had been settled and did not require any immediate Parliamentary action. In that sense the Government was in a position where it could go on until its policy yielded results and in my view it should do so, in preference to scuttling part way through. Our policies were intended to squeeze out inflation and manage the home economy in order to generate export-led growth.

My present judgement was that it was right to fight these policies through, 'and if at the end of the day, after a general election held at the normal time, the country were to return a verdict against the Government, so be it'. Meanwhile, the Government's difficulties chiefly arose from its inability to secure the passage of legislation. This did not necessarily prevent us from carrying out our economic policy but it would obviously be sensible for the Government to recognise that its minority position required it to take into account the views of the smaller Parties in the House when we were framing our legislation. I was therefore enquiring of them in advance of the 'No Confidence' motion whether a basis existed for accommodation.

Whatever the state of United Kingdom politics, the first priority of Northern Ireland's Members is Northern Ireland. Molyneaux and Powell were concerned with two matters: an increase in the number of Parliamentary seats in Northern Ireland, and the return of some form of local government to the Province. They could not promise a positive vote from the Ulster Unionists, but if these issues were conceded there might be up to six abstentions on the 'No Confidence' motion.

Michael Foot had previously urged the need for an increase in the number of Northern Ireland seats, because the average number of electors for each seat was much higher than in Britain. This was an old complaint which had previously been resisted on the grounds that the existence of the elected Assembly at Stormont made a direct comparison invalid. But Stormont had been abolished in 1972 and this had weakened the argument against parity of representation with the rest of Britain. It seemed to me that the Government could legitimately concede that the case for more seats should be looked at again and that the appropriate forum would be an all-Party conference under the Chairmanship of Mr Speaker. I told Molyneaux and Powell I would recommend this, adding that this decision would stand 'even if you are not able to carry your colleagues in the accommodation we are now discussing'. I then probed closely their ideas about a form of local government, particularly with regard to the powers it would have, its staffing and the place of the minority community. I told them that the Cabinet would naturally need to know the reactions of the minority in considering the matter, and I could therefore give no pledge, but I saw enough in their proposals to warrant the Government examining them seriously, and we would do so.

I then informed Molyneaux and Powell that following our meeting David Steel would be calling on me, and I proposed to offer him a form of consultation on the Government's future legislative programme.

Moreover the same offer was open to the Ulster Unionists if they cared to take it up. It would be a tangible recognition of the Government's minority position and a practical way of carrying legislation forward.

I later discovered that my unconditional readiness to refer the question of the Northern Ireland seats to an all-party conference, irrespective of how they voted on the 'No Confidence' motion, had made a favourable impression and improved the atmosphere between us. Without being conscious of it, I had cast my bread upon the waters and later months were to prove the words of the preacher – 'thou shalt find it after many days'. Cooperation between Michael Foot and Jim Molyneaux proved excellent.

David Steel arrived as soon as they had left and I opened the discussion in much the same way as I had done with the Ulster Unionists, emphasising that an accommodation was worth exploring because I wished to pursue the Government's economic policies to a conclusion. My purpose therefore was to construct a Parliamentary majority for future legislation, and I outlined the programme of Bills that lay ahead, naming specifically the Devolution Bill, Industrial Democracy, Post Office Board and Local Authority Works. I told David Steel I had not so far consulted the Cabinet but I would be willing to recommend to them 'the idea of general consultation in return for general support'.

David Steel replied in the rational and realistic manner which I learned to associate with him throughout our relationship. Obviously, he said, we could only agree on policies which lay within the limits of what each side could accept. His colleagues would, on the whole, prefer an election if the alternative was a Parliament that limped along. On the other hand, if accommodation was possible he thought they would prefer such a course to precipitating a Tory landslide. He believed the essence of an arrangement would be regular meetings to discuss future business so that the Liberal Party might make an input. For example, he would propose a separate Bill for Scottish Devolution, and would seek a commitment to hold direct elections to the European Assembly on the basis of proportional representation with a regional base. He acknowledged that the House had already defeated the idea as the means of electing a Scottish Assembly, but he would urge a fresh look at it.

I told him I could see many advantages in regular meetings to discuss future business, and had no difficulty in accepting the idea of a separate Scottish Devolution Bill and direct elections to the European Assembly. This last I had already agreed with my colleagues in the European Council. As he would understand, proportional representation was an animal of a

very different colour, for the Party was against it and so was I. Despite
this he reacted favourably, and the upshot was that we both agreed there
was sufficient in common to make it worth his putting these ideas to the
forthcoming meeting of his Liberal colleagues. He undertook to let me
know the result.

As a result of these meetings, Michael Foot and I could begin to see a
glimmer of light and decided to call a meeting of the Cabinet, which we
arranged for Wednesday 23 March, by which time the result of the
deliberations of the Liberal and Ulster Unionist Parties would be available.

Tuesday 22 March was a day of hectic consultations with the Liberals,
telephone calls, drafts submitted, rejected, amended and rewritten. In all
this Michael Foot played a heroic and tireless role, and when matters
seemed near deadlock I was called in twice to meet David Steel and his
colleague, John Pardoe. Talks went on late into the night and it was
1.20 a.m. in the early morning of Wednesday, the day of the 'No Confidence' debate, before David Steel could finally tell my Private Secretary,
Kenneth Stowe, that the Liberals were in agreement. By this time I had
gone to bed, but it was cheering news to greet me at breakfast. The Cabinet
met at midday, and copies of the Agreement we had negotiated were ready
for Ministers to study. It was quite short and ran as follows:

> We agreed today the basis on which the Liberal Party would work with
> the Government in the pursuit of economic recovery. We will set up a
> joint consultative committee under the chairmanship of the Leader of
> the House [Michael Foot] which will meet regularly. The committee
> will examine Government policy and other issues prior to their coming
> before the House, and Liberal policy proposals. The existence of this
> committee will not commit the Government to accepting views of the
> Liberal Party, or the Liberal Party to supporting the Government on any
> issue.
>
> We agree to initiate regular meetings between the Chancellor and the
> Liberal Party economic spokesman, such meetings to begin at once. In
> addition, the Prime Minister and the leader of the Liberal Party will
> meet as necessary.
>
> We agree that legislation for direct elections to the European Assembly
> in 1978 will be presented to Parliament in this session. The Liberal
> Party reaffirm their strong conviction that a proportional system should
> be used as the method of election. The Government is publishing next
> week a White Paper on direct elections to the European Assembly, which
> sets out the choices among different electoral systems but which makes
> no recommendation. There will now be consultation between us on the

method to be adopted, and the Government's final recommendation will take full account of the Liberal Party's commitment. The recommendation will be subject to a free vote of both Houses.

We agree that progress must be made on legislation for devolution, and to this end consultations will begin on the detailed memorandum submitted by the Liberal Party today. In any future debate on proportional representation for the devolved assemblies there will be a free vote.

We agree that the Government will provide the extra time necessary to secure the passage of the Housing (Homeless Persons) Bill, and that the Local Authorities (Works) Bill will now be confined to provisions to protect the existing activities of direct labour organisations in the light of local government reorganisation.

We agree that this arrangement between us should last until the end of the present Parliamentary session, when both parties would consider whether the experiment has been of sufficient benefit to the country to be continued. We also agree that this understanding should be made public.

At Cabinet, I gave Ministers a full account of our doings during the weekend and since, including the discussions with the Ulster Unionists. I indicated that on present forecasts if the Liberals decided to vote with the Opposition, the 'No Confidence' motion would be carried and a general election would follow. The Government's prospects in such an election would be very slight and a decision by the Cabinet not to support the Agreement would be tantamount to installing a Conservative Government. I therefore sought the authority of the Cabinet to confirm the Agreement and to inform the Liberal Leader. In that event I said, 'I wish to know that I shall be supported by all my colleagues.'

The discussion went to and fro. It was argued that some of the provisions were humiliating; that it was wrong to tread the path of expediency, and it would be preferable to face the consequences of losing the vote, even if the result should be a Conservative Government. I agreed entirely with the view that there should be a Party meeting but the Agreement had been reached in the middle of the night, and the debate on the 'No Confidence' motion would begin within a couple of hours. There was no time to arrange a Party meeting and Labour Members could best show their feelings by how they voted in the Division Lobby. On the other hand, I declared that it was not possible for the Cabinet to be divided on an issue that was central to the very existence of the Government. If Ministers were divided, I would not feel authorised to ratify the understandings with David Steel, and we would have to take the consequences.

I paused for a moment and then went on, 'I understand that all my colleagues will be with me in the Division Lobby tonight.' I paused again but no voice was raised in dissent and on that note I closed the meeting and went to the House to tell David Steel of the Cabinet's agreement, and to scribble some hurried notes for my speech in reply to Mrs Thatcher's attack. Despite her forensic skill, this was an occasion on which she was not at her best, for our new arrangement stole the attention of the House. The speeches of David Steel and myself were punctuated by Tory jeers, but they were cries of rage and frustration which we could easily withstand, and I could not help recalling the old saying that the best rejoinder is a majority. So it turned out, for when the vote was taken, Mrs Thatcher's motion of 'No Confidence' was rejected by 322 votes to 298, a majority of 24, with three Ulster Unionists abstaining, and the remainder, together with the Scottish National Party and Plaid Cymru, voting with the Conservatives. If the Liberals had voted against us and there had been no other changes, the Government would have lost by two votes and a general election would have followed. I was able to leave for a two-day visit to Rome in buoyant and confident spirit.

The relief among our back-benchers was palpable, although forty-eight of them signed a motion saying that whilst they would support the Government in the 'No Confidence' vote, they did not regard themselves as bound to implement the Agreement. In a message to Party workers on the day after we had won the vote, I reassured them that the Agreement was in no sense a coalition and involved the abandonment of not one election commitment. On the contrary, in the matter of Devolution, where the Government had found it impossible to make progress, we would be able to make a fresh start. I repeated that the Government had not committed itself to accept the views of the Liberal Party although we were in honour bound to consider them sympathetically. The central issue was that our Government was in a minority and could make its legislation effective only if we could construct a majority from among the smaller Parties. Our arrangement to consult with the Liberals before we brought legislation forward would enable us to calculate in advance what the prospects would be and give us a stable platform on which to build. For all these reasons there was no justification for the Government to surrender half-way through the life of Parliament and let in the Conservatives.

From the response I received there was no doubt that this represented the views of our supporters, and although the usual group on the National Executive Committee were ready to carp, they were not willing to strike.

This was par for the course during the whole period that I was leader of the Party. A small majority of the NEC was usually opposed to the Cabinet, and some of the Members of Parliament on the NEC appeared to want to set themselves up as an alternative Government. I was only too aware of the need to keep Ministers and members of the NEC running in tandem if possible, for I had observed that Ministers who had never served on the NEC could overlook its importance, and I not only enjoined on Ministers the need to consult, but established a machinery for regular consultation. Ministers did their best to make it work but there was an inadequate response. An advantage held by earlier Labour Governments had been the number of people who were both Ministers and also Members of the NEC, with a resulting cross-fertilisation. Unfortunately, during my period as Leader, there were fewer than usual and although the members of the Government, Fred Mulley and Shirley Williams in particular, regularly sought to explain and defend, when it came to a vote the Government's position was often rejected by a margin of one or two. The Government received more support and understanding from the trade unions at this period than it did from some National Executive members.

Electorally the Party was doing poorly. The cut in real living standards during the previous twelve months, coupled with the fact that the inflation rate was still over 17 per cent a year, was sufficient explanation. It was not yet convincing when we said on the doorstep that the measures we had taken had already arrested the rise in inflation, would dramatically reduce it in the year ahead, and had stabilised living standards, which with improved productivity could begin to pick up again. At such a moment the Government needed maximum support and understanding, for no one on the NEC could have waved a magic wand and swept these issues away.

In Scotland the exciting prospect of substantial oil revenues in the near future lent strength to the Scottish National Party's slogan that Scottish oil was the key to an independent Scotland. Their victories in Glasgow and elsewhere reinforced my view that the growth of a narrow nationalism was a real danger to the unity of the Kingdom and that despite our earlier defeats in the Commons, the Labour Party's concept of devolved powers to a Scottish Assembly should be revived. This view was in accord with the Liberal Agreement, and became the first example of an area where the Government could proceed to bring its legislation before Parliament with some confidence. Another result of the Agreement was that the feverish temperature of the Commons was reduced. The previous uncertainty about the result of each day's vote was largely removed, and the Opposition became resigned to their failure to force an election. Of course the Government still encountered problems; we hit a rock almost immediately when the Liberals refused to vote to increase the tax on petrol in the Budget as an incentive to conserve energy. Accordingly the Government was defeated and had to withdraw the proposal, but although this was a nuisance, it was not fatal to the general progress of the Agreement during the summer.

The month of June 1977 was one of the most exhausting but enjoyable periods I experienced as Prime Minister, bringing together within the space of four weeks the Queen's Silver Jubilee celebrations, a meeting of Commonwealth Heads of Government in London, and a meeting of the European Council, as well as my normal Parliamentary and political functions. The month began with a busy weekend visit to Cardiff, followed on Monday 7 June by a Thanksgiving Service to commemorate the Jubilee in St Paul's, attended by thirty-two Heads of Commonwealth Governments and representatives of other countries. On Tuesday we began the formal proceedings of our ten-day Conference of Commonwealth Heads of Government in Lancaster House, over which I presided, while in the evening the Queen offered a banquet.

On Saturday morning, 10 June, came the traditional Trooping of the Colour to celebrate the Queen's official birthday, and following this I whisked all the visiting Prime Ministers off to Scotland by special High Speed Train for the remainder of the weekend. It was here that the Gleneagles Agreement, severing the Commonwealth's sporting ties with South Africa, was born. We returned to London on Monday 13 June without mishap, all the Prime Ministers being impressed by the speed, smoothness and comfort of the rail journey, which enabled them to pass the time in leisurely conversation as they moved about the train. I thought afterwards how much more agreeable and useful it had been than a faster but much less relaxed journey by aircraft, in which such mobile conversations would have been next to impossible.

As soon as I returned to London, I hastened to a meeting of the Parliamentary Labour Party on the contentious issue of elections to the European Assembly, against which the National Executive Committee was fighting a rearguard action, and then paid another swift visit to Cardiff. I then had four Party engagements in a row – a further meeting of the Parliamentary Party in the House, a joint meeting with the National Executive Committee and representatives of the TUC at Congress House, a separate meeting of the National Executive Committee, and an address to prospective Labour Party candidates.

Some of these activities meant that unfortunately I could not follow the Queen in her progress through Wales, but I was able to join HMS *Britannia* at Barry Docks, and take part in the enthusiastic welcome offered by the people of Cardiff, together with a Thanksgiving Service held in Llandaff Cathedral. The Queen kindly invited Audrey and me to join *Britannia* when she reached my home city of Portsmouth on 27 June for the Naval Review at Spithead. I was determined not to miss this. I had been on board the Admiralty Yacht at the Queen's Coronation Review in 1953 and, even more importantly, my father had served as a seaman in the Royal Yacht *Victoria and Albert* (*Britannia*'s predecessor) when she carried King George V to his Coronation Review in 1912. My father had taken me aboard the *Victoria and Albert* when I was a toddler, but I do not suppose it ever crossed his mind that one day his son would be invited to return as the Prime Minister of the United Kingdom. If ever I visit *Britannia* nowadays I always look for the beautifully ornamented binnacle that was transferred from the *Victoria and Albert* when she was broken up. It is now mounted on the Quarterdeck, and I wonder how many times my father might have given it a polish during his ten years' service aboard the old Yacht.

The Queen held an evening reception aboard *Britannia* and the Royal Marines beat the Retreat, marching and playing as only they can. Once again, I felt my spine tingle as dusk fell and the ceremony drew to an end with the tune 'Sunset' blowing softly on the bugles. The Queen's party was standing on deck in a rather ragged line to watch and at the close, when the deck lights were switched on, I stepped back with the others so that the assembled crowd could see the Queen more clearly. Dickie Mountbatten seized me by the arm and propelled me forward. 'Your place is up there,' he said. It was a kindly gesture, but it was the Queen everyone wanted to see – certainly not me. On the next morning *Britannia* threaded her way through the long lines of ships drawn up for review. Ships of the Royal Navy were in the foreground, but many other countries had sent naval vessels to represent them and their ships' companies cheered loudly as the Queen sailed by. The day concluded with a memorable dinner held in the aircraft hangar of HMS *Ark Royal*, with every ship in the Review sending a representative to the function. This agreeable interlude ended too soon, for I had to hurry back to London to preside at a meeting of the European Council of Heads of Government on 29 and 30 June.

The Cabinet marked the Queen's Silver Jubilee by presenting her with a silver coffee pot and she invited us all to the Palace to mark the occasion. When I presented it to her on behalf of my colleagues she said, 'Oh! I'm so glad you haven't repeated Mr Disraeli's gift to Queen Victoria. He gave her a painting of himself.'

I have given this account of some of the happenings of June 1977 to illustrate that there were many matters on my mind other than the Liberal Agreement. But I could never forget how important it was to the life of the Government and on the last weekend of the month, I sandwiched a Sunday meeting of Cabinet Ministers at Chequers between a flying visit to Cardiff, a speech to Labour Party candidates in London and the Naval Review at Spithead. My purpose was to have a general discussion on the Government's strategy, but it was not a formal Cabinet Meeting and David Owen and Tony Benn both asked that no officials be present, a request I agreed to.

The policy groups had prepared some background material as had Harold Lever, the Chancellor of the Duchy of Lancaster. A conflation of their contents shows that on the monetary and economic fronts they all agreed that the situation had begun to show a marked improvement. Public expenditure had been brought under control for the first time in the 1970s; our sterling reserves had doubled to £10 billions; the sterling exchange rate had recovered from its low point of $1.57 to the pound in the autumn of 1976 to $1.72; our current account on overseas trade was virtually in balance with a surplus forecast for 1978; and if we could keep pay settlements to about 10 per cent, inflation levels would be reduced from over 17 per cent to about 8 per cent by the end of 1978. In addition, the Minimum Lending Rate had been reduced by no less than 6 per cent since the autumn of 1976, to the great benefit of industry and home-buyers, and although unemployment had continued to creep upwards, it was expected to improve again in 1978.

Politically, said the background papers, there had been an attitudinal shift to the right which Mrs Thatcher, aided by the press, was skilfully exploiting with attacks on scroungers and the welfare state and appeals to individual materialism. According to public opinion surveys, those wanting lower taxation outnumbered the rest by ten to one. The conclusion was that no detached observer expected that the Labour Government could hope to win a general election in 1977.

I led into the discussion by saying that unlike the occasion of the vote of 'No Confidence', Ministers now had plenty of time to consider whether the Liberal Agreement should be renewed or whether they believed we should go for a General Election in the autumn of 1977. I asked particularly for the views of those who had been opposed to the original Agreement. Personally, I had no doubt that we should carry on. The proceeds from the North Sea oil would shortly begin to arrive and Ministers should start thinking about how these were to be used to support the country's economic recovery. I asked for Ministers' views on how to resolve the problem that our own supporters were looking for tax cuts, but were also demanding large social benefit increases. The two were incompatible. We must be a Party of movement that stood for more than efficient economic management, and I believed our twin themes should be national recovery together with fairness – the giving of a share to everyone. People were looking for some relief from blood, sweat and tears, and the Chancellor should examine the prospect of easing the tax burden in the next Budget.

Michael Foot, as Deputy Leader of the Party, followed me immediately. He drew an historical parallel with the position of the Attlee Government in 1951, saying that they had erred in going to the country at that time, and that on the present occasion, 'We should absolutely resolve against chucking our hand in, and should go on until autumn 1979 if possible.' He was in favour of trying to secure a further association with the Liberals for a period as long as eighteen months from the end of July 1977, and although another pay agreement with the TUC would be difficult, we should aim for a fall-back position in which the General Council would indicate that although no formal agreement could be reached, they 'understood' the need for the Government's policy. Michael concluded that we should also give our supporters some hope for the future by foreshadowing an improvement in living standards, even though this could not be done at once.

The wish of Ministers to continue quickly made itself felt and I was gratified to find that even those who had opposed the Liberal Agreement in March had subsequently changed their minds. Tony Benn said that the Government, facing both a minority position in Parliament and the worst world slump since the 1930s, had a moral responsibility to the Labour Movement to continue in office. It would never be forgiven for quitting, although there was a danger of defeating ourselves through orthodoxy. There would be dreadful damage to the Party if the Government was defeated and the unions were handed over to Mrs Thatcher still hog-tied to an incomes policy. He then advanced a strange proposition, that Mrs Thatcher might decide after all not to confront the trade unions, but might make up her differences with them. He was nearer the mark when he said that if she won, she could decide to sell North Sea oil in large quantities to overseas countries, and this would lead to large financial surpluses. The Government's course should be to bring forward substantial reflation in the autumn and this, together with a vigorous defence of the national interest, could offer the Government and the country a great future. With this last remark Tony was expressing his opposition to many of the European Community's activities, especially the proposal for direct elections of Members of the European Assembly.

The Chancellor told us that the period of falling living standards was coming to an end, and the Government would be better placed if it continued in office. The country could not pay less tax and at the same time expect social benefits to be increased; the Cabinet must make a choice. He was rather pessimistic about pay prospects, as the 'Neddy 6' (the six TUC leaders serving on the National Economic Development Council) were warning that they would not be able to sell another pay agreement to their colleagues and it was becoming more difficult to hold the twelve-month interval between pay deals. He concluded by supporting strongly the continuation of the Liberal Agreement.

Eric Varley's view was that if there were no guidelines on pay Ford workers would set the stage with a large claim in the autumn. This would be followed by even larger claims by Local Authority manual workers, who would try to leap-frog over Fords and carry us back to the excessive settlements of 1973 to 1975, with serious consequences for inflation. Albert Booth foresaw that if the Government focused too much on holding down pay settlements it would sign its own death warrant, to which Fred Mulley replied that if there was free collective bargaining without restraint, how could the Government be expected to restrain inflation, or to plan any equitable division of the national resources, unless there was heavy unemployment? To this fundamental question no one attempted a reply; it has remained unresolved to this day.

Other matters we discussed as part of our long-term strategy were the best way to reduce the level of unemployment; the next steps needed to carry out party policy on Devolution; the belief expressed by some (which turned out to be accurate) that we were treading a minefield through industrial democracy as the trade unions would be hopelessly split; the problems that pay policy were causing with the police, the prison officers and the Fire Service; and, in view of the divisions in the Party, the difficulties of legislation for elections to the European Assembly.

Every Minister spoke and the mood was vigorous and constructive. In my summing-up I was able to say there was unanimous agreement that we should seek a further arrangement with the Liberal Party for either twelve or eighteen months, and Michael Foot and I would undertake the necessary negotiations. I added that no one must look over his shoulder to make dispositions against the prospect of defeat (I do not recall whether I had any Minister in mind at that moment, but I did later) for when the time came we must all aim to win. It would be difficult to strike the right balance in our discussions with the TUC about the next pay round, but by the end of 1977 the Chancellor would be able to demonstrate the effectiveness of his policy in reducing inflation. The Government's pay policy must be realistic and we might be forced to go ahead on the pay of Local Authority manual workers without having reached agreement with the TUC. On a personal note I added that I would not remain as Prime Minister on sufferance while inflation roared ahead again.

I expressed my strong conviction that the Government must not abandon its objective of full employment, despite our failure to achieve it in 1977, but I was confident if we pursued our existing policies without wavering and without too early reflation the Labour Movement would see a drop in unemployment during the next two years, an opinion that Denis Healey also shared. We should not fritter away the proceeds of North Sea oil when they arrived, but should begin to plan at once to give direction and purpose to their future use.

I concluded by saying that everyone must have been encouraged by the day's proceedings, for it was clear that we were determined not only to survive but also to govern effectively. As a minority Government this could only be done if the country supported our policies because they understood our objectives. Ministers must emphasise the imperative need to bring down inflation, and in addition constantly recall and define in their speeches the kind of society we sought to create.

The following afternoon I met with David Steel who, by coincidence, had also been meeting with his Liberal colleagues on the previous day to discuss a renewal of our Agreement. I had been predisposed to like him from the start for the not very logical reason that thirty years earlier on a visit to West Africa I had stayed with his wife Judy's parents in Sierra Leone. Her father had been a member of the Colonial Civil Service and it is sometimes because of such irrelevant personal contacts that first impressions are formed in politics. In this case, first impressions were lasting. Beneath his quiet exterior, David Steel is a determined man, but one whom I found scrupulous in his dealings with me and always considerate in his understanding of the Government's problems, not least with some of its own supporters. I sometimes had to remind him that there was a net loss to the Government if we won the support of thirteen Liberals but lost the votes of forty Tribunites, some of whom were causing the Chancellor nasty headaches. In the progress of the Finance Bill they had on occasion actually voted with the Tory Opposition in an effort to gain concessions and popularity, whilst the Liberals, sticking to the terms of our Agreement, found themselves on the losing side, voting with Government Ministers. Not unnaturally, the Liberals were unhappy at this, believing it was not their job to support the Government against its own supporters.

I trusted David Steel's discretion and frequently took him into my confidence as a fellow Privy Councillor on a wide range of Government activities, going well beyond the clauses of our Agreement. I wanted him to have as complete a picture as possible of the Government's overall situation so that he would have a better understanding of our limitations. He quickly grasped this, much earlier than his colleagues, who did not enjoy the same advantage and some of whom were quite unrealistic in their expectations. Steel toned down their demands into a manageable package and after a certain amount of to-ing and fro-ing we reached a new Agreement late in July 1977, which we both hoped would carry us through until the autumn of 1978. The major doubt expressed by David Steel about its capacity to endure was his fear that we would not control inflation because of the difficulties the Chancellor was running into in his negotiations with the TUC over the 1977/8 pay round.

Denis Healey had reported to me some months earlier that Jack Jones and Hugh Scanlon, the leaders of the two biggest trade unions, were becoming pessimistic because pressure was building up among their members for a return to free collective bargaining. Some of it was legitimate, they said, but part was being fanned by employers who told their employees they were willing to pay more but were prevented from doing so by agreements made between the TUC and the Labour Government. On 8 July 1977 I called in the CBI to discuss what their members were doing in undermining an agreement which the CBI had approved. Lord Watkinson, the Chairman, said the CBI would be in favour of an effective Phase III (this would be a third year of pay agreements) but then threw up his hands in resignation and told me that the CBI were unable, despite their efforts, to stop medium-sized companies from 'paying the earth', especially for any skilled men they needed. It was a further illustration of the inadequacy of industry's training arrangements.

Both sides of industry knew from experience that the pay agreements of the two earlier years had made an enormous contribution to keeping down costs and restoring a measure of price stability. Industry was not in bad shape. The economy was reviving, and sterling was steady. Interest rates were coming down and capital was flowing in. Earnings in the first nine months of the pay years had increased by 7.5 per cent, which was a great improvement, and unemployment was 1,353,000. The rate of inflation was set to tumble rapidly, and the Chancellor had guaranteed that as a result of the national effort, living standards would not fall during the year. But we were up against the fact that the Conferences of two principal unions, the Transport Workers and the Engineers, had both passed resolutions calling for 'unfettered' collective bargaining, and there were forecasts that big claims were pending from the car workers, dock workers and ICI employees, among others.

I reported to the Cabinet on my disappointing meeting with the CBI leaders who had agreed with the objective of reducing inflation, but could not will the means. Indeed, neither employers nor unions were able to practise a form of self-discipline for a period long enough to have a lasting effect. The Cabinet confirmed that overriding priority was to be given to the continued reduction of inflation. The next step was for me, in company with the Chancellor and the Secretaries for Employment and Industry, to meet the TUC in advance of their Congress in September. At this meeting, a few days later, I expressed the Government's thanks to the trade unions for curbing their bargaining power during the previous two years, which had resulted in a substantial gain to the national welfare, but told them that if the country was to achieve single figure inflation we would need single figure pay settlements, with increases not exceeding 10 per cent for the following year. If this objective was unobtainable the only possible alternatives were depreciation of sterling, and more inflation and unemployment, all of which were unacceptable to the Government. I understood that they still shared the Government's aim of a level of inflation no higher than that of our overseas competitors.

How did the TUC propose that this target should be reached? At this, there was immediate objection by the TUC spokesmen to discussing any target figures for pay. Precision, it was said, in the face of demands for free collective bargaining, would backfire. One or two went further, notably Alan Fisher, the left-wing leader of the National Union of Public Em-

ployees, who argued that the whole policy had been unfair. Coming from
him, this was singularly wrong-headed for his members, who were among
the lowest paid, had benefited more than most other groups as the policy
had been deliberately tilted in their favour. It was in fact Hugh Scanlon's
Engineers who had a relative grievance. Other objections were raised. If
the unions agreed not to press for all they could get at the moment, how
could they be certain that a Labour Government would still be in office
when the time arrived for some improvement? Would not a Tory Government take advantage of their previous abstention? And so on.

I responded by acknowledging their difficulties but re-emphasising
that the Government had a responsibility not to allow a return to the
corrosively high levels of inflation of the early 1970s. We were committed
to that for the sake of everyone, for industrial investment, for maintaining
jobs, for the family, for the pensioner. I continued by putting three
questions to them. First, was the TUC saying that this was the end of the
road, and that no further agreement on pay could be reached? Second,
did the TUC accept that the Government would have to consider issuing
its own policy on pay limits without the agreement of the TUC? Third,
if the Government did this, would the TUC expect open conflict with
Government?

I continued: 'If the answer to these three questions is "yes", then I must
consider whether the Government should continue in office in an atmosphere in which relations between us will be increasingly poisoned. If we
give up now, we are admitting that conflict between the aspirations of the
trade unions and the objectives of the Government is inevitable. In that
event a Conservative Government will have to fight the battle because
a Labour Government, for honourable reasons, cannot carry it through.'

Lionel Murray, as General Secretary of the TUC, at once took up my
challenge. He was cool, conciliatory and practical. The unions wanted
the Government to continue, but they would not be able to make an
exact figure for pay increases 'stick'. Would it be possible to arrive at a
lesser agreement that would be more likely to 'stick'? If so, the TUC
would welcome discussions. Others took up the same theme, especially
Hugh Scanlon, Jack Jones, Alf Allen and David Basnett, who were members of the National Economic Development Council (the 'Neddy 6')
and were leaders of some of the biggest unions. Frank Chapple characteristically parodied himself with the mixture of scorn and arrogance
that so often destroys much of the value of what he says, but generally the mood of the Council was one which recognised the problem,

expressed a readiness to help, but demonstrated an inability to see what could effectively be done.

After the meeting Denis Healey summed up the situation with the comment: 'The unions have too much responsibility and too little power with their members.' The meeting with the TUC had ended with only one firm conclusion and this was negative, namely that the TUC could not deliver a third year of pay agreement, and the Government must anticipate a return to so-called free collective bargaining.

This was a blow, although not unexpected in the aftermath of the results of the various trade union conferences. But all was by no means lost. Unhappy memories of the high inflation of earlier years were still fresh in the minds of trade unionists; there was substantial support among the public for a prices and incomes policy; and we knew that although the activists had forced the pace at some of the union conferences, not all their leaders were happy that they were following the right path. The Government could therefore count on understanding for its policy, if not positive agreement, provided we showed ourselves sensitive to trade unions' attempts to remove the distortions that pay policy had brought about.

My personal position was absolutely committed to a reduction in the inflation level, and the Cabinet quickly agreed that the Chancellor should make a formal statement of our intentions. On 15 July, two days after the abortive meeting with the TUC, the Chancellor went down to the House to announce that the Government's objective for 1978 would be to reduce the inflation rate to single figures for the first time in the 1970s, and that this would require pay settlements also to be in single figures, so that the rate of increase in national earnings should not exceed 10 per cent. This would not reduce living standards, but to ensure this he proposed to increase income tax allowances and child benefits. He further said that Government finance would be available to increase activity in the construction industry, and dividends would be limited to 10 per cent.

Ministers set out to sell this package, and it was at this point that the intimate relations which we had established with the 'Neddy 6' proved their worth. Several months earlier, I had invited the 'Neddy 6' to a small formal working dinner at No. 10 to join two or three Ministers for a general discussion. Both sides had found the occasion useful, and we thereupon agreed to make it a monthly event, and so it continued throughout the remainder of the Government's life. The basic composition of the 'Neddy 6' team was Jack Jones, Hugh Scanlon, David Basnett, Alf Allen, Geoffrey Drain and Lionel Murray, the General Secretary. The Government side comprised Michael Foot, Denis Healey and myself with one or other of our colleagues. This relaxed group, gathering when the day's work was done and sitting around the table for as long as we wished, gave Ministers the chance to explain our problems and prospects, and the 'Neddy 6' the opportunity to respond and in turn to tell us where the shoe was pinching. The 'Neddy 6' worked best while Jack Jones and Hugh Scanlon remained members, and later on was materially weakened by their retirements.

At the critical moment in the 1977 pay talks the old partnership between Michael Foot and Jack Jones and between Denis Healey and Lionel Murray came into play. On 19 July the Economic Committee of the TUC issued a statement which was notable for the moderation with which it put forward the case for a return to free collective bargaining. It said that pay claims must be orderly; a pay explosion must be avoided; it drew attention to the adverse consequences for inflation if pay increases exceeded 10 per cent; it called upon the unions not to return to the damaging practice of reopening pay settlements in less than twelve months; it pointed out that trade unionists shared in the national responsibility to avoid high inflation; and emphasised its desire to continue close cooperation between the trade unions and the Government. In the absence of an agreement, the Government could hardly have asked for more.

In the first week of September I travelled to Blackpool to address the TUC at their Annual Conference. My theme was simple. I expressed genuine appreciation of the way in which they had voluntarily surrendered part of their bargaining power in the national interest, acknowledged the difficulties the pay policy was causing, said the Government could not abdicate its responsibility for reducing inflation, reiterated that a return to free collective bargaining made it even more imperative that pay increases should be moderate in order to improve our competitive position and prevent unemployment from growing, and emphasised that those who said that the Government's policy was opposed to the trade unions misunderstood the situation. On the contrary, the Government was fighting for the real long-term interests of their members.

The delegates listened closely and I felt with considerable understanding. At the end they applauded warmly and in the debate that followed even those who were opposed to the policy spoke more in sorrow than in anger. The upshot was encouraging for the Government; the General Council's statement of 19 July was endorsed with a majority of nearly three million votes. So far, so good.

At the Labour Party's Annual Conference a month later resolutions rejecting the Government's policy were also defeated, thanks to the understanding of the trade union delegations and also to outstanding speeches from Denis Healey and Barbara Castle. Barbara, who wound up the debate, was realistic in describing our economic prospects so that the delegates would have no false illusions, but at the same time she stood aside from the Government, criticising us (as she was entitled to do), and this combination was what the delegates wished to hear. However, I was concerned that while we might win the votes at the Conferences these decisions would be forgotten when the delegates returned home and the pay bargaining started. A Belfast firm with four thousand employees had already conceded a huge pay increase of 22 per cent in the week preceding the Conference and this had been prominently reported.

Certain public sector unions (notably NUPE) were in the vanguard in rejecting the Government's pay policy and a crack was beginning to show between them and the industrial unions. Members of the 'Neddy 6' told me they were losing patience with the NUPE leaders whose approach was, they said, 'totally unrealistic'. They believed that, given a strong lead, it should be possible for the Government to achieve a general run of settlements within a level of 10 per cent. This was very heartening for, as I hope I have made clear, I had no wish to say one thing to the country only to find myself drifting in the opposite direction.

With the inflation rate still as high as 16 per cent my Cabinet colleagues and I were determined that it must come down during 1978. The last thing I wanted was a fudge in which the TUC and the Labour Party passed pious resolutions only to ignore them, so I put the issue bluntly to the Party Conference: 'In the end the people will decide. Meantime I say to both sides of industry – please don't support us with general expressions of goodwill and kind words, and then undermine us through unjustified wage increases or price increases – either back us or sack us. This country has got to make a choice and I have made mine.'

I was extemporising in my speech at this point, and the euphonic phrase 'back us or sack us' came unbidden. It received a lot of publicity and trade union leaders have told me since that these words had a considerable effect for some time afterwards. They needed a return to free collective bargaining, but they also wanted the Labour Government to continue and they knew I was in earnest when I said that I would not remain in office unless the Government could bring down inflation levels.

The concern of the public about high inflation was very high and

opinion polls during the winter of 1977 showed that over 70 per cent of
those questioned supported the Government's pay policy as the best
means of bringing inflation under control. Nevertheless, there were
serious evasions, and these placed a heavy burden on the Ministers who
were monitoring the progress of several different pay claims at the same
time. The Cabinet sub-committee charged with this task met regularly
at least twice a week for several hours. Much of the work was shared between the Chancellor and the Home Secretary, Merlyn Rees, but Merlyn
was carrying a heavy load in his own Department and Denis Healey could
not attempt to do it all. As the winter of 1977/8 wore on it was obvious
that new arrangements were needed, and I called in one of the younger
members of the Cabinet, Roy Hattersley, to become Chairman of the Pay
Committee. He did not have a heavy Department and was therefore able
to devote his time and considerable energy mainly to the monitoring work.

Lionel Murray and his colleagues had been consistently helpful
throughout the whole period and had always sought ways of easing difficulties. Denis Healey found Murray's advice and cooperation invaluable
but by the New Year of 1978, the TUC machine was beginning to feel the
strain, and Lionel Murray complained to the Chancellor that he was
having to take a lot of stick on the Government's behalf from some trade
union activists.

We suffered a further setback at the hands of the power workers, who
in earlier years had shown they were ready to throw the switches if their
pay demands were not met. They made a claim for a 30 per cent pay
increase from 1 January 1978, and Frank Chapple made threatening
noises. I knew that the leaders of the other unions in the electrical industry
believed such a claim was grossly excessive, but they were in the position
in which union leaders sometimes find themselves, of being unable to
dissent openly when they are outflanked by a populist approach. It seemed
that the Government might be faced with a strike involving power cuts,
blackouts in homes, offices and industry, and all the resulting misery that
would fall on the public. Nevertheless, if the power workers succeeded in
winning such an absurd increase, the floodgates would be open for every
other group to follow in their wake and the country could say goodbye
to any hope of reducing inflation. The Chancellor and I talked the matter
over and agreed that he must ensure that both the employers and the
unions understood the Government's strong opposition; the Chancellor
should try to convince them that a settlement of 10 per cent was in everyone's long-term interest.

Because the power workers are a powerful, pace-setting group, we also agreed that we should try to ensure that their negotiations were not unduly hurried, so as to give time for a number of other more moderate claims to be finalised first. At the same time I instructed the Cabinet Office to prepare contingency plans to cope with a strike. This they did. Our January working dinner with 'Neddy 6' was due and I raised the matter with them. They knew better than I the knock-on effect a 30 per cent pay agreement would have on their own members. I therefore said that if the power workers sought a direct confrontation on pay I would have no alternative but to seek the backing of the House of Commons to deal with it, and the trade unions generally would have to live with the consequences.

This last remark referred to the likelihood of the Government being defeated, for neither Mrs Thatcher nor a handful of our own backbenchers were minded to help over pay. The employers in the electrical industry had decided to make an offer of 10 per cent, which was at the top of the limit the Government hoped for, but the union rejected this on 2 February 1978 and a few days later, on 7 February, the Opposition embarrassed us by moving a motion alleging that the Government was misusing its powers on pay. When a discussion took place, eleven Labour members abstained from voting and the Government would have been in serious difficulty had not David Steel and the Liberals voted with us, in accordance with our arrangement. Not unnaturally they told me they saw no reason why they should continue to support the Government if some of its own followers refused to do so.

As was the intention, this debate weakened the Government's stand and the power workers pressed on, wearing down the employers' resistance; they responded by increasing their offer. In the end both sides reached agreement on an average pay rise of 17 per cent, far in excess of the Government's target, and I found little comfort from those who told me it was much less than the original 30 per cent claim. Perhaps the only good was that the settlement did not take place until 2 April, by which time a number of other claims had already been settled and the winter was over.

My brave words to the 'Neddy 6' had had a very limited effect and Frank Chapple and his union had unwittingly taken another step towards creating the conditions that would lead to high unemployment and the weakening of the trade unions in the 1980s. Despite these setbacks, however, we were managing to get through the 1977/8 pay year – admittedly with difficulty, but this was mostly contained. We felt increasing concern about the level of public service pay and the best way of ensuring that this compared fairly with other levels. I had become interested in the West German system of 'concerted action' for the private sector in which two major pay claims near the beginning of a pay round received intensive discussion at all levels of industry and government before they were finalised, and were then generally regarded as setting the pattern for the remainder. Helmut Schmidt had described this to me in some detail, and it seemed a method by which the unions might return to so-called 'free collective bargaining' without ill effects, provided they exercised an enlightened self-interest.

It seemed highly unlikely that the 'acquiescence' of the TUC, on which we had relied during the winter of 1977/8, would endure for the pay year 1978/9 and the Cabinet began a search for a viable alternative. At the final meeting of the Cabinet in 1977, held three days before Christmas, I summed up for Ministers my view about the outlook for 1978. It seemed that if we held as near as we could to our pay objectives the inflation rate would be steadily reduced to about 9 per cent. That would be a note-worthy achievement compared with earlier years, but I urged that the Cabinet should impress upon the country that 9 per cent inflation was simply not good enough when compared with the performance of other countries. It was at this meeting that for the first time I put forward the fateful figure of 5 per cent inflation as our objective for the pay year beginning in August 1978. This would require wage settlements of the same order, recognising that these would mean earnings increases of about 7 per cent.

Everything that has happened since that time *uas* reinforced my con-viction that the trade unions would have been better off, their members would have endured less unemployment, and the country might have escaped the more outrageous attacks on the Social Services if my 5 per cent objective had been accepted and worked for, even if we had not immediately achieved it.

Interminably we discussed alternative approaches and more accept-able solutions, and a different emphasis began to emerge. This showed itself starkly at a meeting at Chequers on a Sunday early in February 1978, to which I had invited Ministers for a relaxed discussion to enable them to inject into the Chancellor's thinking their views about priorities for his forthcoming Budget.

He reported that for the first time for several years inflation had fallen below 10 per cent – actually it was 9.9 per cent – and no doubt he hoped for some congratulations. Instead, he found a number of his colleagues impatiently taking up the cry of employers, unions and the Opposition for a faster rate of growth, and for more public expenditure.

He was told that at 1.5 millions the unemployed figure was a disgrace, and it was said that this figure threatened the whole social fabric of society. Tony Benn argued his case as he did steadily at every opportunity (and I always gave him the chance) for an entirely different policy which he had christened a National Development Programme, but as usual he found no takers among the other Ministers. At the conclusion of one of these expositions, I said to him that I often found myself agreeing with much of his analysis but parted company when he reached his proposed solutions, entirely unconvinced that they would produce a long-term solution.

The Social Services Secretary, David Ennals, demanded an additional £3 billions from the Budget, and others took up the cry. I reminded everyone that this was not necessarily the last Budget before a general election, and there might well be a further Budget in the spring of 1979. The year 1978 would be a test of the Government's continued competence in the eyes of the nation. Loss of that confidence could lead to the loss of the general election.

If this account seems to devote disproportionate space to our pay and economic problems, it is no more than an accurate reflection of the dominant flavour of Government at the time, with pay in particular absorbing Ministers' nervous energies to a greater degree than almost any other issue.

It was always my aim to stand back as much as possible, so as to be able to take a broader view of the scene. Since my period as Chancellor in the 1960s, there had been a number of important changes in world monetary and trade management. National currencies had broken free from the moorings of fixed exchange rates. Currency devaluation and revaluation, despite their bearing on the balance of payments, the competitiveness of exports and the volatility of interest rates, now took place unremarked except in the financial pages of the newspapers. The doctrine of monetarism had come into prominence as the latest cure-all for our economic ills. These changes had propelled the Bank of England into the lead in much of the financial decision-making and its policies were distilled to the Cabinet through the Chancellor.

I had complete confidence in the Chancellor but in view of the importance of Bank policy felt I would like to get a little closer to the Governor's thinking at first hand. Relations between national governments and their central banks varied a great deal. In France the central bank had been totally under the thumb of President de Gaulle and his successors. In post-war Germany the Allies had provided for a legal separation between bank and government, a fact Helmut Schmidt made full use of whenever he was pressed at international gatherings to take action involving the central banks.

The United States Federal Reserve Bank also exercised its role independently of the Administration. In Britain a kind of mid-way position existed. The Bank of England had been nationalised in 1946, but in addition to being the banker for the United Kingdom, it also held the sterling reserves of a number of Commonwealth countries, and it was ever conscious of its obligations to them. In the 1950s and 1960s it could not be said that relations were intimate at all working levels of the Bank and the Treasury, but the events of the ensuing decade broke down much of the distance between them.

Common experience of world economic events had also encouraged informal discussion of monetary matters when leaders of countries met one another, and their importance was formally recognised in November 1975 when President Giscard invited the Heads of State and Government of Germany, the United States, Italy, Japan and Britain to an Economic Summit at Rambouillet. I accompanied Harold Wilson and it seemed to me that the discussions both there and at the second Summit at Puerto Rico in 1976 revealed a gap in our own machinery of government. I therefore decided to set up a group to keep a watch on the interplay of our domestic fiscal and monetary policy with that of overseas countries. It included the Governor of the Bank of England, the Chancellor of the Exchequer and the Foreign Secretary, together with their Permanent Secretaries, Harold Lever (the Chancellor of the Duchy of Lancaster), the Chief Secretary to the Treasury, and the Heads of the Think Tank and of the Policy Unit, Sir Kenneth Berrill and Bernard Donoughue. Gordon Richardson, Governor of the Bank, also brought along his Deputy Governor, Christopher McMahon, of whom I had a high opinion and who had been one of my advisers when I established an earlier economic seminar at Nuffield College during the 1960s. Other Ministers were added from time to time, depending upon the subjects under discussion, and on one occasion in 1978 when the dollar was under attack Ed Streator, the American Minister in London, was invited to join us. I have traced fourteen of these seminars held in the two years 1977 and 1978, an indication that I found them both enjoyable and rewarding.

My practice was to call for papers to be prepared by one or other of the participants on possible developments in certain areas of international finance such as the future levels of the dollar and of sterling, the prospect for interest rates, our use of the sterling safety net, repayments to the IMF, monetary targets and so on. These influential seminars took no formal decisions but the tenor of our discussions led to closer understanding between the Bank and the Government of each other's thinking and undoubtedly influenced both the Bank's policy and the recommendations that the Chancellor placed before the Cabinet.

One subject which we approached with caution was the doctrine of monetarism, and opposing points of view were examined at length, although in the end I do not recall anyone who fiercely embraced the faith. It would be more true to say that we tiptoed around the edges. Monetarism, we were told, would 'burn out' inflation through a twofold policy of rigid monetary restraint and a free-floating pound, whose value would rise and therefore have the effect of reducing import prices. This would not add to unemployment, so it was said, because consumption would be stimulated by the increase in people's money balances brought about by the lower price levels. This seemed somewhat specious and the Treasury having, as I had requested, argued the case at length ended by introducing a strong, sceptical note and a prescient warning: 'Many of us believe that the transitional adverse effects on economic activity and employment [on monetarism] would be both serious and prolonged.' We took heed of that but our successors did not, and as the early 1980s showed, rarely has such a warning proved so deadly accurate in its forecast.

Harold Lever had few Departmental duties and with more time at his disposal than most, issued a stream of stimulating papers from his office, taking what the Americans call 'an overview' of the world economic scene, relating this to Britain's domestic position and challenging us all to rethink our positions. He was among the first to call attention to the threat of imprudent lending by parts of the banking system, because of the unlikelihood that the developing world would ever be in a position to meet its debts. He, like Helmut Schmidt, was impatient with the United States' neglect of its responsibility for the dollar's role as a world currency. He urged the need for international leadership, and on the domestic front kept up a continuous peppering of the Bank and Treasury to force them to justify policies and actions. He sometimes missed his aim, but I do not hesitate to say that over many years his analysis and his predictions have more often proved right than wrong.

I should interpose that our discussions of these matters were made easier by the relaxation of pressure on our domestic economic position following the conclusion of the 1976 IMF negotiations. As the months elapsed we had become almost embarrassed by the inflows of sterling and were able to reduce interest rates steadily. The economy was reviving, our inflation prospects improving; we were in a position to decide whether or not to terminate our 'stand-by' arrangements with the IMF and at the beginning of 1978 we repaid $1 billions to the Fund. The Chancellor could in fact have repaid more, but it was cheap money (we paid 4¾ per cent interest) and although this was not generally appreciated, it was worth our while to keep to part of the loan.

Although it had not been so intended when President Giscard issued his invitation to Rambouillet, the International Economic Summits later took on an existence of their own, and my regular seminar at No. 10 proved highly useful in proposing initiatives that would then be sent back to Departments to be worked up before coordinating our position for summit meetings. Giscard was intellectually restless. Like President de Gaulle, he believed in an active French presence. The West displayed instability and had no vision of its economic future and Giscard thought we should confront the matter. He had spoken of the idea of a high-level meeting for some time and returned to the subject at a lunch given by Harold Wilson at the Helsinki Conference for President Ford, Chancellor Schmidt and President Giscard, at which the Foreign Secretaries of the four countries were also present.

Gerry Ford had seemed rather unenthusiastic about Giscard's proposal, and as we sat in the garden of the British Embassy drinking our after-lunch coffee in the warm July sun, it was to him that Giscard mainly addressed his ideas. Helmut Schmidt too had previously sent us a paper prepared by him, containing a plea for the United States to be less domestic-orientated, urging it to take into account the international repercussions of its policies and suggesting a summit attended by the four of us plus Japan and Italy. Harold Wilson backed the idea and with Henry Kissinger also speaking in favour, the United States President agreed. We decided that each Head of Government should appoint a personal representative to prepare for the conference, and asked France to act as host.

Harold Wilson and I then left the hospitality of the Embassy to visit Tito, and the only hitch in the proposed arrangements occurred when in the hot-house atmosphere of Helsinki the Italians heard a rumour that

they were not to be invited, and uttered a cry of pain which was only stilled
by our reassurance that they would be there. Harold Wilson and I proposed adding Canada and President Ford agreed, but Giscard was adamant and no invitation was sent. We had agreed that such a summit must
be properly prepared in advance, and for this purpose meetings took
place in New York and elsewhere between the Heads of Governments'
personal representatives. These were soon christened 'sherpas' because,
like Tibetan mountaineers, their task was to carry the load to the summit. They worked to a brief which ran as follows: international cooperation in economic matters was as important as in defence matters;
expectations should not be raised too high; it was not the purpose to
produce a perfect blueprint for the future, but we should build on the
personal relationships between the Heads of Government. The intention
was to hold an informal discussion in the broadest political framework
with no holds barred. Each Head of Government was asked to give a
completely candid assessment of the economic prospects of his own
country, to be followed by an examination of future world difficulties as
a whole. To keep the atmosphere informal, attendance was limited to
three from each country – the Head of Government and the Foreign and
Finance Ministers, making a total of eighteen participants. Supporting
staff would not attend the sessions.

The castle at Rambouillet, the location of the summit, was hardly big
enough even for eighteen, and each day helicopters came and went from
Paris, their rotor blades bending the saplings in the park and whirling the
fallen autumn leaves into the air, as if in a snowstorm.

Accommodation was so cramped that the best the French Foreign
Minister could do was to digest urgent telegrams on a table placed in a
corridor, while the officials in the British delegation worked in Napoleon's
bathroom. But none of this detracted from the country house atmosphere
that Giscard had intended and in which he felt so much at home. Thrown
closely together, the coolish atmosphere soon warmed up and President
Ford in particular relaxed. Ford genuinely believed in a cooperative
approach and wished to avoid a confrontation with Giscard, an objective
that was more easily achieved because a French–American dispute on
monetary matters had been partially settled a week or two before the
meeting. In a way this agreement could be counted as a success of the
Rambouillet meeting, for the knowledge that the summit was to take
place spurred the negotiators of both sides to settle.

Two other factors assisted immeasurably: one was that with only one exception, all the Heads of Government, including Takeo Miki, the Japanese Premier, spoke English. The exception was Aldo Moro of Italy. This common language resulted in a quick-fire exchange of views, while the round table around which we sat was small enough to enable interjections to be made easily without interrupting the general flow of argument, and clarifications could be instantaneous. The other favourable factor was that the press was kept at a distance – as far away as Paris. No one indulged in the bad habit of making a contribution and then rushing from the room to tell the press what he had said. This engendered confidence, and genuine dialogue could take place; doubts, hesitations and provisional views could be expressed without the danger that too much significance would be attached to them. During the weekend we enjoyed twelve hours of such relaxed exchanges, in addition to bilateral and other conversations at mealtimes and at night.

Real differences emerged between the participants, notably about the United States' determination to adhere to floating exchange rates, but also on the future of older industries such as textiles and steel, and about the attitudes of the participants to the energy crisis, especially the indexing of oil prices.

Harold Wilson made a powerful and effective contribution, setting out the dire effects of recent oil price increases on the less developed countries. This had sprung from what he and I had learned from the Commonwealth leaders a few months earlier when we had attended the Commonwealth Conference of thirty-four member countries at Kingston, Jamaica. They had convinced us that there was no way they could solve the problems caused by the oil price increases without additional financial help.

Giscard shared our general conclusions, but Helmut, lacking the emotional and historical links of Empire, was more sceptical; Simon, the United States Secretary to the Treasury, argued strongly that developing countries' deficits should be financed by the commercial banking system. He had his way, with the resultant discomfiture to the banks and their Third World debtors that the world has seen.

In the more informal sessions we exchanged views about the prospects for Spain following General Franco's death, the prospects for success of the United States SALT talks with the Soviet Union, how the West should manage its relations with China, as well as public expenditure in the United Kingdom, where some of the others urged the need for caution.

It could not be claimed that much was decided at Rambouillet but we left the meetings more fully informed of the domestic, economic and political factors and of the international factors which governed each other's policies. We educated one another, and in doing so created greater understanding and a conviction that none of the six could solve the problems of recession or unemployment in isolation from the others. Rambouillet paved the way for regular annual summit meetings, largely because it was a forerunner of the mid-1970s view that the economic health of the major industrial nations depended on a coordinated strategy.

A second summit was held at Puerto Rico in 1976 with President Ford as host and Chairman. Canada now joined the summit members, bringing the total to seven. London was the venue for the third, in 1977, and I was intent on holding it at 10 Downing Street in order to preserve the informality of our proceedings. Rarely has London experienced a more crowded and enjoyable summer than in this year of the Queen's Silver Jubilee. The capital was host in quick succession to conferences of Heads of Government of the Commonwealth, the Heads of Government attending a meeting of the European Council, a conference of the NATO Powers and the Downing Street Summit. As Britain was host country, it fell to me to preside on all these occasions during an exhausting but exhilarating year. The Queen, in addition to her other heavy duties, such as an overseas tour of the Commonwealth and her visits to all parts of the United Kingdom, also agreed to entertain those attending this rapid succession of meetings. But arduous though her duties were, she seemed to thrive on the constant procession of visitors and never once did I see her less than sparkling and vivacious at her many public engagements throughout the whole period.

During my first visit to meet President Carter, in the previous March, he had told me in Washington that he would wish to pay a call on the Queen while he was in London and I arranged, in addition, that he should spend a day in the provinces. I wanted to show him something different from the standard tour of London, Oxford and Stratford so I chose the North East, part of the industrial heartland of Britain, where hearts are warm and the people's character, moulded by hardship, is steadfast.

When the President agreed to include a visit to Durham in his itinerary, I placed the oversight of the arrangements in the hands of Ernie Armstrong, Member of Parliament for Durham North East and Parliamentary Secretary to the Department of the Environment. He did his job well and everything went without a hitch, except that the tulip tree which had been sent from Mount Vernon, Virginia, for the President to plant in Washington New Town succumbed on the journey. A replacement was later secured, however, and on my most recent visit, I was glad to see that both the President's tree and the English oak that I planted near it are flourishing, though mine, as I have told him, is the taller of the two! The President naturally paid a visit to Washington Old Hall, the ancestral home of the first President of the United States, but his most tumultuous reception came when he stood on the steps of Newcastle Town Hall, and began his reply to the Lord Mayor's speech of welcome with the famous local rallying cry, 'Hawaay the lads!' The phrase was of course unfamiliar to Jimmy Carter, and he was doubtful about using it, but I coached him during the motorcade procession and as soon as he uttered it, a tremendous cheer went up.

When the short visit was over he was presented with the symbolic miner's lamp and I gave him a copy of Jack Lawson's autobiography *A Man's Life*, the book I had admired for many years. Jimmy Carter wrote to tell me that it had been his reading on his homeward journey across the Atlantic, and it was obvious that the book and his whole visit had given him new insights about Britain. At our first meeting I had formed a clear impression of a man with a well-stocked mind and disciplined approach. He had given considerable thought to his intended initiatives and had a clear idea of what he wished to achieve.

I had reported to Schmidt and Giscard that they would find him earnest, straightforward and without artifice, wishing to improve America's moral standing in the world. This was illustrated when he told me that he intended to raise the question of human rights at the Downing Street Summit, a decision that caused some pursing of lips among German officials who feared that it would raise undue expectations which would not ultimately be fulfilled, with as a consequence greater disappointment in the end. He was anxious that the Soviet Union should take his initiatives seriously, but coming new, as he did, to the international scene, his misplaced belief that the Soviets would accept his gestures and policies at their face value led to disillusion. He had a manifest dislike of horse-trading, and was not ready enough to use tactical skill to overcome the vested interests and powerful Washington lobbies which challenged him. This was a real impediment to getting his programmes through Congress, to whom horse-trading is the way to do business.

The President and his wife worship with the Southern Baptists and their deep moral conviction is evident in their daily lives, without being obtrusive. I recall the President, in the upstairs privacy of his personal apartments at the White House, inviting us to clasp hands with one another before meals, to make a complete circle around the table while he uttered Grace. A gentle and a good man.

Within weeks of President Carter's taking office a problem had arisen about the conditions under which the United States was prepared to supply nuclear fuel to Europe and to other parts of the world. Carter's motives were praiseworthy for he wished to prevent the nuclear fuel exported for peaceful purposes from being subsequently converted into explosives. As part of this, he brought pressure to bear upon Germany and France to halt the export of nuclear reactors to Brazil and Pakistan for which contracts had already been signed. Schmidt in particular took umbrage and told me in vehement tones that Germany would never yield to pressure on these matters from the United States or anyone else. As I was the President of the European Council at the time of President Carter's inauguration, and was also to be the host at the Downing Street Summit, Giscard and Helmut had suggested that I should be the first to visit Washington, and during my stay I attempted to cool the nuclear reactor dispute.

President Carter agreed to place the issue of nuclear fuel policy on the agenda for the forthcoming London Summit in May and I secured the assent of France and Germany for this. But this did not stop Helmut Schmidt coming to London in a smouldering mood, exacerbated by Carter's method of handling discussions. With his precise engineer's mind, the President believed that at the end of a discussion rational people should reach a set of concrete conclusions and an orderly plan of action. He did not at first take on board that when dealing with other Heads of Government it is often counter-productive to force discussion to the point where there is open disagreement accompanied by loss of face. Sometimes of course this will be necessary, but the seven summit members in those early days worked effectively only when there was a consensus, and I have wondered since whether the differences between Schmidt and Carter which emerged in the early weeks of the new Administration coloured Schmidt's later attitude towards United States policies.

However, I must say that Carter candidly acknowledged at the London Summit that the United States might have been guilty of some insensitivity in its handling of the nuclear fuel question, adding in a disarming fashion that the Administration had much to learn. He further improved the atmosphere by a decision to release additional supplies of uranium, but rightly warned that recipient countries must comply with a programme of safeguards to prevent misuse. Carter went on to propose that the Seven should set up a technical group to assess world uranium reserves and the willingness of nuclear suppliers to increase their enrichment facilities, to define the constraints to be placed on consumer countries before they received supplies and to examine the provision of facilities for disposal and other similar problems.

This led to a long and occasionally acrimonious discussion on such questions as the extent to which the world ought to rely on nuclear energy in preference to alternative sources; the future prospects for adequate alternatives; the extent to which supplying countries should apply the same restraints to themselves that they would impose on others, and the anticipated reaction of those countries whose interests were also involved but which would not be part of the proposed study. There was a difference of emphasis as to whether the major purpose of the study was to produce a system of safeguards to prevent the misuse of nuclear fuel, or an examination of future world energy requirements and how they were to be met. But these differences were overcome by some quick footwork during my summing-up and the study went ahead. I refer to this discussion and its outcome to illustrate how a summit meeting could ease bilateral difficulties, lessen misunderstandings and find a useful method of carrying forward policy on a matter of vital importance to the world's future. Discussion on this issue at the summit had not been unduly long, perhaps three hours in all, but it was worth weeks, if not months, of correspondence at the diplomatic level. Most importantly, without a face-to-face meeting, the study to which we committed our officials might never have materialised.

Most of our discussions at the Downing Street Summit were spent reviewing the economic situation of the industrialised countries and the developing world, and exchanging opinions on the policies that should be adopted. Once again, as in previous summits, we educated ourselves and enlightened one another; at the finish we agreed on six conclusions:

1 The most urgent task was to create more jobs, especially for young people, while continuing to reduce inflation which was itself a cause of unemployment.

2 Each Government committed itself to a stated level of growth or a stabilisation programme which when added to the others should provide a

PRIME MINISTER

basis for world-wide growth. If such targets were not likely to be reached, appropriate action was to be taken.

3 In a change from the United States' attitude at Puerto Rico, the Seven committed themselves to securing additional financial resources for the IMF and for the World Bank so that their lending to the Third World should rise and aid levels be increased.

4 The assembled Governments rejected protectionism as not increasing jobs in the long run.

5 Pledges were given to increase conservation and saving of energy, to reduce dependence on oil by diversifying into other energy sources; and while recognising the need to increase nuclear energy as a source of supply, the Heads of Government committed themselves to reduce the risks arising from proliferation.

6 The Governments undertook to give a new impetus to world trade negotiations in view of the fundamental differences in the world economy that had arisen since the oil price rise of 1973.

The success of these summit meetings in terms of productive results depends largely on the thoroughness with which they are prepared. Sir John Hunt, the Cabinet Secretary, who reported directly to me, spared no effort in getting ready for the Downing Street Summit and his standing among his fellow 'sherpas' ensured that the ground was well cultivated by the time we met. Our numbers were small enough to enable us to meet around a large square table in the State Dining Room at No. 10. Denis Healey, David Owen and I sat at one end, facing the Italian Prime Minister, Andreotti, and Germany's Helmut Schmidt, with Pierre Trudeau of Canada and Giscard d'Estaing of France on my left, and Jimmy Carter and Takeo Fukuda, Prime Minister of Japan, on my right. Roy Jenkins, representing the European Community, was seated next to the British delegation.

Once again, the benefit from us all speaking English was apparent. The Japanese were usually noted for their silence at such gatherings but Takeo Fukuda had served in the Japanese Embassy in London prior to World War II and joined fluently in the exchanges. At the end of our discussions, he said that he had been impressed by the evident desire for cooperation: Pierre Trudeau commented on the frankness of our exchanges: Carter, as a first-time attender, had been struck by the friendly atmosphere and by the advantage of having five former Finance Ministers as Heads of Government: Schmidt's conclusion was that each summit meeting had reinforced our confidence in one another, despite the fact that we could obviously not expect to wipe all the world's problems off the face of the earth in two days.

We had decided to monitor the results of the summit, and set up a Nuclear Energy Group under French chairmanship. One report was produced, after which its role was handed over to a wider international body for the purpose of evaluating the complete nuclear fuel cycle. Another group followed up the economic commitments the Seven had entered into and a two-day monitoring session was held in Washington in September 1977. Their reports were noteworthy for the comments of the Japanese and German representatives, both countries reporting that the London understandings had been a real factor in influencing their domestic decisions.

There were, however, problems related to the future. It had been understood that Germany would be the host for the 1978 summit, but friction between Carter and Schmidt continued and David Owen, the Foreign Secretary, reported to me that the United States Secretary of State, Cyrus Vance, had told him that because of this, President Carter was profoundly doubtful about attending a further Summit. This may have been a ploy to put pressure on Schmidt, who, truth to tell, had some justification for his irritation, but voiced his criticism very bluntly.

The cause of the trouble was America's reluctance to act to stabilise the dollar which, because of growing American indebtedness and inflation, was steadily weakening. This had a countervailing effect on other currencies, sterling for example appreciating in January 1978 to $1.93 to the pound, a level I felt was too high for the competitive position of our exports. During the autumn of 1977, Harold Lever had written a series of very perceptive comments on the consequences of the dollar's decline for United Kingdom interest rates, the future of the gilt-edged market and the wider consequences of an unstable monetary system. The Bank of England and the Treasury also prepared papers and I decided to hold one of the Prime Minister's seminars in January 1978. When it took place, general concern was expressed not only by Harold Lever but also by the Governor of the Bank and by Denis Healey at the way the world monetary situation was developing and the absence of an American response.

One reason for this lack of attention was Jimmy Carter's decision to concentrate his energies in repairing a serious decline in the relations between Egypt and Israel, which had worsened after the initial euphoria caused by President Sadat's momentous descent on Jerusalem in November 1977. Carter felt the process of reconciling Jew and Arab had gone into reverse, largely as a result of the Israeli Prime Minister's attitude. I had met Prime Minister Begin some years earlier in Jerusalem before he came to office, when a conversation between us had ended in a fierce dispute, although as always, he never became discourteous. Later, when we were both in office, I decided to invite him to London, a fact that he much appreciated in view of his desperate hostility towards Britain in the period preceding the establishment of the State of Israel. We had then called him a terrorist. He saw himself as a Jewish patriot. His early history had been harsh. When living in Poland as a young man, he had been arrested by the Russian secret police and sent to a concentration camp, and this contribution to his streak of fanaticism. He had a sense of history; when he was shown into the Cabinet Room at No. 10 he made no attempt to disguise his emotion at being present in the room which 'had been the scene of so many great decisions in British history'. He raised both arms above his head: 'How wonderful to be sitting here in the home of democracy.' Then, hardly waiting for a reply, he asked the Brigadier seated next to him to unroll a largish map which he propped on an easel on the Cabinet table and, calling for a pointer, proceeded to give me a lecture on the history of Israel, referring always to the ancient Kingdoms of Israel by their biblical names of Galilee, Samaria and Judah.

This was a rather unorthodox method of conducting a conversation, but I heard him out and after that our conversation proceeded normally. Subsequently, when he had returned to Israel, he would telephone me at regular intervals to tell me of his progress, or lack of it, with Sadat and to ask for my reactions. By his inflexibility, however, he weakened Israel's position in the world. His narrow view of Israel's future failed to bind the people of Israel together, and despite the slaughter, he was later unable to achieve his purpose in Lebanon. Moreover, he was never able, as Sadat was, to take the broad view. Sadat was the bigger man of the two and it must be recorded that Begin left many of the arguments and questions about Israel's best course unresolved when he left office. But this was the man Carter had to negotiate with and early in 1978, he decided to invite both Begin and Sadat to visit him separately in Washington; Sadat to arrive in February and Begin a month later.

While the American President was concerning himself with the Middle East, a series of interchanges and visits was taking place between Giscard, Helmut and myself, which showed that all of us shared similar anxieties about the future of the world's economy, with Helmut the most gloomy.

He was exasperated that the United States Government seemed pre-occupied with viewing economic policy through domestic eyes only, and once again suggested that, in view of my good relations with Carter, I should visit him to encourage the United States to take a broader view.

I called our Ambassador, Peter Jay, home to attend a seminar at which the anxieties I have referred to were repeated by others and it was generally felt the time had come to try to attract President Carter's attention to these matters, despite his preoccupation with the Middle East.

Accordingly, I telephoned the President on 15 February 1978 to tell him that Peter Jay was returning from London with a message covering British and European concerns about the monetary and economic scene, and asking the President to receive him personally. I was not surprised to find Jimmy Carter more eager to talk with me about Middle East prospects, with which I was fairly up to date as Sadat, like Begin, had taken to telephoning me about the current state of affairs. Carter said jocularly that he and I should strike a bargain. If I would make myself responsible for Begin, he could manage Sadat. I told him he would have the easier task. Eventually we got around to my request for him to see the Ambassador and he promised to do so as soon as the latter reached Washington.

Peter Jay took the following message, and in delivering it I told him he was to assume that there was no doubt about the President's intention to attend a Summit in Bonn. He was to say that as a result of our studies, we were concerned that the world economic situation was deteriorating and in the face of that we must act in unison to avoid a break in the solidarity of the Western Powers. There was growing pressure for European protectionism and some weaker countries in the Third World were facing financial collapse. The unstable world monetary system, the OPEC countries' massive dollar holdings, the Japanese and German balance of payments surpluses and continued high unemployment were all inter-related. There was a clear need for a collective approach and I had certain ideas of the way forward that I would like to discuss with him. In view of his important meetings with Sadat and Begin, I proposed that I should make a working visit for a few hours of serious discussion, with no bands, no banquets and no set speeches. My message as conveyed by our Ambassador continued:

> What we have in mind is a series of measures in different fields to be taken
> by different countries, which together might comprise a package which

we could agree at the Summit in Bonn. It would look for contributions
from us all in our different ways in respect of the following five issues:
we could agree at the Summit in Bonn. It would look for contributions
from us all in our different ways in respect of the following five issues:
commitment to growth, the maintenance of world trade, currency
stability, the long-term use of capital surpluses, and conservation of
energy.

In due course these five points bore fruit and became the focus of our
agenda in Bonn. I concluded by saying that I was keeping in close touch
with Helmut Schmidt and dangled the hope that if we were able to agree
on certain of the five points, Schmidt would lead the Federal Republic
to make a positive contribution when we met at Bonn.

The President was as good as his word and saw Peter Jay without delay.
After listening to the proposition, and despite his awe-inspiring self-
imposed schedule of work, he at once agreed to set aside time for my visit.
There had been a constant trickle of criticism about Peter Jay's appointment, some of it motivated by envy, but it is a great advantage to a nation
if the relations between the American President and the Prime Minister
are so close that its Ambassador can have access. This was very true of
David Harlech's relations with President Kennedy, nor do I know of any
other country's Ambassador who would have been received as Peter Jay
was. The President suggested that I should visit Washington on 23 March
which he said would have the additional advantage of allowing us to
discuss the results of his separate conversations with Begin and Sadat and
his proposals for following them up.

In preparation for our own talks, I sent him a paper entitled 'International Initiative on Growth and Currency Stability'. This expanded
the five points that I had referred to in the original message, and in summary suggested that when we met at Bonn there should be agreement on
specific measures by certain countries to increase their growth rates.
These would involve a graded response by the European Community
members, depending on their circumstances; with Germany in the lead,
specific pledges by Japan, and an understanding by the United States to
adhere to its existing growth rate. On capital flows it recommended that
Japan should use its accumulating surpluses to increase aid to the
developing countries: Saudi Arabia and Japan should make additional
funds available to the IMF and the industrialised world should give
assistance to the developing countries to offset the indebtedness caused
by the rise in oil prices. On energy problems, the industrialised countries

should be ready to offer assurances to the oil producers about stability of prices in return for undertakings from them to guarantee supplies.

My aim was to encourage greater exchange rate stability and this required that the United States be less passive about the future level of the dollar. Our paper urged this, bearing in mind that countries like Saudi Arabia would be more inclined to hold their long-term reserves in dollars if they could be reassured that the United States Administration would not wilfully ignore the losses the oil producers would suffer if the dollar dropped in value. There were other technical proposals in this area. Finally, on trade our paper proposed a renewal of the pledge against protectionism, and the setting of a definite date for concluding the current Tokyo round of trade negotiations.

But before the President and I discussed this he had to see Prime Minister Begin, who arrived on 21 March. The Israeli Prime Minister was apparently in a negative mood and during the next forty-eight hours nothing that Carter could say would modify his attitude. Nobody could have worked harder or have been more understanding than the President, but the visit was a failure and I found him rather dejected when I arrived.

He and I began our day's session with a private talk in his room close to the Oval Office and he unburdened himself about the previous two days' harassment. He had found Begin's attitude hard to bear and openly wondered whether he should give up his quest for a Middle East settlement. As happened more than once with the President and others, I found myself cast in the role of sympathetic listener, and as America was the only country with sufficient 'clout' to influence both Israel and Egypt, I urged him strongly not to give up. As is well known, Jimmy Carter did decide to continue with his efforts, and six months later, following an exhausting thirteen-day three-handed discussion, he emerged with the historic Camp David Agreement signed by both Sadat and Begin, a remarkable tribute to the President's persistence, single-minded purpose, good faith and selflessness.

With our preliminary private talks completed, the President took me to the Cabinet Room where both sides were waiting. He had assembled a full team for our discussions: Vice President Mondale, Secretary of State Cyrus Vance, Secretary to the Treasury Blumenthal, National Security Adviser Zbigniew Brzezinski, Ambassador Henry Owen (the President's 'sherpa') and the American Ambassador to London, Kingman Brewster.

I began by commenting on the suggestions contained in the document

I had sent him and outlined our proposals for handling the forthcoming Summit at Bonn. I had wondered whether the President would have had the time to read my paper, but it soon became clear that he had not only done so, but had mastered it. It was another example of his remarkable capacity to absorb facts and arguments. We made an encouraging start as early in our talks he said that he was ready to accept the principle that the Seven should endeavour to act in concert in the five areas I had set out. Further, for this purpose, we should inform and consult one another about proposed changes in our domestic economic policies; for its part, the United States recognised its obligation to take action on conservation of energy and inflation. I had urged upon Carter in our preliminary conversation that uncertainty about the dollar was causing great instability, and while I did not suggest the world could return to a regime of fixed exchange rates, we should aim for less violent swings. I also expressed the view that in the longer term, the United States dollar would not be able to carry the full burden of being the world's reserve currency. We should aim to develop a new reserve currency and in the meantime place some of our reserves into Special Drawing Rights and make them more useable. Mike Blumenthal, as Secretary to the Treasury, was unsympathetic and I made no progress, but I did better with my emphasis that a depreciating dollar was not a matter for the United States to ignore or to treat as a purely domestic issue.

Our discussions continued during a simple, working lunch at the White House, the absence of ostentation suiting both Carter and myself, and at the end of our talks I was well satisfied with the President's summing-up. The meeting, he said, had clarified his thinking. The United States would associate itself with a programme of collective action to which every country should contribute. As the German Chancellor would be the host at Bonn, the President would write to him and set out some areas in which the United States would be willing to act, emphasising that these would be conditional on their being a part of a cooperative venture. These areas he defined as energy conservation, control of internal inflation and action to limit disorderly conditions in the world markets. He also agreed that the 'sherpas' should work out beforehand the details of these and other matters in order that recommendations should be ready for the Summit.

I was happy with the result of this quick 24-hour visit, for however good British ideas might be on the way to improve the world economy, Britain acting alone could not hope to achieve results, any more than

France or Germany. American muscle was needed if our initiative was to succeed, and by securing President Carter's support, the necessary political impetus had been given to the process.

I reported in this vein to Takeo Fukuda, the Japanese Prime Minister, and spoke to Helmut Schmidt and Giscard. Helmut was down in the dumps and while thanking me for my effort, which he had previously encouraged, was pessimistic that anything effective would result. He said that he was about to make one of his regular visits to Paris for bilateral exchanges with Giscard and intended to talk with him about the need for new initiatives in the monetary field: he would let me know the result. Although I did not realise it at the time, these monetary talks were the initial steps that led to the European Monetary System.

A week later, on 4 April 1978, it was not Helmut who telephoned, but Giscard. His purpose was to suggest that the three of us should meet to discuss Helmut's ideas which he also favoured. There were the usual difficulties of coordinating our diaries, but we were all due to be present at the European Council Meeting at Copenhagen on 8 April 1978 and we decided on an early breakfast at the French Embassy. Helmut had recovered from his depression when we met and was in brisk form. He announced that his purpose was to turn German dissatisfaction with the monetary policy of the United States into a practical plan to safeguard Europe's interests. With the partial success of Britain's efforts to disengage sterling from its reserve role, the German Deutsche Mark was itself becoming a reserve currency and, reflecting the strength of the German economy, had become the strongest in Europe.

The morning sun streamed into the breakfast room and as we consumed our croissants and coffee, there evolved the idea of a European-type Bretton Woods, with a European exchange rate fixed against the dollar. Giscard's comments showed that he recognised that this would effectively mean Europe's becoming a Deutsche Mark zone, but was nevertheless ready to go along. I was sympathetic with the general proposal, but had to make clear that as proposed, the effect of the scheme would be disadvantageous to Britain, for the strong Deutsche Mark would have the effect of tugging sterling upwards with deflationary consequences to our economy, unless long-term credit was absolutely unlimited. Helmut did his best to persuade me that membership of a monetary system would assist us, and I undertook to think the matter over. From the drift of Giscard's contributions there seemed little doubt that France and Germany would go ahead even if Britain did not join and their joint decision would almost automatically bring Belgium, Holland and Luxembourg into the scheme.

I favoured the general idea as likely to bring more order into the currency markets of Europe and the world, but quite apart from my technical concerns I could not travel fast. Many people in the Labour Party remained suspicious of what they thought was too close an entanglement with Europe, and this, coupled with my own and the Treasury's belief that sterling was standing too high to make our entry advantageous, led me some days later to tell Schmidt and Giscard that we could not enter the European Monetary Scheme at the outset. On the other hand, I publicly welcomed the scheme in principle, and when it was finally set up the Cabinet agreed to a number of steps to associate Britain with the development of a European Currency Unit (ECU). Sterling was included in the new composite unit for the purpose of determining its value and we agreed to deposit a proportion of Britain's gold and dollar reserves as backing and to accept European Currency Units in their place.

Few people, even in the City of London, know that a European Currency Unit coin actually exists. A very limited number was minted in France and the President presented one to each of the Heads of Government in the Community. It is a large and handsome silver coin, some seventy-two millimetres in diameter, bearing the coat of arms of all the member countries on one side, and the design of the old French écu coin on the reverse.

When I reported to the House that Britain would not become a full member of the European Monetary System, Mrs Thatcher commented sharply that our decision was a sad reflection on the performance of the Government. Nevertheless, as I write this after seven years of Conservative Government, I notice that she has not yet taken the plunge.

The 'sherpas' continued their preparations for the Bonn Summit and by the time we were due to meet, had completed the outline of a series of measures which different countries might undertake in order to present a coordinated package to the world at the conclusion of our meeting. I was pleased that the early British ideas had stood the test, but rather uncertain how the Carter/Schmidt chemistry would react. I had done all I could in telephone and personal conversations to interpret each to the other, and when we reached Bonn on 15 July and I called on Chancellor Schmidt in his 'bungalow', I was relieved to find him in good spirits.

The so-called 'bungalow' was in reality an architecturally pleasing single-storey residence, relatively new and decorated in a mixture of

simple and sophisticated styles. It had a homelike and unpretentious
atmosphere. As living accommodation, it is far more suitable than Downing Street's jumble of downstairs offices, state rooms and an attic flat for
the Prime Minister. Schmidt was in bargaining mood. He told me that the
German banking community was urging him strongly not to stimulate
the economy. Nevertheless, despite his own reluctance, he would be
agreeable to act, provided there was a satisfactory response on energy
conservation from the United States.

He had not discussed this with Carter and asked if I would open the
way. If there was a response, he would arrange to call a German Cabinet
Meeting on the following evening to decide whether the response of the
United States and other countries would justify him in stimulating
Germany's economic growth.

There were several other matters I wished to discuss bilaterally with
Jimmy Carter, including the lack of progress on a Comprehensive Test
Ban Treaty, which had been under negotiation between the United
States, the Soviet Union and the United Kingdom for a long period.
Carter had originally seemed as keen as I was to conclude it, but when I
had seen him a month earlier in Washington he implied that fundamental
questions had been reopened by the Joint Chiefs of Staff and United
States nuclear weapons scientists about the need to test at intervals to
ensure that stocks of weapons did not deteriorate. The Soviets had also
raised questions about the number of seismic verification stations, suggesting that the small land mass of the British Isles needed as many stations
as the whole of the American Continent or the vast area of the Russian
steppes. I had resisted this on grounds of equality.

On the other hand, we had made some progress, for although he preferred a three-year duration for the Treaty, Gromyko had told me he was
ready to accept five years. In order to satisfy him, I had proposed that the
three powers hold a review conference during the fifth year which could
determine whether a revised treaty should be negotiated, and so I was
disappointed when I met Jimmy Carter and he said that we might have
to make the duration no longer than three years. This was a step back-
wards, which was made much worse when I learned that some of the
American experts were suggesting that a three kiloton threshold would
be necessary for proper stockpile testing. I made a deprecating comment
to Carter that this would make a mockery of the treaty, and he agreed
that he would need to take some hard political decisions if the negotiations
were to succeed. I told him of my conversation with Helmut Schmidt and

was glad to find that on the question of energy he was much more forth-coming than earlier, and outlined the measures America would take on conservation. I said I thought they would be sufficient to convince us all that the United States would act firmly, and later briefly saw Schmidt to assure him that we were making progress.

We met in formal session in the Palais Schaumburg on the following morning and Helmut Schmidt, as our host and Chairman, opened the proceedings with an apt simile. It would be hard, he said, for each of us to scale the Summit on his own. What could be more fitting than to tie all our hopes together, as a climbing party was roped together? We could not be satisfied simply by the privilege of taking part in the attempt; each must contribute to the combined effort.

I followed with a plea for fewer general statements in our communiqué and more specific individual commitments to action. It was my impression, I said, that provided we were convinced that each country's individual actions would contribute to the general benefit of the world as a whole, all of us might be willing to take action as part of a collective whole that we would not be willing to take if we acted in isolation. If that were so, the total impact would be greater in psychological terms than the sum of the individual parts. President Carter's contribution was decisive. He reported that America's oil imports had been reduced by one million barrels a day in the first four months of 1978, and firmly undertook to raise the price of oil in the United States to the world level by 1980. If he could not secure the consent of Congress, he would do it by administrative action. Schmidt followed Carter immediately. He volunteered that he too would contribute to a package deal, even though he had some apprehensions. The other Heads of Government one by one followed suit with the result that the communiqué, when finally issued, contained a passage, unique in my experience, in which each individual nation publicly pledged itself to take action of a specified character as its contribution to the threefold objective of higher world economic growth, lower unemployment and reduced inflation. It is worth reproducing the specific undertakings:

A programme of different actions by countries that face different conditions is needed to assure steady non-inflationary growth. In countries whose balance of payments situation and inflation rate do not impose special restrictions, this requires a faster rise in domestic demand. In countries where rising prices and costs are creating strong pressures, this means taking new measures against inflation.

Canada reaffirmed its intention, within the limits permitted by the need to contain and reduce inflation, to achieve higher growth of employment and an increase in output of up to 5 per cent.

As a contribution to avert the world-wide disturbances of economic equilibrium, the German delegation has indicated that by the end of August it will propose to the legislative bodies additional and quantitively substantial measures up to one per cent of Gross National Product designed to achieve a significant strengthening of demand and a higher rate of growth. The order of magnitude will take account of the absorptive capacity of the capital market and the need to avoid inflationary pressures.

The President of the French Republic has indicated that, while pursuing its policy of reduction of the rate of inflation, the French Government agrees, as a contribution to the common effort, to increase by an amount of about 0.5 per cent of Gross National Product the deficit of the budget of the state for the year 1978.

The Italian Prime Minister has indicated that the Government undertakes to raise the rate of economic growth in 1979 by 1.5 percentage points with respect to 1978. It plans to achieve this goal by cutting public current expenditure while stimulating investments with the aim of increasing employment in a non-inflationary context.

The Prime Minister of Japan has referred to the fact that his Government is striving for the attainment of the real growth target for fiscal year 1978, which is about 1.5 percentage points higher than the performance of the previous year, mainly through the expansion of domestic demand. He has further expressed his determination to achieve the said target by taking appropriate measures as necessary. In August or September he will determine whether additional measures are needed.

The United Kingdom, having achieved a major reduction in the rate of inflation and improvement in the balance of payments, has recently given a fiscal stimulus equivalent to rather over one per cent of Gross National Product. The Government intends to continue the fight against inflation so as to improve still further the prospects for growth and employment.

The President of the United States stated that reducing inflation is essential to maintaining a healthy United States economy and has therefore become the top priority of United States economic policy. He identified the major actions that have been taken and are being taken to counter inflation in the United States; tax cuts originally proposed for fiscal year 1979 have now been reduced by $10 billions; government expenditure projections for 1978 and 1979 have been reduced; a very tight budget is being prepared to 1980; steps are being taken to reduce the direct contribution by government regulations or restrictions to rising costs and prices, and a voluntary programme has been undertaken to achieve declaration of wages and prices.

Recognising its particular responsibility in the energy field, the United States will reduce its dependence on imported oil. The United States will have in place by the end of the year a comprehensive policy framework within which this effort can be urgently carried forward. By year end, measures will be in effect that will result in oil import savings of approximately 2.5 million barrels per day by 1985. In order to achieve these goals, the United States will establish a strategic oil reserve of one billion barrels; it will increase coal production by two-thirds; it will maintain the ratio between growth in Gross National Product and growth in energy demand at or below 0.8; and its oil consumption will grow more slowly than energy consumption. The volume of oil imported in 1978 and 1979 should be less than that imported in 1977. In order to discourage excessive consumption of oil and to encourage the movement toward coal, the United States remains determined that the prices paid for oil in the United States shall be raised to the world level by the end of 1980.

Bonn was the last Summit I attended, and with the passage of time their character has changed. The participants of the 1970s have now left the scene, and their successors seem to regard Summits as media events or as opportunities to enhance their election prospects, with thousands of photographers and journalists jostling for the best angle. The leaders make speeches to each other which are intended for public consumption back home. All this is a far cry from our original intention.

Perhaps one reason for this deterioration was the mistaken belief of Governments in the early 1980s that the wisdom of the markets, coupled with strict control of the money supply through the use of high interest rates, was sufficient to produce a healthy world economy.

In reality, there has been increasing poverty in the Third World and record high unemployment in the industrialised world, a combination of low commodity prices and record high interest rates. In more recent days there are glimmers of a return to wiser policies, a recognition of the interdependence of national economies and a growth of international cooperation in the monetary field.

Economic Summits of the kind that took place at Bonn foster a sense of political and economic direction in handling the world's problems. With our growing interdependence it is important that they be continued for they add another dimension to the formal institutionalised exchanges that take place in the IMF, the GATT, the OECD and elsewhere.

I had been able to devote time to international economic problems because of the marked improvement in Britain's domestic economic situation. There had been a surge in overseas confidence in Britain, sterling was untroubled, foreign observers noted that inflation had been brought under control and was coming down steadily, incomes policy had improved our relative export competitiveness, the heavy investment in the North Sea was about to produce results, the first oil would shortly be pumped ashore, and Britain was repaying the IMF loan as the instalments fell due. I should add that by the time the Labour Government left office, the equivalent of the total IMF loan had been repaid.

The Agreement with the Liberal Party had introduced a new stability into the political scene by removing the prospect of an early general election, and both the Opposition and the media became less feverish. I was not sorry to see the Parliamentary spotlight turned away from a constant, morbid obsession with the daily fluctuations of sterling on the foreign exchanges, but of course many other issues, serious and not so, remained. Chief among these, Northern Ireland affairs, Devolution for Scotland and Wales and a Bill to authorise elections to the European Assembly caused most trouble.

The situation in Northern Ireland needed unremitting watchfulness. The abolition of Stormont in 1973 and the inability, despite efforts of both Conservative and Labour Governments, to find an acceptable alternative left a political vacuum in the arena where opposing views could have been thrashed out.

Success ebbed and flowed in the battle fought by police and Army against terrorism, but was not likely to be finally achieved in the near future. I had never forgotten my apprehension that Northern Ireland had reached a fatal watershed when I heard in October 1969 that the first policeman, Victor Arbuckle, had been shot and killed during a visit I was paying to Northern Ireland, in my capacity as Home Secretary.

Since then the killings had mounted, and every time an atrocity took place, it became harder to find appropriate language to give meaning to the horror we felt. Human tragedies were enacted almost daily, bringing sorrow to the families involved, to the police men and women and to the young men in the British Army. The chief suffering was borne by the people of the Province themselves, but Westminster and Whitehall also felt a personal loss with the murder of Airey Neave, the Conservative spokesman for Northern Ireland shortly before the General Election of

1979, and the explosion which killed Christopher Ewart Biggs, our Ambassador in Dublin, and a young civil servant.

Both these events took place whilst I was Prime Minister. There were many other deaths too. I recall particularly the callous explosion of a time-bomb which had been hidden in a restaurant, killing twelve customers and leaving a further thirty with injuries. And there was the unpitying shooting of a young bridegroom in County Meath at the very moment that he was leaving the Roman Catholic Church with his bride at his side. He was killed because he served in the British Army.

I maintained correspondence with the Irish Prime Minister, Jack Lynch, and we met regularly at European Council Meetings, which enabled us to exchange views. In September 1977, I invited him to London for talks, but although our discussions were cordial, I was not satisfied that he was taking sufficiently seriously the vital need for close border cooperation if the IRA threat was to be contained, and I employed the argument that this threat was potentially as grave for the Republic as for the North. Several weeks after Lynch's visit to Downing Street, the Irish Government took steps to stiffen the penalties for conviction on charges of armed robbery, of which there had been a spate, and whose proceeds we suspected went to swell the coffers of the IRA, but even so more police cooperation was needed.

I should add that in recent years it seems that cooperation against the terrorists on the border has greatly improved. A heavy strain fell on the Secretaries of State for Northern Ireland, first Merlyn Rees and later Roy Mason and their supporting Ministers, travelling continuously throughout the Province, moulding and reflecting public attitudes, keeping the machinery of government running, sometimes recalled to Westminster at inconvenient hours by day and night to vote in vital divisions because the Opposition Whips refused to 'pair' them, and all the time conscious of an invisible personal danger. Merlyn Rees bore it with patient goodwill, Roy Mason with stoic realism. The country owes them all, and their successors, a considerable debt. Each Minister was able to record successes among the disappointments, one of the notable occasions being the reduction in the number of violent deaths in 1977, which was the lowest since 1970, and less than half the number of 1976; 111 as against 297.

I gave both Secretaries of State encouragement to put forward ideas and proposals, and they produced a stream of assessments, analyses, minutes, progress reports, meetings which, interspersed with my spas-

modic and fleeting visits to the Province, gave me a snapshot picture of
the community's difficulties and of the wretched conditions under which
police and Army were working. But despite Merlyn Rees's constructive
understanding and Roy Mason's firmness of purpose, we never seemed
in sight of an agreement (much less a settlement) that would be acceptable
to the extremists in both communities, who so often set the tone for the
whole. At no time did I feel we were doing more than breasting the tide.

Since the early 1970s, successive well-intentioned Ministers on this
side of the Irish Sea had put forward differing sets of proposals to end the
bloodshed and give all the people of Northern Ireland a peaceful future,
only to see them dismissed as outrageous by one side or the other, and
sometimes by both. It was frustrating to watch every initiative destroyed
from within, and I can but repeat the opinion I expressed to my Cabinet
colleagues eighteen years ago at the outset of the present troubles in
January 1969: 'The cardinal aim of our policy must be to influence
Northern Ireland to solve its own problems.' It is still my view that there
will be a settlement only when both communities in the Province desire
it, work in cooperation to rid themselves of their extremists, and of their
own free will produce terms that are acceptable to both, with Britain at
hand to urge and to nudge them forward.

I expressed this again in a speech I made in the House on 2 July 1981,
two years after I ceased to be Prime Minister. It was badly received for
my theme was that Britain was incapable of ever offering a settlement that
would satisfy both sides. Britain should bring forward no further solutions, but must continue to fulfill to the limit its responsibilities for the
maintenance of law and order for a predetermined, fixed number of years.
During that period it would be the responsibility of all the political leaders
in Northern Ireland to decide where their future lay, and to enter into
the appropriate constitutional relationships with each other for their own
future. When the predetermined interim period came to an end, Britain
would offer continued British citizenship to all those who wished to
exercise that right so that there might be many dual citizens, but would
withdraw from the Province which would at that time become an independent state. Britain would of course support applications for membership
by the new state of the United Nations, the European Community, the
GATT, NATO, IMF and other international organisations. Britain
would fulfil her financial obligations in all respects in such matters as
pensions, and would offer generous financial aid to the new state.

The broad outline of that speech still represents my view, although I do not necessarily adhere to the precise details (there are different ways of achieving the overall objective). That I proposed a desperate remedy I do not deny; that nothing should be done to hamper any future new initiative by a British Government to find a better solution is unquestioned. But if no one can produce anything that is acceptable, then the time will come when Britain and Northern Ireland must begin to think the unthinkable.

16

Devolution – the Liberals withdraw – a general election postponed – the TUC reject the 5 per cent pay round

There is something about a proposal for reforming the constitution that releases the inhibitions in a Member of Parliament. He is at home in a field in which he is expert. On other subjects (say, on finance) he may be prepared to admit privately that he is foxed when the Chancellor discusses the difference between M_0 and M_3, but when constitutional issues are discussed, his opinion will be as good as the next man's and he is not likely to be convinced otherwise. He may even be right, but in debate the subject lays itself open to inventive minds to spin the most fanciful theories and arguments into wild arabesques that can only be brought to earth by the use of the Parliamentary guillotine. I had been vaccinated against enthusiasm for legislation on constitutional reform by a salutary experience as Home Secretary in 1968 when the Labour Government made an attempt to reform the House of Lords by reducing its powers, confining voting Peers to those of the first generation, in strict proportion to the strengths of the Parties in the Commons. This had been one of Dick Crossman's enthusiasms and he had entered into negotiations with the Conservatives, displaying for him a remarkable discretion and tact. He was encouraged by support from the Conservative Peers, especially Lord Carrington and Lord Jellicoe, but he failed to secure the important backing of Iain MacLeod, who spoke for the Conservatives in the Commons. Nevertheless, a Reform Bill was produced and the Conservative front bench voted for the second reading, although thereafter they gave no active support. From opposite ends of the political spectrum Enoch Powell and Michael Foot made brilliant mockery of the Bill's proposals, and by their tactics held up any serious progress for days at a time. When Roy Jenkins and I changed places, I found myself the Minister in charge of the Bill, but any reluctant admiration I might have felt at the virtuosity of the Bill's opponents was soon smothered beneath increasing bafflement and frustration as we failed to make progress, and lumbered on against a stream of witty, logical and devastating oratory from its two principal, merciless opponents.

Our own Labour Members were unenthusiastic and this may explain the Prime Minister's reluctance to agree to a guillotine motion. Nor was there any pressure for the Bill in the country, where it was regarded as an irrelevance. Eventually it had to be withdrawn.

Crossman was angry with me. At times he lived in a cocoon of conspiracy and believed others did the same. He would not understand that the Bill had no chance once Tory support was withdrawn and their backbenchers were let loose on the floor of the House to talk for as long as they wished, while their front bench smiled quietly at our discomfiture. Crossman alleged that I wanted the Bill to be defeated in order to 'humiliate' the Prime Minister, and thus put myself in a better position to replace him. I never ceased to marvel at his capacity to invent scenarios instead of facing the simple, straightforward facts. To me the occasion was an obvious example of the old military adage, 'Never reinforce failure'.

The lessons were clear. A large Parliamentary majority is not enough by itself to carry a constitutional Bill, for the opportunities for delay by a determined handful of members are infinite. From the outset it is absolutely necessary to have a timetable agreed with the Opposition, or a guillotine motion in reserve to allow sufficient time for proper discussion, but to keep debate within reasonable limits. Finally, even when firmly convinced that the proposed constitutional change ranks with the wisdom of Solomon, do not leave harbour until all other legislative cargoes have arrived safely at their destination, for there is no limit to the uncharted rocks that can wreck this particular freighter during its voyage.

This was graphically illustrated by the Government's difficulties over a period of two years from 1976 to 1978 when we attempted to legislate for the establishment of Elected Assemblies in Scotland and Wales (to which, in the case of Scotland only, certain legislative powers would be devolved from Westminster), with limited executive powers to both Assemblies. The Labour Party had undertaken this commitment in our general election manifesto of February 1974, as a response to the Report of the Kilbrandon Commission issued in the previous November.

Lord Kilbrandon had been Chairman of a Royal Commission appointed in 1969 to consider whether any changes were desirable in the constitutional and economic relationships, primarily of England, Scotland and Wales. His report rejected independence for Scotland, and also turned down a federal solution, but a majority reported in favour of Devolution

to Elected Assemblies in Wales and Scotland through a system of proportional representation in those countries. The Commission also
recommended 'Regional' Advisory Boards for England.

Scottish and Welsh nationalism had long pedigrees going back many
years. Indeed, Keir Hardie had included Home Rule for Scotland in his
election address nearly a century earlier, and Campbell-Bannerman, the
Liberal Prime Minister, had voted for it in the Commons. During my
first twenty years in Parliament, little was heard of it and as late as 1959,
Scottish National Party candidates secured only a derisory 21,000 votes
in a general election.

But the decline in the fortunes of Scotland's traditional heavy industries led to a popular feeling that Scotland was getting a worse deal
than England in the matter of securing new industries. Unemployment
was heavy and sentiment began to grow that she might be better off without the incubus of the English. These ideas were fanned by the discovery
of oil in the North Sea, the exploitation and proceeds of which fervent
nationalists claimed for Scotland's benefit and christened 'Scotland's oil'.
Concern continued to grow about the future of the Scottish economy
among many representative bodies in the country, industry, the trade
unions, the Church of Scotland, the professions, the Scottish press and
the universities. A seemingly unstoppable sentiment developed that
Whitehall decision-making should be replaced by Scottish control of
Scotland's economy, achieved through devolution of power from Westminster to Edinburgh.

This was fertile ground for the Scottish National Party and their
electoral fortunes prospered. In the heady atmosphere of the times they
scored some outstanding bye-election results in the 1960s and although
these were not always sustained in succeeding general elections, their vote
grew dramatically from the microscopic 21,000 of 1959 to no less than
839,000 in the October 1974 general election. This put them second to
the Labour Party, which received a million votes, and well ahead of the
Conservative's 681,000. The Conservatives had won more seats, sixteen
to the Scottish National Party's eleven, but there was no doubt which was
the second party in Scottish politics, especially as they made large gains
in local elections.

A number of members of the Scottish National Party toyed with the
idea of full-scale independence, but the majority knew that the Scots
would reject this. Nevertheless, the Scottish people wanted change, as
the answer to a public opinion poll seemed to show. In December 1976,

22 per cent opted for a 'completely independent Scottish Parliament separate from England', 52 per cent voted for a 'Scottish Assembly as part of Britain, but with substantial powers'; only 20 per cent said they preferred 'no change from the present system'.

There were mixed views in the Scottish Labour Party about the Kilbrandon Commission's proposal of an Elected Assembly. Some believed it should be rejected because it would turn out to be the first slippery step on the road to independence, which they rejected. Others thought it would draw the teeth of those Nationalists whose aim was complete independence. The Scottish Executive Committee of the Labour Party voted against an Elected Assembly by six votes to five, but a wider conference of Labour Party members backed it. The Welsh Labour Party backed an elected Assembly with executive powers, but did not call for it to possess legislative authority.

The new Labour Government proceeded by canvassing opinion and then setting out its ideas in White Papers during 1974 and 1975 under the Chairmanship of Ted Short, later Lord Glenamara, who was Lord President of the Council and Leader of the House of Commons. He did much to create the framework and when he was succeeded by Michael Foot in April 1976, the structure of the scheme was already in existence. Michael made some important amendments during the summer months, notably giving control of the Scottish and Welsh Development Agencies to the Assemblies and establishing that the Judicial Committee of the Privy Council would decide questions of doubt about the use by the Scottish Assembly of its legislative powers.

In the Queen's Speech of 1976 I announced our intention to legislate and moved the Second Reading of the Bill on 13 December 1976. The question had been posed as to whether the people of Scotland and Wales should express their opinion through a Referendum and I undertook that the Government would listen to the weight of opinion in the Debate. The Conservatives had their own plan for Devolution based on a Report produced much earlier by Alec Douglas-Home, which had proposed a Scottish Convention with some legislative powers, but despite this they voted against the Bill which nevertheless was carried by a substantial majority. There were signs of future trouble for the Government even at that early stage as ten Labour Members had voted against the Government and a further twenty-nine abstained. On the other hand, five Conservatives voted for the Bill and about twenty-eight abstained.

Michael Foot set aside thirty days of debate for consideration of the

Bill, which was a generous allowance, but Julian Amery from the Conservative Benches at once warned him that it would not be enough – another sign of difficulties ahead. The debates wore on with progress at a snail's pace, and it became obvious that the Bill could never be finished without the aid of the guillotine. Michael Foot found himself cast in the unenviable role of executioner without any real assurance that a motion to establish a timetable could be carried. The Whips came with the gloomy news that some Labour Members would not support it. But the effort had to be made. If the Government had given up the Bill without testing the House, the Scottish National Party would have had an electoral field-day in Scotland: the demand for independence might begin to grow and even reach dangerous proportions if no effort was made to accommodate the middle ground.

Michael properly insisted that the full thirty days he had originally promised should not be reduced but there was no turning the Bill's opponents. On 22 February 1977, the day of the guillotine debate, the Chief Whip, Michael Cocks, forecast that the Government would lose by thirty votes. He was not far out: the figure was twenty-nine. Some of the Scottish National Party wept crocodile tears but in reality they were delighted, believing they could ascribe the defeat to English obstruction and so sweep Scotland into their camp.

Devolution was the major item in the Government's legislative programme for the year and defeat was a severe blow to the morale of the Parliamentary Party, which was already low enough. Our initial tiny majority had been wiped out, as I have said, by the defection of John Stonehouse, Reginald Prentice and two Scottish Labour Members who had been dissatisfied with the slow progress on Devolution, with the result that the Whips could never guarantee a majority on any issue. We suffered a series of setbacks over the Aircraft and Shipbuilding Industries Bill, while other Bills were badly damaged or totally defeated by the narrowest of margins, sometimes no more than one vote settling the issue.

It was only the agreement we reached with the Liberals a month after the Devolution guillotine debacle that enabled the Government to pull back from the precipice. Although the Liberals had contributed to our defeat by voting against the guillotine, as soon as discussions began about an Agreement, I found that David Steel was anxious that the Devolution Bill should be put to the House once more, subject to certain changes which the Liberals would propose and which I undertook to consider. They were extremely keen on testing the views of Members about proportional representation, and as part of the Agreement, Michael Foot and I undertook to offer the House a free vote on whether the members of the new Assemblies should be elected by this means or not.

It was obvious that even with the support of the Liberal Party, there would not be enough time before the House rose at the end of July 1977 for a controversial Bill of this magnitude to pass through all its stages, and David Steel agreed with my suggestion that we should re-introduce it as a major measure at the beginning of the following parliamentary session in November 1977. We thus had ample time to prepare. Michael Foot was heavily engaged in wrestling with the remainder of our legislative programme and, in his capacity as Leader of the House, had a full-time job fending off the procedural stratagems of the Opposition without a majority to back him. He therefore suggested that the detailed negotiations on Devolution with the Liberals should be undertaken by John Smith, who had assisted him with the earlier Bill. He turned out to be an excellent choice. Despite his name, John Smith was a young Scottish lawyer, a contemporary of David Steel's and they knew each other well. Before he began his work, I asked him to see me and recounted my experience in handling the House of Lords Bill. He has since told me that when I gave him his riding instructions, I said he had a dual task, firstly to work out a Bill that the Cabinet would accept, and secondly to redesign it in such a fashion that it would secure Liberal support without losing any Labour votes. It was a tall order but John Smith was equal to the task, a fact he has since demonstrated in becoming one of the most formidable of Labour's front bench team. When his work on the Devolution Bill was done, I had no hesitation in inviting him to join the Cabinet as Secretary for Trade in 1978 at the age of thirty-nine. He was one of the group of able younger people including David Owen and Roy Hattersley who, with an eye to the future, I wished to gain Cabinet experience in case we should be defeated at the following election.

Our second attempt at Devolution in November 1977 was more successful than the first. The Bill was split into two with separate legislation for Scotland and Wales, and both new Bills were guillotined from the first day. The Liberal Party voted for the guillotine, and taking into account the time spent in discussion of a similar Bill in the previous session, the number of days allocated for further debate was not unreasonable – namely seventeen days for the Scottish Bill and eleven days for Wales. We soon found that the House had become uninterested in long, repetitious speeches, with hardly a new argument to be heard, and the debates were carried on by a handful of zealots. Despite the limitations of the guillotine, there was plenty of opportunity for procedural manouevring and the Whips reported that there were up to fifty Labour Members on whom we could not rely for support.

It was a precarious legislative voyage with many cross-currents eddying one way and another. John Smith proved he was a skilful navigator and assembled a majority from among the disparate elements who were in favour of the principle of the Bill, but had varying degrees of enthusiasm about its details. Inevitably the Government suffered a number of defeats, beginning with the very first clause which was of a declaratory nature and affirmed a truism, namely that the unity of the United Kingdom and the supreme authority of Parliament were not impaired. We had not anticipated any difficulty with this, but an assorted rag-bag of Conservatives, Liberals, Ulster Unionists and Nationalists, supported by Tam Dalyell, voted against the clause and it was defeated. This was embarrassing but no real damage was done.

Not so our next defeat which was instigated by another Labour sceptic, George Cunningham, with the support of Labour and Conservative opponents. He proposed that if the consultative referendum contained in the Bill resulted in less than forty per cent of the total electorate voting in favour of Devolution, then the Secretary of State for Scotland would be required to lay an order before Parliament, wiping out the whole Act. This provision was carried by a majority of fifteen, with as many as thirty-four Labour Members voting against the Government. On the other hand, a small number of Conservatives and the Liberal Party supported us.

I have since wondered whether those thirty-four Labour Members would have voted as they did if they had been able to foresee that their vote on that evening would precipitate a General Election in 1979, at the least favourable time for their Government.

During other important debates, a number of free votes took place on proportional representation as the Liberals had suggested as part of our Agreement. The question was debated in both Houses with the result that the House of Lords voted in favour of proportional representation, while the House of Commons, on every occasion that the Members were asked to decide on a free vote, rejected the proposition by large majorities drawn from both sides of the House. Fortunately, David Steel was satisfied that Michael Foot and I had fully discharged the undertakings we had given him.

The lengthy debate was full of uncertainties, but eventually, thanks to the guillotine motion, both the Scotland and Wales Bills were passed by both Houses, receiving the Royal Assent on 31 July 1978, twenty months after the first introduction of the original Bill. The manner in which it was amended and reshaped during its passage was a reflection of the power of the back bencher and demonstrated that on an issue like this he is not lobby fodder as some of the pundits contemptuously aver. This is more in evidence when a Government is without a majority, but even a Government which possesses a working majority can be compelled to modify or withdraw its proposals if enough of its supporters are sufficiently in earnest.

The attempt at Devolution was important for its own sake, but I am bound to admit that it had other incidental advantages. So I did not complain unduly about the tactical manoeuvres of the opponents or their procedural ambushes (although I knew they placed a strain on Michael Foot, John Smith and the Whips), for they helped to distract parliamentary attention from a morbid preoccupation with the state of the economy. The Government needed time above all to show that the measures we had taken during 1976 would indeed bear fruit in a reduction of inflation, lower unemployment and a resumption of growth and investment.

A by-product of the long drawn-out devolution battles was that as long as these continued, they secured for the Government the support of the Welsh and Scottish Nationalist Parties, as well as of the Liberals. The Government was accorded the solid underpinning it needed to enable its economic policies to bring results, and Ministers were given a breathing space to turn to other affairs.

But over and beyond this I have no doubt that legislation on Devolution was an historical necessity in the mood of Scotland at the time. Even sober observers had been somewhat carried away by the noisy clamour of a small minority to believe (in the words of one serious commentator) that 'the ending of the Union far from being unthinkable was a possibility'. Even those in Scotland who were not swept along on this tide felt that a move must be made to change the status quo, by giving Scotland more control over its own affairs. The long debates were well reported in Scotland and Wales and had an educational effect: as people became better informed they understood that devolution would have costs as well as benefits. It was noticeable that there was a trend away from extreme attitudes and towards a more sober approach at the end of the deliberations on the Bill than there had been before the debates began. Discussion successfully drew the teeth of the separatists; the process helped to re-inforce belief in the unity of the United Kingdom, which it was my overriding concern to preserve.

The Devolution Acts would have had the advantage of democratising the large measure of devolution that already existed by making it more accountable, but many remained unconvinced that we had been successful in solving such difficult questions as future sources of finance, relations between the Assemblies and local government, or the adverse effect (exaggerated in my view) on the English regions. So when the referenda were held seven months later on 1 March 1979, the electorate in Wales decisively rejected the Welsh Act. In Scotland, a majority of those voting were in favour of setting up an Elected Assembly, but the Act failed on the forty. per cent test, with disastrous results for the Government as it precipitated a general election at a time not of our choosing. Nevertheless, it seems probable that the call for devolution will revive in due time and the Government's abolition of the English Metropolitan Counties may add new weight to it when the issue is reconsidered. My own experience in South Wales is that close-knit, well-defined communities possess some advantage if they can exercise a measure of self-control over regional economic development, and there is a strong case on democratic grounds for making some of the existing powerful quangos accountable. When the time comes, what we did between 1974 and 1979 will provide a useful bedrock on which a future Parliament can build.

The Scottish and Welsh Development Acts had received the Royal Assent on 31 July, and this effectively ended the session for the House rose two days later for the long summer recess. I was glad to be able to leave 10 Downing Street for the farm, which I had been able to visit only twice during the preceding three months, although I had of course enjoyed the hospitality of Chequers in between times. The pace had been furious, and consulting my diary, I note that in the five weeks before the House rose I visited New York to receive the Hubert Humphrey International Award, paid two visits to Germany to attend the European Council and then the Economic Summit of the Seven, spoke at the Durham Miners' Gala, at Conferences of the National Union of Railway-men and the Shipbuilding and Engineering Unions, met the Council of the TUC and the CBI, received Chancellor Kreisky of Austria, and attended the Welsh National Eistedfodd, in addition to holding meetings of the Cabinet, speaking to the Parliamentary Party, answering questions twice a week in the House, opening a major debate on the economy and much else. I was ready for a break and decided to spend the month of August at home, leading a regular life and not moving base.

A small skeleton staff moved from Downing Street to Lewes, the county town nearest the farm, and a communications network was established so that we were in instant contact with London. Official papers and telegrams were brought to me every day which I disposed of as quickly as possible and then joined in the busy routine of the farm and the harvesting of the crops. We were cheerful when the weather allowed the combine to make an early start; we watched anxiously if heavy clouds gathered; and we fretted when it rained. The pace quickened each evening as we hurried the last trailer-loads to the barn before the dew formed and halted work for the day. Then came the closing ritual of producing ice-cold bottles of lager and we walked across the stubble estimating the yield and the acres we still had to cut. Every season has its own delights, but few exceed the satisfying completion of many months of work as the harvest comes home. I am indebted to the editor of the *Economist* for a quotation from Socrates – 'Nobody is qualified to become a statesman who is entirely ignorant of the problems of wheat.'

I have some idea of what was meant. To grow wheat successfully you must plan ahead, select the seed well, cultivate the land thoroughly, be patient with breakdowns and other unexpected problems you will encounter, be hardened to disappointment and grateful for uncovenanted benefits like good weather. You must be ready to wait for results and always remain optimistic that next year's harvest will be better than the present. In the late summer of 1978, my feelings about the political scene were not dissimilar. There was no doubt about the extent of our improvement, politically and economically. We had achieved a remarkable reduction in the rate of inflation. It stood at 8 per cent whereas a year earlier it had been over 17 per cent, and in the years before that as high as 27 per cent. Let me add also that it stood at only half the rate we had inherited from the Conservative Government in 1974. Living standards were rising again as we recovered from the fall brought about by adjusting to the five-fold increase in oil prices in 1973. We had protected the weakest in the country during our period of office, and in some areas had increased benefits, notably those of children, as well as bringing in new benefits to help the disabled, coupled with invalid car allowances and a mobility allowance. This was practical Socialism – ensuring that the nation met the needs of those who were unable to help themselves even if others suffered a temporary reduction in their own standards. The beginning of the recovery had enabled the Chancellor to reduce the rate of income tax on the first £750 of taxable income to 25 pence in the pound, although the Tories wanted more and had assembled a majority in the House to reduce the standard rate for everybody by one penny in the pound. Our sterling reserves had grown substantially; the exchange rate was floating easily; industrial production and investment were increasing; exports were growing faster than imports, and the balance of payments was not in deficit.

With public concern about high inflation beginning to recede, the level of unemployment was replacing it as the principal source of worry, but even the numbers of the unemployed were being slowly reduced. Another favourable factor was that North Sea oil was beginning to flow. Britain had borrowed heavily abroad to finance the 1973 oil price increase. Never would we have a better chance than in the years ahead to repay those debts from our own oil revenues and rebuild Britain's industrial strength.

During the latter part of 1977 the Cabinet had made a detailed study of the expected impact of this welcome bonus, and in the spring of 1978, the Government published a White Paper, 'The Challenge of North Sea Oil'. It pointed out that although large in itself, the revenue would be only a relatively small addition to Britain's Gross National Product, and its consequential effect should be kept in perspective. We did not intend that the proceeds should be wholly used as a quick fix for a large tax reduction or an increase in social benefits. Instead, the White Paper proposed six major causes to which this addition to our national wealth should be devoted: reinvigorating the inner cities; training young people and retraining their elders; developing energy conservation and new sources of energy; supporting the National Enterprise Board; increasing aid to those Third World countries which had suffered from the oil price increases; and some reduction of personal taxation.

The Chancellor had rightly resisted the attractive idea of establishing a Special Fund for the oil revenues, as it would have been unrealistic to try to identify the expenditure increases arising from our proposed projects and attribute them solely to such a Fund. On the other hand, it was right to call attention to the ephemeral nature of the oil revenues, and it was our intention to publish an annual report commenting on the general direction of their use. Like other things, this idea vanished after we left office.

One other important area of policy was the Government's industrial strategy, which had been launched in November 1975. We had made some progress, but it was too early to look for results from such a long-term project of reform and regeneration. Its purpose was to persuade management and unions in the private sector to put their own house in order so as to achieve a high output, high wage economy. Unlike the National Plan of 1965, there was no attempt to impose a strategy from above. Instead, each industrial sector was invited to review its own future and to rework its plans accordingly.

For this purpose, management, unions and government had established by agreement thirty-nine separate tripartite working parties, one for each major sector of British industry. These varied in quality but by the summer of 1978, most of them had done a lot of good work in analysing, identifying and forecasting their shortcomings and their future prospects. Some of them reported that the very fact of discussion had been enlightening; it assisted in formulating better understanding and a sense of common purpose when they agreed about the nature of their problems. But in Government we could begin to see that the next phase would be more difficult for although the sector working parties could make recommendations, they were not in a position to implement them. It was a problem we would need to tackle.

Progress had been made in establishing and funding the National Enterprise Board, giving it commercial objectives. Unfortunately, before it got into its stride, we saddled it with two awkward problems – loss-makers British Leyland and Rolls Royce – both private enterprise firms which had been forced to turn to the State for assistance in order to survive. In my view by absorbing too much of the National Enterprise Board's energy, these unwelcome responsibilities diverted it from its intended role. Nevertheless, as I sat at home in the relative quiet of August 1978, I was not unhappy with the result of my political stock-taking. Before leaving London, I had asked Sir John Hunt, the Cabinet Secretary, to prepare a list of the items that the Government would need to deal with in the period up to April 1979. His summary showed that we would have a number of difficulties, but that we had also made a lot of progress. Despite our occasional defeats in the House, the tide was coming in and we had taken maximum advantage of it.

A summer announcement by the Liberal Party that they would withdraw from their Agreement with us when the new session began in November 1978 inevitably increased the Government's vulnerability to defeat on major issues. The first test would come at the conclusion of the Queen's Speech, which would be the first business of Parliament when it resumed work in the autumn. This had naturally started a buzz of speculation about the prospects of a general election and, fanned by the press which always enjoys the fun at such times, the gossip in the Lobbies grew louder. By the time the House rose at the end of July, some Members who were not standing again had so convinced themselves that the House would not reconvene that they cleared out their filing cabinets and I was told that some held farewell parties. At that time my own inclination was to delay a decision on an autumn election until I had a clearer idea about whether the Government could secure a majority in the House for the Queen's Speech. If we could, then in parliamentary terms I estimated there would be no other mortal challenge in the Division Lobbies before the spring of 1979, by which time I hoped we should have consolidated our successes of the previous eighteen months in the minds of the electors, and so improved the chance of winning. On the other hand, if we were likely to be defeated on the Queen's Speech, then we should not wait beyond October.

I began to receive advice and opinions from many quarters. Michael Foot came to see me and urged that we should put the idea of an autumn election out of our minds and concentrate on preparing for the next session. The Chief Whip, Michael Cocks, came separately and also expressed a strong preference for embarking upon another session. He said we would have a bumpy ride, but he believed we could reach the journey's end. He reported that the Whips' Office had met privately to discuss the options for the timing of the election, and by a clear majority (I believe it was seven votes to two) had declared against an autumn election. Among the diverse opinions they garnered were that Scotland and Wales were safe, but the English marginal seats still remained to be won, and they could not see any substantial Labour gains either in the North or in the Midlands in the autumn. Some thought that the electors might believe that an autumn election meant the Government was 'running away' before the situation worsened, but others argued that if there was no autumn election, we would be said to be 'hanging on' without cause.

Those in favour of going to the country argued that Parliamentary defeats, even on small issues, would be damaging and that the prospect of uncertainty about the behaviour of the unions during the winter meant it was preferable to go to the country while things were in reasonable shape, even though our prospects were uncertain. In terms of whether or not we could win votes in Parliament, the Deputy Chief Whip, Walter Harrison, who was a genius at conjuring majorities out of thin air, was characteristically robust. 'We have lived on next to nothing for years and should have a go at carrying on.'

Amongst my advisers there was general agreement that Party morale was good and that an autumn election would find our active supporters in good heart. But welcome news though this was, it would not necessarily be sufficient for victory. I found myself recalling an earlier election in 1959 when the Party fought with great enthusiasm and went through the campaign believing we had a splendid chance of victory, but when the results were declared we found the Conservatives had gained a number of seats, and the Labour vote had actually fallen. One reason for this was the Party's attitude at the time of Suez in 1956 which still rankled three years later with some of our own supporters and this had cost us votes.

Action should have been taken earlier to offset the five-fold increase in the price of Middle East oil in 1973, but for the first two years until 1975 we had sought, by borrowing abroad, to stave off the effects. In due course in 1976 came the recourse to the IMF and although that loan was being steadily repaid and the inflation rate was lower than when the Conservatives had left office, it seemed to me that not enough time had elapsed for the traumas of 1976 to sink into the background of the public memory. There is usually a time gap between current economic reality and public awareness of it and this was such an occasion. The text which every Government should pin up in the Cabinet Room is: 'Take the disagreeable medicine as soon as you come to power. The sweets can follow later.'

A number of Cabinet colleagues wrote to tell me their views. Most were in favour of an appeal to the country although their letters conveyed very little conviction that we could win outright. They based themselves on such arguments as the prospect of defeats in the House sapping our morale: the damage if we appeared to be 'hanging on'; we would have no reliable allies in the House; (flatteringly) my personal reputation was high: industrial problems were awaiting us: the Party workers were ready to go and in the case of Scotland, were enthusiastic. But while all these arguments were important, only one member of the Cabinet expressed a belief that we could win. Even he hedged his bet: 'We cannot be certain of winning. But we would start at least evens and I believe we would pull ahead during the campaign.' This was hardly a trumpet call, especially as he added that in his judgement the conclusive argument was that the

Government could not survive the Parliamentary scene until the spring.

Bernard Donoughue sent me a summary of the pollsters' figures. They showed that the Conservative lead over Labour in the early months of 1978 had dwindled, although they were still ahead by a small margin. They also indicated that the incomes policy was still popularly approved by 66 per cent of the electorate with no more than 24 per cent dissatisfied.

I continued taking soundings during the first fortnight of August 1978, consulting a number of colleagues in different parts of the country by telephone; they were generally agreed that our electoral situation was much better than it had been a year earlier. Opinions differed, but a realistic view came from the West Midlands where I was warned that Labour's results in Council bye-elections, although showing a dramatic recovery from our low point, were not good enough to hold on to a number of the Parliamentary seats that we had won in 1974.

I did my own amateur calculations and came up with 303 Labour seats and 304 Conservatives – which if I were anywhere near being right would have left us with a small loss of seats, but with a Conservative gain of more than twenty. Such a result would have been a tremendous psychological fillip for the Tory Party and the situation would have resembled 1950/51 when a Tory Party with its tail up because of its gains in the 1950 election, harried the Attlee Government until it lost its authority and fell. My estimate was that the most probable result would be another 'hung' Parliament, a prospect I did not relish. While I would have been ready to carry on at the head of a government with a reasonable majority, I had no wish to undergo once again the frustration and uncertainty of having no Parliamentary majority. Moreover, the polls showed that as the country began to understand what we were trying to do, an increasing number liked what they saw. There was still another twelve months to run before the life of Parliament must come to an end. Why run the risk of a very doubtful election result in October 1978 if we could convert it into a more convincing majority in 1979? I made up my mind. The Government should aim to consolidate the progress we had made and then ask the country to confirm us in office on a progressive manifesto in the spring. I looked at the 1979 calendar. A new electoral register would come into force in February; British Summer Time would begin on 18 March; Good Friday was on 13 April. I drew a ring around Thursday 5 April 1979, the last day of the income tax year. This seemed as auspicious as any other day. Having decided, I telephoned the Chancellor who was my near neighbour in Sussex and invited myself to tea on Friday 18

August. I recall it was a lovely summer's afternoon, and we sat in the garden while I told him what I had decided. We then reviewed the winter's prospects.

Before the Cabinet had dispersed for the summer recess, I had informed them that they would be the first to know my decision and we had arranged to hold a Cabinet Meeting on 6 September, which was the first occasion when we should all be in the country at the same time. Before that meeting I had an earlier engagement to address the Congress of the TUC at Brighton and I took the opportunity to invite the 'Neddy 6' to dinner at the farm on Friday 1 September. They came, David Basnett, Geoffrey Drain, Terry Duffy, Moss Evans and Lionel Murray, led by the Chairman Lord Allen. My wife's reputation as a cook was well known and she presided over a splendid table at which our guests were served by my eldest granddaughter, Tamsin Jay. Now that the August holidays were over and with the approach of the TUC Congress, the press had resumed its speculation about an autumn election, and it was obvious that my guests had convinced themselves that it must be held in October. Without revealing my decision, I argued the alternative case for the spring quite strenuously, but apparently not convincingly.

Afterwards I heard that some members of the General Council felt they had been misled about the date, but no one who was present at dinner on that evening has ever said as much to me, and I doubt if they would, in view of my vigorous advocacy that a genuine alternative did exist, for which valid reasons could be advanced. But I made a mistake in allowing the speculation to build up to an almost feverish crescendo without uttering a word to cool it. My reason was my promise to the Cabinet that they should be the first to hear, but on reflection, I could have found a means of informing most of them earlier and so killed the speculation before it had become a 'certainty' in the mind of the media. When I finally made the announcement, the astonishment and in some places (like Conservative Central Office, which had already spent a lot of money on propaganda) the consternation, I was told, was awesome.

I met the Cabinet on Thursday morning 7 September and informed them of the announcement to be made later that day. They received the news in a matter of fact way and at once turned to government business. Later in the day I made a television broadcast:

> The benefit the country is experiencing today is a result of your efforts and the Government has eased the situation because we thought the economy could stand it and for no other reason.

This can be a lasting, not a temporary, improvement if we follow
through with consistent policies, so I am not proposing to seek your votes
because there is some blue sky overhead today. Obviously all parties'
want to win a General Election when it comes, but let us think for a
moment of the great domestic issues the country faces now, and ask
ourselves whether a General Election now would make it any better this
winter.

Would a general election now make it easier to prevent inflation going
up once more? Would unemployment be any less this winter? Would a
general election now solve the problem of how to deal with pay increases
during the next few months? Would it bring a sudden dramatic increase
in productivity? No. There are no instant solutions. Advertising slogans
are no substitute. The Government must and will continue to carry out
policies which are consistent and determined, which do not chop and
change, and which have brought about the present recovery in our
fortunes.

We shall face our difficulties as we come to them. I can already see
some looming on the horizon. I cannot, and do not, promise we shall
succeed. I can say we shall deserve to. Basically, I want to say we go on
because we are doing what is best for Britain. So, I shall not be calling
for a general election at this time. Instead, I ask every one of you to carry
on with the task of consolidating the improvements now taking place in
our country's position. Let us see it through together.

After people had recovered from their surprise it was apparent that the
decision had done us no harm. Indeed, if the polls were to be believed,
Labour was riding high in November 1978 after the season of party
conferences had been held, when our standing had so far improved that
we had drawn ahead with a lead of 5.5 points over the Conservatives.

Taking one month with another, the Opinion Polls were oscillating,
pointing in no consistent direction, but it seemed not unreasonable to
assume that the Government, having made such a remarkable recovery
in public estimation from our abysmal showing of two years earlier, would
have good hopes of consolidating public confidence by the spring of 1979
and even prospects of scoring an outright victory.

But the winter of discontent intervened, and I must retrace my steps
and give some account of those events that were to shatter our hopes and
antagonise the country beyond recall.

The seeds had been sown twelve months earlier in December 1977
when, shortly before Christmas, two Cabinet Meetings were held on 19
and 22 December. At the first we held a general discussion on future

prospects for the economy, including a paper submitted by Tony Benn entitled 'A National Development Programme'. I have already referred to the second Cabinet. This was more sharply focused on the problems caused by the incomes policy, which were both administrative and substantive. In work terms, the task of monitoring major pay claims was throwing a heavy burden on Ministers, and particularly on the Chancellor, who as soon as New Year 1978 arrived would need to devote much time to preparing his Budget.

Denis Healey and I had previously discussed what steps would be needed after August 1978 when the current incomes policy would expire, and although we recognised the strength of the unions' demand for a return to so-called free collective bargaining, both of us were in agreement that we could not simply throw the reins on the horse's back and allow it to gallop away. It was the familiar story of every Incomes Policy; impossible to emerge from without pain and tears. Some restraint would be needed, and we were reinforced by our knowledge that a number of senior trade unions leaders understood this.

On the basis of the settlements being made in the autumn of 1977, the current pay round with its 'norm' of 10 per cent was forecast to produce earnings increases as high as 14 per cent, although because of other factors, such as increased productivity and the lower price of imported raw materials, the inflation rate for late 1978 was forecast to be no more than 7 or 8 per cent. This would be a vast improvement on earlier years, but even so it was too high when compared with the inflation rates of other major industrial countries and would have had the effect of further eroding our competitive position.

Accordingly, at the Cabinet Meeting on 22 December, I threw out the idea that from August 1978, we should aim to get pay settlements down to 5 per cent for the following year which, given the phenomenon known as 'wage drift', might result in earnings increases of 7 or 8 per cent. This would be roughly in line with our hoped-for inflation level. In the event, for several months settlements actually ran at between 8 and 9 per cent. As far as I can recall, because no formal proposal was before the Cabinet, there was no discussion of my 5 per cent suggestion and Ministers probably assumed I was thinking aloud – as indeed I was.

However, when I made my New Year Broadcast on Sunday 1 January 1978 from the Hawtrey Room at Chequers, the 5 per cent idea hardened and popped out when the interviewer tempted me to outline my hopes for the coming year. I replied that I was already looking beyond 1978 to 1979, and added that I wanted to work for an inflation rate no higher than 5 per cent for that year. So the figure of 5 per cent swam into the public ken.

During the following weeks, the Chancellor, together with other members of his team, Roy Hattersley, Albert Booth, the Secretary for Employment, and Eric Varley, Secretary for Trade and Industry, had desultory talks with TUC leaders, but at the end of February before we held our regular monthly dinner with the 'Neddy 6' at No. 10, Denis Healey had to report that he was making little progress.

Our difficulties in trying to come to some agreement with the TUC were compounded by the fact that the leadership of the two largest unions, the Transport Workers and the Engineers, was in the process of changing hands. Jack Jones retired in March 1978, and Terry Duffy was elected to succeed Hugh Scanlon in May 1978. These changes materially weakened the influence of the 'Neddy 6'. Terry Duffy was strongly supportive, but had not then acquired Hugh Scanlon's background knowledge or experience. Moss Evans, who succeeded Jack Jones, had declared only two months earlier that he was opposed to any policy about pay, whether it was imposed by the Government or reached through voluntary agreement. David Basnett of the General and Municipal Workers Union moved more into the leadership of the group, and together with the Chairman, Alf Allen of the Shopworkers Union, struggled hard to find some common ground with the Government, but Moss Evans was obdurate, whilst always insisting that he wished to see a Labour Government victory whenever an election was held. I had no doubts about his sincerity, only of his methods. At one of our monthly dinners in the early months of 1978 there was a tart exchange between him, Alf Allen and Hugh Scanlon. Moss Evans had said that when the election came, the attitude of the trade unions should be critical of the Government's mistakes but friendly to our re-election. Hugh Scanlon at once pounced on him. Such an attitude would be useless. There must be massive support for the Government if we were to win.

Alf Allen was one who was open in his desire that the TUC should respond to the Government on pay, but unfortunately the members of the 'Neddy 6', unlike previous years, were divided and increasingly ineffective. I was under no illusions about the difficulties these divisions would cause for the next round of incomes policy and at an early meeting in February 1978, told the 'Neddy 6' that if they could not reach agreement among themselves or with the Government, Ministers must reach their own conclusions. I pointed out that we could not avoid this in view of our responsibility for public sector pay and went on, 'the Government would have to take decisions with or without the help of the trade unions', adding in an ominously accurate forecast that in such an event, 'in my view we shall not be able to get through another year [from July 1978] without your support'. Everyone worked hard to try and reach an accommodation with great help from Len Murray, but Moss Evans remained adamant. At our regular monthly dinner in April 1978, he told me that the Government should 'back off' and let the unions get on with the job of securing the best settlements they could. He said that the Government could rely on the union leaders to behave responsibly. How remote his optimism was from reality can be judged by his union's claim for a 30 per cent increase on behalf of over 150,000 motor car workers in Ford and British Leyland in the autumn of 1978 and for a 40 per cent increase (and in some local cases, an even higher sum) for the road haulage industry.

It was my vain hope during the early months of 1978 that we might move to a long term understanding. Influenced by the West German experience I preferred tripartite discussions to take place each year between the Government, unions and employers, in an attempt to create a consensus about the national level of earnings that would be compatible with keeping inflation at a low level; both sides would then work within such an understanding in their pay negotiations. There were no takers for this idea. Cabinet became restless as the summer wore on without any sign of an understanding with the TUC, and to make matters worse, in June 1978 Ministers were faced with recommendations from the Top Salaries Review Board to pay large salary increases to senior civil servants, judges and chairmen of nationalised industries, some of whom admittedly had not received increases for a number of years.

Because of this, the recommendations were frighteningly large when compared with what the Cabinet had in mind for the next pay round. Ministers were fully aware of the potential danger if these large awards were implemented for it was not in human nature for the unions to accept that the gross figures represented a topping-up over a period of years. What the rank and file members would see was large increases being given to groups who already enjoyed substantial salaries. It presented a dilemma for the Government which I had seen played out on several previous occasions, and to which I never discovered a satisfactory answer. The Cabinet was so evenly divided that it could not come to a conclusion and in the end I myself had to make the decision to implement the report. I did so with my eyes open to the dangers of what I was doing.

July is invariably a fractious Parliamentary month, and 1978 was no exception. The Cabinet was not in the best of moods when I set out a timetable of meetings to consider both our economic prospects and the future of pay. Several Ministers wished us to increase the level of public expenditure, demanding that it take precedence over tax reductions even if, as one or two Ministers argued, 'the price was electoral unpopularity'. Others were worried that unemployment was too high and called for selective import controls and quotas on imports as part of a fundamental alternative to our existing strategy, although there was never more than a small minority of Ministers in favour of such measures. A number of Ministers regarded another year of pay policy as a regrettable necessity and approached it without enthusiasm, but they argued that defeating inflation was crucial to the nation's future and to the Labour Party's prospects of electoral success. The official estimates showed that the tax reliefs given in the Budget, when added to child benefit increases, were worth over 8 per cent to a family of four, and those in favour of a further round of incomes policy declared that these rising living standards would create a more favourable climate for wage negotiations, especially among the rank and file trade unionists who, unlike the activists, were not opposed to pay policy on grounds of principle. The view of some other Ministers was that we should abandon pay policy and rely on trade union moderation in their pay claims. These Ministers argued that whatever the Government did, the unions would ignore another pay round, especially as there was a growing feeling of irritation among industrial workers that the public sector had been receiving more favourable treatment. This was a reference to recent settlements for the Services and the police which (like the top civil servants and judges) were part of 'catching up' increases. Although justified in themselves, they tended to result in leap-frogging pay claims from other groups. A different group of Ministers who believed another pay round was necessary, nevertheless argued that 5 per cent was too small and pressed for a 'norm' of 7 per cent in the belief that the higher figure would be more acceptable. Michael Foot, together with Albert Booth, the Secretary for Employment, also urged that a bigger increase should be available to the lowest paid and to this the Cabinet agreed. The Chancellor put in hand a White Paper setting out the Government's policy and while this was being prepared, I went through a series of consultations with the CBI and the TUC to acquaint them with what we had in mind and to gain some idea of their reactions. A little later I sent a draft copy of our proposals privately to David Steel, whose response was generally favourable. He suggested that I make some acknowledgement of Liberal assistance as that would make it easier for him to rally votes for the Government when the issue was debated in the House.

The TUC was conciliatory and helpful when we met. Lionel Murray said that they and the Government shared the same objectives and they acknowledged that without the efforts we had made unemployment and inflation would have been higher. They were anxious to avoid a wages explosion, but employers were increasingly blaming the Government for their failure to pay higher wages, with the result that beating the 'norm' was becoming a challenge. In addition, the Government underrated the anomalies and distortions that had built up in the wages structure. I replied that the Government recognised the difficulties and did not wish to place impossible burdens on the shoulders of the TUC. But they had acknowledged that existing policies had been a success in bringing down inflation, and if these were continued then unemployment also would continue to fall. The ending of high wage settlements in 1975 had markedly improved Britain's industrial reputation with our overseas customers and it was imperative to adhere to the policies which had brought this about. It was ridiculous to talk (as some trade union leaders had) of a 10 per cent 'norm' for wage increases as being a 'wage freeze'. I emphasised that expectations had risen too high and must be more realistic but concluded that I had no desire for controversy with the trade unions whose help the Government needed, and once again reminded them that I would decline to hold on to office if the price was to shoulder responsibility for a return to the excessive rates of inflation and unemployment of earlier years.

David Basnett on behalf of the TUC emphasised that because they were facing demands for a return to voluntary collective bargaining, they were unable to reach a formal agreement with the Government but repeated that they shared our objectives. He kept the door open by saying that they would reserve further comments until they had seen the White Paper. We parted without rancour.

When the CBI came to see me on the next day, I repeated that an inflation rate in double figures was unacceptable – a statement with which they agreed – and questioned them about the TUC's concerns about the distortions caused by incomes policy on differential pay structures. Their estimate was that perhaps 25 per cent of firms had made progress in correcting such pressures and more would be able to do so in the coming year if there was a policy of 'flexible moderation' on pay. The CBI be-

lieved that a figure of 7 per cent on earnings would enable them to do
so and would keep inflation in single figures, although they were unwilling formally to recommend such a figure. Seven per cent was of
course in line with the 5 per cent 'norm' that the Government intended
to propose in the White Paper.

It was obvious from these meetings that there would be no possibility
of pinning down an exact agreement, but the question that remained
unanswered was how far would the unions carry their opposition? A
number of conferences had called for a return to free collective bargaining.
On the other hand, reports (and the opinion polls) showed that incomes
policy was popular among the public and acceptable to a big majority of
rank and file trade unionists. If resistance in 1978 turned out to be no
greater than it had been in the winter of 1977, when we also had no formal
agreement with the TUC, we would stand a good chance of keeping
inflation within single figures, even with some wage drift. I hoped we
could minimise opposition by emphasising the paragraph in the White
Paper about the Government's intention that low-paid workers should
receive special treatment and not be confined to 5 per cent.

I did this in opening the debate in Parliament which took place shortly
before the House rose for the summer recess, and I further intimated
that wage negotiations should not discourage self-financing pay deals at
a higher level than 5 per cent, provided they were based on genuine productivity increases and did not increase the unit costs of production. In
the debate that followed some Labour speakers expressed their open
opposition to the Government's policy and when a vote was called, a
number of them refused to vote. However, the Government managed to
secure a respectable majority of fifteen, thanks to support from several
members of the minor parties. During August there was little overt
political or industrial activity until matters hotted up in September when
the TUC Congress was held in Brighton, followed by a confrontation a
month later at the Labour Party Conference.

The TUC was, as always, more restrained than the Party Conference,
but both bodies strongly rejected the 5 per cent figure – or any other. The
majority mood was encapsulated in a resolution at the Party Conference
from a Liverpool constituency, which 'whilst recognising the value of
cooperation between trade unions and the Government, rejects totally
any wage restraint by whatever method, including cash limits, and
specifically the Government's 5 per cent'. Michael Foot wound up the
debate and tore the logic of that resolution to pieces. 'If we were to see

inflation going upwards, ten per cent, fifteen per cent, twenty per cent, it certainly would not assist the low-paid workers . . . everybody in his heart knows that to be the truth.' And, he continued, 'If you have a Tory Government, what sort of wages policy do you think you are going to have? You can have a wages policy imposed by mass unemployment, far worse unemployment than anything we have experienced – that is the Keith Joseph–Thatcher policy.' Well, in the light of what has happened since 1979, no one can complain that Michael did not warn them.

But despite his warnings, the resolution was carried by a large majority in a heated and emotional atmosphere. The result confirmed that the temperature on pay was much higher than it had been a year earlier and I decided to try and lower it in the course of my Parliamentary report to the Conference on the following day. This had been prepared before the Conference began, but I inserted a long, extempore passage (I called it a parenthesis) speaking my mind as the words came and restating the dire consequences of abandoning an incomes policy, in an effort to win the understanding of the delegates, even if we could not reverse the vote of the previous day. What I said was sympathetically received by the delegates and had a cooling effect at the time. The new pay year had started off well for the Government's policy when 5,500 process workers in the British Sugar Corporation had accepted a pay increase of 5 per cent plus a scheme for additional payments in exchange for higher productivity. This was in line with government policy, but this success was offset a few days later when several thousands of Ford motor car workers went on strike in support of a 30 per cent wage increase. This strike was in progress when my Conference appeal was made and I invited those Ministers primarily concerned with pay to my hotel suite in Blackpool to discuss how we should handle the Ford claim, which if successful would not only wreck our pay policy but also undo our success in reducing inflation which was then at its lowest level for six years. I also wanted to discuss our response to the Conference's rejection of any form of pay policy.

I began the discussion by saying that to accept the views of Conference would mean the Government abandoning an anti-inflation policy which was demonstrably successful. We ourselves had made it the touchstone of success in reducing unemployment and if we gave it up, we would lose all credibility. However, we should try to meet the genuine feeling of Conference delegates about the low paid and I asked Ministers to examine ways of hardening up the general statements in our White Paper which permitted flexibility in reaching settlements for the purpose of increasing low rates of pay. Albert Booth pointed out that by itself this would not solve the problem as discontent had built up among higher-paid workers precisely because their pay differentials had already been narrowed as a result of increases to the low paid, and this proposal would accentuate the squeeze. However, we agreed that he should take informal soundings with some of the trade union leaders attending the Party Conference and report back.

Denis Healey reported that some Ministers had privately discussed the prospect of increasing the 'norm' from 5 per cent to 7 per cent, but I took the view that in the existing atmosphere there was no prospect of the unions agreeing to any precise figure. I realised that it would be difficult to adhere to the five per cent figure but in my view we should do so as nearly as possible, and to the extent that we failed, the Chancellor would have to take off-setting action in the spring Budget of 1979 in order to restrain a rise in inflation. I recognised that with an election due in 1979 a poor budget would be unpopular, but inflation must be kept down and the unions could surely understand that if they wished to keep a Labour Government, they must cooperate on pay.

We further discussed what should be done if Ford, the first big pay claim and the pace-setter for others, flagrantly ignored the guide-lines. In view of the wide publicity such a settlement would receive and the consequential repercussions throughout industry, all present reluctantly agreed that sanctions against Ford would need to be invoked by the Government. We decided to meet again as soon as we were all back in London on Monday 9 October.

I then set about rescuing the talks with the TUC which had earlier ended in stalemate. From Blackpool I sent a message to Lionel Murray, suggesting that we hold one of our regular dinners with the 'Neddy 6' at Downing Street on Tuesday 10 October. The gist of my message was that free collective bargaining had been thrown down as a challenge to the pay guidelines, but the Government could not withdraw from pay issues at this stage. Nevertheless, we were ready to try with the TUC to resolve the problems of low pay, prices and squeezed differentials if this would help in keeping down the general level of settlements.

With David Basnett, Geoffrey Drain, Moss Evans, Terry Duffy and Lionel Murray arriving at the dinner, the representatives of all the biggest unions were present. Michael Foot and Denis Healey were with me. On this occasion all of them without exception tried to be helpful and constructive. The TUC representatives said at the outset that they wished to see inflation held below ten per cent during 1979 and David Basnett added that there was no disposition on the part of those present to break with the Government although some who were not present wanted to make a dash for freedom.

Alf Allen repeated that although the union leaders were under directions to pursue free collective bargaining, they were anxious to help keep inflation below ten per cent. Each side was locked into its position and both should try to find a way out. I said that the Government had given a clear answer to the question of how single figure inflation could be achieved during 1979. The trade unions had declared that they shared the same aim. It was now their turn to answer the question of how they could reconcile this declared objective with free collective bargaining. 'If you are saying that pay is outside any possible agreement, then what remains inside it in order to get the right answer on inflation? The Government is entitled to a reply from the TUC.'

Moss Evans took up the challenge. He said that most negotiators in the TGWU were thinking of settlements below ten per cent because they recognised that if wage increases generated price increases, inflation would take off again. If employers could demonstrate this during pay negotiations then the trade union representatives would take it into account and might instead negotiate a productivity deal.

Denis Healey said that the Treasury conclusion was that a 5 per cent guideline meant that with the addition of 'wage drifts' plus assistance to the low paid, the outcome on pay would be a national increase of nine per cent. If the final figure went above this, double figure inflation would be certain to return. Roy Hattersley had put forward a useful proposal about the role of the Price Commission which had been established by the Conservative Government in April 1973. Its role had been continued and extended by the Labour Government. Hattersley's idea was that trade unions might give evidence and bring their opinions to bear at the Price Commission's hearings. Firms seeking price increases would be required to show the effect of increased labour costs.

Moss Evans took this up but turned the proposition round the other way. He suggested we should have a common goal, namely not to increase prices by more than an agreed percentage figure, but should they exceed that figure, the unions would then be free to go back with a further wage claim. This resembled the Italian *scala mobile* with its disadvantage that if the target figure turned out to be too low, we would return to the pernicious system of two or more settlements in a year from which we had, by the efforts of the TUC, recently escaped.

Nevertheless, I was encouraged by the obvious desire of those present to find a means of escape from the dilemma and I assured them once more that the Government would be happy to see an improvement in the position of the low-paid, and to put even greater emphasis on ways to restrain price increases.

The dinner table discussion proceeded with an open and friendly interchange of views and the evening ended with Lionel Murray agreeing to report the discussion to the influential Economic Committee of the TUC with the object of getting them to agree to fresh talks about a new understanding for 1979. The Economic Committee agreed and the upshot was a series of meetings between the 'Neddy 6' and the Chancellor's team. Michael Foot joined the talks and he and Denis Healey tried hard to find a way forward. It seemed that all was not lost and I reported in this sense to the Cabinet in mid-October. The Chancellor told Ministers that the inflation rate for September 1978 had fallen to 7.8 per cent and that the slow fall in unemployment was continuing, while domestic production was growing by 3 to 4 per cent and new private investment was improving.

These tangible gains had been won by intensive effort from the Government with great help from the trade unions and assistance from a fall in world prices, and when I summed up the Cabinet discussion that followed Denis Healey's report I emphasised that any new agreement with the TUC must be of a character that would enable us to continue our progress. The ground we had gained could not be sacrificed for the sake of a cosmetic arrangement. Both sides worked hard and Denis Healey and Michael Foot employed impressive ingenuity and showed great resilience. The TUC negotiators too were genuinely anxious to avoid a rift and Lionel Murray worked closely with the Chancellor to try and produce a meaningful document.

Unfortunately, future events were to show that the goodwill of the TUC was not sufficient and that our critics in some of the unions and in the Party would be satisfied with nothing less than a complete abandonment of any incomes policy. This I was not prepared to do.

17

The Government loses vote on pay – referendum on Devolution –
discussions on defence at Guadaloupe – Government defeated on vote
of confidence

The Government faced the opening of the new session of Parliament on
1 November 1978. The purpose of the Queen's Speech which begins the
Parliamentary year is to set out the Government's programme for the
ensuing twelve months, and by convention any Government whose programme is rejected is expected to resign at once. November 1978 was a
particularly piquant occasion as it was the first test of our ability to secure
a majority following the withdrawal of the Liberals from their Agreement
with the Government. It was not a propitious moment. The debate took
place against the background of the well-publicised strikes by the motor
car workers at Ford and Vauxhall, and the Opposition harried Ministers
about what action would be taken by the Government in the event that
the Ford management conceded a pay increase in excess of 5 per cent.
Would the Government follow the precedent of previous years when
other firms had been blacklisted? Would the Government refuse to
purchase Ford cars and vans?

In reality the Government did very little business with Ford, but that
did not deter the opponents of incomes policy who seized on the issue as
a matter of principle, some Labour Members as well as the Conservatives
keeping up a running fire against the Government. I was able to avoid a
direct answer during the debate as no settlement was in sight but during
the weeks ahead the Ford issue was to embarrass us; eventually it contributed to the Government's undoing. When the vote was called, the
Whips proved once again their ability to forecast the result correctly. The
Liberals celebrated their new-found freedom by voting against the
Government, but thanks to the aid of the smaller Parties we emerged
with a majority of ten, a cushion that was almost luxurious in days of
hard-won victories.

There were other preoccupations at the time. President Carter was
concerned about the West's relations with the Soviet Union and the
prospects for the Strategic Arms Limitation Talks (SALT II).

Since Gromyko's visit in March 1976 Britain's bilateral relations with the Soviet Union had been on an even keel, but there were growls from Moscow when they learned that the Chinese were interested in purchasing the Harrier Jump Jet to deploy on their sparse and under-modernised airfields close to their long border with the Soviet Union. The Harrier was basically a defensive weapon, but the Soviets neverthe-less took great exception to any deal. Brezhnev wrote letters to Carter, Giscard, Helmut Schmidt and myself, going so far as to imply that unless the United States pressurised Britain and France not to supply arms to China, the SALT II Agreement would be in danger. None of us wanted such an outcome and I suggested that the four of us should discuss the Brezhnev letter at our next meeting, which was then being arranged for the following January at Guadaloupe.

At that meeting I said that Britain could not permit the Russians to determine our relations with China, a point strongly supported by Helmut Schmidt. The outcome was general agreement that we should all pursue our existing policies and we should send similar replies to Brezhnev making clear that improving our links with China did not imply that we were 'playing the China card' against the Soviet Union. Prior to this I had indicated to the Chinese that I had every desire to deepen relations with that great country, but these could not be limited to arms purchases. We would be ready to consider selling the Harrier but our relations needed to be deepened in all aspects – economic, political and cultural. After much discussion, the Chinese Government accepted this and the Chinese Vice Premier arrived in London. At the end of his visit a major seven-year economic agreement was signed between our two countries, but the Chinese did not pursue the purchase of the Harrier, mainly, they said, because the price was too high. Our improved relationship had another spin-off: for the first time in thirty years the air service between the Chinese mainland and Hong Kong was resumed.

On the African continent, the situation in Southern Africa was de-teriorating as the guerrilla war in Rhodesia intensified. This was accom-panied by a series of half-hints from Salisbury that it might be possible to reach an accommodation if I were willing to act as Chairman of an all-party conference in London. David Owen, the Foreign Secretary, who was working closely with the United States, was always alert to any prospect of bringing an end to the illegal regime in Rhodesia on the basis of majority rule, but neither he nor I had any desire to be used by Ian Smith as a device for postponing the inevitable end. On the other hand, although President Carter was continuing to put pressure on the regime by way of sanctions, he faced strong countervailing pressure in Congress in view of Ian Smith's declared intention to hold some kind of elections of a limited character. It was necessary to help President Carter hold the line on the Anglo-American partnership, and it seemed that the best way to decide whether Smith was serious was to send someone who was not a Minister to visit Southern Africa and report on the attitudes of those he met. President Carter agreed and was also willing to send someone to accompany our emissary. I asked Cledwyn Hughes to go. He was suited in every way. Not only did he have previous experience as a former Commonwealth Minister, but he had a cool head and a shrewd appreciation of his fellows, and I placed great reliance on his judgement. Only a few days earlier he had moved the reply to the Address in the Queen's Speech in a manner that won general applause, and he possessed the confidence of both sides of the House. He spent several weeks in Africa, accompanied by President Carter's representative, visiting Ian Smith in Salisbury, talking with Presidents of the Front Line States, holding discussions with Robert Mugabe in Mozambique and Joshua Nkomo in Zambia, and going down to Cape Town to test Prime Minister Botha's opinions. There were many others to see, too, such as General Obasanjo in Nigeria.

On Cledwyn's return to London he concluded that although all the major parties would probably be willing to attend a conference in London, such a gathering would stand no chance of success. Smith was not ready to face the inevitable, and up to the present, circumstances had not forced him to do so. Reluctantly I accepted his conclusion and put the idea on one side. Writing to President Carter, I suggested that our next step in Rhodesia should be determined at an early meeting between us.

The Government was not given long to enjoy the stabilising effect of our victory at the end of the debate on the Queen's Speech. The negotiations conducted by Denis Healey, Michael Foot and their team with the TUC representatives were brought to an end at almost the same moment in early November, and as soon as I saw the final draft it was obvious that its terms reflected little more than an agreement to differ.

It was strong on objectives but weak on the methods by which they would be reached. It restated our agreement that inflation must be reduced still further but contained no practical proposals for doing so except to enjoin pay negotiators to reach settlements that would not lead to price increases. It called on negotiators not to absorb all the benefits that flowed from increased productivity in higher pay, but to take into account the interests of the consumer and the need for new investment. The principle of comparability in certain occupations was given a more central role: the Price Commission would examine both labour and capital costs in deciding on price increases. Finally, there would in future be an annual discussion between Government and unions on a whole range of issues 'including a common understanding on pay and prices'.

The sentiments were admirable. The TUC declared its belief that 'adherence to its guidance within the system of free collective bargaining would result in settlements consistent with bringing down inflation'. I could agree with the conclusion, but had little faith that the advice would be followed in the absence of more concrete action; already the road haulage workers were putting forward a claim for a 20 to 30 per cent pay increase (which was later revised upwards), the engineers for 33 per cent, the local authority workers and the miners for 40 per cent.

I was disappointed that the document made no precise proposals for helping the low paid, as this was a point the Party Conference had been rightly concerned with. When I questioned the Chancellor he told me that he had proposed an underpinning increase of three pounds a week for the low paid, but the TUC negotiators had been divided and the proposal was dropped. I summed up the situation to my Private Secretary, in a verse I am apt to quote when faced with a thicket of procedure but little substance. It is by Roy Campbell, the South African poet:

> You praise the firm restraint with which they write –
> I'm with you there of course;
> They use the snaffle and the bit all right,
> But where's the bloody horse?

However, it was argued that the very fact that an agreed document was in existence would keep open the lines between the Government and the TUC; admittedly there was an explicit recognition of the link between pay and price increases, and the document might ensure a helpful neutrality from the TUC as a whole (similar to their stance in 1977) when the going became rough later on.

But the Government was to be denied even this modest support. We had anticipated that when the 'Neddy 6' presented the document to the full Council of the TUC on 14 November 1978 it would be accepted. Their own negotiators had spent five weeks hammering it out and expected no real difficulty. All of us were wrong. There was strong resistance, some of it very misguided. The opponents argued that comparability studies to determine pay levels would bring no advantage, and that pressure would intensify to keep wage settlements down if the negotiators were encouraged to concentrate on price increase effects. (I had thought that keeping down inflation was a major object of the exercise.) At the end of a long discussion the document was put to the vote and the result was a tie – 14-14. The Chairman, Tom Jackson, was in favour of the document but by TUC convention was reluctantly forced to give his casting vote against it. And so it was lost.

The Chancellor had arranged to give a press conference to launch the new understanding, and when the news of the adverse decision reached him he was bowled over. He put on a brave face, and I do not remember ever seeing him as downcast and disappointed: five weeks' hard work had disappeared in a twinkling. His black mood did not last for long. With Denis it never does, and almost at once, in conjunction with Albert Booth, he began thinking about the alternative methods that might be found to help the low-paid and to develop longer-term treatment of pay issues. But the political impact of the TUC's rejection was serious and totally offset the beneficial effect of our victory in the Queen's Speech debate. Conservative spokesmen mocked the end of the partnership; the Liberals called for a general election; the Government's moral authority on pay issues was undermined.

For the first week or two after the breakdown things did not go too badly and on 6 December I received a report that of the early pay agreements, no less than half a million workers had settled within the Government's guidelines. This seemed encouraging until it was viewed against the mass of claims for sums far in excess of the 5 per cent which still remained to be settled. As the season of pay negotiations gathered momentum, Ministers found themselves more and more embroiled: Peter Shore was dealing with the repercussions of the Local Authority manual workers' claim for a 40 per cent increase; David Ennals with the National Health Service auxiliary workers; Shirley Williams with the teachers; Merlyn Rees with the BBC; Fred Peart with the TUC; Eric Varley with British Leyland; Bill Rodgers with oil tanker drivers, road haulage drivers and so on, in an apparently never-ending stream.

We had an early foretaste of what was to come in the public sector when three members of NUPE were dismissed for allegedly switching off the heating boilers at the London hospital at which they worked. If true, this was a callous act, but those concerned had a right of appeal under pro-

cedures agreed by their union. Instead of using this, local officials immediately called a strike of workers at the hospital. This kind of unreasonable
behaviour was resorted to by only small groups of public sector workers
who were sometimes influenced by politically motivated trade union
officials, but although they were not typical, such examples when highlighted by press and television brought the good name of trade unionism
into disrepute.

However, the heaviest blow, which did much to determine the wretched
course of events in the winter of 1978, came not from the public services
but from the private sector. The Ford motor car company had made a
substantial profit in the previous year and had resisted a nine-week strike
of car workers. At the end they surrendered and to finish the strike offered
a pay increase of 17 per cent which the union representatives immediately
accepted. The Ford pay claim was the bellwether of the flock, watched
by other unions and highlighted by the press. Where Ford would go the
others would follow, and such a flagrant breach of the guidelines could
not be ignored if the policy was to be left with any content.

In earlier years smaller firms than Ford had been told that they could
expect no Government orders if they paid more than the Government's
guidelines and when the Cabinet met, Ministers decided Ford could not
be treated in a different manner. We were at once attacked from both
sides. The Conservative Party called for an early debate on a misuse of
the Government's powers; Moss Evans reinforced his union's opposition
by threatening to appeal publicly to Labour Members of Parliament
sponsored by the TGWU, calling on them to vote against the Government when the debate was held. Stanley Orme, the Minister of Social
Security and a left-wing member of the Cabinet, offered to meet the
Tribune Group composed of back-bench left-wing Members to explain
the seriousness of a Government defeat. He worked loyally and hard, but
reported that he could make no impression.

Two days later the Tribune Group made an urgent request to meet me,
which I complied with, in company with Michael Foot, an erstwhile
member of the Group. A tense meeting was held in my room at the House
of Commons. Some of the delegation were hard and unforgiving; others
were anxious to find an accommodation. All complained that the Government had failed to accept the decision of the Labour Party Conference to
abandon any form of incomes policy. In the past, they said, they had
supported the Government, despite Conference decisions and against
their consciences. This was now the parting of the ways. Jo Richardson,

who led them, said that they intended to place their own amendment to the Government's proposals on the Parliamentary Order Paper and call for it to be debated and voted upon. I replied that when a Labour Government was in power it was neither feasible nor was it the intention of the Party Constitution that an Annual Conference could determine the executive actions of Labour Ministers in the month-by-month conduct of affairs. The purpose of Conference was to lay down long-term policy, which in this case meant a return to free collective bargaining. Ministers would work towards that, but it was impossible to abandon an incomes policy immediately and simply drift without guidance or control.

Two members of the delegation, Frank Allaun and Martin Flannery, argued that the Government would not be able to prevent a series of massive wage claims, and as many of them would succeed, the best policy would be for the Government to let them go through without objection. Michael Foot argued strenuously that if the Tribune Members abstained or voted against the Government, they would fall into a trap set by the Tory Party, giving them their greatest triumph, but even he was unable to shake the Group's resolve, although they volunteered that if their own proposal was not carried, they would abstain from voting for the Conservative Party's amendment.

Someone then proposed that the Government should announce that we would 'suspend' the policy, and the atmosphere became heated when I replied that this would amount to abandoning it and would make the Government a laughing stock. I emphasised that Ministers were actively working on proposals to meet one of the concerns of the Annual Conference, namely how to improve the lot of the low paid, but I was not willing to take responsibility for the higher levels of inflation and unemployment which would be the price to be paid if there was a general run of massive pay settlements. I wound up by saying that abstention from voting by the Group would be as bad as voting against; it would not save the Government from defeat and if that happened and the Parliamentary Party was shown to be seriously divided, the question would arise as to whether the Government's life should be ended. One member, who certainly had the courage of his convictions, said he would prefer this. Later when the election came he lost his seat. I concluded by again reminding the group that the future life of the Government lay in the hands of its supporters in the Commons and that they must make up their minds.

In the event, thirty of the group signed the so-called Tribune Amendment, but Speaker Thomas decided not to select it and the debate took place on a Conservative call to abandon any sanctions against companies which broke the 5 per cent guidelines. In one respect sanctions resembled the nuclear deterrent, in that they were most effective when they were not used. In another respect they were totally different, for when used would hardly have caused Ford a scratch. They were a gesture of disapproval and as such, no one in the Cabinet was enthusiastic about employing them. When the vote was taken both Liberals and Scottish Nationalists voted with the Conservatives and against the Government. On the other hand, nearly all the Tribune Group voted with the Government, although a few abstained. We were defeated by the narrow margin of two votes – 285 to 283.

Strangely enough, when the result was declared there was no wild outburst of joy from the Opposition benches – only a muted cheer. It was as if they knew they had delivered a blow against pay moderation. I at once rose to face a crowded and expectant House and declared that in view of this narrow defeat on an important issue, I would place the future of the Government in the hands of the House. I would put down a vote of confidence at once which would be debated on the next day. I did this in order to make the Scottish Nationalists face the consequences of their actions, for they knew that if the Government lost the vote of confidence and a general election took place, the result would be to postpone the referendum on Devolution for which they had been eagerly waiting, and might indeed lead to its abandonment. This move had the expected effect: on the following day the Scottish National Party changed sides. We emerged with a majority of ten.

During my speech in the confidence debate, I defended the Government's policy as the best way to hold down inflation and to prevent a rise in unemployment, and once again I repeated my forecast that if the policies of the Conservative Party were adopted they would lead to a multitude of bankruptcies and would put tens of thousands of men and women out of work. Experience was to show that this estimate was a modest one.

The CBI came to see me to thank the Government for dropping the threat of using sanctions against their members, adding that there would not be a pay explosion in the private sector of industry provided the Government was resolute in resisting excessive pay claims from the public sector. This was all very well, but even as they spoke road haulage and oil tanker drivers, with encouragement from the TGWU, were striking in support of 25 to 30 per cent pay increases. Moss Evans washed his hands of any responsibility for the long-term effect of his actions, affirming, 'My responsibility is to look after my members' pay claims', and made the strike official, thus ensuring that it would be a long struggle.

The next downwards step was for the shop stewards to enforce second-ary picketing – a pernicious system that brought pressure to bear on workers in industries totally unconnected with the original dispute, call-ing on them to cease work themselves in solidarity. Some pickets even had the effrontery to issue so-called permits to owners and drivers, with the pretence of authorising what goods could or could not be moved. Mrs Thatcher exploited this attempted usurpation of authority with gusto and the leaders of the TGWU could not have been surprised at the growing dislike they engendered.

There was alarmist talk of a shortage of food, some of which was exaggerated for political advantage and led to panic buying, but John Silkin, the Minister in charge of food supplies, kept a cool head through-out and was justified in his denials of rumours. The contagion spread to other industries and services, and during January 1979 unofficial strikes erupted every week, with workers in one industry inflicting hardship on their fellows in other industries. Public service workers were in the van. Some union officials did nothing to discourage them although we were actively discussing with their leaders means of relieving their members' grievances through the medium of those same comparability studies which the Government had suggested earlier and which the TUC had then rejected. Even with the passage of time I find it painful to write about some of the excesses that took place. One of the most notorious was the refusal of Liverpool grave-diggers to bury the dead, accounts of which appalled the country when they saw pictures of mourners being turned away from the cemetery. Such heartlessness and cold-blooded indifference to the feelings of families at moments of intense grief rightly aroused deep revulsion and did further untold harm to the cause of trade unionism that I, like many others, had been proud to defend throughout my life. What would the men of Tolpuddle have said? My own anger increased when I learned that the Home Secretary Merlyn Rees had called upon Alan Fisher, the General Secretary of NUPE, to use his influence to get the grave-diggers to go back to work, and Fisher had refused.

Merlyn was Chairman of the Cabinet's Contingencies Unit and was a tower of strength and commonsense, but as the pressure grew during January and February he needed assistance and I detached Gerald Kauf-man, one of Labour's rising stars, from his work at the Department of Industry, to be full-time in the Cabinet Office. Together with Bill

Rodgers, the Secretary for Transport, he worked with considerable success to ensure that essential supplies continued to move.

Indeed, the only redeeming features that I could discern throughout the whole affair were the remarkable ingenuity with which those affected set about improvising arrangements to beat its adverse effects, and the stoicism with which the general public met the hardship and inconvenience to which they were subjected. Ministers considered whether we should declare a state of emergency. My instinct was in favour of doing so as a demonstration of our determination, but it was argued that it was very uncertain whether a declaration would do much practical good. The Conservative Government of 1970–74 had declared five such states of emergency, and it was pointed out that none of them had made any significant difference.

After a time signs began to appear that the fever was running its course. The TGWU grew apprehensive at the backlash of public opinion against the excesses of some of their shop stewards, and told the Home Secretary that if the Government would inform them where essential foodstuffs or other materials were held up, they would try to unblock the channels.

During the dispute the TUC had stood by helplessly watching, the influence of the General Council washed away by the tide of industrial irresponsibility, but Ministers had kept in touch with their officials and by the end of January they judged that the time had come to pick up the threads once again.

I discussed with Michael Foot, Denis Healey, Albert Booth and Eric Varley what line the Chancellor and his team should take when they met the TUC. We agreed that two main propositions should be put to them. There must be an agreed code of trade union practice dealing with the conduct of disputes and drafted to eliminate the excesses of picketing; secondly, we should aim for a three-year policy to reduce inflation to below 5 per cent by the end of 1981, to be supported by the development of institutions such as a new Pay Board, while the Government would undertake a fresh examination of price regulation. Ministers met the Economic Committee of the TUC to put forward these propositions and found the atmosphere sufficiently encouraging to warrant my calling all forty members of the General Council to Downing Street on Monday 29 January.

I opened the discussion. The current scenes were doing great damage to the country, to the Government's standing and to the trade unions themselves. If the present situation continued, a general election might be forced on us before the end of April, especially as the referendum on Devolution would be held on 1 March. Such an election would take place at a most unfavourable moment, when the Government's achievements in other areas would be overshadowed by the present crop of strikes. If the present situation continued 'it could well be a Conservative Government you will have to deal with and their approach will be through public expenditure cuts and legislation to reduce the strength of the unions!' I reminded them that this was the Government's third attempt to secure a worthwhile agreement with the unions and the last chance for everyone. The minimum that was required was a period of industrial calm; the unions should guarantee that strikes would not disrupt essential services; they should be more active to protect and defend their own members from verbal intimidation and harassment by unofficial strikers; and they should disavow unofficial strikes which were called while pay negotiations were proceeding.

The General Council heard me quietly; indeed, many of them privately agreed with what I had to say. Lionel Murray acted as their spokesman. They wished for a positive understanding with the Government for this would be in the best interests of working people. It was true that the difficulties of the situation were compounded by the possibility of a Conservative victory, but even so the TUC should not promise more than it could deliver. The TUC was unable to agree to a percentage figure for pay increases, but on the other hand it was wholly opposed to some of the bad practices that were being employed in the current disputes. Harry Urwin, the Deputy General Secretary of the TGWU, followed up. The TUC had never agreed with or supported violence on the picket lines but some left-wing political forces were at work, fomenting the situation. The unions were actively seeking improvements in three areas of concern to the Government, namely secondary picketing, the maintenance of essential services and greater flexibility in the closed shop. Provided the approach was voluntary and not legislative, he hoped a worthwhile understanding could be reached on each point.

David Basnett then made an appeal to other leaders around the table whose unions were engaged in industrial action to heed what had been said, and the meeting drew to a close, with an undertaking by the TUC to work urgently to produce a new understanding. Knowing that a general election could not be far away, I had insisted that any agreement must be concluded within a fortnight, and after much burning of midnight oil, two documents were ready for issue by mid-February – the first, a joint statement by the Government and the TUC, the second a guide on negotiating procedures and the conduct of disputes issued on the TUC's own authority. This second document was clear and forthright: strikes, it said, are a measure of last resort; ballots should be held when strikes are contemplated; essential services should be maintained together with plant and machinery during a strike; pickets should act in a disciplined and peaceful manner; there should be no question of intimidation; demonstrations should not convey the impression that the object is to blockade a workplace; and much other good sense, which if it had been followed earlier would have enhanced the reputation of the unions and perhaps saved the Government. Now the question was whether there was time to salvage it.

The Government–TUC joint statement accepted the objective of reducing inflation to 5 per cent within three years; recognised the fundamental importance of increasing productivity and the need for training and retraining for skills; agreed to a national assessment of economic prospects (including pay) by Easter of each year with the possibility of synchronising pay settlements in certain areas; and undertook to examine the possibility of new pay arrangements in areas where public health and safety were involved.

The two statements contained a lot of good sense but before there was time to test whether they could be translated into action, they were submerged in the general tide of disillusionment and dislike that had been generated by the events of the previous six weeks, and which now swept the country. Both the Labour Government and the trade unions had become widely unpopular. It was but the latest demonstration of a truth we have all uttered to the effect that the fortunes of the unions and the Labour Party cannot be separated. As one trade union leader told his colleagues during the worst of our troubles, 'The TUC can either have a Labour Government with some unpalatable policies, or a Conservative Government with disastrous ones.' The serious and widespread industrial dislocation caused by the strikes of January 1979, short-lived though they were, sent the Government's fortunes cascading downhill, our loss of authority in one field leading to misfortune in others just as an avalanche, gathering speed, sweeps all before it.

A fortnight later the Devolution referenda were held and public dislike of the Government undoubtedly contributed to the poor result in Scotland where only 51.2 per cent voted in favour, while in Wales the proposals were overwhelmingly defeated. From this it was but a step to the decision of the Scottish National Party to put forward a motion of censure on the Government for failing to bring Devolution into being immediately. The opportunity to defeat us, which had been snatched from the Conservatives so many times before, was now at hand. Even if the Scottish National Party wished to, it could not back away from its own censure motion which was staring at them from the Order Paper, and the Liberals made clear that they too would vote against the Government. The Opposition seized their opportunity to unite like with unlike in a strange alliance of those opposed to Devolution voting with those in favour. I had said in the course of the debate that the Scottish National Party would walk through the division lobby like turkeys voting for an early Christmas and, sure enough, in the general election of 3 May which followed our defeat they lost nine seats out of eleven.

Several weeks before these events reached their climax I had taken part in talks with President Carter, President Giscard and Chancellor Schmidt on the French island of Guadaloupe in the West Indies on 5 and 6 January 1979.

I first learned that a meeting was in the offing while I was attending the Labour Party Conference at Blackpool the previous September, wrestling with Conference's rejection of the incomes policy. During one of the sessions I received a message that President Carter's National Security Adviser Zbigniew Brzezinski wished to come to Blackpool to see me, and asking that his visit be kept from the press. I detached myself from the Conference wondering what crisis was about to break.

Fortunately, when he arrived I discovered that it was only the exigencies of his timetable which had prevented him from waiting until I returned to London, together with the fact that the purpose of his mission was not known to the United States State Department. He told me that President Carter was once again concerned about the difficulties that were growing between the United States Administration and the Federal Republic of Germany on certain aspects of nuclear arms control and modernisation: Carter wished to ease the situation. Would I be willing to take part in a discussion between Carter, Schmidt and Giscard, with the minimum number of staff attending, perhaps meeting in a relaxed atmosphere in the Caribbean after Christmas? I too had some problems, notably the disappointment of learning that the American Administration had cooled off on the proposal for a Comprehensive Test Ban Treaty and the need to talk over the Anglo-American initiative on the future of Rhodesia. I accepted at once, and Brzezinski departed for Bonn and Paris without the eagle eyes of the press once alighting on him, although Blackpool was swarming with them. At that time Carter was hopeful that the long-drawn-out negotiations on SALT II which had begun under President Nixon as early as 1972 and had been continued by his predecessor, President Ford, would shortly come to a successful conclusion. Indeed, he hoped that Brezhnev would visit America for a signing ceremony in February 1979. Later that date receded to the end of March, then to May, and finally the two men met in Vienna on 15 June 1979.

The purpose of SALT II was to establish equal ceilings in the strategic missile forces of the Soviet Union and the United States. Also it would begin the process of reducing nuclear weapons numbers and was intended to limit their qualitative improvement. Carter was deeply and rightly convinced that both sides possessed far too many nuclear weapons for the purpose of deterrence, and he was ready to begin a new round of negotiations for a SALT III Treaty as soon as the American Congress had ratified SALT II. I shared both his conviction and his objective but there would be more than one important difficulty to overcome in the next round of negotiations.

As so often in arms negotiations the timing of the modernisation of existing weapons by the two alliances did not coincide. Sometimes one was ahead and sometimes the other. This applied both to longer range weapons – the subject of SALT negotiations until now – and those of medium range. In the case of the latter weapons, in 1979 the Russians were well under way with their modernisation programme, replacing their older SS4 and SS5 weapons by the alarmingly mobile SS20s, more accurate, targetted against the European cities of the Alliance members, and with a range of 5,000 kilometres so that they could be based far back in the heart of Russia and still threaten the West. The phasing of NATO's European modernisation programme ran later in time than the Russians, but discussions on its future shape had already taken place between the military and scientific experts. It was conceivable that decisions on types of weapons and their deployment would come forward from Defence Ministers to their Governments at the exact moment when President Carter might be beginning his talks on SALT III. Already technical opinion was crystallising around various modes of weapon, and the question was whether building and deploying them would destroy the prospect of a successful SALT III negotiation, although they might not be directly relevant to that.

There was a further difficulty to which Helmut Schmidt had given voice in a speech in London in October 1977. Speaking of the possible conclusion of the SALT II talks between the two great powers, Schmidt had commented, 'SALT neutralises their strategic nuclear capabilities. In Europe this magnifies the significance of the disparities between East and West in nuclear, tactical and conventional weapons.' He went on to argue that unless this nuclear superiority of the Soviet Union in medium and short-range nuclear weapons and their conventional superiority could be removed in parallel with a SALT II Agreement, the consequences would be destabilising and Europe would be in greater danger than before. His criticism was not taken up at the time, both Russia and America possibly believing that they had enough complications to deal with. But Schmidt's concern could be met in one of two ways, either by agreement on the part of the Soviets to reduce their European superiority (if they acknowledged its existence) or by the West attempting to match it. Obviously, any sensible person would opt for the first.

Someone invented the term 'Grey Area' as a generic description of all the US and Soviet nuclear delivery systems not included in the SALT II negotiations. Included in the Grey Areas were United States aircraft based in Europe, and aircraft carriers capable of striking targets in the USSR. On the Warsaw Pact side they included, in addition to the SS20, and the earlier SS4 and 5, the 'Backfire' bomber. These weapons added substantially to the existing Soviet overkill: clearly, a SALT III negotiation would be of more direct concern to Europe, both East and West, than the earlier SALT II negotiations had been. The Russians also claimed that the British Polaris, French nuclear submarines and other medium range forces fell into the Grey Area.

A number of questions were coming together which merited a meeting between the four of us. First, President Carter was seeking reassurance, in view of Helmut Schmidt's earlier criticism, that he could rely on his major Allies to back him when SALT II went before the Senate for ratification. He told us that he knew it would be a hard struggle, although he was hopeful of getting the sixty-seven votes he needed in the Senate. Next, assuming SALT II was ratified and Carter succeeded in moving to SALT III, the West would need a clear and united position on our objectives. Carter was anxious to avoid another fiasco like the neutron bomb. In particular he wished to know whether we should deploy any modernised weapons prior to negotiations (which was the preferred American military position), or should we negotiate before deploying?

As long as the American and Russian talks had been about their own nuclear arsenals, as in SALT II, the Europeans were content to watch from the sidelines, providing they were fully consulted and informed at each stage. But once European interests and weapons became directly involved, the Allies obviously would want to make a full contribution to the negotiations. Further, given the French attitude, was there any possibility of her being willing to join in the negotiations? Finally, from the British angle, what effect would SALT III talks have on the future of the British nuclear deterrent, in view of the necessity to decide whether to replace Polaris – a decision which would be needed by about 1980? A meeting at Guadaloupe could not reach decisions but it would enable us to understand each other's problems, and perhaps reach some common understanding.

Our host President Giscard issued a statement about the meeting, saying that he had invited us 'to take part in personal and informal discussions on political matters and international developments of special interest'. His first intention was to hold the meeting in Martinique, but this was abandoned in favour of Guadaloupe, as it was easier to keep the journalists at bay and so encourage an informal exchange of views. In personal terms, our gathering was a success. We spent forty-eight hours together without interruption and with the minimum staffs, living cheek by jowl in adjacent simple holiday accommodation. We gossiped on the grass outside our huts, ate together informally, and even when our formal discussions took place they were held in an open, round thatched hut. For recreation Carter jogged, Giscard played tennis and I sailed a small dinghy. We all spoke English. There were no position papers, no fixed agenda, no communiqué, and only one reception, given by Giscard as our host. The frigate HMS *Scylla* was in the Caribbean at the time and the Ministry of Defence met my request that she should sail to Guadaloupe and act as guardship while we were there. Jimmy Carter (a very knowledgeable former Commander in the United States Navy) and I stole some time aboard and spent a happy couple of hours sitting in the captain's cabin while the President learned something of the Royal Navy and we retold old stories. The press was kept at a distance throughout the talks, and some of the differences they described were pure fabrications.

Our discussions began with an exchange of views on the problems of the Pacific area, notably the perennial problem of how to secure a more balanced trade with Japan, followed by the question of arms supplies to China, to which I have already referred. We discussed our attitude to the

Soviet Union. There was general agreement that as Brezhnev reached the end of his career, we should act in such a way that his successor, whoever he might be, should come to power aware that the West preferred to work with the Soviet Union and not against her. To that end, we ought to make clear that we had no intention of playing China off against the Soviet Union, and to ensure that the Russians were kept informed of Western intentions in relation to all aspects of detente.

We turned to Iran, where Britain had assumed responsibility for coordinating contingency evacuation plans for Western expatriates in the event of the Shah's abdication or removal. The United States had no Congressional approval for such a step, and we had stepped into the breach. It was a gloomy discussion. All our reports agreed that the Shah would be forced to leave within the next few days, but we could see no improvement from any possible successors. Giscard had been ready at an earlier stage to expel Khomeini from France in view of his activities, but the Shah had asked him not to do so. Now it seemed that the Shah was no longer capable of taking action and there was uncertainty about the position of the military. There was some suggestion that Khomeini should be contacted, but this was not followed up and the discussion petered out.

Among other matters, we felt it would be valuable if Germany took the lead in assistance to Turkey, a responsibility which Schmidt shouldered with reluctance. I urged him not to overlook the possibility of using this assistance to secure progress on the Cyprus dispute.

There was a long discussion on Southern Africa in which Carter and I ran in double harness for most of the time. On the question of sanctions against South Africa it was said that public opinion in the United States and France was strongly opposed to any implementation, and that German opinion was divided. We were agreed, with the French President expressing most caution, that further pressure must be brought to bear. I told them that Britain had made a secret study of the effect of sanctions on our supplies of raw materials, and of the possibilities of finding alternative sources, and I was ready to put it at their disposal.

Eventually, I volunteered that Britain would call together experts from all our countries to prepare a paper setting out the kind of evolution we believed South Africa should follow, with recommendations as to how such developments could be actively encouraged, and an agreed attitude towards sanctions. France was given the task of briefing the European Community on our intentions, and the United States was to brief the other NATO members. We agreed that the four countries would meet again on this issue later in the year. Jimmy Carter's religious convictions gave him genuine concern about Southern Africa and strengthened his opposition to Apartheid. He stoutly defended the role of Andrew Young, the black pastor and Congressman whom he had appointed as America's Ambassador to the United Nations. Young was a controversial character who, as Carter once remarked to me, seemed to have offended everybody, but at the same time had been successful in giving a new slant to African perceptions of the United States.

I felt more in tune with Jimmy Carter about Africa than with the others, and I believe this was reciprocated. He urged me always to pick up the telephone and call him if Britain needed any help or had any doubts about America's African policy. Whilst we were at Guadaloupe I gave him a copy of the Cledwyn Hughes Report with its conclusion that the time was not ripe for a London conference, and after discussing it, we agreed that the key to further progress probably lay through South African pressure on Smith. Carter was keen to invite Prime Minister Botha to visit the United States and we agreed that subject to events not turning for the worse in Namibia, we should both endeavour to see him in March 1979. Unfortunately, this proposal, like others, became submerged by the tidal wave of events in Britain during the rest of the winter.

It was the SALT II negotiations and their aftermath that took most of our time and we spent some part of three of our four sessions discussing how to proceed. Carter began by reporting on the outstanding issues that were still in dispute: the date by which excess launchers over the number agreed in SALT II should be dismantled; the final formula setting out what modifications of intercontinental ballistic missiles would be permissible; agreement on the transmission of telemetry in such a manner as not to impede verification by either side of the provisions of SALT II; the limitation of the number of pilotless vehicles to be carried in heavy bombers, and agreement that not more than thirty 'Backfire' bombers be built annually.

This seemed a formidable list to settle in advance of the proposed United States/Soviet Union Summit which the President told us was expected in late February 1979, but he expressed his confidence that they would be solved.

I followed the President and at once offered Britain's support for the outlines of the Agreement. With an eye on Helmut Schmidt's earlier criticisms, I urged that when we returned to Europe, Britain, France and

Germany should all voice their hopes that the Agreement would be ratified by Congress once the outstanding issues had been settled. The German Chancellor at once took up my remarks and responded positively. He made clear that he had no apologies for the reservations he had publicly expressed but was of the opinion that once the negotiations were complete, Germany and all European Governments should back the final Agreement. Giscard enquired whether we should declare ourselves at an early or late stage in the Senate's ratification process, to which Carter replied 'Both'. The President was obviously gratified by this support for his position and remarked that whatever else happened at Guadaloupe, our assurances had made his visit worthwhile.

We moved to other defence questions and these discussions exposed the differences that existed, with President Carter and Chancellor Schmidt taking the lead. If President Carter had hoped that the three European leaders would arrive in Guadaloupe with a clear position and a united voice he was soon disillusioned. France was as always somewhat reserved, but the basic problem soon emerged as the German Chancellor recapitulated his view that the SALT II Agreement might have the unintended effect of increasing European (and especially German) insecurity.

I understood Helmut Schmidt's argument to be that SALT II might undermine a basic assumption on which the defence of the Alliance rested. This was that a Soviet attack would be directed against the territory of the United States as well as against Europe. But if the effect of SALT II was to create a nuclear stalemate between the United States and the Soviet Union, the territories of the two Superpowers might tacitly become inviolate while the advent of the SS20, based deep in the Soviet Union, increased the prospect of an attack on Germany. NATO's strategy for defending Europe was based on the doctrine that its response to a Soviet attack would be flexible and graduated in severity, starting with the use of conventional weapons but, if they seemed insufficient to repel attack, as was likely, stepping up the use of nuclear weapons, with the hope that sufficient time would have been gained for a rational exchange of views between the adversaries that would end hostilities before the final holocaust overtook the world.

It was by no means a wholly convincing scenario, but it was the current doctrine and Schmidt applied himself to it. I had sympathy with his proposal that as the disparity in conventional forces between the two sides was weighted in favour of the Warsaw Pact, the West should strengthen its own conventional forces, but I had to point out to the

Chancellor that Britain's percentage of our Gross National Product assigned to arms expenditure was higher than that of Germany or France, and that the foreign exchange costs of keeping British forces in Germany was £600 millions a year. I reminded Helmut that he had said on earlier occasions that it was in Europe's interest for Britain to remain a nuclear power. Did he still say so? It would not be possible for us to do so and at the same time to increase our conventional arms still further. How was the gap to be filled? Chancellor Schmidt replied at once. He had never doubted the value of Britain's strategic nuclear weapons to Europe, but Germany was the country most at risk. The German people had not so far come face to face with the consequences of current NATO strategy, which postulated their country as the sole or even main battleground. The impact of this might not make itself felt until a few more years had elapsed and he had gone from the scene, but he had gloomy forebodings of the effect on his fellow countrymen if at that time there existed a continued Soviet preponderance in medium-range nuclear weapons. But, he concluded, having raised the question, he had no clear idea about how to resolve it.

President Carter took him up at this point. We were all agreed, he said, on the disparity between the theatre nuclear weapons of East and West, and on the threat posed by the SS20s. The United States would be willing to build and deploy both Pershing II and ground-launched cruise missiles in order to procure the necessary leverage for negotiations about the SS20. Provision already existed in the United States Budget for Pershing II weapons, but he would not be willing to spend the funds merely in the hope that someone would agree to their deployment. There must be a commitment before he did so and the onus rested on the Europeans. It was the Germans who had raised the issue and if Europe was so concerned for its safety that it wished to have meaningful negotiations about the SS20 with the USSR, then the Europeans should be ready to deploy cruise missiles as a bargaining counter.

Chancellor Schmidt replied that he was not seeking a review of NATO strategy, but neither could he postulate a situation in which fighting took place only on German soil. He realised the difficulties and he supposed that if there was no alternative, Germany would be ready to take cruise missiles, but she could not be alone and he must make it a condition that one other European ally would do so too. President Carter visibly stiffened. If, he said, Germany was not prepared to accept the necessary deployment, it was difficult to see why others should do so on her behalf.

This was somewhat unjust to Helmut, who had personally never shrunk from doing whatever was necessary in defence matters, but he had laid himself open to Carter's remarks by an unusual lack of logic on his part.

Both Giscard and I poured oil on the troubled waters. I reminded Helmut that Germany was not alone. Britain already shared certain risks in the interests of common security through the American submarine base in Scotland and also the F-111 planes based in our country. Helmut acknowledged this gracefully. President Giscard introduced a new element into the discussion by suggesting that the United States should rest on its achievements in the SALT I and II Agreements, but if there was to be an early SALT III, then his inclination was to exclude the so-called Grey Areas. Any agreement with the Russians on these would have a decoupling and unbalancing effect, unless something was developed on the Western side which could be traded for the SS20.

As things stood, there could be no cruise missiles deployed in Europe for some time ahead, and the SS20 was in no sense the equivalent of the French and British strategic deterrents. The Russians had told him that they had never attempted to include either these or the United States forward-based systems in any SALT negotiations. (My recollection of the Russian attitude was different.) In one sense, said President Giscard, France had no interest in the matter, as in no circumstances would she be willing to include the French nuclear force in a SALT Agreement. France would have its own capability to develop cruise missiles although there was no final French decision to do so. I said that like France, Britain had been consistently opposed to including the Grey Areas in strategic arms limitation talks because of the impact on the British nuclear deterrent. This remained our official position, but new systems had been developed by the Soviets and the SS20 could devastate London as readily as Bonn, Hamburg or Paris. I was personally beginning to modify my thinking and was ready to have the Cabinet's Defence Committee examine a proposition that the whole range of weapons on the Western side, including both strategic and Grey Areas, should be brought under one negotiating umbrella for SALT III. Jimmy Carter was very disturbed by the course of the discussion. He was to see Brezhnev at the end of February and intended to raise the question of a new SALT III round of talks. European interests were inevitably involved and he complained that he had received no clear message as to what we wanted. He would prefer to work towards deploying cruise missiles in due course and then include them and all other Grey Areas in the next round of negotiations.

I resisted an attempt by Giscard to sum up the discussion to the effect that there was a consensus against the inclusion of Grey Areas. If Giscard's forecast was correct and the Russians wished to exclude Grey Areas from the talks, we could take a decision on whether to deploy cruise against the background that there was no prospect of negotiating them away. On the other hand, if Brezhnev showed interest in Grey Area negotiations, we would each then have to decide whether we should agree to their inclusion, and in particular whether to deploy cruise missiles in advance of the talks. But we should leave any final conclusion until after Carter and Brezhnev had met. Our meeting then broke up with the issue unresolved, and we spent an agreeable evening together. It was a feature of our relationship that the afternoon's sharp discussion cast no shadow over a relaxed conversation in which we expanded on the nature of politics, our domestic problems and our methods of handling them.

When we met in our thatched hut the next morning, with staffs kept carefully out of earshot and only the sound of the sea to distract us, President Carter at once returned to the charge. He had made up his mind and was in brisk form. He intended, when Brezhnev visited Washington, to tell him of his concern about the increasing deployment of the SS20 in Europe. The United States would be ready to open negotiations about this as well as about the American Forward Base systems in Europe. Further, the negotiations should be on the basis that some of the West's systems would be modernised, and not on the assumption of the *status quo*. In his talks he would do nothing to jeopardise European interests, nor would he agree to the inclusion of any European-owned weapons in the United States–Soviet discussions.

The President emphasised that he would want a clearer view from Europe before he began and he therefore proposed to send David Aaron, who was Brzezinski's Deputy, to visit European capitals in the first week of February for bilateral talks that might clarify the options prior to his meeting with Brezhnev. Giscard responded at once that there was no prospect of the French nuclear force being included in the discussion. But apart from that, there was no dissent by any of us from the President's proposed line of action and we moved almost at once to a discussion about our reaction to the serious developments in Iran.

I did not see Aaron when he came to London, but I settled the guidance he was to be given. It was to the effect that I had reported our discussions at Guadaloupe on Grey Areas to the Cabinet, which had not been asked to take any formal decision. In due course, subject to the result of the

Brezhnev–Carter meeting, I would be ready to recommend to my colleagues that Grey Area systems should be included in SALT III negotiations. If the Cabinet agreed, this decision would be subject to certain conditions. First, Britain would regard it as necessary to be a direct participant in the negotiations. Second, Germany, whose interests would be vitally affected, should also agree to the negotiations and preferably should take part in them. Otherwise, if Germany preferred Britain to represent a wider European interest than our own, I would be ready for us to do so. It would be essential to reach prior agreement within the Alliance on a credible negotiating position. The Cabinet had reached no decision on either arms control or modernisation, and I saw these issues as being two sides of the same coin. Finally, in the absence of Cabinet decisions, the President's discussions with Brezhnev must be noncommittal and exploratory as far as our interests were concerned.

When Aaron arrived he told the Cabinet Secretary that matters were not going as the President had intended. Brezhnev had put back his visit by a month to the end of February (the first of a number of postponements) and the President had decided on a change of tactics. He had concluded that the most important consideration in the months ahead was to secure the ratification of the SALT II Treaty by the Senate, and he did not expect this process to be completed until the autumn. In these circumstances he would not open up with Brezhnev the prospect of SALT III talks and would delay planning a strategy for them until the end of 1979. This would give the European members of the Alliance sufficient time to reach a consensus, but he would need to know by then how he was to proceed. I formed the impression from this report that, because of the lack of agreement among the European Allies, the Americans had decided to go ahead speedily with their modernisation programme during 1979, while hanging back on arms control negotiations.

I accepted the validity of the President's position because of his difficulties with Europe and with Congress, but the decision was a disappointment because it meant that modernisation of Europe's nuclear weapons and arms control negotiations, which we had intended to proceed in parallel, would now get out of phase. Preparations for modernisation would proceed without halt, and once completed, there was no reason to doubt that pressure would be exerted for the deployment of cruise and Pershing II in Europe. If our domestic circumstances in February 1979 had been better I would have taken up the issue with the President at once, but my time was almost completely occupied with the winter's industrial disputes and I did not raise the matter.

A few days later, I learned that the German view was the same as ours and they had suggested that a working group of the Alliance be set up to consider the timetable of events and make recommendations. Like me, Helmut Schmidt was anxious to pursue modernisation and arms control in parallel, and the underlying purpose of the working group was to ensure that progress on one aspect did not outstrip the other.

The American Administration agreed to the German proposal, but our Government was defeated on a vote of confidence shortly afterwards and this ended my involvement in a troublesome problem that engulfed the domestic politics of Belgium, Holland, Germany and Britain during the early 1980s. It is quite possible that even in the most favourable atmosphere the West would not have succeeded in negotiating the withdrawal and destruction of the SS20s until the cruise and Pershing IIs had been deployed, but we shall never know because we did not try. At the time we met at Guadaloupe, our information was that fewer than fifty SS20s had been deployed. Three years later the figure had built up to 441. A SALT II Agreement was eventually reached between Jimmy Carter and Brezhnev but the failure of the United States to ratify it affected the atmosphere on arms control negotiations and heightened mutual distrust. The Soviet Union's response was to take measures that were doubtfully within the provisions of the SALT II Treaty and some of them, in my judgement, were certainly outside its intentions.

After I left office President Reagan put forward a 'zero zero option', by which was meant that both sides should withdraw all the SS20s, cruise and Pershing II weapons. Ironically, the Americans then found that some European countries which earlier had been reluctant to deploy cruise were now opposed to its withdrawal.

To add to the confusion, a belief was growing in Western circles that the Soviet Union was revising its military doctrine about the most effective means of launching an attack on Western Europe. It would thrust its conventional forces forward rapidly in the early stages of a war to interpenetrate with Allied forces, so that the Allies, whose conventional forces are fewer, could not use their nuclear weapons without endangering their own armies.

Whether this theory is correct or not, it is impossible to believe that the security of any one of us was enhanced by the developments of the early 1980s.

During the visit to Guadaloupe I took the opportunity of having a discussion with President Carter about Britain's future as a strategic nuclear power, including whether or not we should continue in that role. Polaris was getting older but would remain serviceable until the 1990s and this had prompted the Government military advisers to come to me early in 1978 with the opinion that because of the long building time, a decision would be needed by 1980 if Polaris was to be replaced.

I decided to have a study made by officials of the factors that would affect the future of the United Kingdom deterrent. The terms of reference were strict and limited. The preamble stated that no decision on the future of the deterrent would be needed during the lifetime of the present Parliament, which could conceivably have ended in the autumn of 1978, or at the latest 1979. The study should examine and report on all the factors which the next Government of whatever Party would need to take into account in reaching a decision. It was instructed not to make recommendations, but to put forward the facts and balanced arguments on which Cabinet decisions could be taken. Its sole purpose, said the terms of reference, was to provide the basis on which a fully informed decision could be taken. Officials were given a year in which to complete the study.

I received the report eight months later, in December 1978, and it was clear that the authors had fulfilled my remit exactly. The paper examined the strategic environment in the 1990s and beyond and considered the nuclear programmes of the Soviet Union, the United States, France and China against the background of possible arms control negotiations such as SALT III. It set out a series of options in their international, political and military aspects but, as instructed, it took no account of domestic political considerations. It examined various alternative possibilities if Britain did not continue with its ballistic missile system, but decided to opt for something else.

In the first instance, I decided to circulate the document to those Ministers most immediately concerned, namely the Defence Secretary, the Foreign Secretary and the Chancellor of the Exchequer, suggesting that we have a preliminary discussion at a meeting which had been arranged for 21 December to brief me in advance of Guadaloupe. When we met, I said that there had been little time since the report was received for preparation of views or for consultation with the Cabinet. Moreover, the intention of the Guadaloupe meeting was to focus on other aspects of nuclear weapons policy, but the British strategic deterrent was related in subject matter and the meeting would afford an opportunity to have a preliminary discussion with the President. What were my colleagues' views about such a talk? A long discussion ensued about the essential nature of Britain's future defence strategy and whether it could be sustained without radical change, and the conclusion was reached that our own studies could not go much further without consultation with the United States.

At the second briefing meeting, held on 2 January 1979, just forty-eight hours before I left for Guadaloupe, it was apparent that opinions had crystallised in favour of my having a talk with the President provided it took place without commitment on my part: I should work out with him the best way of exploring Britain's nuclear options more fully. I should ascertain the views of the President on whether and in what form American help could be forthcoming if the Cabinet were to decide upon the replacement of Polaris. We were all aware that a decision would not be necessary for the next twelve months and I suggested that in the intervening period there would be advantage in more public discussion of the issue. The Labour Party Conference had expressed itself very clearly against the replacement of Polaris, and while a decision would not come before the existing Cabinet, if I eventually concluded that it was in the national interest to go ahead there would be a difficult decision for colleagues in the next Labour Cabinet to take and a major argument would ensue in the Labour Party. To prepare for such an eventuality it would be wise to have an informed public opinion, so that the choices as well as the dilemmas were well understood. At that moment, I told my colleagues, if our eventual decision turned out to be that Polaris should be replaced, on the basis of the information we had before us I would favour the C4 Trident submarine.

My opportunity to talk with the President came in a break between the sessions on the afternoon of 5 February. Rosalynn Carter and Audrey had gone with the other ladies to visit a neighbouring island and I knew he would be alone. I walked the few yards across the grass to his hut next door and found him resting. No one else was present during our talk, but when it was over and I had returned to my hut I called for Sir John Hunt, the Secretary to the Cabinet, and repeated the substance of the conversation to him. I told the President the nature of the report I had commissioned and said I was speaking with him at this stage because the Ministers immediately concerned were of the view that we could not proceed further with exploring the options about the future of our nuclear deterrent until we received some indication of America's attitude towards the supply of weapons. I then gave an outline of my view. For Britain, as a nation, the balance of advantage in procuring a successor to Polaris would be no better than marginal. There was a good case for arguing that any available resources could be used to better effect in strengthening our conventional forces and my own approach was that any chosen successor weapon must be shown to be cost-effective. But another factor weighed with me, namely that Britain had a responsibility not only for her own defence, but also shared a responsibility for the defence of Europe.

It was for this reason that I had put a question about Germany's attitude to Britain's nuclear deterrent to Helmut Schmidt during our earlier session and had received a reply similar to others he had given me when I had discussed the matter on earlier occasions. His consistent view was that Germany would prefer that France was not alone as the sole European power possessing strategic nuclear weapons, and that he would feel more comfortable if Britain also were in the field. I continued: since my first visit to Russia in 1945, in the aftermath of the Second World War, I had always realised that it was Germany that lay at the heart of the Soviet Union's concern about Europe, and this had shown itself in many ways, not least in the post-war division of Germany which remained as an un-solved problem. Relations between the two Germanies were not likely to cause trouble, but the rest of us could never afford to overlook the political strains that might be developed in a divided state, and should not dismiss the sensitivities of the West German Government.

I could not estimate what decision Britain would arrive at on the future of the deterrent, and my views might not find a ready echo in all my Party, but when the time arrived to reach a conclusion it would be necessary to take into account not only Britain's own security but also the extent to which Germany felt the need for reassurance, and whatever our decision, it must contribute to the total security of Europe.

The President heard me out. He said that like Helmut Schmidt, he also was glad that Britain possessed the nuclear deterrent. He did not take up my comments about Germany directly, but said that he hoped that Britain as well as France would remain a nuclear power. In his view, it was better that there should be a shared responsibility in Europe, rather than that America should go it alone, as he would not wish the United States to be the only country in confrontation. He was disturbed that the four of us had not reached a common position about the modernisation of the intermediate range weapons, as it would make his intended talks with Brezhnev more difficult. But in view of the traditional French attitude, it would be necessary for him and me to talk in the near future about how Britain might be associated with the SALT III talks when they got underway.

The Soviet Union, he added, argued that the more they agreed with the United States on a mutual reduction of nuclear armaments the more significant the smaller numbers of nuclear arms of other countries would become. In saying this, the President probably had in mind Helmut Schmidt's view that if the SALT III talks produced a further limitation in long-range United States/USSR systems without a parallel reduction in Soviet SS20s, this would undermine Germany's confidence in the commitment of the United States and have a destabilising effect. Carter said further that the Soviet Union was concerned about China's developing arsenal and this influenced their attitude to the possession of the SS20s. This led us on to a discussion of nuclear systems and the President enquired what systems we were thinking of. I replied that we were at this stage not committed, even in principle, to a successor to Polaris, but on the technical issue the Ministers most directly concerned were divided about which would be the best weapon. Hitherto the option I thought most likely to meet our requirements, if we decided to go ahead, was the Trident C4 submarine which would carry multiple independent re-entry vehicles.

The President said that he could see no objection to transferring this technology to the United Kingdom and it would assist the United States to meet the unit costs of production. I picked up this point. Cost would be one of several factors in our decision, and I remarked that I had seen a figure of $10 billions mentioned. This would be beyond our means. The President responded that he thought it should be possible to work out satisfactory terms and I suggested that I should send two officials to Washington to discuss technical and financial aspects further. I named Professor Mason and Sir Clive Rose for this purpose. Both of them were very experienced. Mason, a Merthyr-born boy, had risen by sheer ability to become the Chief Scientist in the Ministry of Defence, and Clive Rose was a Deputy Secretary in the Cabinet Office who had previously been head of the British negotiating team on Force Reductions in Central Europe.

The President at once consented to the visit and said that he would nominate Harold Brown, the United States Defence Secretary, to discuss the matter. Before our *tête à tête* ended, I repeated that I hoped he had understood that I had not been stating a final British position. The Cabinet had not begun to consider the matter and it might turn out that as a result of successful SALT III negotiations there could be an advantage to world peace and to the strength of the Alliance if Britain gave up her nuclear capacity. Such a possibility should not be ruled out. The President replied that he understood I had not been putting forward policy positions, but raising matters that we would need to consider together later on, order to reach decisions. With that, we ended our discussion on nuclear matters and turned to other questions.

On my return to Britain, I found that Professor Mason was to be in the United States in mid-February 1979 in connection with a test-firing at Cape Canaveral by Britain's Polaris submarine HMS *Repulse*, and I authorised him and Clive Rose to go to Washington to begin 'exploratory' talks. By this time other domestic matters had assumed major proportions, and I sensed that the Government's life might come to a sudden end. Accordingly, on my birthday, 27 March 1979, I sat down and wrote a letter to the President.

I told him that the Government was facing a crucial vote of confidence on the following day and I could not tell which way the vote might go. But whether we won or not, a general election could not be far off and I therefore wished to put on record my understanding of what had passed between us at Guadaloupe. I had informed him that I had recently begun to think about the options for the next Government in deciding whether it should develop a successor to Polaris, in view of the fact that a decision would be needed within twelve months. I then repeated that I understood the United States was willing to receive Mason and Clive Rose to discuss the technical and financial aspects of a successor weapon, such as the Trident C_4, and concluded: 'I thought it right to put our conversation on record in view of certain eventualities here, although the onus of suggesting a visit would of course still lie with me or my successor. I hope my understanding is the same as yours.'

I had my letter to the President placed on file and there it rests. On 4 May, the day following the general election, before I left Downing Street for the last time I wrote my final minute on the subject. This authorised that my correspondence with the President on the future of the nuclear deterrent, together with the report I had received the previous December, should be made available to the incoming Prime Minister to prevent her from being at a disadvantage in any future exchange she might have with President Carter about the replacement or otherwise of Polaris.

Since Guadaloupe, a number of accounts of our meetings have appeared in press articles and television programmes. They have been of varying degrees of accuracy, including one serious allegation that I had committed my colleagues further than I was free to do on the future of Britain's nuclear deterrent. The record shows that this is untrue.

Whatever my personal views about a successor for Polaris, the position of the Cabinet was fully safeguarded. Guadaloupe committed Ministers to no course of action, nor would I have attempted to do so before any Cabinet discussion on the matter. It has always been the role of the Prime Minister of the day to take the lead in discussing nuclear matters with the President of the United States, and my intention was that the Cabinet should have all the available information in front of it when the time arrived to consider the question and take a decision. It was my practice that Ministers should have the fullest opportunity to state their views and argue for them in any important matter that it fell to the Cabinet to decide. When the time came to take a decision on Britain's nuclear future, I too would have argued strongly for the course of action I believed best served the national interest.

It will happen from time to time that decisions on secondary issues will be taken by the Cabinet with which the Prime Minister disagrees. If he is wise, he may decide to let such matters go. At any rate he should never insist on having his own way on everything. But no Prime Minister can abdicate his overriding responsibility to safeguard national security, and once his mind is made up on the best course for the country, he must do what he believes is necessary, fight for his decision, and if he cannot get support then he should stand down.

It was the adverse result of the two Devolution referenda in Scotland and Wales that finally ended the Government's life. Both were held on 1 March 1979, St David's Day, for John Morris, the Secretary of State for Wales, had hoped that the compliment would strike a patriotic chord in Welsh hearts. But the valleys were deaf to the sound of our music, and rejected the blandishments by a huge majority of four to one. The Scottish result was better, with a slim majority voting in favour, but this counted as a defeat as the Devolution Act had provided (against the Government's will) that 40 per cent of the total electorate must vote in favour, so with those who abstained added in, the total fell well below the required figure.

On the surface this was a surprising result and I concluded that in the back of people's minds, the merits of the case had become entangled with a vote on the Government's popularity, which was not high even in

Scotland because of the recent industrial disputes.

Michael Foot telephoned me at home on Sunday 4 March to discuss the results. He was deeply disappointed for he had made Devolution his cause, and had overcome every obstacle to get the Bills through Parliament. These results required the Government, in accordance with the two Acts, now to lay an Order before Parliament for their total repeal.

Michael is a fighter and he still thought the day could be saved. Why not, he said, lay the Repeal Order before Parliament, but invite the House to reject it? This would leave the Scottish Act on the statute book in accordance with the wish of the majority of those who had voted. But it would not come into force until a second Order, known as a Commencement Order, was laid, and this should be postponed until after a general election. It was an imaginative proposal, but from the start I did not approach it with an open mind. Ten years earlier, when I had been Home Secretary, I too had laid an Order before the House to bring about constituency boundary changes, and on that occasion had urged its defeat on behalf of the Government. I secured a majority, but had been pilloried for my action, reckless charges of impropriety and unconstitutional behaviour being thrown around. I could envisage the same kind of abuse being hurled at Michael's head and although the charges would be unfounded the mud would stick, especially in view of the battering the Government had taken during the preceding weeks. I reasoned that we would have a hard job to recover from our unpopularity without handing a further stick to our opponents. In fairness to Michael, I promised to consider the idea although he detected a lack of enthusiasm, and we met in the Prime Minister's room in the Commons late on the evening of 5 March. In addition to the two of us there were present the Chancellor, the Home Secretary, the two Secretaries for Scotland and Wales, the Chief Whip, Gregor Mackenzie, who was not only the Minister of State for Scotland but had worked with me for many years, and Ron Hayward, the General Secretary of the Labour Party.

Michael put his case, coupling it with a further suggestion that the Government should call for a general vote of confidence. Ron Hayward reported that the Party in Scotland was pretty shell-shocked, but a meeting of the Scottish Labour Council had urged that while Devolution should remain in the forefront of Labour's programme, the well-being of the Government must be a priority in considering what to do next in Parliament. I had received other reports from Scotland to the effect that the Scottish National Party leadership would do a lot of sabre-rattling, but would play for time, although this could not be counted on, as behind the leadership stood 'a lot of mad men in kilts'. If accurately reported, the leadership's attitude would suit us.

Michael Cocks, the Chief Whip, had spoken with some of Labour's Devolution rebels. In his view the difficulty within the Party was much greater than any from the Scottish National Party and the Whips' judgement was that the Government could not rely on the votes of Labour Members from Merseyside or the North if we moved to reject the Repeal Order. The Chief Whip's advice was that there was no prospect of mustering a sufficient number of votes. Denis Healey took the view that the Government had neither the moral authority nor the political ability to move ahead on the Act, and more time was needed before the next move. Bruce Millan, the Scottish Secretary, responding to suggestions that the Act should be changed, did not believe a weakened Devolution Act would be worthwhile, but he wished to keep the Liberals and the Scottish National Party with us on the basis of a commitment to the principles of the existing Scotland Act. He thought there was a case for discussions with the minor Parties.

Gregor Mackenzie's view was that Michael Foot's manoeuvre would be too complicated for people to understand, and they would suspect bad faith. He believed that some Labour Party supporters had voted for Devolution mainly out of Party loyalty. Nevertheless, in view of the referendum result, we must keep faith with the majority, and it would be best if we began by talking with the other Parties. Gregor has a keen political sense and I always listened carefully to him. Our discussion was interrupted by a vote in the Chamber and as we walked through the Division Lobby, I had a further word with the Chief Whip. What he had to say that night remained firmly fixed in my mind and was a major factor in determining my course of action. It was this. The Whips were pessimistic about being able to muster enough votes from the minor Parties to be sure of carrying the vote of confidence that Michael Foot had in mind. The Chief Whip was firmly opposed to the Government putting down such a motion. We would lose. It was two years since he had last brought me such a fateful forecast. Then, however, Devolution still lay ahead and this had enabled us to come to an arrangement with the Liberals. March 1979, with the referendum completed, was very different from March 1977. A general election was approaching and if the Scottish National Party members were bent on electoral suicide, no one could stop them from jumping off the Forth Bridge. If Michael Cocks was right and

it were the case that the Government was unable to win a vote of confidence
initiated by itself, then indeed our days were numbered.

For three years we had believed in ourselves and in our capacity to
govern and to win, despite all the odds against us. Now I sensed this was
no longer true. Nearly thirty years earlier, as a junior Minister in the
Attlee Government, I had watched demoralisation set in and a thick pall
of self-doubt begin to envelop Ministers as they and the increasingly
paralysed Government Departments and Civil Service waited for the
inevitable election.

In 1979 seven months of life still lay ahead before a general election
need be called, but I did not wish my administration to drag out the next
few months, surviving only by wheeling and dealing. From the moment
I knew we could not win a vote of confidence I preferred to put the issue
to the test of a general election. Michael Foot also agreed that the Government could not go ahead making deals solely designed to keep us in office,
but having lived with the Devolution issue for such a long period, he was
deeply concerned to find ways of avoiding the repeal of the Scotland Act.
I too had no doubts that the Government must remain committed to the
broad concept of Devolution. Nor did I have any desire to see two years'
work wiped out in a single afternoon's debate on the Repeal Order,
although I did tell Michael that in practice a different Act might later be
necessary.

When the issue came to the Cabinet, Ministers did not reject Michael's
proposal – which was known among ourselves as 'the Frankenstein
solution' – but decided to leave it on one side for the time being, in
favour of an alternative course, namely that I should publicly propose
that since a majority of those voting in Scotland had been in favour, there
should be a short interval for reflection. This period would be used for
talks between the Parties, the minor Parties as well as the Conservative
Opposition, to see if any accommodation could be reached on how to
carry Devolution forward. I coupled this with an announced intention to
offer the House a vote on the Repeal Order not later than 30 April, in the
light of the results of the talks.

In the meantime positions were hardening and I was flooded with
advice from all quarters. The Tories were hesitating about putting down
a vote of no confidence, having had their hopes dashed on similar occasions in the past, but Michael Foot could see the trap closing and, in
company with the other Ministers concerned, worked like a Trojan to
prevent it. If we could have avoided defeat, the credit would have gone

to him and to the Whips, but it was not to be. The result was in effect decided when the Scottish National Party decided to put down their own vote of censure. The Conservative Party gratefully latched on to it, recognising that this would make it impossible for the Scottish National Party to back off, and the stage was set for a debate on 28 March. The few days preceding the debate were full of rumours and offers. It was even suggested by the Ulster Unionists that they would support the Government if we would agree to build a gas pipeline across the Irish Sea between England and Northern Ireland, but I ruled that out.

On the other hand, I readily agreed that we should press ahead at full speed to place on the statute book a measure announced in the Queen's Speech several months previously for the purpose of compensating Welsh slate quarrymen who suffered from respiratory diseases brought on by their work. Several slate quarries had closed down and had left some of the victims without compensation. I had seen the painful suffering caused by these dust diseases as far back as 1945, when one of the major departments engaged in preventive and remedial research for the South Wales miners had been based in Llandough Hospital in my constituency. When I learned that a speeding-up of the Bill would gain us the votes of the Welsh Nationalists, I felt we were assisting two good causes at the same time.

The result of the vote of confidence was in doubt up to the last minute. One of our Members, Alfred Broughton, was seriously ill and it would have been inhuman to bring him to Westminster in an ambulance; in fact he was to die only a few days later.

Gerry Fitt, the SDLP Member from Northern Ireland, who had consistently supported the Government in previous vital votes, spoke and voted against us despite desperate efforts by a number of Labour Members to persuade him otherwise. He objected to the proposed increase in the number of Northern Ireland constituencies which he felt would benefit the Ulster Unionists at the expense of the SDLP. Gerry was a brave man and a warm-hearted, impulsive character but he took the wrong turning on that night.

His vote, together with the absence of our dying colleague, decided the issue. I had never seen the Chamber as crowded, and when the vote was called at the moment Big Ben struck ten o'clock, the Division Lobbies bulged and heaved with Members. I voted and returned to my seat on the front bench with Michael Foot and Denis Healey sitting each side, and we waited while the slow procession of Members recorded their names and were counted by the Tellers from each Party. The wait seemed never-ending. At last one of the Government Whips, Jimmy Hamilton, a Scot from Bothwell, emerged from the Lobby which had counted the Members who had voted for the Government. He struggled through the almost impassable crowd of Members herded together at the Bar of the House waiting to hear the result, and as he went to the clerk's table he gave me an almost imperceptible thumbs up. For one moment I wondered whether, as in *The Perils of Pauline*, we had escaped once more, a prospect I would have greeted with mixed feelings, but then the whole House saw the clerk hand the voting slip to the Conservative Whip to announce, and a great roar went up from their benches at the sign they had awaited for the last three years.

The margin of defeat could not have been smaller – 311 votes to 310 – but one was enough and a general election was inevitable. I left the Chamber with my Parliamentary Private Secretary, Roger Stott, who had been my constant companion, advisor and eyes and ears during the previous three years. He seemed more depressed than I as we sat talking in my room until nearly midnight, quietly reviewing the prospects. I had seen many setbacks in earlier years but it was hard for him as a younger man to see our hopes dashed. However, he has great resilience and later became a most effective front bench Spokesman for the Party. For my part, I slept well that night, for the uncertainty was over and the die was cast.

Even if the vote had gone in our favour I did not expect the election to be long delayed. Since Christmas the Government had suffered severe set-backs on incomes policy and on Devolution, and we could command a majority in the House of Commons for neither. On the morning after our defeat, I called the Cabinet together to fix the date of the general election, which was complicated by the forthcoming Local Authority elections and by the first election of Members of the European Parliament. Our meeting concluded, I went immediately to Buckingham Palace to acquaint the Queen formally of the position and seek a dissolution of Parliament to be followed by a general election on 3 May.

The Government's defeat had been the first time since 1924 that a Government had lost a confidence vote. That occasion had seen the ending of a short-lived minority Labour Government and its replacement by a big Conservative majority.

Contrary to the myths which have sprung up since 1979, Labour did not lose support in the general election – our national vote was in fact slightly higher than it had been nearly five years earlier in October 1974, when we had won more seats than the Tories. It demonstrated how much steady understanding and support existed for what we had tried to do. But, tempted by promises of lower taxation and with memories of the winter, the abstaining Tories of 1974 had flocked back to their Party's colours and this gave Mrs Thatcher a large majority of seats.

It was a miracle that we had governed as long and effectively as we had and carried out as much of our programme. The Labour Government of 1974 to 1979 had no reason to feel ashamed, and much to be proud of.

POSTSCRIPT

---◆---

Had I followed my personal inclination in May 1979 I would have resigned as Leader of the Party in order that a new Leader might be elected who would face the Conservative Government without the taint of defeat. Given the size of Margaret Thatcher's majority it seemed likely that Parliament would run its full course. I would then be in my early seventies and the Party would be demanding a younger Leader.

To carry out the onerous responsibilities of Party Leader properly requires superhuman stamina, strict personal discipline and an ability to endure tedium as well as cope with crises, leaving precious little time for family or private life. For more than thirty continuous years as a member of Labour Governments, Shadow Cabinets and the National Executive Committee I had willingly embraced this existence. By 1979 I was ready for a little more freedom. On the other hand I was told that the Parliamentary Labour Party was ready to re-elect me unanimously and I felt that if I resigned it might appear that I was leaving at the very moment of defeat, unwilling to account for myself at the inevitable inquest which always follows. I therefore decided to remain as Leader for one session of Parliament in the vain hope that by then some of the bitterness of defeat would have drained away. It was not a happy period. I was ready to accept criticism and to defend the Government's record when it was unfairly attacked, but I deeply resented the charges of 'betrayal' made by the left and used as an excuse to fetter the Parliamentary Party and to organise factions to replace Members of Parliament with whom they did not agree. The tactic nearly always failed but it fomented an atmosphere of mistrust and cynicism in which the motives and actions of Party Leaders were continually questioned.

Accordingly, when my self-chosen retirement date arrived in October 1980 I had no wish to change my mind, despite pressure to stay from Michael Foot, the Chairman of the Party Alex Kitson and others, and I retired willingly to the back benches. In 1983 I became Father of the House as the longest serving Member and it dawned on me that I was the only surviving Minister of Clement Attlee's post-war Government to remain in the House. There is a convention that the Father of the House may speak when he wishes, so I was able to play an active role and felt immeasurably pleased when I was named Back-Bencher of the Year by a panel of political correspondents in the *Spectator*'s 1985 Parliamentary Awards.

I enjoyed being free to take up long-standing invitations to visit several countries and so keep alive friendships which had been formed in earlier years, and I took on some new tasks: a Governor of the Rajaji Institute in Delhi, Chairman of the London end of the Hubert Humphrey Institute at the University of Minnesota, Trustee of Cambridge University's Commonwealth Scholarships and, last but by no means least, President of University College, Swansea. There were other satisfactions too: time at last to read for pleasure and listen to music and time to win the Challenge Cup for growing the best field of corn in the district of the local Agricultural Society.

Michael Foot, who succeeded me as Leader, inherited a bed of nails and was never given a fair chance. It was deeply disappointing that shortly after my resignation some prominent former members of the Labour Cabinet should have deserted to form the Social Democratic Party instead of remaining to fight the battle against the unrealistic and often malignant factions which plagued the Labour Party at that time. This made Michael's task doubly difficult. His resignation after the 1983 election bought a new generation to the fore and the vigorous leadership of Neil Kinnock, Roy Hattersley and others met the Militant faction head on and defeated them, thus strengthening the Party's prospects for victory at the next election.

The Labour Party Neil Kinnock leads today is very different from the one in which I was first elected to Parliament, over forty years ago. But so too is society, and it is not for those of us who have exceeded our allotted span to bemoan the fact that things are not what they used to be. Harold Wilson understood this. Explaining his retirement to me, he said that when he saw the same problems recurring and realised that he would give the same answers, he knew it was time to go. There will never be final answers so long as mortal man is fallible, but the satisfaction of a political life lies in searching for the solutions. Democratic politics is more than manipulation, and leadership more than the efficient management of affairs. In a civilised society both rest on ethics and on consent.

It was Clement Attlee who said that the British have the distinction of putting new wine into old bottles. The vintage of the early 1980s was not one of our best, either for Britain or for the rest of the world. The hopes we nurtured in the 1970s of conquering unemployment, achieving détente, relieving Third World poverty and debt have all been thwarted. But we must not reconcile ourselves to failure or futility. New discoveries in many fields – biotechnology, communications and others – are opening up immense possibilities for the benefit of mankind. We have hardly begun to grasp these. Provided we do not allow our scientific and technological virtuosity to outrun our moral sense and provided we harness progress to morality there will be room for reasoned optimism about the future. In the Labour Party it is now the task of the new generation which has climbed into the saddle to discover how to apply the socialist ethic; to reconcile individual freedom with the general welfare, to settle the limits of the state's reach, to grapple with and overcome racial discrimination, and to assist the great mass of poor people who make up the world's population to free themselves from poverty and ignorance.

I began by stating that memory is a capricious companion. More constant is experience. Make of it what we will, it cannot be undone. I have set down some of my experiences; time and chance have given me others, but this is a memoir, not a history, and some things must remain untouched. The general election of 1979 seemed a natural point at which to finish. But 1979 was not the end, although if I may misquote a famous phrase it was probably the beginning of the end, and in any event it is the end of my beginning.

INDEX

———◆———

What They Don't Teach You at Harvard Business School

Mark H. McCormack

Mark McCormack, founder of the sports management industry and now manager and marketer of achievement in such diverse forms as Martina Navratilova, Sebastian Coe and Jack Nicklaus, is a legendarily successful entrepreneur. His knowledge of selling, marketing and management is second to none.

Now, for the first time, he reveals the secrets of his business success in a book which – like him – is sharp, precise and very much to the point. It fills the gap between a business school education and the street knowledge that comes from the day-to-day experience of running a business and managing people.

The collected wisdom, golden rules and unorthodox advice he offers is guaranteed to make anyone's professional life more successful. As he himself says: 'It's all based on my experience, so I know it works.'

FONTANA PAPERBACKS

Maxton

Gordon Brown

James Maxton's political story is one of the great episodes in the history of the Labour Movement. Britain's most charismatic socialist politician of the inter-war period and the best known orator of his time, Maxton was seen by many as a potential Labour Party leader and future socialist Prime Minister.

From Conservative student to socialist teacher in slum-ridden Glasgow, to street corner orator, political prisoner and eventual leadership of the Independent Labour Party his political career spanned the great events which shaped modern Britain – the two world wars, the general strike, mass unemployment in the twenties, the hunger marches in the thirties and the rise and eventual triumph of the modern Labour party in 1945.

With unique access to Maxton's unpublished letters and correspondence, Gordon Brown's important and highly readable biography argues that Maxton's ultimate failure to capture the Labour Party for a programme of socialist change to end mass unemployment foreshadowed the failure of an entire political generation.

FONTANA PAPERBACKS